Netscape Communicator™

Windows® Version

NETSCAPE COMMUNICATOR™

Windows® Version

Bryan Pfaffenberger

University of Virginia
Charlottesville, Virginia

AP PROFESSIONAL
AP PROFESSIONAL is a division of Academic Press

Boston San Diego New York
London Sydney Tokyo Toronto

This book is printed on acid-free paper.

AP PROFESSIONAL
1300 Boylston Street, Chestnut Hill, MA 02167, USA
http://www.apnet.com

An imprint of ACADEMIC PRESS
A Division of HARCOURT BRACE & COMPANY

ACADEMIC PRESS LIMITED
24–28 Oval Road, London NW1 7DX, UK
http://www.hbuk.co.uk/ap/

Library of Congress Cataloging-in-Publication Data

Library of Congress CIP data pending.

ISBN 0-12-553164-8

Printed in the United States of America
97 98 99 00 IP 9 8 7 6 5 4 3 2 1

Contents

Introduction

Welcome to the definitive book on Netscape Communicator, Professional Edition. Whether you're interested in browsing the Web, sending and receiving e-mail, posting to Usenet, chatting live with other Internet users, or even creating and publishing your own Web pages, Netscape Communicator is the ideal tool. And this book comprehensively covers every part of this huge, fantastic program. If you want to do *any* of the marvelous things that Communicator can help you accomplish, you've come to the right place!

What is Netscape Communicator?

The successor to Netscape Communication, Inc.'s wildly popular Netscape Navigator browser, Netscape Communicator is a collection of Internet programs that all share the same, well-designed interface. Communicator includes the latest version of Netscape Navigator, version 4—and much, much more. Here's what you'll find after you've installed Netscape Communicator, Professional Edition:

- **Netscape Navigator version 4** The world's most popular Web browser, with tons of cool new features. Navigator enables you to access the World Wide Web (as well as information made available on an internal corporate intranet).

- **Netscape Messenger** This is an *outstanding* e-mail program—the only one you'll need. With this program, you can send and receive e-mail to anyone on the Internet (more than 50 million people, at last count), as well as anyone on any of the on-line services (such as America On-line). You can use Messenger for simple, text-based e-mail—it's easy. If you'd like to get fancy, there's no limit: Messenger enables you to compose and send rich messages using HTML (but without forcing you to learn HTML). You can also encrypt your messages so that nobody but the intended recipient can read them.

- **Netscape Collabra** Here again, this is the best program you can use for its purpose—namely, accessing Usenet newsgroups (or a corporate news server). Like Messenger, Collabra enables you to send and receive messages in rich HTML, but without forcing you to learn HTML. And for convenience when you're reading or posting to Usenet, this excellent program can't be beat.

- **Netscape Conference** Free Internet telephone calls? Yes—it's possible, and what's more, you can talk to people anywhere in the world, for as long as you like. (They need a computer that's properly equipped, though.) Netscape Conference is all the software you'll need to take full advantage of this glorious freebie.

- **Netscape Page Composer** Like to publish your own Web documents? Don't have time to learn HTML? Don't have time to *code* HTML? You're going to love Composer, which is (in my opinion) the best "what-you-see-is-what-you-get" HTML program available, at any price. It creates standard Web documents that can be accessed by any browser, and it's as easy to use as a word processor. Wonderful program—I use it every day.

- **Netscape Calendar** This is a workgroup scheduling program that's useful mainly to corporate intranet users. If you fall into this category, you're really going to like Calendar, a standards-based program that enables groups to create and share common schedules.
- **IBM Host-On-Demand** This is a cool Java applet that enables you to access all that data housed on legacy mainframe systems.

If you're using the Standard Edition, you've got all of the above except Calendar and IBM Host-on-Demand.

Why should you read this book?

You've probably heard that Netscape is easy to use. It is, up to a point. But Netscape is a tool for accessing the World Wide Web (and indeed, the whole Internet). When you learn Netscape, you learn the Web and you learn the Internet. That's a lot to learn, and you'll need some help. You've come to the right place.

This isn't just a book about learning Netscape Communicator, although we somewhat immodestly feel that it does a pretty good job in that department. It's about mastering Netscape Navigator, becoming a flat-out master of e-mail, learning how to extract the maximum value from Usenet, taking advantage of free Internet phone calls, bringing live content to your desktop, designing and publishing your own Web pages, and—if that's not enough—learning how to apply Netscape to enterprise computing. It's *seven* books in one—and you need all five. Anything short of that means that you wouldn't be getting the maximum out of this amazingly full-featured program.

No matter whether you're a beginner with Netscape or a seasoned vet of all-night surf sessions, you'll find that this book is packed with knowledge, strategies, techniques, and cunning tricks. It presents a comprehensive strategy for total mastery of the Internet and of Web content creation.

How This Book Is Organized

This book is designed for a fast start with Netscape Communicator. Each of the parts of this book begins with the basics, clearly explained. As the need arises, you can use the additional chapters to round out your knowledge of this fantastic program, the Web, and the Internet.

Part I Netscape Navigator: Browsing the Web

Here's the ideal introduction, tutorial, and reference for mastery of Netscape Navigator version 4, the latest version of the world's most popular browser. Get started in Chapter 1, which explains the basics, including all the new version 4 features —so it's worth reading even if you've used previous versions of Navigator. From there, you can learn to surf with the best of them in Chapters 2 and 3, which also serves to introduce the wonders of the World Wide Web.

Once you've learned the basics, you learn essential skills, including searching for information-and actually finding it (Chapter 4), dealing with problems you encounter while browsing (Chapter 5), changing the default start page (Chapter 6), improving Navigator's performance (Chapter 7), creating bookmarks to store your favorite sites (Chapter 8), dealing with document management tasks such as printing (Chapter 9), understanding the security and privacy dimensions of Web browsing (Chapter 10), and customizing Navigator so that it works just the way you want (Chapter 11).

You'll also learn how to make Navigator work smoothly with additional software and goodies, such as plug-ins (Chapter 12), sounds and movies (Chapter 13), Adobe Acrobat documents (Chapter 14), Java applets (Chapter 15), and dynamic HTML, including fonts and layers (Chapter 16).

Part II Netscape Messenger: Staying in Touch with E-mail

Here's everything you need to get started with e-mail — even if you've never sent or received e-mail before — and take your e-mail skills to the max. After reading Part II, people will think you've been an Internet expert for years and years.

You'll get started with Chapter 17, which introduces e-mail and shows you how to configure Messenger. You'll get to know the program and customize it for maximum efficiency. Chapter 18 fully surveys all the knowledge you'll need to make e-mail a mainstay of your personal and professional life. Chapter 19 goes for flat-out e-mail excellence; you'll learn how to create an address book containing frequently-used e-mail addresses, how to filter incoming messages into folders, and how to send and receive encrypted e-mail with complete confidence. This stuff may sound advanced, but it's easy, and what's more, every Netscape Communicator user should learn how use all of these features.

Part III: Netscape Collabra: Joining On-line Discussions

Some people think Usenet is a waste of time, but don't tell that to the millions of people who find it to be an indispensable resource for their profession or hobbies. In Chapter 20, you learn how to configure Collabra and get started with reading Usenet newsgroups. Chapter 21 shows you how to get involved in Usenet discussions yourself—and without getting burned.

Part IV: Netscape Conference: Chatting It Up On-line

Free long distance phone calls? Yes, it's true—as long as the person you're talking to has a computer, an Internet connection, and a standard Internet telephony program, such as Netscape Conference. That's a lot of people, actually, so there's a good chance someone in your family or one of your business contacts can talk to you by means of your net connection. In Chapter 22, you learn how to configure Conference and get started making free calls. Chapter 23 shows you how to take advantage of cool Conference extras, such as collaborative (directed) browsing, text chat, and the shared whiteboard space. Very cool stuff!

Part V: Netscape Netcaster: Subscribing to Live Content

With the Web, you have to go to content. With Netcaster, content comes to your desktop, automatically. This is a great way to enrich your enjoyment of the World Wide Web and, what's more, keep track of fast-breaking developments in world news, sports, weather, and much more. In Chapter 24, you learn how to get started with Netcaster Chapter 25 shows you how to take full advantage of Netcaster's advanced capabilities, which enable you to schedule information delivery as you please.

Part VI: Netscape Page Composer: Creating High-Impact Web Pages

I love Composer. As I mentioned earlier, I use it every day—and so do thousands of professional Web designers. Why? It's simply the fastest, easiest, and most convenient way to knock out Web pages in short order. We don't make money sitting around fussing with HTML. We make money by getting pages out on the Web, and Composer is a fabulous way to do it.

Did I say it's loved by professional Web designers? Don't let that scare you off. The reason we love it is because it's so darned easy! In Part VI, I'll show you every trick I know for creating fantastic Web pages, beginning with the very basics. Incidentally, Part VI isn't just a tacked-on part of this book; you'll find ten very thorough chapters that fully explore every aspect of this fantastic program.

Part VII: Netscape Communicator in the Enterprise

If you're using Communicator (Professional Edition) in a corporation, Part VII shows you how to make use of the new tools Netscape provides for corporate intranets. Chapter 36 provides an overview of Communicator's uses in the enterprise, while Chapter 37 introduces Calendar and IBM Host-On-Demand.

How to Read This Book

With Netscape Gold close by, naturally. Also, I recommend Mountain Dew for those all-night sessions (yawn). Check out the From Here section at the end of every chapter of this book for pathways to follow.

In addition, keep your eye out for icons. They provide cues and clues that help you find your way through this book. Here's a quick overview of this book's icons:

Here you'll find tips, shortcuts, suggestions, insights, and other helpful information about Netscape Gold.

We've tried to anticipate the problems you'll run into—and this icon shows where to look for solutions.

The Treasure Trove icon marks a cool Internet resource of some kind. Check it out!

Look here for inside information on the way the Web works and for fairly advanced information that might be of interest to you if you'd like to master Netscape Gold.

ACKNOWLEDGMENTS

Writing a book such as this one isn't a solitary job for which an author should take sole credit—we get lots of help. I'd like to thank Mike Williams (Acquisitions Editor), Cindy Kogut and Andrew Williams (Managing Editors), and everyone else who helped—including Dmitri Nerubenko and all the unsung people who helped out with production and design. I would also like to thank my agent, Carole McClendon of Waterside Productions, for linking me up with AP Professional, and the great people at Netscape for making such a fantastic program!

NETSCAPE COMMUNICATOR™

Windows® Version

Part I

Netscape Navigator: Browsing the Web

Getting Started with Netscape Navigator

On screen, Netscape Navigator looks like most other Windows applications—with a few strange twists. What's the big "N," and why do comets shoot past it sometimes? And what's that funny open lock thing?

Whether or not you've already started surfing with Netscape (I'll bet you have), sooner or later you will want answers to such questions. You'll find them here, arranged for quick look-up. And if you're really busy, just scan "For the Time-Challenged," at the beginning of each chapter. This section hits the high points succinctly.

Are you a seasoned Windows user? You'll find lots of important stuff in this chapter about the features that differentiate Netscape from other Windows applications, such as the

lenged

is preset to display the Netscape welcome page as its default home ou can change this if you want, as explained in Chapter 6.)

t spend too much time trying to learn all the options on the menu bar. u won't use them frequently. With the exception of Bookmarks, the options you'll frequently use are available on the Toolbar.

The Netsite box displays the URL (Uniform Resource Locator, the Web address) of the document you are currently viewing. (This box is called Location if you're accessing a server other than those made by Netscape Communications.)

- The lock icon tells you whether you're accessing a secure server (if it's open, you're not).
- Hyperlinks, generally shown in color and underlining, enable you to access another Web document. Just move the pointer to the hyperlink, and click the left mouse button once.
- The big "N" (the status indicator) displays an animation while Netscape is downloading a document you've requested. At the bottom of the screen, the status bar tells you what you're downloading, and the progress bar tells you how much of the job is finished.

toolbar's navigation buttons, the directory buttons, the open lock, and the hyperlinks. You can skim this chapter to get the information you need.

Are you a beginning Windows user? I'm going to assume that you know the fundamentals of using Windows 3.1 or Windows 95, such as how to start a program. But you'll find plenty of help for getting started with Netscape.

Some of the pages I'm seeing look different than the ones in this book's screen shots! Good Web authors keep their pages fresh, and that's especially true of the Netscape pages you're about to see in this chapter: In fact, some of them change daily. Don't worry if what you're seeing on screen doesn't exactly match the screen shot. In later chapters, you'll almost certainly find that a page or two mentioned by this book has disappeared from the Web. This can happen for many reasons. Again, it's nothing to worry about. It's nothing you're doing wrong. It's just the way the Web is.

Which Version of Windows Are You Using?

This book covers both Windows versions of Netscape, the 16-bit version for Windows 3.1 and the 32-bit version for Windows 95. The two versions of the program are almost identical, so all the instructions work for both versions of Netscape Navigator. If you're using Windows 3.1, don't be put off by the screen illustrations in this book—your version of Netscape will look almost exactly the same, except that you'll see the old, familiar Windows 3.1 interface.

Starting Netscape Navigator

Assuming you've already installed Netscape Navigator and are connected to the Internet, you're ready to surf the Web.

To start Netscape Navigator:

1. Click the icon that connects you to your Internet service provider or the Microsoft Network.
2. Double-click the Netscape Navigator icon. If you're using Windows 95, you can choose Netscape from the Program menu, which you can access through the Start menu.

You'll see Netscape on screen (Figure 1.1). To find out what you're looking at, read on.

What's on the Screen?

When Netscape Navigator starts, you'll see the program's window on screen. The program icon (the big "N") displays an animation, informing

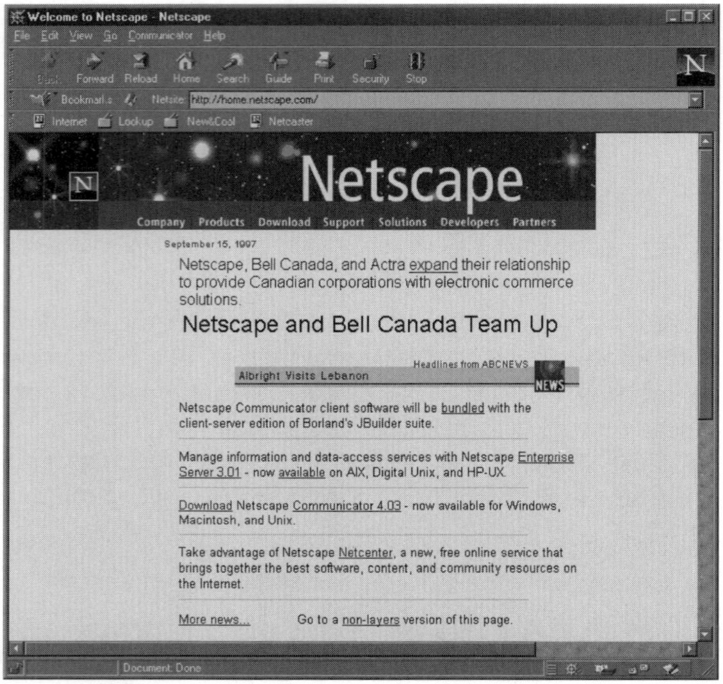
Welcome to Netscape - Netscape
File Edit View Go Communicator Help
Back Forward Reload Home Search Guide Print Security Stop
Bookmarks Netsite: http://home.netscape.com/
Internet Lookup New&Cool Netcaster
Netscape
Company Products Download Support Solutions Developers Partners
September 15, 1997
Netscape, Bell Canada, and Actra expand their relationship to provide Canadian corporations with electronic commerce solutions.
Netscape and Bell Canada Team Up
Headlines from ABCNEWS
Albright Visits Lebanon
NEWS
Netscape Communicator client software will be bundled with the client-server edition of Borland's JBuilder suite.
Manage information and data-access services with Netscape Enterprise Server 3.01 - now available on AIX, Digital Unix, and HP-UX.
Download Netscape Communicator 4.03 - now available for Windows, Macintosh, and Unix.
Take advantage of Netscape Netcenter, a new, free online service that brings together the best software, content, and community resources on the Internet.
More news...
Go to a non-layers version of this page.
Document: Done

Figure 1.1 Netscape Navigator.

you that Netscape is downloading information. In about a minute (or less, if you have a fast connection), you'll see the default *start page,* the page that appears when you start Netscape (or click the Home button).

Appearing within Netscape's application workspace, the default start page (see Figure 1.1) comes to you from Netscape Communications Corporation's headquarters in sunny California. In Netscape, as in any graphical Web browser, the default home page (also called the *start page*) is the Web document that the program is preset to display when started.

Help

My start page isn't Netscape's home page! If you obtained Netscape from an Internet service provider (ISP) such as EarthLink TotalAccess, you may see a different start page. To see Netscape's home page, open the Directory menu and choose Netscape's Home.

If you don't like the default Netscape start page, you can change it to something more to your liking. Find out how in Chapter 6.

The following sections detail the rest of the Netscape window, shown in Figure 1.2.

Title Bar

At the top of Netscape's window is the title bar, a standard Windows feature. Here, Netscape displays its own name. In addition, you see the title of the document you are currently viewing.

Where Does the Title Come From?

Web documents are written in the HyperText Markup Language (HTML), which enables Web authors to identify specific parts of the document, such as the title, headings, body text, and lists. The title bar displays the text that's marked with the <TITLE>...</ TITLE> tags. If the document you're displaying contains the title "Sailing Page," you'll see "Netscape – [Sailing Page]" on the title bar.

Menu Bar

Below the title bar is the menu bar, which is just down the street from the neighborhood bar—but it's not five yet, is it? On the menu bar, you'll find the titles of Netscape's menus, from which you can choose additional options. Frankly, you won't use the menu bar very often—most of Netscape's most useful tools are available on the toolbars (see the next sections).

Here's a very quick overview of what's on these menus:

- **File** This menu enables access to a grab bag of display, storage, and printing options.
- **Edit** This menu contains the standard Windows editing options, including Undo, Cut, Copy, Paste, and Find. The keyboard shortcuts are faster and easier. To use them, you hold down the Ctrl key and

press the indicated key (for example, if you press Ctrl + F, you see the Find dialog box).

- **View** From this menu, you can choose options controlling the way Netscape obtains documents, but most of them can be chosen more quickly by using the toolbar (discussed in the next section).
- **Go** Like the View menu, this menu contains several commands that are more easily accessed by clicking buttons on the toolbar. But there's one gem: At the bottom of the menu, you see a list of the documents you've accessed recently. To go back to any of them, you just choose the document's name from the menu.

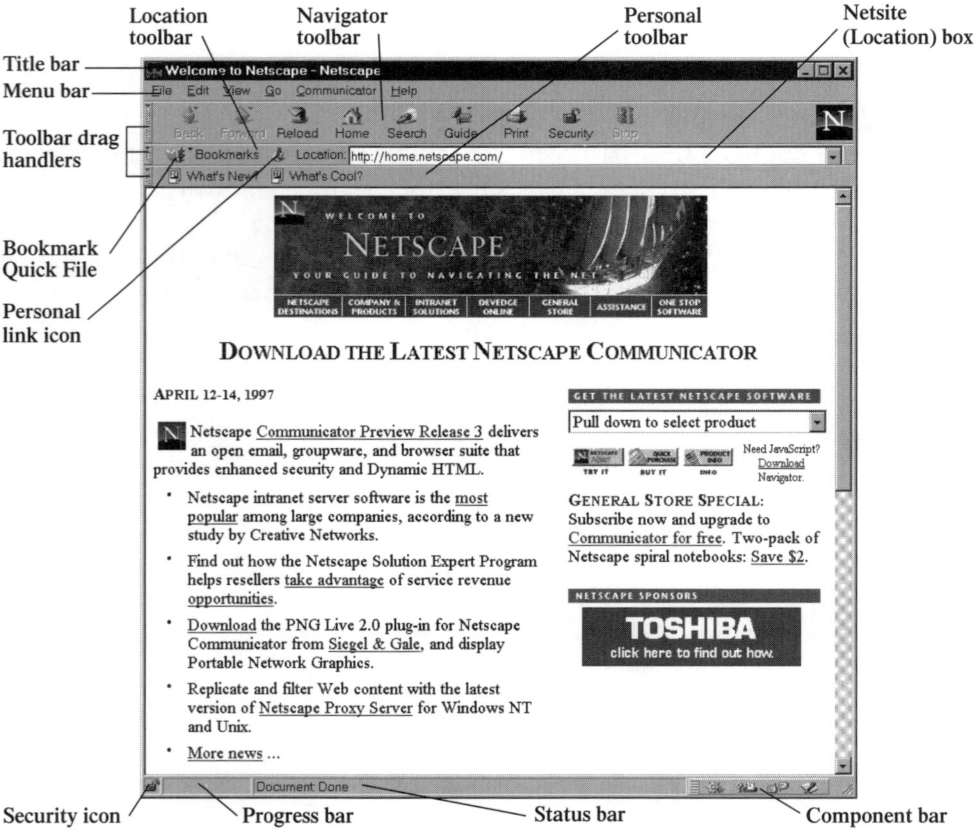
Location toolbar
Navigator toolbar
Personal toolbar
Netsite (Location) box
Title bar
Menu bar
Toolbar drag handlers
Bookmark Quick File
Personal link icon
Security icon
Progress bar
Status bar
Component bar
Welcome to Netscape - Netscape
File Edit View Go Communicator Help
Back Forward Reload Home Search Guide Print Security Stop
Bookmarks Location: http://home.netscape.com/
What's New? What's Cool?
WELCOME TO NETSCAPE
YOUR GUIDE TO NAVIGATING THE NET
DOWNLOAD THE LATEST NETSCAPE COMMUNICATOR
APRIL 12-14, 1997
Netscape Communicator Preview Release 3 delivers an open email, groupware, and browser suite that provides enhanced security and Dynamic HTML.
Netscape intranet server software is the most popular among large companies, according to a new study by Creative Networks.
Find out how the Netscape Solution Expert Program helps resellers take advantage of service revenue opportunities.
Download the PNG Live 2.0 plug-in for Netscape Communicator from Siegel & Gale, and display Portable Network Graphics.
Replicate and filter Web content with the latest version of Netscape Proxy Server for Windows NT and Unix.
More news ...
GET THE LATEST NETSCAPE SOFTWARE
Pull down to select product
Need JavaScript? Download Navigator.
GENERAL STORE SPECIAL:
Subscribe now and upgrade to Communicator for free. Two-pack of Netscape spiral notebooks: Save $2.
NETSCAPE SPONSORS
TOSHIBA
click here to find out how.
Document: Done

Figure 1.2 The parts of Netscape Navigator's program window.

New for 4

- **Communicator** This menu provides a way to get to other components of Communicator (including your Messenger mailbox, Collabra discussions, Page Composer, and Conference). You can also use this menu to show or "dock" (hide) the Component Bar—more about that in a minute—and to display a number of special-purpose Communicator windows, including the Message Center, Address Book, Bookmarks window, the all-important History window, and the seldom-used Java Console (something that's only needed for testing or exploring Java programs). At the bottom of this menu you'll find a list of the current windows that you've opened; you can switch from one window to another by choosing the window from the list.
- **Help** This menu offers access to Netscape Navigator's on line help directory—but hey, you've got this book. Much of the rest of this menu is a rather thinly disguised marketing tool.

Help

Where are the Bookmarks and Windows menus? Ah, you've used previous versions of Navigator. The Bookmarks menu now lives on the Location toolbar. The chief functions of the Windows menu have now been taken over by the Communicator menu. Many experienced Netscape uses aren't too happy about this change—they have to go hunting for something and don't understand why—but you'll love the new Bookmark capabilities.

Help

I've got tennis elbow from using this darned mouse! I like to keep the use of my mouse to the minimum—and to do so, I make full use of keyboard commands. Look for the underlined letter in menu and option names. You can use these letters with the Alt key to select commands and options—without touching the mouse! To choose the View menu, hold down the Alt key and press V (uppercase or lowercase). To choose the Reload option in this menu, just press R. For a complete list of keyboard shortcuts.

Navigation Toolbar

The Navigation toolbar contains buttons, or tools, that enable easy access to frequently used Netscape commands. Here's a very quick once-over-lightly (you'll learn how to use these buttons in this chapter and the next):

Back Go back to the document you just viewed.

Forward Return to the document you went back from. This button isn't available unless you've displayed a document and then clicked the Back tool.

Reload Gets a new copy of the document from the network.

Home Redisplay the default home page.

Search Display a page of search engines for searching the Web.

Guide Displays a menu of cool places to go.

Print Print the document that Netscape is currently displaying.

Security Shows security information for this page.

Stop Reloads the current document. If the document is still downloading, this button says "Stop." Click it to stop downloading.

New for 4

Location Toolbar

The second toolbar, called the Location toolbar, contains the Bookmark menu and the Netsite (Location) box.

I don't see this toolbar! That's because somebody hid it when they configured Netscape for you. Chances are, they were trying to be nice, so don't get mad. Anyway, you can easily display it. From the View menu, choose toolbars, and choose Show Location toolbar. While you're at it, make sure the other toolbars are displayed by choosing Show Navigation Toolbar and Show Personal toolbar, if necessary.

The term *bookmarks* refers to favorite sites that you've saved so you can get back to them easily. To display current bookmarks and to access the bookmarks window, you just click the little bookmark icon (which is called the Bookmark QuickFile), and a pop-up menu appears. This menu has lots of options, which we'll discuss in Chapter 8.

The Netsite box indicates the Web address (the URL) of the document you are currently viewing. When you access a non-Netscape Communications server, this box is called Location instead of Netsite. When you type a Web address into this box directly, it changes its name to Go To.

New for 4

Personal Toolbar

This is one of the best new features of Navigator 4.0. You can load up this toolbar with the sites you most frequently visit, and access any of them simply by clicking its icon. To add a favorite site to the Personal toolbar, just click the Bookmark QuickFile—the little bookmark icon on the Location toolbar—and choose File Bookmark. From the pop-up submenu, choose Toolbar Folder, and Presto! the item appears on your Personal toolbar. To access this item, just click its icon.

I added all sorts of junk to my Personal toolbar and now I want to get rid of it! No problemo. Just flip to Chapter 8, where you'll learn how to edit your bookmarks. It's as easy as selecting the one you don't want and pressing Delete.

Bookmark Calisthenics

You can show or hide bookmarks by clicking View on the menu bar, and choosing Toolbars. But there's an even better way. Each toolbar has a drag handle—a little rough-looking thing with an arrow on it, located at the far left of the toolbar. Here's what you can do with the drag handle:

- To hide a toolbar, just click the drag handle. The toolbar collapses so that all you see is the drag handle. To display the toolbar again, click the drag handle.

- To change a toolbar's location within the toolbar area, drag the drag handle to the place you want the toolbar to appear, and release the handle.

Should you hide the toolbars? I don't think so. The toolbars provide the quickest and easiest way to access Navigator's commands. You'll use them all the time. You might want to hide them temporarily if you're viewing a particularly large graphic or something, but I'll bet you redisplay them soon afterward.

New for 4

The Component Bar

To enable you to quickly access Netscape Communicator components, you can display the Component bar (Figure 1.3). (If you don't see the Component bar, click Communicator on the menu bar, and choose Show Component bar.) Here's a quick guide to the icons:

Click here to display Navigator and browse the Web.

Click here to display your e-mail inbox.

Click here to join Usenet or Collabra discussion groups.

Click here to create a new Web document with Composer.

If you hide the Component bar, it pops up on the status bar (at the bottom of the window). You still can access components by clicking the icons.

Status Indicator

The big "N" lets you know when Netscape is downloading a document from the Web—it plays an animation (currently, comets shooting over the earth). When the document is finished downloading, you see "Document Done" on the status bar (at the bottom of the screen).

To return to Netscape's home page, just click the status indicator.

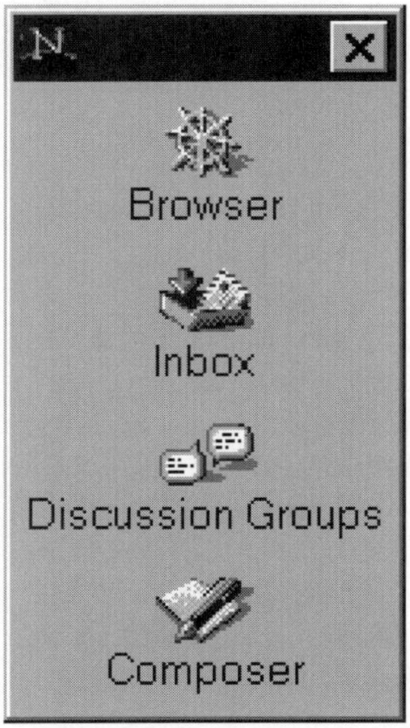

Figure 1.3 The Component bar provides quick access to other Communicator components.

Application Workspace

Here, Netscape displays the document you're currently viewing. You'll see text and hyperlinks, and you may also see inline images (graphics that appear along with the text). If the document is bigger than the available window space, the scroll bars activate. You can click the scroll arrows, or drag the scroll bars, to bring hidden portions of the document into view.

Status Bar and Progress Bar

Next to the doorkey icon, there's a panel called the *status bar.* Netscape uses the status bar to display messages about what the program is doing.

Most of the time, you can ignore these messages, unless you're curious to know what the program is doing.

What's in a URL?

A URL has three parts. The first part (http://) indicates the type of resource you're viewing. If you're viewing an FTP file archive, the first part of the URL reads "ftp://," while a Gopher menu's URL reads "gopher://." The second part of the URL indicates the name of the computer you're accessing (such as home.netscape.com).

The third part of the directory indicates the path that Netscape must take to locate the document, and it also includes the document name (/home/welcome.html). Sometimes the third part of a URL is missing, which tells Netscape to look for and obtain the default document.

Do you really need to know all this? Not really, but sometimes you'll need to type URLs and it's important to do so correctly. For more information, check out Chapter 2.

Next to the status bar, you see a blank panel called the *progress bar.* When Netscape retrieves a document from the Internet, you'll see a graphical display indicating how much of the document has been obtained.

New for 4

Component Icons

Did you hide the Component bar? If so, the icons pop up on the status bar, in the panel on the right end of the bar. You can click the icons to access your inbox, discussions, or Composer. To zoom the Component bar to full size, just click the drag handle.

HYPERLINKS: THE BASICS

Note that some of the words and phrases you see are highlighted with colors and underlining (if you're using a monochrome monitor, you'll see only underlining). These are *hyperlinks* (also called *anchors* or just *links*).

When you click on a hyperlink, Netscape locates the Web document that is linked to this hyperlink and initiates the transfer.

Try clicking one of the hyperlinks now:

1. Move the tip of the mouse pointer so that it's positioned over the hyperlink, and take a look at the status bar at the bottom of the screen. This displays the URL of the document to which this anchor is linked. Also, note that the pointer changes shape to a hand.
2. With the left mouse button, click the link. Forget all that double-clicking stuff; you just click once.

Several things happen now:

- The big "N" displays an animation (shooting comets). This tells you that Netscape is obtaining the document you requested, through a process called *downloading*. Incidentally, the official name for the big "N" is *status indicator.* (I like "Big 'N'" better.)
- The status bar indicates that Netscape is downloading a document.
- You see the new document within Netscape's application workspace.

What does *downloading* mean? When downloading occurs, Netscape transfers an entire document to your computer's memory, along with any associated graphics. This is called "downloading" because the information is coming from a distant computer to your computer. (As you might guess, the term *uploading* means sending information from your computer to a distant computer.) Once the document is in your computer's memory, you can scroll through it quickly. In addition, Netscape stores recently accessed documents in memory so that you can redisplay them quickly, should you wish to return to them.

Now try going back to the document you displayed previously. To do so, just click the Back button on the toolbar. Take a look at the hyperlink you just clicked.

If you're viewing Netscape on a color monitor, note that the hyperlink you just clicked has changed color. This is a *visited* hyperlink, a hyperlink to a document that you've already seen. You can still click the hyperlink to redisplay the visited document, but Netscape wants you to know that you've been down that road before.

Basic Window Calisthenics

Like the window of any fine Windows application, Netscape's window can be adjusted until it suits your fancy. You can also minimize the program to an icon or maximize it to full size. The following instructions quickly detail these procedures; Figure 1.4 shows the on-screen window controls.

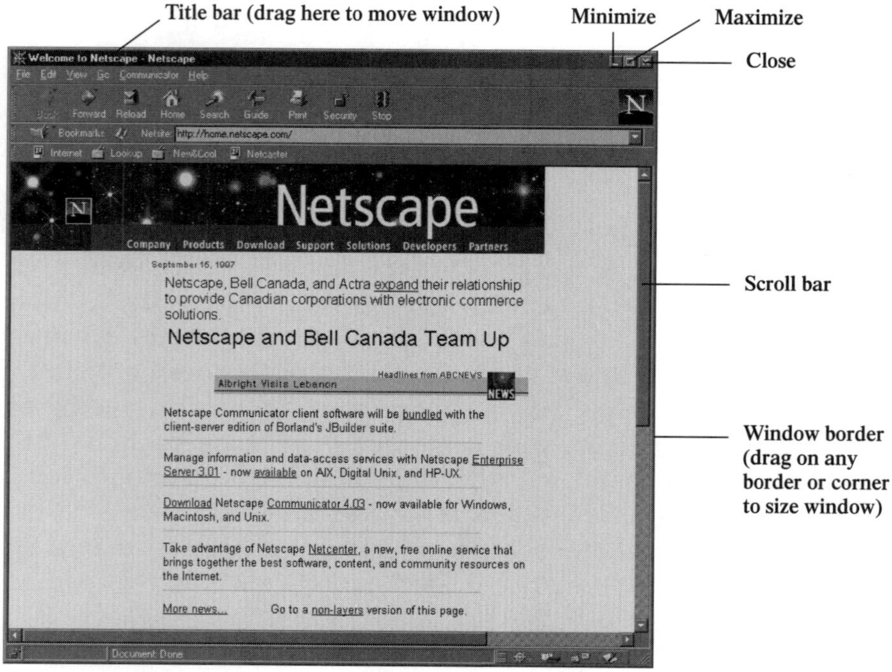

Figure 1.4 On-screen window controls.

Moving the Window

To move Netscape's window on the screen:

1. Move the mouse pointer to the title bar, hold down the left mouse button, and drag. You'll move the whole window.
2. When you've moved the window to where you want it to appear, release the mouse button.

Sizing the Window

To size Netscape's window:

1. Move the mouse pointer to one of the window's borders until the pointer changes shape, and drag the border.
2. When you've sized the window the way you want, release the mouse button.

Here's a neat trick: To size two borders at once, click on one of the corners and drag.

Minimizing the Window

To minimize Netscape's window:

1. Click the Minimize button. This shrinks Netscape down to an icon on the desktop (Windows 3.1) or a button on the taskbar (Windows 95).
2. To redisplay Netscape, double-click the minimized program icon (Windows 3.1) or the taskbar button (Windows 95).

Maximizing the Window

To maximize Netscape's window:

1. Click the Maximize button.
2. After you've maximized the window, you can restore the window to its previous size by clicking the same button.

Here's a neat trick. To maximize or restore the window, just double-click the title bar.

Quitting Netscape Navigator

So, you're done. It's about 5 A.M., isn't it? Hope you had fun.

To quit Netscape Navigator:

- From the File menu, choose Exit.

  or

- Press Alt + F4.

From Here

- Surf's up! Learn the basics in Chapter 2.
- Explore the Web in Chapter 3.
- Learn how to search the Web in Chapter 4.
- Running into problems—like that horrible "403—Access Forbidden" message? Check out Chapter 5, "When the Surf Gets Rough."

Chapter 2

The Gentle Art of Web Surfing

Wouldn't it be cool to learn how to surf the Web with the best of 'em, and in just an hour or two? If you agree, read this chapter. Sure, there's more to learn than this chapter covers, but you'll learn 90 percent of what you need to have some serious fun with Netscape. Plus, this chapter serves as a guide to much of the rest of this book. Later chapters explore its topics in more detail. By reading this chapter, you can learn which subjects you'd like to explore more deeply.

Just what does surfing the Web mean? It means exploring, discovering, navigating—and, above all, being swept away by a series of awesome hyperlinks that you can ride all over cyberspace.

Netscape's your surfboard. You start by finding a cool Web document, one that's loaded with hyperlinks, and then begin exploring. As you navigate link after link, you'll connect with computers all over North America, Europe, Australia, and even more remote places. You can look forward to countless hours of discovery, fun, and even enchantment, with a bit of boredom thrown in (admittedly, not every Web site is worth accessing).

The surfing metaphor is darned appropriate: Sometimes you'll put your "board" on an amazing series of hyperlinks, and they'll carry you off to who-knows-where. And sometimes, admittedly, the hyperlinks you'll ride aren't very interesting, although (happily) some of them are so stupid that they are truly hilarious. But there's gold in those links, as you'll surely agree. Have fun, and be sure to cancel tomorrow's appointments.

This chapter will benefit every reader of this book, and that's true even if you've already done some Web surfing with Netscape. In this chapter, you'll find a Web-savvy approach to Netscape, the approach that experienced Netscape mavens use every day. Working through this chapter, even the stuff that seems obvious, will reveal the Netscape secrets and strategies that make this program the Web browser of choice.

A Word about Web Terminology

The Web's grown so fast that there hasn't been time to develop a consistent nomenclature—which doesn't help people who are trying to learn how to use it. Here are a few definitions to help you get started.

Page A Web document. Of course, many of these documents are longer than one page.

Home page A Web document that's a "home" or a headquarters for a certain type of information. People like to set up home pages containing information about themselves, for example. Netscape has its own home page, the one you see every time you start the program.

Start page The Web document that you see every time you start Netscape (or click the Home button). By default, this is Netscape's home page. You can change this, as explained in Chapter 6.

For the Time-Challenged

- Remember to click just once when you click a hyperlink.
- A graphic with a blue border contains a hyperlink.
- Some graphics contain hyperlinks but don't have blue borders. To tell whether a graphic contains a hyperlink, move the mouse pointer over the graphic. If it changes to a hand shape, the graphic contains a hyperlink.
- To return to a document you've previously displayed, click Back or choose the document's name from the Go menu. To redisplay the document you were just viewing, click Forward.
- If you've accessed a multipart Web page that has internal navigation buttons, learn how to use them. For finding your way around this Web site, these buttons are much better than Netscape's Back and Forward buttons.
- When you access a document that contains frames, Netscape's window splits into two or more independently scrollable panels. To work with one of the panels, click within it.
- To access a Web page by typing its Web address directly, type it in the Location box and press Enter.
- If you get lost, click the Home button.
- To view movies, you need to install a helper application (see Chapter 13). Netscape is preset to play certain sounds.
- To locate documents on the Web, learn how to use search engines and subject trees.

Web browser A program that enables you to surf the Internet in search of Web pages.

Web server A program that makes Web pages available to people who are browsing the Web.

Web site A computer that's running a Web server. A Web site may contain lots of pages—maybe thousands of them. Many people use the term *site* as if it were synonymous

	with *page* ("That's a cool site" usually means "That's a cool page").
URL	The Web address of a Web page. I'll use the terms *Web address* and *URL* interchangeably.

There are more Web terms to learn, but these are more than sufficient to get you going.

Starting Netscape

Assuming you've already installed Netscape and configured your Internet connection, you're ready to go. Unless you or somebody else (such as an Internet service provider who gave you a copy of Netscape) modified the default start page, you see Netscape's home.

Starting Netscape with Windows 3.1

In Program Manager, locate the Netscape Communicator program group, and double-click the Netscape Navigator program icon.

Starting Netscape with Windows 95

In the Start menu of Windows 95, click Programs, and then click Netscape Communicator. Choose Netscape Navigator from the pop-up menu. You'll see Netscape on screen, and the program displays the default start page (see Figure 2.1).

Netscape likes visitors—they help it sell advertising space on its home page—but you should eventually change the default start page to something more tailored to your needs. It's really easy to do. For the lowdown, see Chapter 6.

The Fundamental Maneuvers of Web Surfing

What makes the Web so much *fun* is its unpredictability—you start out clicking links from Netscape's home page (suggestion: click the What's Cool button to see a list of neat sites), and who knows where you'll wind up?

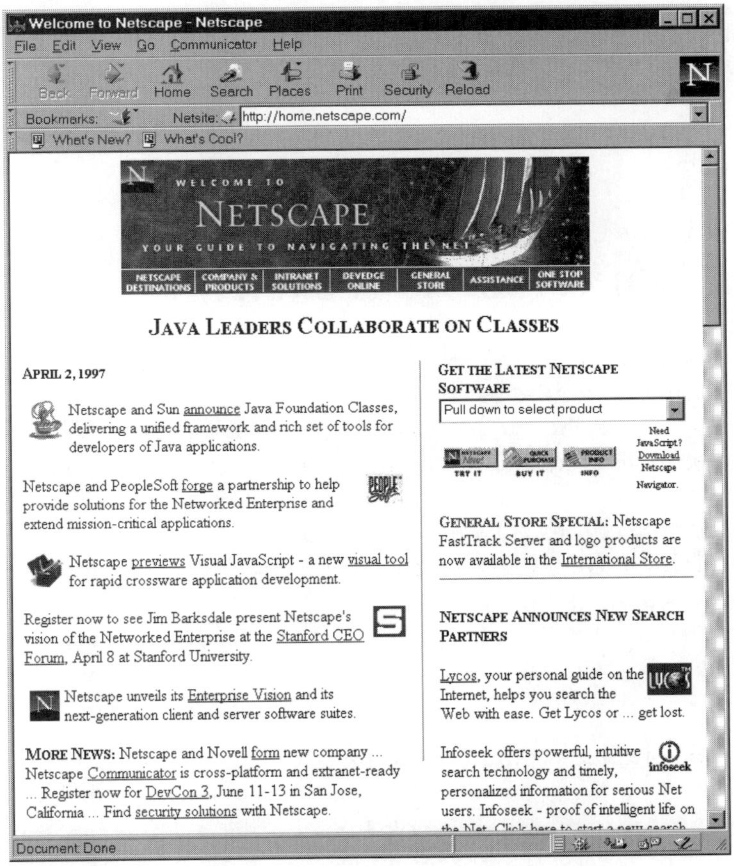
Welcome to Netscape - Netscape
File Edit View Go Communicator Help
Back Forward Home Search Places Print Security Reload
Bookmarks: Netsite: http://home.netscape.com/
What's New? What's Cool?
WELCOME TO
NETSCAPE
YOUR GUIDE TO NAVIGATING THE NET
NETSCAPE DESTINATIONS
COMPANY & PRODUCTS
INTRANET SOLUTIONS
DEVEDGE ONLINE
GENERAL STORE
ASSISTANCE
ONE STOP SOFTWARE
JAVA LEADERS COLLABORATE ON CLASSES
APRIL 2, 1997
Netscape and Sun announce Java Foundation Classes, delivering a unified framework and rich set of tools for developers of Java applications.
Netscape and PeopleSoft forge a partnership to help provide solutions for the Networked Enterprise and extend mission-critical applications.
Netscape previews Visual JavaScript - a new visual tool for rapid crossware application development.
Register now to see Jim Barksdale present Netscape's vision of the Networked Enterprise at the Stanford CEO Forum, April 8 at Stanford University.
Netscape unveils its Enterprise Vision and its next-generation client and server software suites.
MORE NEWS: Netscape and Novell form new company ... Netscape Communicator is cross-platform and extranet-ready ... Register now for DevCon 3, June 11-13 in San Jose, California ... Find security solutions with Netscape.
GET THE LATEST NETSCAPE SOFTWARE
Pull down to select product
TRY IT
BUY IT
INFO
Need JavaScript? Download Netscape Navigator.
GENERAL STORE SPECIAL: Netscape FastTrack Server and logo products are now available in the International Store.
NETSCAPE ANNOUNCES NEW SEARCH PARTNERS
Lycos, your personal guide on the Internet, helps you search the Web with ease. Get Lycos or ... get lost.
Infoseek offers powerful, intuitive search technology and timely, personalized information for serious Net users. Infoseek - proof of intelligent life on
Document: Done

Figure 2.1 Default start page (Netscape Communications Corporation).

Experienced surfers know, though, that there are two kinds of surfing:

- **Grooving** This is good. Seriously good. When you're in a groove, you just can't seem to do anything wrong—you keep finding these *tremendous* sites, and the links from these sites take you to even more tremendous sites.
- **Thrashing** Everything you see is junk. On top of that, you're lost. You click and click, but there's nothing worth seeing.

Caught in a thrash? Get out of it by clicking the What's Cool button. You'll see Netscape's What's Cool page again. Try surfing from there—you can't go wrong. Check out a page, and click the Back button to go back to the What's Cool page again.

THE SUBTLE MYSTERIES AND FINER POINTS OF HYPERLINKS

You already know that hyperlinks appear in distinctive formatting (color and underlining, if you're using a color monitor). In addition, visited hyperlinks (ones you've clicked before) appear in a different, distinctive color. Here are a couple of additional points you need to know about hyperlinks:

- **Click *once*.** To activate a hyperlink, you just move the pointer to it, and click. Yes, that's right—click once. Because many Macintosh and Windows functions are initiated by double-clicking something, you may have to unlearn the tendency to double-click. That second click may activate an unwanted hyperlink on the page that's about to be displayed, taking you to who-knows-where.
- **Some graphics contain hyperlinks.** You can click these pictures to display a Web document. Here's how to tell whether an inline graphic is a hyperlink: Look for a border around the graphic. With most browsers, the border appears in blue. Note, though, that Web authors are increasingly hiding the blue border (there's a way you can do this), since they believe that it's unaesthetic. When this is done, though, there's usually some indication on the graphic itself that it's really a hyperlink. In Figure 2.1, for example, the Netscape Now graphic is a button—just the sort of thing you'd want to click.
- **Learn to use image maps.** Some Web pages include graphics that have clickable regions, each associated with its own hyperlink. Such graphics are called *image maps*, although they don't necessarily look like a map. An example is the beautiful graphic at the top of Netscape's home page, which has a number of distinct areas. If you click one of these areas, Netscape displays the linked document. A great example of an image map is White House for Kids (Figure 2.2). Much of this screen is a clickable image map. (You can access this page from www.whitehouse.gov.)

I can't tell whether this graphic contains a hyperlink or not! No blue border? It might still contain one or more hyperlinks. To find out, move the mouse pointer over the graphic. If it changes shape to a hand with one finger extended, then you know that the graphic contains a hyperlink.

I'm Lost! (Navigation Fundamentals)

Two exclamations are heard from beginning Web surfers: "Cool!" followed shortly by "Where am I!!?" Here's a very quick mini-course in Web navigation.

Going Back

At any time, you can go back to see a document you previously viewed. To go back, you click the Back button. If you just love toying with Windows' menus, you could choose Back from the Go menu, but mouse-haters are cheerfully invited to use the Alt + < keyboard shortcut. (< is the less-than symbol, which you'll find to the right of the letter M on your keyboard.)

Mouse lovers, here's a neat trick. To go back, just click the *right* mouse button anywhere within the document. From the pop-up menu, click Back.

If you're displaying a document in which the page has been broken up into two or more independent panels, called *frames*, clicking Back displays the previous document in the selected frame. For more information on frames, see "It's a Frame-up," later in this chapter.

If you're trying to redisplay a document that you viewed several clicks ago, don't waste time by clicking the Back button repeatedly. Instead, open the Go menu and look for the document's name at the bottom of this menu. Note that some-

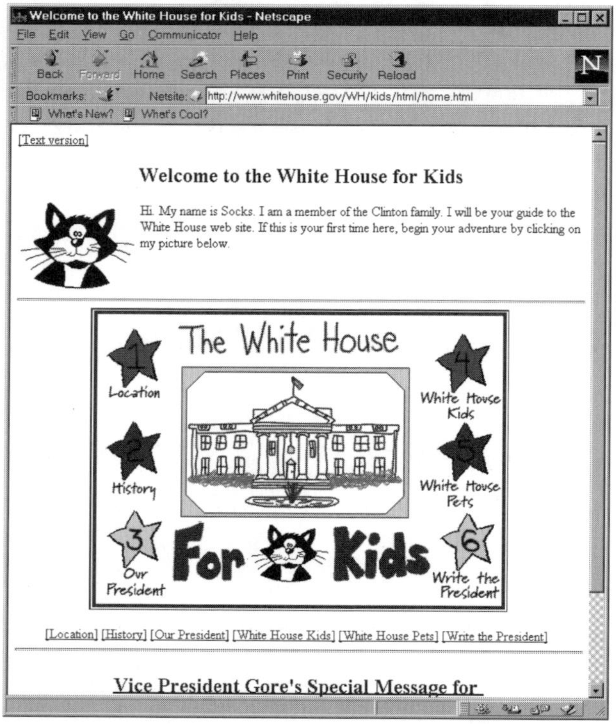

Figure 2.2 White House page for Kids (http://www.whitehouse.gov/WH/kids/html/home.html).

times Netscape doesn't save the names of all the documents you've visited. To find out why, see "There's a History to This," in Chapter 7.

Notice that going back is a lot faster than downloading the document in the first place? That's because Netscape stores a copy of recently accessed documents in a special memory area called a *cache*. The program can retrieve documents from the cache much faster than it can retrieve them from the network.

New for 4

Going Back More than One Page

Sometimes you may wish to go back more than one page. If so, don't just sit there clicking Back—it takes time to reload each page, one by one, as you go back. Instead, click the Back button, but hold down the mouse button. The Back button suddenly sports a drop-down menu, listing sites you've recently visited. Just choose the one you want from the list! (Cool feature, Netscape!)

Going Forward

Once you've gone back by clicking the Back button, the Forward button becomes available. Try it now (or press Alt + >).

If you like using the mouse, try this: Right-click anywhere within the document, and choose Forward.

If you're displaying a document with frames, clicking Forward displays the next document in the frame (but only if you've gone back in this frame).

So what does the Forward button do? It lets you return to the document you just went Back from. Oh, heck, it's easier to do than talk about.

The Forward button is dimmed! You're viewing the most recent document you downloaded, which means that you can't go forward. You can go back, or you can access a new Web document by clicking a hyperlink or typing a Web address.

New for 4

Going Forward More than One Page

Did you go *way* back? Want to go forward more than one page—or all the way forward? The Forward button also has a drop-down menu. To use this menu, click Forward, but hold down the mouse button until the menu appears. Choose the page you want from the menu.

Look for Internal Navigation Buttons!

Many Web sites offer more than just a page; they offer a *web*, and within this web each page has navigation buttons to help you find your way. A web (as opposed to *the* Web, the World Wide Web) is a collection of related Web documents, all stored on a single site; each document explores one facet of the topic at hand. Internal navigation aids help you find your way around in a web. Ideally, navigation buttons appear on every page of the web and look just the same, so you quickly learn how to navigate within the web.

If the web you're browsing has internal navigation buttons, by all means use them! Internal navigation buttons always give you the best way of navigating within a multidocument web. That's because the web's author knows just how the web is structured. The navigation buttons have been designed to help you navigate the web logically. You can use Netscape's Back and Forward buttons to redisplay pages you just accessed, if you wish, but the internal navigation buttons are your best bet.

You'll quickly learn to recognize navigation buttons, which are of two kinds:

- **Graphical buttons** These are popular because they look neat, but they take forever to download on slow SLIP/PPP lines using modems. See Figure 2.3 for an example.
- **Text buttons** These navigation aids download much more quickly because they're made from ordinary characters. See Figure 2.4 for an example.

I don't know what this darned navigation button does! Too many Web authors use button graphics that don't really suggest what's going to happen when you click on the navigation buttons—so don't feel bad, it's not you. Thoughtful Web authors include explanatory text along with the buttons, unless the buttons' meanings are so clear that it's obvious what they do.

It's a Frame-up (Using Frames)

A very nice new feature of Netscape is support of *frames*, a set of HTML tags that enable Web authors to divide a page into several independently

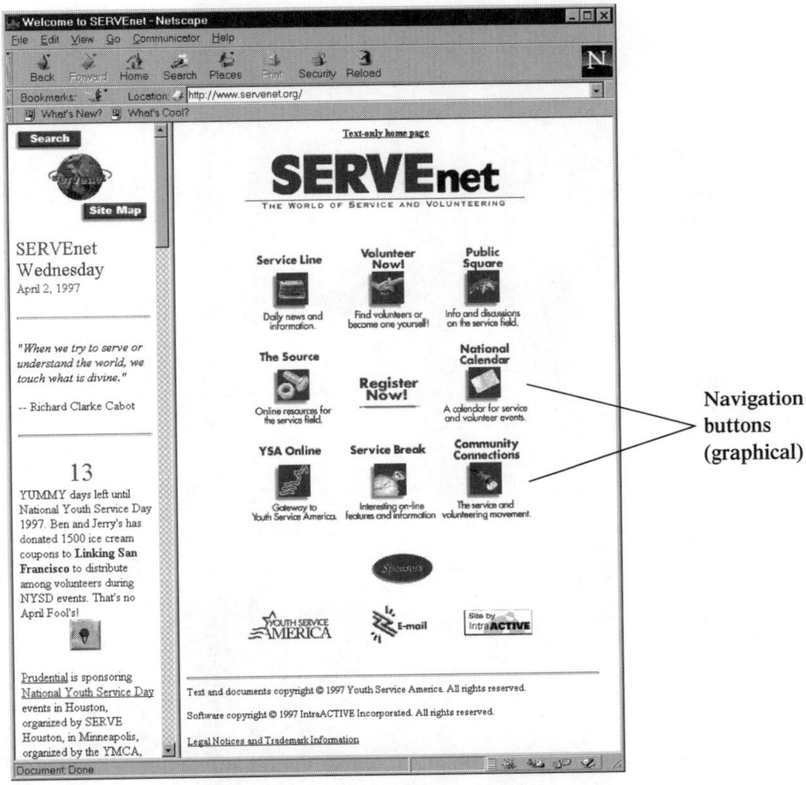

Figure 2.3 Graphical navigation buttons.

scrollable panels. When you access a document that contains frames, Netscape divides the application workspace into two or more panels. If there's more text in one of the panels than Netscape can display, the program automatically includes a scroll bar. You can use the scroll bar to bring the hidden parts of the panel into view.

Some Web authors may give you the option of repositioning the frame borders. If you'd like to do so, move the pointer to the border. If the pointer changes shape to a bidirectional arrow, you can adjust the border's position.

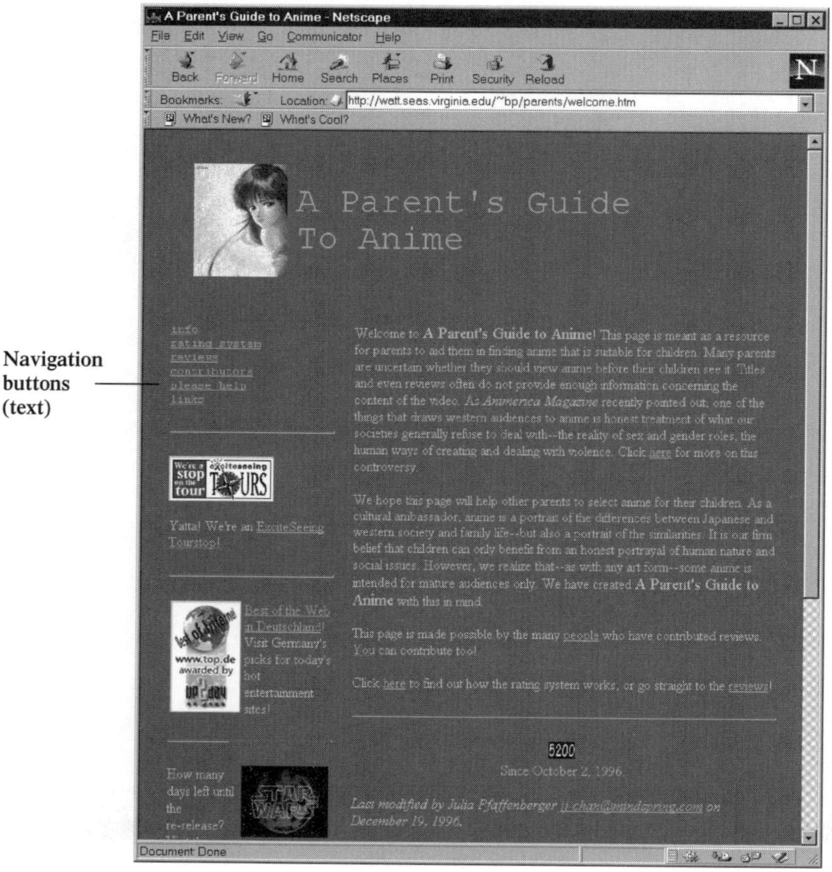
Navigation buttons (text)
A Parent's Guide to Anime - Netscape
File Edit View Go Communicator Help
Back Forward Home Search Places Print Security Reload
Bookmarks Location: http://watt.seas.virginia.edu/~bp/parents/welcome.htm
What's New? What's Cool?
A Parent's Guide To Anime
info
rating system
reviews
contributors
please help
links
Welcome to A Parent's Guide to Anime! This page is meant as a resource for parents to aid them in finding anime that is suitable for children. Many parents are uncertain whether they should view anime before their children see it. Titles and even reviews often do not provide enough information concerning the content of the video. As Animerica Magazine recently pointed out, one of the things that draws western audiences to anime is honest treatment of what our societies generally refuse to deal with--the reality of sex and gender roles, the human ways of creating and dealing with violence. Click here for more on this controversy.
We hope this page will help other parents to select anime for their children. As a cultural ambassador, anime is a portrait of the differences between Japanese and western society and family life--but also a portrait of the similarities. It is our firm belief that children can only benefit from an honest portrayal of human nature and social issues. However, we realize that--as with any art form--some anime is intended for mature audiences only. We have created A Parent's Guide to Anime with this in mind.
This page is made possible by the many people who have contributed reviews. You can contribute too!
Click here to find out how the rating system works, or go straight to the reviews!
Yatta! We're an ExciteSeeing Tourstop!
Best of the Web in Deutschland! Visit Germany's picks for today's hot entertainment sites!
www.top.de awarded by
How many days left until the re-release?
5200
Since October 2, 1996
Last modified by Julia Pfaffenberger on December 19, 1996.
Document: Done

Figure 2.4 Text-based navigation buttons.

An obvious and appropriate use for frames is to keep navigation buttons on screen at all times. With a one-page display, the buttons scroll out of sight as the user reads the document. With frames, a Web author can position the frame in a panel that stays put, even if the user scrolls the other panel (see Figure 2.5). Another obvious application of frames lies in computer-aided instruction. In Figure 2.6, you see an interesting explanation of the human eye; when you click on one of the features of the eye, you see an explanation in the right-hand panel.

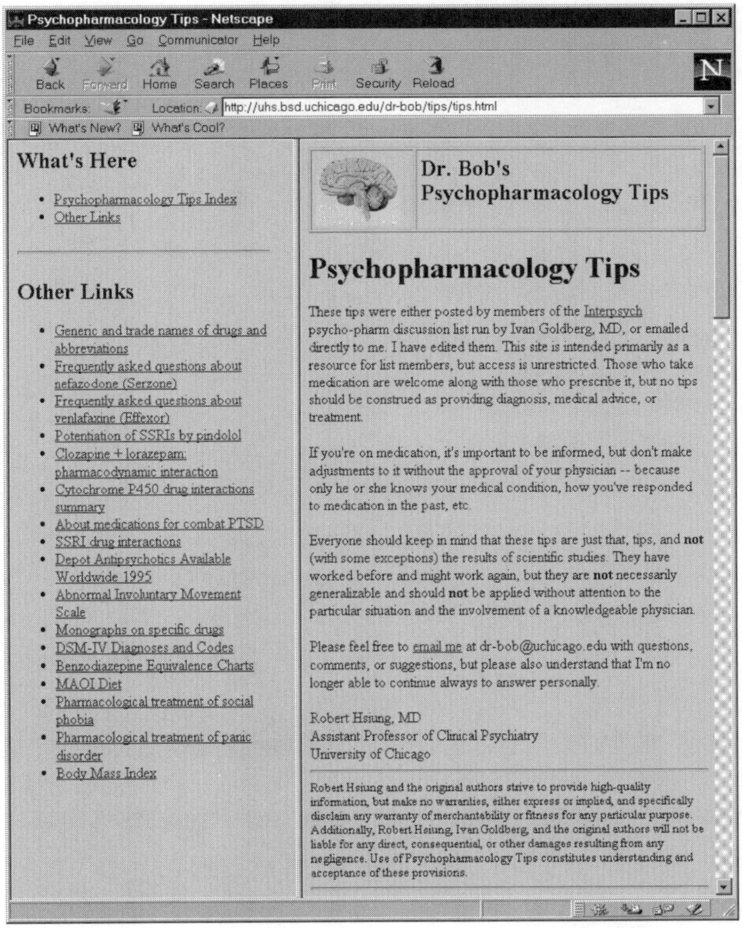

Psychopharmacology Tips - Netscape
File Edit View Go Communicator Help
Back Forward Home Search Places Print Security Reload
Bookmarks: Location: http://uhs.bsd.uchicago.edu/dr-bob/tips/tips.html
What's New? What's Cool?
What's Here
Psychopharmacology Tips Index
Other Links
Other Links
Generic and trade names of drugs and abbreviations
Frequently asked questions about nefazodone (Serzone)
Frequently asked questions about venlafaxine (Effexor)
Potentiation of SSRIs by pindolol
Clozapine + lorazepam: pharmacodynamic interaction
Cytochrome P450 drug interactions summary
About medications for combat PTSD
SSRI drug interactions
Depot Antipsychotics Available Worldwide 1995
Abnormal Involuntary Movement Scale
Monographs on specific drugs
DSM-IV Diagnoses and Codes
Benzodiazepine Equivalence Charts
MAOI Diet
Pharmacological treatment of social phobia
Pharmacological treatment of panic disorder
Body Mass Index
Dr. Bob's Psychopharmacology Tips
Psychopharmacology Tips
These tips were either posted by members of the Interpsych psycho-pharm discussion list run by Ivan Goldberg, MD, or emailed directly to me. I have edited them. This site is intended primarily as a resource for list members, but access is unrestricted. Those who take medication are welcome along with those who prescribe it, but no tips should be construed as providing diagnosis, medical advice, or treatment.
If you're on medication, it's important to be informed, but don't make adjustments to it without the approval of your physician -- because only he or she knows your medical condition, how you've responded to medication in the past, etc.
Everyone should keep in mind that these tips are just that, tips, and not (with some exceptions) the results of scientific studies. They have worked before and might work again, but they are not necessarily generalizable and should not be applied without attention to the particular situation and the involvement of a knowledgeable physician.
Please feel free to email me at dr-bob@uchicago.edu with questions, comments, or suggestions, but please also understand that I'm no longer able to continue always to answer personally.
Robert Hsiung, MD
Assistant Professor of Clinical Psychiatry
University of Chicago
Robert Hsiung and the original authors strive to provide high-quality information, but make no warranties, either express or implied, and specifically disclaim any warranty of merchantability or fitness for any particular purpose. Additionally, Robert Hsiung, Ivan Goldberg, and the original authors will not be liable for any direct, consequential, or other damages resulting from any negligence. Use of Psychopharmacology Tips constitutes understanding and acceptance of these provisions.

Figure 2.5 Navigation aids positioned in left panel.

Frankly, frames haven't been too popular among Web authors, and with good reason: In version 2.0, clicking Back propelled you backward, completely out of the site. Version 3 fixed this problem by restricting the effect of the Back and Forward buttons to the selected frames. This works very nicely, as you'll see. Display a frame document and then navigate around within one of the panels. Then click Back until you've gone back to the first

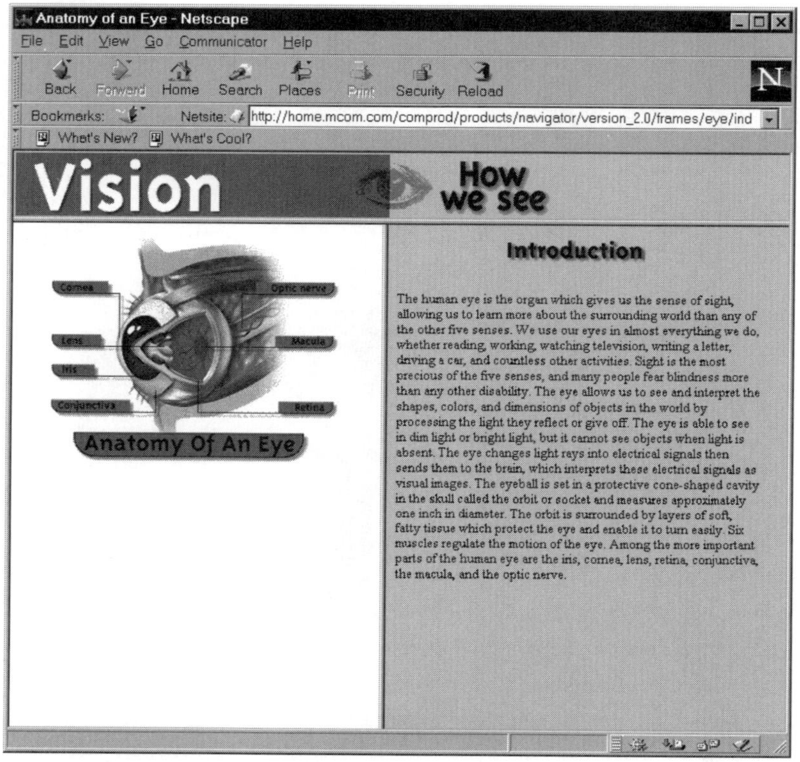
Anatomy of an Eye - Netscape
File Edit View Go Communicator Help
Back Forward Home Search Places Print Security Reload
Bookmarks: Netsite: http://home.mcom.com/comprod/products/navigator/version_2.0/frames/eye/ind
What's New? What's Cool?
Vision
How we see
Cornea
Optic nerve
Lens
Macula
Iris
Conjunctiva
Retina
Anatomy Of An Eye
Introduction
The human eye is the organ which gives us the sense of sight, allowing us to learn more about the surrounding world than any of the other five senses. We use our eyes in almost everything we do, whether reading, working, watching television, writing a letter, driving a car, and countless other activities. Sight is the most precious of the five senses, and many people fear blindness more than any other disability. The eye allows us to see and interpret the shapes, colors, and dimensions of objects in the world by processing the light they reflect or give off. The eye is able to see in dim light or bright light, but it cannot see objects when light is absent. The eye changes light rays into electrical signals then sends them to the brain, which interprets these electrical signals as visual images. The eyeball is set in a protective cone-shaped cavity in the skull called the orbit or socket and measures approximately one inch in diameter. The orbit is surrounded by layers of soft, fatty tissue which protect the eye and enable it to turn easily. Six muscles regulate the motion of the eye. Among the more important parts of the human eye are the iris, cornea, lens, retina, conjunctiva, the macula, and the optic nerve.

Figure 2.6 Frames used for computer-aided instruction.

document in that frame. If you click Back once more, you'll leave the site and see the previously displayed site.

JAVA!

Here's the latest and probably the neatest thing on the Web. Java is a new programming language that is being developed by Sun Microsystems. Based on the popular C++ language, widely used by professional programmers,

Java enables professional programmers to prepare mini-programs called *Java applets*. New HTML tags enable Web developers to embed Java applets into Web pages—when you access such a page, things happen!

On pages containing Java applets, you'll see action where there was once nothing but static text and graphics—for example, words will whirl, blink, and fade. One of the coolest demonstration sites shows a simulated stock ticker tape, which scrolls past the screen at an impressive clip.While it does, three charts track your favorite stocks' price movements throughout the day. Most exciting, though, is a whole range of planned Web applications that will enable you to interact with a Web page and see the results immediately.

Netscape version 4 can run Java applets, and does so automatically. You don't need to do anything special, or learn any new commands. You'll just notice that the pages you download have added functionality.

This Java applet is taking forever to load! Some Java applets require downloading graphics and sounds in addition to the Java code, and this might require a minute or two. Be patient—chances are that the wait will be worth it!

While we're on the subject of Java, you should also know about JavaScript. JavaScript is an easier version of Java that's designed for nonprogrammers. Like Java applets, JavaScript programs execute without your needing to do anything. They produce animations and enhance interactivity.

Are Java and JavaScript secure? There's still some debate about this. Some people think that computer hackers could write rogue Java applets or JavaScript programs that could damage data on your computer. If you'd prefer to be on the safe side, you can disable them. From the Edit menu, choose Preferences. Click Advanced. In the Advanced panel, make sure there's no check mark next to Enable Java and Enable JavaScript. Click OK to confirm. If you visit a page that has Java or JavaScript and you think it's trustworthy, you can turn these options on by following these steps again and selecting these two options. Click Reload to reload the page—and this time you'll get the Java or JavaScript.

Stop That!

Did you just start downloading a huge page, and regret that you clicked on the hyperlink? You can stop the download: Just click the Stop button.

New for 4 After you click Stop, or after a document stops downloading, the Stop button changes to Reload.

Play It Again, Sam

Sometimes you may wish to reload a document. Here are two occasions:

- You clicked Stop, but then decided you wanted to see the whole document. Click Reload to do this.

- You clicked a link before the document had fully downloaded, went off somewhere, and then returned. The document isn't complete, because Netscape stopped downloading it when you zoomed off. Click Reload to get the whole document.

Typing a Web Address Directly

You've picked up your copy of *Netguide*, and you've read about this seriously cool Web site. The only problem is, there's no hyperlink to this site on Netscape's default home page. How do you get there? You can type the Web address directly and go straight to the site, as this section explains.

Understanding Web Addresses

A Web address (URL) has three parts:

- **Protocol Name** This is the first part of the URL. It specifies the type of Internet communication standard (protocol) that's used to obtain this document. Web documents use the HTTP (World Wide Web) protocol, so you'll see *http://* at the beginning of Web addresses. You may also encounter *gopher://, ftp://,* and other protocol names.

- **Internet Address** In the second part of the URL, you see the Internet *domain name* of the computer that stores the resource you're accessing. The parts of the domain name are separated by dots, as in *www.yahoo.com.*
- **File Location** The third part of a URL specifies the location of the resource within the file system of the computer you're accessing. You may see one or more subdirectory (folder) names in this section. The final component of the URL is the file name of the resource you're accessing. If it's a Web document, the file will end in *.htm or *.html.

A URL looks like this:

http://dmf.culture.fr/files/imaginary_exhibition.html

You don't have to type the "http://" part of a Web address. To locate the above URL, you could type dmf.culture.fr/files/imaginary_exhibition.htm.

Using the Open Page Dialog Box

To access a Web address by typing it directly, follow these steps:

1. From the File menu, choose Open Page, or use the Ctrl + O keyboard shortcut.
2. In the Open Page dialog box (Figure 2.7), carefully type the URL. Be sure to copy the URL exactly, including the exact pattern of capitalization. Don't include any spaces.
3. Click Browser, if necessary, to open the file in the browser. (The other option opens the file in Composer.)
4. Click Open.

I typed the URL, but it didn't work! Whoops. Well, there are several possible reasons. Here's a rundown:

- **You may have typed the URL wrong.** Even a little tiny mistake, like putting a period at the end of the

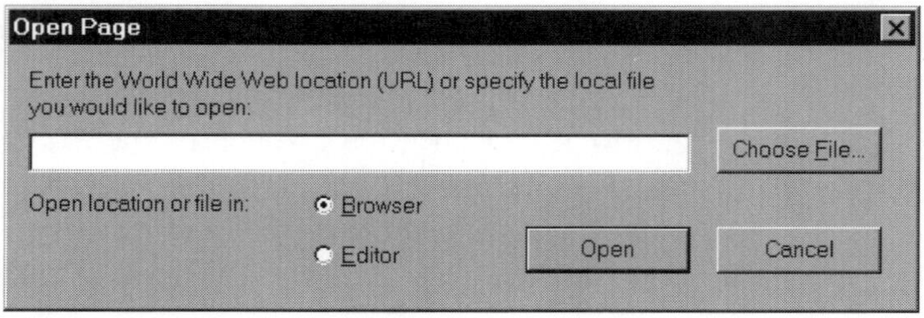

Figure 2.7 You can open a page with this dialog box, but it's easier to just type a URL in a Address box.

URL or adding a space, can mess things up. Remember, too, that URLs are case-sensitive (uppercase and lowercase letters are different). If you find a mistake, just edit and correct it within the Location box, and press Enter to try again.

- **The author or site administrator may have pulled the plug on this site.** That wasn't very nice, was it? But it happens. Incidentally, some of the URLs in this book may have gone bye-bye in the interval between my writing and your reading—if you run into any of these, let me know (bp@virginia.edu).
- **Too many people are trying to access the site.** Netscape is trying, trying, trying to access the site; the comets keep shooting, but nothing appears . . . minutes go by, fruitlessly. Give up, and click Stop. Try again later—like 2 A.M. So many people are surfing the Web that it's sometimes hard to get through to popular sites during prime daytime hours (10 A.M. to 4 P.M.).

Typing the URL in the Location Box

Here's a faster way to type the URL:

1. Click within the Location box. Netscape selects the current Web address.
2. Just start typing the new URL. The name of the Location box changes to Go to.
3. Press Enter when you're done typing the URL.

You can sometimes tell a lot about a Web resource by looking at its URL. For example, the URL on page 35 tells me that the document is located in a computer in France (the "fr" part of the domain name is a code name for France). I'll bet that the document is stored on a UNIX machine, too, since UNIX computers can handle long file names ("imaginary_exhibition.html"). A short file name with the *.htm extension is a dead giveaway that the computer is a Windows 3.1 system. Some more tips: In domain names, "edu" indicates a college or university, while "com" indicates a private company, "org" indicates a nonprofit organization, and "gov" indicates a government office of some kind.

Don't retype a URL if you want to revisit a site that you previously accessed by typing the URL directly—Netscape remembers the last ten URLs that you directly typed in the Location box. To choose one of them, click the down arrow at the right edge of the Location box.

How I Got Here, I Haven't a Clue (Go Home)

If you're really lost, you'll know it: hyperdisorientation sets in. (Hyperdisorientation is a well-documented malady of cyberspace, a recently discovered syndrome with distressing symptoms: Patients do not know how they got to where they are, haven't the foggiest idea how to retrace their steps, and babble incessantly about lost URLs.) Netscape provides a quick cure: Click the Home button. You'll see the Netscape welcome page again.

SOUND OFF!

Netscape can't do everything by itself, although it does a great job of displaying GIF and JPEG graphics. Sounds, movies, and animations are dinosaurs of a different color, though—the program needs helper applications, programs that start when they're needed in order to play a movie or sound.

Netscape comes with LiveAudio, a sound plug-in that's already installed automatically and ready to go, so let's give it a whirl. How about a selection from Neil Young's *Sleeps with Angels*? To access the *Sleeps with Angels* page, type the following URL directly:

http://www.iuma.com/Warner/html/Young,_Neil.html

By the way, note the comma and underline after "Young"—you need to type this URL exactly. (If this page isn't available, access IUMA's home page at www.iuma.com, and listen to something else.)

This is legit, incidentally; it's a 30-second excerpt from "Change Your Mind," one of the cuts from the album, and it's offered by Warner Brothers—for promotional purposes, obviously.

To hear the mono version of "Change Your Mind," click the Sun-AU (271K) option. (The other option, an 800K-plus stereo MPEG file, requires a custom sound player.) Netscape downloads the sound (this takes a while), and then displays the LiveAudio plug-in (Figure 2.8). You'll see VCR-like controls; just click the Play control to start the sound.

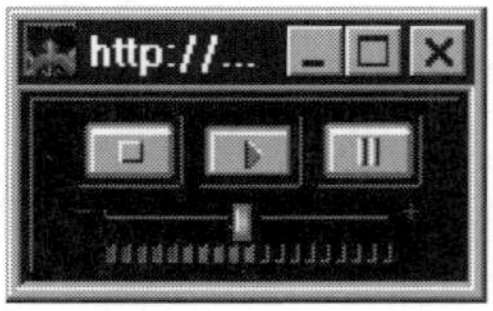

Figure 2.8 Netscape can play sounds—try it!

It won't play through my PC's little speaker! To hear the sound, your system must be equipped with a sound card and speakers.

When you're finished listening to the sound, you can "rewind" it and play it again, or just quit by clicking the LiveAudio close box.

I Want to See You Again, or, Setting Bookmarks

You've found a cool Web site, haven't you? And you want to know how to get back without having to click for six months, or type the URL, don't you? That's why Netscape lets you set bookmarks.

A bookmark is a URL that you've saved to a special list of ultra-cool Web sites, a list you have constructed yourself. Whenever you run across a Web site you like, just set a bookmark, as explained here.

To set a bookmark:

1. Display the Web page that you want to mark.
2. On the Bookmarks toolbar click the Bookmark QuickFile button.
3. Choose Add Bookmark from the pop-up menu.

Netscape adds the name of the document you're displaying to the Bookmarks QuickFile menu. To visit this document again, click Bookmark QuickFile and choose the document's name.

I've added too many documents to my Bookmarks QuickFile menu! This happens pretty fast, you'll find. Once you've added one or two dozen documents to your Bookmarks QuickFile menu, it isn't very much fun to use anymore. Time to get organized! Netscape provides a cool way to create submenus, so that you can pack dozens and dozens of bookmarks in this menu without creating something overwhelming to the eye. Flip to Chapter 8 for the lowdown on organizing your Bookmarks menu.

I Want This One on My Personal Toolbar!

You found something that's *really* cool? Something you'll access over and over, almost every time you use Netscape? Perhaps it's a candidate for adding to your Personal toolbar. It's easy! Just follow these steps.

To add a Web page to your Personal toolbar:

1. Display the page you want to add.
2. On the Location toolbar, click the Bookmarks QuickFile icon.
3. Choose File Bookmark from the pop-up menu.
4. Choose Toolbar Folder from the pop-up menu.

That's all you have to do! The item appears on your toolbar. (If you would like to delete a Personal toolbar item, flip to Chapter 8.)

Excuse Me, Where's the Subject Catalog? (Subject Trees and Search Engines)

Let's start with the bad news. It's really difficult to find information on the Web. Here's why. You've probably heard that the Internet is an experiment in controlled anarchy—there's no central headquarters of Internet, Inc. You don't have to get anyone's permission to hook up your computer or network to the Internet. So the Internet just grows and grows, hooking up an estimated 35 million people so far.

Because the Web uses the Internet for its communication base, the Web's just as gloriously disorganized—you don't have to ask anyone's permission to put documents on the Web. There's no single, central repository of records concerning Web documents.

With some 8 million Web documents now in existence (make that 12 million by the time you read this), we're talking about an information retrieval nightmare. There's stuff on the Web concerning the chardonnays of Western

Australia, the role of community networks in improving health care delivery, or the history of punk rock in the funkier districts of London—but good luck finding it, unless you're lucky enough to stumble on a trailblazer document that summarizes all the relevant links. (A trailblazer document, discussed in Chapter 15, stems from some charitable individual's attempts to sum up a number of interesting links, often on a single subject area such as gardening.)

Although there's no official, central database of Web documents, lots of clever computer people have been trying to solve the information-retrieval problem. They've taken two approaches, called *subject trees* and *search engines*.

- **Subject trees** A subject tree is a subject-oriented catalog of URLs, organized by topic (such as "Astrology," "Astronomy," "Astrophysics," etc.). The *tree* part of the name comes from the catalog's hierarchical organization; under "music," for instance, you find branches of the tree, such as classical music, folk music, and techno-rave music. No subject tree is complete; it is a really big pain to keep one of these things updated. Most of the work is done by civic-minded volunteers, who have only so much time for such things. Out of some 2 million Web documents, for example, Yahoo—one of the best subject trees—indexes only about 32,000. On the bright side, though, Yahoo contains 32,000 *good* URLs. There's a lot of junk out there, but it doesn't pass the subject tree's screening mechanisms.
- **Search engine** A search engine provides keyword searching of a database that has been compiled by a spider or worm (a program that automatically "crawls" the Web, finding Web documents and recording information about them). A search engine enables you to type in one or more search words (such as "Neil" and "Young"). The search engine then tries to match these search terms against a database of URL names and topics. Search engines and spiders are helpful tools, but bear in mind that they retrieve the chaff as well as the wheat: A search for CDs, for instance, will retrieve Kenny Z's useless list of his CD collection along with some online compact disc vendors and an unbelievable assortment of other stuff.

Chapter 4 fully explores both types of search tools. For now, try a quick search.

Doing a Quick Search

New for 4

Looking for something? Try this. Click the Location box, and select the whole URL, if necessary. Then type some words that describe the subject you're looking for, and press Enter.

Try typing five or six words that describe your interests. The more specific you are, the better. For example, suppose you're interested in spending some time exploring the Chesapeake Bay, and you'd like to stay in bed-and-breakfasts—particularly romantic inns. Try typing "Chesapeake Bay bed breakfast romantic inn," and see what you get.

What will you see after you press Enter? I'm not sure, and here's why. Using this feature is sort of a gamble; you can't be sure which search engine or subject catalog is going to get your search terms. You get a different one every time, until you finally come to the end of the circle. Currently, the search services include Yahoo, Magellan, Lycos, Excite, and InfoSeek. Figure 2.9 shows what comes up with Lycos.

Search didn't work out? Try it again—you'll get a different search service, and maybe it will do a better job.

When you get the search results, scroll down the page and examine what's been retrieved. If the search didn't go very well, don't get discouraged—it's par for the course. You'll need to learn some tricks to search effectively. Then again, you might find something useful on the first page or two—if so, you're in luck. To go to a page that looks interesting, just click its title.

To really get the most out of the Web, you need to master more advanced searching skills. This "quick and dirty search" sometimes comes up with a useful page or two, but advanced searching skills enable you to pinpoint the information you're looking for. Flip to Chapter 4 for more information.

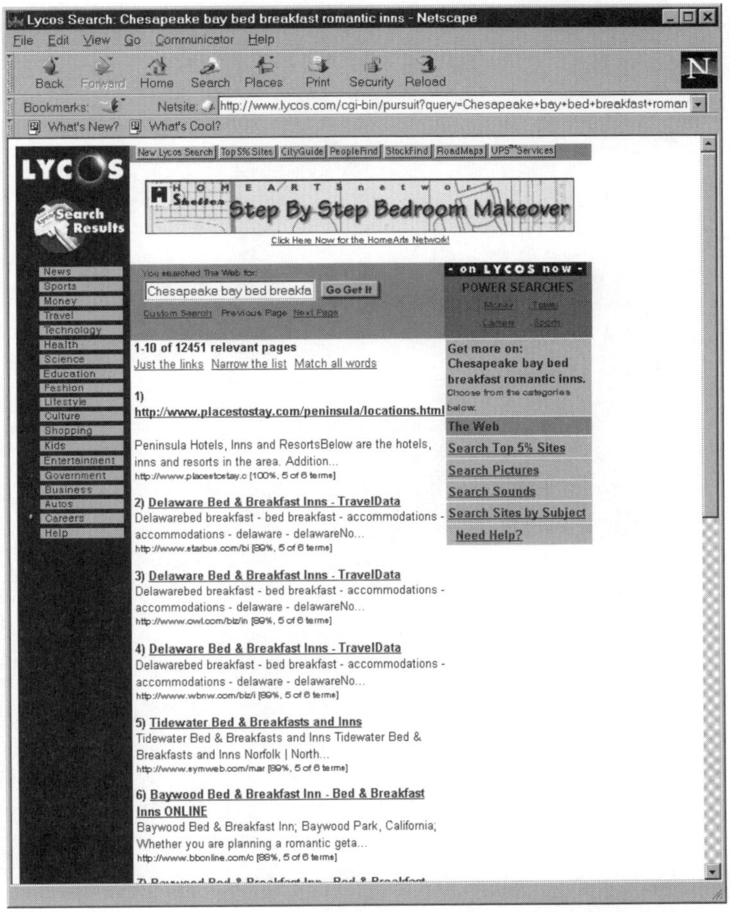

Figure 2.9 A quick Location box search may give you good results.

From Here

- Change the default start page. To do so, flip to Chapter 6.
- Run into some trouble navigating the Web? Check out Chapter 5.

- Deal with an unwieldy Bookmarks menu in Chapter 8—or better yet, install SmartMarks or Smart Bookmarks and learn how to use these much-improved bookmark organizers (Chapter 7).
- Learn how to save and print the documents you display on the Web (Chapter 9).

Chapter 3

Exploring the Web

It's a big Web out there, with several hundred million documents. One thing's for certain: You're going to need help finding information. Surfing alone won't do it.

Fortunately, there are plenty of people who are trying to help. In this chapter and the next, you'll learn how to make full use of Web documents that people have created in an attempt to help you find your way. I call these *trailblazer pages*. They don't attempt to be complete, up-to-date, or even 100 percent accurate—those URLs come and go—but they can be invaluable. Chapter 4, on subject trees and search engines, covers Web information resources that *do* try to be comprehensive. But for now, you're looking for good places to launch your exploration of the Web, and this chapter points the way to some very useful resources.

For the Time-Challenged

- Trailblazer pages point the way toward Web information resources.
- Use starting points pages to begin your exploration of the Web.
- Locate metapages in your areas of interest.
- Check out "Best of the Web" pages to see what's cool.
- Use "What's New" pages to keep up with new Web developments.

Please note that some of the URLs mentioned in this chapter may have joined the dead byte heap of history by the time you read this. Still, I've chosen most of these documents because they appear to be more or less stable, so most of them should be up and running when you read this book.

Introducing Trailblazer Pages

Pioneers, explorers, adventurers, helpful souls—whatever you want to call them, they're the saints of the hour. Often on a purely voluntary basis, they've gathered the best of the Web (and sometimes the weirdest of the Web) into collections of hyperlinks. I divide this fast-evolving class of documents into the following categories:

Starting Points These are Web documents that are intended to help neophytes get started with the World Wide Web. Some are created and maintained by organizations, but the better ones are voluntary efforts by individuals.

Metapages These pages attempt to summarize all the links in a particular subject area. If you can find one in your area of interest, you will find it very helpful.

Most Popular Links What everyone is accessing, largely because people read pages like this to find out what everyone is accessing.

Best of the Web What some people (or more likely, one person) think the best sites are—a cyberspace Top Ten.

Cool Links I'm not sure what the difference between "Best" and "Cool" is, but see for yourself by checking out these pages. Be prepared to waste at least five hours.

Worst of the Web A relatively new and praiseworthy development, these pages list sites singled out for wasting Internet bandwidth with unnecessary junk (such as a list of some guy's T-shirts).

Weird Links Compilations of links to the Web underground. Forget sex, incidentally; there are too many dateless geeks out there looking for sex sites. When one appears, it gets inundated with several million accesses per day, which overloads the server and brings the computer to a halt. The service provider screams bloody murder, and the site gets shut down. A *Sports Illustrated* swimsuit site made a brief appearance, but after getting 7.2 million accesses in the space of 48 hours, it was withdrawn.

What's New These resources try to keep track of the deluge of new Web documents.

Starting Points Pages

Starting points pages stem from the ancient past (maybe two years ago) when the Web was completely unfamiliar to people. They provide a good point of entry for people accessing the Web for the first time.

The Starting Point

A very good place to start your exploration of the Web is The Starting Point (www.stpt.com), shown in Figure 3.1. This site isn't loaded with links—but that's the good thing about it. There's a nice selection of links in areas sure to appeal to you. Spend some time here; you'll get a good overview of some of the better material that's available on the Web.

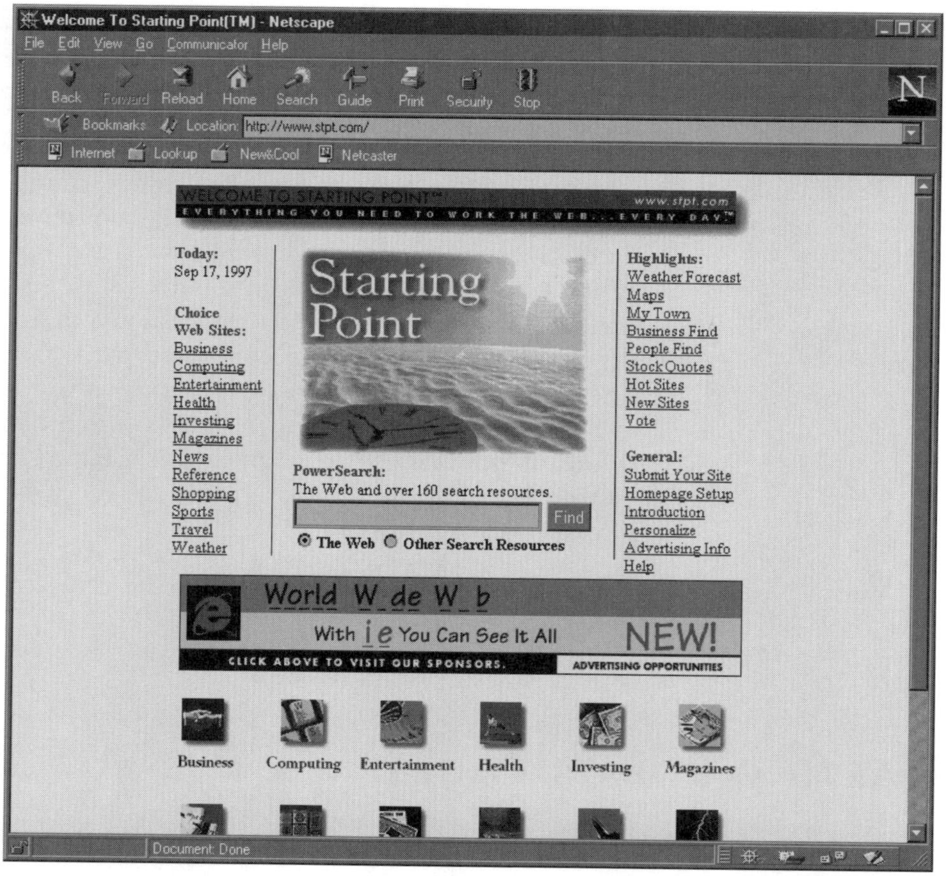

Figure 3.1 The Starting Point is—you guessed it, a great place to start surfing.

Netscape's Internet Guide

To access one of the best starting points on the Net, just click the Guide button, and choose Internet. You'll see the Destinations page, shown in Figure 3.2. There's lots of cool stuff, including today's news and links drawn from a variety of topical areas. Note that these pages are intended to showcase Netscape technology, so there's a bit of a bias. Still, it's a great site.

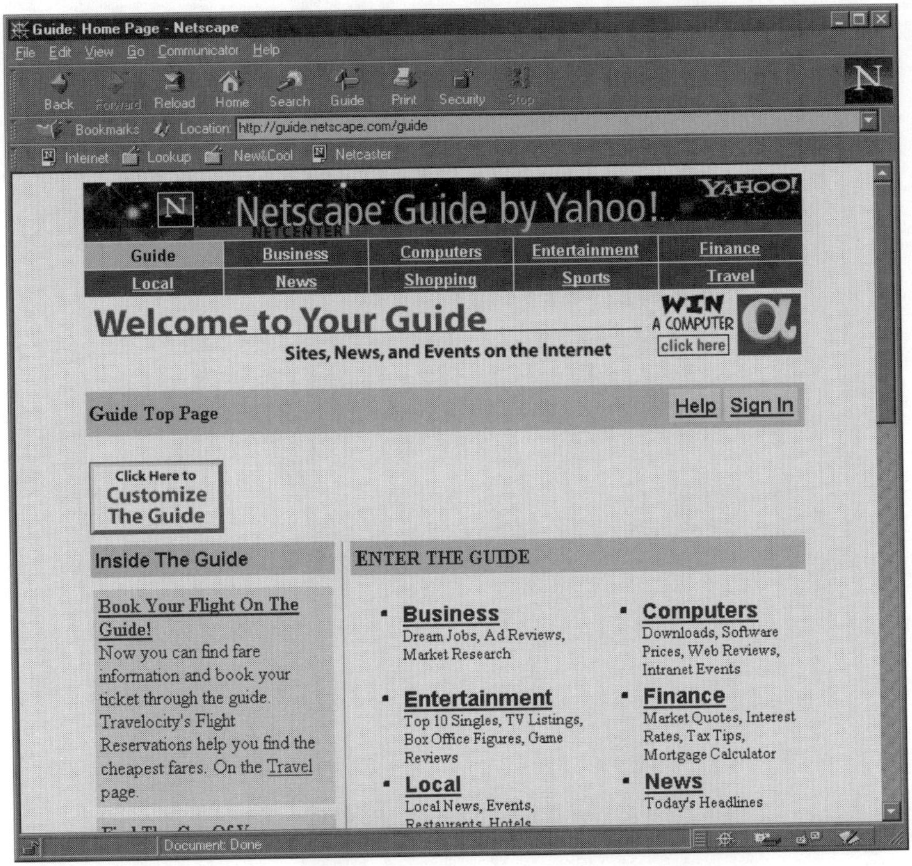

Figure 3.2 Netscape's Guide page has links to high-quality sites that show off Netscape's technology.

Excite Reviews

Excite not only offers one of the Web's better search engines, but also offers reviews of Web sites—more than 60,000 of them—in a variety of topical areas (http://www.excite.com/Reviews/; see Figure 3.3). On the title page, WebWatch offers pointers to some of the most interesting pages around. This makes it a good starting point. The Reviews menu is on the left.

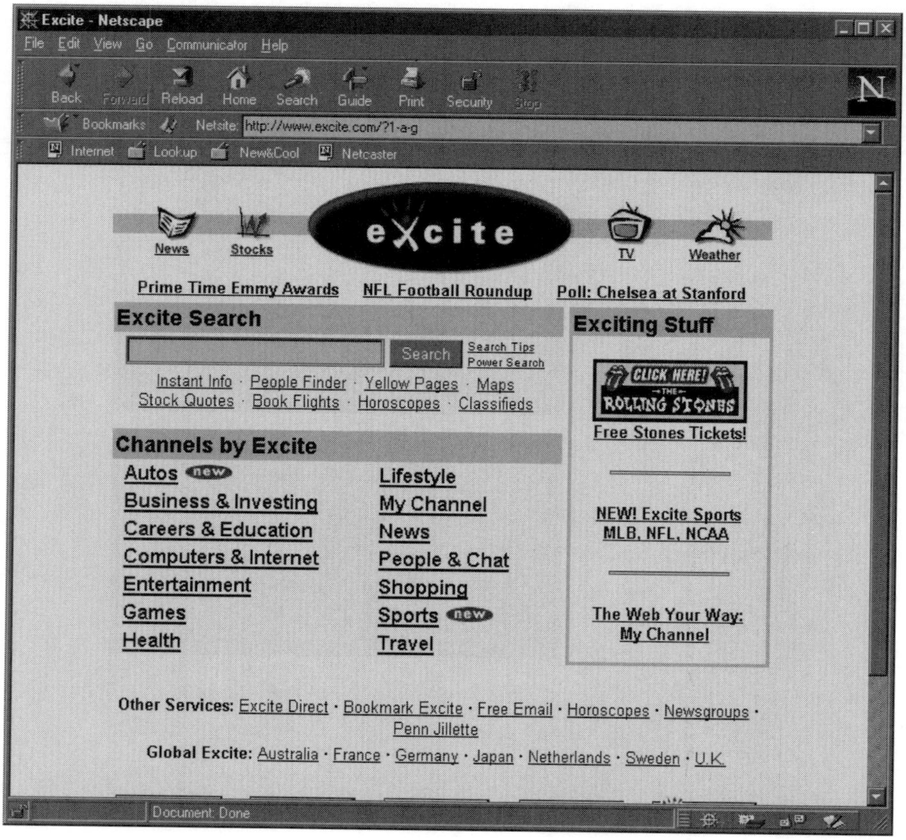

Figure 3.3 Excite offers rated reviews of 60,000 Web sites.

Lycos Sites by Subject (a2z)

Another search engine, Lycos, offers a starting point (http://a2z.lycos.com) that you'll want to visit (Figure 3.4). Called a2z, this service offers a subject guide to hundreds of popular pages in a variety of subjects. The reviews aren't as critical or helpful as Excite's, however.

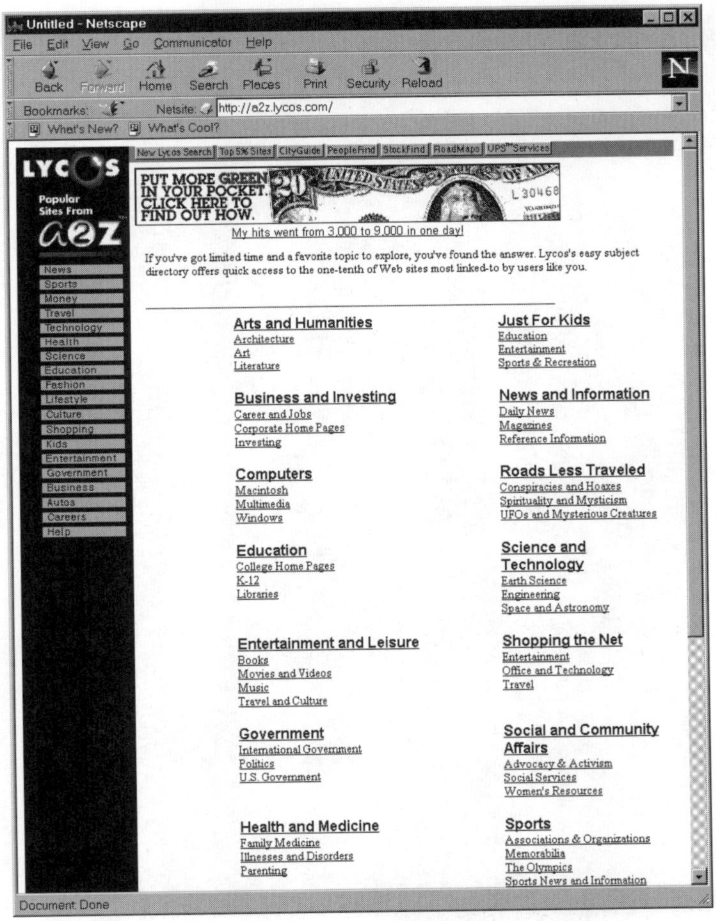

Figure 3.4 Lycos a2z home page starts you off with hundreds of popular sites.

DisInformation

You've probably heard that the Web is loaded with propaganda, paranoia, conspiracy theories, UFO sightings, catastrophe scenarios, and other forms of craziness. Thanks to DisInformation (http://www.disinfo.com), there's now a starting point for the disturbed side of the Web (Figure 3.5). This site is critical of the irrationality it indexes, so it's a learning experience as well as a useful subject guide.

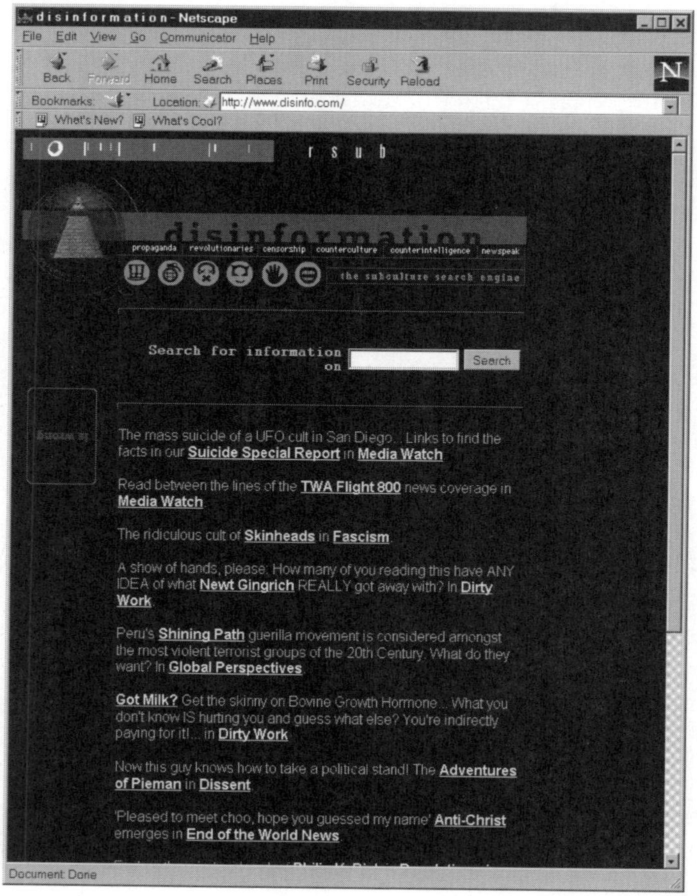
disinformation - Netscape
File Edit View Go Communicator Help
Back Forward Home Search Places Print Security Reload
Bookmarks Location: http://www.disinfo.com/
What's New? What's Cool?
propaganda revolutionaries censorship counterculture counterintelligence newspeak
the subculture search engine
Search for information on
Search
The mass suicide of a UFO cult in San Diego... Links to find the facts in our Suicide Special Report in Media Watch.
Read between the lines of the TWA Flight 800 news coverage in Media Watch.
The ridiculous cult of Skinheads in Fascism.
A show of hands, please: How many of you reading this have ANY IDEA of what Newt Gingrich REALLY got away with? In Dirty Work.
Peru's Shining Path guerilla movement is considered amongst the most violent terrorist groups of the 20th Century. What do they want? In Global Perspectives.
Got Milk? Get the skinny on Bovine Growth Hormone... What you don't know IS hurting you and guess what else? You're indirectly paying for it!... in Dirty Work.
Now this guy knows how to take a political stand! The Adventures of Pieman in Dissent.
'Pleased to meet choo, hope you guessed my name' Anti-Christ emerges in End of the World News.
Document: Done

Figure 3.5 DisInformation indexes the zany side of the Web.

TVGuide

Here's a great starting points page for anyone interested in entertainment: It's called iGuide (http://www.tvguide.com; Figure 3.6). You'll find links to the online version of *TV Guide*; reviews of books, films, and recent CDs; and a search engine for entertainment-related areas. A cool feature: Search for TV shows on subjects you like.

Figure 3.6 iGuide.

Let's Get Academic

Looking for some serious information, at the college level or higher? There's no better place to start than Argus Clearinghouse (www.clearinghouse.net). You'll see the welcome page shown in Figure 3.7. Listed are general subject categories; go in a little further and you'll find many more.

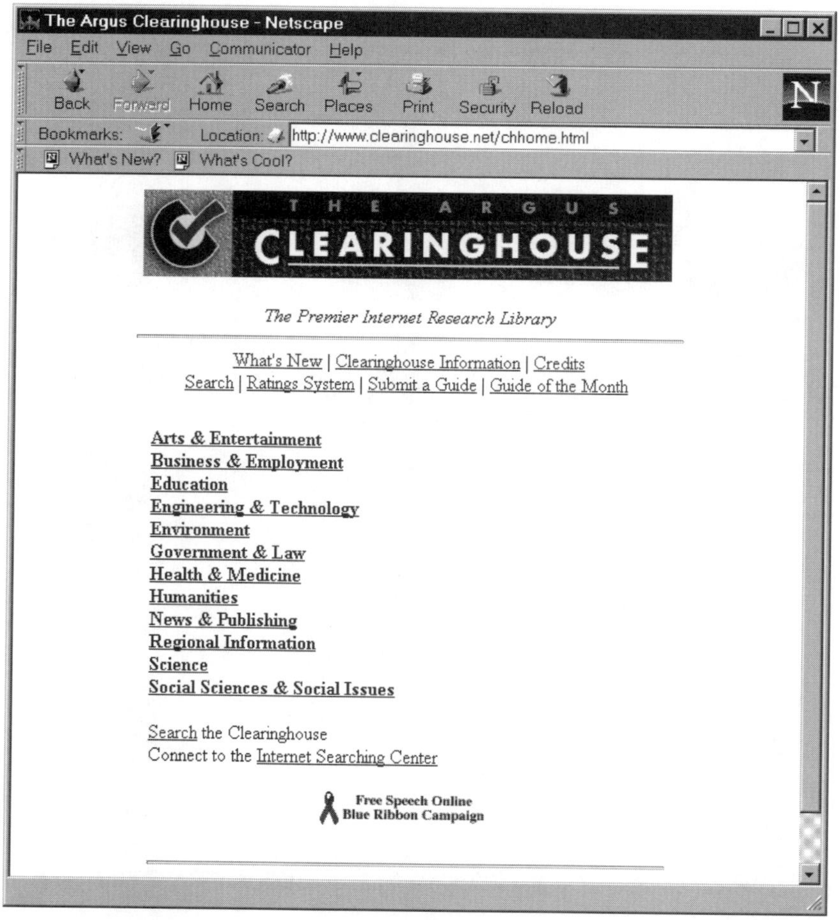

Figure 3.7 Argus Clearinghouse's general subjects.

Each page in the Clearinghouse is maintained by a subject specialist. Just to pick one at random, here's a really nice one on archaeology (Figure 3.8)—an amazing amount of stuff.

Like the Clearinghouse? A similar service—with some overlap with the Clearinghouse's coverage—is provided by the WWW Virtual Library (www.w3org/pub/DataSources/bySubject/Overview.html).

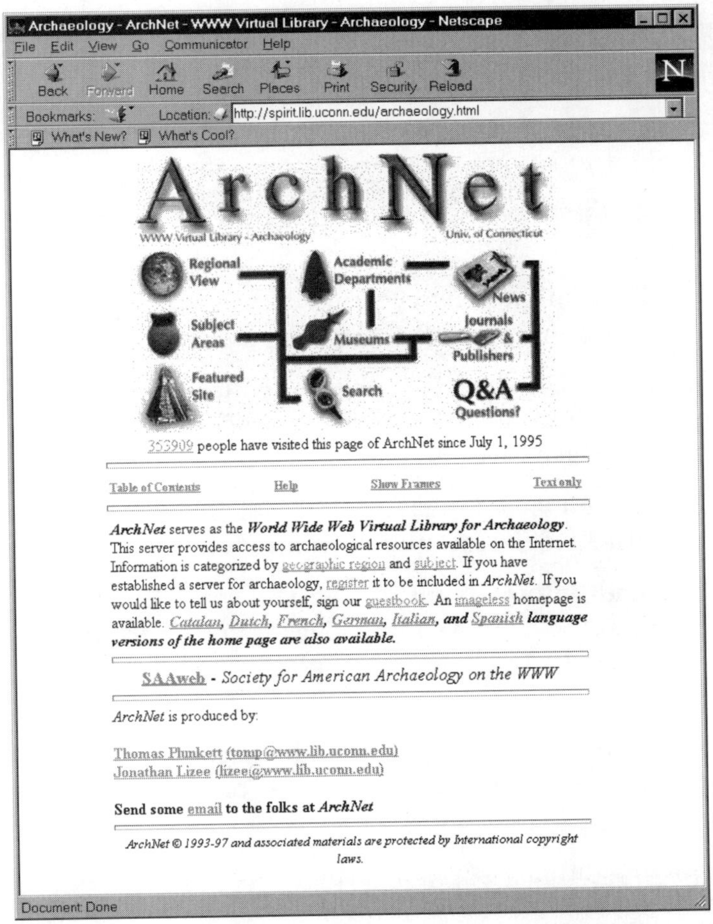
Archaeology - ArchNet - WWW Virtual Library - Archaeology - Netscape
File Edit View Go Communicator Help
Back Forward Home Search Places Print Security Reload
Bookmarks: Location: http://spirit.lib.uconn.edu/archaeology.html
What's New? What's Cool?
ArchNet
WWW Virtual Library - Archaeology
Univ. of Connecticut
Regional View
Academic Departments
News
Subject Areas
Museums
Journals & Publishers
Featured Site
Search
Q&A Questions?
353909 people have visited this page of ArchNet since July 1, 1995
Table of Contents
Help
Show Frames
Text only
ArchNet serves as the World Wide Web Virtual Library for Archaeology. This server provides access to archaeological resources available on the Internet. Information is categorized by geographic region and subject. If you have established a server for archaeology, register it to be included in ArchNet. If you would like to tell us about yourself, sign our guestbook. An imageless homepage is available. Catalan, Dutch, French, German, Italian, and Spanish language versions of the home page are also available.
SAAweb - Society for American Archaeology on the WWW
ArchNet is produced by:
Thomas Plunkett (tomp@www.lib.uconn.edu)
Jonathan Lizee (lizee@www.lib.uconn.edu)
Send some email to the folks at ArchNet
ArchNet © 1993-97 and associated materials are protected by International copyright laws.
Document: Done

Figure 3.8 A Clearinghouse-linked subject guide.

METAPAGES

Metapages seek to sum up all the hyperlinks pertaining to a particular subject. Put together by volunteers who have personal interests in the area, they are gold mines of information. The following list provides some examples of useful metapages. Unfortunately, there's no real index of them; nobody's even sure what to call them (some people call them "home pages," while others call them "pointers pages," and still others call them "indexes"). You can try to discover a metapage in your area of interest by using the search techniques introduced in the next chapter.

- **Backcountry Home Page** (http://io.datasys.swri.edu/Overview.html) Fishing, hiking, backpacking, climbing—and the "distilled wisdom" of the experts.
- **Chronic Fatigue Syndrome** (http://metro.turnpike.net/C/cfs-news/) Tons of information about this disabling disease.
- **FedWorld** (http://www.fedworld.gov/) A very impressive list of U.S. government Web resources.
- **Games Domain** (http://www.gamesdomain.co.uk/) Everything you would ever want to know about computer games.
- **Human Languages Page** (http://www.willamette.edu/~tjones/Language-Page.html) A treasure trove of information about human languages, past and present.
- **Legal Links on the Internet** (http://ssnet.com/~james5/business.html) Emphasizing federal law and litigation.
- **Rockhounds Information Page** (http://www.rahul.net/infodyn/rockhounds/rockhounds.html) Everything on the Internet pertaining to rock collecting, including links to rock shops and photos of cool rock formations.
- **Science Fiction Links** (http://www.abdn.ac.uk/~u01rpr/sci-fi.html) Tons of links to *Star Trek*, *Star Wars*, and science fiction sites.
- **CineMedia** (http://www.gu.edu.au/gwis/cinemedia/CineMedia.tv.html) Grand Central Station for TV and film-related hyperlinks on the Web.

- **The Froggy Page** (http://www.cs.yale.edu/HTML/YALE/CS/HyPlans/loosemore-sandra/froggy.html) An unbelievable assortment of frog-related items: pictures, songs, sounds, links to scientific studies, lists of famous frogs. Wow!
- **The Web as a Learning Tool** (http://www.cs.uidaho.edu/~connie/interests.html) A very nice effort to bring together Web resources for K–12 education.
- **Ultimate Band List** (http://american.recordings.com/wwwofmusic/) Links to all the rock bands—over 1,200 of them, from the 3D House of Beef and Cling to Trendy Wednesday and Weeping Tile—represented on the Web. There are some bands you've heard of here, too, somewhere.
- **Wine Home Page** (http://www.speakeasy.org/~winepage/wine.html) Dozens of links concerning wines, wineries, wine collecting, and wine accessories.
- **WWW Tennis Server** (http://www.cs.utoronto.ca/~cwong/tennis/tennis.html) Get the pun? Everything for the tennis fan, including ATP and WTA rankings, the code of tennis, and lots of tennis-related hyperlinks.

By far the best resource for subject-oriented metapages is the Virtual Library, a subject tree that is actually a compilation of volunteers' metapages. For more information on the Virtual Library, check out the next chapter.

What's Popular

Want to know what everyone else is doing with their Web browsers? Here's how to find out:

- **Most Popular Links at EINet Galaxy** (http://galaxy.einet.net/most-popular.html) EINet Galaxy is a subject tree/search engine hybrid. This page links the most popular sites directly accessed from Galaxy.

- **The WebCrawler Top 25** (http://webcrawler.com/WebCrawler/Top25.html) The top 25 most popular pages accessed by means of the WebCrawler search engine, discussed in Chapter 4.
- **WebCrawler Select Top 50** (http://www.webcrawler.com/select/top.new.html) The 50 most-accessed links in WebCrawler Select.
- **Yahoo What's Popular** (http://www.yahoo.com/popular.html) The most popular sites accessed from the Yahoo subject tree, also discussed in Chapter 4.

Best of the Web

What are the best sites available on the Web? Everyone has an opinion, but some have pages:

- **David Siegel's High Five** (http://www.highfive.com/) "The Carnegie Hall of Web Sites."
- **Best Webs of the World** (http://www.sct.fr/net/ubest.html) A French view, and a nice, succinct list.
- **Top 5% Sites** Lycos' rated list of Web pages worth a visit.

Cool Links

Frankly, I'm not sure what differentiates a "Best" site from a "Cool" site. You figure it out.

- **Cool Site of the Day** (http://cool.infi.net/) Glenn Davis selects a new site every day for this coveted distinction. You can browse a voluminous list of previous cool sites.
- **Yahoo Cool Links** (http://www.yahoo.com/Entertainment/COOL_links/) Definitely cool.

- **What's Hot and Cool on the Web** (http://kzsu.stanford.edu/uwi/reviews-l.html) A collection of cool sites, organized in a somewhat hard-to-figure-out table.

Don't forget Netscape's own What's Cool page. View it by clicking the Places button and choosing What's Cool.

Worst of the Web

It had to happen. With all those "Best of the Web" pages, somebody, somewhere, would have had to come up with this idea.

- **Useless Web Pages** (http://www.go2net.com/internet/useless/) This is actually one of the Web's best sites. With additions made on a daily basis, you'll find plenty of hysterically funny stuff here. Latest editions: A penis length chart, a dissertation on barbecue potato chips, and a shocking exposé of the lesbian Barbie doll scene.
- **Enhanced for Netscape Hall of Shame** (http://www.meat.com/netscape_hos.html) Too many blinks spoil the broth.

Weird Links

It's the fringe. The edge. And if you're looking for it, here are the starting points:

- **Anders' Weird Page** (http://www.nada.kth.se/~nv91-asa/weird.html) Discordiana, very substantial collection of links to the Church of the Subgenius, Geek-related mysteries, and more; you figure it out, you let me know, OK?
- **The Web's Edge** (http://kzsu.stanford.edu/uwi.html) This is apparently the leading edge of some kind of worldwide conspiracy.

What's New Pages

As if there weren't enough stuff on the Web to wade through, there are dozens—possibly hundreds—of new Web documents created daily. Here's how you can find out what's new:

- **Automatic News HREFs** (http://www.cs.cmu.edu/afs/cs.cmu.edu/user/bsy/www/auto_news/auto_news.0.html) URLs culled automatically from Usenet postings.

Click the Places button, and choose What's New, to see Netscape's list of new sites.

From Here

- Take advantage of subject trees and search engines to find information on the Web. Both subjects are covered in Chapter 4.
- Choose a start page that's more to your liking. Find out how in Chapter 6.
- Manage those Web documents—print 'em, save 'em, and cache 'em. Find out how (and what cache means) in Chapter 9.

Chapter

4

Find It on the Web!

Search Engines and Subject Trees

Looking for information on the Web? Let's start with the bad news. No single, up-to-date catalog of Web documents has ever been created. To do so would require a staff of hundreds of subject indexers working 'round the clock. Perhaps we'll see a Web Library someday, a service that would exhaustively catalog everything that's on the Web, but nothing like it exists right now.

Now here's the good news. To find information on the Web, you can make use of the following tools:

- **Subject trees** A subject tree is an alphabetically organized list of selected Web resources that is usually organized with major headings such as Arts and Humanities, Business, Economy, Government, and the like. Within each category are found subheadings, which in turn display pages listing specific hyperlinks. Because subject trees are manually updated, they cannot hope to cover all of the Web—these services aren't the Web Library, or anything close. But they are very useful because they are selective; they list only those documents that would likely prove useful to you.

- **Search engines** A search engine enables you to search a database of Web documents using keywords (such as "frogs" or "wine"). The search engine ransacks a database of Web documents. Where does this database come from? In most cases, the databases are created by Web-roaming programs called *spiders*. These programs seek out new URLs and add them to the database. Searching one of these search engines will very likely produce a lot of useless, junk URLs, but you may find some gold amidst the gravel.

This chapter shows you how to construct an effective Web search using Netscape Navigator, subject trees, and search engines. If it's out there, you'll know how to find it after reading this chapter. You should use the information in this chapter with that in Chapter 3, which discusses trailblazer pages, metapages, and other subject-specific Web resources.

The distinction between subject trees and search engines is starting to erode, as you'll discover. Infoseek, one of the most technologically interesting and advanced search engines, tries to link your search terms with subject tree headings, which are displayed in a frame on the left of the retrieval list. If your search didn't work out very well, you can find some high-quality documents under these headings, one or more of which might be relevant to your interests.

Understanding Search Techniques

In both subject trees and search engines, you can make use of keyword searches. In subject trees, you search the subject tree entries. In search engines, you search a huge database of URLs. In either case, you will find it helpful to understand a few basic concepts:

- **Choosing keywords** Try to think of one or more words that best describe the subject for which you're searching. The more general the term, the more likely it is that you'll find something useful.

For the Time-Challenged

- Subject trees try to classify Web documents according to subject. You can browse the subject tree. You can also search the subject headings and document titles. But bear in mind that subject trees classify only a small percentage of the total number of documents available on the Web.
- Search engines compile huge databases of Web documents, and you can search the databases using keywords. The trouble is, you'll retrieve a lot of junk amidst the useful documents.
- A good search strategy uses both subject trees and search engines. To make sure you've found all the useful documents in a given subject area, you should repeat your search in several subject trees and search engines.

- **Choosing portions of the document to search** Some of the search tools discussed in this chapter let you specify which part of the document to search. For example, Yahoo enables you to search the document title, the URL, and the document description. It searches all three by default. You can perform a more focused search by restricting the search to the document title. This will eliminate irrelevant documents that just happen to include the keyword in their descriptions.
- **Case sensitivity** Most of the search tools discussed in this chapter are case-insensitive, which means that they ignore the capitalization pattern you type. However, some offer the option of case-sensitive searching. If you choose this option, the search tool will match only those documents containing keywords with the capitalization pattern you typed (if you type "MRI," the software will match "MRI" but not "mri").
- **AND operator** Most of the search tools you use will use the Boolean AND operator by default. If you type more than one keyword, the software will not retrieve a document unless it contains all of the words you type. This is a very restrictive search and may not produce good results. However, it's a good approach when your initial search produces too many documents.
- **OR operator** Some search tools enable you to use the Boolean OR operator. If you type more than one keyword, the software will retrieve documents that contain any of the words you typed.

- **Phrase search** A few search tools let you specify that the software should match the keywords you type only if they occur in the precise order you typed them, with no other words in between. For example, if you type "Mesoamerican archaeology," the software will retrieve only those documents that contain these two words in this exact order, without any other words between them.
- **Substrings and whole-word searches** By default, most of the search tools discussed in this chapter search for substrings. A substring is a series of characters that might be embedded in a longer word. For example, if you search with the substring *very*, the software will retrieve documents that contain *every* as well as *very*. To restrict the search to whole words only (*very* only), you can sometimes choose a "whole word" or "complete word" option. If you choose this option, the search software will not retrieve documents in which the keyword appears as a substring.

If the search doesn't produce any results, click the Back button to redisplay the search page, and check your spelling! This is the most common cause of search errors. If the search retrieves too many documents, try using more specific keywords—and be sure to use the AND rather than the OR operator. To cut down on false drops, use whole-word searches instead of substring searches.

To access most of the Web's search services, including subject trees and subject engines, just click the Search button on the Toolbar. You'll see a panel of subject tree and search engine offerings. From this panel, you can choose (currently) Infoseek, Lycos, Magellan, Excite, or Yahoo. If you scroll down, you'll find links to the rest of the services discussed in this chapter (including AltaVista), and many more.

A Guide to the Web's Subject Trees

There are several excellent subject trees available on the World Wide Web. Each has its own plusses and minuses, as you'll see in the pages to follow. We'll survey the top three: Yahoo, the Virtual Library, and WebCrawler Select.

Yahoo

Yahoo—short for Yet Another Hierarchically Odiferous Oracle—is the work of David Filo and Jerry Yang, two Stanford University graduate students who abandoned their Ph.D. work to make their subject tree the centerpiece of a private company. It's the best place to start your quest for Web information.

To access Yahoo, just click the Net Search directory button and click the Yahoo hyperlink, or enter the URL (http://www.yahoo.com/) directly. You'll see the Yahoo page, shown in Figure 4.1. Listed are Yahoo's main subject classifications, followed by second-level headings in each category.

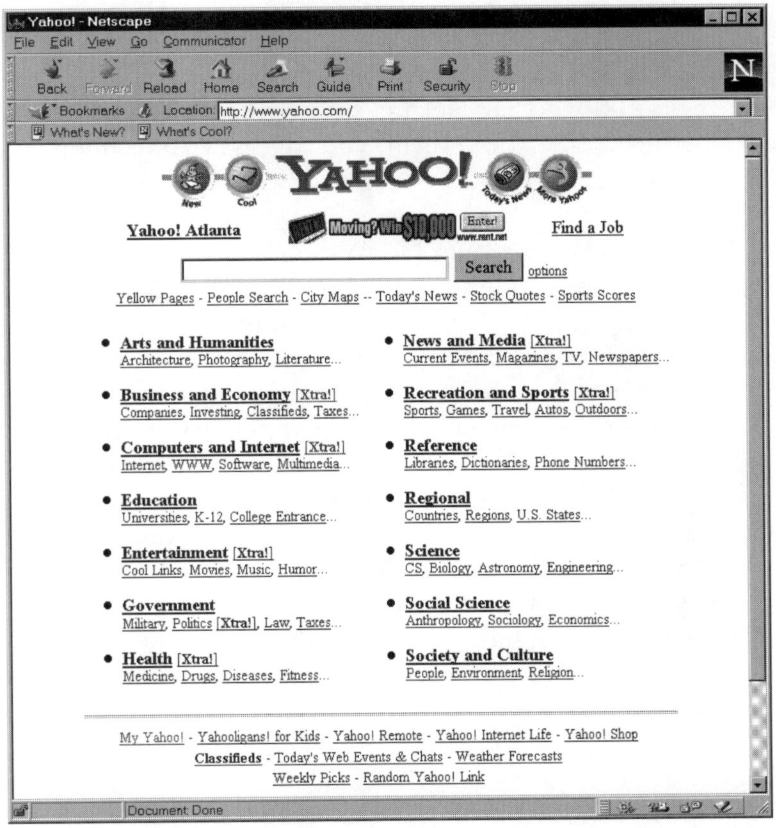

Figure 4.1 The main Yahoo page.

The word *Xtra!* next to a subject classification signals the existence of a page of hyperlinked headlines pertaining to that category.

What's up with all these academic sites becoming private companies? The Web started as an academic phenomenon—and then the general public caught on. It makes sense that the best academic resources break free of their academic incubators and make a go at it in the private sector, and that's what's happening. All the major academic search tools, including Lycos and WebCrawler, have "gone .com," and other resources are doing the same with regularity. It's part of the trend toward privatization on the Web.

Listing over 34,000 documents (at this writing), Yahoo offers a rich library of hyperlinks. To explore them, you can use two techniques, exploring the tree and searching.

Exploring the Tree The first way to use Yahoo is to navigate the subject tree by clicking on hyperlinks. To do so, just click on one of the subject classifications, such as "Entertainment." You'll see an additional page of second-level subject headings, such as the one shown in Figure 4.2. These headings are followed by the number of hyperlinks in each category in parentheses. The word "New" signals categories to which new hyperlinks have been added. If you keep clicking, you'll eventually reach a page that includes hyperlinks to Web documents. Unlike Yahoo's internal links, hyperlinks to Web documents aren't followed by a number, and many of them include descriptions (see Figure 4.3). To access a hyperlink to a Web document, just click it.

Look for hyperlinks that have a picture of a little pair of sunglasses next to them. These are the cool links—the ones that Yahoo recommends!

Yahoo's Toolbar, positioned near the top of the screen, provides handy navigational aids. Here's what the options do:

YAHOO! Displays Yahoo's opening (top-level) page.

Displays the What's New At Yahoo page—the most recently added links.

Takes you to The Cool Links page.

Brings up Yahoo's Reuters news feed.

Displays a page of more specific search engines, such as National and Metro Yahoos.

Searching for Information Another way to access the information in Yahoo is to perform a keyword search. To do so, go back to the Yahoo welcome page. You'll see a text box for entering keywords at the top of the page. That's a pretty basic search. If you need a more flexible search, click the Options

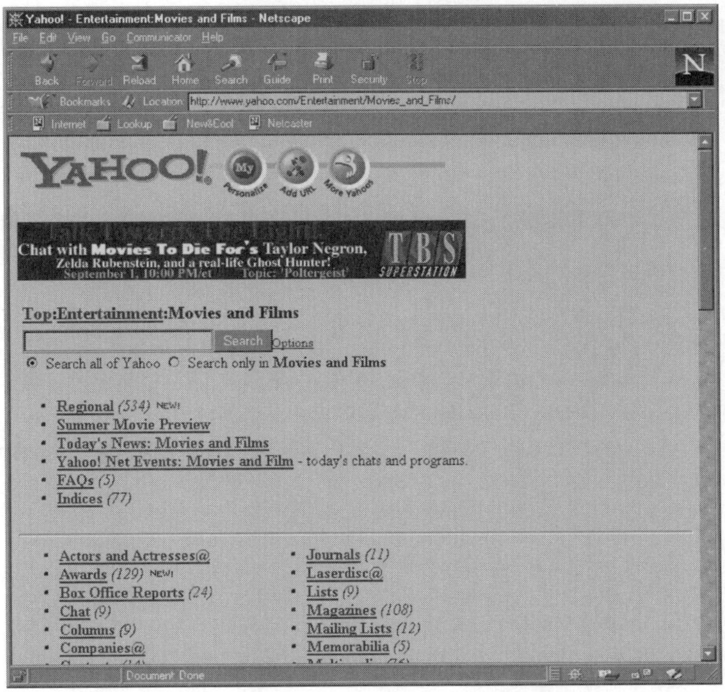

Figure 4.2 A page of second-level subject headings in Yahoo.

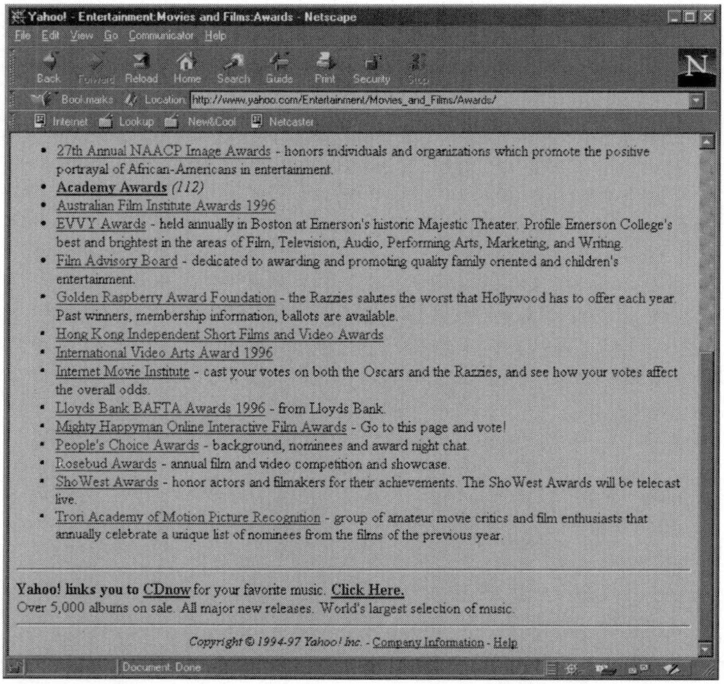
Yahoo! - Entertainment:Movies and Films:Awards - Netscape
File Edit View Go Communicator Help
Back Forward Reload Home Search Guide Print Security Stop
Bookmarks Location: http://www.yahoo.com/Entertainment/Movies_and_Films/Awards/
Internet Lookup New&Cool Netcaster
27th Annual NAACP Image Awards - honors individuals and organizations which promote the positive portrayal of African-Americans in entertainment.
Academy Awards (112)
Australian Film Institute Awards 1996
EVVY Awards - held annually in Boston at Emerson's historic Majestic Theater. Profile Emerson College's best and brightest in the areas of Film, Television, Audio, Performing Arts, Marketing, and Writing.
Film Advisory Board - dedicated to awarding and promoting quality family oriented and children's entertainment.
Golden Raspberry Award Foundation - the Razzies salutes the worst that Hollywood has to offer each year. Past winners, membership information, ballots are available.
Hong Kong Independent Short Films and Video Awards
International Video Arts Award 1996
Internet Movie Institute - cast your votes on both the Oscars and the Razzies, and see how your votes affect the overall odds.
Lloyds Bank BAFTA Awards 1996 - from Lloyds Bank.
Mighty Happyman Online Interactive Film Awards - Go to this page and vote!
People's Choice Awards - background, nominees and award night chat.
Rosebud Awards - annual film and video competition and showcase.
ShoWest Awards - honor actors and filmakers for their achievements. The ShoWest Awards will be telecast live.
Troi Academy of Motion Picture Recognition - group of amateur movie critics and film enthusiasts that annually celebrate a unique list of nominees from the films of the previous year.
Yahoo! links you to CDnow for your favorite music. Click Here.
Over 5,000 albums on sale. All major new releases. World's largest selection of music.
Copyright © 1994-97 Yahoo! Inc. - Company Information - Help
Document: Done

Figure 4.3 Descriptions of sites in Yahoo.

hyperlink to the right of the search box. You'll see a complete search page, as shown in Figure 4.4. The instructions below explain how to use the expanded search page you see after clicking the Options hyperlink.

Yahoo offers excellent search capabilities, allowing all of the search options discussed in "Understanding Search Techniques," earlier in this chapter. To search Yahoo, follow these steps:

1. You should see the Yahoo search box on every Yahoo index page. If you don't see it—if, for example, you're looking at the Information page—click the large "Yahoo" at the top of your screen. To the right of the search box is the Options hyperlink. Click it to bring up the complete search page.
2. In the text box, type one or more keywords. Check your typing and spelling carefully.

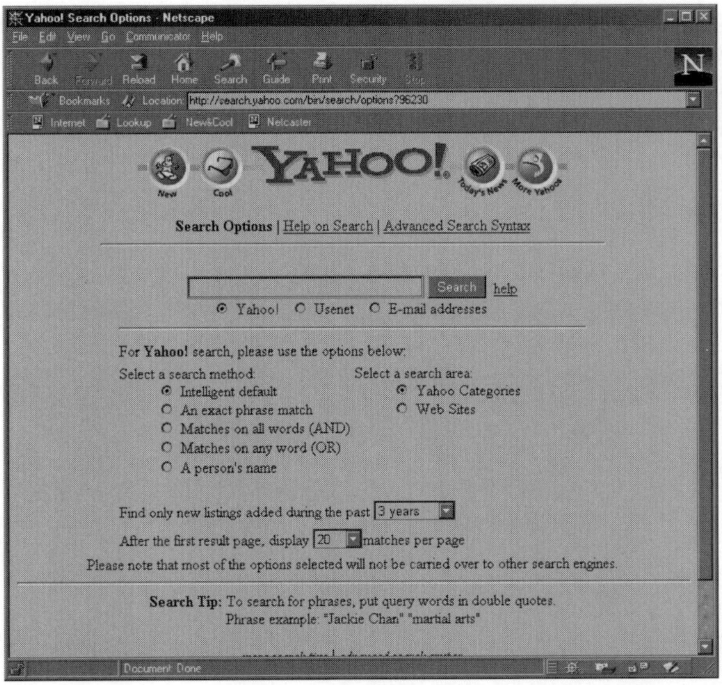

Figure 4.4 The Yahoo search page.

3. If you would like to restrict the search to Yahoo, click the leftmost radio button. By default, Yahoo searches its entire subject tree. You can also choose to search Usenet articles or e-mail addresses.
4. To perform a Boolean search, click the OR or AND button.
5. To perform a phrase search, click an exact phrase match.
6. To search for a person's name, click a person's name.
7. Click Yahoo categories to restrict the search to categories, or Web Sites to restrict the search to Yahoo Sites.
8. To start the search, click Search.

The result of a Yahoo search is a list of Yahoo entries that match your keywords (Figure 4.5)—or, if there aren't any matches, a message that no match was found. You can browse the list and click the links as you please. To redo the search, erase your previous search, click the Back button, and try again.

"It says the information I am submitting is not secure!"
By default, Netscape displays a warning dialog box when you try to send unencrypted text over the Internet. Basically, sending this text is like sending a postcard—anyone can read it. But this isn't really something to worry about when you're

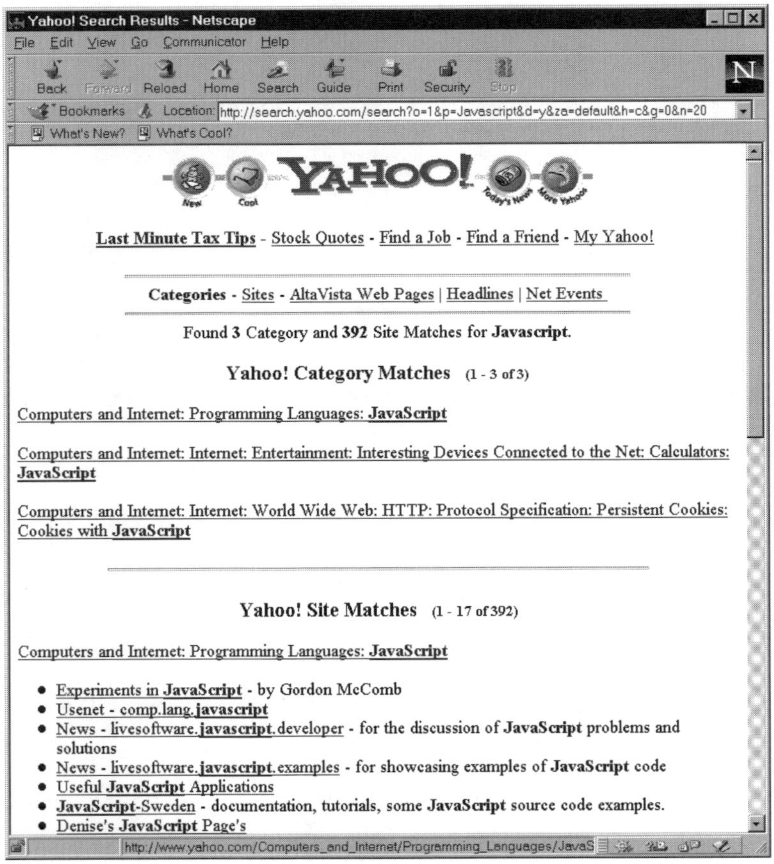

Figure 4.5 The results of a Yahoo search.

uploading text to search engines. Take this warning to heart, but do click the option that stops displaying this warning. You'll get sick of seeing it if you don't.

The Virtual Library

CERN, a center for particle physics research located in Geneva, Switzerland, is the birthplace of the Web. Among its many contributions to the Web is the Virtual Library, one of the first subject trees to be developed and still one of the most useful and comprehensive. So that CERN can focus on high-energy physics, the Virtual Library is now maintained by the W3 Organization (W30), headquartered in Cambridge, MA.

Unlike Yahoo, whose staff takes upon itself the arduous task of adding new URLs to the subject tree, the Virtual Library is a *distributed subject tree*. This means that the responsibility for maintaining the pages is distributed among individuals, each of whom possesses expertise in one area.

The Virtual Library's links point to pages maintained by these individuals, who have been chosen to maintain only the page for which they are responsible. Figure 4.6 shows the Anthropology page.

Many of the Virtual Library's pages got their start as metapages. They were incorporated into the Virtual Library after it became obvious that they had succeeded in achieving the most comprehensive collection of links in a given area.

You can browse the list of subject headings in numerous ways. The default list is more compact and somewhat easier to browse. If you click the Category Subtree hyperlink, you see a lengthier list of subject headings and subheadings. The Category Subtree gives you more of a sense of the riches stored within the Virtual Library's hyperlinks. In addition, you can display the subject headings according to Library of Congress subject classifications (to do so, click the Library of Congress Classification hyperlink; see Figure 4.7). Alternative listings include Statistics, which orders subject fields according to their popularity, and Service Type, which orders the Library's resources by type of service (Web servers, Gopher, WAIS databases, etc.).

To access the Virtual Library, just click the Virtual Library icon in this book's home page, or use the following URL:

http://www.w3.org/hypertext/DataSources/bySubject/Overview.html

To access one of the pages in the Virtual Library, just click one of the subject hyperlinks.

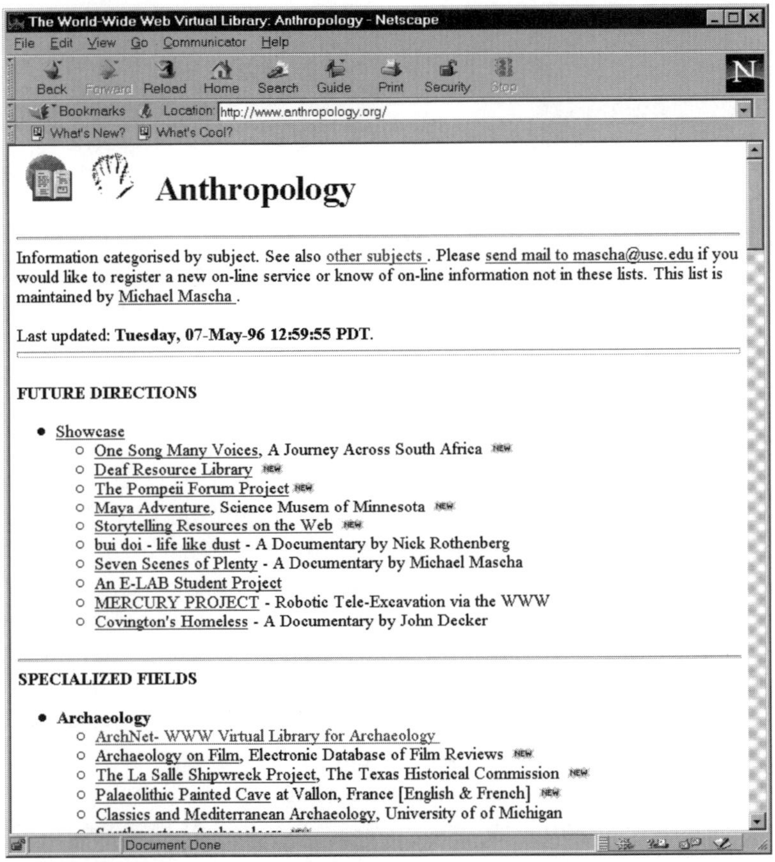

Figure 4.6 The Virtual Library Anthropology page.

Magellan

Another comprehensive subject tree is Magellan (http://www.mckinley.com), shown in Figure 4.8. One of the neat things about Magellan is that each site is rated using a four-star system, with the best sites appearing at the top of each list (see Figure 4.9 for an example).

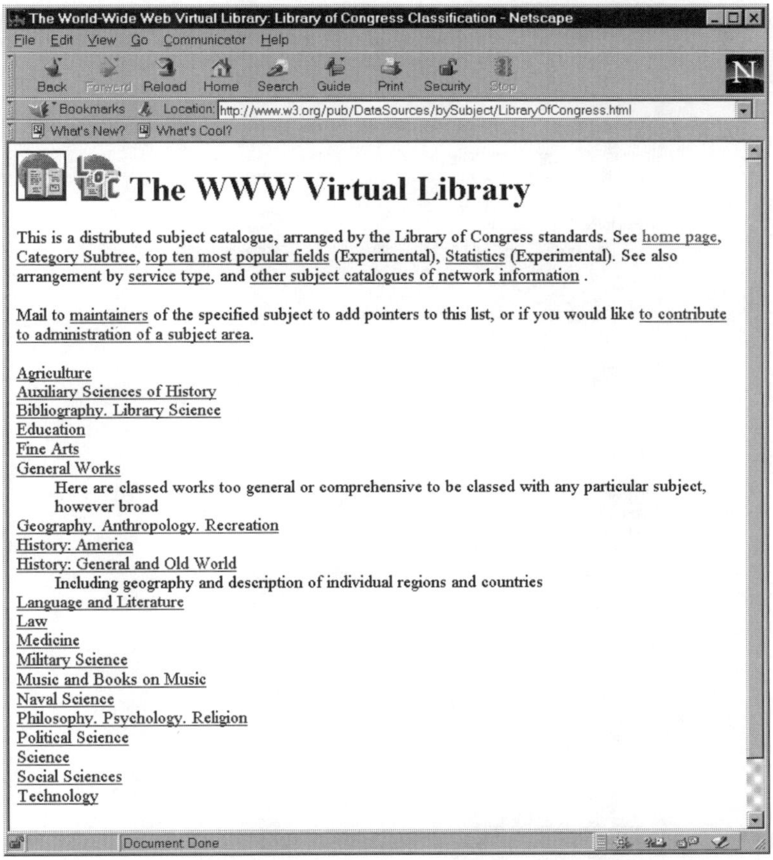

Figure 4.7 The Virtual Library listings arranged by Library of Congress classification standards.

Are your kids surfing the Net? Find kid-safe sites by looking for the green light in Magellan reviews. This indicates that the site doesn't contain adult content, such as nudity, adult language, violence, or sexual situations.

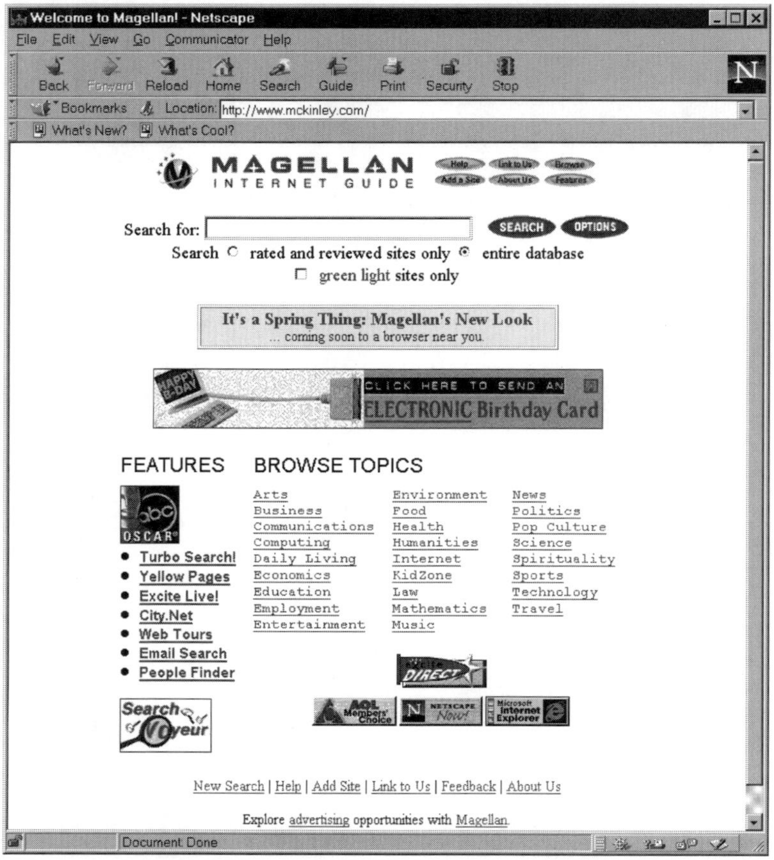

Figure 4.8 Magellan offers a searchable subject guide to the Web.

WebCrawler

One of the most impressive publishing phenomena of the 1990s was the success of Ed Krol's *The Whole Internet*, published by O'Reilly & Associates. Formerly a sleepy, strictly low-volume publisher of obscure books on obscure UNIX topics, O'Reilly hit the jackpot with Krol's excellent book. The revenue led to all sorts of ventures, and the Whole Internet Catalog—based on the useful appendix included in Krol's book—is one of them. Now there's an on-

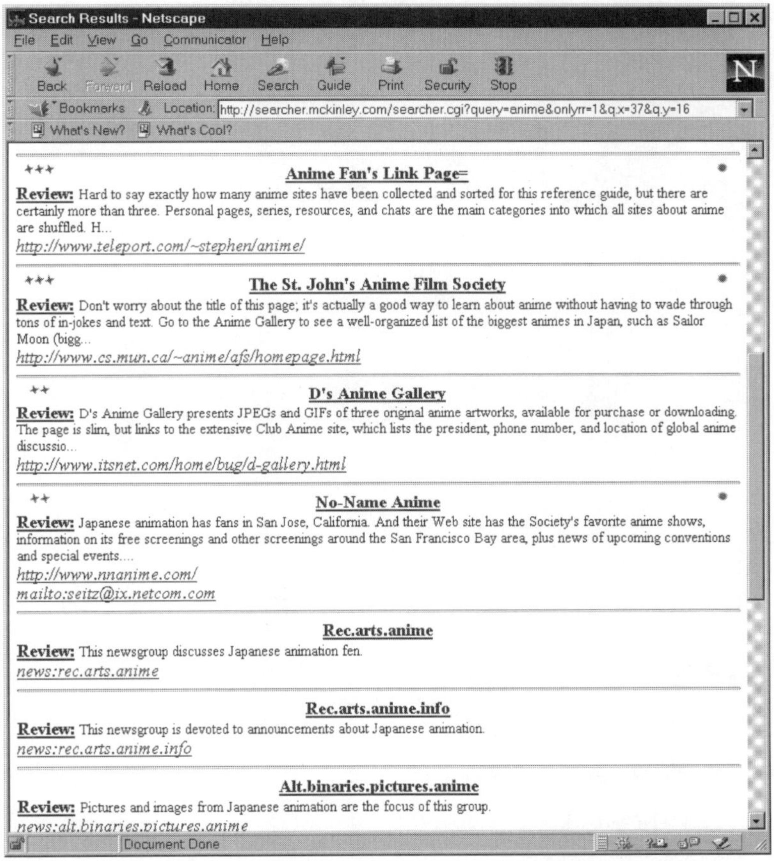
Search Results - Netscape
File Edit View Go Communicator Help
Back Forward Reload Home Search Guide Print Security Stop
Bookmarks Location: http://searcher.mckinley.com/searcher.cgi?query=anime&onlyrr=1&q.x=37&q.y=16
What's New? What's Cool?
Anime Fan's Link Page=
Review: Hard to say exactly how many anime sites have been collected and sorted for this reference guide, but there are certainly more than three. Personal pages, series, resources, and chats are the main categories into which all sites about anime are shuffled. H...
http://www.teleport.com/~stephen/anime/
The St. John's Anime Film Society
Review: Don't worry about the title of this page; it's actually a good way to learn about anime without having to wade through tons of in-jokes and text. Go to the Anime Gallery to see a well-organized list of the biggest animes in Japan, such as Sailor Moon (bigg...
http://www.cs.mun.ca/~anime/afs/homepage.html
D's Anime Gallery
Review: D's Anime Gallery presents JPEGs and GIFs of three original anime artworks, available for purchase or downloading. The page is slim, but links to the extensive Club Anime site, which lists the president, phone number, and location of global anime discussio...
http://www.itsnet.com/home/bug/d-gallery.html
No-Name Anime
Review: Japanese animation has fans in San Jose, California. And their Web site has the Society's favorite anime shows, information on its free screenings and other screenings around the San Francisco Bay area, plus news of upcoming conventions and special events....
http://www.nnanime.com/
mailto:seitz@ix.netcom.com
Rec.arts.anime
Review: This newsgroup discusses Japanese animation fen.
news:rec.arts.anime
Rec.arts.anime.info
Review: This newsgroup is devoted to announcements about Japanese animation.
news:rec.arts.anime.info
Alt.binaries.pictures.anime
Review: Pictures and images from Japanese animation are the focus of this group.
news:alt.binaries.pictures.anime
Document Done

Figure 4.9 Magellan reviews use a four-star system.

line version (Figure 4.10), called WebCrawler, and you'll certainly want to make it part of your document-hunting strategy.

Like Yahoo, WebCrawler is maintained manually, but the staff doesn't even try to put in thousands of links. On the boundary between a starting points resource and a subject tree, the Catalog offers only about 2,000 links—but they're good links.

To access WebCrawler, use this URL:

http://webcrawler.com/

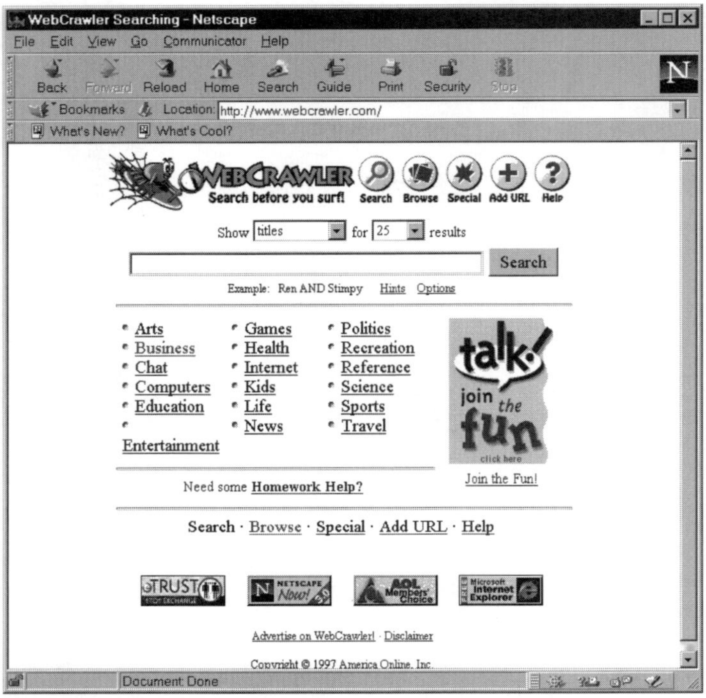

Figure 4.10 WebCrawler.

To access one of WebCrawler subject pages, just click the hyperlink. You'll see a page such as the one shown in Figure 4.11.

Search Engines

With more than two million documents on the Web and hundreds more arriving daily, there's no chance that Yahoo, the Virtual Library, or WebCrawler Select can keep up. That's why your search strategy should include search engines.

Most search engines are based on robotlike programs called *spiders* (also called *worms*), which roam the Web looking for new URLs. Most of them

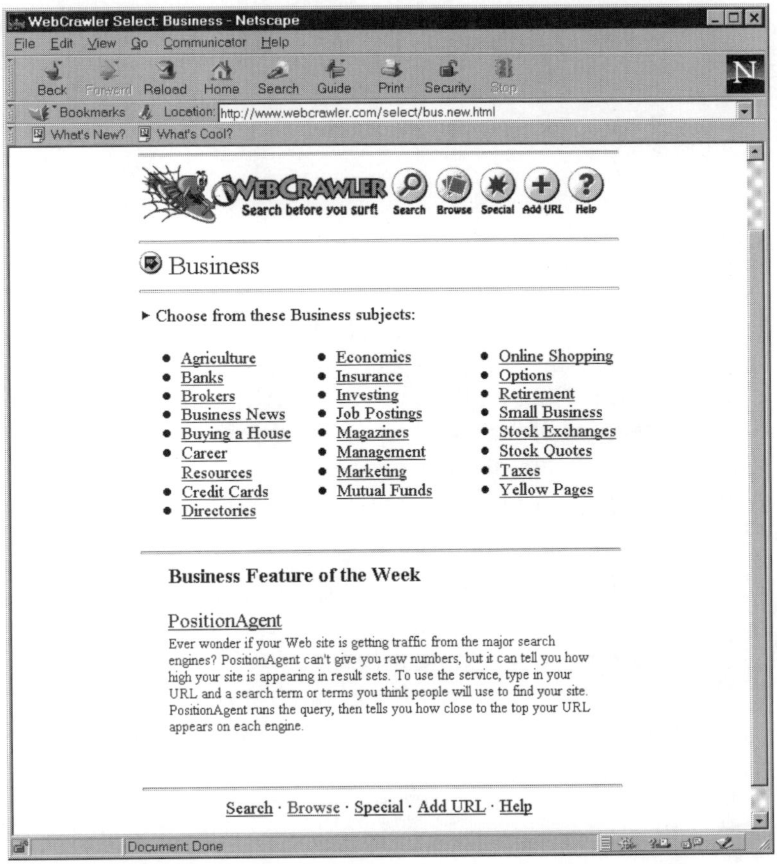

Figure 4.11 WebCrawler Select Business page.

do little more than catalog the words in the URL and the document's title and move on. Some spiders index the first few dozen words in the document itself, and a few index all the words in the entire document.

There's a tradeoff here. If the spider indexes only the title and words in the URL, it can index a lot of documents—the search goes quickly. But don't expect good results from your search. Web authors don't give much thought to their document titles, unfortunately, and URL words may have little or nothing to do with the document's content. Searching the database created by such a spider is sure to produce a lot of false drops, documents that aren't relevant to your interests. On the other hand, if the spider indexes the full text of the document, don't expect the database to include more than a few hundred thousand documents—the search takes a long time. However, searching the database produces better results. Now that you know about this tradeoff, you can make a more informed choice among the various search engines that are available.

Searching from the Location Box

New for 4

New to Netscape Communicator is a very cool feature that enables you to initiate a search from the Location box. To find something on the Web, simply type two or more search words, separated by spaces, within the Location box (the one that normally shows a URL), and press Enter. When Netscape has determined that what you've typed couldn't possibly be a domain name, the program sends the words you've typed to a search service, such as Infoseek, Yahoo, or Magellan, and you see a retrieval list.

My Location box search didn't retrieve anything! When you use this new feature, Netscape selects a search engine at random—and it might not be the right one for your needs. For example, it's great to search Yahoo if you've typed general concepts (such as desktop publishing or Windows 95 shareware), but it's better to use AltaVista or Lycos if you're hunting down something more obscure. If your Location box search doesn't work out, try choosing the right search engine for your needs and access it directly.

AltaVista

A service of Digital Equipment Corporation, AltaVista indexes the full text of more than 16 million Web pages at this writing. It's one of the best major-league Web search engines.

To access AltaVista, use this URL:

http://altavista.digital.com/

You'll see the AltaVista welcome page and search form, shown in Figure 4.12.

To search AltaVista:

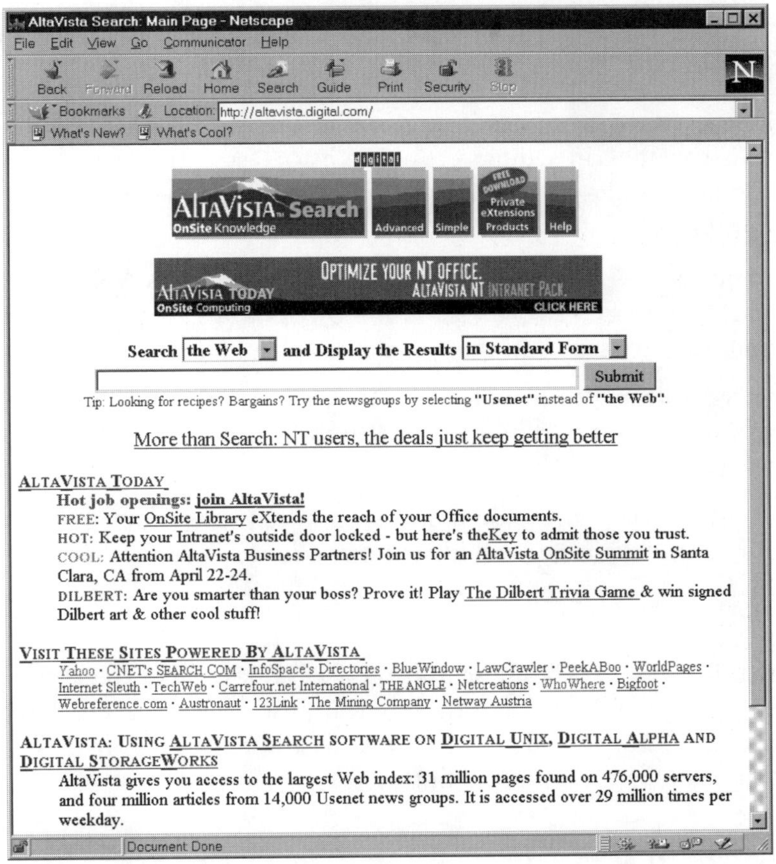
AltaVista Search: Main Page - Netscape
File Edit View Go Communicator Help
Back Forward Reload Home Search Guide Print Security Stop
Bookmarks Location: http://altavista.digital.com/
What's New? What's Cool?
AltaVista Search
OnSite Knowledge
Advanced Simple
FREE DOWNLOAD Private eXtensions Products
Help
OPTIMIZE YOUR NT OFFICE.
ALTAVISTA NT INTRANET PACK.
AltaVista TODAY
OnSite Computing
CLICK HERE
Search the Web and Display the Results in Standard Form
Submit
Tip: Looking for recipes? Bargains? Try the newsgroups by selecting "Usenet" instead of "the Web".
More than Search: NT users, the deals just keep getting better
ALTAVISTA TODAY
Hot job openings: join AltaVista!
FREE: Your OnSite Library eXtends the reach of your Office documents.
HOT: Keep your Intranet's outside door locked - but here's theKey to admit those you trust.
COOL: Attention AltaVista Business Partners! Join us for an AltaVista OnSite Summit in Santa Clara, CA from April 22-24.
DILBERT: Are you smarter than your boss? Prove it! Play The Dilbert Trivia Game & win signed Dilbert art & other cool stuff!
VISIT THESE SITES POWERED BY ALTAVISTA
Yahoo · CNET's SEARCH.COM · InfoSpace's Directories · BlueWindow · LawCrawler · PeekABoo · WorldPages ·
Internet Sleuth · TechWeb · Carrefour.net International · THE ANGLE · Netcreations · WhoWhere · Bigfoot ·
Webreference.com · Austronaut · 123Link · The Mining Company · Netway Austria
ALTAVISTA: USING ALTAVISTA SEARCH SOFTWARE ON DIGITAL UNIX, DIGITAL ALPHA AND DIGITAL STORAGEWORKS
AltaVista gives you access to the largest Web index: 31 million pages found on 476,000 servers, and four million articles from 14,000 Usenet news groups. It is accessed over 29 million times per weekday.
Document: Done

Figure 4.12 The AltaVista search form.

1. In the large text box at the top of the page, type your search terms.
2. Tell AltaVista to search either Web documents or Usenet news by selecting an option from the list box.
3. Opt for Standard, Compact, or Detailed (long) site descriptions.
4. Click the Submit button.

AltaVista offers one of the most customizable search interfaces out there. Here are some useful tips for Alta Vista searches:

- Putting words in quotes requires that the search engine find those words together, in sequence. A search for "scientific calculator," for example, would not return a site containing the words *scientific graphing calculator.*
- The plus symbol means AND; the minus sign means AND NOT. For example, a search for *cleveland+ohio-columbus* (without the italics) would return sites containing *cleveland* and *ohio*, but not *columbus*.
- Use the asterisk as a wildcard. A search for *fly* would return sites containing that word by itself; a search for **fly** would return *flypaper*, *flygirl*, and *barfly*.
- Use the modifier *title*: to specify words that must appear in a document's title. *title:Jones* would return sites with *Jones* in the title.

You'll see the results of your search on a new page, like the one shown in Figure 4.13. If you selected Standard output, the title of the site, hyperlinked to the site itself, appears at the top of its description. The URL, also hyperlinked to the site, appears at the bottom.

There's an advanced search form at AltaVista, too. Access it by clicking the Advanced button on the toolbar on the AltaVista welcome page. The advanced search form appears in Figure 4.14.

The advanced search form lets you construct searches with the Boolean operators AND, OR, NOT, and NEAR. NEAR specifies that one word must be within 10 words of another.

For example, an advanced search for the following:

grapes AND raisins AND NOT walnuts

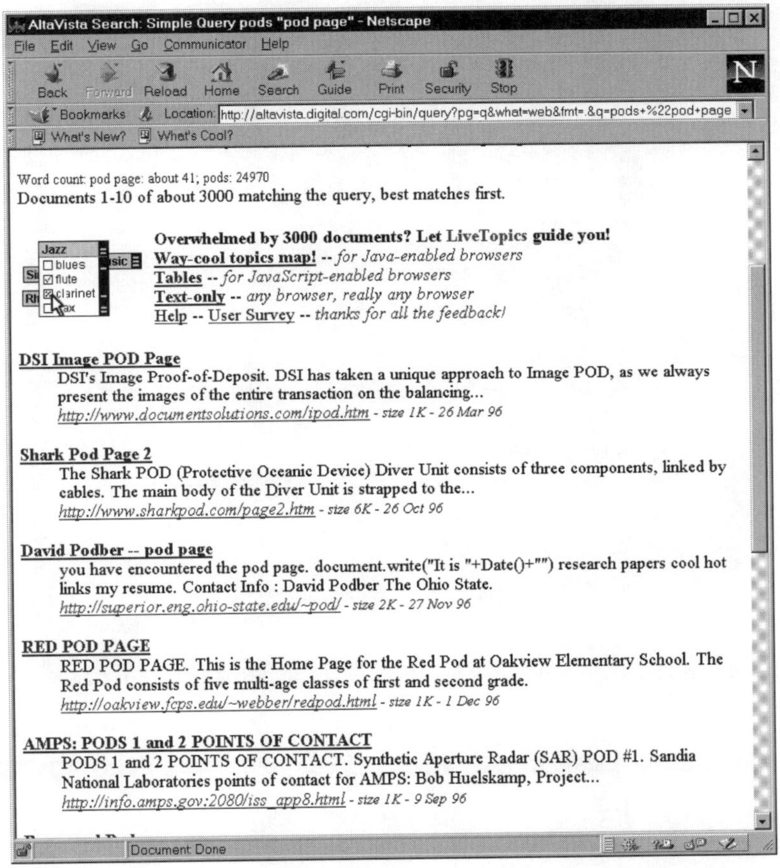
AltaVista Search: Simple Query pods "pod page" - Netscape
File Edit View Go Communicator Help
Back Forward Reload Home Search Guide Print Security Stop
Bookmarks Location: http://altavista.digital.com/cgi-bin/query?pg=q&what=web&fmt=.&q=pods+%22pod+page
What's New? What's Cool?
Word count: pod page: about 41; pods: 24970
Documents 1-10 of about 3000 matching the query, best matches first.
Jazz
blues
flute
clarinet
Overwhelmed by 3000 documents? Let LiveTopics guide you!
Way-cool topics map! -- for Java-enabled browsers
Tables -- for JavaScript-enabled browsers
Text-only -- any browser, really any browser
Help -- User Survey -- thanks for all the feedback!
DSI Image POD Page
DSI's Image Proof-of-Deposit. DSI has taken a unique approach to Image POD, as we always present the images of the entire transaction on the balancing...
http://www.documentsolutions.com/ipod.htm - size 1K - 26 Mar 96
Shark Pod Page 2
The Shark POD (Protective Oceanic Device) Diver Unit consists of three components, linked by cables. The main body of the Diver Unit is strapped to the...
http://www.sharkpod.com/page2.htm - size 6K - 26 Oct 96
David Podber -- pod page
you have encountered the pod page. document.write("It is "+Date()+"") research papers cool hot links my resume. Contact Info : David Podber The Ohio State.
http://superior.eng.ohio-state.edu/~pod/ - size 2K - 27 Nov 96
RED POD PAGE
RED POD PAGE. This is the Home Page for the Red Pod at Oakview Elementary School. The Red Pod consists of five multi-age classes of first and second grade.
http://oakview.fcps.edu/~webber/redpod.html - size 1K - 1 Dec 96
AMPS: PODS 1 and 2 POINTS OF CONTACT
PODS 1 and 2 POINTS OF CONTACT. Synthetic Aperture Radar (SAR) POD #1. Sandia National Laboratories points of contact for AMPS: Bob Huelskamp, Project...
http://info.amps.gov:2080/iss_app8.html - size 1K - 9 Sep 96
Document: Done

Figure 4.13 Results of an AltaVista search.

would return a document containing the phrase, "How to make raisins from grapes," but would ignore one that contained the phrase "Grape-Raisin-Walnut Salad."

The NEAR operator is useful in searching for someone's name. The search

richard NEAR jones

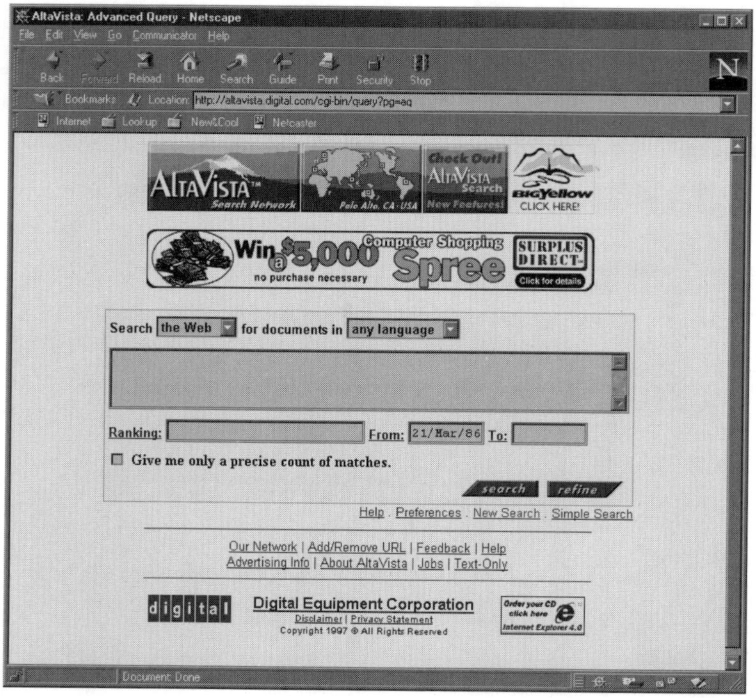

Figure 4.14 The AltaVista advanced search form.

would return references to “Richard Jones,” “Richard A. Jones,” and “Richard Allison Jones, M.D.” Unfortunately, that search would also return hits on documents containing phrases like “Richard Krinklemeyer and Joyce Jones are pleased to announce . . . ,” since “Richard” and “Jones” are within 10 words of each other in that phrase, too.

The advanced search form also lets you specify the order in which your search results appear. Enter the most important words in your search in the second text box. AltaVista will rank documents containing these words ahead of documents that satisfy the search criteria but do not contain the words you put in the second box.

Infoseek

One of the easiest-to-use services on the Web, Infoseek, combines a big database with lots of useful starting points, arranged by subject. The Infoseek page appears in Figure 4.15.

To access Infoseek, type the URL directly:

http://www.infoseek.com

To search Infoseek:

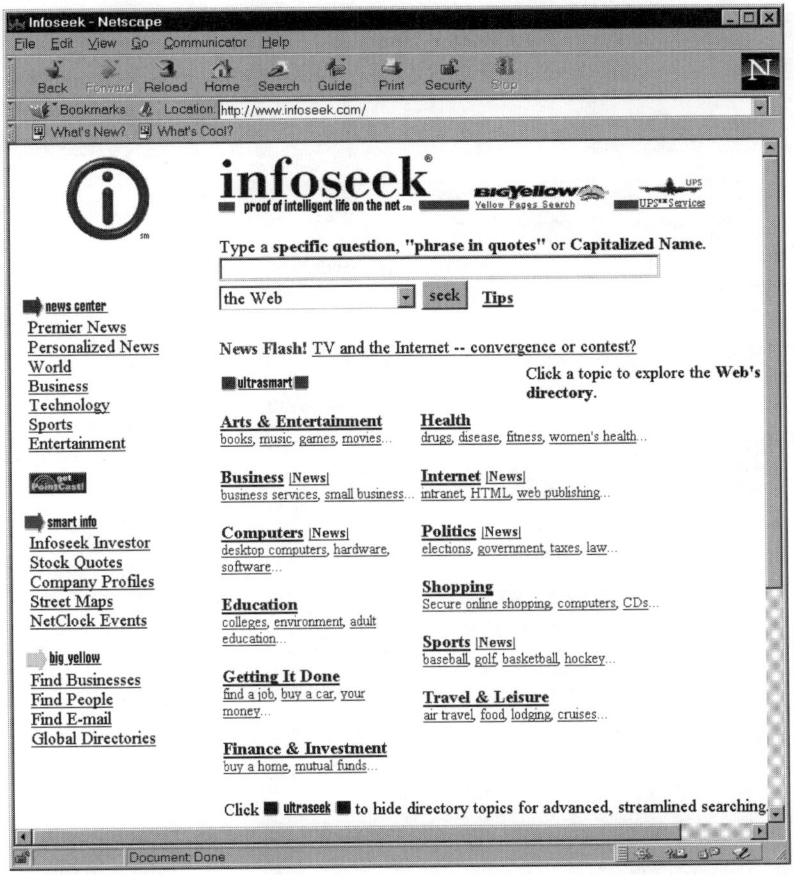

Figure 4.15 Infoseek.

1. Type your search terms or query into the text box.
2. Specify, using the list box under the text box, whether you want to search Web pages, FAQs, or whatever.
3. Click the Seek button.

Infoseek will display the results of your query on a page like the one shown in Figure 4.16. Click the heading of a page's listing to jump to that page.

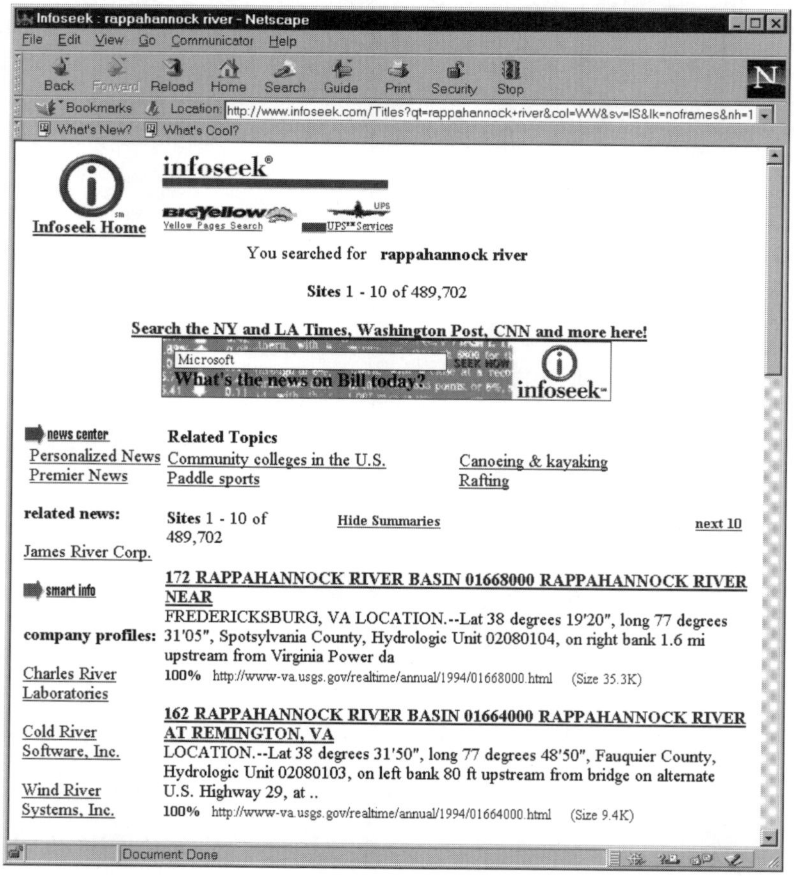

Figure 4.16 Results of an Infoseek Ultrasmart search.

Infoseek offers advertisers a nifty bonus for advertising on Infoseek pages: When users enter a search term, the search software examines the list of advertisers and tries to match the search subject to a pertinent ad. Try searching for "Netscape." You'll almost certainly see an ad from Netscape Communications, Inc. Clever, huh? Advertisers pay more for this type of advertisment, since it's more likely to generate a response. In Figure 4.16, for example, a search for "wine" netted an ad for Virtual Vineyards. Personally, I think this is great. Virtual Vineyards is one of the best wine sites on the Web. If I didn't already know about it, I'd be delighted to discover it, thanks to the ad. Nice job, Infoseek!

Look at the side of the result page to see a list of Infoseek subject headings that are relevant to your search topic. If you see one that looks dead-on, click it to see a list of high-quality (reviewed) links. Look in the left panel for news stories related to your topic. As you can see, Infoseek combines a search engine and subject tree in a very appealing way.

At the bottom of the Ultrasmart result listing is another search box so that you can narrow the original search. For example, if you started searching by typing "wine," you could narrow the search by typing "California" in this box and clicking the "Search only these results" button. A new list of sites that include both search terms will be returned.

Lycos

The Web search engine that started it all, Lycos left Carnegie-Mellon University in 1995 to form the centerpiece of a private company. Though it competes with such wonderful search engines as Infoseek and AltaVista, Lycos still offers excellent capabilities and belongs in everyone's search repertoire. Like Infoseek, Lycos is breaking down the boundaries between search engines and subject trees, thanks to the firm's acquisition of Point (which reviews the "top 5% of Web sites").

To access Lycos, use this URL:

http://www.lycos.com/

You can work with that simple form, or click the Custom Search hyperlink to see a search form like the one shown in Figure 4.17. These instructions deal with using the advanced form (the best choice for serious searching).

To search Lycos using this form:

1. From the list box next to "Search," choose whether to search the entire Web or Lycos' site list, or search directly for sound and image files on the Web using Lycos' multimedia index, Pictures & Sounds.

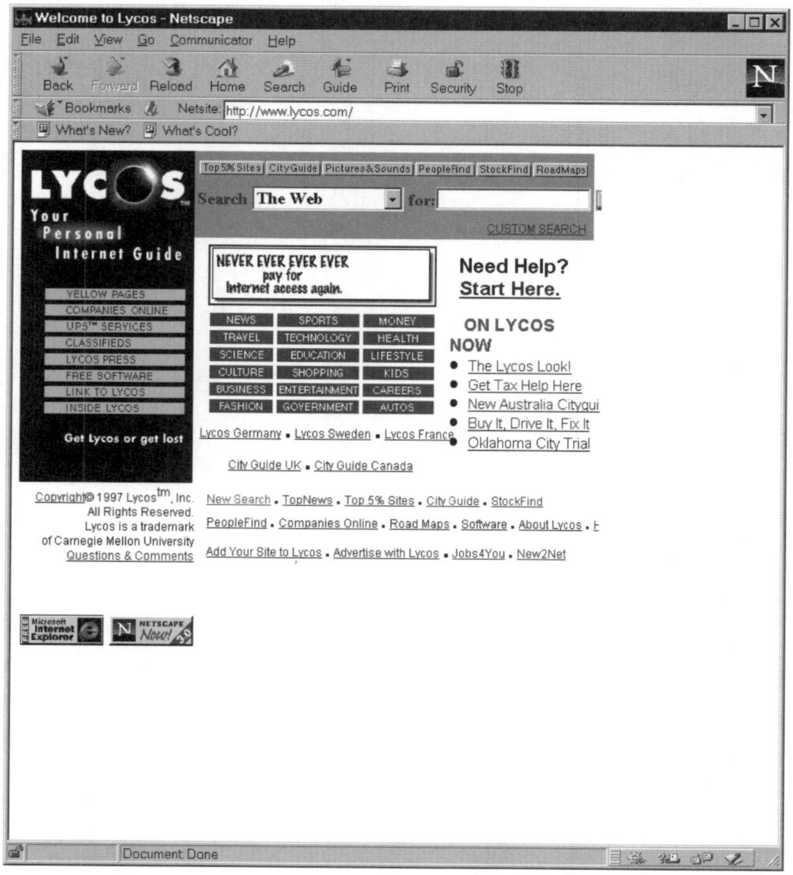

Figure 4.17 The Lycos advanced search form.

2. In the text box next to "for," type one or more keywords.
3. To initiate the search, click the Go Get It button.

The results of your Lycos search appear in a new window (Figure 4.18). You see your keywords, plus a list of the words in Lycos' database that match the keywords you typed. Following are the hyperlinks that Lycos

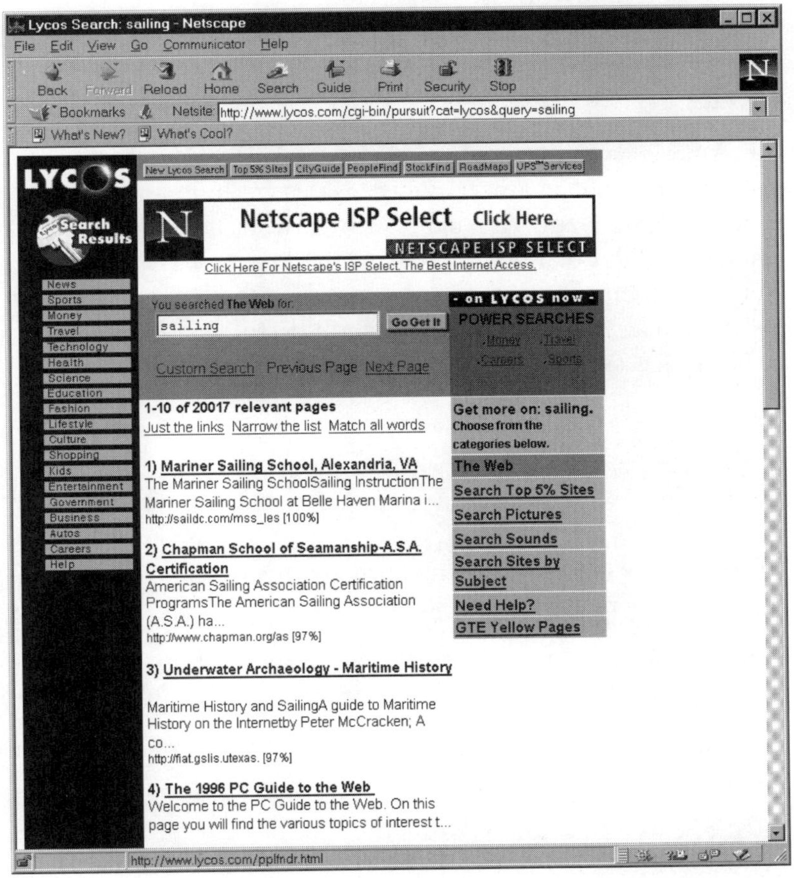

Figure 4.18 The results of a Lycos search.

retrieved, if any. If you find an interesting hyperlink, click it—or click the Back button to revise your search strategy.

This document's at the top of the list, but it isn't relevant to my interests! Just because a document scores high in Lycos' ranking system doesn't mean that it's going to contain material of interest to you. This ranking is done by mindless computers, blindly following their programming. They can't read the documents or understand the content—they can just match characters. Sometimes the result is laughably off the mark.

WebCrawler

Owned by America Online, the spider-based WebCrawler doesn't have a very large database, but it amply compensates by indexing the full text of the documents it analyzes. As such, WebCrawler is much more likely to retrieve that valuable document in which the keywords appear only at the end of the document, buried deeply within the document's text. Even though its database isn't very big, you should still include WebCrawler in your search. To access WebCrawler, use the following URL:

http://www.webcrawler.com/

You'll see the WebCrawler page, shown in Figure 4.19.

To search WebCrawler, follow these steps:

1. Type one or more keywords in the text box.
2. If you would like to perform a Boolean OR or AND search, include those terms with your search terms. For example, you can search for "beer or ale," or "netscape and plug-ins."
3. If you would like to see more than 25 documents, choose a larger number next to "results."
4. Click Search to initiate the search.

The result of your WebCrawler search is a page of hyperlinks, such as the one shown in Figure 4.20. Like the results of a Lycos search, the documents are ranked in order of relevance, with the top-scoring document at the top.

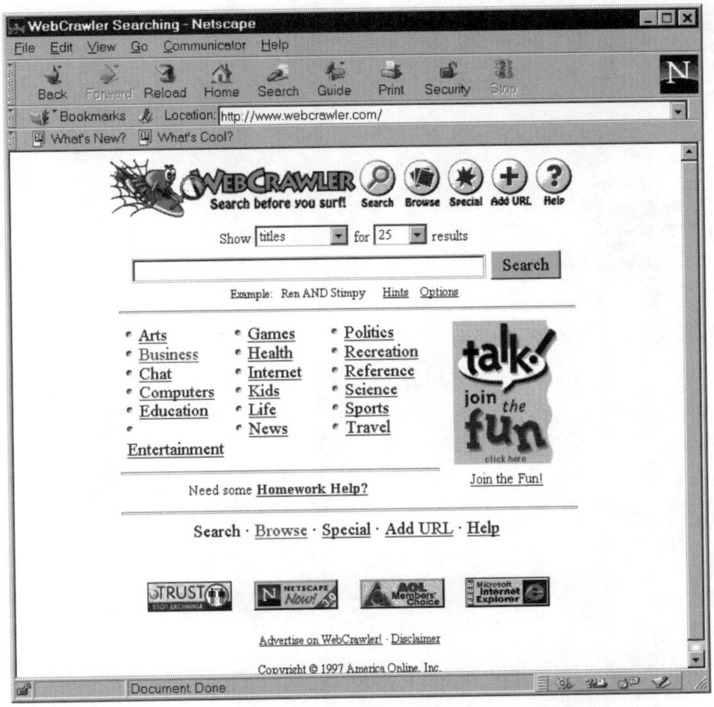

Figure 4.19 The WebCrawler welcome page.

HotBot

It's the newest kid on the block, and maybe the best. HotBot, offered by the same folks that bring you *Wired* magazine (www.wired.com), combines ease of use with exceptional accuracy. If you don't want to get into advanced search techniques, but also don't want a retrieval list loaded with irrelevant stuff, HotBot's for you.

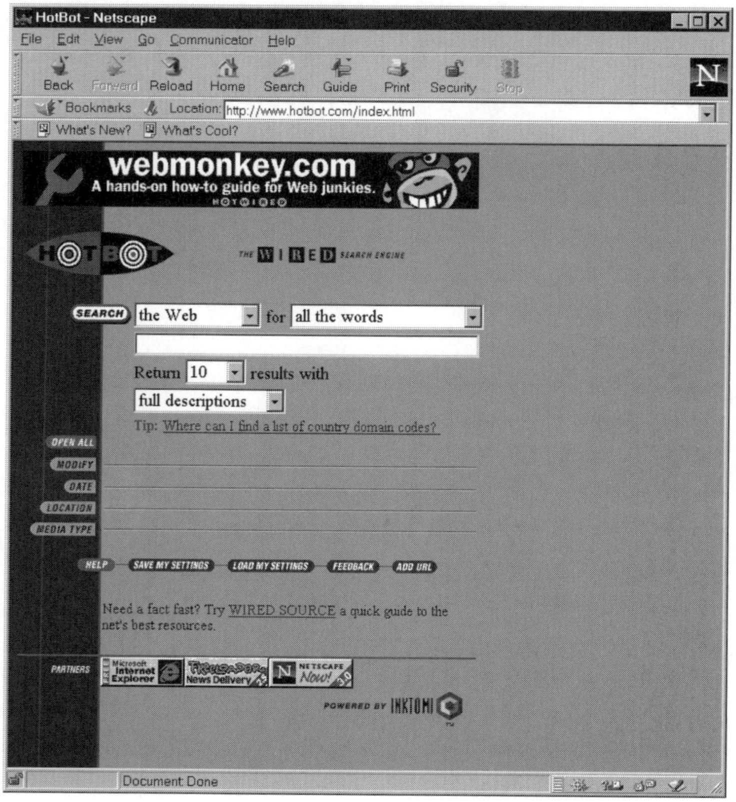

Figure 4.20 The results of a WebCrawler search.

Access HotBot at www.hotbot.com (Figure 4.21). To initiate a search, do the following:

1. In the text box, type one or more search words.
2. Choose The Web or Usenet from the first pull-down box.
3. Choose how HotBot matches the words. You can choose from all the words (AND operator), any of the words (OR operator), the exact phrase, the person, links to this URL, or a Boolean expression (use AND, OR, or NOT between each two search terms).
4. Click Search.

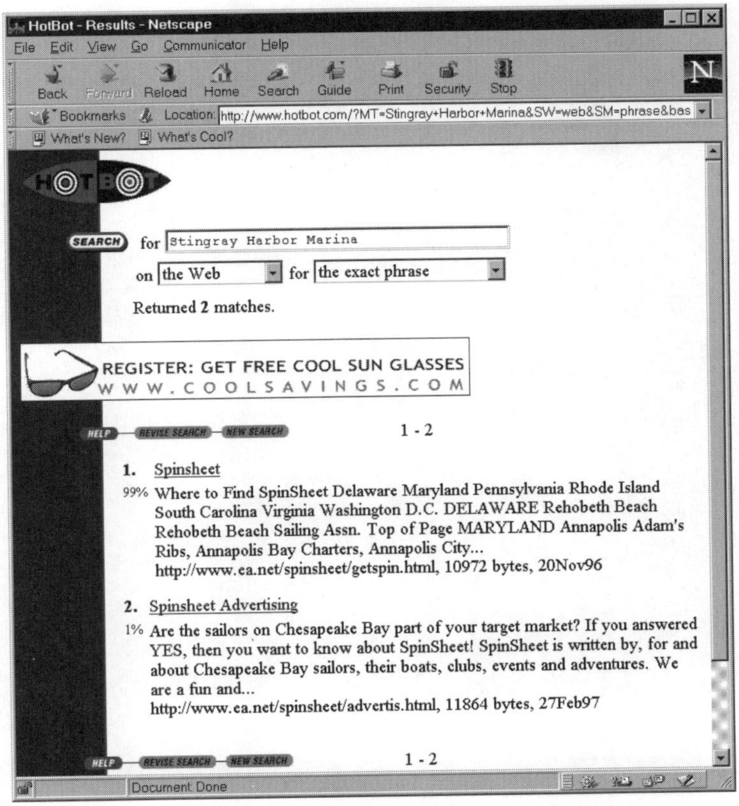
HotBot - Results - Netscape
File Edit View Go Communicator Help
Back Forward Reload Home Search Guide Print Security Stop
Bookmarks Location: http://www.hotbot.com/?MT=Stingray+Harbor+Marina&SW=web&SM=phrase&bas
What's New? What's Cool?
SEARCH for Stingray Harbor Marina
on the Web for the exact phrase
Returned 2 matches.
REGISTER: GET FREE COOL SUN GLASSES
WWW.COOLSAVINGS.COM
HELP REVISE SEARCH NEW SEARCH 1 - 2
1. Spinsheet
99% Where to Find SpinSheet Delaware Maryland Pennsylvania Rhode Island South Carolina Virginia Washington D.C. DELAWARE Rehobeth Beach Rehobeth Beach Sailing Assn. Top of Page MARYLAND Annapolis Adam's Ribs, Annapolis Bay Charters, Annapolis City...
http://www.ea.net/spinsheet/getspin.html, 10972 bytes, 20Nov96
2. Spinsheet Advertising
1% Are the sailors on Chesapeake Bay part of your target market? If you answered YES, then you want to know about SpinSheet! SpinSheet is written by, for and about Chesapeake Bay sailors, their boats, clubs, events and adventures. We are a fun and...
http://www.ea.net/spinsheet/advertis.html, 11864 bytes, 27Feb97
HELP REVISE SEARCH NEW SEARCH 1 - 2
Document: Done

Figure 4.21 HotBot produces good results—give it a try!

The retrieval list is nicely organized, with a brief abstract that gives you a feeling for what's in the documents (Figure 4.22).

Summing It Up: Top Search Tricks

Here's a brief summary of some hot search tricks:

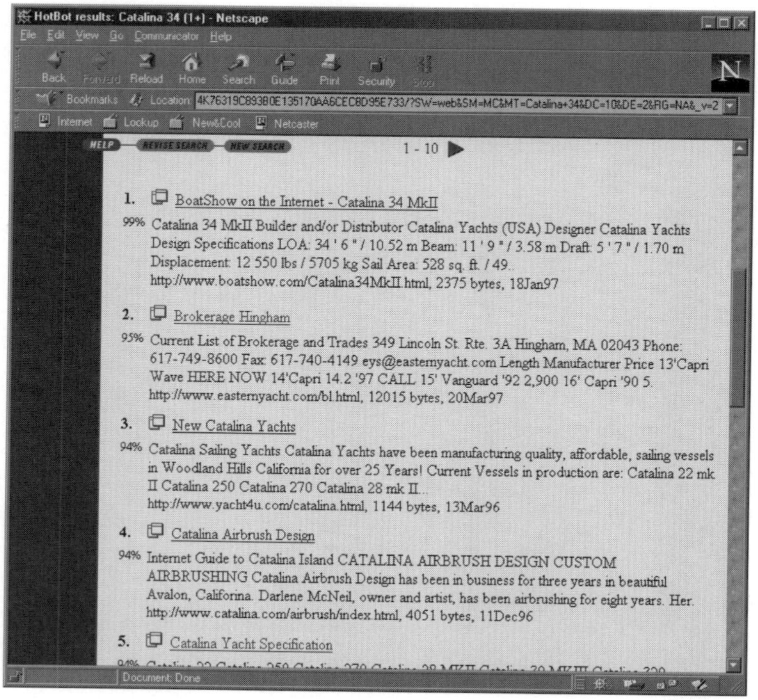
HotBot results: Catalina 34 (1+) - Netscape
1 - 10
1. BoatShow on the Internet - Catalina 34 MkII
99% Catalina 34 MkII Builder and/or Distributor Catalina Yachts (USA) Designer Catalina Yachts Design Specifications LOA: 34 ' 6 " / 10.52 m Beam: 11 ' 9 " / 3.58 m Draft: 5 ' 7 " / 1.70 m Displacement: 12 550 lbs / 5705 kg Sail Area: 528 sq. ft. / 49..
http://www.boatshow.com/Catalina34MkII.html, 2375 bytes, 18Jan97
2. Brokerage Hingham
95% Current List of Brokerage and Trades 349 Lincoln St. Rte. 3A Hingham, MA 02043 Phone: 617-749-8600 Fax: 617-740-4149 eys@easternyacht.com Length Manufacturer Price 13'Capri Wave HERE NOW 14'Capri 14.2 '97 CALL 15' Vanguard '92 2,900 16' Capri '90 5.
http://www.easternyacht.com/bl.html, 12015 bytes, 20Mar97
3. New Catalina Yachts
94% Catalina Sailing Yachts Catalina Yachts have been manufacturing quality, affordable, sailing vessels in Woodland Hills California for over 25 Years! Current Vessels in production are: Catalina 22 mk II Catalina 250 Catalina 270 Catalina 28 mk II...
http://www.yacht4u.com/catalina.html, 1144 bytes, 13Mar96
4. Catalina Airbrush Design
94% Internet Guide to Catalina Island CATALINA AIRBRUSH DESIGN CUSTOM AIRBRUSHING Catalina Airbrush Design has been in business for three years in beautiful Avalon, California. Darlene McNeil, owner and artist, has been airbrushing for eight years. Her.
http://www.catalina.com/airbrush/index.html, 4051 bytes, 11Dec96
5. Catalina Yacht Specification
Document: Done

Figure 4.22 A HotBot retrieval list includes informative abstracts.

- Too many documents retrieved and not enough of them relevant? Try a phrase search in AltaVista or HotBot.
- Find some good stuff but there's a particular subject that's getting in the way? Suppose you're searching for links on sailing, but you don't want to see pages on sailing schools. Try an AltaVista search in which you type a hyphen (minus sign) before the unwanted term (such as *sailing -school*). You can also try a Boolean search in HotBot using the NOT operator, as in *sailing NOT school*.
- Too few documents? Think of some synonyms for your search topic, and try searching again using the synonymns.

- Nothing good out there? Check your spelling—you may have mistyped one or more of the search words.

From Here

- If you've gotten this far in this book, congratulations! You're a darned good Netscapist by now, and what's more, you know how to retrieve information in an orderly way. You'll be getting tons of useful documents, so you'd better learn how to share them with others by electronic mail, the subject of Part III.
- What, electronic mail isn't fast enough for you? Learn about real-time chat with IRC in Chapter 18.
- Reach out and touch someone—but without paying long-distance charges! Find out how in Part V.

Chapter 5

When the Surf Gets Rough

Netscape is loads of fun to use, but the Web isn't perfect. You will encounter many network-related problems while you're surfing. These aren't Netscape's fault, but part of Netscape mastery involves knowing what to do about them. This chapter discusses the things that can go wrong while you're surfing the Web—the black holes, the forbidden zones, the unplugged sockets, and more.

Even if you haven't run into the problems discussed in this chapter, it's still a good idea to skim it.

For the Time-Challenged

- If a site doesn't respond after a minute or two, give up and try again later.
- If you type a URL directly, make sure you type it correctly. A typing error could produce a DNS error message (the domain name is incorrect) or a 404 Not Found message (the document name is incorrect). Correct your typing and try again.
- Still getting a DNS or 404 error message? The site's down or the document's gone. Sorry.
- A 403 Forbidden message means that the document is not available to users from your Internet domain. This might mean the document is for local use only.
- Socket error messages generally indicate a temporary problem: Try clicking the hyperlink again.
- The other stuff discussed in this chapter falls into the minor nuisance category.

I Clicked the Hyperlink – and Nothing Happened!

The site you're trying to access is busy, busy, busy—so busy in fact, that it can't even transmit a message that it's too busy! Pathetic. Try again later—like at 2:30 A.M.

If you're determined to get through to a site, open a new window in Netscape and let the original window keep on tryin'. Maybe the document you want will appear after a few minutes. Maybe not.

A site that just never responds is known to Web surfers as a Black Hole. If you've never had this experience, but would like to give it a try, there is a Black Hole simulation at the following URL:

http://ravenna.wwa.com/blackhole.html

Please do not click the Black Hole link (Figure 5.1). You will be caught in the Hole and be unable to get out. Somehow, resist the temptation! (Actually, you can just click Home to get out of the Hole.)

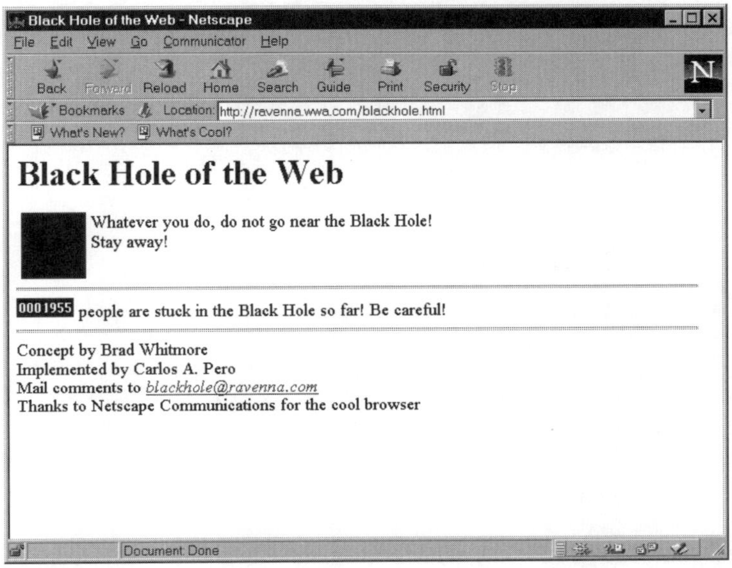
Black Hole of the Web - Netscape
File Edit View Go Communicator Help
Back Forward Reload Home Search Guide Print Security Stop
Bookmarks Location: http://ravenna.wwa.com/blackhole.html
What's New? What's Cool?
Black Hole of the Web
Whatever you do, do not go near the Black Hole!
Stay away!
0001955 people are stuck in the Black Hole so far! Be careful!
Concept by Brad Whitmore
Implemented by Carlos A. Pero
Mail comments to blackhole@ravenna.com
Thanks to Netscape Communications for the cool browser
Document: Done

Figure 5.1 The Black Hole.

It Says "Connection Refused by Server"!

The server's too busy. Try again later!

It Says "A Network Error Occurred! Unable to Connect to Server!"

This means that there's some kind of network problem along the way. The server seems to exist, but Netscape couldn't get through. Perhaps the server is down temporarily, or perhaps part of the network is down. Try again later!

It Says "There Was No Response!"

Netscape tried to connect to the server, but the server didn't respond. The server might be down temporarily—probably due to too many people trying to access the server at the same time. Try again later (Is this starting to sound like a broken record?)

It Says "Document Contains No Data!"

Several things can cause this message. The author of the page might be in the midst of updating it. This message might also be caused by a network problem of some kind. Almost always, you can solve the problem by clicking the Reload button a few times.

It Says the DNS Lookup Failed!

Netscape tried to access a Web site, but nothing happened, and then you see a dialog box with the message that the DNS lookup went awry (Figure 5.2). There are several possibilities here:

- Are you using a SLIP or PPP dialup connection? Check to make sure that you're still connected. Many dial-in systems are set up to hang up on you if there is no activity for a specified period of time, such as 10 minutes. (After all, other people are trying to access the system, and as far as anyone knows, you've probably gone fishing or something.) Use your SLIP/PPP dialer to reestablish the connection, and click the hyperlink again.
- Did you type the URL? You may have mistyped the domain name part of the URL (the part that contains the name of the computer you're trying to access).
- The computer you're trying to answer may have gone "Whoomp!" (That's the noise a computer makes when it's taken out of service and permanently disconnected from the Internet, in case you were wondering.)
- The DNS server might be overloaded. Try again later.

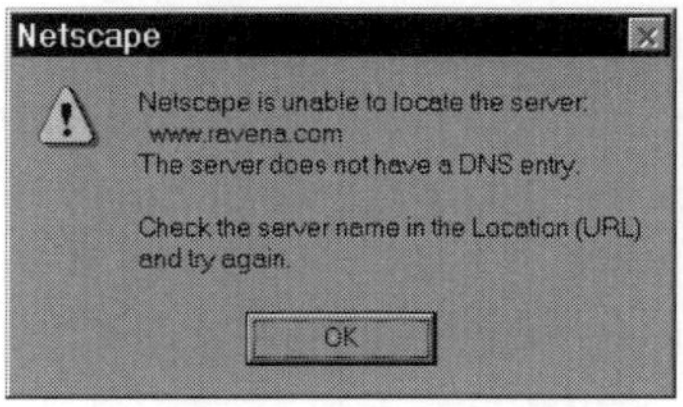
Netscape
Netscape is unable to locate the server:
www.ravena.com
The server does not have a DNS entry.
Check the server name in the Location (URL) and try again.
OK

Figure 5.2 A DNS lookup gone astray.

It Says "Not Found"! (Error 404)

The domain name's all right—Netscape was able to contact the computer you're looking for—but, sorry to say, there's no document by that name located on the machine you've accessed (Figure 5.3). Did you type the URL yourself? If so, carefully check your typing and make any corrections, if necessary, right in the Location box. Press Enter to try again.

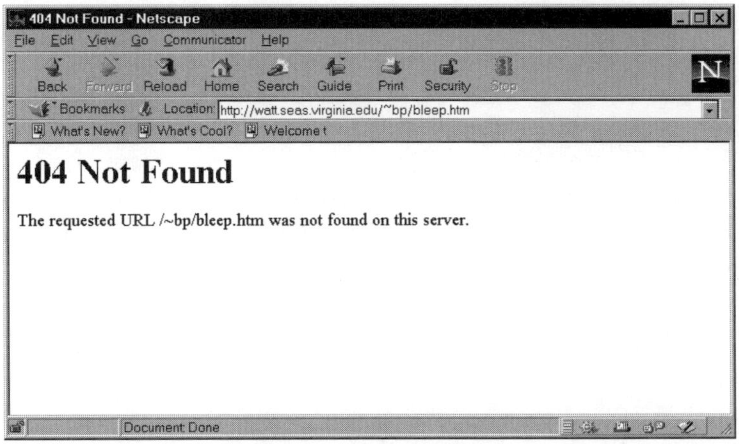
404 Not Found - Netscape
File Edit View Go Communicator Help
Back Forward Reload Home Search Guide Print Security Stop
Bookmarks Location: http://watt.seas.virginia.edu/~bp/bleep.htm
What's New? What's Cool? Welcome t
404 Not Found
The requested URL /~bp/bleep.htm was not found on this server.
Document: Done

Figure 5.3 404 Not Found.

If you get the 404 Not Found message again, the document has probably been withdrawn from the server.

Here's a great tip. If you get a 404 message, there's some good news—you've managed to contact the server. There's a good chance that the document you want is still there—the Webmaster may have moved it or renamed it. Here's how to find it.

To find the page you're looking for, you can try a technique known as "backing up the URL." Here'show this works. Suppose you're looking for the following document:

http://www.hotserver.com/multimedia/movies/cool.html

You get a 404. But don't despair—there may still be hope. In the Location box, place the cursor at the end of the URL, and press the Backspace key to erase the last item (here, "cool.html"). Then press Enter. If you get another 404, erase another item, and press Enter again. Sooner or later, you'll see a page—probably the site's welcome page, from which you can search or navigate for the information you want.

Wow! "Forbidden"! (Error 403)

Naughty, naughty! You weren't trying to access a sex site, were you? Sites with naughty pictures and stories tend to get restricted or shut down by system administrators, thanks to the fact that there are, apparently, about 20 million Web users with nothing better to do than hunt down erotic Web sites. With so many people trying to access the document, its host system can't function. Irate, the system administrator restricts access to the local domain only, and you see the "403 Forbidden" message. (Figure 5.4).

Sometimes you'll get this message when you're trying to access a non-naughty site. It probably means that the document you're looking for is of strictly local interest.

Horrors! A Network Error

Something went wrong with the network connection (Figure 5.5). Chances are good it's a temporary problem. Just click the hyperlink again.

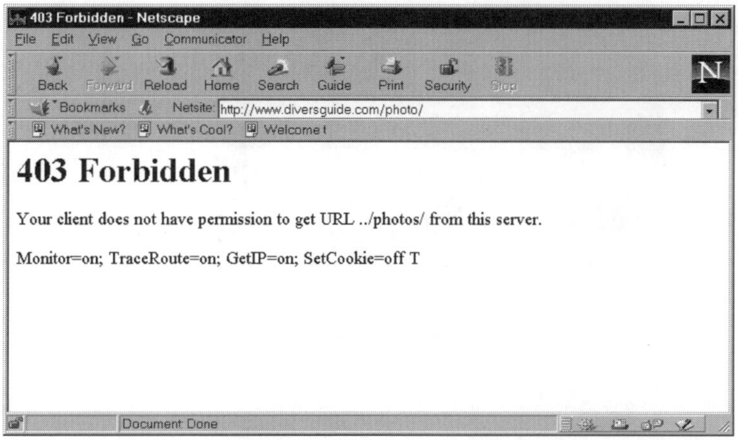
403 Forbidden - Netscape
File Edit View Go Communicator Help
Back Forward Reload Home Search Guide Print Security Stop
Bookmarks Netsite: http://www.diversguide.com/photo/
What's New? What's Cool? Welcome t
403 Forbidden
Your client does not have permission to get URL ../photos/ from this server.
Monitor=on; TraceRoute=on; GetIP=on; SetCookie=off T
Document: Done

Figure 5.4 403 Forbidden.

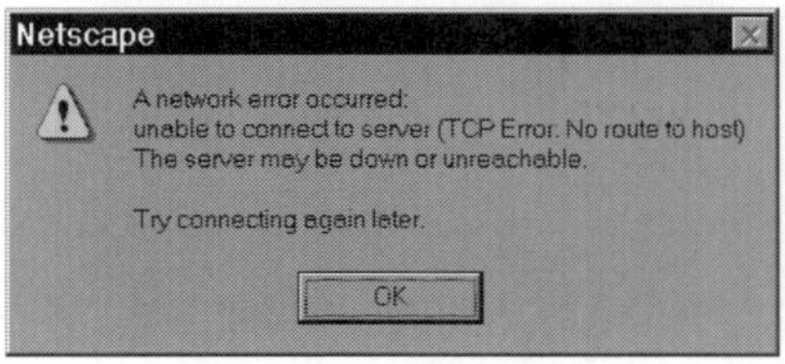
Netscape
A network error occurred:
unable to connect to server (TCP Error: No route to host)
The server may be down or unreachable.
Try connecting again later.
OK

Figure 5.5 Socket disconnected.

If that doesn't work, check to see whether you're still on line. High-speed modems are sensitive creatures—if there's a big-time error transmitting data, usually caused by a noisy line, they may down the connection without giving you any warning (thanks). Try reconnecting and accessing the site again.

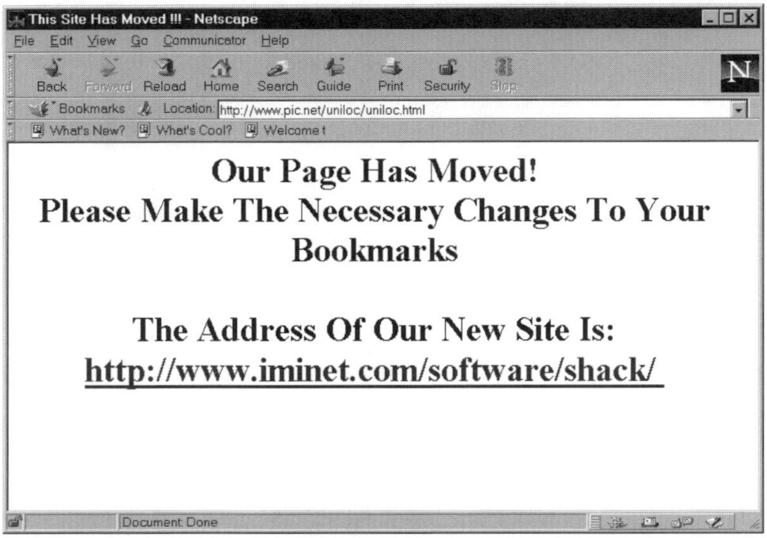
This Site Has Moved !!! - Netscape
File Edit View Go Communicator Help
Back Forward Reload Home Search Guide Print Security Stop
Bookmarks Location: http://www.pic.net/uniloc/uniloc.html
What's New? What's Cool? Welcome t
Our Page Has Moved!
Please Make The Necessary Changes To Your Bookmarks
The Address Of Our New Site Is:
http://www.iminet.com/software/shack/
Document: Done

Figure 5.6 Forwarding address.

It Says "This Site Has Moved"!

Well, make a note of the new hyperlink. Usually, pages such as this one include something you can click to get to the right place (see Figure 5.6).

They're Demanding a Password!

They can do that, if they like. And you can't access the page unless you type the correct login name and password (Figure 5.7). Probably there's information on how to register—if you want to gain access to the site, do it.

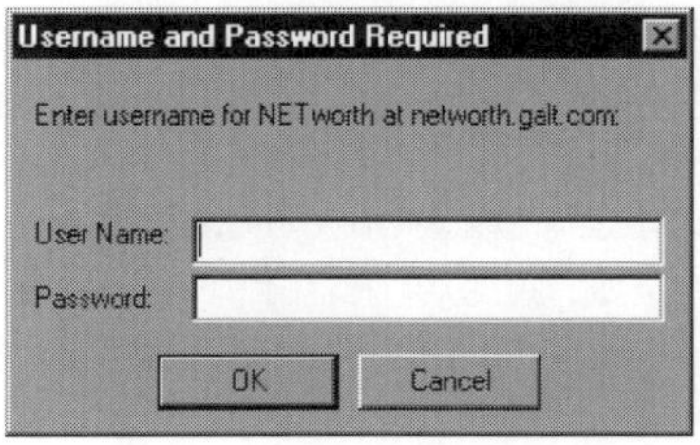
Username and Password Required
Enter username for NETworth at networth.galt.com:
User Name:
Password:
OK
Cancel

Figure 5.7 Login name and password required for access.

It Says "The Information You Have Submitted Is Not Secure"!

And it isn't (Figure 5.8). Any message you send on the Web can be quite easily intercepted and read. That's why you should never, never, never send your

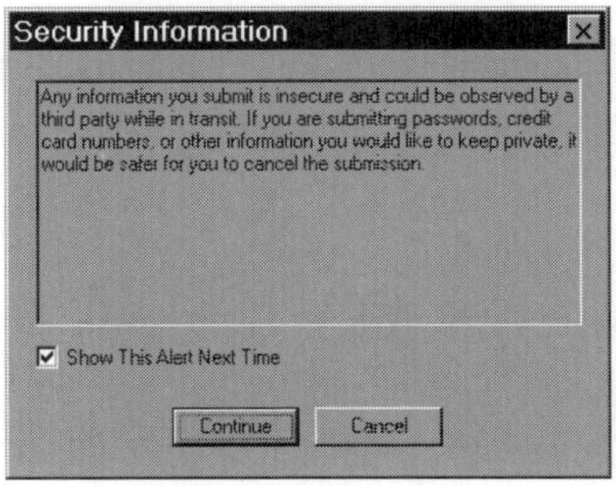
Security Information
Any information you submit is insecure and could be observed by a third party while in transit. If you are submitting passwords, credit card numbers, or other information you would like to keep private, it would be safer for you to cancel the submission.
Show This Alert Next Time
Continue
Cancel

Figure 5.8 Warning about uploading information.

credit card information, or any other personal information, via forms that you fill out in Web documents—unless, that is, you're accessing a secure document (see Chapter 10). This message is telling you that you're uploading (sending) information to a server that isn't secure. (Netscape knows.)

This message gets a bit boring after a while. If you're tired of seeing it, and know better than to upload sensitive information to servers that aren't secure, you can stop Netscape from displaying it. From the Options menu, choose Security Preferences. In the General area, deselect Submitting a Form Insecurely. Click OK to confirm the change.

IT SAYS "JAVASCRIPT ERROR!"

You may see this alert box (see Figure 5.9) if you access a page that's got some sloppy Java or JavaScript programming. Just click OK to see the rest of the page, *sans* the Java applet or JavaScript stuff that's not working correctly.

Alert - Netscape
JavaScript Error: http://www.pbs.org/boatworks/, line 180:
unterminated string literal.
window.status = 'Sign on for some lobste<A HREF=
................^
OK

Figure 5.9 Just click OK if you run into this—it's a sign of sloppy Java or JavaScript programming.

From Here

- Make the Web more accessible by changing your start page. Find out how in Chapter 6.
- Is Netscape running too sluggishly for your taste? Soup it up in Chapter 7, "Improving Netscape Navigator's Performance."
- Can't find your way back to a favorite site? Check out Chapter 8, "Creating and Using Bookmarks."

Chapter 6

Change That Start Page!

You start Netscape, and every time you do, you see Netscape's default start page, at Netscape's headquarters in Menlo Park, California. Wouldn't you like to see something more useful, something more tailored to your Web-browsing needs? If so, you've come to the right place: This chapter shows you how to change the default start page, the page you'll see every time Netscape starts. (You also see this page when you click the Home button.)

What's the point of changing the start page? The improvement is more than cosmetic. A good start page gives you instant access to a huge variety of resources: starting points, subject trees, search engines, news, weather, sports, time-wasting diversions, humor, entertainment, and more.

You can choose any home page you like—this chapter shows you how to hunt down cool home pages and make them your own.

For the Time-Challenged

- A start page is what you see when you start Netscape or click the Home button. You should change the default start page (Netscape's welcome page), substituting something of more personal value to you.
- You can create a customized start page by clicking PowerStart on Netscape's home page. If you like news, though, you'll prefer My Yahoo.
- You can save your bookmark list and make it your home page. For more information, see Chapter 8.

Every reader of this book should check out this chapter and change Netscape's default home page. It's easy, and you don't need to know any HTML. You'll get a lot more out of the Web!

Making Any Page Your Default Start Page

It's easy to make any Web page your default Web page. Like to start your Web sessions with the AltaVista search engine? You can make this your default start page. Here's how to do this.

To make a Web page your default start page:

1. Display the page you want to use as your default start page.
2. From the Edit menu, choose Preferences.
3. In the Category panel, click Browser.
4. In the Browser panel, click Use Current Page in the Home page area.
5. Click OK.

Now that you've redefined your start page, you'll see this page every time Netscape starts. You'll also see this page when you click the Home button.

I'm sick of my start page! Made a bad choice, huh? You can easily change it again. Just repeat the above steps, and choose a different page. If you'd like to restore the default start page, access http://home.netscape com, and then follow the above steps.

Creating a PowerStart Page

How would you like to start each Netscape session with a custom start page, one that contains your very favorite links? With Netscape's PowerStart page, you can, and this section tells you how to do it.

PowerStart is an option on Netscape's home page. Although Netscape has no public plans to change PowerStart, you can bet that somebody's going to say, "Hey, let's totally redesign our home page!" PowerStart might be renamed, or moved, or both, which will force you to hunt around a bit in order to find it. For now, PowerStart works the way I've described. If you can't find PowerStart on Netscape's site, skip to the next section.

Accessing PowerStart

To access PowerStart, look for the PowerStart link on Netscape's home page (to display Netscape's home page, click the Home button on the navigation toolbar). Currently, the link's at the bottom of the page. If you can't find the link, use the following URL: http://personal.netscape.com/custom/index.html.

You'll see Create Your PowerStart Page, the framed document shown in Figure 6.1. Click the Continue button to go on to the PowerStart page builder, shown in Figure 6.2.

Understanding How PowerStart Works

The PowerStart builder page is easy to use. In the right-hand panel, you see the current contents of your page. By default, Netscape gives you the items shown, which include links to the daily news, business and finance sites, sports sites, technology-related sites, search services, and more. Also included is a nifty little Java-based notepad utility, which actually lets you

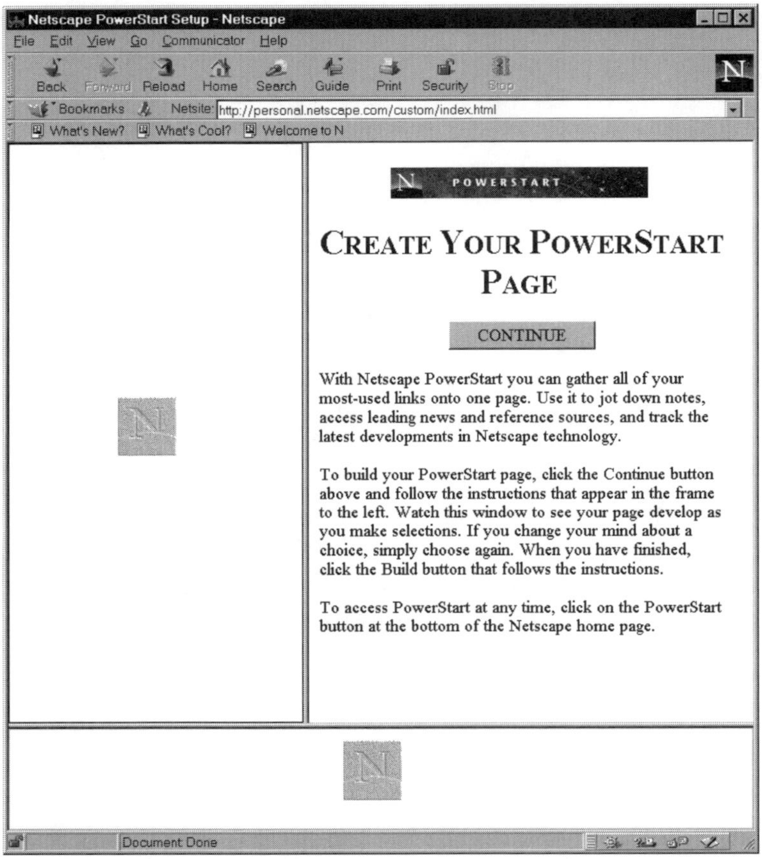
Netscape PowerStart Setup - Netscape
File Edit View Go Communicator Help
Back Forward Reload Home Search Guide Print Security Stop
Bookmarks Netsite: http://personal.netscape.com/custom/index.html
What's New? What's Cool? Welcome to N
POWERSTART
CREATE YOUR POWERSTART PAGE
CONTINUE
With Netscape PowerStart you can gather all of your most-used links onto one page. Use it to jot down notes, access leading news and reference sources, and track the latest developments in Netscape technology.
To build your PowerStart page, click the Continue button above and follow the instructions that appear in the frame to the left. Watch this window to see your page develop as you make selections. If you change your mind about a choice, simply choose again. When you have finished, click the Build button that follows the instructions.
To access PowerStart at any time, click on the PowerStart button at the bottom of the Netscape home page.
Document Done

Figure 6.1 Begin your PowerStart page here.

write notes to yourself ("Don't be a dummy, remember our anniversary!") To select your own sites, scroll down the left panel, select a topic, and choose the options you want by clicking a choice in the bottom panel. As you build your page, Netscape updates the right-hand panel.

Adding Your Stocks or Funds

If you know the ticker symbol of your stocks or funds, you can add a delayed-quote stock ticker to your PowerStart page. Click Stock Ticker. The bottom panel will ask you if you'd like to include a stock ticker. Click Yes,

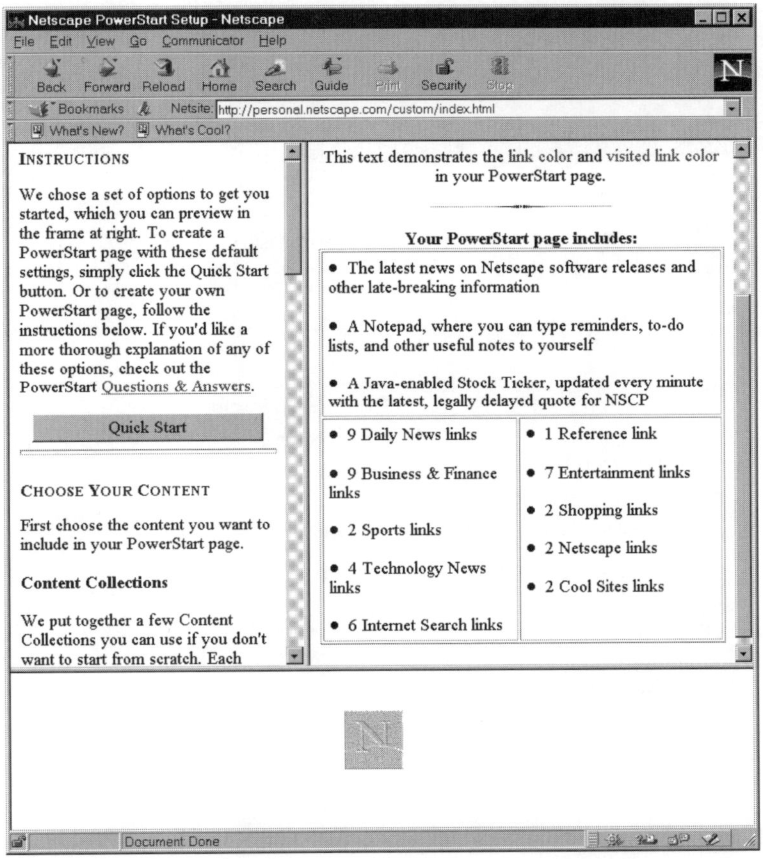
Netscape PowerStart Setup - Netscape
File Edit View Go Communicator Help
Back Forward Reload Home Search Guide Print Security Stop
Bookmarks Netsite: http://personal.netscape.com/custom/index.html
What's New? What's Cool?
INSTRUCTIONS
We chose a set of options to get you started, which you can preview in the frame at right. To create a PowerStart page with these default settings, simply click the Quick Start button. Or to create your own PowerStart page, follow the instructions below. If you'd like a more thorough explanation of any of these options, check out the PowerStart Questions & Answers.
Quick Start
CHOOSE YOUR CONTENT
First choose the content you want to include in your PowerStart page.
Content Collections
We put together a few Content Collections you can use if you don't want to start from scratch. Each
This text demonstrates the link color and visited link color in your PowerStart page.
Your PowerStart page includes:
• The latest news on Netscape software releases and other late-breaking information
• A Notepad, where you can type reminders, to-do lists, and other useful notes to yourself
• A Java-enabled Stock Ticker, updated every minute with the latest, legally delayed quote for NSCP
• 9 Daily News links
• 9 Business & Finance links
• 2 Sports links
• 4 Technology News links
• 6 Internet Search links
• 1 Reference link
• 7 Entertainment links
• 2 Shopping links
• 2 Netscape links
• 2 Cool Sites links
Document: Done

Figure 6.2 The three panels enable you to build your PowerStart page.

and type the ticker symbol of the stock you'd like to track. If you don't know the symbol, click the link that enables you to search for it.

Adding Your Own Links

To add your own links to your PowerStart page, you need the URLs. Look 'em up and write 'em down. When you're ready, scroll down the left panel until you find Personal Links, and click this link. In the bottom panel, you see text boxes that enable you to add personal links (see Figure 6.3).

To add links, do the following:

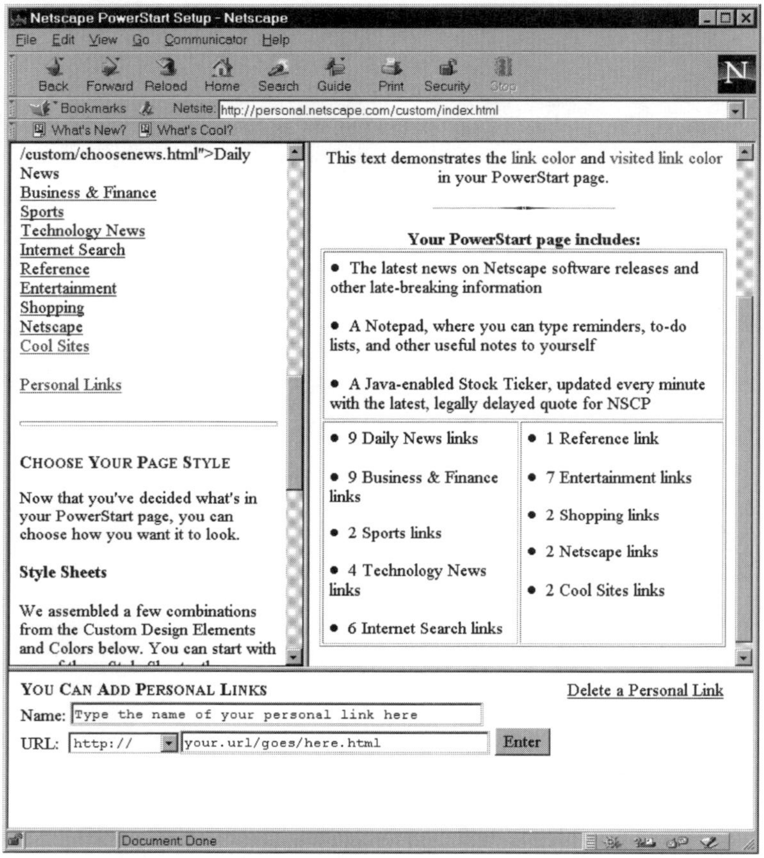
Netscape PowerStart Setup - Netscape
File Edit View Go Communicator Help
Back Forward Reload Home Search Guide Print Security Stop
Bookmarks Netsite: http://personal.netscape.com/custom/index.html
What's New? What's Cool?
/custom/choosenews.html">Daily News
Business & Finance
Sports
Technology News
Internet Search
Reference
Entertainment
Shopping
Netscape
Cool Sites
Personal Links
CHOOSE YOUR PAGE STYLE
Now that you've decided what's in your PowerStart page, you can choose how you want it to look.
Style Sheets
We assembled a few combinations from the Custom Design Elements and Colors below. You can start with
This text demonstrates the link color and visited link color in your PowerStart page.
Your PowerStart page includes:
• The latest news on Netscape software releases and other late-breaking information
• A Notepad, where you can type reminders, to-do lists, and other useful notes to yourself
• A Java-enabled Stock Ticker, updated every minute with the latest, legally delayed quote for NSCP
• 9 Daily News links
• 9 Business & Finance links
• 2 Sports links
• 4 Technology News links
• 6 Internet Search links
• 1 Reference link
• 7 Entertainment links
• 2 Shopping links
• 2 Netscape links
• 2 Cool Sites links
YOU CAN ADD PERSONAL LINKS
Delete a Personal Link
Name: Type the name of your personal link here
URL: http:// your.url/goes/here.html Enter
Document: Done

Figure 6.3 In the bottom panel, you can add personal links to your PowerStart page.

1. In the Name box, delete the existing text and type the text that you want to appear on your PowerStart page. This text should briefly describe the link.
2. In the box just to the right of "URL," leave the setting as it is (http://) if you're planning to access a Web page. Otherwise, choose another option (for example, choose ftp:// if you're planning to access an FTP site).

3. In the box to the right, type the rest of the URL. Check your typing carefully. Note that some Web documents have the extension *.htm, while others use *.html.
4. Click Enter.
5. Repeat steps 1 through 4 to add as many personal sites as you wish.

Making It Pretty

Finished adding links? Now you can choose color and design options.

The easiest way to design your page is to choose one of the predesigned Style Sheets. Click the Style Sheets link. You'll see the Style Sheet options in the bottom panel (Figure 6.4).

After choosing a style sheet, you can change individual layout or color options by clicking one of the following links in the left panel (Layout, Personal greeting or headline, Headline image, Horizontal lines, Background color or pattern, Text color, Link color, Visited link color). Frankly, the predesigned style sheets are OK for most purposes—you don't really need to choose any of these customization options. One exception, perhaps, is Personal greeting or headline; you could use this to say hello to yourself.

How to I get rid of stuff I don't want? Don't want some of PowerStart's default options? To get rid of an unwanted link, just click the link topic (such as "Sports" or "Entertainment," and locate the item list in the bottom window. Just deselect the ones you don't want.

Building Your Page

When you're done choosing the options you want, scroll down to the bottom of the left panel, and click Build. You'll see the results on your screen (Figure 6.5).

Cool, but I Want to Change It!

No problemo. Just click Change PowerStart, one of the navigation options at the top of the page. You'll see pretty much the same PowerStart build page you worked with earlier, except that this one "knows" all your previous choices. You can add or delete as much content as you like. When you're done, click the Build button again.

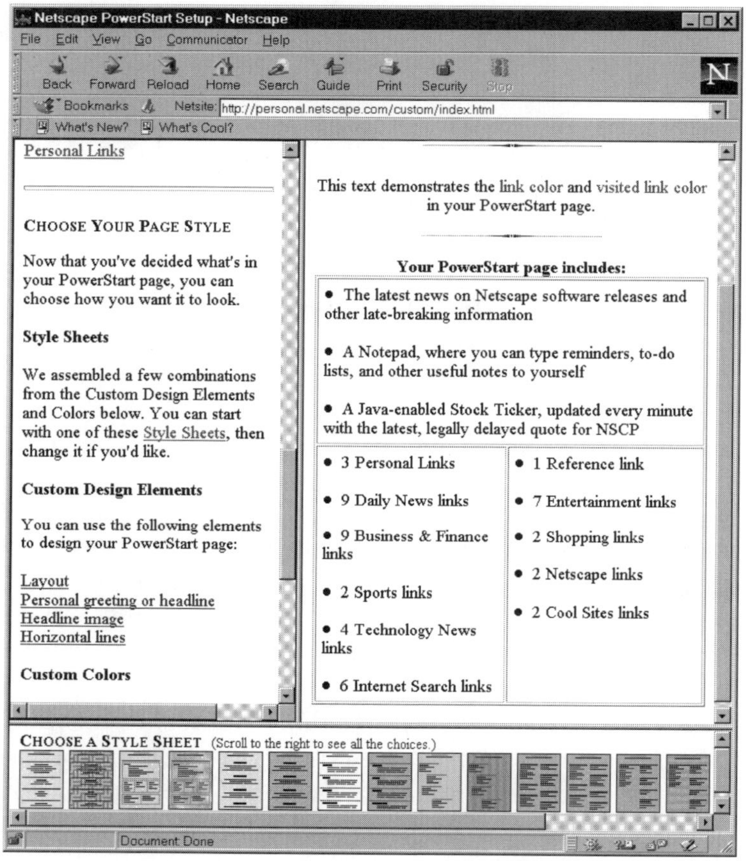
Netscape PowerStart Setup - Netscape
File Edit View Go Communicator Help
Back Forward Reload Home Search Guide Print Security Stop
Bookmarks Netsite: http://personal.netscape.com/custom/index.html
What's New? What's Cool?
Personal Links
CHOOSE YOUR PAGE STYLE
Now that you've decided what's in your PowerStart page, you can choose how you want it to look.
Style Sheets
We assembled a few combinations from the Custom Design Elements and Colors below. You can start with one of these Style Sheets, then change it if you'd like.
Custom Design Elements
You can use the following elements to design your PowerStart page:
Layout
Personal greeting or headline
Headline image
Horizontal lines
Custom Colors
This text demonstrates the link color and visited link color in your PowerStart page.
Your PowerStart page includes:
• The latest news on Netscape software releases and other late-breaking information
• A Notepad, where you can type reminders, to-do lists, and other useful notes to yourself
• A Java-enabled Stock Ticker, updated every minute with the latest, legally delayed quote for NSCP
• 3 Personal Links
• 9 Daily News links
• 9 Business & Finance links
• 2 Sports links
• 4 Technology News links
• 6 Internet Search links
• 1 Reference link
• 7 Entertainment links
• 2 Shopping links
• 2 Netscape links
• 2 Cool Sites links
CHOOSE A STYLE SHEET (Scroll to the right to see all the choices.)
Document: Done

Figure 6.4 It's easy to design your page's appearance using the preconfigured style sheets (visible in the bottom panel).

Adding Your PowerStart Page to Your Personal Toolbar

To add the page you've just created to your Personal toolbar, just click the icon next to the Netsite box and drag this icon to the Personal Toolbar. Presto! The site's added.

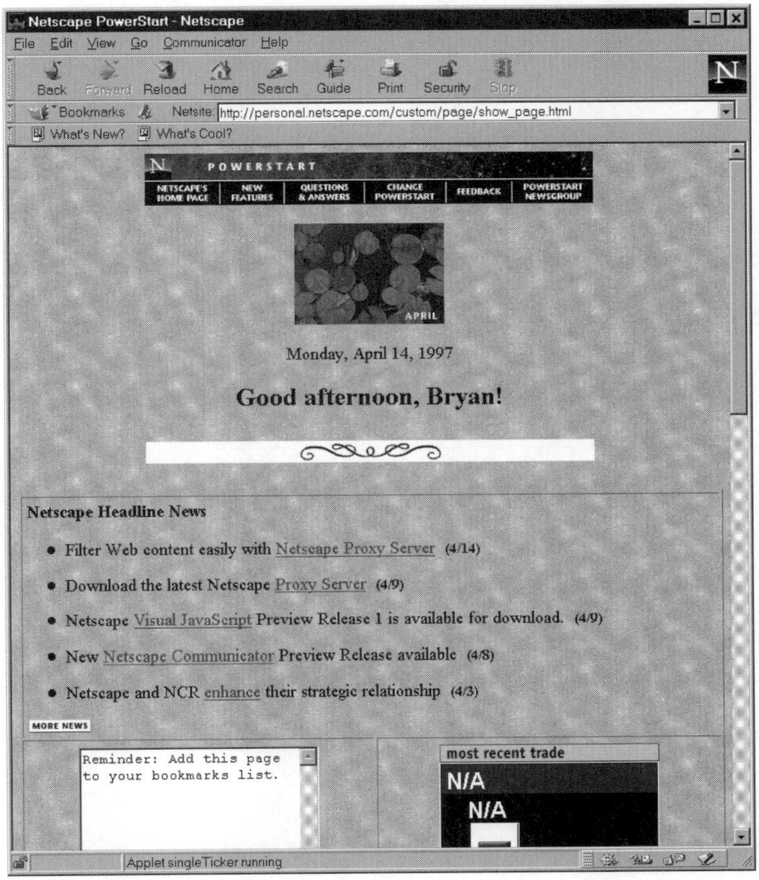

Figure 6.5 Here's my customized PowerStart page.

Making Your PowerStart Page Your Default Start Page

Would you like to make your PowerStart page appear automatically every time you start Netscape or click the Home button? It's easy. Just display the PowerStart page, and then flip to the section of this chapter called "Making Any Page Your Default Start Page."

My Yahoo!

If you like PowerStart, but you'd like more news, you're going to love My Yahoo!. This works exactly like PowerStart—you build your page by making choices. Unlike PowerStart, your My Yahoo! displays content as well as links (see Figure 6.6 to give you an idea of what's possible).

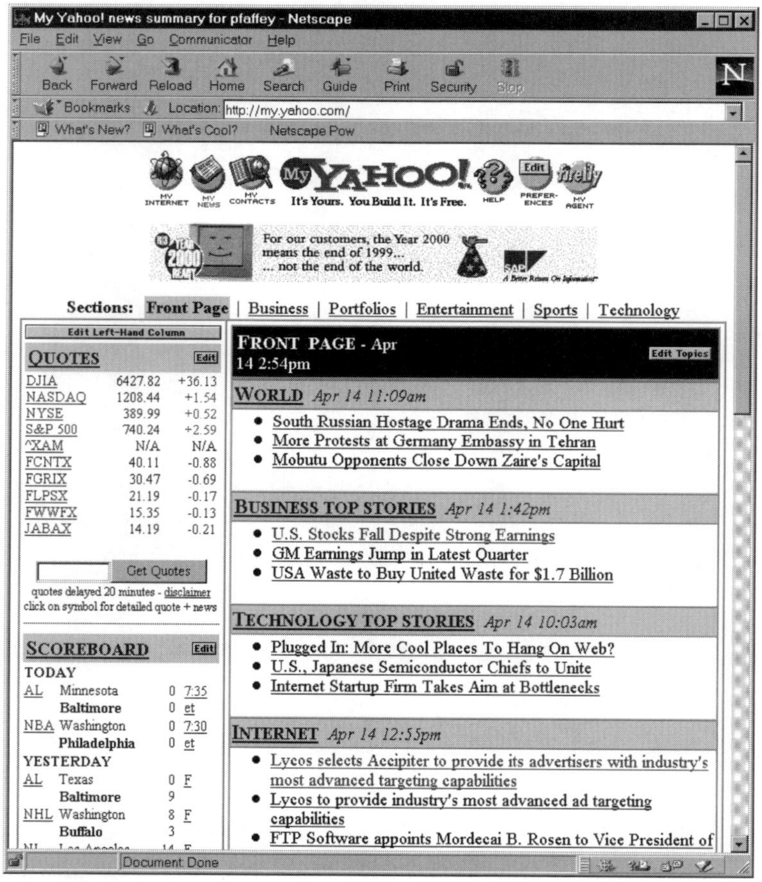

Figure 6.6 My Yahoo! enables you to create a customized news page, replete with current stock quotes, a sports scoreboard, and weather.

To create your My Yahoo! page, access Yahoo (www.yahoo.com), and click the My Yahoo link. Click the Start Your Own button, and just follow the on-screen instructions to make your page. As with the PowerStart page, you can add the finished product to your Toolbar (see "Adding Your PowerStart Page to Your Personal Toolbar," above), or make it your default start page (see "Making Any Page Your Default Start Page").

More Great Start Page Ideas

You'll find lots of great start pages on the Web. Does one of these work as your default start page?

- **AltaVista** (altavista.digital.com) Do you typically start with a search? Why not make AltaVista your default start page?
- **Christian Science Monitor** (www.csmonitor.com) Would you like to start the day with one of the most respected national newspapers in the U.S.? It's the online edition of the *Christian Science Monitor*, and it has many very attractive features—including a free archive search going all the way back to the late 1960s. (In case you're not familiar with this newspaper, it's obviously sponsored by a religious organization, but the reporting is secular and highly respected for its objectivity.) Figure 6.7 shows the *Monitor's* front page. Among the many wonderful features: A Reference Links page that links outstanding Web sites related to today's stories. This is one of the Web's very best sites, period.
- **CNNfn** (www.cnnfn.com) This is the Cable News Network's financial news page, and you might really like having this as your start page if you're into investing or business. You get hot stories, current market reports, columns, and tons of great links (see Figure 6.8).
- **Nerd World Media** (http://www.nerdworld.com/) Here's a fun starting point (Figure 6.9) that divides more than 150,000 sites into two major categories, Leisure and Knowledge; these categories are further broken down into a variety of subject headings. Hip and fun.
- **Point** (http://www.pointcom.com/) Point is famous for its "top 5% of the Web" awards, which purport to identify the cream of the Web

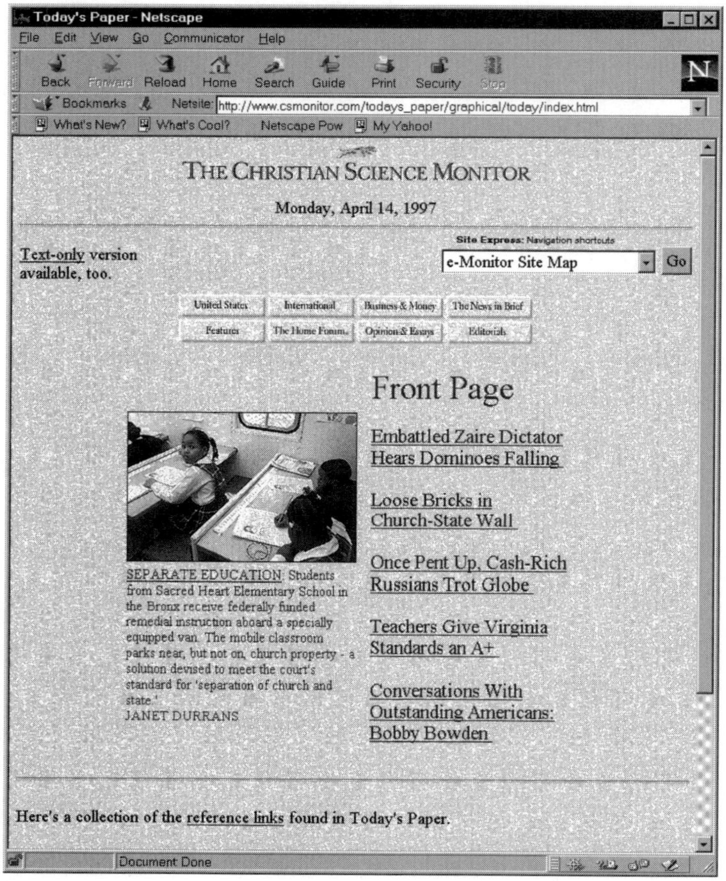

Figure 6.7 Start each day with the *Christian Science Monitor.*

crop. A subject-oriented starting points page containing high-quality Web sites, Point indexes sites in the following subject areas: education, business/finance, entertainment, news/info, leisure activities, government and politics, science/technology, computers/Internet, shopping, arts/humanities, health/medicine, social and community affairs, kids, and "the road less traveled."

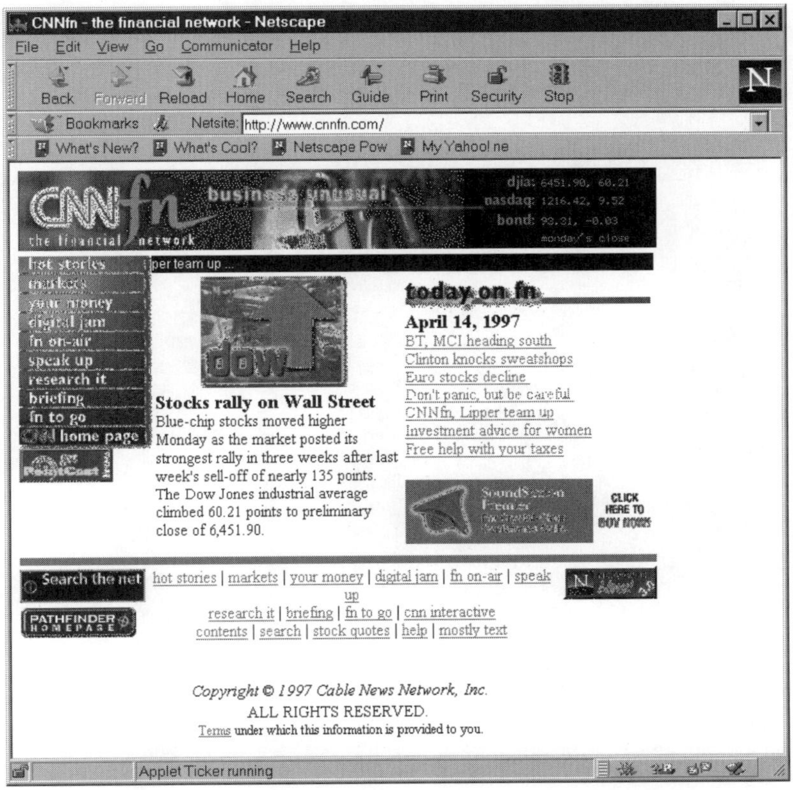

Figure 6.8 CNNfn has the right stuff for investors.

- **Washington Post** (www.washingtonpost.com) So you're a newspaper junkie, huh? Welcome to the club. You're going to love the *Post's* Web page, which features the latest news and in-depth *Post* features and columns.

To make any of these great pages your default start page, just type its URL in the Home Page Location box in the Appearance page in the Preferences dialog box, as described in the previous section.

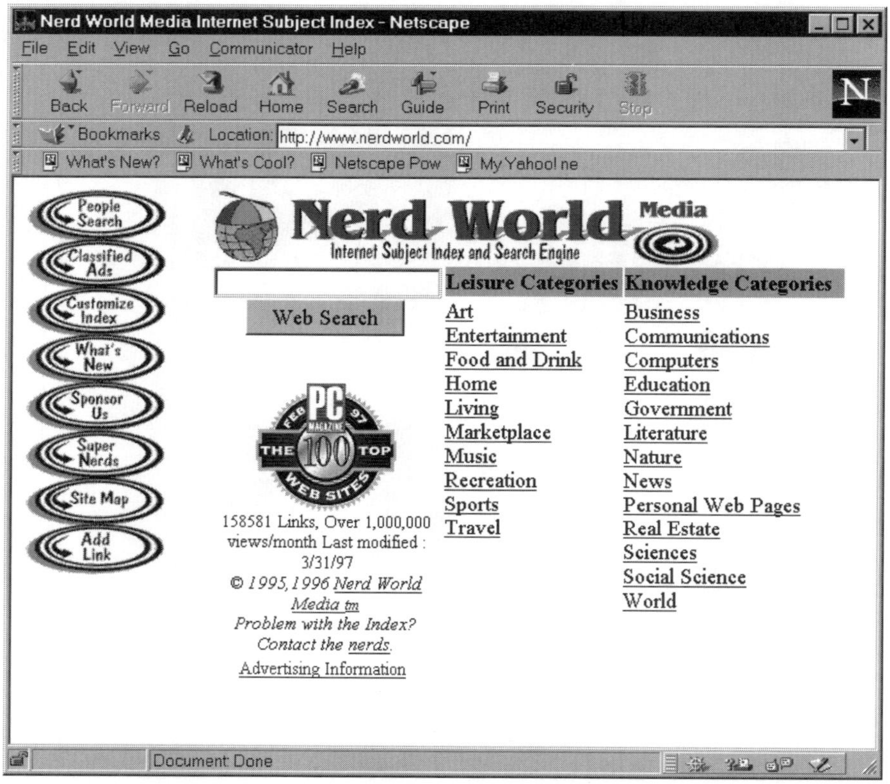

Figure 6.9 Nerd World Media packs more than 150,000 sites into a cool starting point.

FROM HERE

- Is Netscape Navigator too slow for your tastes? Speed up the program's performance considerably by following the tips and strategies in the following chapter.
- Learn how to save bookmarks in Chapter 8.

Chapter

7

Improving Netscape Navigator's Performance

By now, you've mastered the essentials of Netscape Navigator, and I'll bet you've had some fun exploring the Web. In this chapter, you go beyond the basics. You learn the time-saving tricks and fine points that Netscape mavens use to make Netscape run faster, work more smoothly, and in general cause less stress.

Use the Pop-Up Menus

Here's a great time-saving trick. Instead of using the menus, keyboard, or toolbar, try pointing at something and right-clicking the mouse. You'll see a pop-up menu, such as the one shown in Figure 7.1. These menus group all the relevant options for whatever you're pointing at. For example, the menu shown in Figure 7.1 pops up when you point to a graphic and click the right mouse button. Among the various nifty things you can do: Save the image to your hard disk and set the image as wallpaper for your computer!

Try pointing to different things within the document to see what's on the menu. You'll usually see the basics:

- **Back** Same as clicking the Back button on the toolbar.
- **Forward** Same as clicking the Forward button on the toolbar.
- **Reload** Same as clicking the Reload button on the toolbar.
- **Stop** Same as clicking the Stop button on the toolbar.
- **View Source** Displays the HTML code that underlies the document. This is the same as choosing Page Source from the View menu.
- **View Info** Displays information about the document. This is the same as choosing Page Info from the View menu.
- **Add Bookmark** Adds the current page to your Bookmark list.
- **Create Shortcut** In Windows 95 or Windows NT, creates a desktop shortcut for the current document.
- **Send Page** Sends the current page's URL to somebody via e-mail. This is the same as choosing Send Page from the File menu.

These are the basic options when you click on a document's background. Try right-clicking links and images; you'll see additional options that are relevant to what you're doing. For example, when you right-click a hyperlink, you see the following additional options:

- **Open in New Window** Opens this link in a new Navigator window.
- **Open in Composer** Opens this link in a Composer window for editing.
- **Save Links As** Saves the link as an HTML or text file.
- **Copy Link Location** Copies the URL to the clipboard, so that you can paste it elsewhere.

Right-clicking is cool. Learn it, use it.

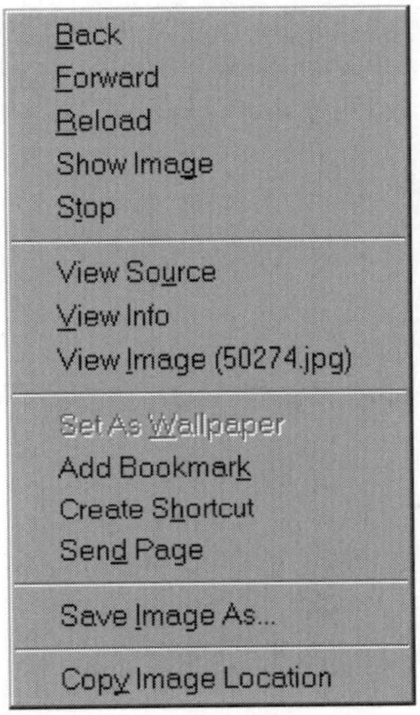

Figure 7.1 Pop-up menu.

WHERE THE HECK IS THAT TEXT? (FINDING TEXT IN A DOCUMENT)

AltaVista says the document you're reading really does contain the phrase "The history of disestablishmentarianism." Only, your poor, tired eyes can't find this phrase in what turns out to be an 80-pager! Don't wear yourself out needlessly: Let Netscape do the hunting for you.

To find text in a document, do the following

1. From the Edit menu, choose Find Text in Page, or use the Ctrl + F shortcut. You'll see the Find dialog box, shown in Figure 7.2.
2. In the Find What box, type the text you're trying to match. Be sure to check for typos or spelling errors.
3. If you're trying to match a certain pattern of capitalization, click Match case.

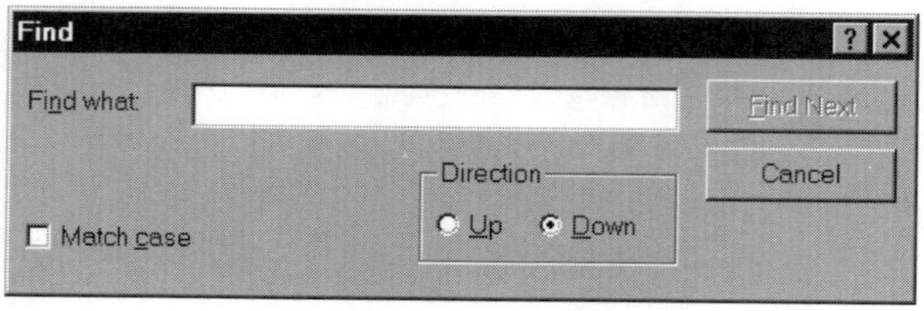

Figure 7.2 Don't go blind hunting for text manually—use the find command.

4. Click Down to search from the cursor's current location to the end of the document, or Up to search from the cursor's current location to the beginning of the document.
5. Click Find Next. If Netscape finds a match, the program highlights the match and displays the matching text in reverse video. To find another match, click Find Next.

   If there's no match, you'll see an alert box that says, "Search string not found!" This means that Netscape couldn't find any text that matches what you typed.
6. When you're done searching—either you've found the text you're looking for or you've given up—close the Find dialog box by clicking Cancel or by clicking the close box.

After you close the Find dialog box, Netscape "remembers" the last search text you typed. To search again for the same text, even in a different Web page, click the Edit menu and choose Find Again (or press Ctrl + G).

I'm Going Blind Reading This! (Increasing Font Size)

Font too small? Some pages really strain the ol' eyeballs (for an example, see Figure 7.3). You can make the font size bigger (see Figure 7.4), although doing so might mess up the layout a bit.

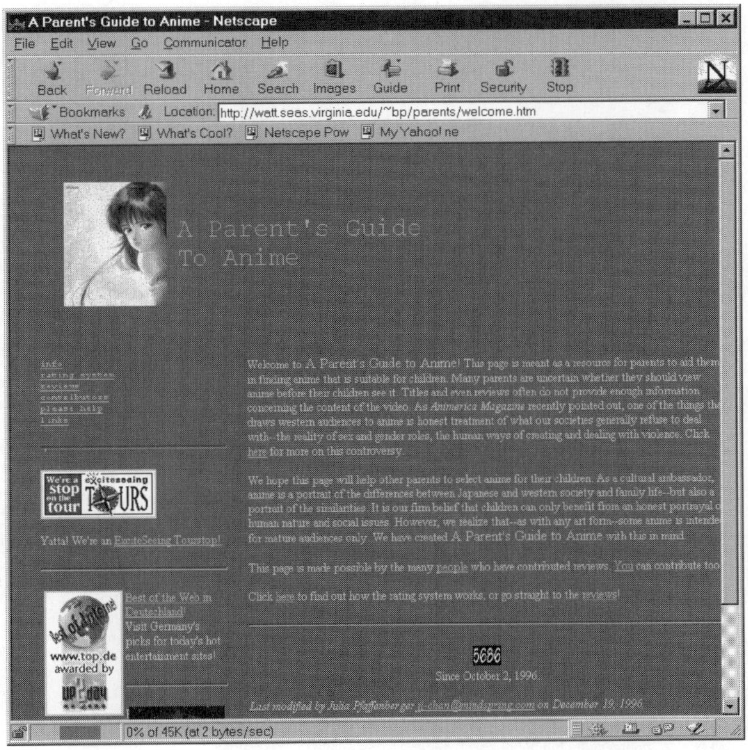

Figure 7.3 Web page with small font size.

To make the font size bigger, do the following:

- From the View menu, choose Increase Font

  or

- Press Ctrl +] (right bracket).

The more times you press this command, the bigger the font gets—until it gets *ridiculously* big (see Figure 7.5). There doesn't seem to be any limit to how many times you can use this command—the font just keeps getting bigger and bigger until you get sick of doing this.

A Parent's Guide to Anime - Netscape
File Edit View Go Communicator Help
Back Forward Reload Home Search Images Guide Print Security Stop
Bookmarks Location: http://watt.seas.virginia.edu/~bp/parents/welcome.htm
What's New? What's Cool? Netscape Pow My Yahoo! ne
A Parent's Guide To Anime
info
rating system
reviews
contributors
please help
links
We're a stop on the tour excitseeing TOURS
Yatta! We're an ExciteSeeing Tourstop!
Welcome to A Parent's Guide to Anime! This page is meant as a resource for parents to aid them in finding anime that is suitable for children. Many parents are uncertain whether they should view anime before their children see it. Titles and even reviews often do not provide enough information concerning the content of the video. As Animerica Magazine recently pointed out, one of the things that draws western audiences to anime is honest treatment of what our societies generally refuse to deal with--the reality of sex and gender roles, the human ways of creating and dealing with violence. Click here for more on this controversy.
Document: Done

Figure 7.4 Web page with large of font size.

To make the font size smaller, do the following:

- From the View menu, choose Decrease Font

  or

- Press Ctrl + [(left bracket).

You can use this command more than once, too. Every time you choose Decrease Font, the font gets smaller, until you reach another point of absur-

Figure 7.5 Font enlarged to point of utter absurdity.

dity (Figure 7.6). This is some program, isn't it? Netscape gives you enough power to totally destroy somebody's painstaking Web page design. Still, it's nice to be able to make the fonts a bit bigger if you're having trouble reading.

STOP! *PLEASE* STOP!

You just clicked a hyperlink. It looked interesting. But now you can see that it's going to be a pain. There are at least 50 pictures of the Brady Bunch. And it's taking forever to download. Stop the madness! Here's how:

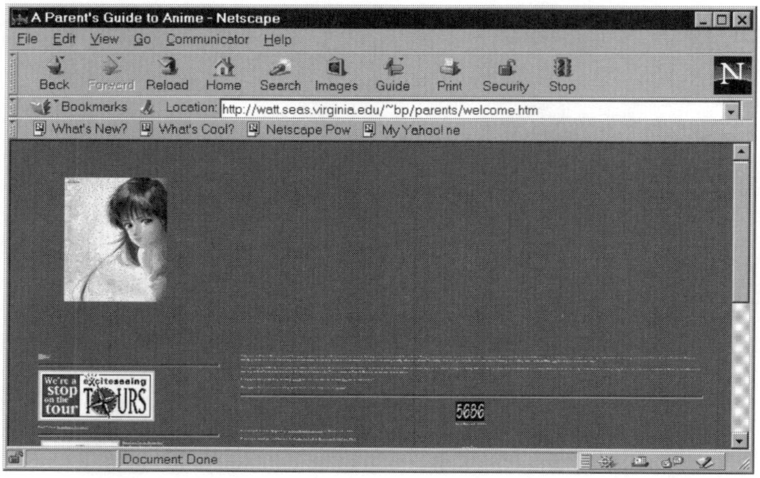

Figure 7.6 Font decreased in size so that it's totally illegible.

- Click the Stop button

  or

- Press Esc

  or

- From the View menu, choose Stop Page Loading

After you stop downloading, you may see part of the document on-screen, but it may show signs of its brutal treatment (for example, inline images that didn't download will be shown with placeholders, like the ones in Figure 7.7). Just click the Back button to abandon this battle scene. If you feel sorry for the document and would like to give it an opportunity to live once again, click the Reload button.

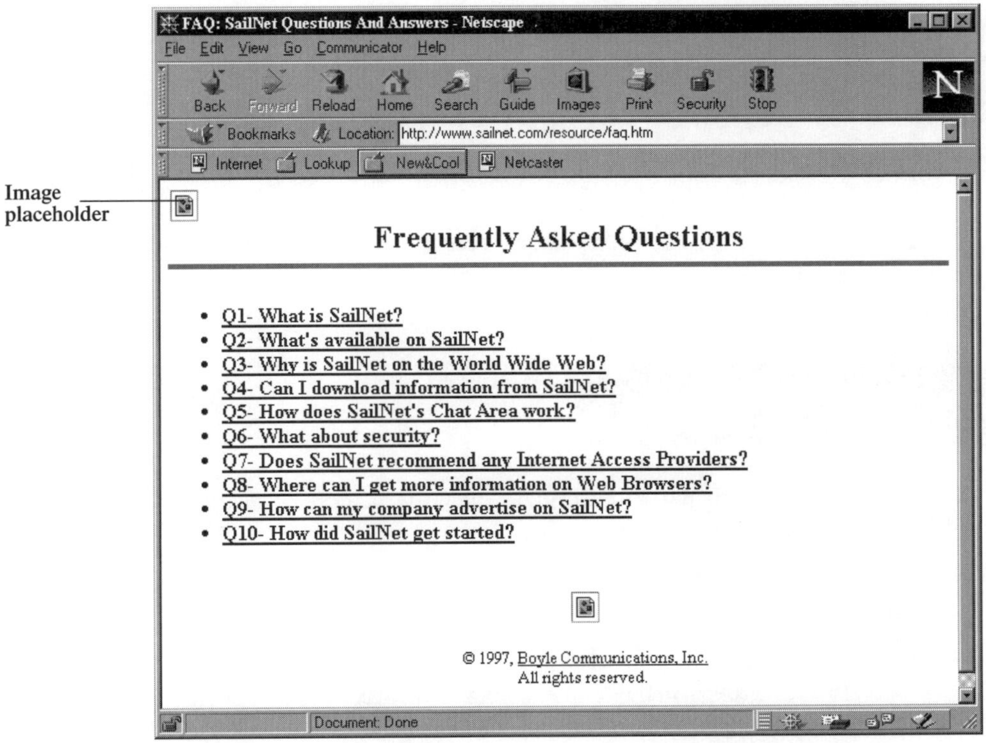

Figure 7.7 Document with image placeholders (produced by interrupted transfer). Thoughtful Web authors include text explaining what the graphs would show.

This Document's Too Slow! (Too Many Images)

If you're accessing the Web over a SLIP or PPP connection, documents stuffed with in-line images can take forever to download. That's OK, if you're really interested in the pictures; after all, why else would you access the *Playboy* Home Page? (Of course, I only read the interviews.) Often, though, you're searching for some specific information, and the graphics—however pretty—serve only to delay your journey. For such Web ventures, you'd be wise to turn off the automatic downloading of in-line images. Here's how.

Turning Off Automatic Image Downloading

To turn off the automatic downloading of in-line images, do the following:

1. From the Edit menu, choose Preferences. You'll see the Preferences dialog box.

For the Time-Challenged

- Try right-clicking various objects on your screen. You'll see a pop-up menu that conveniently groups options.
- If you've inadvertently clicked a hyperlink and Netscape begins downloading a huge, unwanted file, click the Stop button.
- To speed document downloading considerably (a plus if you're using a slow SLIP/PPP connection), turn off the automatic display of in-line images. You can selectively display an individual graphic by right-clicking it and choosing Show Image.
- Don't go nuts trying to get back to a document by clicking the Back button—use the Back button's drop-down list instead. While you browse, Netscape keeps a record of the documents you've visited in the current lineage (a series of documents that are all linked outward from a single, beginning document). While you're still within the lineage, you can go back to any of these documents by choosing a document name from the Go menu. If you begin a new lineage, however, Netscape erases the previous lineage's history list and begins a new one.
- Because Netscape erases a lineage's history list when you start a new lineage, you should begin the new lineage in a new window. (Each window's history list is separate.)
- If Windows messes up Netscape's screen display, choose Refresh from the View menu. If you've redisplayed a previously accessed document and suspect that the original may have changed, click the Reload button.

2. In the Category list (the left panel), click Advanced. You'll see the Advanced options.
3. De-select Automatically load images.

Hey, I turned off images! Why do I still see some of them? Netscape still displays in-line images if there's a copy in the cache. For more information on the cache, see "Increasing the Cache Size," in the next section.

You've turned off automatic image downloading. Great! Documents load quickly, but they aren't much visual fun anymore, are they? In place of the in-line images, you see *placeholders*, which to some people look like little crying robots. Well, read on.

Selectively Loading In-Line Images

After you've turned off automatic image downloading, you can view any single in-line graphic, just as you please. This is very cool. The technique uses that sophisticated right-clicking maneuver that gives a certain distinguished body language to your computer usage.

To view an individual in-line graphic (when automatic image downloading has been turned off):

1. Point to the image's placeholder, and click the right mouse button.
2. From the pop-up menu, choose Show Image (to display the image within the current document) or View Image (to view the graphic in a new, separate document). Netscape will download the image you've clicked (Figure 7.8).

After you turn off automatic image downloading, you'll see a new button—Image1—on the Navigation toolbar. To download the current page's image, just click this button.

How do I know which image to download? The better Web authors provide text that explains what the image is for. Look for this text next to the placeholder.

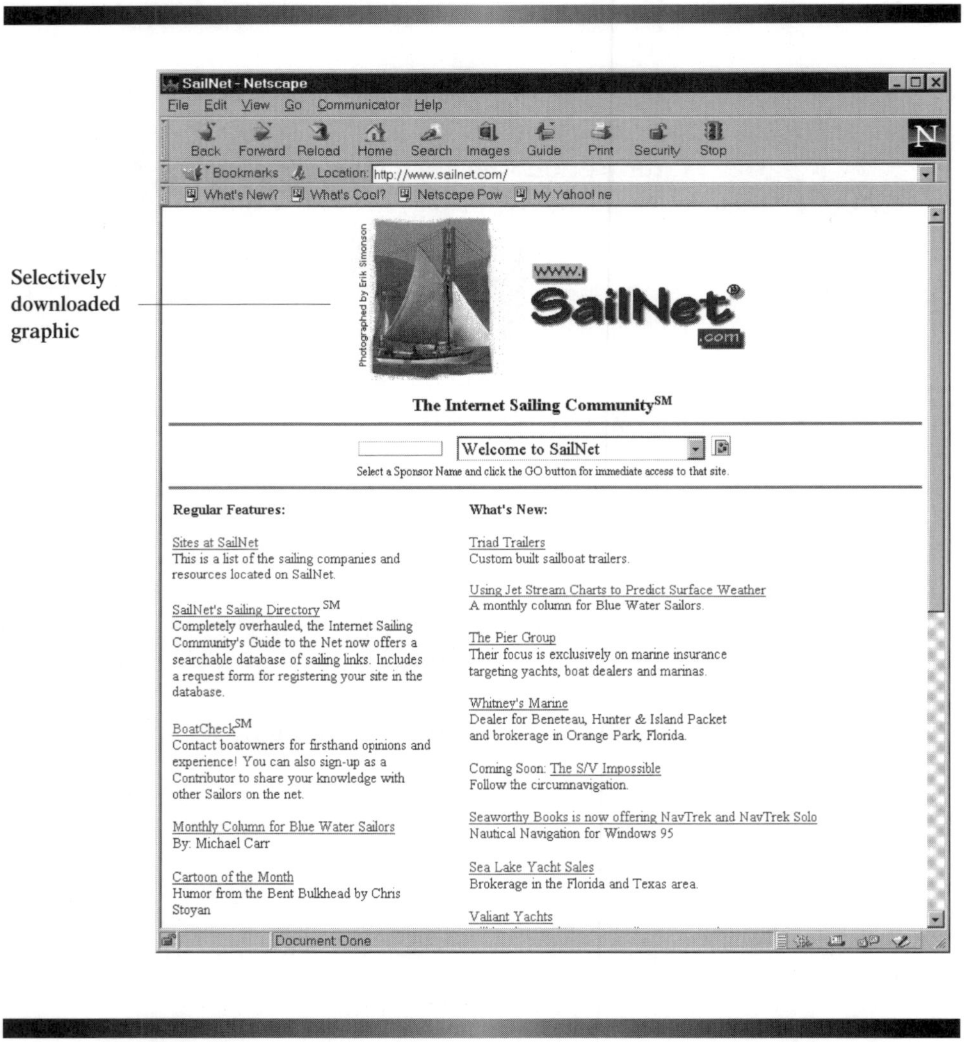

Figure 7.8 Image selectively downloaded.

Downloading All the Images in a Document

You can also download all the images in a given document:

- From the View menu, choose Show Images

I don't care how long it takes to download the pictures! I want images on by default! No problem. From the Options menu, choose Preferences. Click Advanced, and select Automatically load images.

These animations are driving me crazy! One of the latest innovations in Web publishing is the GIF animation, which allows almost any Web publisher to include cute little animations on their Web pages. No programming is required. This is nice, and often adds a lot, but more than a few Web authors overdo it, and the animations become distracting. If they're bugging you, you can turn them off. To do so, click View on the menu bar, and choose Stop Animations.

Increasing the Cache Size

A *cache* is a temporary storage location, like the ones thieves use to stash the loot until they get out of the pen. By the way, cache is pronounced "cash." Netscape uses cache memory to store recently accessed documents—and as you'll learn in this section, one of the best things you can do to increase Netscape's speed is to increase the size of the disk cache.

How the Cache Works

When you download a document, Netscape places the document in the cache. Should you wish to go back to a document you have viewed previously, Netscape locates and displays the document in the cache rather than retrieving it again from the network. Since cache retrievals are many times faster than network retrievals, this produces an impressive gain in Netscape's speed.

Where Does Netscape Store Cached Documents?

Netscape employs two caches, a memory cache and a disk cache.

- **The Memory Cache** This cache is a portion of your computer's random-access memory (RAM) that has been set aside for storing the most recently accessed documents. In comparison to network retrieval, retrieval from the memory cache is very fast; compare, for instance, how long it takes to download a new document and how long it takes to redisplay the same document by clicking the Back button. By default, Netscape sets aside 1024 Kilobyte, abbreviated KB, for the memory cache. (1024 KB is equal to one megabyte.) Just how many documents the memory cache holds depends on the average size of the documents you've retrieved; a text-only document may require as little as 32 K, while a document loaded with inline images may consume the entire cache. As you retrieve additional documents, older documents are flushed (removed) from the cache. At the end of your Netscape session, the memory cache is erased as you quit Netscape.

- **The Disk Cache** This cache is a portion of your computer's hard disk that, like the memory cache, has been set aside for storing the most recently accessed documents. By default, Netscape sets aside 7680 KB for this purpose. As you retrieve additional documents, older documents are flushed from the cache. Unlike the memory cache, the disk cache retains documents between Netscape sessions. About 7.7 megabytes of previously accessed Web documents are present on your disk, ready for fast retrieval should you access these documents again.

When Does Netscape Use the Caches?

The two caches come into play in the following situations:

- **When you access a visited hyperlink** As you know, Netscape keeps track of visited hyperlinks, hyperlinks to documents that you have previously accessed. These hyperlinks appear in a distinctive color. When you access a visited hyperlink by any means (choosing a bookmark, clicking a visited hyperlink, or typing the URL directly), Netscape contacts the server and attempts to verify whether the document has been altered since its last retrieval. If the document has been altered, Netscape retrieves a new copy. If not, Netscape retrieves the document from the disk cache. By default, Netscape verifies visited hyperlinks every time you access one.

- **When you click the Back button** If you click Back, you're returning to a document that you have accessed in the current Netscape session. For this reason, it's probable that the document has not been altered since its last retrieval, so Netscape does not contact the server to see whether the document has changed. Instead, the program retrieves the document from the memory cache or, if it has been flushed from the memory cache, from the disk cache.

Should You Increase the Size of the Caches?

If you can, yes. Take the following quick quizzes to find out whether increasing the size of the caches is for you.

- **Increasing the size of the memory cache** Do you frequently find yourself clicking the Back button to go back to previously accessed documents? Do you run Netscape all by itself, with no other big programs running at the same time? Do you have 16 or 32 MB of RAM? If your answer to all these questions is "Yes," you can improve Netscape's performance dramatically by increasing the size of the memory cache. A cache that's 2048 KB will hold almost twice as many documents as the default 1024 KB cache, but it will leave less memory for other applications. With a 2048 KB cache, there's a better chance that Netscape will be able to retrieve a redisplayed document from the memory cache, which is faster than the disk cache and much faster than network retrieval.
- **Increasing the size of the disk cache** Do you have at least 50 MB of free hard disk space? Do you frequently access documents that have lots of in-line images, and redisplay them in subsequent sessions? If your answer to both these questions is "Yes," you may wish to increase the size of Netscape's disk cache. You won't notice any difference until you try to redisplay a document you accessed several weeks ago; the larger the cache, the less chance there is that this document has been flushed from the cache. If it's still in the cache, retrieval will be much faster than network retrieval, which is Netscape's only option if the document isn't present in either cache.

For information on modifying the size of the caches, see the next section.

Changing Cache Size Defaults

If you've decided to change the default size of the caches, follow these instructions:

1. From the Edit menu, choose Preferences.
2. Click the Advanced tab. If necessary, click the plus sign (+) next to Advanced so you can see the options under Advanced.
3. Click Cache. You'll see the Cache options shown in Figure 7.9.
4. To change the size of the memory cache, type a new number in the Memory Cache box. The default size is 1024 KB. If you have lots of free memory, change this to 2000 KB or more.
5. To change the size of the disk cache, type a new number in the Disk Cache box. Don't type a number that exceeds half of your available disk space.
6. Click OK to confirm your preferences and exit.

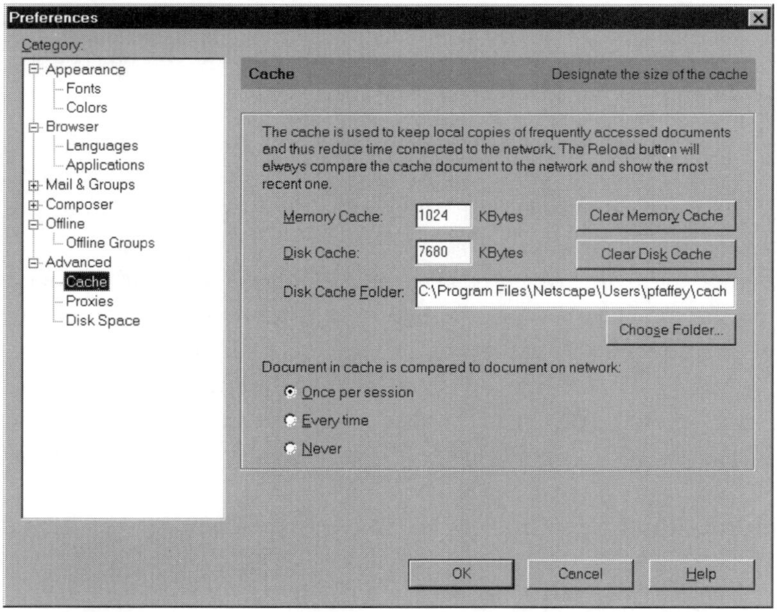

Figure 7.9 Cache options.

I'm out of hard disk space! After you increase the size of your disk cache and use your system for a while, you may run out of hard disk space—believe me, it happens. Just bear in mind that you can free up space—maybe a lot of space—by reducing the size of Netscape's cache.

Changing the Verification Frequency (A Super Speed Trick)

As you've just learned, Netscape stores a copy of visited documents in the disk cache. When you reaccess one of these documents, the program *verifies* the document. In brief, this means that the program contacts the original site to determine whether the document has changed since it was last downloaded. If the document has changed, Netscape downloads a new copy.

Verification is time-consuming—in fact, it cuts down the cache's performance considerably. Recognizing this fact, Netscape's designers set up the program so that it verifies documents only once per session. If you revisit the document later in the same session, the program loads it directly from the cache without verification—try it. As you can see, the second load is much faster. The speed is limited only by the data transfer rate of your hard disk drive.

So here's the super speed trick: You can change the verification setting so that Netscape *never* checks to see whether the document has changed. You can choose this setting in the Cache page of the Preferences dialog box—but before you do, consider whether you really want to do this.

What's the effect of changing the reload checking frequency to "Never"? A super speed improvement—you won't believe it. When you access a document that's in the cache, it loads very quickly because Netscape does not have to send a message out over the network.

But here's the danger. If the document you're accessing really *has* changed, you won't know it. Netscape will show you the copy that's in the cache. There might be some important new information in the new version of the document, the one that's available out on the Web—but you're in the dark. To be sure, you can manually initiate a check by clicking the Reload button (discussed later in this chapter), but you might forget to do so.

Because you might miss important new information by using the "Never" setting, you should think twice before changing the default setting (Once per Session). If you decide to go ahead and make the change, please put a big sign by your computer that says, "Remember to click Reload if you suspect the document has changed!"

To change the default verification setting:

1. From the Exit menu, choose Preferences.
2. Click Advanced, and then Click Cache.
3. Click Never.
4. Click OK to confirm your preferences and exit.

Should you use the "Every Time" verification option? Only if you're working with important, time-sensitive information, such as stock quotes. With this option, Netscape always verifies whether documents have changed before loading them from the cache. The result is sluggish operation, but you'll be certain that you'll never miss a change in an important document you're using.

When Should You Flush the Caches?

Netscape provides commands, found in the Cache page of the Preferences dialog box, that permit you to flush the memory cache and disk cache manually. The only reason you'd want to do this is for security. Put bluntly, the cache provides an electronic trail, readable by a knowledgeable snooper, that tells where you've been browsing lately.

To flush the memory cache, click Clear Memory Cache in the Cache page of the Preferences dialog box.

To flush the disk cache, click Clear Disk Cache. *Note:* This operation may take a few minutes.

Remember that deleting files doesn't destroy them beyond recovery—deleted files can be undeleted. To eradicate your traces totally, obtain a program that can "wipe" your hard disk so that all areas containing deleted files are overwritten with garbage data.

Finding a Document in the Cache

As you've just learned, Netscape downloads and saves a copy of the documents you've visited, up to the limits of the disk storage space that has been set aside for this purpose. Saved are every component of these documents, including the HTML text, GIF and JPEG graphics, and text files. And I do mean *every* component—every little button and rule, the cool icons and banners, the works

Since these documents are stored in the cache, can't you go into the cache with File Manager (Windows 3.1) or Windows Explorer (Windows 95) and open them individually? Yes, but there's just one catch: Netscape renames all these files using a coding scheme that makes perfect sense to the browser but no sense at all to humans. The cache is full of files with names such as M0B8V1.gif and M0OB56LO.html. What's in 'em? Who knows? There are hundreds or even thousands of these files, and you'd go nuts going through all of them.

The Document Info dialog box contains lots of interesting information about a document. Listed are not only the document's URL, but also the URLs of all the Web resources included in the document (hyperlinks, graphics, the works). You can access any of these by clicking the URL, which is an active hyperlink.

If you'd like to see one of these documents again, the easiest way is to use Netscape to locate the document on the Web, and let Netscape find and redisplay the cached version. Once you've done so, you can determine the cached file's name.

To determine the file name of a cached document:

1. Locate the document on the Web and display it using Netscape.
2. From the View menu, choose Page Info. You'll see the Document Info dialog box, shown in Figure 7.10.
3. In the lower panel, look at the Local Cache File area and note the name of the file. That's it!
4. Close the window.

There's a History to This (The History List)

After a good, long Web surf, you'll be wondering, "Where am I?" And after spending five hours at the Babylon 5 page (www.babylon5.com), you'll be thinking, "How do I get back to that *useful* page I saw half an hour ago?" You've surfed so many sites, you'd have to click the Back button six zillion

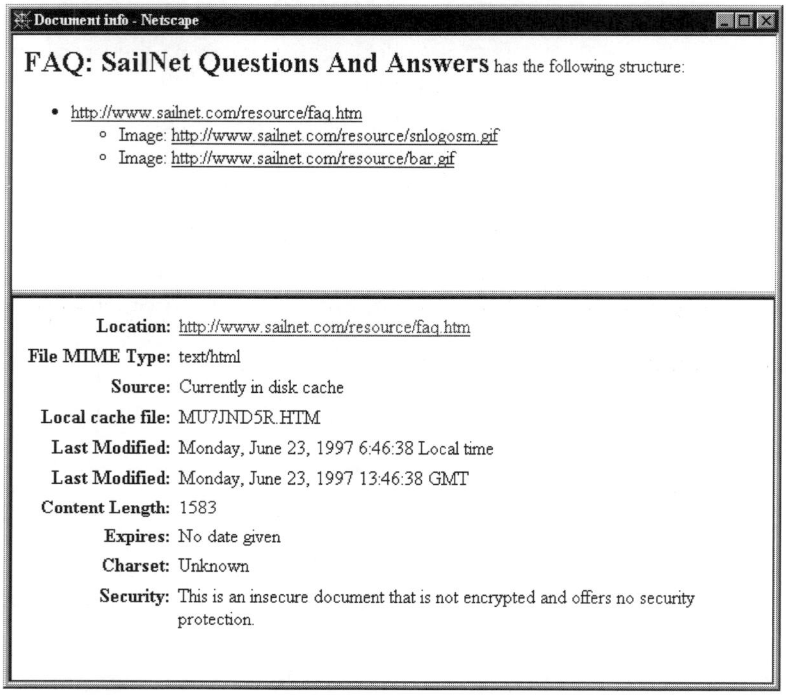

Figure 7.10 Document Info dialog box.

times. But there's a better way, maybe. You may be able to use the history list to go back quickly to previously accessed sites.

Unbeknownst to you, Netscape has been keeping a record of your travels. The program knows where you've been. It just keeps a record of the URLs you've visited, with certain important limitations, which I'll explain in a minute.

Using the Go Menu

You'll find a list of recently visited sites on the bottom portion of the Go menu. To go back to a document you've visited previously in the current Netscape session, do the following:

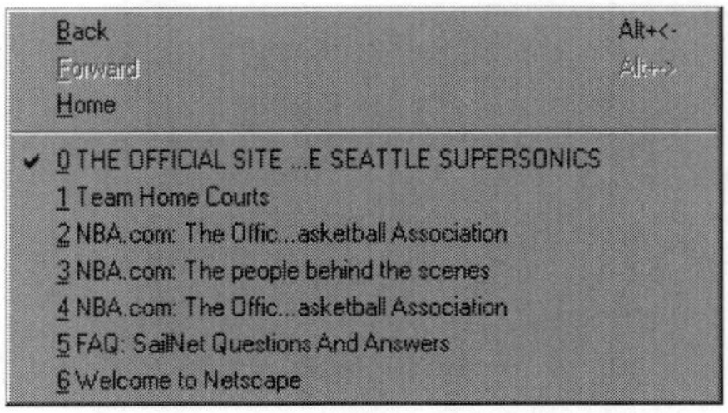

Figure 7.11 Recently visited sites on the Go menu.

- From the Go menu (Figure 7.11), choose the title of the document to which you want to return.

  or

New for 4

- Right-click the Back button, and choose the document from the list (Figure 7.12).

Using the History List

You can also go back to a document by using the History dialog box, as explained in the following:

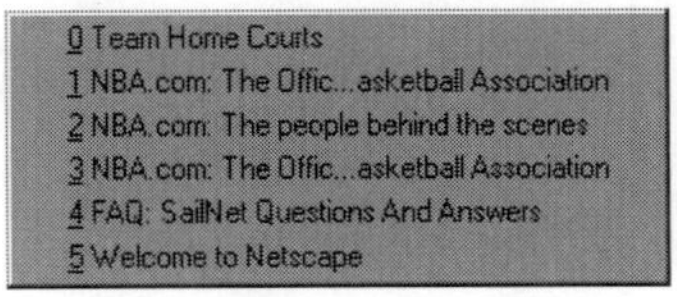

Figure 7.12 Back button drop-down list.

1. From the Communicator menu, choose History, or use the Ctrl + H keyboard shortcut. You'll see the History dialog box, shown in Figure 7.13.
2. Highlight the document to which you want to return, and click Go To (or just press Enter).
3. Click Close.

In Windows 95 and Windows NT, the History window has all the attributes of a standard Explorer window. For example, to sort the history list by page title, just click the Title button at the top of the Title column. You can also sort by location, date of first visit, date of last visit, expiration, and visit count. You can also search the history list. To do so, click the Edit menu, and choose Search History List. In the Search History List dialog box, indicate which column you want to search on, how you want Netscape to match the term, and type the terms you're looking for. For example, you can search for that pesky missing URL that you know contains the word "csmonitor" in the URL (Location). This is a very nice feature and well worth remembering when you're wasting time paging through the history list manually.

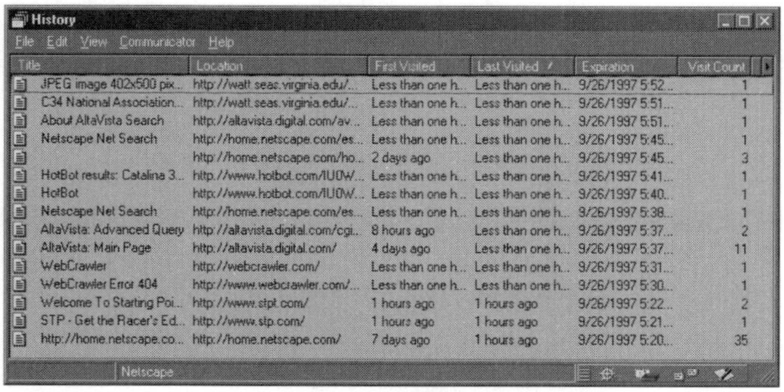

Figure 7.13 History dialog box.

Why the History List Erases Some of the Sites You've Visited

I just visited that site! I know I did! Why isn't the site listed in the darned history list? Sooner or later, you'll look at the history list, hoping to return to a site you visited a few clicks ago—and it's gone. This is very frustrating, and you'll probably think it's a bug. It isn't a bug. There's a logic to it. That doesn't mean I like it, but at least there's an explanation—so here goes. Netscape's history list records only a single lineage of sites. A *lineage* is a series of hyperlinks that all extend outward from a single, source document.

Here's an example of a lineage. Let's say you start with Yahoo, and click the Virtual Library link. From the Virtual Library, you select the Wine page. From the Wine page, you select Napa Valley. From the Napa Valley page, you select Napa Valley Wineries, and so on. For this lineage, Netscape keeps all the links.

But then you get tired of browsing in this area, and go back to Yahoo. You select Stock Quotes to check out how your stocks are doing. They're doing fine, but check out the Go menu. Hmmm! All the previous links have been erased. That's because you're in a new lineage.

Don't trust the history list to keep an exact record of every site you've visited. If you see a Web page that you definitely want to keep, choose Add Bookmark from the Bookmarks menu, and flip to Chapter 8 for more information.

Looking for something in the history list? Flip to chapter 9 for some.

Going Back to a Previously-Visited Site

Using the Go menu, the Back button, or the History list, you can return to a previously-visited *page*. But there's another way to go back. You can also return to a previously-visited *site*. (A site, if you remember our vocabulary lesson in Chapter 1, is an Internet computer that houses many different Web pages.)

When is this useful? Suppose you've been nosing around c|net (www.cnet.com), looking for fast-breaking news about computing. Then you go to Yahoo to do some searching, and from there you surf off to who knows where. This gets boring, so you decide to go back to c|net. Rather than messing with the History list, try clicking the down arrow on the Location box. This drop-down list contains a record of the sites you've recently visited. Look for www.cnet.com, and choose it from this list—and presto, you're back. Cool!

When – and How – to Open a New Window

Now that you know how history lists work, there's another important thing to realize about Netscape: The program keeps a separate history list for each window.

Well, so what? Here's what: Whenever you start a new lineage, open a new window. If you do this, Netscape won't erase the history list in the last lineage's window, enabling you to go back to previously accessed documents (in case you get tired of the current lineage).

Just remember my motto: "New lineage, new window."

Working with a New Window

When you open a new window for Netscape, you see what appears to be a new, independent copy of the program—and as far as you are concerned, it is. In the new window, Netscape automatically displays the home page that you've chosen, just as if you were launching the program at the beginning of a new Netscape session.

The new window's history list is a copy of the previous window's list, but the window shows you the *oldest* document in this list—a veritable invitation to launch off in a new lineage, wouldn't you say?

Your subsequent actions in this window will not affect the history list in other Netscape windows.

To open a new window, do the following: From the File menu, choose New Navigator Window.

Use this great trick to open a hyperlink in a new window. Point to the hyperlink, and click the right mouse button. From the pop-up menu, choose Open in New Window. Netscape opens a new window. Instead of displaying the home page, the program displays the document you've chosen.

Here's another good reason to open a new window. If you suspect that you'll have trouble accessing a hyperlink, perhaps because it's lengthy or the site is situated on a 56 Kbps network in Tasmania, use the pop-up menu to open the link in a new window. While the new window is stalled pending retrieval of the document, you can switch back to the original window and continue enjoying the Web.

Managing Multiple Windows

When more than one Netscape window is open, you can switch between them as you please. When you're done with a window, you can close it without quitting Netscape, as long as at least one other Netscape window is open. The following instructions detail these procedures.

To switch from one Netscape window to another:

- Click on the window you want to activate. This shouldn't be difficult, since Netscape cascades new windows (each new window is slightly offset from the others, enabling you to read the title bar of each open window).

To close a Netscape window:

- From the File menu, choose Close

  or

- Press Ctrl + W

When more than one Netscape window is open, the window-closing procedures just described close the window without quitting the program. When you're down to the last window, these procedures quit the program.

When to Reload, When to Refresh

On the View menu, you'll find options called Reload, Reload Frame, and Refresh. Here's what they do:

Reload	When you choose this command, Netscape goes back to the network and determines whether the document you're viewing has changed—and if so, a new copy is downloaded.
Refresh	When you choose this command, Netscape retrieves a fresh copy of the current document from your computer's memory. The program doesn't check to see whether the document has changed.

When Should You Reload?

Only when you think there's a chance the document has changed since you last downloaded it. Here's why.

Netscape saves a copy of recently accessed documents in its *memory cache* (a special storage area designed for fast re-retrieval of documents). When you click a previously visited hyperlink, Netscape checks to see whether there's a copy of the document in the cache, and if there is, the program loads the cache's copy rather than retrieving the document from the network. In most cases, that's fine—the document appears much more quickly. But what happens if the original, network-based version of the document has changed? You wouldn't know this, because Netscape is showing you the old copy. If you suspect that the network version has changed, choose Reload from the View menu, or press Ctrl + R, or just click the Reload button.

If you decided to select the "Never" verification frequency (see "Changing the Verification Frequency," earlier in this chapter), bear in mind that the document you're viewing may not be the most recent version. To find out, click Reload.

When Should You Use Refresh?

Sometimes your Microsoft Windows system will fail to update the screen properly. This isn't really Netscape's fault. Windows is notoriously susceptible to screen update problems attributable to low memory or system resources. For example, the fonts might not look right, or the background color may have changed in a weird way. If this happens, choose Refresh from the View menu.

From Here

- The next set of skills you'll need to master involves Netscape's bookmarks features. Check them out in Chapter 8.
- Want to save or print a document or graphic? Find out how in Chapter 9.

Chapter 8

Creating and Using Bookmarks

You've just found the most awesome Web site. It holds the key to your dreams—nay, your job. And then, following links, you surf off in a zillion directions—only to find, to your dismay, that you've started a new lineage, somehow, and the darned history list has erased that awesome site's URL. (For the lowdown on lineages and history lists, see Chapter 7.) No matter what you do, you can't find it again. You give up in frustration, and late that night you sob softly into your pillow.

Don't let this happen to you: Set bookmarks.

In Netscape, a *bookmark* is a document title that you've added to the Bookmarks menu. In addition to the document title, Netscape saves the URL. To return to the document, you just choose the bookmark name from the Bookmarks menu.

This chapter presents indispensable Netscape skills. In particular, you'll learn what to do when your Bookmarks menu gets overstuffed—a malady, you will find, that befalls every Netscape user, including you. A plus: This

For the Time-Challenged

- When you set a bookmark, the title of the Web page you've bookmarked appears on the Bookmarks menu, which is accessible via the Bookmarks QuickFile on the location toolbar.
- Very soon, your Bookmarks menu becomes too crowded. To alleviate this problem, you can create folders for your bookmarks. You do this within the Bookmarks window. After creating folders, you can organize your bookmarks by dragging them into the folders you've created.
- After you organize your bookmarks into folders, the folders appear on the menu and the bookmark items appear in pop-up submenus.
- By choosing What's New from the Bookmarks window's File menu, you can find out whether any of your bookmarked pages have changed since you last visited them.
- To add new bookmarks to a specific folder, open the Bookmarks window, highlight the folder, open the Items menu, and choose Set to New Bookmarks Folder.

chapter's tutorials will prove invaluable in learning how to reorganize bookmarks, a crucial Netscape skill.

New for 4

In previous versions of Netscape, bookmark functions have been one of the program's weakest features. Microsoft Internet Explorer 3.0 charted the way with a much more convenient bookmark utility, called Favorites, which enables users to file bookmarks in folders as they're stored. Taking the cue, Netscape Communicator incorporates a similar feature, and there are many more improvements. In fact, bookmark features have been so thoroughly revised that I'll let this one "new for 4" icon stand for the whole chapter! If you've used Netscape bookmarks before and found them somewhat frustrating, read on.

Adding and Choosing Bookmarks

The simplest way to use bookmarks is to add them to the Bookmarks menu, which you access by clicking the Bookmark QuickLink on the Location toolbar. To return to a bookmarked item, you simply choose it from the Bookmarks menu. The drawback of this technique, as you'll quickly discover, is an overly lengthy Bookmarks menu. When you get to that point, you'll want to organize your bookmarks, as discussed later in this chapter.

Adding a Bookmark to the Bookmarks Menu

You can add a Web document to your Bookmarks menu in three ways:

- **Using the Bookmark QuickLink** To add the current page to your bookmark menu, click the Bookmark QuickLink, and choose Add Bookmark from the pop-up menu.
- **Right-clicking a hyperlink** Point to a hyperlink and click the *right* mouse button. From the pop-up menu, choose Add Bookmark.
- **Press Ctrl + D.**

After you add a bookmark, the bookmark you've added appears on the lower portion of the Bookmarks menu (see Figure 8.1).

Choosing a Bookmark

After you've added a bookmark, you can choose it easily. Just click the Bookmark QuickLink, and choose the bookmark from the pop-up menu. Netscape will download the document you've requested.

Introducing the Bookmarks Window

One of the most common complaints about Netscape, typically voiced by people who have been using the program for two weeks or so, is that the Bookmarks menu has become glutted with items. It's disorganized, out of order, too lengthy, and—for all these reasons—close to useless Figure 8.1 shows mine—what a mess! The solution? Organize your bookmarks using the Bookmarks window.

Accessing the Bookmarks Window

To access this window, do one of the following

- From the Communicator menu, choose Bookmarks, and choose Edit Bookmarks from the pop-up menu.

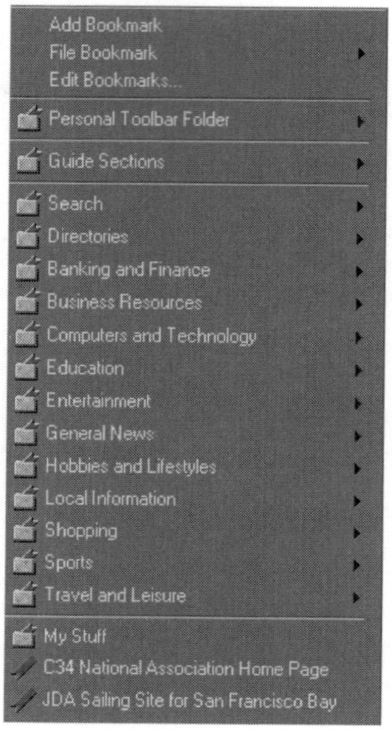

Figure 8.1 Bookmarks appearing on Bookmarks menu.

or

- On the Location toolbar, click the Bookmarks Quick File icon.

or

- Press Ctrl + B.

What You Can Do in the Bookmarks Window

The Bookmarks window (Figure 8.2) provides tools for doing the following:

- **Organizing bookmarks** When you create a folder, a new submenu shows up on Netscape's Bookmarks menu. To place bookmarks into

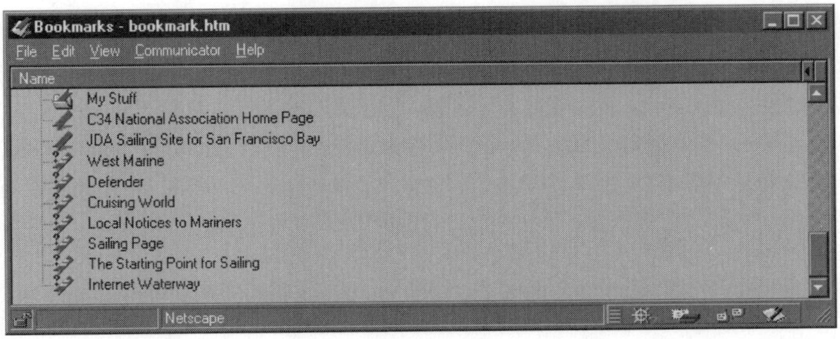

Figure 8.2 Bookmarks window with unorganized bookmarks.

a folder, just drag the bookmark into the folder. This bookmark will then appear on a pop-up submenu in the Bookmarks menu. In this way, you can quickly customize the Bookmarks menu so that it contains dozens or even hundreds of your favorite documents. Within a folder, you can sort your bookmarks so that they appear in alphabetical order. Additionally, you can change the title of a page to something that's more descriptive.

- **Accessing bookmark pages** Just double-click any Web page's title. Netscape will display the page. If you can't find the bookmark in a lengthy list, the Bookmark Window's Edit command contains a Find in Bookmarks command that helps you look.
- **Adding new bookmark items to a folder you've created** After you've organized your bookmarks list, you can choose which of the folders you've created that you want to display on the Bookmarks menu, and you can also choose the folder to which you'd like Netscape to add new bookmark items.
- **Importing and exporting bookmarks** You can easily exchange bookmark lists with other Netscape users by exporting your list and importing lists that people give you.

- **Sort and display your bookmarks** From the View menu in the Bookmarks window, you can sort your bookmarks by name, location, date of creation, or date of last visit. You can sort in ascending or descending order.
- **Determine the storage location for bookmarks** By default, Netscape places new bookmarks on the Bookmarks menu. If you wish, you can store new bookmarks in your personal toolbar (not a very good idea, since it will quickly become overcrowded), or a Bookmark folder of your choosing (you'll have to create one first). After you've set up your folders, the best way to store bookmarks is to use the new QuickFile feature, which enables you to choose a storage folder at the time you save the bookmark. I'll explain how to do this later in this chapter.
- **Find out whether any bookmark items have changed** To see whether any changes have occurred in the pages you've stored, click View on the Bookmark windows' menu bar and choose Update Bookmarks. Netscape contacts the server. If any of the documents contain new material, you'll see an icon that tells you the content has changed.
- **Organize and edit your personal toolbar** As you know, you can add Web pages to your personal toolbar just by dragging them to the toolbar and releasing the mouse button. In the Bookmarks window, you can edit and reorganize the toolbar items.
- **Add a bookmark to the toolbar** To do this, just select the bookmark, click the File menu, and choose Add Bookmark to Toolbar.

The contents of the Bookmarks window are stored in a file called BOOKMARK.HTM, which you'll find in Netscape's directory. This file is actually a valid HTML document, which Netscape automatically creates. As you'll learn later in this chapter, you can open any valid HTML file using the File Open command in the Bookmarks window, and all the hyperlinks that this document contains will appear as bookmarks in this window. You can also give your bookmark file to anyone who uses Netscape or any other browser, so that others can open it and make use of the links you've found.

Organizing Your Bookmarks

Chances are that you have a lengthy, disorganized list of bookmarks, which you've saved directly to the Bookmarks menu. In the Bookmarks window, these appear in a list like the one shown in Figure 8.2. To organize your bookmarks, you'll want to create and name folders, and then drag the bookmarks into the appropriate folder. You may also wish to create *separators*, lines that appear on the Bookmarks menu, so that the menu looks neater. The following sections detail these procedures.

Creating Folders

To get your bookmarks organized, the first thing you need to do is to create and name folders. A folder is a storage place for your bookmarks.

Give some thought to how you want to organize your folders. Bear in mind that you can put folders within folders. Currently my disorganized Bookmarks list contains pages about three subjects:

Research Tools
Sailing
Weather

These are the folders I'll create.

To create a folder, do the following:

1. In the Bookmarks window, select the top item ("[Your Name]'s Bookmarks"). You need to do this because Netscape always creates the folder beneath the level you've selected.
2. From the File menu, choose New Folder. You'll see the Bookmark Properties dialog box, shown in Figure 8.3.
3. In the Name area, type the name for your new folder. This name also shows up on the menu.
4. In the Description area, type a brief description, if you wish.
5. Click OK. You'll see the folder positioned beneath the selected item.

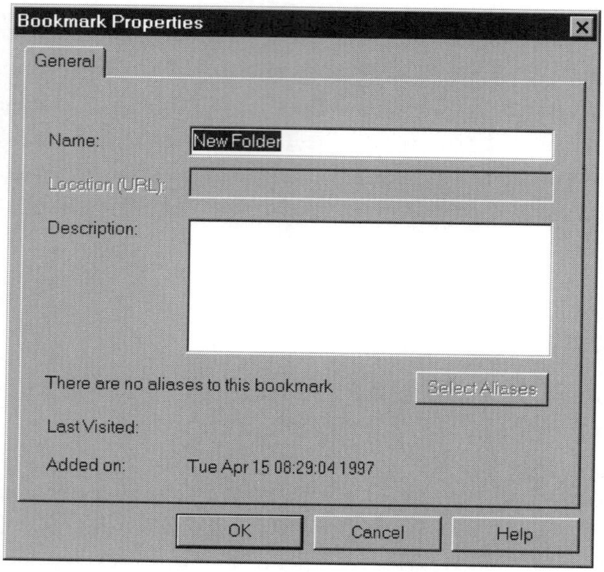

Figure 8.3 Bookmark Properties dialog box.

Adding Bookmarks to a Folder

It's easy to add bookmarks to a folder. Just select the bookmarks and drag them to the folder until the folder changes color, then release the mouse button.

After you add bookmarks to a folder, you'll see that the Bookmarks window uses a tree-like diagram to show the list's logical organization (see Figure 8.4).

What do the little minus signs mean—the ones that are positioned next to the folder's name? Click on one to find out. This collapses the folder's contents, so that these contents aren't visible on-screen. You see a plus sign, indicating that there's something hidden. To view these contents again, click the plus sign.

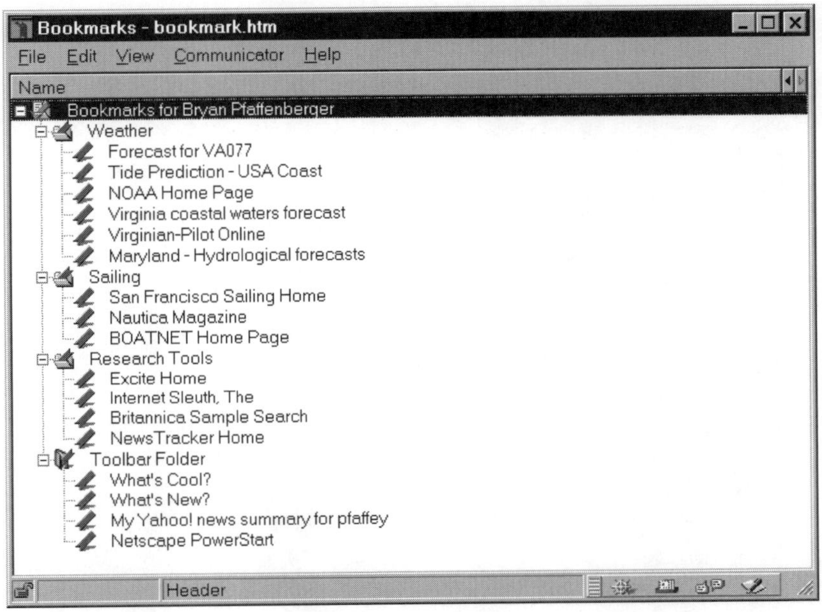

Figure 8.4 Tree structure of bookmarks list.

Adding Folders within Folders

Add additional folders and subfolders to flesh out the list's organization, as shown in Figure 8.5. (I added "Chesapeake" and "Charlottesville" folders under "Weather.") To add a folder within a folder, just select the folder into which you would like to insert a folder. Then choose New Folder from the File menu, and name the folder as described in the previous section.

Making an Alias

If you'd like a bookmark to appear in more than one folder, you can do so quickly by making an alias. To do so, follow these steps:

1. Select the bookmark item.

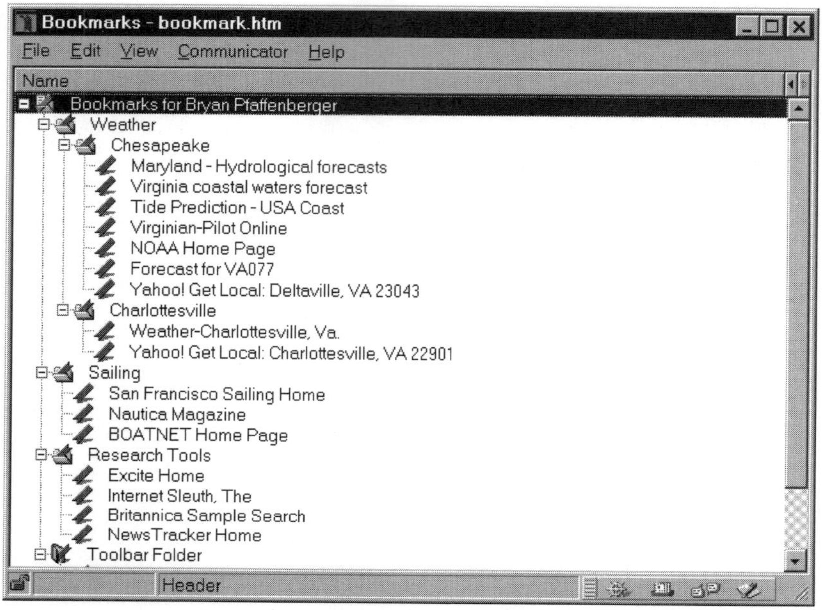

Figure 8.5 Bookmarks list after adding additional folders.

2. Click the right mouse button, and choose Make Alias from the pop-up menu. You'll see a copy of the item in the same folder.
3. Drag the copy to its new location in another folder.

Deleting an Item

To delete a bookmark item, simply select it and press the Delete key. (This just deletes the bookmark, by the way—it doesn't delete the original document out there on the Web.)

Looking at the Bookmarks Menu

The changes you're making in the Bookmarks window will be reflected in the Bookmarks menu. Top-level folders appear as items on the menu; when you click one of them, you see a pop-up menu containing the items you've added (see Figure 8.6). If you've added folders within folders, you get pop-up menus within pop-up menus.

Adding Separators

To clarify the logical organization of your Bookmarks menu, you may wish to add separators (lines that appear on the menu).

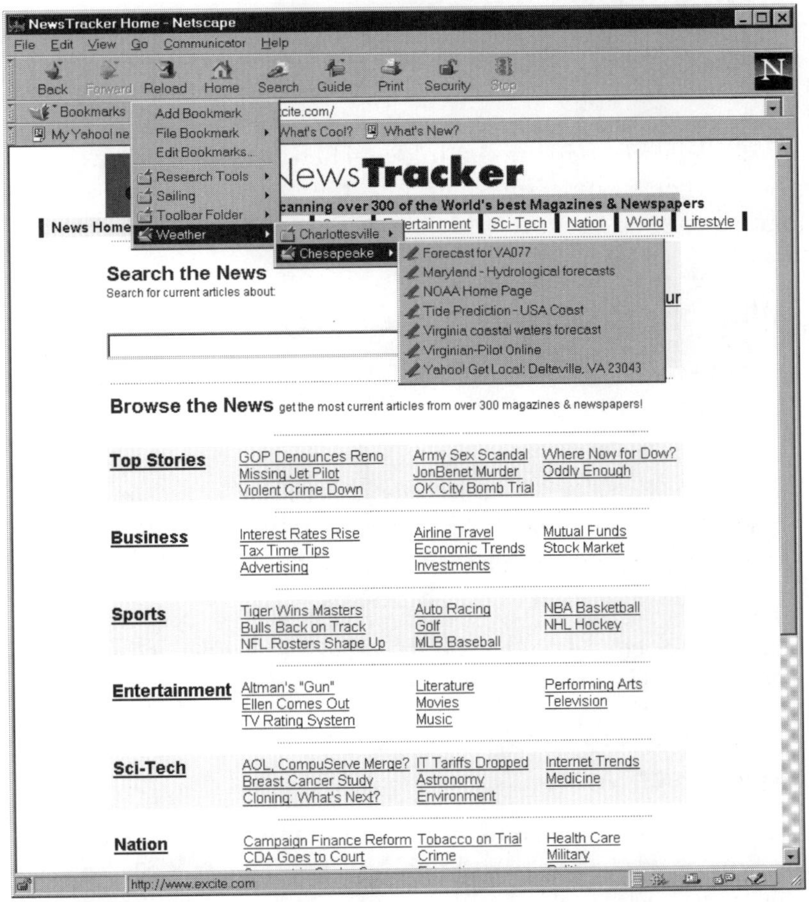

Figure 8.6 Pop-up menu containing added items.

To add a separator, do the following:

1. Select the item or folder above the place you want the separator to appear.
2. From the File menu, choose New Separator.

If you don't like the placement of the separator, you can drag it to a new position within the Bookmarks window. To get rid of the separator entirely, select it and press Delete.

Reorganizing Folders

Once you've created your folders, you may wish to reorganize them. It's easy to do so. For example, suppose I've decided to create a new folder called Recreation, and I want to put Backpacking and Sailing Stuff into this new folder. To do so, I create the folder. Then I select the Backpacking and Sailing Stuff folders, and drag them into the new folder. Netscape includes the bookmark items, and any folders within folders, in the move.

Controlling the Bookmark List Display

Within the Bookmarks window, you can use the following techniques to control the way the list appears:

- To close a folder, so that only the folder name appears, double-click the folder icon. Alternatively, you can click the minus sign next to the folder. After the folder closes, you'll see a plus sign indicating that the folder contains items.
- To open a closed folder, double-click the folder icon. Alternatively, you can click the plus sign next to the folder.

Adding a Description

If you would like to make some notes about a bookmark item, you can do so in the Bookmark Properties dialog box (see Figure 8.3). You may want to do this so you can add a few key words to the item. Later, you'll learn how you can search for an item, including the description. Adding a few key words increases your chance of finding the item in a lengthy bookmark list.

To add a description, do the following:

1. In the Bookmarks window, select the item to which you would like to add a description.
2. From the Edit menu, choose Bookmark Properties.
3. In the Description box, type a description.
4. Click OK to confirm your comments.

Accessing Bookmarked Pages

You can use the Bookmarks window as well as the Bookmarks menu to access the bookmarks you've created.

To go to any bookmark listed in the Bookmarks window, just double-click it. The document appears in Netscape's window, not in the Bookmarks window. To see the document, switch back to Netscape's window.

Finding a Bookmark

In a lengthy bookmark list, you may have trouble finding a bookmark—especially if you've closed the folder in which it's stored. Let Netscape do the hunting for you.

To search for a bookmark item:

1. Select the folder where you want the search to begin (it proceeds downward from there). To search the entire bookmark file, select the top item.
2. From the Edit menu, choose Find in Bookmark1, or press Ctrl + F. You'll see the Find Bookmark dialog box, shown in Figure 8.7.
3. In the Find area, type the text you want to find. Choose where to search (Name, Location, or Description). Capitalization doesn't matter, unless you click Match Case. If a match is found, the program selects the item (if necessary, it opens the folder that contains the item). To turn of substring matching, click whole word.
4. To find the next matching item, click the Find Again button.

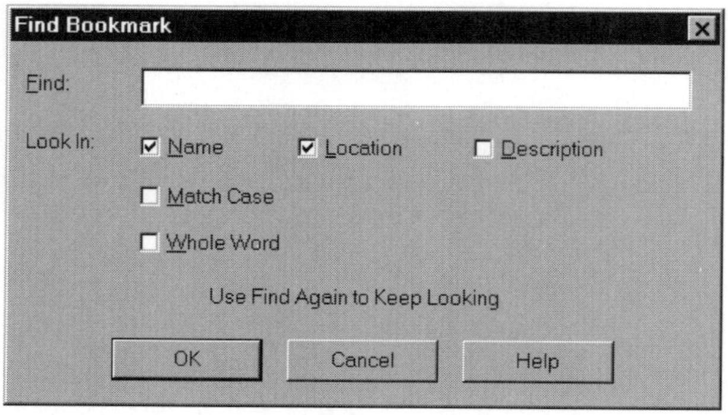

Figure 8.7 With this dialog box, you can search for bookmarks.

After you've exited the Find dialog box, you can still repeat the search with the same settings—just choose Find Again from the Edit menu, or press Ctrl + G.

Finding Out Whether Source Documents Have Changed

Chances are that the documents you've marked as bookmarks are pretty important to you—so naturally you'll want to know whether they've changed. Netscape can check the documents to find out whether they've changed. If any of them have, the Bookmarks menu will contain marks that indicate which of your bookmark items contain new material.

To determine whether source documents have changed:

1. Select one or more items.
2. From the View menu, choose Update Bookmarks. You'll see the What's New dialog box (Figure 8.8), which enables you to look for changes in all the bookmark items or just the ones you selected.

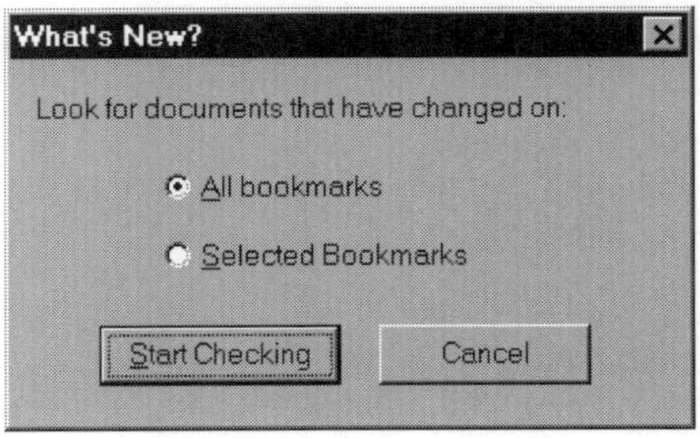

Figure 8.8 Use this dialog box to search for bookmarked pages that have changed.

3. Choose All Bookmarks to check out all the items, or Selected Bookmarks to check out just the ones you selected.
4. Click Start Checking. You'll see a dialog box that informs you how much time this operation will take. When it's finished, you'll see another dialog box informing how many documents, if any, contain changes.
5. Click OK to confirm, and look at the Bookmarks window. Documents that have changed are shown with a distinctive flag.

Adding New Bookmarks to a Specified Folder

Once you've created folders for your bookmarks, you can select a new default folder to serve as the destination for new bookmark items. To do so, follow these steps:

1. In the Bookmarks window, select the folder you want to use as the destination for new bookmark items.
2. From the View menu, choose Set to New Bookmarks Folder. In the bookmark item list, you'll see a distinctive icon next to this folder's name.

This isn't the best way to route bookmarks. It's a lot better to file them when you store them, something you couldn't do with previous versions of Netscape. To learn how, skip to the section titled "Filing Bookmarks When You Save Them," later in this chapter.

Restricting the Menu Display

After you've added lots of folders and subfolders, your Bookmarks menu can seem cluttered again. If there's just one folder that you tend to use frequently, you can restrict the Bookmarks menu so that just this folder appears. To do so, follow these steps:

1. In the Bookmarks window, select the folder that you would like to appear on the Bookmarks menu, to the exclusion of all others.
2. From the Item menu, choose Set to Bookmark Menu Folder. In the bookmarks item list, you'll see a little menu icon on top of this item's folder icon. Only the items in this folder will appear on your Bookmarks menu. You can access the other items by opening the Bookmarks window, however.

Note that your choice of a folder as the Bookmark menu folder does not affect into which folder Netscape inserts new bookmark items. That's controlled by the Set to New Bookmarks Folder command, discussed in the previous section.

Where did all my bookmarks go? If you choose Set to Bookmark Menu Folder, as just described, the Bookmarks menu contains only the bookmarks in the currently-selected folder. To access the rest of your bookmarks, you'll have to open the Bookmarks window.

Frankly, I don't recommend that you use this command. It's a throwback to the bad old days of Netscape's bookmarks menu, when it was much more difficult to use. If you tried it, you can undo its evil effects by selecting the top-level folder (the one that says "Bookmarks for So-and-So"), clicking the Edit menu, and choose Set to Bookmark Menu Folder. This re-displays your entire contents on the bookmark menu.

Exporting Bookmarks

One of the nicer points of Netscape is the program's ability to export bookmarks to a bookmark file, which you can then give to friends and colleagues (or whomever). These fortunate persons can then import the bookmark file, and your bookmarks will magically appear on their Bookmarks menu. This has created a certain amount of Internet traffic in bookmark files.

Another reason to export your bookmark file is that this enables you to create and store more than one bookmark file on your system. For example, you could create one bookmark file for your research on Civil War memorabilia, and another for your collection of hot Web sites. To learn how to open one of the bookmark files you've created, see the next section.

To export your bookmarks to a bookmark file:

1. From the File menu in the Bookmarks window, choose Save As. You'll see the standard Windows Save As dialog box.
2. Type a name for the file (be sure to use the extension .htm), and click Save.

Don't try to edit a bookmark file directly. It contains lots of secret, weird codes and other information that enables Netscape to import the file properly.

Opening a Local Bookmark File

If you've saved a bookmark file as just described, or if someone has given you one, you can open it. The new bookmark file replaces the previous one, so you'll see different options on the Bookmarks menu.

To open a bookmark file, do the following:

1. From the File menu in the Bookmarks window, choose Open Bookmarks File. You'll see a standard Open dialog box.
2. Locate and select the file you want to open, and click Open. Netscape replaces the current bookmark file with the one you just opened.

I want my old bookmark list back! No problem. Just open it using the instructions just given. It's still called Bookmark.HTM. This file is in the Users folder, inside Netscape's folder.

Filing Bookmarks When You Save Them

Now that you've set up your folders, here's how to store bookmarks in folders at the same time you save them. This is really a great feature—you'll love it.

To store a new bookmark item in a folder at the same time you save it:

1. Display the page.
2. Click the Bookmarks QuickFile.
3. Choose File Bookmark.
4. From the pop-up menu, choose the folder in which you want to store the bookmark.

That's it! Easy, isn't it?

Editing the Toolbar Folder

As you've probably already gathered, the Toolbar folder is just another Bookmarks folder. The difference is that the Toolbar folder's contents appear on the Personal Toolbar.

You can edit Toolbar folder items the same way you deal with bookmarks. To delete an unwanted item, select it and press Delete. If you don't like the name Netscape automatically assigned to the item when you created it, click Edit and choose Bookmark Properties.

You can move a bookmark item into the Toolbar folder. After you do, the bookmark will appear on your Personal Toolbar. To do this, simply select the item and drag it to the Toolbar folder. If you'd like to keep the item in the bookmark folder, don't drag it—click File, and choose Add Bookmark to Toolbar instead.

The Best Toolbar Trick Ever

Have you created a bookmark folder that would make a great Personal Toolbar for a special job? In the bookmark window, select the folder, click Edit, and choose Set to Personal Toolbar. This becomes the toolbar! Cool, huh? To reverse this later, just repeat these steps, but choose Toolbar Folder to restore the usual toolbar items.

Yet Another Bookmark Window Trick

Like to see the location, creation date, and the time of your last visit to all your bookmark and Personal Toolbar items? Click the little right arrow at the extreme right edge of the button bar (the one that contains "Name"). You'll see the additional columns, as shown in Figure 8.9.

Now you can sort this list any way you want, and the results will actually make some sense. Here are some tips:

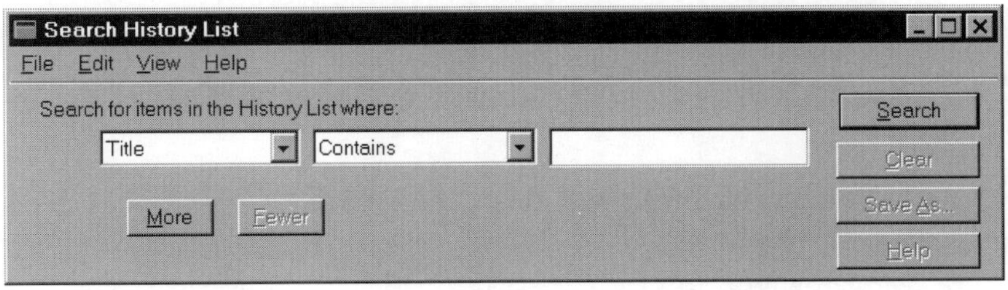

Figure 8.9 Bookmark window with additional columns displayed.

To see which sites you accessed most recently, click View and choose Sort Descending, and then click View and choose By Last Visited (or just click the Last Visit button in the bookmark window).

To group sites by location, click View and choose Sort Ascending, and then click View and choose By Location (or just click the Location button in the bookmark window).

To view sites by the date you saved them as bookmarks, click View and choose Sort Descending, and then click View and choose By Created On (or just click the Last Visit button in the bookmark window).

Importing Links from an HTML File

Here's a cool trick: With the Import command on the Bookmarks window's File menu, you can import all the links from any HTML document that you've saved on your local disk. They'll appear as bookmark items. The document headings will appear as folder names. This is pretty cool—try it out.

To import the links in an HTML file, do the following:

1. From the File menu in the Bookmarks window, choose Import. You'll see the Import Bookmarks dialog box.
2. In the Files of Type box, choose HTML files.
3. Locate and select the file you want to open, and click Open.

Netscape imports all the headings as folders and all the links as bookmark items. Note that the organization may not be ideal; you may have to rearrange the folders to make the list useful.

Creating Internet Shortcuts

If you're using the Windows 95 version of Netscape, you can easily create shortcuts to your favorite Web documents. The shortcuts will appear on your Windows desktop, where you can access them quickly.

To create an Internet shortcut:

1. In the Bookmarks window, select the item that you want to become an Internet shortcut.
2. Drag the item to the desktop, and release the mouse button. If you can't see this desktop because you have too many windows open, Click File and choose Create Shortcut.

You'll see the shortcut icon on the desktop. To access this document quickly, just double-click the icon.

From Here

- Want to print or save the documents you're downloading—and how about those neat graphics, too? Find out how in the next chapter.
- Learn how to choose Netscape's Preferences! Get the lowdown in Chapter 11.

Chapter 9

Managing Documents with Netscape Navigator

While you're viewing Web documents with Netscape, you can select and copy text from the screen to the Clipboard, search for text, save the document to your hard drive (in HTML or plain text), save inline images to your hard drive, print documents, and view the source HTML. This chapter fully discusses these document-handling aspects of Netscape Navigator. You'll also learn how to make full use of the History window.

Copying Text or Graphics to the Clipboard

You can easily select and copy any text or inline graphic image that you see on screen in Netscape Navigator. The copied text goes to the Clipboard, where you can paste it using other applications.

For the Time-Challenged

- You can copy text and graphics from any document that Netscape displays. The copied text or graphic goes to the Clipboard, where you can paste it using other applications.
- If you need to find text within a document you're displaying, click the Find button, type some search text, and click OK.
- To open a local document, use the Open File command.
- To save an inline image to your hard drive, right-click it and choose Save This Image As.
- To print the document you're currently displaying, click the Print button.
- To view information about a document, choose Document Info from the View menu.
- To view the source HTML, choose Document Source from the View menu.

To copy text to the Clipboard, follow these steps:

1. Using the mouse, select the text on screen.
2. From the Edit menu, choose Copy, or just use the Ctrl + C keyboard shortcut.
3. To paste the text using another application, use that program's Edit Paste command, or press Ctrl + V.

I tried to copy the darned text but I clicked a hyperlink instead! If the text you're copying contains a hyperlink, the copy operation can sometimes inadvertently turn into a hyperlink click. If this happens, click the Back button to return to the document. Try selecting the text again, but start by clicking *just outside* the text you want to copy, and carefully drag all the way over the text and release the mouse button just beyond the edge of the text.

To copy graphics to the Clipboard:

1. Point to the graphic with the mouse, and click the right mouse button. You'll see the pop-up menu shown in Figure 9.1.
2. Click Copy this Image Location.
3. To paste the text using another application, use that program's Edit Paste command, or press Ctrl + V.

I can copy, but I can't cut or clear this text! That's right. The Cut and Clear commands are enabled only when you've positioned the cursor within an editable text area.

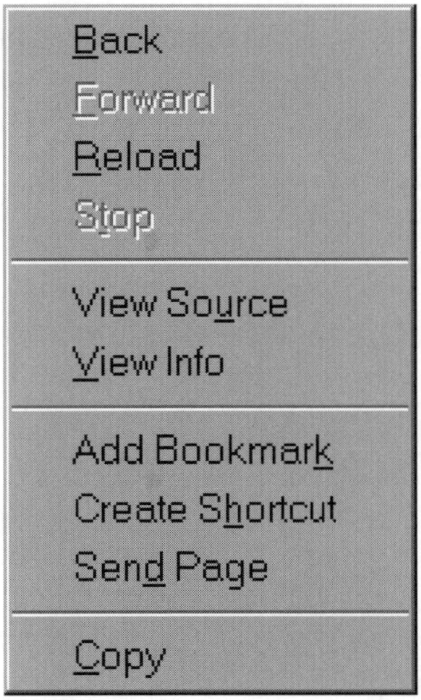

Figure 9.1 Pop-up menu (right-click).

Saving Documents and Graphics

You can save any document or frame that Netscape can display. It's easy to save documents in native HTML or plain text. But be aware that Netscape doesn't automatically save inline images. To save a document with inline images, you're in for some work, as the following sections explain.

Saving Documents in Plain Text

If you've downloaded a document that contains lots of interesting text that you'd like to save for future reference or use, you can save the document as plain text. With this option, Netscape removes all the HTML codes and hyperlinks.

If you just want a clean printout of the document, print it instead of saving it as plain text. Netscape's Print command produces an attractive-looking printout of the document, just as you see it on screen—no ugly HTML codes.

To save a document as plain text:

1. From the File menu, choose Save As, or press Ctrl + S. You'll see the Save As dialog box (Figure 9.2).
2. In the Save as Type box, choose Plain Text (*.txt).
3. In the Directories list, choose the directory to which you would like to save the document.

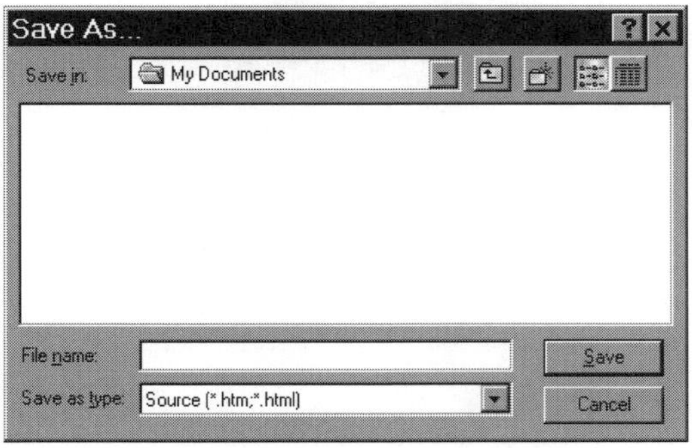

Figure 9.2 Save As dialog box.

4. In the File Name box, type a name for the document. Netscape suggests a name using the document's current title. Be sure to use the extension .txt.
5. Click Save.

Saving Documents in HTML

The Web documents that Netscape displays are written in HTML, as you know. If you save a document in HTML format, you can reopen the document using Netscape's Open File command (File menu), and you'll see all the text formatting and hyperlinks that the document contains. But you may not see the inline graphics, as explained below.

When should you save HTML documents? There's really only one good reason: You're learning HTML and you want to study the HTML coding. But why learn HTML? You don't need to with Composer (see Chapter 33). Frankly, I can't think of a good reason to save pages in HTML, but in case you want to, here's how.

To save the document in HTML format:

1. From the File menu, choose Save As, or press Ctrl + S. You'll see the Save As dialog box, shown in Figure 9.2.
2. In the Save as Type box, choose HTML.
3. In the Directories list, choose the directory to which you would like to save the document.
4. In the File Name box, type a name for the document. Netscape suggests a name using the document's current title.
5. Click Save.

Viewing and Saving Inline Graphics

Netscape's pop-up menu enables you to save graphics to your hard disk.

To save an inline graphic:

1. Point to the graphic.
2. Click the right mouse button. You'll see the pop-up menu shown in Figure 9.1, earlier in this chapter.

Why don't you see inline images when you open an HTML file you've saved? To understand, you need to know the difference between a relative link and an absolute link.

- A *relative link* displays a graphic or document that's stored in the same directory as the document; it doesn't contain any path information other than, in effect, "Look in the same directory for this."
- An *absolute link* displays a graphic or document that's stored on some other computer, and contains complete instructions on where it should be obtained.

Now let's say you download an HTML file to your \docs directory, and open the file. Almost certainly, all of the inline images were created with relative links. Netscape goes hunting for the graphics in the \docs directory, but they're not there, so you see lots of placeholders. Web authors are loath to use absolute links for inline images and for good reason: If you link to an image on somebody else's computer, what happens if that someone else decides to erase the image? Since you can't control this, it's easier and safer to use relative links for inline images.

The moral of the story here is that Netscape doesn't do a very good job of letting you save documents to your disk for local, offline browsing.

3. Choose Save Image As. You'll see the Save As dialog box. Netscape has automatically placed the graphic's name in the File Name box.
4. In the directories list, select the Directory where you want to save the graphic.
5. Click Save.

I can't save the background graphic! That's right. Click as hard as you might, you can't download the background graphic. However, where there's a will, there's a way. From the View menu, choose Document Info. You'll see the information page for this document. The Background image is located right at the top. To save it, right-click it and choose Save Link As. Cool, huh?

Saving Frames

To save a frame, position the cursor in the frame you want to save, click the File menu, and choose Save Frame As. In the Save As Type box, choose HTML or Plain Text.

Opening Local Documents

With Netscape, you can open any HTML or text file that's present on a disk in your computer. To do so, follow these instructions:

1. From the File menu, choose Open File, or just press Ctrl + O (the letter). You'll see the standard Open dialog box.
2. Use the folder tree commands to locate the disk and directory containing the file that you want to open.
3. In the Files of Type box, choose the type of file you want to open.

Printing Documents

By far the best way to produce a permanent record of a Netscape-accessed document is to print it. Netscape prints all the fonts and graphics just as you see them onscreen.

If you're printing a document that has frames, you can only print the current frame. Reflecting this, the Print command changes to Print Frame when you're viewing a document that has frames.

Choosing Page Setup Options

The Page Setup command on the File menu enables you to choose a number of print output options, including margins. To use the Page Setup dialog box, open the File menu and choose Page Setup. You'll see the Page Setup dialog box, shown in Figure 9.3.

In the Page Options area, you can make the following choices:

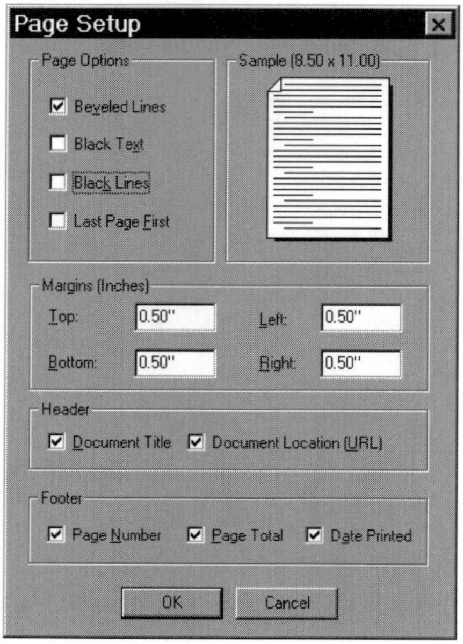

Figure 9.3 Page Setup dialog box.

Beveled Lines	Click here to print the beveled rules you see on-screen.
Black Text	If you have a color printer, click here to suppress color printing of hyperlinks.
Black Lines	Click here to print rules as a solid black line.
Last Page First	Click here if you need this option to avoid having to hand-collate the printed output.

In the Margins area, you can change the margins by typing new measurements in inches.

In the Header area, you can choose to print the document title and the URL. It's a great idea to leave both of these selected—they're on by default—so that you can return to the Web location of a page you've printed.

In the Footer area, you can control page numbers, the printing of a total number of pages with the page numbers, and the date printed.

Previewing Print Output

To see what your document's printed output will look like, you can use the Print Preview command (File menu):

1. From the File menu, choose Print Preview. You see the Print Preview window, shown in Figure 9.4.
2. To see the next page, click Next Page. To return to the previous page, click Previous Page.
3. To view two pages in the same window, click Two Page.

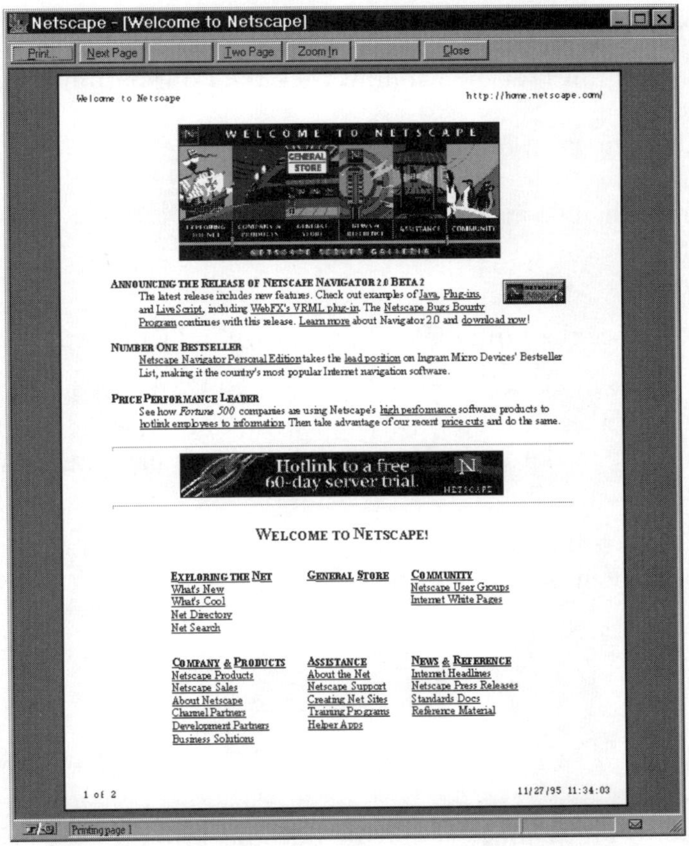

Figure 9.4 Print Preview window.

4. To zoom in for a closer look, click Zoom In once or twice. Click Zoom Out once or twice to return to full-page view.
5. To exit Print Preview, click Close. If you would like to print, click Print, and see the next section for printing instructions.

Choosing Print Options and Printing Your Document

Depending on your printer's capabilities, you can choose from a variety of printing options before printing. Options found in most printers include selecting the page range and the number of copies to print. After you choose your options, Netscape prints your document.

To choose print options and print your document:

1. Do one of the following:

   In the Print Preview window, click the Print button
   or
   Click the Print button on the toolbar
   or
   From the File menu, choose Print
   or
   Press Ctrl + P
2. You'll see the Print dialog box, shown in Figure 9.5.
3. If you would like to print just some of the pages in the document, select Pages in the Print Range area, and type the beginning page number in the From box and the ending page number in the To box.
4. To make more than one copy, type the number of copies you want to make in the Copies box.
5. Choose OK to initiate printing.

Viewing Document Information

If you'd like to know more about the document you're viewing, open the View menu and choose Page Info, or press Ctrl + I. You'll see the Document Info about the document you're currently viewing, as shown in Figure 9.6. You'll find information that may prove helpful in certain situations; for

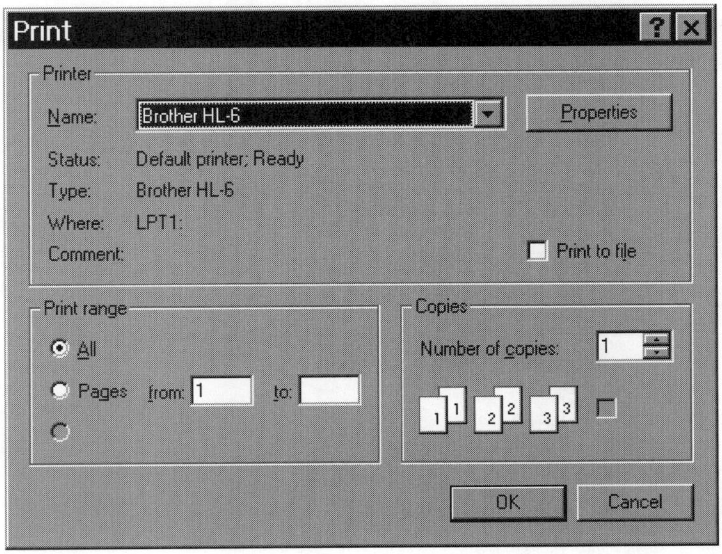

Figure 9.5 Print dialog box.

example, you can find out from this window which file name Netscape has used to store the document in the disk cache.

Note that the Document Info page contains a list of all the hyperlinks in a document, including links to graphics. You can click any of these links to access the links and graphics referenced in the document. If you'd like to access and save all the graphics referenced in a document, this is the most convenient way to do so.

Viewing the Source HTML

If you're learning HTML, the language used to code Web documents, you'll sooner or later access a particularly cool site and exclaim, "How did they *do* that!" Here's how you can find out. From the View menu, choose Page Source (or press Ctrl + U), and you'll see a colorful view of

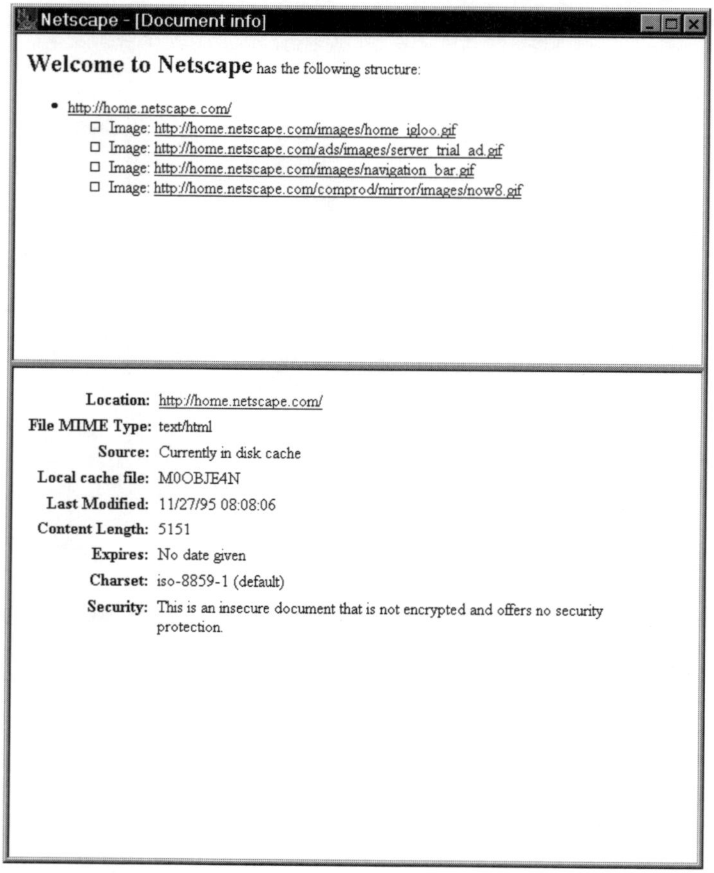

Figure 9.6 Document Info.

the underlying HTML code (Figure 9.7). The colors help the eye to separate the code from the text.

From this screen you can select and copy snippets of HTML code verbatim, and paste them into HTML documents with which you're experimenting. Try varying some of the attributes to see what effect the variations have on the result.

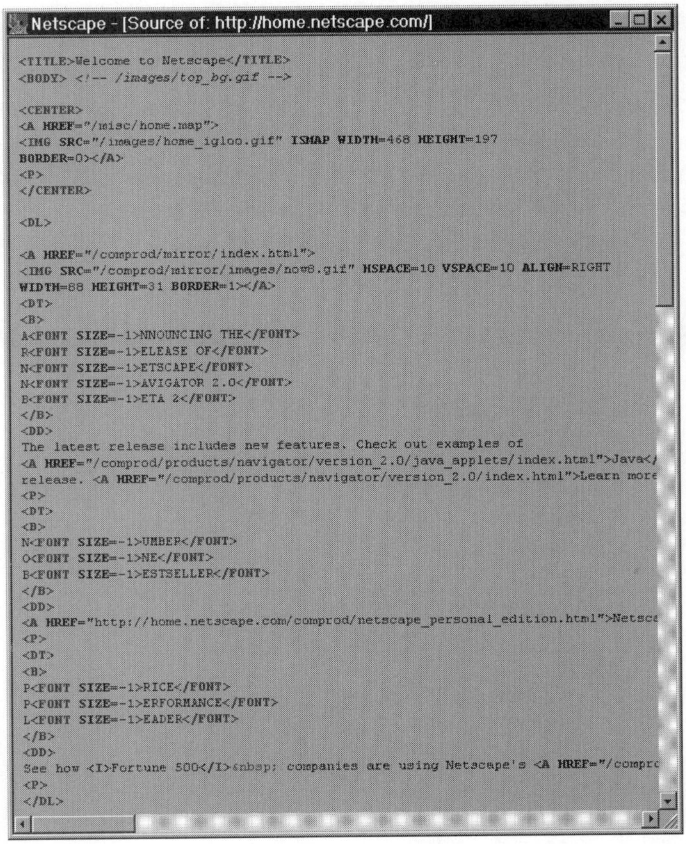
Netscape - [Source of: http://home.netscape.com/]
<TITLE>Welcome to Netscape</TITLE>
<BODY> <!-- /images/top_bg.gif -->
<CENTER>
<A HREF="/misc/home.map">
<IMG SRC="/images/home_igloo.gif" ISMAP WIDTH=468 HEIGHT=197
BORDER=0></A>
<P>
</CENTER>
<DL>
<A HREF="/comprod/mirror/index.html">
<IMG SRC="/comprod/mirror/images/now8.gif" HSPACE=10 VSPACE=10 ALIGN=RIGHT
WIDTH=88 HEIGHT=31 BORDER=1></A>
<DT>
<B>
A<FONT SIZE=-1>NNOUNCING THE</FONT>
R<FONT SIZE=-1>ELEASE OF</FONT>
N<FONT SIZE=-1>ETSCAPE</FONT>
N<FONT SIZE=-1>AVIGATOR 2.0</FONT>
B<FONT SIZE=-1>ETA 2</FONT>
</B>
<DD>
The latest release includes new features. Check out examples of
<A HREF="/comprod/products/navigator/version_2.0/java_applets/index.html">Java</
release. <A HREF="/comprod/products/navigator/version_2.0/index.html">Learn more
<P>
<DT>
<B>
N<FONT SIZE=-1>UMBER</FONT>
O<FONT SIZE=-1>NE</FONT>
B<FONT SIZE=-1>ESTSELLER</FONT>
</B>
<DD>
<A HREF="http://home.netscape.com/comprod/netscape_personal_edition.html">Netsca
<P>
<DT>
<B>
P<FONT SIZE=-1>RICE</FONT>
P<FONT SIZE=-1>ERFORMANCE</FONT>
L<FONT SIZE=-1>EADER</FONT>
</B>
<DD>
See how <I>Fortune 500</I> companies are using Netscape's <A HREF="/compro
<P>
</DL>

Figure 9.7 Web page displayed using Document Source.

Mailing Documents to Others

If you run across a page that you'd love to share with somebody, here's how you can do it electronically. You don't actually share the whole page, just the URL. If the person to whom you're sending the URL has a reasonably Internet-savvy mail reader, the URL will appear as a hyperlink. The recipient can click this link, which will then appear in the window of the browser this person is using.

To mail a document to someone:

1. Display the document.
2. From the File menu, choose Save Page (or Save Frame, if you're viewing a frame). You'll see a Composition window, such as the one shown in Figure 9.8. Note that Netscape has automatically placed the document's title in the Subject line. The program has also placed the document's URL in the message body area.

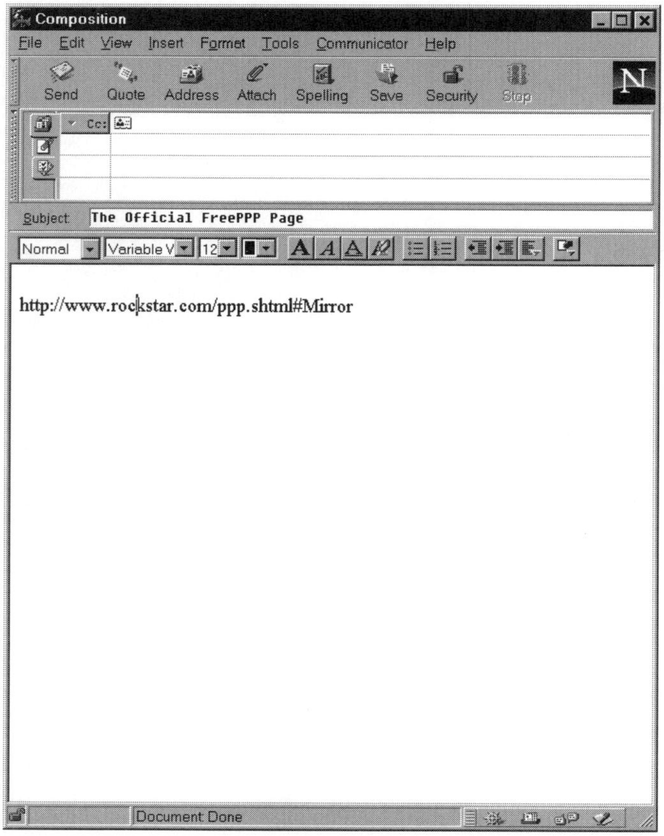

Figure 9.8 It's easy to mail a URL to somebody.

3. In the To box, type the recipient's e-mail address.
4. Edit the Subject line, if the page's title isn't self-explanatory.
5. Add a short note explaining why you're mailing this URL to the person.
6. Click Send.

Amazing History List Tricks

You learned about the history list in Chapter 7. As you know, Netscape keeps a list of all the sites you've recently visited. In the History window, you can view this list—and do some nifty things with it, as this section explains.

To display the History window, do one of the following:

- From the Communicator menu, choose History

  or

- Press Ctrl + H.

You *Know* That Link Is In There Somewhere!

Trying to get back to a site you visited a while ago? Frustrated by searching through zillions of History list items by hand? Well, don't bother. You can search the history list using an especially powerful and useful search utility.

To search the History window, do the following:

1. Open the History window, if necessary.
2. From the Edit menu, choose Search History List. You'll see the Search History List dialog box, shown in Figure 9.9.
3. In the first list box, choose the part of the History list item that you want to search for. You can choose from Title (the default choice), Location, First Visited, Last Visited, Expires, or Visit Count.
4. In the second list box, choose the comparison you want. Depending on what you've chosen in the first box, your choices include

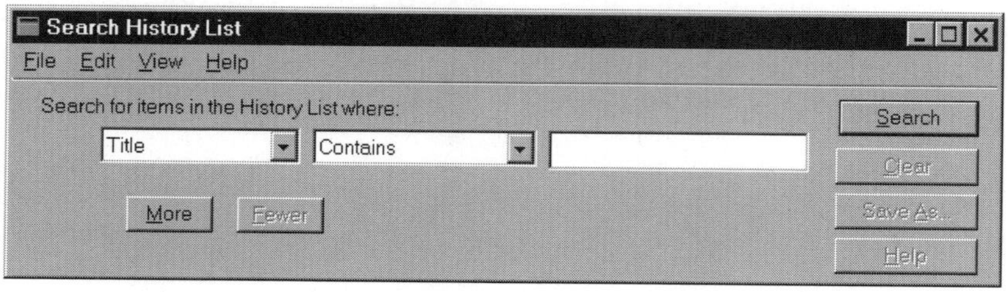

Figure 9.9 The History window gives you supple tools for searching your history list.

Contains, Doesn't Contain, Is, Isn't, Is Before, Is After, Is Less Than, or Is Greater Than.

Note that "Is" requires you to type the matching text or date in full. If you're searching for "A Parent's Guide to Anime," you have to type this entire title if you're using the Is comparison. It's better to use Contains. With "Contains," you can type "A Parent's," or "Guide to Anime," and you'll get a hit. When should you use Is? When the Contains search produces too many documents to go through conveniently.

5. To add an additional condition, click More. You'll see an additional row of text boxes, just like the one you just filled out.

   Bear in mind that each new row further restricts your search, because Netscape connects them using an AND operator. This means that a page won't be found unless it matches *both* of the conditions you've specified—that is, both lines. You should use more than one condition line only if an initial one-line search produced too much stuff.

   Figure 9.10 shows a three-line condition and the resulting matches. Cool, huh?

   To reduce the number of conditions, click Fewer.

6. To perform the search, click Search. If Netscape finds any matches, you'll see them in the mini–History list at the bottom of the window (see Figure 9.10).

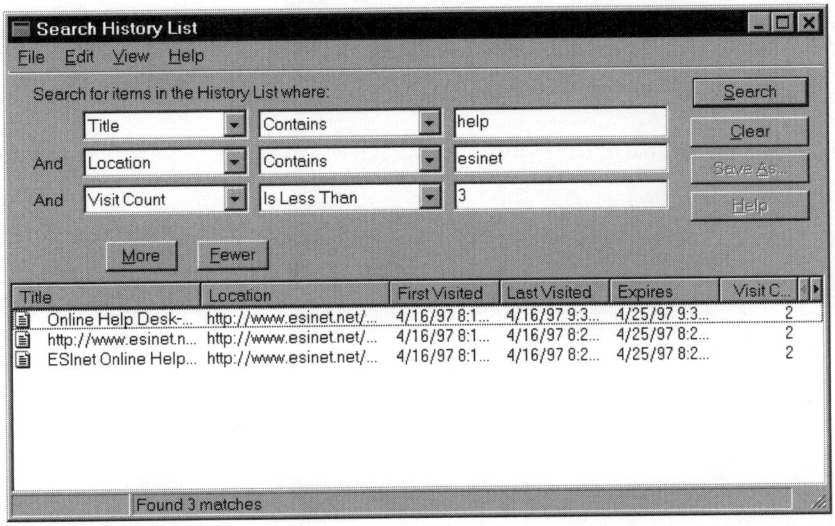

Figure 9.10 A multicondition search enables you to zero in on a missing link.

If you'd like to start over with a new search, click Clear.

To go to one of the pages you've retrieved, just double-click it.

More Tricks

Here are some more nifty things you can do in the History window.

- To add a history list item to your Bookmark menu, select the item, click File, and choose Add to Bookmarks.
- To add a history list item to your Personal toolbar, select the item, click File, and choose Add Page to Toolbar.
- Using Windows 95 or Windows NT? To create a desktop shortcut for a history list item, select the item, choose File, and choose Create Shortcut.

FROM HERE

- You've mastered all the Netscape Navigator fundamentals. Now it's time to choose some configuration options, as explained in the next chapter.
- Get into multimedia, Java, and VRML! Get the lowdown in Part II.

Chapter 10

Understanding Security Issues

Is a revolution under way? Will millions of people buy things through the Web, the way they do on the phone? It hasn't happened yet. Although a few businesses have been able to establish a business on the Web, online shopping is growing only at a slow pace. The reason that it's growing so slowly isn't so much that there's no solution to the problems of security on the Net, but rather that there isn't enough standardization to encourage both vendors and shoppers to leap into the fray.

This chapter provides an introduction to the security issues facing the would-be Web shopper.

For the Time-Challenged

- Security actually involves three different aspects: authentication (knowing who's sending you something), confidentiality (knowing that no third party can intercept and read the information you exchange with someone), and integrity (knowing that your message has not been tampered with or altered while en route).
- Public key cryptography, the technology that underlies Netscape's security features, enables any two people to exchange undecipherable messages without needing to exchange decoding keys via a secure channel.
- Netscape's security standard, called Secure Socket Layer (SSL), uses public key cryptography to enable you to establish a secure connection with a Web server.
- There is no single Web security standard yet; in fact, there are several competing standards. In the years to come it is likely that a single standard will emerge.
- Your credit card information cannot be intercepted en route, but you still need to use common sense when ordering via the Web. Order from trusted, well-established firms, and make sure you understand their policies.

What Is Security?

In the computer world, security has three distinct shades of meaning: authentication, confidentiality, and integrity, as the following sections discuss.

Authentication

In brief, *authentication* ensures that you are really who you say you are when you log on to a server. There's a flip side to this one: It also ensures that the site you're logging on to is actually the site that you think it is.

Authentication is very important. If criminals got hold of your credit card, they could log on to a commercial site that lacks authentication and order like crazy. By the same token, a criminal could set up a fake Web site, one that poses as a bona fide compact disc store, say, and get people's Visa numbers and expiration dates. They could then go on a phone shopping spree. Scary, huh?

Authentication is poorly developed. Most Web servers demand no authentication at all—they just let you in. However, virtually all Web servers support simple protection by password: You must type a login name (user name) and password to access the service. An example of a Web service that requires password authentication is HotWired, the online version of *Wired* magazine.

When you access HotWired for the first time, you're asked to create a login name and password and to supply your e-mail address. You then receive an automatically generated e-mail message that includes an authorization number. You must then supply this authorization number to access the system. What's gained from this? A modicum of assurance that you aren't accessing the site using someone else's name and e-mail address. But it's only a modicum. Computer criminals called crackers are notorious for getting past password-based authentication schemes.

And how do you know that the Web site you're accessing is really a bona fide site?

Confidentiality

Confidentiality refers to the protection of information while it is en route to its destination. It's not nice to think about, but none of the information you are transmitting via the Web is free from prying eyes. Hackers, criminals, or investigators can easily intercept, record, and print all the information you transmit.

It says anything I upload isn't secure! This alert box appears when you upload text to a non-secured Web page. It's a good reminder that the Web isn't secure, but even so, it's a pain. Learn the lesson, but click the option that hides this warning in the future.

Integrity

Integrity refers to the exact preservation of the transmitted data so that it reaches its destination without any alteration, accidental or deliberate. As with confidentiality, the Web provides absolutely no means of ensuring the integrity of transmitted data. It could be altered while en route, either by chance or deliberate interference, and the receiving computer would have no way of knowing.

It says this file might contain viruses! I'm sure you've seen this warning, too. It appears when you're about to download or open a file that you've retrieved from the network. This is one of the biggest concerns in the integrity area: The Internet is a sort of happy hunting ground for virus authors. Be very careful about downloading any executable program (any program that can run on your computer) from the Internet! Download only from really trustworthy sites, such as Download.com (www.download.com) or the software publisher's home page. But wait! Are you sure it's really the software publisher's home page? There's a trick called Web site spoofing that enables saboteurs to set up phony sites. Be very careful, and don't download anything if you don't feel 100 percent confident that it's OK.

A Solution: Encryption

The solution to the Web's security problems lies in the use of encryption. In essence, *encryption* is the process of converting a plain-text message (a message that could be read by anyone) into an unreadable ciphertext by means of a key (a method of transforming the message so that it appears to be gibberish). The message can be read only by the intended recipient, who possesses the key and uses it (in a process called *decryption*) to make the text readable again.

Understanding Encryption

A simple encryption technique is ROT-13, which "rotates" all letters in the alphabet 13 characters to the right. The ciphertext looks like gibberish, but it is easily decrypted by rotating the letters 13 characters to the left. Encryption ensures integrity as well as confidentiality; if anyone or anything has altered the message en route, it won't decode 100 percent correctly, so you'll know that something has gone wrong.

ROT-13 is a poor encryption technique because its key is so simple. In fact, it's used on Usenet only to keep adult-oriented material away from the eyes of children or those who would rather not have such material thrown in their faces. More complicated keys are needed to ensure confidentiality and integrity. With more complicated keys, though, another problem arises:

how to transmit the key to the recipient. Traditionally, this has been done by courier, but this is costly and time-consuming.

Public-Key Cryptography Explained

A new cryptographic method called *public-key cryptography* eliminates the need to deliver the key and raises the possibility that people who have never previously exchanged messages could send encrypted messages to each other that could not be intercepted by a third party. In public-key cryptography, there are two different keys, an encryption key and a decryption key:

- **Public Encryption Key** You make your encryption key public; people use it to send an encrypted message to you.
- **Decryption Key** This key is kept private. You use it to decode the messages sent to you. Nobody else can read the message without this key.

With public-key cryptography, there is no need to establish a secure channel to exchange the decryption key; the person who wishes to send an encrypted message to you merely obtains the public encryption key, encrypts the message, and sends it to you. Nobody along the way can decode the message, even if they have intercepted the encryption key; they would need the decryption key, and you keep that secret. Rightfully, public-key encryption has been described as a revolution in cryptography. It will make cryptography available to ordinary people.

Introducing the Secure Socket Layer Security Protocol

To provide secure transactions via the World Wide Web, Netscape Communications Corporation has proposed a standard called the Secure Socket Layer (SSL) protocol. This proposed Internet standard seeks to provide secure public key encryption capabilities so that people can exchange information securely via any established Internet protocol, including not only the Web but also Gopher, FTP, Telnet, and others. What's more, SSL seeks to do this without placing undue demands on users; much or all of the SSL processing goes on in the background, without requiring any intervention from the user.

An SSL session begins when an SSL-capable client (such as Netscape Navigator) contacts an SSL-capable server (such as Netscape's secure Web servers). A brief exchange of public keys occurs; from that point on, the client and server can exchange secure, encrypted messages, and no third party can intercept them. In addition, SSL includes integrity-checking features that assure both parties that the message has not been tampered with or altered during its transmission.

I read that somebody cracked the security scheme! Due to limitations stemming from Cold War–era export restrictions, Netscape's security can indeed be cracked—but only by running several expensive workstations for days on end. That's worth doing to make a point, perhaps, but not to decode your $29.95 order to Victoria's Secret.

Why Encryption Isn't Enough

OK, we're going to encrypt our messages. Security problem solved, right? Nope—wrong. There's still the authentication problem. As just mentioned, can you be absolutely certain that the site you're contacting is actually the site you think you're contacting? What if a criminal sets up a phony commercial site, and starts taking all kinds of credit card orders on a bogus basis? Perhaps he'll use some recognized brand name to lend credibility to what he's doing. And on the other end, how does a business know that you are really the person you say you are? What if you're using a stolen credit card? They might not get paid.

For these reasons, a total security solution has to involve some kind of digital authentication. And that's precisely why Web-based commerce has been so slow to develop. Only now are the details being worked out to everyone's satisfaction. Netscape Communicator comes very close to offering a complete security solution, as the next section explains.

Netscape Communicator's (Almost) Complete Security Solution

Netscape Navigator tackles the security problem in the following ways:

- **Secure servers** Netscape's server programs incorporate a security scheme that enables secure, encrypted communication between you, the Web user, and an online vendor. That takes care of the confidentiality and integrity problems pretty well. When you access a secure server, the open lock icon becomes locked, and you can proceed with the confidence that no individual could intercept your credit card information while it's en route.

- **Site certificates for vendors** These certificates establish that the vendor you're contacting is really a bona fide online vendor. To prevent people from forging certificates, they're issued and validated by independent certificate authorities, which do the job for a fee. When you first contact a vendor, Netscape examines the certificate to see whether it has been digitally signed by a recognized authority. Subsequently, Netscape stores the certificate (to see a list, click the Security button and click Sites).
- **Signed objects** To protect you when you're downloading Java applets and other software components from the Internet, you'll be able to view and approve a software publisher's signed digital certificate. The certificate is issued by an independent verification agency, which attests that the software publisher is really the software publisher, and not some imposter. This certificate is encrypted so that it can't be forged or altered while it's en route. You view the certificate, decide whether it's trustworthy, and on this basis continue or abandon the download.
- **Personal certificates** These certificates establish that you're actually the person you say you are. Your digital certificate is something like showing your driver's license when you buy something with your credit card. The recipient of a message signed with your digital certificate can verify that the message actually originated from the person who signed it, and what's more, that it hasn't been altered en route. To get a personal certificate, you need to obtain one from a certificate agency, such as Verisign. I'll show you how later in this chapter.

Does Netscape's solution make everyone happy? Nope. It's still not quite a complete solution. From the vendors' standpoint, there still isn't an agreed-upon mechanism for validating credit card purchases, the way clerks do at stores when they swipe your card through a validation reader.

Credit card companies aren't completely happy with this solution, either. The largest source of credit card fraud occurs on the vendor's end; peoples' credit card numbers and expiration dates are freely available to employees, and a lot of them get stolen and misused. Credit card companies want a system that simultaneously obtains validation and keeps the credit card number encrypted, so that the vendor never has access to it. Such a system would be very much in the consumer's interest.

The SET Standard

Credit card companies themselves have taken the leadership to resolve the standardization issue. Visa International, working with MasterCard, Netscape, Microsoft, and other corporations, has recently proposed a single standard for dealing with all the issues of credit card security over the Internet. SET also includes standards for personnel certificates—the electronic equivalent of showing your ID when you use a credit card. This standard, called Secure Electronic Transactions (SET), still isn't finalized, but it offers the best hope yet that digital commerce will really take off.

SET directly addresses the remaining issues of Internet security by enabling merchants to obtain online validation, while at the same time protecting credit card numbers from the prying eyes of unscrupulous employees. With SET, nobody but the credit card company itself ever sees your credit card number, and validation is automatic and instantaneous.

The SET standard is good news for Web users because it resolves a major standardization issue. Previously, Visa had been working with Microsoft on one security standard, while MasterCard and Netscape had been working on a competing standard. Getting all four of these parties to agree and work together is in everyone's best interests; without cooperation at this time, Web commerce might not develop at all.

Getting Your Digital Certificate

To get started with secure network use, including secure e-mail, you need a personal certificate—a digital ID. At this writing, Verisign (digitalid.verisign.com/id_pick.htm) is offering a free, one-year Class 1 digital ID. Normally, the fee is $6 per year.

What's a Class 1 certificate? A Class 1 digital ID is the lowest level of identification that Verisign provides. There's not that much assurance that you are who you say you are—the only assurance is that you get the certificate by e-mail reply. Class 2 IDs are verified by matching your name, mailing address, and other personal information against a consumer database.

There's a two-phase mailback process to ensure that nobody else can obtain a digital ID using your name. Class 2 certificates run $12 per year.

Get started with a free Class 1 certificate while the offer's still valid. To enroll, access digitalid.verisign.com/id_pick.htm, and follow the on-screen instructions. You'll supply your name and e-mail address. Subsequently, a Netscape Communicator wizard will appear, and it will guide you through the steps needed to create your private key. When this is done, the program automatically submits this to Verisign, and Verisign sends information back to your e-mail account instructing you how to download your certificate. You then reaccess Verisign's site, and Netscape downloads your certificate. You can view this, if you wish, as shown in Figure 10.1.

To make sure your digital certificate was installed correctly, click the Security button on the Toolbar. You'll see the security information for this page. On the right panel, under Certificates, click Yours; you should see your new certificate listed (see Figure 10.2).

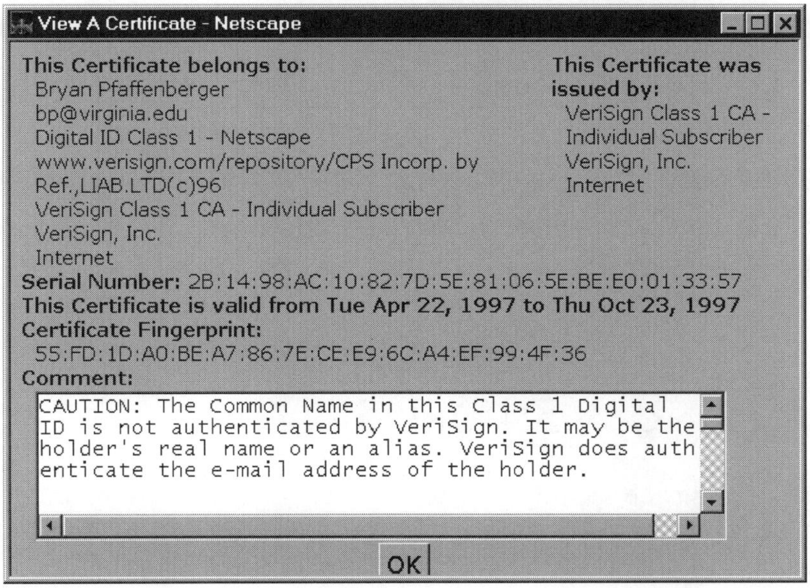

Figure 10.1 My very own digital certificate (Class 1).

Figure 10.2 Your new digital certificate appears in Netscape's security dialog box.

Accessing a Secure Server

Notwithstanding the security and validation problems that are still holding back many would-be Web vendors, a few pioneers have gotten into the act (for some samples, see "Let's Go Shopping," later in this chapter). They're using Netscape's secure servers to implement Netscape's security scheme, sans SET.

You'll know when you access a secure server because you'll see the dialog box shown in Figure 10.3. This dialog box informs you that you are accessing a secure document. Also, the Security button's open lock icon becomes locked.

Figure 10.3 Secure server.

If you don't want to see this warning again, deselect the check box next to Show This Alert Next Time.

To get more security information about the document you have accessed, click the Security button. This command displays the dialog box shown in Figure 10.4.

When you access a secure document, Netscape checks the site's certificate, to see whether it's verified by an agency that Netscape trusts. This tells

Netscape that you really are accessing the service you think you're accessing (and not some clever hacker's "mock" service).

It says the certificate can't be authenticated! A security certificate ensures that the service you're accessing is actually what it says it is, and not some fly-by-night imposter. In order to authenticate the site, Netscape examines the site certificate to see whether it has been signed by an independent certification authority (CA) that Netscape trusts. If not, you see a wizard that warns you that the certificate isn't fully trustworthy. This probably just means that the firm hasn't completed the security system—only a few on-line vendors have done so. It might also mean that Netscape hasn't inked a deal with the certificate authority.

Managing Site Certificates

The more secure sites you visit, the more security certificates you collect. Netscape stores them so that you don't have to confirm them on subsequent visits. If you'd like to see the site certificates, click the Security button on the Navigation toolbar, and click Sites. For each certificate, you can choose the following options: Edit (enables you to view the certificate and choose trust level options), Verify (initiates a verification check), Delete, or Select Expired (identifies the certificates that have expired, so you can delete them).

Why would you want to edit the certificates? To change the trust level for a given site. Suppose you're absolutely confident that a given site is trustworthy—you've dealt with them successfully, and received shipments. You can modify this site's certificate so that Netscape automatically trusts the site, instead of hitting you with a warning. For other sites, you can set the trust level lower, so that you see a warning when you access the site.

Managing Certificate Authorities

Netscape also keeps a list of trustworthy certificate authorities. To see these, click the Security button, and click Certificate Authorites. As with site certificates, you can choose the following options: Edit (enables you to view the certificate and choose verification options), Verify (initiates a verification check), Delete, or Select Expired (identifies the certificates that have expired, so you can delete them).

Why would you want to edit the certificate authorities? Again, to change the trust level. By default, Netscape automatically accepts connections with any secure site that's certified by one of these agencies. Should you wish to lower the trust level so that you see a warning when you access these sites, or if you'd like to disallow connections to any site that's verified by a given certificate authority, click the certificate, and choose Edit. You can change the trust level for each certificate authority in this way.

Changing Security Alerts

If you're tired of seeing those irritating security alerts all the time, you can disable them. Just be sure that you fully understand the risks of Internet use before you do so.

To disable security alerts, click the Security button, and click SSL Browsing in the Security window (see Figure 10.4). You can change the following alerts:

- Entering an encrypted site
- Leaving an encrypted site
- Viewing a page with an encrypted/unencrypted mix
- Sending unencrypted information to a site

You can also choose the certificate that's requested when you access a secure server; by default, this is set to Ask Every Time—and that's where you should leave it.

At the bottom of this panel you'll find buttons enabling you to configure the encryption level of SSL, but you'd be well advised to leave these alone, unless you know what you're doing. The default settings are fine.

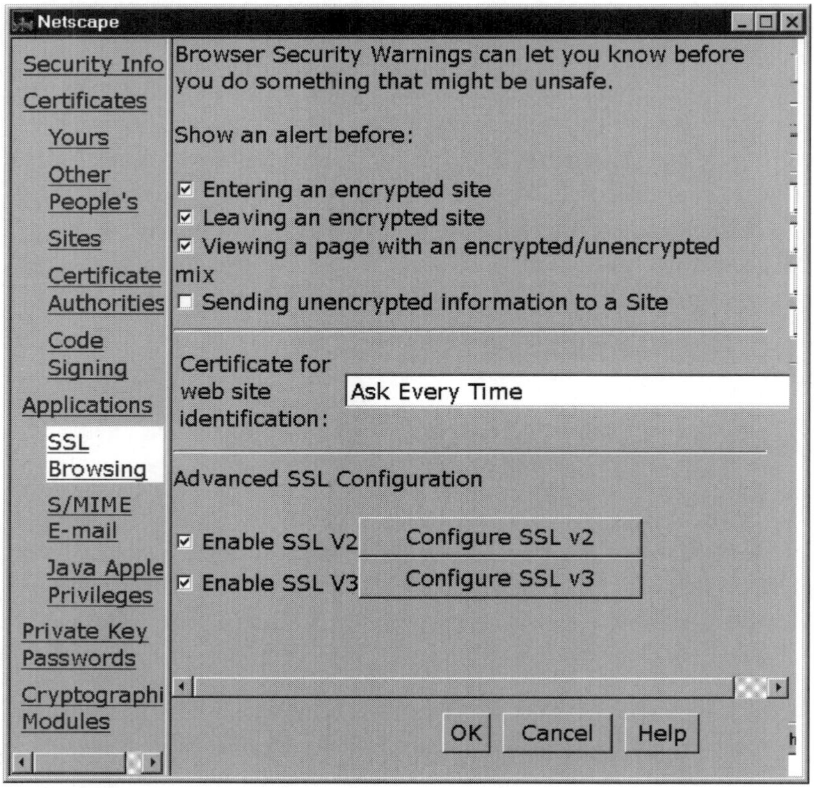

Figure 10.4 In this dialog box, you can stop the display of those annoying (but important) security alerts.

Is My Credit Card Information Really Safe?

Once you've accessed a secure server, you can transmit your credit card number without fear of its being intercepted along the way. Does that mean your credit card information is safe? With Netscape's security features, you can be assured that nobody can obtain your credit card number by tapping

VeriFone/Netscape Deal Makes It Easier to Offer Online Ordering

When you charge something at a store, the clerk takes your card and swipes it through a little verifying machine. It's actually an online device; the card reads your information, contacts the verification service, and determines whether your card's valid and how much credit is available. Right now, there's no software available that does this automatically when you order online, unless vendors develop the software themselves—an expensive proposition. So somebody has to manually check all the orders before they can be processed. But that's about to change.

The maker of about 75 percent of those "swiping" devices, VeriFone, announced an agreement with Netscape to develop automatic verification for Netscape's Commerce Server. One of the Web-based vendors that welcomes this development is the Internet Shopping Network, of Palo Alto, CA, which currently processes some $1.4 million in credit card orders each month.

your Internet connection. But sending your credit card number via a secure link is very much like giving it to somebody over the telephone: You're still dependent on the honesty and integrity of the person on the other end. In the end, ordering on the Web won't be any safer than any other form of mail or telephone order.

If you're thinking about ordering something by credit card on the Web, use all the common-sense rules that you would when ordering by telephone or mail. Order from well-established firms with good reputations. Make sure you fully understand the firm's policies regarding the delivery of ordered goods, returns and exchanges, and refunds.

LET'S GO SHOPPING!

Web commerce is still in the experimental phase. Many questions remain unanswered. What's going to sell on the Web? Are there some types of merchandise that aren't well suited to the Web commercial idiom? Do you offer just a few high-profile items or your whole catalog? Are Web commercial sites best deployed for one-of-a-kind, special-interest items or for huge shopping enterprises on a department store scale? As of yet, nobody knows, but there are plenty of experiments in all directions.

This section provides an in-depth look at a few of the most interesting commercial Web sites that were online at the time of this book's writing; the Showcase page will certainly list additional vendors, so take a look.

Don't be shy about browsing these sites—there's no obligation. You can even fill out order forms, and then change your mind and cancel at the last moment.

The Grapevine

Here's a challenge. You own a winery. But most of your visitors and customers aren't young. How do you reach the younger generation and introduce them to the pleasures of fine wine?

The Grapevine (http://www.winery.com/) is one answer. It's a complete guide to wine, featuring the creations of more than 30 vineyards (Figure 10.5). To keep things fresh, the site features current news and events, such as the catalog from a recent Sonoma County wine auction. By means of an online toteboard, people browsing the site could relay their bids to the auctioneers!

The Grapevine relies on heavy-duty equipment: Several Sun workstations and Netscape's Commerce Server, which enables secure online ordering. Once within the site, you can navigate by means of well-designed icons (Wineries, Maps, Products, Events, What's New, Travel, Reviews, Judging, and On-Wine, an online wine newspaper).

What about the wineries? One of the things that's worrisome about Web commerce is that the vendors might not represent the best of the lot. But you'll find some of California's best wineries on Grapevine, including the superb Matanzas Creek Winery, makers of what many wine aficionados believe is one of the finest Merlots in the entire world. And it's not just California that's represented. You'll find Oregon, Australian, and even Texas wineries in Grapevine—and doubtless more by the time you read this book.

software.net

As an indication of what software retailing might be like in the future, software.net (Figure 10.6) goes the whole nine yards—not only can you

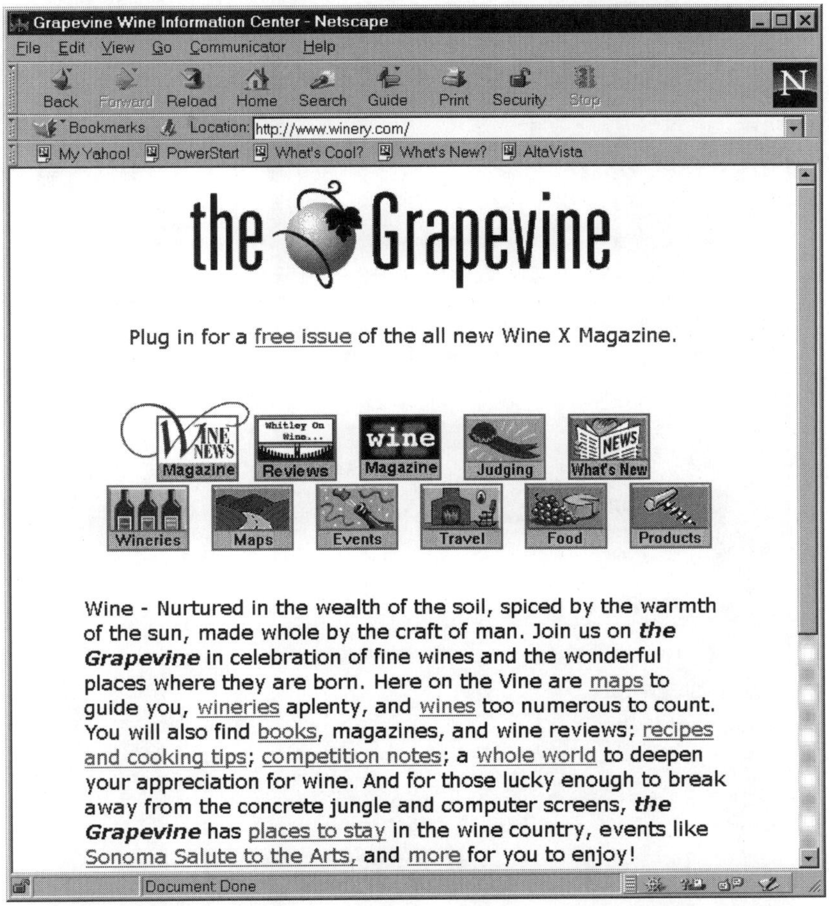

Grapevine Wine Information Center - Netscape
File Edit View Go Communicator Help
Back Forward Reload Home Search Guide Print Security Stop
Bookmarks Location: http://www.winery.com/
My Yahoo! PowerStart What's Cool? What's New? AltaVista
the Grapevine
Plug in for a free issue of the all new Wine X Magazine.
Magazine Reviews Magazine Judging What's New
Wineries Maps Events Travel Food Products
Wine - Nurtured in the wealth of the soil, spiced by the warmth of the sun, made whole by the craft of man. Join us on the Grapevine in celebration of fine wines and the wonderful places where they are born. Here on the Vine are maps to guide you, wineries aplenty, and wines too numerous to count. You will also find books, magazines, and wine reviews; recipes and cooking tips; competition notes; a whole world to deepen your appreciation for wine. And for those lucky enough to break away from the concrete jungle and computer screens, the Grapevine has places to stay in the wine country, events like Sonoma Salute to the Arts, and more for you to enjoy!
Document: Done

Figure 10.5 The Grapevine (www.winery.com).

take advantage of online ordering via secure Netscape transactions but you can also obtain some programs via electronic links. No packaging to fill up landfills, no old buggy versions to worry about, no truck making its way across the United States, no week-long delay—just instantaneous, environmentally responsible delivery. Don't think that the software distributed electronically is strictly no-name, low-quality stuff: For those taxing moments before April 15, for example, you can obtain H&R Block's TaxCut or Novell's TaxSaver.

Figure 10.6 software.net (www.software.net).

software.net (http://www.software.net/index.htm) illustrates the First Rule of Web Marketing: Provide some freebies that make the site attractive to people. Not a site to mince words, software.net offers a Free Stuff page full of genuinely interesting stuff. At this writing, you could obtain the latest version of the Norton virus scanning software and a half-dozen sampler programs (full-featured but with built-in expiration dates). There's even a Usenet-like discussion system for software.net's products and services. To help you make the best selection, you can search a database of over 50,000 magazine articles from 16 major computer publications.

Internet Shopping Network

It had to happen: Cable TV's Home Shopping Network was one of the first commercial ventures on the Internet, and it figures (Figure 10.7). After all,

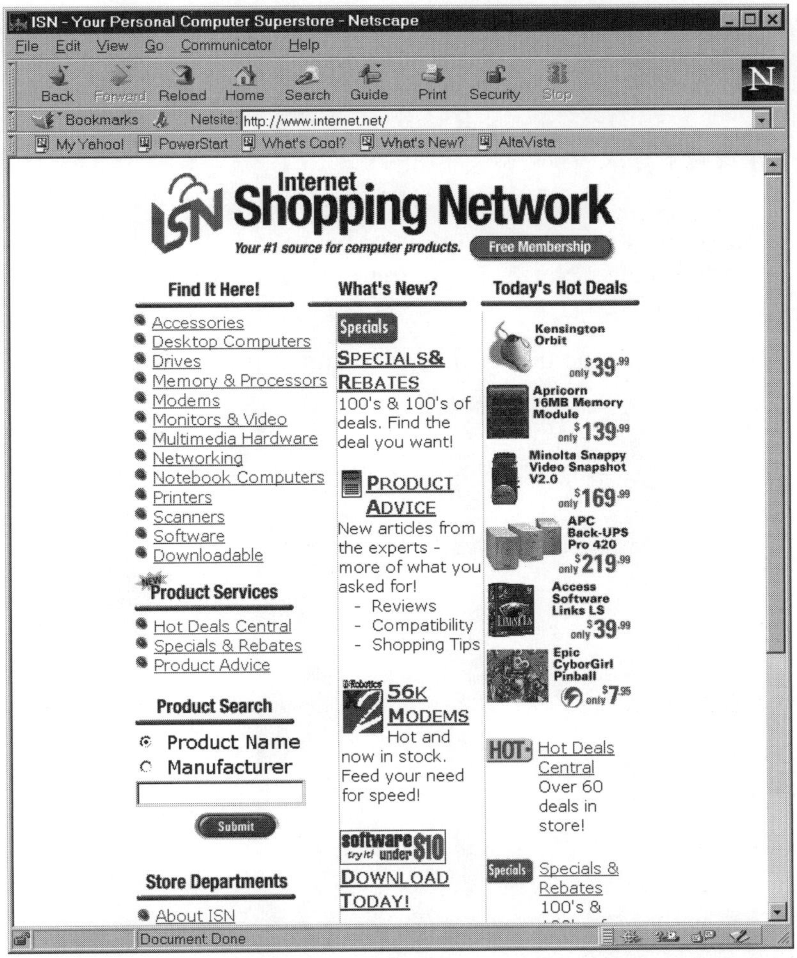

Figure 10.7 Internet Shopping Network (www.internet.net).

who else has more experience in high-tech marketing? Don't expect to find everything under the sun at ISN, though—the site specializes in the stuff its youthful browsers like to buy. Specifically, you'll find software, computer and electronics gear, photo and video stuff, equipment for home offices, and—naturally—flowers for those with romantic yearnings.

So how do you order? It's easy. When you find something you like you click the Buy button, and the server shifts into the secure mode. You'll see a page inviting you to become a member of ISN, if you're not already. If you don't feel comfortable about giving your credit card information online, despite the security protection, or if you're accessing ISN from behind a firewall that disables security, you can call an 800 number, or fax the membership form. There's no charge for the membership.

From Here

- You've mastered the essentials of browsing the Web. Now configure and customize Netscape so that it works your way, as shown in Chapter 11.
- Get into multimedia and live contents. Find out how in Part II.

Chapter

11

Customizing and Configuring Netscape Navigator

Netscape Navigator is more fun when it works the way you want. You can choose the fonts you like, and you can also paint the screen with colors and even graphic backgrounds. On the Options menu and the Preferences dialog boxes, you'll find many more options that will make Netscape run your way. In addition, you'll find many essential configuration options.

This chapter discusses all the configuration options available in the Options menu, but you'll find more detailed discussions of some of them elsewhere in this book:

For the Time-Challenged

- If you would like to view text in foreign languages, choose the language's encoding scheme, and then associate a font with this encoding.
- Many Web documents contain font choices. For those that don't, you can choose fonts other than the boring old default fonts that Netscape uses. I like Verdana, a free font you can download from Microsoft.
- I don't recommend that you change the default color settings for text, background, and links, except maybe you'd want to change the default background to white. Happily, most Web authors make good color choices these days; let them be.
- Turn off Java and JavaScript until you've read Chapter 15 and fully understand the security risks.
- Turn off cookies unless you want to do some on-line shopping.
- If more than one person uses your copy of Netscape, set up individual user profiles for each user. That way each person will see his or her own e-mail messages, bookmarks, and configuration choices.

- For an in-depth discussion of cache configuration options, see Chapter 7, "Improving Netscape Navigator's Performance."
- For information on installing the helper applications and plug-ins, see Chapter 12.
- For information on configuring e-mail, see Chapter 17.
- For information on configuring Collabra discussions and news, see Chapter 20.
- For information on configuring Conference, see Chapter 24.
- For information on configuring Netcaster, see Chapter 25.

Choosing Options on the View Menu

The View menu contains several options that you can use to configure Netscape. Here's a quick overview of these options, some of which I've mentioned earlier.

Controlling the Toolbar Display

I really like the toolbars—all three of them. I recommend that most Netscape users keep them displayed. If you're working with a really tiny screen, or if you want to see more of a document, you may wish to hide them. You can do so using the following options on the View menu:

- **Hide Navigation Toolbar** This option hides the Navigation Toolbar (the one with the big navigation buttons, such as Back and Forward). After you choose this option, it changes to Show Navigation Toolbar.
- **Hide Location Toolbar** This option hides the Location Toolbar, which contains the Netsite/Location box and the Bookmark QuickLink. After you choose this option, it changes to Show Location Toolbar.
- **Hide Personal Toolbar** This option hides the Personal Toolbar, which contains your personal toolbar items (see Chapter 7 for information about adding items to this toolbar). After you choose this option, it changes to Show Personal Toolbar.

I want my toolbars back! No problem. Just click the View menu, and choose one of the Show Toolbar options. You might have to drag the toolbars around to get them in the order you want.

Changing the Font Size

If you're like me, you're going blind from staring at computer screens. A bigger font really comes in handy. To increase the size of the fonts in any page you're viewing, click View and choose Increase Font, or just press Ctrl +]. You can decrease the font size by clicking View and choosing Decrease Font (or press Ctrl + [).

Displaying Non-Latin (Foreign Language) Character Sets

Do you read a language other than English? If so, you can take advantage of non-Western character encoding schemes. These character encoding schemes display text in a variety of foreign languages that don't use Latin characters, including Russian, Turkish, and Japanese. To change the character encoding scheme, click the View menu, choose Encoding, and choose an encoding scheme from the menu.

I changed the encoding scheme but I can't see Japanese characters! That's right. Changing the encoding isn't quite enough. You also need to install the right font on your computer, and then tell Netscape which font to use for that encoding. For more information, see "Choosing Fonts," later in this chapter.

A really great source of free font links is the Free Fonts page, located at jeff.cs.mcgill.ca/~luc/freefonts.html. By the way, if you're interested in displaying Japanese, the way to go is KanjiKit, created by Pacific Software Publishing (www.pspinc.com). You can download KanjiKit and use it for free for 45 days.

Some Web pages display more than one language. If you would like to choose the order of appearance in which Navigator displays languages, you can do so. From the Edit menu, choose Preferences, and click Browser. Click the plus sign, if necessary, to show the pages under Browser. Click Languages (one of the Browser subpages), and click Add to add a language. Use the up and down arrows to change the order, if you wish. Click OK to confirm.

Choosing Options in the Preferences Dialog Box

As just mentioned, the most frequently chosen options are available on the Options menu—but there are loads more on the several pages of the General Preferences dialog box. This dialog box has the following tabbed pages:

Appearance	In this page, you can choose options for the fonts and colors.
Browser	In this page, you choose general options for Navigator, including the start page location. You can also change the preference order for languages (discussed earlier in this chapter), and specify helper applications for different file types (discussed in Chapter 12).

Mail and Groups This page enables you to choose options forNetscape Messenger (e-mail) and Netscape Collabora discussions (newsgroups). These options are discussed in Chapters 16 and 20.

Composer This page enables you to choose options for Composer. These options are discussed in Chapter 33.

Offline This page enables you to set up options for offline reading of newsgroups, a useful option if you're connecting via modem. You'll learn more about this option in Chapter 21.

Advanced In this page, you choose many important customization and configuration options for Navigator. This chapter discusses all of these options.

Controlling Netscape's Appearance

You can change Netscape's on-screen appearance by choosing Toolbar options, fonts, and colors.

To choose appearance options, open the Edit menu and choose Preferences. In the Preferences dialog box, click Appearance. You'll see the Appearance options, shown in Figure 11.1.

To see additional options under Appearances, click the plus sign next to Appearances.

Choosing Startup Options

By default, Netscape starts with a browser page that shows Netscape's home page. You can change the page that Netscape displays when the program starts. If you prefer, the program will start with a mail, news, or computer window instead of the browser window.

To start the program with a mail or news window, choose Messenger Mailbox or Collabra discussions in the On Startup Launch area. The default option is Navigator. You can select more than one startup window, if you wish.

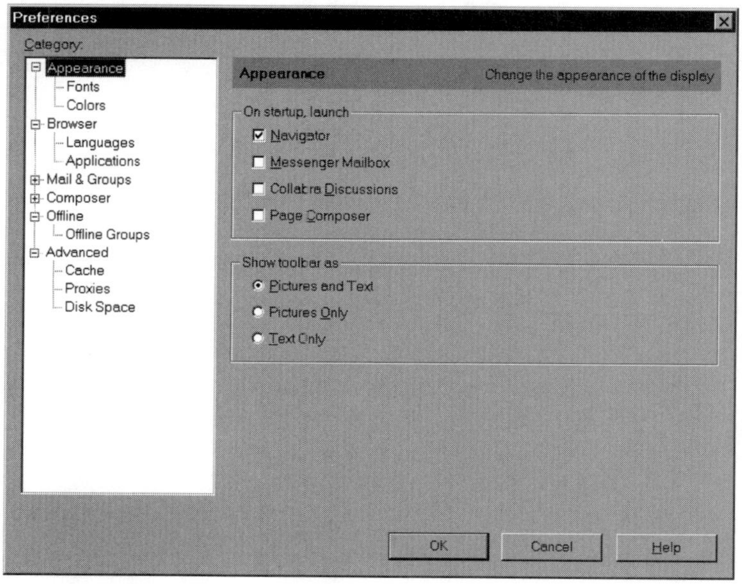

Figure 11.1 Appearance page (General Preferences).

Choosing Navigation Toolbar Options

Netscape's Toolbar is preset to display *pictures* (the cute little drawing of the house, for example, on the Home button) and *text* (the button's name). If you prefer, you can display only the pictures, or only the text. To choose one of these options, click the appropriate option button in the Show as toolbar area.

To conserve space onscreen, try the Text option; this hides the pictures. making the Toolbar buttons compact.

CHOOSING FONTS

Tired of those same old typefaces when you browse the Web? Get ready for some visual excitement. Thanks to advances in HTML, Web authors can choose fonts for their documents. For example, a Web author can choose to display text in Verdana, a free TrueType font (see Figure 11.2).

There's a big problem here, though. A Web author's font choice appears onscreen only if the needed font is installed on your system. If the needed font isn't found, Netscape uses the default fonts for the character encoding that the document uses. So what's the point here? Simple: To see the best of the Web, install lots of fonts on your system.

To stimulate the use of fonts on the Web, Microsoft makes a suite of attractive TrueType fonts available for free: Verdana, Trebuchet, Georgia, Comic Sans, and Arial Black. Many Web authors use these appealing, free typefaces, which have been

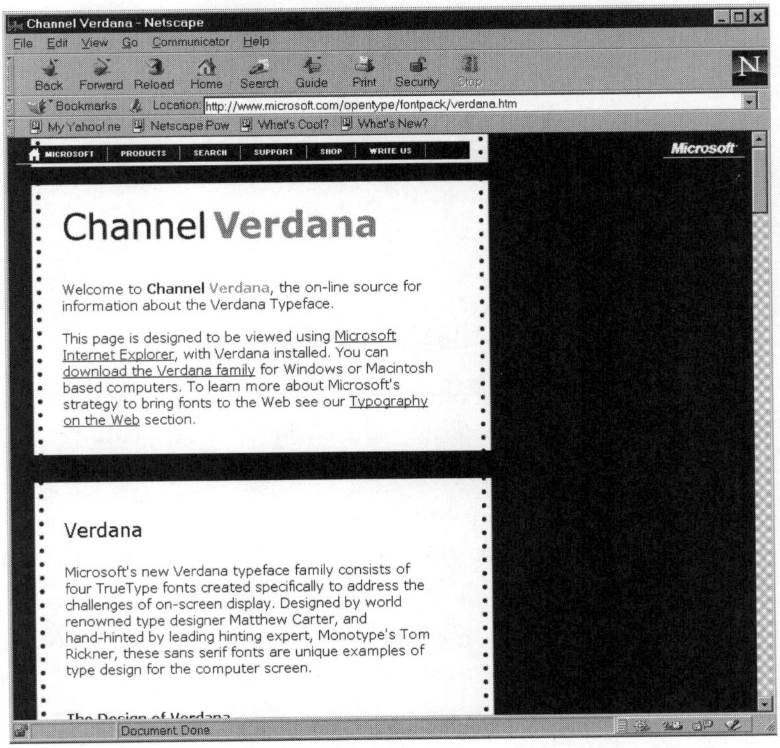
Channel Verdana - Netscape
File Edit View Go Communicator Help
Back Forward Reload Home Search Guide Print Security Stop
Bookmarks Location: http://www.microsoft.com/opentype/fontpack/verdana.htm
My Yahoo! ne Netscape Pow What's Cool? What's New?
MICROSOFT PRODUCTS SEARCH SUPPORT SHOP WRITE US
Microsoft
Channel Verdana
Welcome to Channel Verdana, the on-line source for information about the Verdana Typeface.
This page is designed to be viewed using Microsoft Internet Explorer, with Verdana installed. You can download the Verdana family for Windows or Macintosh based computers. To learn more about Microsoft's strategy to bring fonts to the Web see our Typography on the Web section.
Verdana
Microsoft's new Verdana typeface family consists of four TrueType fonts created specifically to address the challenges of on-screen display. Designed by world renowned type designer Matthew Carter, and hand-hinted by leading hinting expert, Monotype's Tom Rickner, these sans serif fonts are unique examples of type design for the computer screen.
Document: Done

Figure 11.2 You can see an author's font choices—but only if your system contains the required font.

optimized for Web use. To obtain these fonts for free, access www.microsoft.com/opentype/fontpack/.

Even if you're viewing a page that doesn't make a font choice, you can still jazz up its appearance by choosing your own default font. If you've downloaded the freebie Microsoft fonts, for example, you could make the beautiful Verdana font the default for all the documents you browse. (If you're in a more formal mood, choose Georgia.)

If you're planning to use an encoding other than Latin, be sure to obtain and install fonts that have all the characters needed to display foreign languages. For more information, see "Displaying Non-Latin (Foreign Language) Character Sets," above.

To change the default fonts for a given encoding, do the following:

1. In the Preferences dialog box's Categories panel, click the Fonts option. (If you don't see this, click the plus mark next to Appearances.) You'll see the Fonts page, shown in Figure 11.3.
2. In the For the Encoding box, choose the character set you want to change. In the English versions of Netscape, the default is the Latin1 character set.

   The choices you make in the next two boxes affect only the character set you choose in the For the Encoding box.
3. In the Variable Width Font box, choose the variable width font you want to use for the encoding you've chosen. You can choose a font size, too.
4. In the Fixed Width Font box, choose the fixed width font you want to use for the encoding you've chosen. You can choose a font size, too.
5. If you would like to override Web authors' font choices, click Always use my fonts, overriding document. I don't recommend this, though.
6. Some documents automatically download their fonts, but this takes time. To prevent fonts from downloading, choose Use document fonts when it does not increase download time. Otherwise, choose Use document fonts whenever available (this is the default).

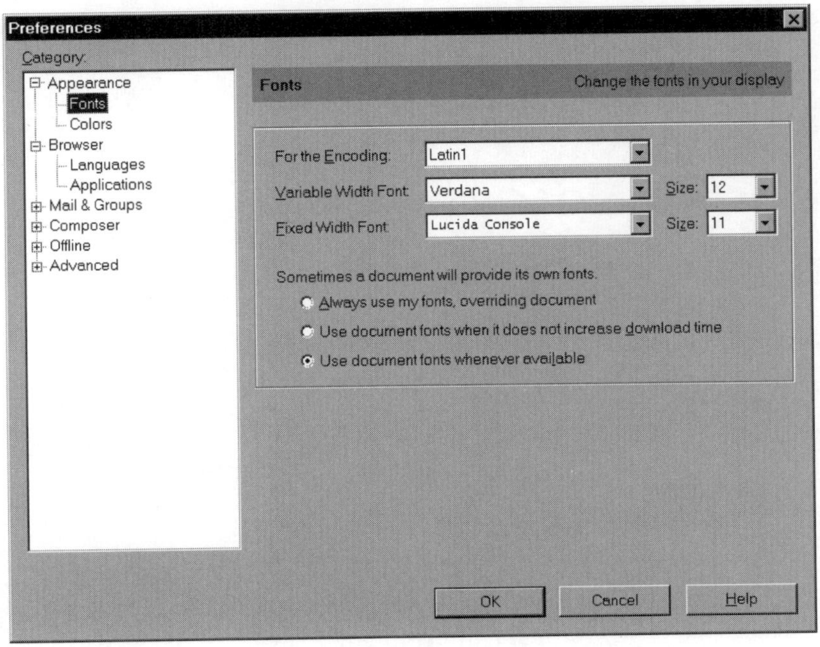

Figure 11.3 For each character encoding, you can choose a font. You must do this if you want to display foreign languages correctly.

7. Click OK to confirm your font choices.

Netscape is designed to work with a number of standardized character set encodings. These encodings enable Netscape to display foreign languages. For each chararacter set, you can choose the following fonts:

- **Variable Width Font** This is the font used for almost all of the text you'll see onscreen. In a proportionally spaced font, each character is given a width proportional to its size ("m" gets more space than "l"). The default proportionally spaced font is Times Roman.
- **Fixed Width Font** This is the font used for plain-text documents (such as README files in FTP file archives) and text marked with

the <CODE> tag in HTML. (The <CODE> tag is used to give examples of computer programming code.) In a fixed-width (monospace) font, each character gets the same amount of space, producing the effect of a typewriter. The default monospace font is Courier.

Choosing Colors

Netscape provides several options for choosing colors:

Text	All nonlink document text. By default, it's in black.
Background	The default background is battleship gray. You can choose colors or, to make things even more visually confusing, a background graphic.
Unvisited Links	Hyperlinks you haven't visited appear in this color. By default, they're blue.
Visited Links	Hyperlinks you've already visited. By default, they appear in lavender.

Should you change color options? Frankly, I don't think so. If you choose weird colors for text, background, and links, you'll soon get sick of them. One exception might be to change the default background color from battleship gray to white.

To change color options:

1. In the Preferences dialog box's Categories panel, click the Colors option. (If you don't see this, click the plus mark next to Appearances.) You'll see the Colors page, shown in Figure 11.4.
2. In the Colors area, deselect Use Windows Colors to enable text and background color options.
3. To change the default Text color, click Text. You'll see the Color dialog box, shown in Figure 11.5. Choose one of the colors, or click Define Custom Colors to display the custom color chooser. To make a custom color, click on the color map, and click Add to Custom

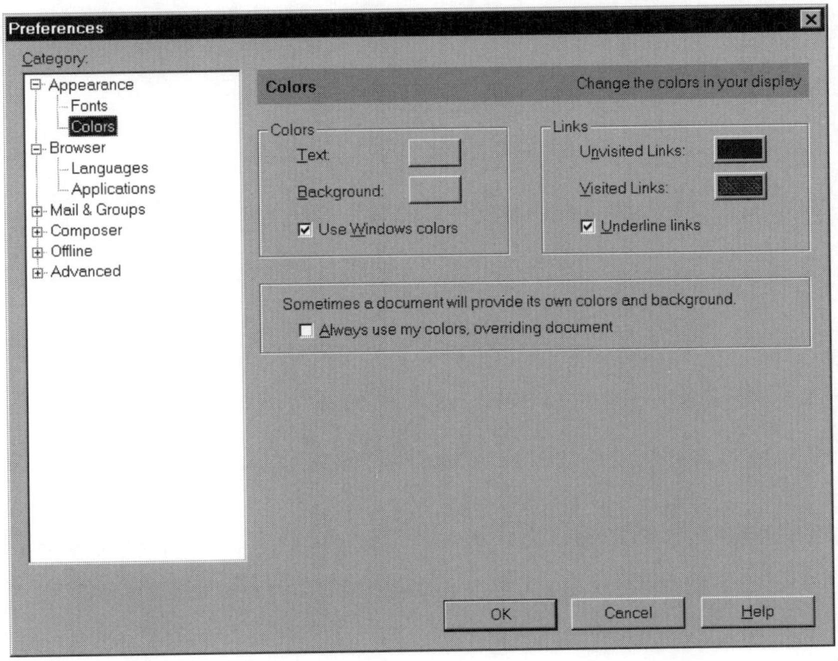

Figure 11.4 You can choose your own colors for text, background, and links, but it really isn't a very good idea.

Color. Click the color you've added. When you've chosen your color, click OK.

4. To change the default Background color, click Background. See step 3 for instructions on using the Color dialog box.
5. To choose an unvisited link color, click Unvisited Links. See step 3 for instructions on using the Color dialog box.
6. To choose a visited link color, click Visited Links. See step 3 for instructions on using the Color dialog box.
7. If you would like Netscape to display hyperlinks with underlinin (the default setting), be sure to click Underline links. I don't recommend

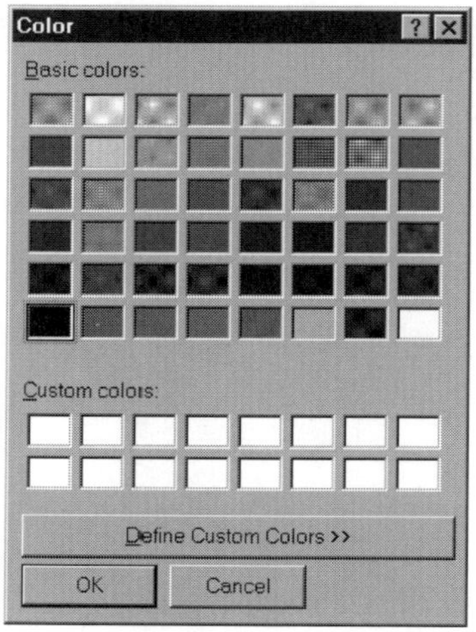

Figure 11.5 The Color dialog box enables you to choose colors.

deselecting this option; you may not be able to tell which text is a hyperlink.

8. Sometimes—very frequently, actually—Web authors provide their own colors and background. If you'd like to override this choice, click Always use my colors, overriding document. I don't recommend this unless you have some special reason for choosing a custom color scheme, such as color blindness.
9. Click OK to confirm your color choices.

This background is so busy that I can't read the text! Sometimes Web authors make terrible background and text color choices, to the point that you can't read the text. Although I believe you're best off viewing authors' color choices, sometimes you need to hide them in order to read the content. To override an author's color choices temporarily, do this: From the Edit menu, choose Preferences. Click Colors, and click Always use my colors. Click OK, and then click Reload. Hah! Now you can read this document. To restore the default setting after viewing the formerly unreadable document, repeat these steps, except deselect Always use my colors.

I'm sick of this! I want the defaults back! Didn't follow my advice, huh? Sick of that purple background? No problemo. Just open the Colors preferences again, and click Use Windows Colors.

Choosing Start Page and History Options

In the Browser page, you can specify what Netscape Navigator displays when the program starts, and you can also choose options for your history list. You've already learned how to change the default start page (see Chapter 6), so here's a quick look at the options you haven't explored.

Drawing a Blank

Would you like Netscape to display *nothing* when the program starts? Well, it can. In the Preferences dialog box, click Browser. You'll see the Browser page, shown in Figure 11.6. Click Blank page, and click OK.

Are you the type of person who likes to take up where you left off? A cool option in the Browser page is Last page visited, which automatically displays the last Web page you were viewing. This could be sort of embarrassing, though, if you last visited Lingerie Land and then start up Netscape with somebody looking over your shoulder!

Starting with Your Bookmark Page

As Chapter 6 explained, you can use the Home Page area to choose a new default start page for your document. A neat trick is that you can use any local file (that is, a Web page that's stored on your system). Well, guess what? Your bookmark file (bookmark.htm) is a valid Web page. If you'd like to start browsing with your bookmark page, click the Browse button to

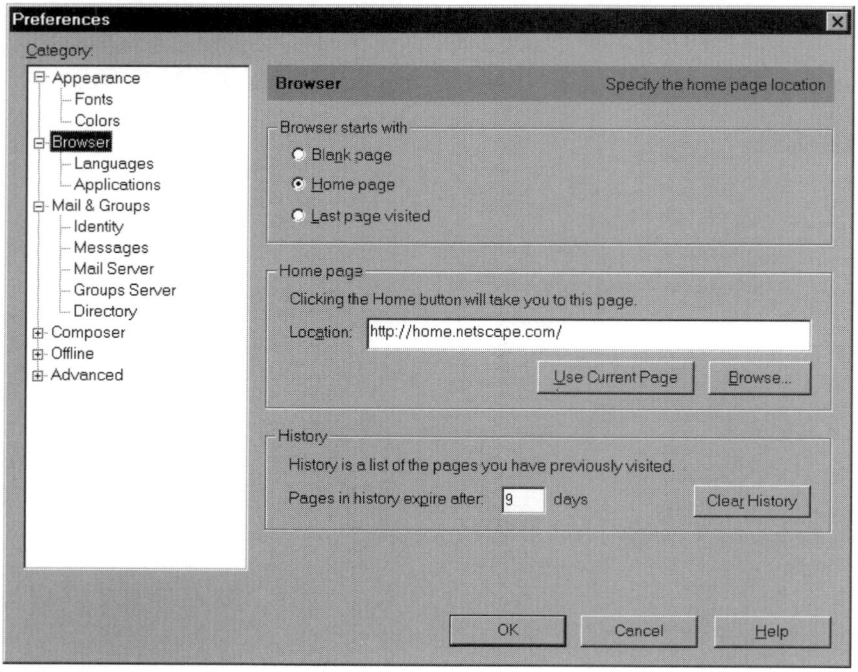

Figure 11.6 In this dialog box, you can choose which page appears when you start Netscape.

locate bookmark.htm (you'll find it in the Users folder within Netscape's folder). Figure 11.7 shows what my bookmark page looks like. Cool trick!

How Much History Can You Handle?

How long would you like to keep items in your history list? In the History area, you can change the number of days that Netscape keeps these items. The default is 9 days. (Why 9? Beats me.) You can make this longer or shorter. Making it longer enables you to find more previously viewed documents, while making it shorter enables you to conserve disk space.

If you'd like to clear your history list, click Clear History.

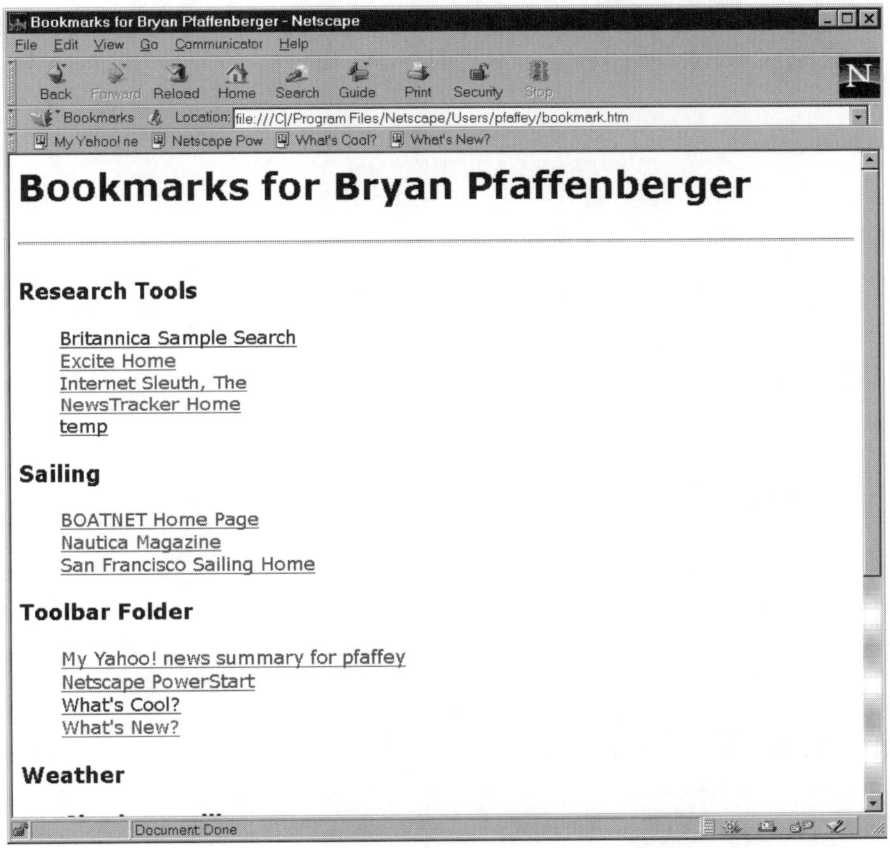

Figure 11.7 If you like, you can start browsing with your bookmark page, which is, after all, an HTML file.

Why Clear History? Suppose you've just finished a research project on something, like Controlling Gophers in Your Garden. You've discovered there's no way you can do this, so you don't care to go back to these sites. To make room for history list items pertaining to a new research project, you can clear your history list by clicking Clear History.

Concerned about privacy? Do you think that somebody might snoop into your history list to find out where you've been browsing? Set the number of days to zero. This will effectively blank the History list window. The bad thing about this is that you won't be able to see which links you've recently visited—they won't appear in a distinctive color. Also, this doesn't affect the list of recently visited sites in the Netsite/Location box's drop-down list box. Also, bear in mind that many companies track employee surfing at the network level. You might be able to hide your tracks by clearing the history list, but your trail's traceable at another level. Don't do any surfing at work that's not connected to your responsibilities in a clear way.

Choosing Advanced Options

In the Preferences dialog box, the Advanced page presents you with a number of important configuration choices. This section goes over these choices, some of which you'll want to consider.

Controlling What Netscape Downloads and Sends

On the main Advanced page (Figure 11.8), you'll find a number of very important options that control what Netscape downloads and sends. Many of these options have important security and privacy implications. This is just a quick overview of these choices; you'll find fuller discussions of these issues elsewhere in this book (for example, Chapter 15 discusses the security risks of Java and JavaScript).

- **Automatically Load Images** I've mentioned this option previously; it's a good choice if you're using a slow modem. Personally, I like the pretty pictures. My recommendation: Keep this option checked.
- **Enable Java** If you're concerned about the security of Java applets, deselect this option. You'll miss out part of the active content of Web pages, though. My recommendation: Keep this option deselected until you've had a chance to learn about the risks of Java.
- **Enable JavaScript** Again, you can deselect this option if you're concerned about JavaScript security, but you'll miss out on part of

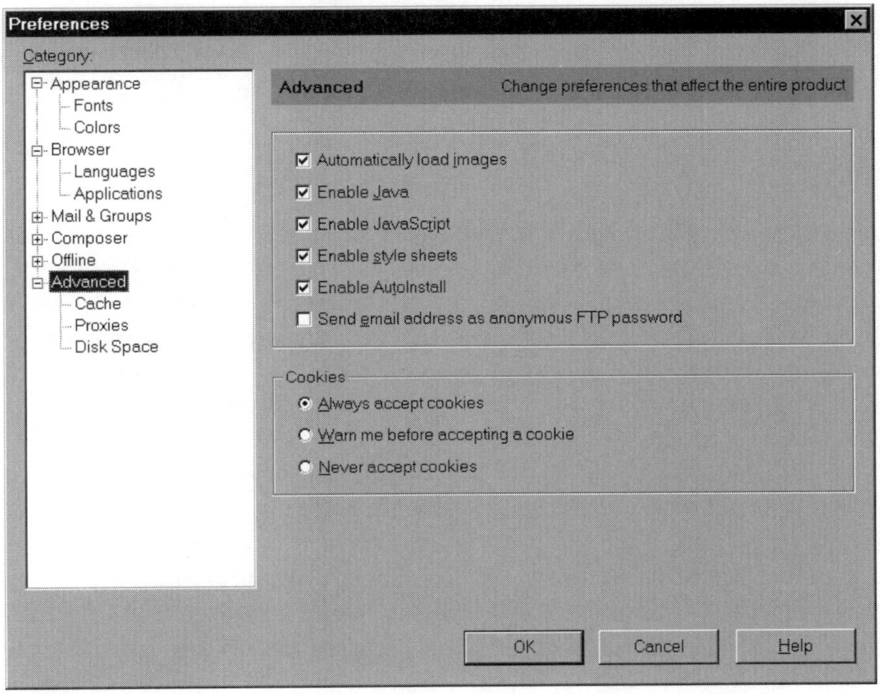

Figure 11.8 The Advanced options enable you to turn off Java, JavaScript, and other features, if you're concerned about security.

the fun. My recommendation: Keep this option deselected until you've had a chance to learn about the risks of JavaScript.

- **Enable Style Sheets** This option enables Netscape to read the font, font size, and formatting instructions in HTML style sheets. This is a cool feature of the newest version of HTML. If you disable this option, you'll miss out on the best new layout practices on the Web. My recommendation: Check this option.
- **Enable AutoInstall** This option enables Netscape to install software that you download. If you download only from trustworthy download sites (such as www.download.com), leave it checked. If you download from untrustworthy sites, and want to run a virus checker on downloaded programs before you use them, deselect this item.

- **Send e-mail address as anonymous FTP password** When you download software from public FTP sites, it's the custom to provide your e-mail address as a password. However, hackers have learned that they can obtain your e-mail address this way. My recommendation: To avoid harassment and junk mail, deselect this item.

Have a Cookie?

Cookies are small text files that Web servers give to Netscape, which then obligingly stores them on your hard disk (in the file cookies.txt, located in your Users folder). Later, a server can ask Netscape to upload one or more of these stored cookies. In short, cookies provide a way for servers to store information temporarily on your system. Using cookies, a server can tell whether you've visited the site before, which pages you've seen, and which options you've chosen.

Are cookies good or bad? Both. A lot of the interactivity you'll find at many sites depends on cookies, and it's quite innocent. For example, when you visit a shopping site, cookies are used to store information about which items you've "purchased" and placed in your "shopping basket." Without cookies, on-line shopping wouldn't be as convenient.

But there's a downside to cookies, too. Direct marketing companies want to track your movements through the Web so that they can learn more about your personal interests. The idea is that they can then give you custom advertisements, which are of more appeal to you and more likely to generate revenue for the advertiser. Cookies can be used to track your movements from site to site in this way. Chances are, you've already been tracked.

Is this a violation of your privacy? The direct marketing companies that are involved in this type of monitoring claim that they aren't trying to associate your clickstream with your name—they just give you a numerical ID, which identifies you as some unique user somewhere. The problem is that the information they're collecting about you is valuable, and some firm, someday, is going to be tempted to link it to your name and sell it. In the absence of laws to the contrary, this is virtually certain to happen.

Even if these companies don't try to associate your browsing activities with your name, it's still sort of unsavory. Imagine going to a supermarket and finding out that there was a camera tracking your every move, looking at which items you selected and how long you looked at certain areas of the shelf. That's essentially what cookies enable these marketing firms to do, and it's all done without your consent or knowledge. To add insult to injury, your own computer system is used to store the data! Personally, this infuriates me.

New for 4

If you're concerned about cookies, I suggest you click Never Accept Cookies in the Cookies area (Advanced page). You'll miss out on a lot of the Web's interactivity, but at least you won't be subjected to monitoring that's undertaken without your consent.

I chose "Warn me before accepting cookies," but all the dialog boxes are driving me crazy! I don't recommend this option. Ideally, it would enable you to accept cookies selectively—for example, you could accept them while you're shopping at Amazon.com (www.amazon.com), the Web's best on-line bookstore, and reject them if you think they're coming from a direct marketing firm. However, servers pelt you with as many as a dozen cookies per page, so you'll have to click No many times before you finally see the page's content. You'll get sick of this pretty quickly. Your only real options now are to accept cookies (and cave in to the direct marketing industry) or reject them (and miss out on some valid uses of cookies).

Other Advanced Options

Here's a quick look at the options you'll find on pages stored under Advanced. (If you don't see these pages in the Categories panel, click the plus sign next to Advanced.)

- **Cache** For an explanation of these options, see Chapter 7, "Improving Netscape Navigator Performance."
- **Proxies** If you're using Netscape at home and connecting via a modem, you don't need to worry about this page. It's for people using Netscape at work, where they connect using a local area network (LAN) that's secured by a *firewall* (a computer that tries to keep hackers from gaining unauthorized access to the company's resources). You'll need your network administrator's help to configure this dialog box correctly, so I'm going to skip it.
- **Disk Space** This is a mail and news thing, so see Chapter 17 or Chapter 21.

Configuring Netscape for Multiple Users

New for 4

Does more than one person use your computer? Are you tired of sitting down at your computer, only to find that another user has changed all your e-mail account information, bookmarks, address book entries, stored e-mail messages, and preference settings? Then read on! With Netscape Navigator 4.0, you can set up multiple user profiles. When you log on using your personal profile, you see your settings, and no one else's. The same goes for the other users, too! Cool, huh? This section explains how to set up profiles for yourself and other users.

Actually, you've already used Profile Manager. You set up your own, personal profile when you used Netscape for the first time. You need to follow the steps in this section only if you want to set up profiles for additional users.

Before you get started, you'll need the following information for each profile you set up: e-mail address, outgoing mail (SMTP) server, incoming mail (POP3 or IMAP).

Creating a New Profile

To create a profile:

1. Exit Netscape Communicator, if it's running. You can't set up profiles with Netscape on screen.
2. From the Start Menu, choose Programs, and choose Netscape Communicator. From the pop-up menu, choose Profile Manager. You'll see Profile Manager on screen, as shown in Figure 11.9.
3. Click New. You'll see the first page of the Profile Setup Wizard.
4. Click Next, and supply the requested information.
5. Keep supplying the requested information until you get to the Finish page. Click Finish to create the profile and exit.

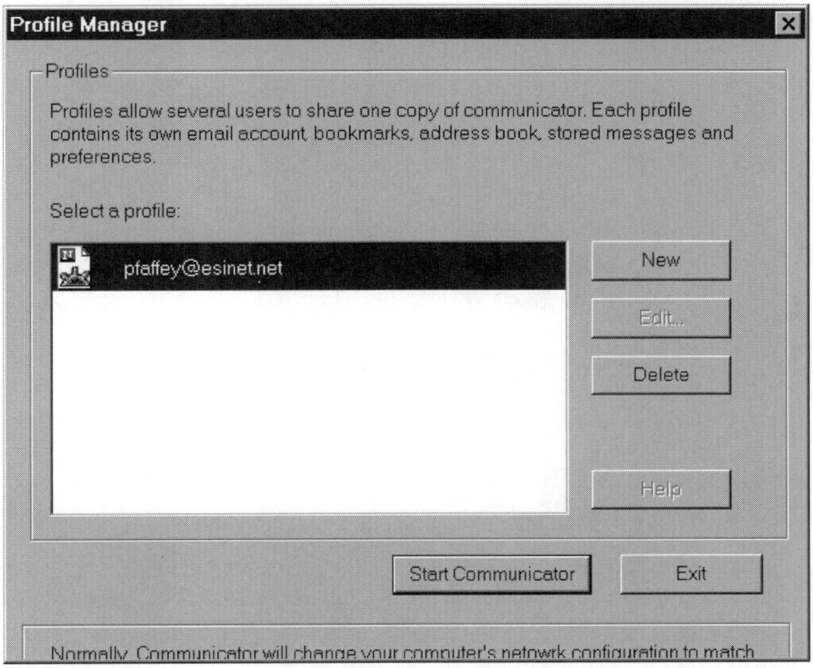
Profile Manager
Profiles
Profiles allow several users to share one copy of communicator. Each profile contains its own email account, bookmarks, address book, stored messages and preferences.
Select a profile:
pfaffey@esinet.net
New
Edit...
Delete
Help
Start Communicator
Exit

Figure 11.9 With Profile Manager, you can set up multiple user profiles.

Starting Communicator after Creating Two or More Profiles

After you've created more than one profile, Netscape Communicator automatically starts with Profile Manager. Just select your profile, and click Start Communicator.

Deleting a Profile

If one of the profile users is no longer accessing your computer, you can delete that user's profile.

To delete a profile:

1. From the Start Menu, choose Programs, and choose Netscape Communicator. From the pop-up menu, choose Profile Manager.
2. Select the profile you want to delete.
3. Click Delete.

Editing a Profile

If a user's information changes (for example, if the person changed service providers and has a new e-mail address and server information), you can edit the profile.

To edit a profile:

1. From the Start Menu, choose Programs, and choose Netscape Communicator. From the pop-up menu, choose Profile Manager.
2. Select the profile you want to edit.
3. Click Edit. You'll see the Profile Wizard.
4. Edit the information as necessary, clicking Next to move along to the next wizard page.
5. Click Finish when you're done.

Chapter 12

Getting and Using Plug-ins

Netscape can't handle all the types of data out there on the Web—at least, not without help. Sure, Netscape can read HTML, and the program can handle GIF and JPEG graphics natively. (By *natively*, I mean on its own, without any outside help.) It can also decode Java instructions (see Chapter 15 for more information about Java). But there's much more out there—so much, in fact, that Netscape couldn't possibly include enough program code to handle everything the Web is capable of slinging at a browser. Linked to Web pages are sounds, movies, animations, live radio broadcasts, live TV broadcasts, spreadsheets, virtual reality worlds, and even a model railroad (I am not making this up—check out http://rr-vs.informatik.uni-ulm.de/rr/).

For the Time-Challenged

- Helper applications are separate programs that start automatically when Netscape encounters a certain type of data, such as a compressed file. You only need one helper application: WinZip, which decompresses the files you download from the Internet.
- Plug-ins modify Netscape so that the program can deal directly with specific types of data, such as video, audio, and 3-D files.
- Netscape's default plug-ins can cope with most of the multimedia you'll encounter on the Web.
- If you run into a link to a helper app or plug-in that you don't have installed, you'll see a dialog box informing you that you need additional software. Click More Info to get the software you need.
- Some plug-in links start AutoInstall, a new Netscape feature that automatically downloads, configures, and installs the needed plug-in.

Here's something fun: A collection of links to pages that connect bizarre devices to the Web, including clocks, coffee machines, pets (!), robots, spy cameras, and more. Check out

http://www.yahoo.com/Computers_and_Internet/Internet/Interesting_Devices_Connected_to_the_Net/

In order to deal with all the data that's accessible on the Web, Netscape needs two kinds of help:

- **Helper applications** These are programs that Netscape starts when it encounters a type of data that it can't handle directly. All versions of Netscape can work with helper applications. Helper applications are separate programs that run in their own windows, which isn't very convenient.
- **Plug-ins** These are programs that modify Netscape so that it can deal directly with data of a certain type. For example, the Live3D

plug-in enables Netscape to directly display virtual worlds—and you can navigate inside of them in three dimensions! Some plug-ins run right in Netscape's windows, which is much more convenient than using a helper app.

Netscape includes a great suite of plug-ins. These include LiveAudio (sounds), LiveVideo (movies), Netscape Media Player (streaming video), and Live3D (VRML virtual reality worlds). Distributed with Netscape, these plug-ins are installed and configured automatically—which means, happily, that you start using multimedia resources immediately.

Here's a list of the data types that Netscape's plug-in suite can deal with automatically:

- MIDI sounds
- MPEG movies
- MPEG sounds
- Netscape streaming audio sounds
- QuickTime (MOV movies)
- Silicon Graphics/Apple sounds (AIFF sounds)
- Sun/NeXT sounds (AU sounds)
- Video for Windows (AVI movies)
- VRML (3-D) worlds
- Windows (WAV) sounds

That's a lot of data types. In fact, these cover about 90 percent of the multimedia data that you'll encounter on the Web.

So Why Do I Need to Read This Chapter?

New for 4

In the bad old days (say, Netscape Navigator version 2.0), you couldn't access multimedia until you had downloaded and installed a suite of helper applications. It was a tedious business, requiring all sorts of configuration and technical smarts. For the most part, those days are gone. Since version 3.0, Netscape provides help when you encounter a type of data for which you've no helper application or plug-in installed. And with Navigator 4.0, there's a new feature called AutoInstall, which automatically downloads and installs any components, plug-ins, or Java applets that you might need.

For all these reasons, this chapter is a lot shorter than it was in previous editions—a good thing, you'll surely agree. Still, it's worth reading pretty carefully. There's still one helper application that you really need to have (WinZip), and you should learn what to do if you encounter a data type that's not currently supported by your installed applications.

Help Me, Helper Apps

In brief, a helper app is a separate program that's designed to start automatically when data of a certain type is encountered.

For example, suppose you click on the name of a file that was compressed by WinZip, a popular compression utility. Your browser looks for WinZip—and if the program is present on your disk, the browser starts WinZip and the file downloads. Netscape starts WinZip, and you see WinZip on screen. Just click Next to install the program you've downloaded.

When you've configured your browser to work with helper applications and they work correctly, it's cool. Here's an example. Suppose you click on a hyperlink for an MPEG video. If everything's working smoothly on your system, your browser starts an MPEG helper application, downloads the video, and you see it on screen (Figure 10.1).

What If I Don't Have the Needed Helper Application?

If you try to access a data type for which there's no installed helper application or plug-in, you'll see the dialog box shown in Figure 12.2. You have the following options:

- **More Info** To get Netscape's help in locating the needed helper application or plug-in, click this option. You'll see a Plug-in Finder page, such as the one shown in Figure 12.3. If Netscape knows of a helper application or plug-in for the data type you've accessed,

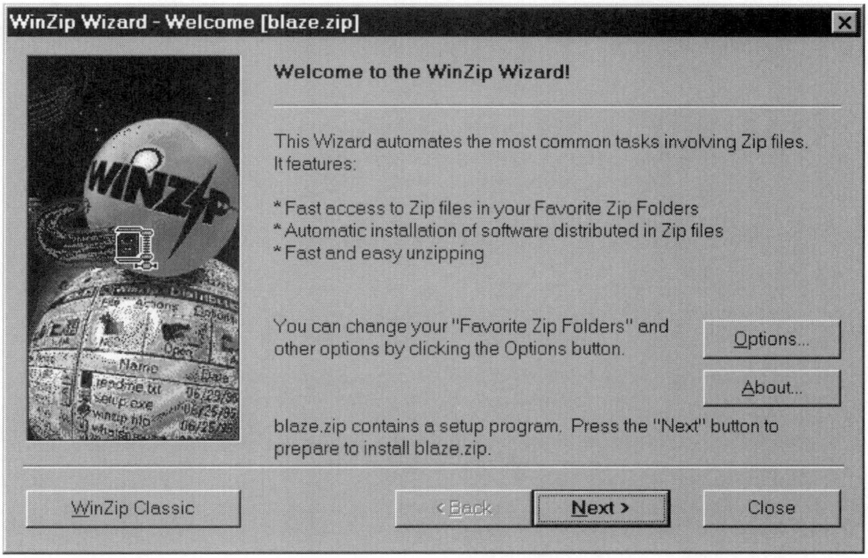
WinZip Wizard - Welcome [blaze.zip]
Welcome to the WinZip Wizard!
This Wizard automates the most common tasks involving Zip files. It features:
* Fast access to Zip files in your Favorite Zip Folders
* Automatic installation of software distributed in Zip files
* Fast and easy unzipping
You can change your "Favorite Zip Folders" and other options by clicking the Options button.
Options...
About...
blaze.zip contains a setup program. Press the "Next" button to prepare to install blaze.zip.
WinZip Classic
< Back
Next >
Close

Figure 12.1 If you've installed a helper application such as WinZip, Netscape starts the program automatically when it encounters the application's data type.

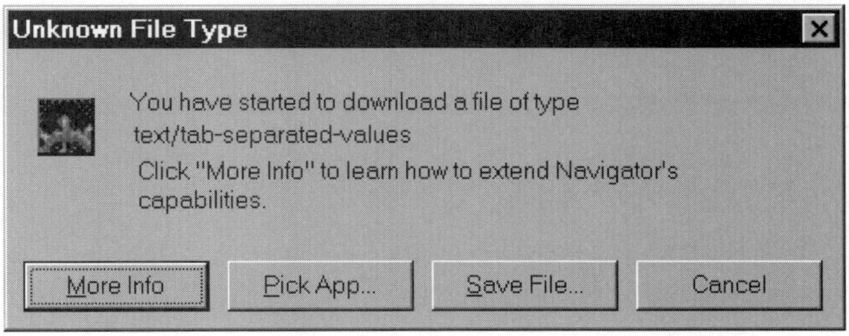
Unknown File Type
You have started to download a file of type text/tab-separated-values
Click "More Info" to learn how to extend Navigator's capabilities.
More Info
Pick App...
Save File...
Cancel

Figure 12.2 You see this dialog box if you try to access a data type for which there's no installed helper application.

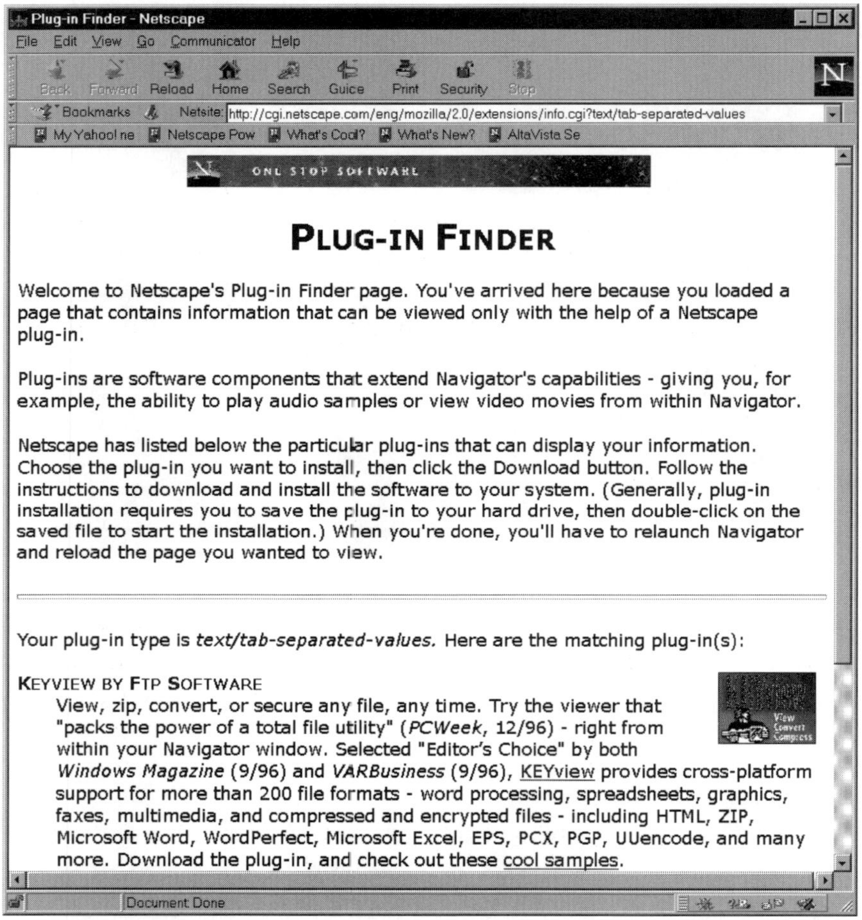
Plug-in Finder - Netscape
File Edit View Go Communicator Help
Back Forward Reload Home Search Guide Print Security Stop
Bookmarks Netsite: http://cgi.netscape.com/eng/mozilla/2.0/extensions/info.cgi?text/tab-separated-values
My Yahoo! ne Netscape Pow What's Cool? What's New? AltaVista Se
ONE STOP SOFTWARE
PLUG-IN FINDER
Welcome to Netscape's Plug-in Finder page. You've arrived here because you loaded a page that contains information that can be viewed only with the help of a Netscape plug-in.
Plug-ins are software components that extend Navigator's capabilities - giving you, for example, the ability to play audio samples or view video movies from within Navigator.
Netscape has listed below the particular plug-ins that can display your information. Choose the plug-in you want to install, then click the Download button. Follow the instructions to download and install the software to your system. (Generally, plug-in installation requires you to save the plug-in to your hard drive, then double-click on the saved file to start the installation.) When you're done, you'll have to relaunch Navigator and reload the page you wanted to view.
Your plug-in type is text/tab-separated-values. Here are the matching plug-in(s):
KEYVIEW BY FTP SOFTWARE
View, zip, convert, or secure any file, any time. Try the viewer that "packs the power of a total file utility" (PCWeek, 12/96) - right from within your Navigator window. Selected "Editor's Choice" by both Windows Magazine (9/96) and VARBusiness (9/96), KEYview provides cross-platform support for more than 200 file formats - word processing, spreadsheets, graphics, faxes, multimedia, and compressed and encrypted files - including HTML, ZIP, Microsoft Word, WordPerfect, Microsoft Excel, EPS, PCX, PGP, UUencode, and many more. Download the plug-in, and check out these cool samples.
View
Convert
Compress
Document: Done

Figure 12.3 This page helps you find plug-ins for Navigator.

you'll find a link to the program's home page, from which you can download the application.

- **Pick App** If you believe you already have a program installed on your system that can handle this data type, click Pick App. You'll see an Open dialog box that enables you to type the program's location or browse for it.

- **Save File** If you'd rather not view the data right now, click this option to save the data to a location on your hard disk. You can obtain the needed program and view it later.

What Helper Applications Do I Need?

There's one helper application that you absolutely *must* have in order to get the most out of the Web: WinZip for Windows (www.winzip.com). If you haven't already installed WinZip on your computer, do so right away. After you install WinZip, Netscape automatically associates a variety of compressed data file formats with WinZip, and Netscape starts WinZip automatically when the browser encouters one of these files.

But Don't I Have to Configure These Things?

New for 4

In previous versions of Netscape Navigator, you had to configure helper applications. With version 4.0, you don't need to do this, in most cases. That's because Netscape Navigator version 4.0 associates data types with programs by using the current Windows associations. To view these associations, open any file in My Computer, choose Options from the View menu, and click the File Types tab. Normally, programs modify this list automatically when you install them. For example, WinZip automatically modifies this list so that WinZip is associated with any file with the *.zip extension. If you're trying to use a really old helper application that doesn't come with an installation program, though, you may still need to configure Netscape manually.

Shouldn't I Get Dozens of Helper Applications?

If somebody tells you that you can't use Netscape unless you've downloaded and installed dozens of helper applications, please don't believe this! Doing so could actually harm Netscape's functionality, because installing these older programs could wipe out Netscape's default plug-in configuration. Plug-ins are much better than helper applications because they run seamlessly from within Netscape. Plug-ins are good; helper applications are bad, for the most part—except WinZip, of course.

Plug In to This!

Netscape Navigator's program architecture enables you to install *plug-ins*. A plug-in is a program that, after installation, extends Netscape's capabilities. What's really cool about plug-ins is that, unlike with helper apps, there's no separate program to fuss with—the plug-in becomes part of Netscape, seamlessly extending its capabilities.

Compared to a helper application, a plug-in program is a pleasure to use. There's no configuration hassle, and the plug-in operates automatically. With many plug-ins the action takes place right on the Web page you're viewing, not in a secondary window such as the ones that helper applications use. In Figure 12.4, you see the very impressive results you'll get after installing a virtual reality plug-in. Such a program enables Netscape to display three-dimensional spaces, which you can explore using the special controls that the program adds to Netscape.

What Plug-ins Do I Already Have?

Find out right now. From the Help menu, choose About Plug-ins. You'll see a Web page that lists the plug-ins that are already installed in Netscape's folder (see Figure 12.5).

What Happens if I Don't Have a Needed Plug-in? Unless the plug-in has been set up to start Netscape's AutoInstall, which I'll discuss in a moment, you'll go through the same drill that you'd go through for uninstalled helper apps (see "What If I Don't Have the Needed Helper Application?" earlier in this chapter). Click More Info to go to Netscape's plug-in page, where—chances are—you'll see a link to the type of plug-in you need.

New for 4

Using AutoInstall A new and needed feature of Netscape Navigator 4.0 is AutoInstall, a utility that automatically detects when you need to download components, such as plug-ins and Java applets. AutoInstall works only if the plug-in link contains the right coding; since this feature is new, very few links are set up that way currently, but you'll run into more of them.

When you try to access a plug-in that's not installed, and the link has been set up for AutoInstall, you'll see the Safe Download dialog box informing you that you don't have the needed plug-in. From this dialog box, you can begin downloading the needed plug-in. When the downloading's fin-

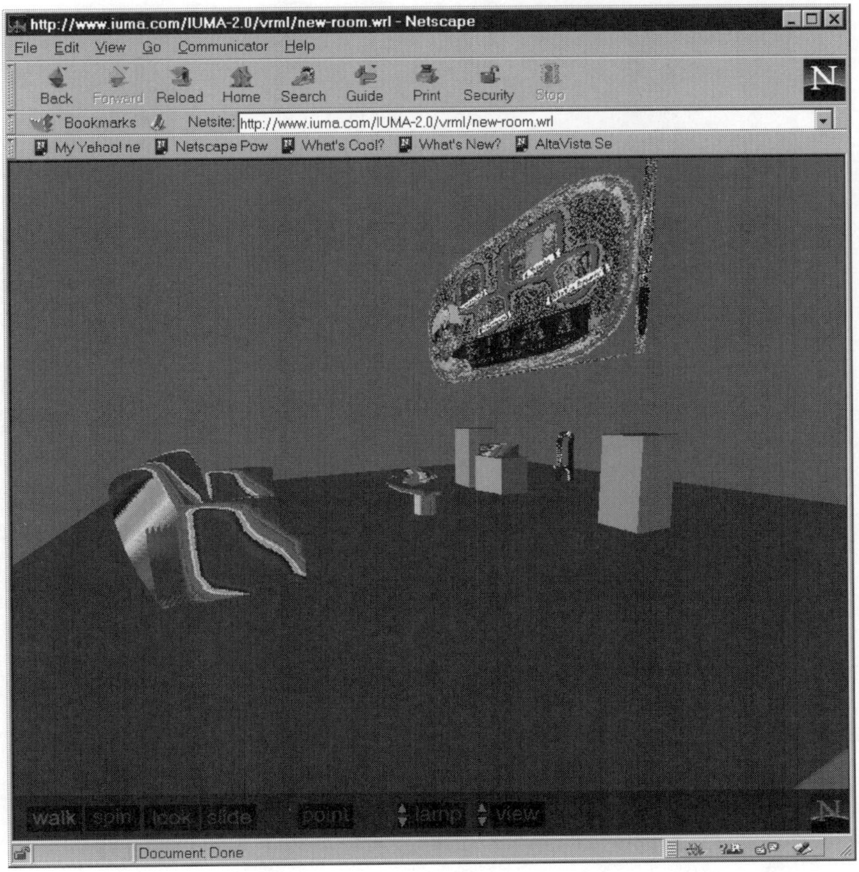

Figure 12.4 Data display within Netscape's window via plug-in (Live3D).

ished, you'll see a Security dialog box reminding you that you shouldn't install the plug-in unless you believe it's from a trustworthy source. Some plug-ins come with signed digital security certificates, which means that they're trustworthy. Click Install if you decide that it's safe to install the software.

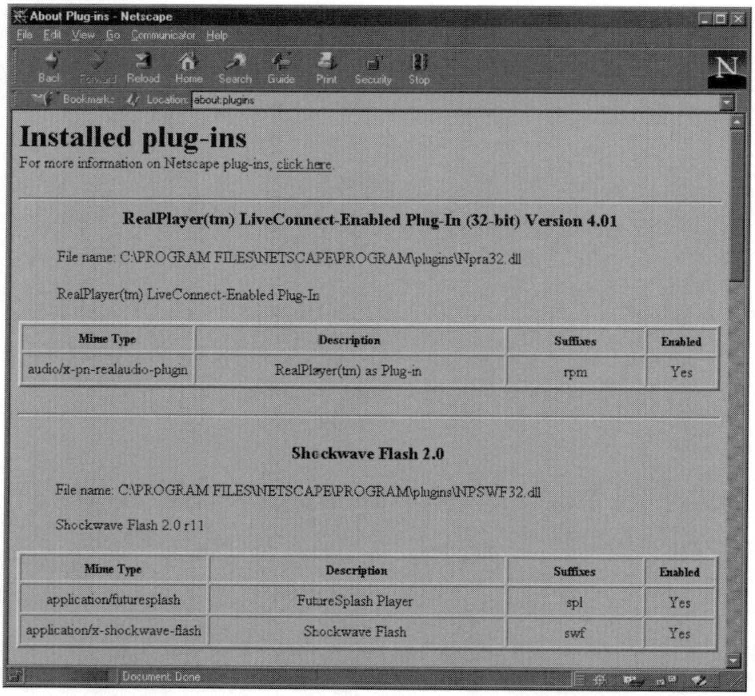

Figure 12.5 To find out which plug-ins are already installed, choose About Plug-ins from the Help menu.

Getting Huge Quantities of Additional Plug-ins

Dozens of plug-ins are available that do lots of additional things, and you can download many of them for use during a free evaluation period (or just for free).

The best place to look for plug-ins is Netscape's plug-ins page, currently accessed by clicking the Software button and following the links for downloadable components. Another excellent place to look is Stroud's Consummate

Winsock Apps List, which has pages for Windows 95 and Windows 3.1 plug-ins. There are several places where you can find Stroud's nifty page; try http://www.hkstar.com/cwsapps/.

Installing Plug-ins

Plug-ins are easy to install. Generally, you download them to a temporary directory on your hard disk. With File Manager (Windows 3.1) or Windows Explorer (Windows 95), display and double-click the downloaded file's icon. This will start an installation program that automatically installs the plug-in in the correct directory (the PLUGINS directory in Netscape's folder) and configures Netscape to use it. When you start Netscape, the program examines this directory and loads all the plug-ins it finds there. Compared to helper applications, what could be simpler?

Using Plug-ins

Plug-ins are also very easy to use. When you click a link to a multimedia resource that a plug-in recognizes, Netscape downloads the file and starts the plug-in.

This is taking too long! There are those who feel that Netscape's plug-in technology is pushing the technological envelope too far, especially for people who are using slow 14.4 Kbps modem lines. Downloading a huge VRML world that has lots of linked sounds and graphics can be an exercise in frustration, unless you really like sitting around for 10 minutes, anxiously watching the status line for the long-awaited "Document Done" message. If you find the wait too frustrating, think twice before accessing pages that are rich in multimedia resources (or if you do, click Stop).

From Here

- Have you installed and configured your helper apps yet? Do not collect $200, and most of all, don't go to the next chapter—the stuff that's described there won't work until you've installed the helper apps.

- You did install the helper apps? OK. Check out Chapter 13 for the lowdown on sounds, movies, and animations.
- In Chapter 14, you'll find a thorough discussion of Adobe Acrobat, including the use of the new Amber reader.

Chapter

13

Playing Sounds and Watching Movies

It's hypermedia time! You click links to sounds, movies, and animations—and things start to happen. In this chapter, you'll learn how to work with the many types of sounds, videos, and animations you'll encounter on the Web.

Listening to Sounds

Listening to sounds is pretty simple—you just click on the link to the sound, and Netscape starts the player that's associated with the type of sound you're downloading. For a quick introduction to the different types of sounds you'll encounter on the Web, see the next section. If you'd prefer to

For the Time-Challenged

- After Netscape downloads a sound, you'll see the sound player. Look for a VCR-type Play button to initiate the sound, unless it starts playing automatically. You can use the VCR-type controls to pause, stop, "rewind," or "fast-forward" the sound. When you're finished listening to the sound, exit the sound player.
- After Netscape downloads a movie, you'll see the movie player. Look for a VCR-type Play button to start viewing the movie. When you're finished watching the movie, exit the movie player.

skip the technical details, go to the sections discussing the LiveAudio and RealAudio sound players, the two you'll use most often.

To listen to sounds on your Microsoft Windows system, you must equip your computer with a sound card and speakers. The applications discussed in this section won't play through your computer's tinny little standard speaker.

Understanding Sound File Formats

Here's a list of the sound file formats that you're most likely to encounter on the Web.

- **Silicon Graphics/Apple sound (audio/x-aiff)** These sound files have the extension *.aif, *.aiff, or *aifc. You don't often encounter these sounds.
- **Sun/NeXT sound (audio/basic)** This is a Sun/NeXT (*.au or *.snd) sound. *.au sounds are fairly compact and generally of low quality; they're often used, though, to provide a small-size "sampler" of a much bigger MPEG sound file.
- **WAV sound (audio/x-wav)** This is a standard Microsoft Windows sound. The sound quality depends on how the recording was done—there are a number of options, ranging from low-quality

monoaural to high-quality stereo—but it's probably going to be very good.

- **MPEG sound (audio/x-mpeg)** This may prove to be of very high quality—at best, near-CD quality in stereo. But MPEG files are huge.
- **MIDI sound (audio/midi)** MIDI sound files are compact—they consist only of ASCII text. What you hear depends on the quality of your sound card. If you've got a wave-table synthesis card, the sound might actually be pleasing to the ear. If your sound card uses FM synthesis, it will sound like some kid playing a $29 electronic organ.
- **RealAudio sound (audio/x-pn-realaudio)** When you access a RealAudio sound, Netscape looks for the RealAudio plug-in. You need this plug-in to listen to RealAudio sounds. RealAudio sounds begin playing almost immediately after you access them, but don't expect good sound quality—it's OK for voice but barely acceptable for music.

Using LiveAudio

LiveAudio, one of the plug-ins that comes with Netscape, can play just about any type of sound you encounter on the Internet, except RealAudio sounds.

To play a sound, just click the Play button. You can also pause the sound, adjust the volume (with the slider control), stop the sound, and play it again (by clicking Play once more).

Here's a quick guide to the controls you'll find on Netscape Audio Player's control panel:

 Stop

 Play

 Pause

In addition to these controls, you'll see a slider control (see Figure 13.1) that enables you to control the sound's volume.

Using the RealAudio Player

You'll find two kinds of RealAudio sound files on the Web:

- **RealAudio Version 1** You can download and listen to these files using a 14.4 Kbps modem.
- **RealAudio Version 2** To listen to these files, you'll need a Pentium computer and a 28.8 Kbps modem. These files are often flagged with a RealAudio 28.8 icon. To play them, you'll need to install the RealAudio plug-in, which is available from Netscape's plug-in download site.
- **RealAudio Version 3** This format requires a super-fast connection, such as ISDN, but delivers excellent quality.

When you access a RealAudio sound file (*.ra), Netscape starts the RealAudio sound player, shown in Figure 13.2, and you hear the sound almost immediately. The RealAudio dialog box shows the title of the sound being played, the author, and the copyright holder, if any. You'll also find the following controls:

Figure 13.1 LiveAudio.

Figure 13.2 RealAudio player.

Play/Pause

Stop and return to beginning of sound

Rewind

Fast Forward

Adjust the volume using the slider control.

It sounds really garbled! If you've heard some good sound, but all of a sudden the quality goes way down, chances are the data stream has run into a roadblock on the Internet. (It happens.) Just be patient—the quality will probably come back up in a few moments. If not, you'll see a dialog box informing you that the quality is unacceptable. Try accessing the site later, when the Internet's not so busy.

One of the most valuable resources to be found anywhere on the Internet is National Public Radio's Web site (www.npr.org). You'll find gazillions of RealAudio files, including the latest news broadcast, and archives from the following programs: *All Things Considered, Morning Edition, Sounds Like Science, Weekend Edition, Fresh Air, Talk of the Nation, Science Friday,* and many more.

Other Sounds You May Encounter

Besides the sounds already discussed, you may run into a few additional streaming audio formats. Netscape has its own, actually, and there's even a player included with your copy of Communicator, but Netscape streaming audio sounds aren't much in evidence on the Web. They're designed mostly for corporate intranet use.

Another streaming audio format you may encounter is Macromedia's Shockwave Streaming Audio, which does a better job of playing music than do other streaming audio technologies. If you encounter one of these sounds, Netscape will help you download the Macromedia plug-in.

VIEWING MOVIES

You'll find thousands of movies on the Web, but don't expect too much in terms of quality. Every movie, digital or otherwise, is simply a succession of still images (called *frames*); in a high-quality movie, the frames go by quickly enough that the brain is tricked into seeing smooth motion. To keep file sizes down, the creators of most of the digital movies you'll find on the Web kept the number of frames per second to a minimum, which results in a very jerky presentation that won't trick your eye, your brain, or anything else.

It's taking a half hour to download this movie! Unfortunately, movie files tend to be big and bigger—the one I'm downloading right now is about 2.5 MB. On a 14.4 Kbps modem line, a file that large will take many minutes to download. If it's taking too long, remember that you can switch back to Netscape and browse elsewhere while the file's downloading—or you can cancel the download, skip the whole thing, and go down to your video store and rent a real movie.

The best movie formats offer sound as well as video. As with the digital sound just discussed, you'll need to equip your Windows system with a sound card and speakers if you wish to hear these sounds.

Understanding Movie File Formats

Like sounds, the digital movies you'll find on the Web are stored in a variety of file formats, so you'll need more than one movie viewer. Here's a quick overview of the movie file formats you're most likely to find on the Web. Netscape's plug-ins can handle all of these.

- **MPEG (video/mpeg)** MPEG is short for the Motion Picture Experts Group, an industry consortium that meets periodically to define digital video standards. At present the MPEG-1 standard defines a relatively low-quality video standard. MPEG movies, stored in *.mpg files, aren't much to write home about, you'll find, and they require huge files.
- **QuickTime (video/quicktime)** Originally created by Apple Computer, the QuickTime format is now an international standard, and it's better than MPEG. In addition to offering good compression and performance, QuickTime offers near-CD-quality digital stereo sound. Stored in *.mov and *.qt files, QuickTime movies are played by the QuickTime plug-in that's distributed with Netscape.
- **Video for Windows (video/x-msvideo)** The Windows movie format (*.avi) offers another high-quality movie standard with digital stereo sound. Not as efficiently compressed as QuickTime movies, the files are very large but the quality is good. Windows movies are played by LiveVideo.

I just downloaded an 8-megabyte movie, and it plays for only three minutes! And the picture's the size of a postage stamp! Don't say I didn't warn you. Is network video here yet? Use your own judgment, but I'd say no. Right now, it's an amusing diversion at best. Movies aren't going to become a significant attraction on the Web until better compression techniques are developed and people have much faster Net connections.

Using LiveVideo

When you access a link to a Windows (*.avi) or MPEG movie, Netscape displays a new page and starts downloading everything on it, including the video file. Unfortunately, this could take quite a while. Check the status line; you'll see an estimate for how much longer it will take to finish downloading the file. Whatever you do, don't exit the page by clicking Back, because that will stop the download!

When the movie has finished downloading, you see the finished page. The movie looks like an inline image, but when you double-click on it, the movie starts playing. It's cool to see the movie on the same page, without an intrusive, separate window starting. To see the movie again, just click it.

Using the QuickTime Plug-in

Like the LiveVideo plug-in, the QuickTime plug-in displays the movie inline (along with the text and graphics of a Web page). When you access a link to a QuickTime (*.mov) movie, Netscape displays a new page and starts downloading the file. As with Windows movies, this could take a while; it's a good time to get a cup of coffee or chat with a co-worker! Where the movie will appear, you'll see a QuickTime logo while the movie is downloading. Finally, the movie appears in the window, framed within the QuickTime player. Here's an overview of the VCR-type tools you'll find in the player:

 Volume

 Play/pause

 Rewind

 Fast Forward

In addition to these controls, you can use the slider to position the start of the film where you want.

USING NETSCAPE MEDIA PLAYER

New for 4 Packaged with Netscape Communicator is Netscape Media Player, a new plug-in that enables Netscape Navigator users to view streaming audio as well as synchronized multimedia, delivered by Netscape's Live Media Server.

When you access a Netscape Media Player audio link, the page downloads, and you soon see a control bar like the one shown in Figure 13.4. Just use the controls to adjust the sound as you like. You'll see synchronized multimedia—that is, pictures—in the page you're viewing.

Figure 13.3 Netscape Media Player control bar.

From Here

- Learn how to view Adobe Acrobat documents in Chapter 14.
- Try out some Java sites in Chapter 15.
- Getting Dynamic HTML in Chapter 16.

Chapter 14

Viewing Adobe Acrobat Documents

When you view HTML documents with Netscape, you'll see Netscape's interpretation of the underlying HTML tags. The formatting is simple and effective. Unfortunately, HTML does not include tags needed for more complex document formats, such as multiple-column text or footnotes.

To provide richer document formatting, some document authors prefer to encode their documents using a proprietary document format. One such format is the PostScript page description language, familiar to users of laser printers. PostScript can also generate richly formatted screen displays, but this requires a reader capable of decoding the PostScript commands. Such readers exist—GhostScript is an example—but Adobe, the originator of PostScript, has developed a set of extensions to PostScript, called Adobe Acrobat, that produce superior results on screen. You will encounter growing

For the Time-Challenged

- Acrobat enables you to download and view richly formatted documents, no matter on which brand of computer they were created.
- Once you've downloaded a document, you can easily navigate through it by using the Acrobat toolbar.

numbers of Acrobat documents on the Web (for an example, see Figure 14.1), and you can read them with the Adobe Acrobat Reader software included with this book.

In Adobe's nomenclature, Acrobat documents are *portable documents*—and it's a great term. Unlike richly formatted documents created with word processing programs such as Microsoft Word, Acrobat documents can be viewed and read on any computer system for which an Acrobat reader has been provided (and there are Acrobat readers for almost all commonly used types of computers). Acrobat is a major plus for large organizations, in which people using many different types of computers must be able to exchange richly formatted documents and don't have time to translate them. And it's a natural for publishing on the Web.

Adobe has added lots of new features to the basic Acrobat design, by means of plug-ins. The coolest of the lot is Weblink, which enables Acrobat authors to incorporate Web links into their Acrobat documents. And with Weblink installed in the Reader, you can access Web documents by clicking links, just as you would within Netscape.

If you're using the Windows 95 version of Netscape, you can take advantage of the amazing new Acrobat Amber plug-in, which enables you to view Acrobat presentations within Netscape's window. What's more, you can view one page at a time—there's no need to wait for the whole presentation to download before you can start viewing.

This chapter begins by discussing the Adobe Acrobat helper application, which runs in a separate window. If you're using Windows 95, you can take advantage of the Amber plug-in, which is discussed later in this chapter.

Friday
January 12, 1996

Internet Edition

Eight pages
© 1996 The New York Times

TimesFax
FROM
The New York Times

FROM THE FRONT PAGE

Budget Battle Turns To Campaign Fodder

WASHINGTON — There was little mourning among political consultants when the budget talks were suspended this week. The strategists were already planning Congressional campaigns that revolved around the great, unresolved differences between the two parties on balancing and reconfiguring the Federal budget; the lack of a deal just makes those differences sharper.

"I haven't lost a lot of sleep over it," said Stan Greenberg, who polls for the Democratic National Committee. After weeks of surveys and voter research, Democrats are convinced that their party can prosper mightily if it presents itself as the last line of defense against Republican cuts in Medicare, education and environmental protection.

As Democratic consultants see it, Republican incumbents enter the 1996 campaign with a crippling record of votes on those issues, and the lack of a budget deal means they have no overarching accomplishment to outweigh those votes.

Republican strategists counter with a very simple theme that takes into account the lack of a budget deal, (or, perhaps someday, a less-than-perfect budget deal) as well as the stalling of other high-profile parts of their legislative agenda: Their party tried to bring about the fundamental change the voters demanded in 1994, but the Democrats blocked them.

By ROBIN TONER

Gingrich Hits Clinton on Budget Plan

WASHINGTON — Insisting that a balanced budget plan was "within our grasp," President Clinton called on Congressional Republican leaders to renew the drive for an agreement Thursday. But he was instantly rebuffed by Speaker Newt Gingrich, who accused him of misleading the public in "a political game."

The deep difference between the two sides in the drawn-out budget battle was made starkly clear when the President held a televised news conference to declare his own optimism that a deal can be reached "if we set aside partisanship and work to seize this moment."

"We shouldn't let our fundamental agreement on a balanced budget," Mr. Clinton declared, "be held hostage to a narrower agenda that seeks to prevent America from giving Medicare to senior citizens or quality nursing home care or educational opportunity for young people or environmental protection to all of us."

Mr. Clinton was soon castigated by Mr. Gingrich for accusing the Republicans of seeking excessive "cuts" in Medicare, Medicaid and other social welfare spending when the financing of these programs, Mr. Gingrich said, would actually be increasing.

"It was a very disappointing press conference," Mr. Gingrich commented in Seattle after watching the President on television during a West Coast fund-raising trip. "It does not give me much encouragement."

By FRANCIS X. CLINES

Peru Convicts American Woman of Treason

LIMA, Peru — Lori Helene Berenson of New York was convicted of treason Thursday by a secret Peruvian military court and sentenced to life in prison for aiding Marxist guerrillas who prosecutors said were planning to seize the Peruvian Congress and abduct lawmakers.

The widely expected verdict was announced six weeks after Ms. Berenson was arrested in an anti-terrorist police operation that also led to the capture of 22 other people after an all-night shootout in a Lima suburb. But the sentence came as a surprise, especially since prosecutors had requested a 30-year prison term, the minimum penalty for treason in Peru, and reflects the Government's tough policy toward insurgent groups.

Ms. Berenson is expected to be moved soon to Yanamaygo Prison in Puno, a special prison for terrorists situated in the Andes. Lawyers for Ms. Berenson, 26, said a treaty between the United States and Peru allows her to serve her sentence in the United States after all judicial appeals have been completed. But the lawyers said their client had indicated no desire to serve her time in the United States.

By CALVIN SIMS

Fear of Diseases Drives Britons From Beef

LONDON — For centuries, beef has held pride of place at the British table. All that may change. Despite pledges by Government ministers that British beef is safe, consumers by the droves are giving it up for fear that meat from diseased cattle could cause a degenerative brain disease.

The Government emphasizes that no link has been established between bovine spongiform encephalopathy, commonly known as mad-cow disease, and Creutzfeldt-Jakob Disease, a rare brain disease fatal to humans.

Since November, when the scare erupted, the Ministry of Agriculture, Fisheries and Food has trotted out scientists and reports suggesting that it is unlikely for a disease to cross the "species barrier" and that even if it did, regulations are in place to keep the diseased portions of cow carcasses out of the human food chain. But the scare refuses to go away. For every scientist who says beef is safe, there is one who says it may not be. The debate over a possible link rages in British medical journals.

The public is voting with its fork. According to a research organization, 1.4 million households have stopped buying beef.

The decline began in November and by mid-December, sales were down 25 percent.

By JOHN DARNTON

Figure 14.1 *New York Times* (TimesFax) displayed by Adobe Acrobat .

Downloading an Acrobat Document

Adobe Acrobat documents are stored in *.pdf files (the "pdf" is short for Portable Document Format).

When you click a link to an Adobe Acrobat document, Netscape downloads the document and starts the Acrobat Reader. When the downloading is complete, the Acrobat Reader starts and appears in its own window. You use the Acrobat Reader's controls to page through the document.

Understanding the Acrobat Reader Window

The Acrobat Reader window has its own toolbar, which offers the controls discussed in the following sections. You'll rarely use the menu commands.

Choosing a Display Mode

Acrobat enables you to view the document three different ways. The default mode is the Page Only display mode, and it's the one you'll probably want to use most often.

Page Only Display Mode In this mode, the default mode shown in Figure 14.1, the Adobe Acrobat document fills the window.

Bookmarks and Page Mode In this mode, you'll see a vertical list of bookmarks in the left panel of the page, with the document displayed in the right panel. These bookmarks are like hyperlinks. You can click them to display a page other than the one you are viewing. You may encounter some Acrobat documents that take advantage of this feature.

Thumbnails and Page In this mode, you see a vertical list of thumbnail (postage-stamp-sized) images of the document's pages in the left panel, while the document is displayed in the right panel (Figure 14.2). To go to one of the pages, click the thumbnail image.

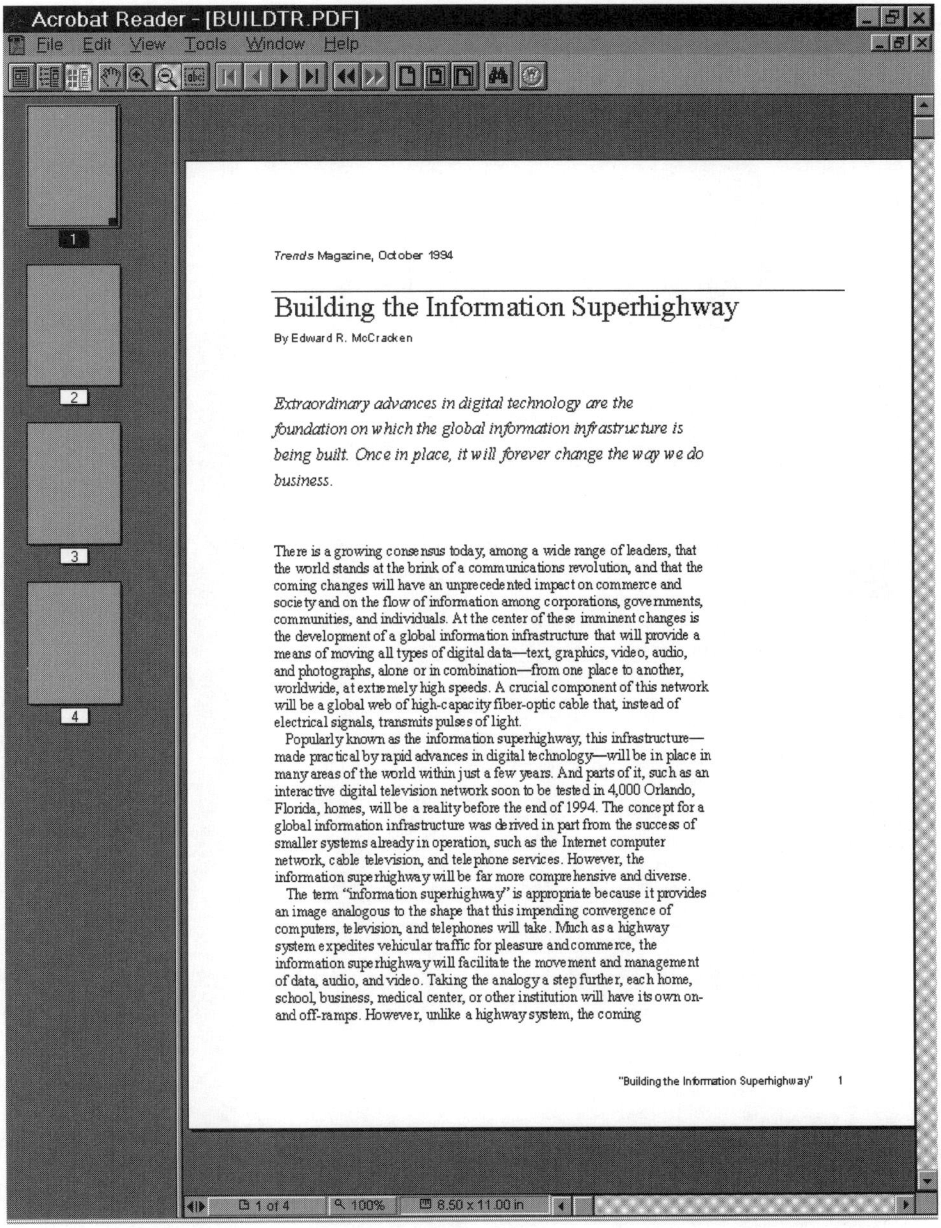

Trends Magazine, October 1994

Building the Information Superhighway

By Edward R. McCracken

Extraordinary advances in digital technology are the foundation on which the global information infrastructure is being built. Once in place, it will forever change the way we do business.

There is a growing consensus today, among a wide range of leaders, that the world stands at the brink of a communications revolution, and that the coming changes will have an unprecedented impact on commerce and society and on the flow of information among corporations, governments, communities, and individuals. At the center of these imminent changes is the development of a global information infrastructure that will provide a means of moving all types of digital data—text, graphics, video, audio, and photographs, alone or in combination—from one place to another, worldwide, at extremely high speeds. A crucial component of this network will be a global web of high-capacity fiber-optic cable that, instead of electrical signals, transmits pulses of light.

Popularly known as the information superhighway, this infrastructure—made practical by rapid advances in digital technology—will be in place in many areas of the world within just a few years. And parts of it, such as an interactive digital television network soon to be tested in 4,000 Orlando, Florida, homes, will be a reality before the end of 1994. The concept for a global information infrastructure was derived in part from the success of smaller systems already in operation, such as the Internet computer network, cable television, and telephone services. However, the information superhighway will be far more comprehensive and diverse.

The term "information superhighway" is appropriate because it provides an image analogous to the shape that this impending convergence of computers, television, and telephones will take. Much as a highway system expedites vehicular traffic for pleasure and commerce, the information superhighway will facilitate the movement and management of data, audio, and video. Taking the analogy a step further, each home, school, business, medical center, or other institution will have its own on- and off-ramps. However, unlike a highway system, the coming

"Building the Information Superhighway" 1

Figure 14.2 Thumbnails and Page mode.

Navigating through the Document

Use the following buttons to navigate through the Acrobat document:

Click this button to display the next page.

Click this button to display the previous page.

Click this button to display the last page.

Click this button to display the first page.

Click this button to go back to the previously displayed page.

Click this button to redisplay the page you were just viewing.

Sizing the Document on Screen

To get a closer look at a portion of the page, use one of the following tools:

Click this button to increase the magnification.

Click this button to decrease the magnification.

Click this button to turn on the hand tool, which lets you bring hidden portions of the document into view.

Note that some Acrobat documents contain author-defined articles, which are designed so that you can page through them almost automatically. To find out whether the document has articles, open the View menu and choose Articles. You'll see a list of the articles the document contains, if any. To read an article, select it and click OK. The Reader will display the beginning of the article. Just click the mouse button to page through the article automatically.

You can also size the document by clicking one of the three page size buttons, which are situated near the right end of the toolbar:

Click this button to display the page at 100 percent magnification.

Click this button to fit the page to the window.

Click this button to fit the width of the page to the window.

Reading the Document in Full-Screen Mode

You can also read Acrobat documents in full-screen mode, in which the page takes up the whole screen. From the View menu, choose Full Screen. To view the next page, press Enter, the right arrow key, or the down arrow key. You can also click the left mouse button. To view the previous page, press the left arrow or up arrow key. When you are finished paging through the document, the program switches back to the normal display mode (you see the Adobe Acrobat Reader in a window).

Finding Text in an Acrobat Document

If you would like to search for text in an Acrobat document, click the Find tool (the button with binoculars). In the Find dialog box, type the text for which you want to search. Click the Whole Word option to avoid retrieving embedded strings, and click Match Case, if desired, to match the capitalization pattern you have typed. To search backward, click the Find Backwards option. Click Find to initiate the search. If the program finds a match, it highlights the matched text on screen. Press F3 to find the next occurrence of the same text.

If no match is found, you'll see a dialog box asking whether you want to continue searching from the beginning of the document. If you click OK, the program continues the search. Should this search fail to retrieve a match, you'll see an alert box informing you that the text could not be found.

Copying Text and Graphics to the Clipboard

If you find text in an Adobe Acrobat document that you would like to copy to another document, click the Select button (the one with "abc" on the button face), and select the text. Then open the Edit menu and choose Copy, or press Ctrl + C.

You can also select and copy graphics. To do so, open the Tools menu and choose Select Graphics. Then drag a selection box around the graphic you want to copy. From the Edit menu, choose Copy, or just press Ctrl + C.

Printing the Document

To print the Adobe Acrobat document you are viewing, follow these steps:

1. From the File menu, choose Print.
2. In the Print dialog box, choose printing options, if you wish. You can print all the pages (the default setting), the current page, or a range of pages. You can also choose to print more than one copy. Additional options may be available, depending on your printer's capabilities.
3. Click OK to start printing.

I can't save this document! You're right—there's no Save option on the Reader's File menu. What gives? Simple—there's no need. Netscape has already downloaded the Acrobat document to the directory listed in the Temporary Directory box (Apps page of the General Preferences menu item). Unless you deliberately erase it, there it will stay. Even after you quit Netscape, you can open the Adobe Acrobat Reader and load this document using the Open command in the File menu.

For an introduction to the extremely cool things that can be done with Adobe Acrobat and the Web, check out the following URL:

http://www.adobe.com:80/Acrobat/PDFsamples.html

You'll find Acrobat versions of Shakespeare's plays and sonnets, the Declaration of Independence and other historical documents, Aesop's fables, and lots of other very interesting things. Don't miss Sun Tzu, *The Art of War.*

From Here

- Take a look at the most exciting thing to hit the Internet since Netscape itself—Java. You'll find a complete introduction in Chapter 15.

Chapter 15

Taking a Sip of Java

Java is many things—a programming language, a key innovation in the history of computing, even a step into a new technological world. For Netscape users, though, it's fun, most of all. With Java, those static Web pages come alive with action, which can include sound, animation, and video. And these pages also provide *inter*action, enabling you to make choices or input data and see the results immediately, right on the page you're viewing.

In this chapter, you'll take a tour of some of today's best Java sites, and you'll learn more about what lies behind Java—and why some people think that Java will change the face of computing forever.

For the Time-Challenged

- Helper programs aren't a very good solution for Web multimedia. They run in a separate window. Worse, if you don't have the helper software, you're out of luck—you can't use the multimedia file. Java solves both problems by downloading the needed software (called an *applet*) along with the multimedia material. You then see the multimedia presentation within Netscape's window.
- Java is a new programming language that's beautifully suited to the Web environment. Unlike other programming languages, a Java program generates a *byte code*, which is expressed in plain ASCII characters that any computer can read. A Java interpreter, designed for a particular computer, transforms the byte code into instructions designed for that computer.
- Although Java contains many measures to safeguard computer security, users have been somewhat rattled by a continuing string of discoveries concerning security loopholes, and malicious Java applets are appearing on the Web. Until these problems are solved, you may wish to restrict your Java browsing to recommended sites or even turn off Java altogether.
- Netscape 3 contains a built-in Java interpreter, so you don't need to do anything special to run Java programs. When Netscape accesses a Web page containing a Java applet, Netscape downloads the code and runs it.
- JavaScript is a subset of Java that enables amateur programmers to bring rich, interactive features to their Web pages.

Java – What's the Big Deal?

You've done some serious surfing now, and I'll bet you've run into this problem: You've clicked on something, but Netscape tells you that it doesn't recognize the file you're trying to access. What's going on? The problem: You don't have the right helper program. So you've got two choices, neither of which is terribly satisfactory: You can skip the file, or you can download it and then try to find a helper program that will run it.

What's so cool about Java is that, when a Web page includes Java code, Netscape automatically downloads the program, called an *applet,* that is needed to make things happen. Your computer then executes (runs) the applet, producing action—and interaction—right on the Web page you're viewing.

Helper programs aren't about to go away, though. Java's very useful, but it works best when the programs being downloaded are relatively small. As you'll see in the next section, where you'll take a look at some excellent Java sites, these programs do simple things, such as displaying an interactive crossword puzzle or a real-time clock. For now, you'll still need helper programs to play sounds, watch movies, and run animations.

What about Security?

Java's a great idea, but it has raised concerns about computer security. For example, what if someone wrote a destructive prank program that masqueraded as a legitimate Java applet? The original Java language specification sought to prevent this by ensuring that Java applets can't do destructive things, such as erasing files.

Unfortunately, these measures weren't sufficient, and researchers have unearthed a series of holes in Java that could enable malicious programmers to do nasty things. As each of these problems has been discovered, Netscape and Sun have developed solutions and implemented them in the latest versions of Netscape.

It's something of a pain to upgrade to the latest version of Netscape—you have to download and install the program, which can take about a half hour—but it's wise to do so. The latest version incorporates the latest security fixes!

Hey, this applet is consuming all my computer's memory! Welcome to reality. Hostile Java pages are appearing on the Web. Some of them consume memory or system resources maliciously, forcing the user to quit and restart. A particularly evil one paints the screen black and prompts for your password to restore access (a blatant attempt to steal passwords). Efforts are under way to remove such sites from the Web, but the antisocial mentality of a small minority of computer programming enthusiasts virtually ensures that they'll pop up time and again. If you're curious to see what kind of damage malicious Java applets can do, check out http://www.match.gatech.edu/~mladue/HostileApplets.html—but please, don't click any of the links!

Because of the potential for Java security leaks, you may wish to consider turning Java off entirely, at least until you're satisfied that the problems have been solved. To do so, open the Options menu and select Network Preferences. Click the Language tab, and deselect Enable Java and Enable JavaScript. If you subsequently find a site that you believe to be authentic and wish to view the Java applet in action, turn these options on again and reload the page.

For the latest on Java security problems (and their solutions), see Java Resources (http://www01.ix.de/ix/raven/Web/Java/Security.html). Also, take a look at the Java Frequently Asked Questions—Applet Security page (http://java.sun.com/java.sun.com/sfa/index.html).

It says "Type your user name and password to restore service"! Please, please, please, *don't fall for this trick!* Computer criminals want your user name and password so that they can carry out crimes such as unauthorized access, vandalism, and theft on line. If you access a Web page that demands the user name and password you use to gain access to the Internet, quit Netscape immediately and do not return to the site. *Note:* This doesn't apply to bona fide Web pages that require you to type a special user name and password, different from those you type to access the Internet, in order to access services to which you have subscribed.

A Tour of Java Sites

You don't need to do anything special to run Java programs—with Netscape, it's all automatic. When you access a site that contains Java code, you'll know it—there are placeholders where the Java action will take place, and it takes a while for the code to download and execute. Once it does, things start happening!

If you're nervous about Java security, browsing these sites is a great way to experience Java without fear. These are bona fide sites that don't contain any malicious applets.

Taking a Tour of Gamelan

The best place to start your exploration of Java is Gamelan, the Web's official Java directory (Figure 15.1). Here, you'll find tutorials (in case you'd

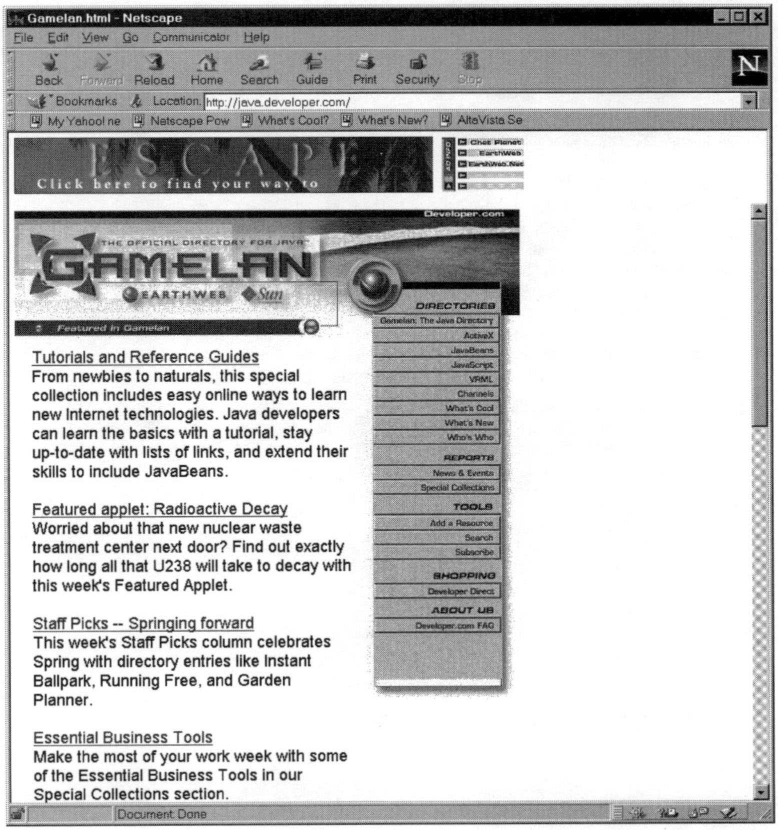
Gamelan.html - Netscape
File Edit View Go Communicator Help
Back Forward Reload Home Search Guide Print Security Stop
Bookmarks Location: http://java.developer.com/
My Yahoo! ne Netscape Pow What's Cool? What's New? AltaVista Se
ESCAPE
Click here to find your way to
Developer.com
THE OFFICIAL DIRECTORY FOR JAVA
GAMELAN
EARTHWEB Sun
Featured in Gamelan
DIRECTORIES
Gamelan: The Java Directory
ActiveX
JavaBeans
JavaScript
VRML
Channels
What's Cool
What's New
Who's Who
REPORTS
News & Events
Special Collections
TOOLS
Add a Resource
Search
Subscribe
SHOPPING
Developer Direct
ABOUT US
Developer.com FAQ
Tutorials and Reference Guides
From newbies to naturals, this special collection includes easy online ways to learn new Internet technologies. Java developers can learn the basics with a tutorial, stay up-to-date with lists of links, and extend their skills to include JavaBeans.
Featured applet: Radioactive Decay
Worried about that new nuclear waste treatment center next door? Find out exactly how long all that U238 will take to decay with this week's Featured Applet.
Staff Picks -- Springing forward
This week's Staff Picks column celebrates Spring with directory entries like Instant Ballpark, Running Free, and Garden Planner.
Essential Business Tools
Make the most of your work week with some of the Essential Business Tools in our Special Collections section.
Document: Done

Figure 15.1 Gamelan is the Web's premier Java directory.

like to get into Java programming) and lots of example applets, which you can run.

Garden Planner

One of the most impressive Java applets I've ever seen is Garden Planner, accessible via Garden Escape (www.garden.com). This applet lets you

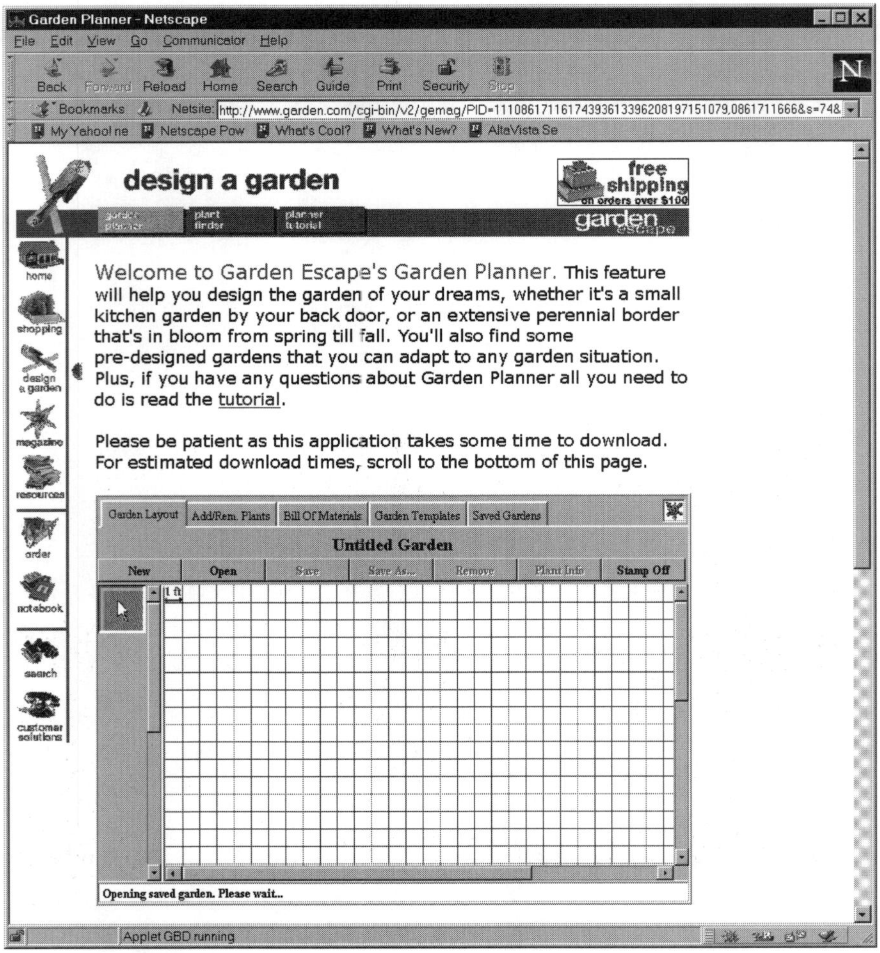
Garden Planner - Netscape
File Edit View Go Communicator Help
Back Forward Reload Home Search Guide Print Security Stop
Bookmarks Netsite: http://www.garden.com/cgi-bin/v2/gemag/PID=1110861711617439361339620819715 1079,08617116668s=748
My Yahoo! ne Netscape Pow What's Cool? What's New? AltaVista Se
design a garden
free shipping on orders over $100
plant finder
planner tutorial
garden escape
home
shopping
design a garden
magazine
resources
order
notebook
search
customer solutions
Welcome to Garden Escape's Garden Planner. This feature will help you design the garden of your dreams, whether it's a small kitchen garden by your back door, or an extensive perennial border that's in bloom from spring till fall. You'll also find some pre-designed gardens that you can adapt to any garden situation. Plus, if you have any questions about Garden Planner all you need to do is read the tutorial.
Please be patient as this application takes some time to download. For estimated download times, scroll to the bottom of this page.
Garden Layout
Add/Rem. Plants
Bill Of Materials
Garden Templates
Saved Gardens
Untitled Garden
New
Open
Save
Save As...
Remove
Plant Info
Stamp Off
1 ft
Opening saved garden. Please wait...
Applet GBD running

Figure 15.2 The Garden Planner enables you to design your own garden.

design a garden in line with professional recommendations concerning such matters as planting proximities. Each square on the chart represents a square foot; incidentally, in case you're curious, *gamelan* is the name of the traditional gong orchestral ensemble of the Indonesian archipelagos of Java and Bali.

Robert's Online Loan Pricer

Like to know how much that new sailboat is going to cost you every month? Here's a great demonstration of Java's ability to create interactive pages: It's a loan payment calculator, but with a twist—you type in any four of the five needed lines of information, and the Java applet does the rest (Figure 15.3). To access this site, use http://www.ripley.org/~robertl/option-pricer.html.

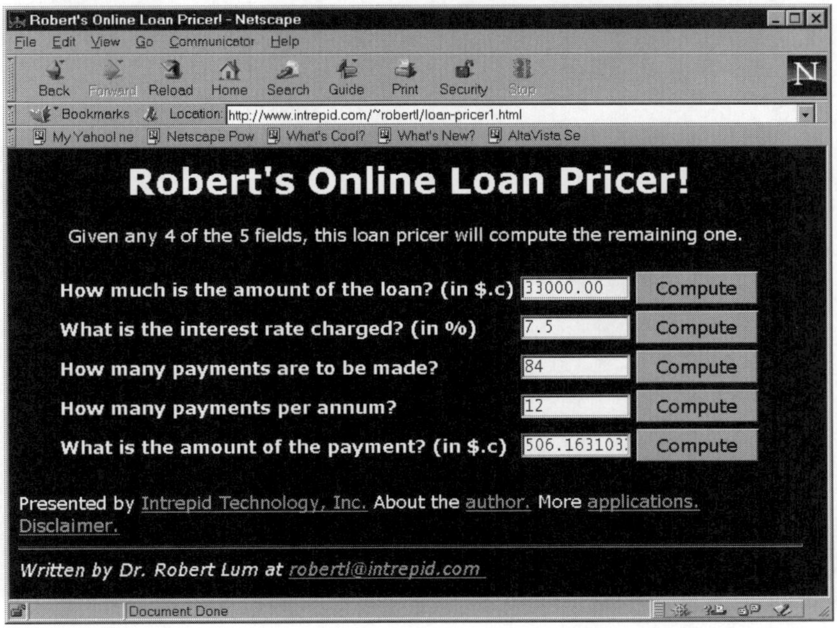
Robert's Online Loan Pricer! - Netscape
File Edit View Go Communicator Help
Back Forward Reload Home Search Guide Print Security Stop
Bookmarks Location: http://www.intrepid.com/~robertl/loan-pricer1.html
My Yahoo! ne Netscape Pow What's Cool? What's New? AltaVista Se
Robert's Online Loan Pricer!
Given any 4 of the 5 fields, this loan pricer will compute the remaining one.
How much is the amount of the loan? (in $.c) 33000.00 Compute
What is the interest rate charged? (in %) 7.5 Compute
How many payments are to be made? 84 Compute
How many payments per annum? 12 Compute
What is the amount of the payment? (in $.c) 506.163103 Compute
Presented by Intrepid Technology, Inc. About the author. More applications.
Disclaimer.
Written by Dr. Robert Lum at robertl@intrepid.com
Document Done

Figure 15.3 Robert's Loan Pricer enables you to calculate you monthly payment.

Solitaire

If you're wondering whether Java applets can have enough functionality to really *do* something, check out Solitaire (http://w3.gwis.com/~thorn/BetaSol.html). Shown in Figure 15.4, this site displays an impressive Solitaire game, which is bound to keep you busy for a while!

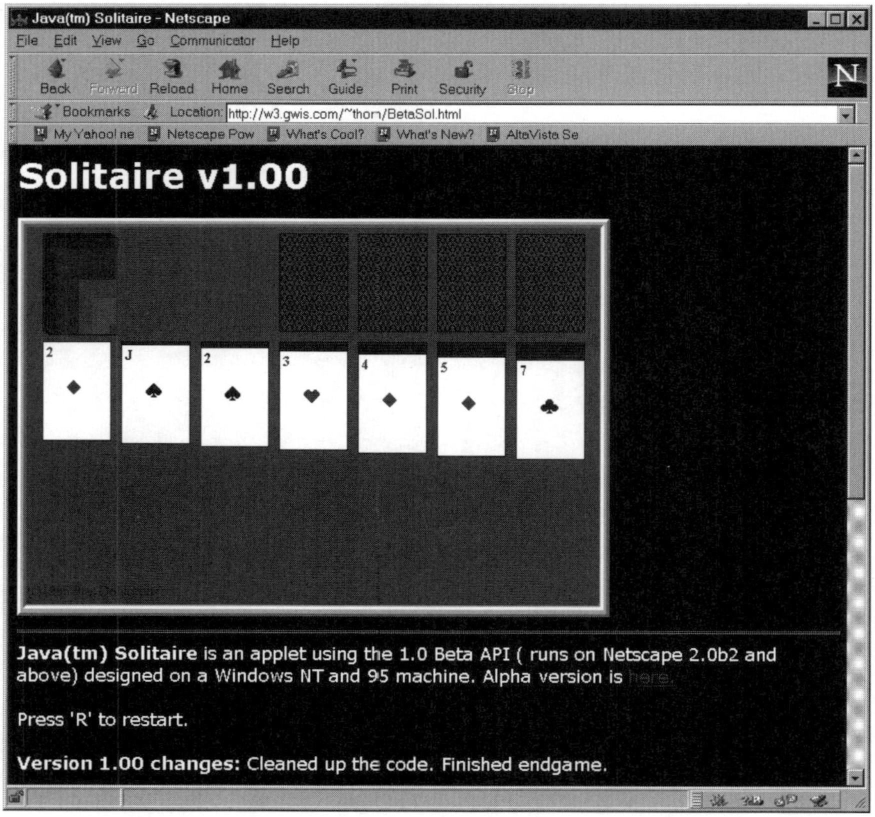
Java(tm) Solitaire - Netscape
File Edit View Go Communicator Help
Back Forward Reload Home Search Guide Print Security Stop
Bookmarks Location: http://w3.gwis.com/~thorn/BetaSol.html
My Yahoo! ne Netscape Pow What's Cool? What's New? AltaVista Se
Solitaire v1.00
Java(tm) Solitaire is an applet using the 1.0 Beta API (runs on Netscape 2.0b2 and above) designed on a Windows NT and 95 machine. Alpha version is here.
Press 'R' to restart.
Version 1.00 changes: Cleaned up the code. Finished endgame.

Figure 15.4 Solitaire.

Where Did Java Come From?

You may be surprised to learn that Java got its start before the Web did. Java creator James Gosling, a programmer at Sun Microsystems, conceived of Java in early 1991—and at that time, Gosling thought that Java would be used to program consumer electronic devices. Specifically, Java would be used to create programs for TV set-top devices which, from the early 1990s and pre-Web perspective, were a sure bet to bring the Information Age into the home.

As Gosling initially conceived Java, the language would have to work with any kind of computer processing unit, since consumer electronic devices would surely have lots of different processors installed. Thus Java was intended to be *platform-independent* from the beginning, meaning that it would work with just about any processor made. As you'll see, that's one of the reasons it works so well with the Web—but we're getting ahead of the story.

The TV set box idea didn't work out—it seems that interactive television is always about to happen, but never quite makes it—but Java didn't die. Looking at the rapid growth of the World Wide Web, Gosling and his colleagues quickly realized that the Web, not interactive television, provided the perfect vehicle for disseminating Java applets. They created the first Java-enabled browser, called HotJava, to demonstrate what Java could do in tandem with the Web. Then Netscape Communications Corporation announced that the next version of their browser would include a Java interpreter—and the rest, as they say, is history!

Ironically, something like the TV set-top box is appearing in stores right now—but it's not designed for interactive television. On the contrary, it's a small computer (sans disk drives), priced at about $500, that enables you to access the Web!

What's JavaScript?

One of the most wonderful things about the World Wide Web is that just about anyone can learn HTML and put up a Web page. Java's great, but many Web enthusiasts fear that Java will raise the technology bar, preventing nonprogrammers from creating interactive Web sites. Thanks to JavaScript, a subset of Java designed for use by nonprogrammers, this pessimistic scenario may not occur.

Gosling and his team started with a programming language called C++, but quickly found that it was too quirky to serve their purposes. Taking the best ideas from C++ and other programming languages, they devised a new language from the ground up. Java would have the following characteristics:

- **Simplicity** Reacting against the oddly named key words and other deficiencies of previous programming languages, Java's developers wanted the language to be easy to learn and use.
- **Object-Oriented** In an *object-oriented* programming language, programmers create and polish small program modules, each of which accomplishes a certain task, such as displaying a dialog box on the screen. Once this module (called an *object*) is tested, it can be copied and used in any program. As an object-oriented language matures, programmers create hundreds and even thousands of objects, which can be put together to construct new applications in short order.
- **Robustness** Java eliminates some of the programming traps that bedevil users of C++ and other programming languages. By encouraging good programming habits, Java helps to ensure that the Java programs you run will be bug-free.
- **Architecture Neutral** This is probably the most amazing thing about Java—its ability to run on any kind of computer ever made. Unlike all previous programming languages, a compiled Java program doesn't generate binary code, which is tied to the instruction set of a particular processor. Instead, it generates a *byte code*, a list of intermediary instructions that can be expressed in ASCII characters that any computer can deal with.
- **Interpreted** To translate the byte code into instructions that a specific computer can read, you need a Java interpreter. Netscape has its own, built-in Java interpreter, so you're ready to go!
- **High Performance** All these innovations wouldn't add up to much if Java performed sluggishly. To ensure high performance, Java introduces a number of important innovations. Among them is the Java *garbage collector*, a program that runs in the background, cleaning up disused memory so that a program always has the maximum amount of memory to run.

- **Multithreading** A good program can do two or more tasks at once, so Java incorporates multithreading. In multithreading, two or more separate program processes, called *threads*, can execute at the same time.
- **Security** Programs bandied about over the network pose security problems, but Java incorporates a number of advanced protection measures to safeguard your system.

JavaScript enables anyone who's able to learn HTML to create rich, interactive sites. The cool thing about JavaScript is that it enables you to become the master of ceremonies for the events on a Web page. For example, when a user clicks a button, a portion of the script jumps into action and performs a function, such as searching a database for information or running a prepackaged Java applet.

In Figure 15.5, you see JavaScript in action. This page's greeting, showing the time of day and the date, as well as the scrolling banner in the box (you can't see it scrolling, I know, but take my word for it) are both created by simple JavaScripts.

What About ActiveX?

While we're talking about Java and JavaScript, it's appropriate to mention ActiveX, which is Microsoft's answer to Java. Unlike Java, ActiveX isn't a programming language; on the contrary, it's a way of packaging programs (which could be written in any of a variety of programming languages) so that they can talk to the applications you've installed on your system. To do this, ActiveX controls make use of Microsoft's Object Linking and Embedding (OLE) technology, which is built into Microsoft Windows.

The last sentence of the preceding paragraph contains the key to understanding ActiveX—as of right now, it's really not a cross-platform technology. The thing that's made the Internet so wildly successful is that you can access it no matter what type of computer you're using. Java is cross-platform—it doesn't matter whether you're running Netscape on a Mac, UNIX box, or a Windows system. Any of these systems can run Java applets, as long as you're running Netscape. With ActiveX, though, you really need to be using Windows. Reportedly, OLE is being added to other operating systems, but nobody expects this to happen very quickly. The reality is that ActiveX assumes that just about everyone is using Windows, and if they aren't, they should be. Well, what else would you expect from Microsoft, given that they make most of their money by selling Windows and Windows applications?

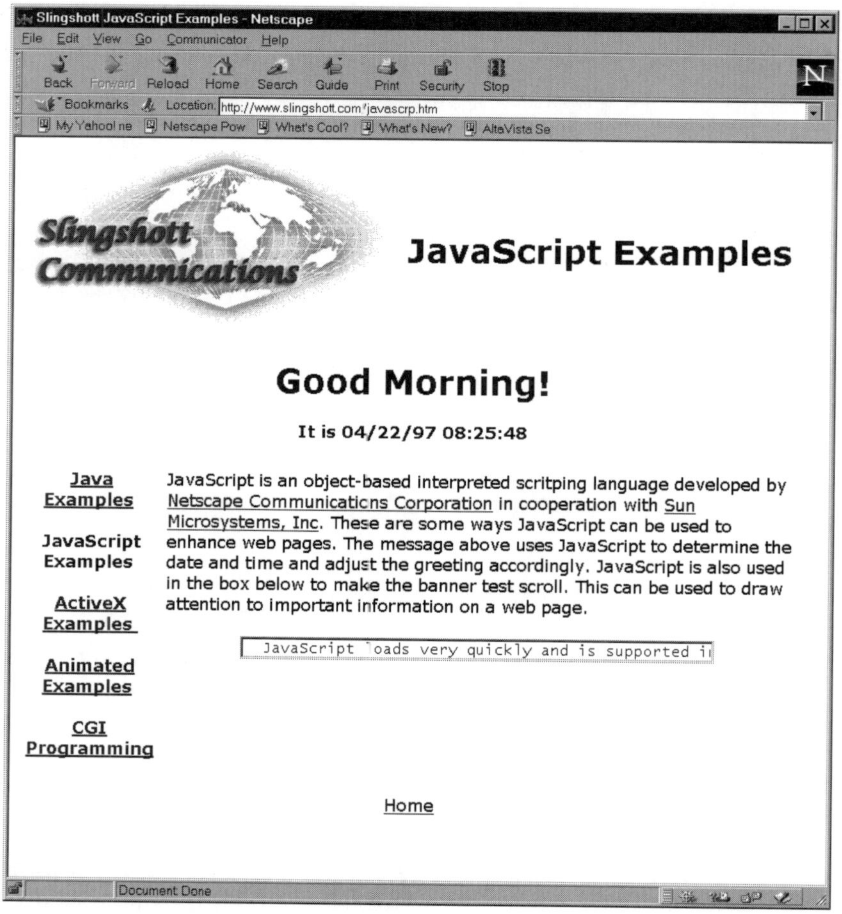

Slingshott JavaScript Examples - Netscape
File Edit View Go Communicator Help
Back Forward Reload Home Search Guide Print Security Stop
Bookmarks Location: http://www.slingshott.com/javascrp.htm
My Yahoo! ne Netscape Pow What's Cool? What's New? AltaVista Se
Slingshott Communications
JavaScript Examples
Good Morning!
It is 04/22/97 08:25:48
Java Examples
JavaScript Examples
ActiveX Examples
Animated Examples
CGI Programming
JavaScript is an object-based interpreted scritping language developed by Netscape Communications Corporation in cooperation with Sun Microsystems, Inc. These are some ways JavaScript can be used to enhance web pages. The message above uses JavaScript to determine the date and time and adjust the greeting accordingly. JavaScript is also used in the box below to make the banner test scroll. This can be used to draw attention to important information on a web page.
JavaScript loads very quickly and is supported i
Home
Document Done

Figure 15.5 JavaScript provides an easy way to add interactive, attention-getting features to Web pages.

ActiveX gives Internet users qualms for other reasons besides its built-in favoritism to Windows. Another problem lies in the technology's security. Unlike Java and JavaScript, ActiveX programs, called *controls*, have full access to your computer's file and operating systems. A rogue ActiveX control could wipe out your hard disk in a flash—in fact, it's trivial to write an ActiveX control that could do this.

To deal with the security issues, Microsoft employs digital certificates. These appear when you're about to download an ActiveX control. The digital certificate, provided by an independent certification agency, attests that the program you're about to download was indeed created by a bona fide software publisher, and hasn't been altered in any way. If you choose to accept the certificate, downloading proceeds and the needed software is installed automatically.

If you're a Netscape user, you naturally don't want to be shut out of the ActiveX content that's out there—and Netscape agrees. The company plans to integrate ActiveX technology into the release version of Netscape Communicator. Netscape 3.0 users can get ActiveX functionality by installing Scriptactive, a plug-in created by NCompass (www.ncompasslabs.com).

Chapter 16

It's Dynamic!

New for 4

It's the latest, hottest thing in Netscape land—Dynamic HTML. Potentially, it's the ultimate in multimedia, the key to transforming the Web into a highly effective presentation medium. With Dynamic HTML, you can view documents that have rich, downloaded fonts, style sheets that enable Web designers to specify layout formats that will make magazine designers envious, and *layered* documents, which enable you to select different "leaves" of a page without having to download more data. Sounds great, right?

There's just one problem with Dynamic HTML. As of right now, there's no single standard for doing these things (the exception is style sheets, which are supported by HTML version 3.2). Competitor Microsoft has its own version of Dynamic HTML that has been submitted to the relevant standardization body, the World Wide Web Organization (W3O). Just which version will win out is anyone's guess. For now, Web designers are likely to hold back on developing Dynamic HTML sites—they don't want to restrict their audience to users of just one browser.

For now, then, Dynamic HTML—at least, Netscape's version of it—is likely to remain something of a curiosity, something you can play with at Netscape's demonstration sites and a few additional Web sites that have decided to exclude people using other browsers. By the next version of Netscape, one hopes that the standards will have materialized, and that all the major browser publishers will adhere to them.

One thing's for certain—by looking at Dynamic HTML, you're looking at the future of the Web. As HTML has evolved from an academic presentation language into a commercial designer's tool, Web designers have been clamoring for more control over document formats (including fonts, absolute page positioning, and style sheets). They're not going to give up, and they're going to get what they want—eventually. The only thing standing in the way is the standardization process, which takes time. Take a look at Netscape's demo site (home.netscape.com/comprod/products/communicator/index.html), and you'll see what's up.

Let Them Have Fonts!

Right now, Web designers can include font specifications in their documents, and both popular browsers—Netscape Navigator and Microsoft Internet Explorer—will display them. Trouble is, you have to have the font installed on your system. Earlier, I pointed out that you'd be wise to equip your system with as many fonts as you can, in the hope that just possibly you'll have one of the fonts the designer chose to use. (If you don't have the needed font, the browser reverts to the default fonts for the character set you're using.) Obviously, that's not very satisfactory.

What's the Solution for Fonts?

According to Netscape, it's the company's Dynamic Font Support, a feature of Netscape Communicator. Dynamic Font Support enables designers to include the needed fonts with their HTML files. When you download the page, you also download the font. Amazingly, it doesn't take too much more time to do this, and the results are really beautiful (see Figure 16.1). As you can see, this is an inevitability—the only thing that's needed is a universal standard for delivering fonts dynamically.

Bitstream TrueDoc Announcement - Netscape
File Edit View Go Communicator Help
Back Forward Reload Home Search Guide Print Security Stop
Bookmarks Location: http://www.bitstream.com/world/demo.htm
My Yahoo! PowerStart What's Cool? What's New? AltaVista
The PFR for this document includes characters from 10 fonts. The PFR is only 25 KB.
Netscape Communicator to Use TrueDoc for Font Portability
See the New World of Web Publishing
世界を見ます
Netscape Communicator with Bitstream TrueDoc lets users see the world from their desktops.
If you are a web author, you can create a home page with any font you own - including international fonts, such as Cyrillic and Kanji - without worrying if users viewing your document have the same fonts on their systems.
Netscape to include award-winning TrueDoc in Communicator
Netscape Communicator with Bitstream TrueDoc gives authors complete control over the look and feel of documents created for the World Wide Web. Documents retain complete font fidelity.
If an author uses Kuenstler 165 or Zurich Bold Extended for a headline font, that is what readers see. With Bitstream TrueDoc, What You See Is What THEY Get.
S E E T H E
W O R L D
Document: Done

Figure 16.1 Dynamic Font Support in action (Bitstream's TrueDoc technology).

Introducing Bitstream's TrueDoc

To implement Dynamic Font Support, Netscape has hitched its corporate wagon to strategic ally Bitstream, a font publisher. Bitstream has developed a dynamic font downloading standard called TrueDoc. Trouble is, there's a competing standard, called OpenType, which is being pushed by—you guessed it—Microsoft.

For the Time-Challenged

- Netscape's Dynamic HTML is pre-standards, so don't expect to run into a lot of sites that make use of the new font downloading and layering features. Microsoft is pushing different standards for both of these functions. For now, developing a site with one standard means excluding a big part of your potential audience.
- Bitstream's TrueDoc technology is very impressive—with this technology, supported by Communicator, needed fonts download quickly and display beautifully. Plus, it's truly cross-platform.
- Netscape's support for the HTML 3.2 style sheet standard enables Web designers to create quality, magazine-style layouts for Web documents. Since this is also supported by Microsoft Internet Explorer, you can expect big improvements in Web document design soon.
- Communicator's layering technology enables Web designers to create multiple layers on a single page. They take some time to download, but after they are, you can view the different layers quickly because they don't have to be retrieved from the network. But layers aren't standardized yet, so don't expect a lot of sites to use them.

Bitstream's TrueDoc has a lot of advantages over OpenType, according to Bitstream's press releases. Unlike OpenType, which Bitstreams claims to be Windows-centric, TrueDoc is a truly cross-platform technology; it will work with any computer that's capable of running Communicator (or any other TrueDoc-enabled browser). For font designers, TrueDoc offers protection of intellectual property, too. Unlike OpenType, TrueDoc doesn't download the entire font and install it on your system—it just downloads the specific information needed to display a page, such as the one shown in Figure 16.2. This information is really compact; in Figure 16.2, for example, it's only about 30K, which is less than an average GIF graphic. This is pretty cool technology.

Where's that font? I want it! If you're hoping you can snare TrueDoc fonts for your own use after viewing a Web page, you're out of luck. TrueDoc doesn't download all the technology that's needed to install the font in your computer. Instead, it downloads just enough to display the font in Communicator.

Anti-aliased text and background texture - Netscape
File Edit View Go Communicator Help
Back Forward Reload Home Search Guide Print Security Stop
Bookmarks Location: http://www.bitstream.com/world/textest2.htm
My Yahoo! PowerStart What's Cool? What's New? AltaVista
Quality
This is a demonstration of anti-aliased text over a background texture
The anti-aliasing in the text is keying to the background color specified in the html document, not to the color in the background texture. The background color is #336600 (green).
The typefaces used in this document were embedded with HexWeb Typograph,
a BBedit extension by
Document Done

Figure 16.2 TrueDoc fonts displayed over complex background.

Wow, That Looks Like a Magazine Layout! (Style Sheets)

Another thing about HTML that bugs designers is the lack of precise control over just how page elements appear. *Style sheets* enable Web designers to do this, finally. With style sheets, Web designers can specify a number of formats for each of the standard page elements, such as headings. These formats include fonts, spacing, indentation, and alignment. Figure 16.3 shows a newsletter format that's created with style sheets.

Unlike Dynamic Font Support, style sheets are already standardized, so look forward to much more attractive page designs on the Web. Still, style sheets aren't a complete solution for the font problem. Designers can specify

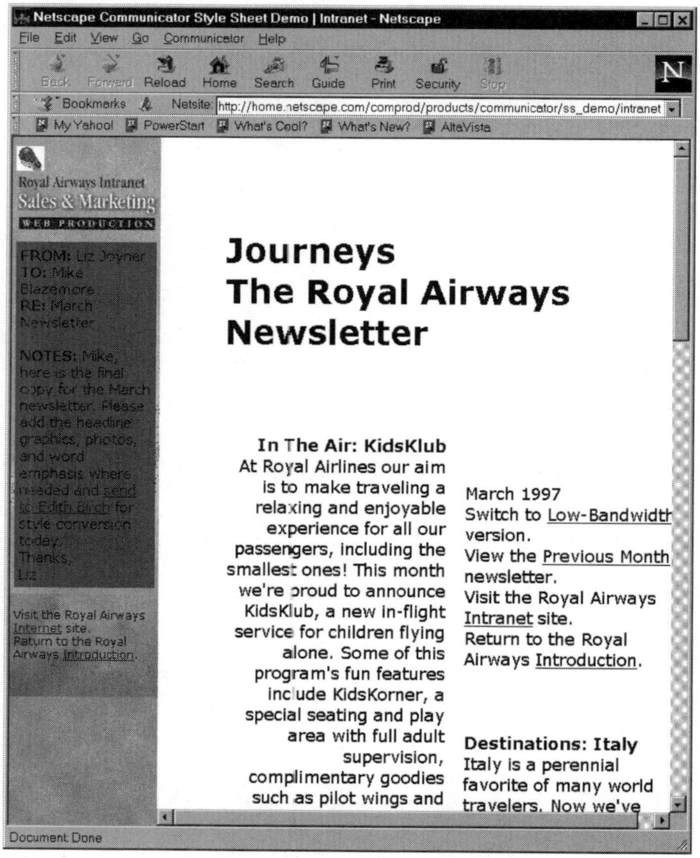
Netscape Communicator Style Sheet Demo | Intranet - Netscape
File Edit View Go Communicator Help
Back Forward Reload Home Search Guide Print Security Stop
Bookmarks Netsite: http://home.netscape.com/comprod/products/communicator/ss_demo/intranet
My Yahoo! PowerStart What's Cool? What's New? AltaVista
Royal Airways Intranet
Sales & Marketing
WEB PRODUCTION
Journeys
The Royal Airways
Newsletter
In The Air: KidsKlub
At Royal Airlines our aim is to make traveling a relaxing and enjoyable experience for all our passengers, including the smallest ones! This month we're proud to announce KidsKlub, a new in-flight service for children flying alone. Some of this program's fun features include KidsKorner, a special seating and play area with full adult supervision, complimentary goodies such as pilot wings and
March 1997
Switch to Low-Bandwidth version.
View the Previous Month newsletter.
Visit the Royal Airways Intranet site.
Return to the Royal Airways Introduction.
Destinations: Italy
Italy is a perennial favorite of many world travelers. Now we've
Document: Done

Figure 16.3 Style sheets enable magazine-style layouts.

fonts, but you're back to the old problem of having to install the needed fonts on your system in order to view them in the Web page. Something like Dynamic Font Support is needed.

There's More Than One Layer to This!

The most advanced—and possibly the most controversial—of Netscape's HTML innovations is layering, a technology that enables Web designers to create multilayer pages.

A multilayer page is just that—a page that has several different "leaves," which you can view by clicking on a navigation aid. From the user's perspective, this is something like using a framed page, where you can click links to see different things in another frame. But there's an enormous difference in performance: A layered page downloads with all of its leaves, so Communicator doesn't have to go back to the network to show you another layer. As a result, layer changes happen lickity-split. Plus, the layers can fit on top of each other, like the layers in a computer graphics application.

Sound confusing? The best way to see how this works is to try it by accessing the demo site mentioned at the beginning of this chapter. Short of that, you can take a look at Figure 16.4, which shows a Netscape demo. This is an architect's presentation, showing off "Millennium Plaza," an office complex. By clicking the navigation aids to the right, you can turn the various layers on and off. Figure 16.5 shows what this site looks like when you've turned off everything but the landscaping.

How is this done? With JavaScript, in case you're curious, and a new spate of Netscape extensions to HTML. Will they become part of the HTML standard? It's anyone's guess. For now, you won't find very many layered sites, unless the site designers really want to exclude users of other browsers.

This layered page is taking forever to download! "Forever" is an exaggeration, but you'd best be aware that, when you access a layered page, you're downloading a lot more data than you usually download. Thoughtful Web authors will tell you how long this will take—generally, a couple of minutes over a modem line, depending on the presentation's complexity. Remember, once all of this stuff is downloaded, you can

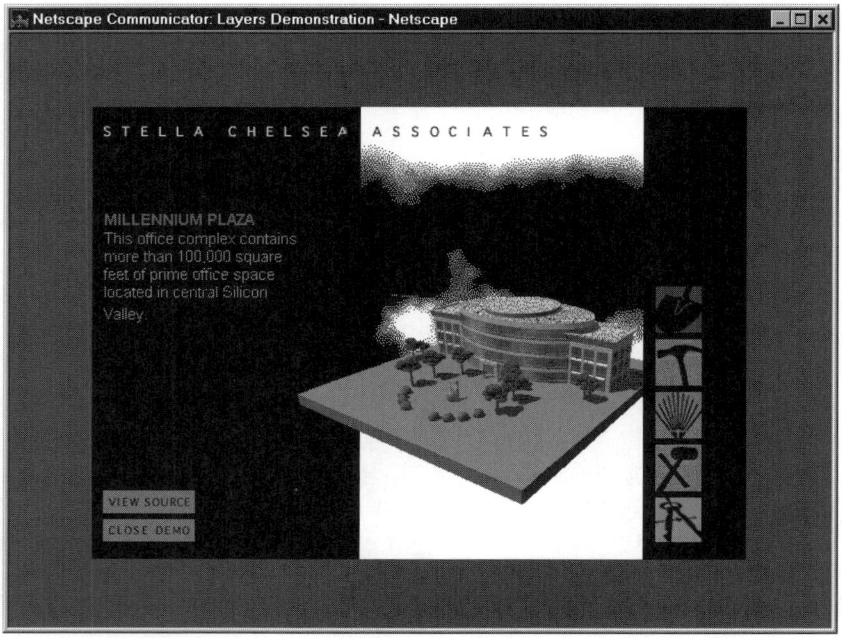
Netscape Communicator: Layers Demonstration - Netscape
STELLA CHELSEA ASSOCIATES
MILLENNIUM PLAZA
This office complex contains more than 100,000 square feet of prime office space located in central Silicon Valley.
VIEW SOURCE
CLOSE DEMO

Figure 16.4 Netscape's layer demonstration shows an architect's presentation.

navigate around within the layered presentation at your computer's top speed (not the network's).

Taking the Layers Tour

A few Web sites offer layer demos, so you can explore this new technology, if you'd like. Premiere WorldLink (www.worldlinkservices.com), a phone card company, offers an interesting layers demo; it's essentially an advertising presentation, replete with a little JavaScript window—containing their

Taboca Transpray Example ...
TranSpray example
Welcome to Taboca Transpray. I mean, transictions and spray like effect over HTML layer. It examples you how layer can be used to provide dynamic artwork content. Dynamic Artwork is when your business don't need to recall the website artist

Figure 16.5 Taboca Entertainment (www.taboca.com) offers a number of interesting layer effects, including this dynamic spray-paint font effect.

800 number, naturally—that wanders around the screen, irritatingly defying your attempts to close it (hint: Use Alt + F4). The downside of all this dynamic stuff, unfortunately, is that commercial sites will find even more ways of sticking themselves in your face.

Taboca Entertainment (www.taboca.com) demonstrates a number of nifty uses of layering, including the "spray" font fill-in shown in Figure 16.5. This is hard to see in the figure, but the black font has been filled in from the bottom by what appears to be black spray paint; the screen shot shows the window as the spraying process nears completion.

Kazuhiro's JavaScript Games (www1.nisiq.net/~jimmeans/) uses layers and JavaScript to create some cool games, including the JavaScript version of Tetris shown in Figure 16.6. If you'd like to find out how this was done, you can view the document's source.

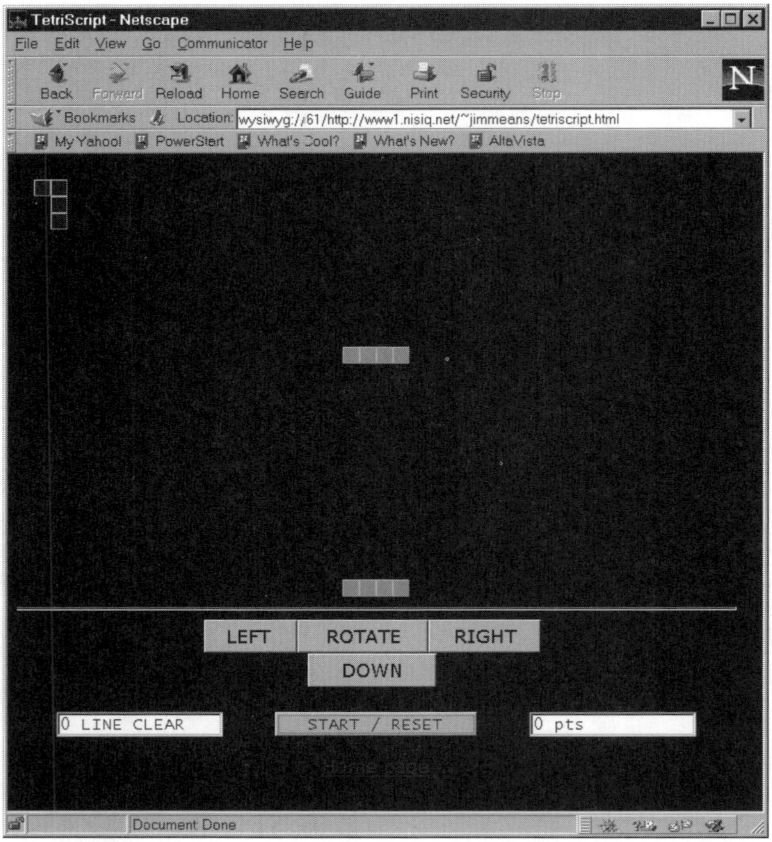

Figure 16.6 Kazuhiro's JavaScript Games uses layers and JavaScript to create a series of Web-based games.

From Here

- You've mastered Netscape Navigator! In Part III, you learn how to use Netscape Messenger. And you're in for a treat. I believe Messenger is the best e-mail program you can get anywhere. You'll find out why in the chapters to come.

Part II

Netscape Messenger: Staying in Touch with E-mail

Chapter

17

Getting Started with Netscape Messenger

New for 4

Netscape Messenger is a separate module of Netscape Communicator that's devoted to e-mail and news messages. Combining both types of messages in a single, easy-to-use message manager, Messenger enables you to stay in touch using one-to-one (e-mail) and one-to-many (news) communication methods. Part II of this book focuses on Messenger e-mail; you'll learn how to use Messenger for news purposes in Part III.

This chapter introduces Netscape Messenger and e-mail, and shows you how to configure your copy of Communicator to access your mail. In the next chapter, you'll learn how to send and receive your first e-mail messages.

Introducing Messenger E-mail

As an e-mail program, Netscape Messenger is impressive—it includes all the basics you need for e-mail and a lot more. Netscape Messenger offers the following advanced features:

- **Rich mail formatting** You can create messages with HTML, using the formatting options in the Compose window. If the recipient is using an e-mail program that can decode HTML-based e-mail messages, your recipient sees this formatting.
- **Mail directory support** Messenger knows how to read corporate X.500 mail directories. If you're using Messenger inside an organization that has such directories, it's easy to find somebody's e-mail address. For e-mail addresses outside an organization, Messenger directly searches e-mail databases such as Four11 and Bigfoot.
- **Secure, encrypted e-mail** Sending e-mail with most programs is like writing a postcard—anyone can read it. With Netscape Messenger, you can encrypt your mail so that nobody can read it en route.
- **Spell checking** Don't ever send a mistake-riddled e-mail message or Usenet post again. Messenger's spelling checker corrects your mistakes before you send your messages.
- **Folders and filters** You can easily write filtering rules that will direct incoming mail to named folders, which you can organize as you please. Don't let a chatty mailing list fill up your Inbox, obscuring important mail.
- **Search message text** Looking for an e-mail message you received long ago, and just can't find it? Use Messenger's Find in Message command, which enables you to search the entire text of every message you've received. In moments, you'll see the "lost" message on screen.

These are features that users of the best standalone e-mail programs have enjoyed for years. That's right—Messenger is just about the best e-mail program you can possibly use. In the chapters that follow, you'll learn how to take your use of e-mail to the max—and you'll find out why a full-featured e-mail program such as Messenger is an indispensable asset to one's professional and personal life.

Introducing E-mail

When you establish an account with an Internet service provider (ISP), you'll get an electronic mailbox. This mailbox is stored on the ISP's *mail server*, an Internet-connected computer with special mail software and a very large hard disk. The mail server stores your mail temporarily until you log in to the system. At that time, Netscape looks for new mail—if there's any waiting for you (and if you've set up Netscape Mail Notification), you'll see an on-screen notice that there's mail waiting for you. Think of the mail server as a temporary parking place for your mail.

When you compose and send e-mail to others, what happens is the reverse of the above process: Netscape sends your mail to the server, which relays it on to its Internet destination.

How do I know whether someone's read my message? If you don't get a reply from somebody, don't assume you're being ignored—the person may not have logged on! If you want others to have confidence in sending mail to you, be sure to log on to your server frequently and check your mail.

About E-mail Addresses

To exchange e-mail with someone, you'll need your own e-mail address, as well as the e-mail address of the person with whom you'd like to correspond. You'll receive your e-mail address when you establish an account with an Internet service provider.

Internet e-mail addresses have three parts:

- **User name** The first part of the e-mail address identifies your personal mailbox. For example, if your name is David Smith, you may be assigned a mailbox name of *dsmith*.
- **At sign (@)** The second part of the e-mail address is a separator: It separates the first part from the third part, so those dumb computers can tell the difference.
- **Mail server's domain name** The third part of the e-mail address gives the domain name of your e-mail server.

A complete, correct e-mail address looks like the following fictitious ones:

dsmith@asteroid.chv.va.us

bpod@dehiscent.org

rfang@wolf.net

Please note that you can't place any spaces in an e-mail address.

E-mail addresses aren't case-sensitive, the way URLs are. Most people use lowercase letters for e-mail addresses, though, and it's a good practice because it prevents confusion (if you type part of your address in capital letters, people might think they need to do so).

CONFIGURING E-MAIL

To get started with Netscape's e-mail, you need to configure your copy of Netscape so that it knows where your mail server is located. Before you do this, call your ISP and ask the following questions:

- What is the address of the SMTP server for outgoing mail?
- What is the address of the POP3 server for incoming mail?
- What is my user name?
- What is my mail password?

Often, the addresses for the outgoing and incoming mail are the same. Be sure to write all this information down, but keep your password from prying eyes.

Filling in Server Information

To configure Netscape's e-mail:

1. From the Edit menu in any Netscape window, choose Preferences. You'll see the Mail & Groups page.
2. Click the Mail & Groups category.

For the Time-Challenged

- An e-mail address begins with the sender's mailbox name, and continues with an "at" (@) sign and the name of the computer where the person has an e-mail address (such as galadriel@lothlorien.org).
- You need to configure Messenger before you can send and receive e-mail. You'll need information given to you by your service provider, including your e-mail address, the name of the computer that stores your incoming mail, and the name of the computer that sends your outgoing mail.
- The Message Center groups all your mail and news messages. The Messenger Mailbox window displays the contents of a mail or news folder.
- The Messenger Mailbox shows your Inbox, which contains your incoming mail. When you read your mail, it's best to start with Messenger Mailbox, rather than Message Center.
- Before you send any e-mail, take a few minutes to create a signature (a text file containing contact information that's automatically appended to each message you send).

3. Click the Identify category (under Mail & Groups). If you don't see this category name, click the plus sign next to Mail & Groups. You'll see the Identity page, shown in Figure 17.1.
4. In the Your name box, type your name. You don't actually have to type your real name, but you should do so if you plan to use e-mail for professional purposes.
5. In the Email address box, type your e-mail address. Please check this carefully against the address your ISP gave you.
6. Just leave the Reply To box blank unless you've been told by your ISP that you need to fill this in.
7. In the Organization box, type your company or organization's name. This is optional, but you should fill it out if you're using e-mail for professional purposes.
8. If you created a signature file for another e-mail program, you can use it with Netscape. A signature file is a text file containing text (such as your name and telephone numbers) that is automatically

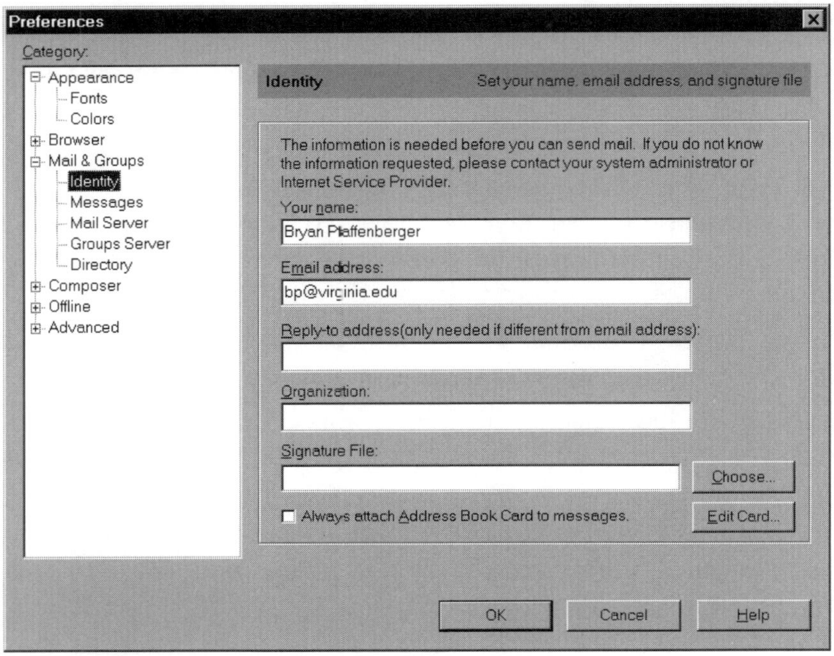

Figure 17.1 The Identity page enables you to enter your name, e-mail address, and organizational affiliation.

attached to outgoing messages. For now, just leave this box blank—you'll learn how to create a signature file later.

9. If you would like to automatically attach your Address Book Card to outgoing messages, click the check box, and click Edit Card. You'll see your Address Book Card, like the one shown in Figure 17.2. (The Address Book enables you to store names and contact information for the people with whom you correspond.) Fill out the card with as much information as you're willing to make public, including contact information (click the Contact tab to fill out this information). Click OK when you're done.

Now that you're done with the Identity page, go on to fill out the next one, as explained in the following section. If you'd like to take a break, just click OK; you can later open the Edit menu, choose Preferences, and continue.

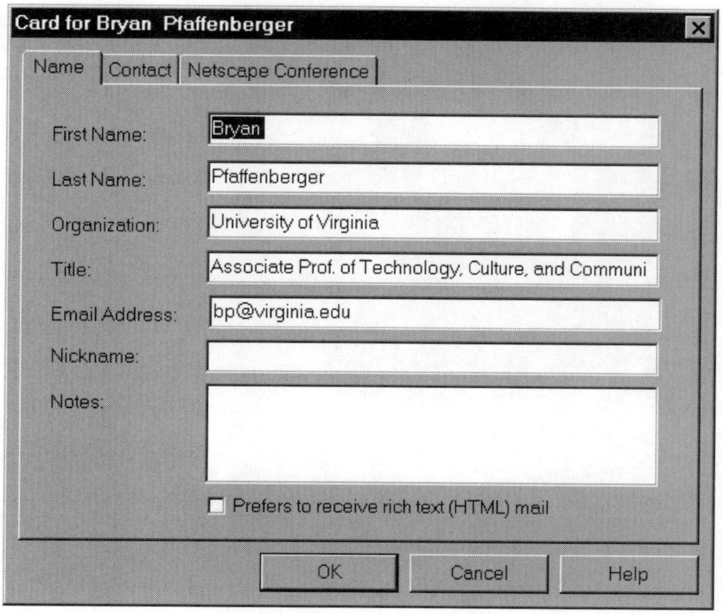

Figure 17.2 Here you choose important options concerning the way Netscape handles your mail.

Choosing Message Options

Now that you've finished filling out the Identity card, click Messages. You'll see the Messages page, shown in Figure 17.3.

Message Properties In the Message Properties area, you choose options for how Netscape sends your mail. Here are my suggestions:

- **Don't send HTML messages by default.** Many people are still using mail packages that can't read HTML. You can optionally send HTML to people whose e-mail programs can decode HTML tags.
- **Don't automatically quote original messages when replying.** Often, you don't need to quote the whole original message, and sometimes you don't need to do so at all. You can always add the quote when you compose your reply, as you'll learn in the next chapter.

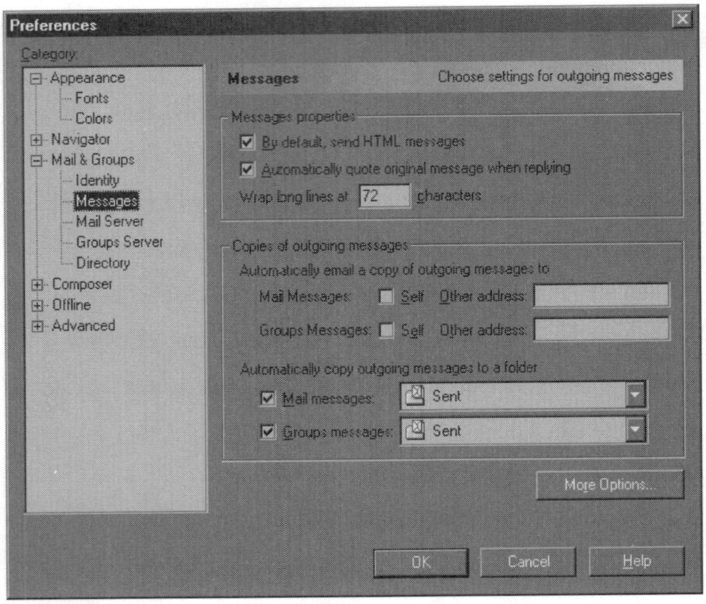

Figure 17.3 Here, you choose options for handling messages.

- **Wrap long lines at 72 characters.** Some people's e-mail programs send really long lines—you may not be able to read their messages conveniently without this feature.

Copies of Outgoing Messages In this area, you choose how Netscape makes and stores copies of the messages you send. Here are my suggestions:

- **Don't automatically mail copies of your messages unless you really need to.** There's no need to mail copies of your messages to yourself, since Netscape can store your sent messages automatically.
- **Copy your mail and group messages to the Sent folder.** This is the default setting, and it's a good one. You'll have a record of every mail and news message you sent.

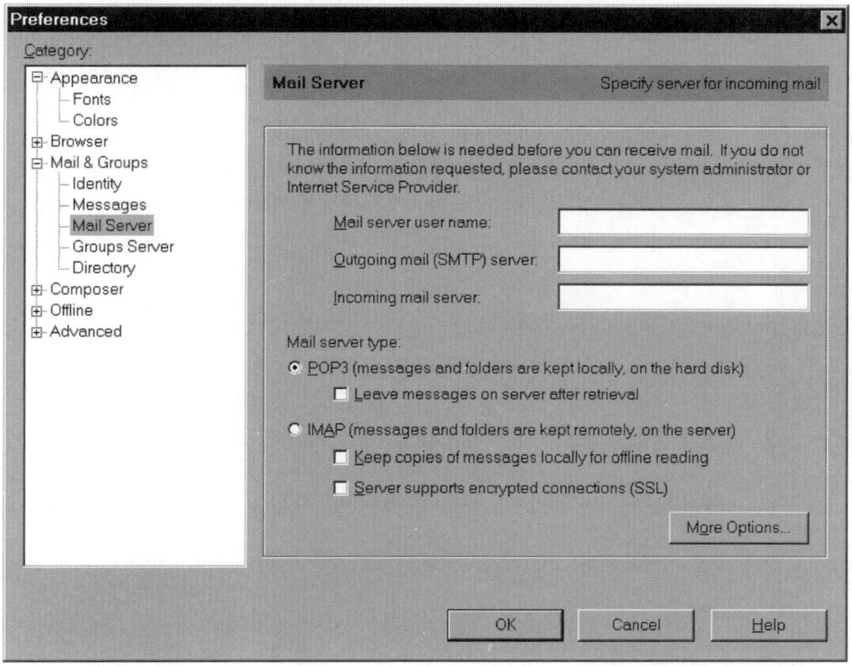

Figure 17.4 You need to fill in your mail server options in order to send and receive mail.

There are more options accessible with the More Options button, but we'll get to these later. Let's get your mail server information recorded.

Configuring Your Mail Server

In the Preferences dialog box, click Mail Server (under Mail & Groups) to configure your mail server options. You can't send or receive mail unless you've filled in the needed information on this page, shown in Figure 17.4.

Adding the Server Information Here's the important part. Please make sure that you type this information correctly, based on what your ISP gave you.

To fill out your server information:

1. In the Mail server user name box, type your user name or mailbox name, exactly as your ISP gave it to you. This probably isn't the same thing as your real name, but rather a nickname that might include part of your name or initals and some other stuff (like mcp4e or barnaby9). If you're not sure what your user name is, call your ISP.
2. In the Outgoing Mail (SMTP) server box, type the name of your ISP's outgoing (SMTP) server. This will be a computer name, with the parts of the name separated by dots (such as mail.earlysville.net). Don't include any spaces.
3. In the Incoming Mail server box, type the name of your ISP's incoming (POP or POP3) mail server. This will also be a computer name. It probably is the same as the Outgoing Mail server name, but it could be different. Even if the Incoming Mail server name is the same as the Outgoing Mail server name, type it here. You have to fill in this box.

Choosing the Mail Server Type Messenger can work with two different types of mail servers:

- **POP3** With this type of server, your mail is stored temporarily on your service provider's system. When you get your mail, the server downloads the mail to your hard disk, and that's where it's stored. The bad thing about POP3 servers is that, once you've accessed your mail, it's downloaded to your computer, and that's the only place you can read it. If you access your server from a notebook computer or somebody else's system, the only messages that you'll see are the ones that have come in since you last downloaded your mail. To be sure, you can check Leave messages on server after retrieval, but I don't recommend this. Many service providers place an upper limit on how many messages you can store in a POP3 server. If you exceed this limit, the mail server will reject your incoming mail and you'll never see it. That's bad.
- **IMAP** With this type of server, your mail is stored permanently on your company's mail server system. You can choose to keep copies of messages locally for offline reading. Some IMAP servers enable SSL encryption of mail messages while they're en route; check with your company to find out.

By default, Netscape is set up to work with POP3 servers. If you're not sure which type of server you're working with, call your service provider or your company's network support staff.

Choosing More Mail Server Preferences When you're finished filling out the server information in the Mail Server page, click More Options, the button at the bottom of the page. You'll see the More Mail Server Preferences dialog box, shown in Figure 17.5.

The default settings for mail storage are fine. What's of concern here are the following two options:

- **Check for Mail** If you would like Messenger to check your server for new mail automatically, click this option and supply a time interval (such as every 5 or 10 minutes). What happens if you don't check this option? You'll have to click Get Msg (in the Messenger window) to see whether any new mail has come in.

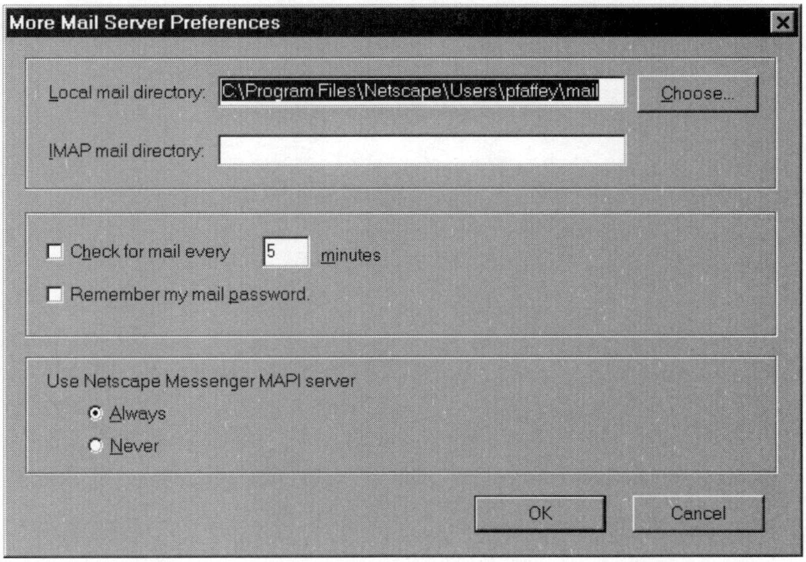

Figure 17.5 Here you can tell Messenger to check your mail automatically.

- **Remember My Mail Password** By default, Netscape prompts you to supply your mail password. If you check this option, Netscape "remembers" your password and you don't have to supply it every time the program accesses your mailbox. However, you shouldn't choose this option if somebody else uses your computer. With this option checked, anyone can read your mail.

My service provider is angry because I've been connected for 48 hours straight! Although ISPs offer "unlimited access," they actually have fewer modems than subscribers. If you stay online all the time, you make it more difficult for others to access the service. Chances are pretty good your computer was unattended most of that time. Normally, ISPs log you off after a set period of inactivity, such as 30 minutes, but setting up automatic mail checking disables this—so far as your ISP knows, you're sitting right there at your computer, clicking Get Msg every five minutes. Moral: If you click Check for Mail, be sure to log off when you're not going to be using your computer for a while. Be nice.

Choosing Message Formats

Now that you've finished setting your server options, go back to the Mail & Groups page. There's no real need to change any of the default settings, which are fine, but you can if you wish. The first area controls how Messenger displays quoted text when you make a reply. You can choose the style, size, and color. The second section enables you to choose a fixed or variable width for displaying your mail.

Some people like to include cute little ASCII art pictures in the signature they append to their messages. However, these won't look good if you choose a variable width font. If you're viewing your mail with a variable width font, don't make yourself look dumb by writing back to somebody and saying their picture is scrambled! Switch to a fixed width font. Chances are the picture will look a lot better.

The third section of the Mail & Groups page enables you to choose options about reusing windows and sounding alerts when new mail arrives. Try working with all of these options switched on, for now.

Understanding How Messenger's Windows Work

Now that you've configured Netscape for your e-mail account, it's time to open the e-mail window and log on to your server. In this section, you learn how the various Messenger windows work together.

The Message Center

The Message Center (Figure 17.6) is a Grand Central Station for all of your communications, including e-mail and newsgroups. Within the window, you see the mail and news servers that you've linked to (here, there's one mail server and two news servers). Let's leave the news part aside for now—we'll get to that later—and look more closely at the e-mail portion of Messenger. To display the Message Center, click Communicator on the menu bar, and choose Message Center, or press Ctrl + Shift + 1.

The Local Mail item stores all of your mail in named folders. Under Local Mail, you see the following folders:

- **Inbox** Here's where incoming messages go. When you contact your mail server, Messenger downloads all the new messages to your Inbox, where you can read and respond to them.
- **Outbox** Outgoing messages are stored here temporarily until Messenger sends them to your mail server.
- **Drafts** Here's where you can store messages temporarily while you're working on them.
- **Sent** This folder contains copies of all the messages you've sent.
- **Trash** This folder contains messages that you've deleted. It's emptied when you quit Netscape Communicator.

To see the contents of any of these, just double-click the folder name. For example, to see the contents of the Inbox, just double-click this folder's name. You'll see an Inbox with new messages, such as the one shown in Figure 17.7.

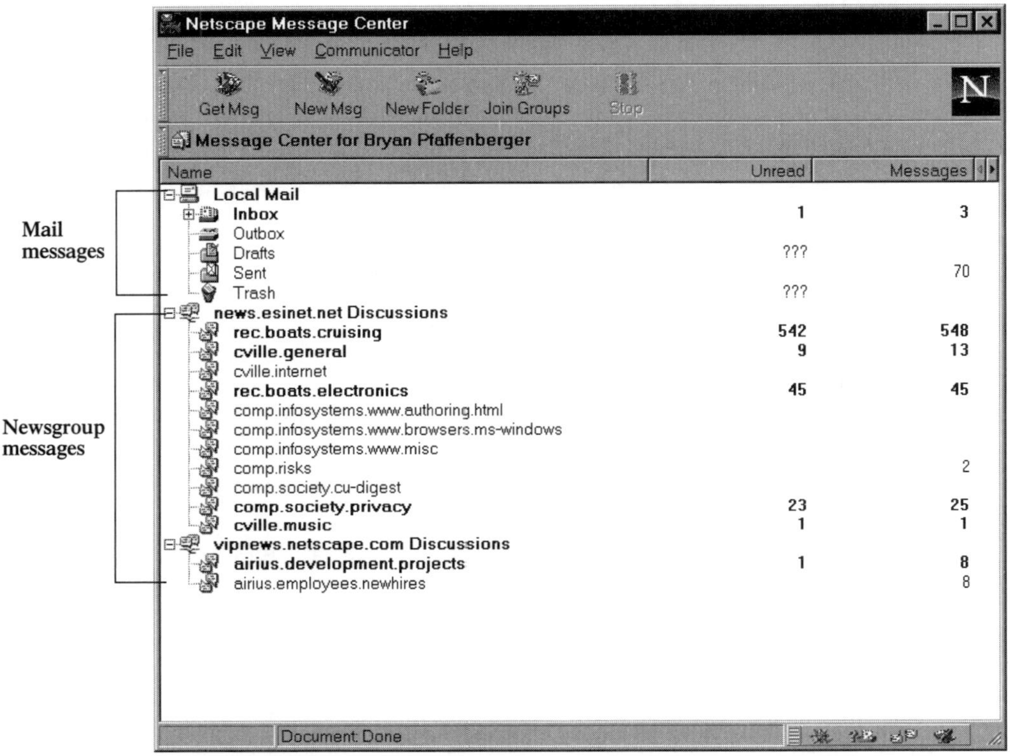

Figure 17.6 The Message Center groups all your e-mail and newsgroup messages, both incoming and outgoing.

The Messenger Mailbox Window

When you're accessing your mail, it's better to start with the Messenger Mailbox, rather than the Message Center—doing so saves you a step, since you don't have to click Inbox to see your mail. To open your Inbox directly without having to go through the Message Center, click the Communicator menu on any Communicator menu bar, and choose Messenger Mailbox (you can also press Ctrl + 2).

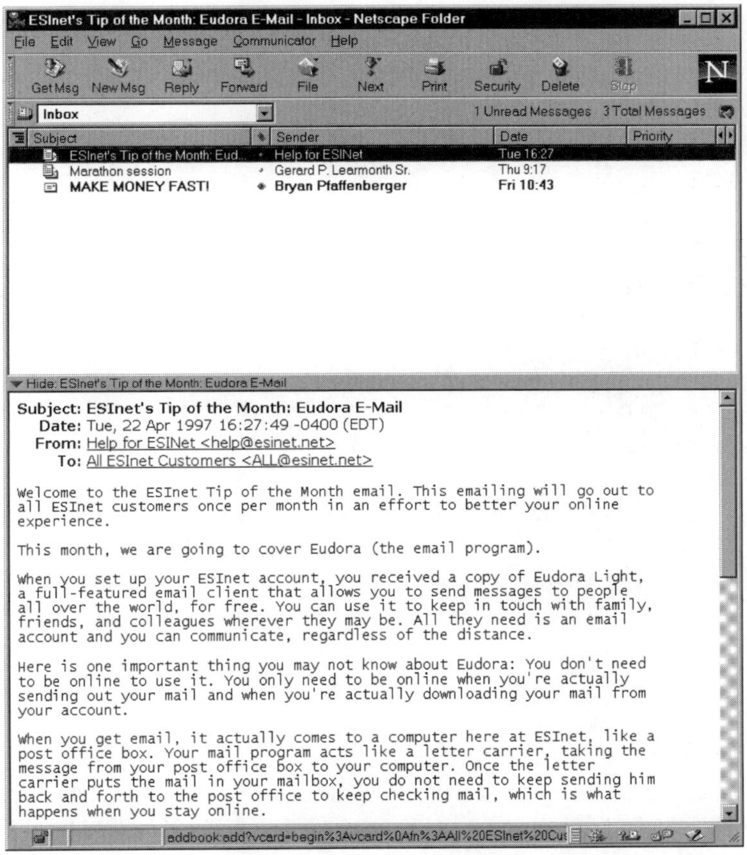
ESInet's Tip of the Month: Eudora E-Mail - Inbox - Netscape Folder
File Edit View Go Message Communicator Help
Get Msg New Msg Reply Forward File Next Print Security Delete Stop
Inbox
1 Unread Messages 3 Total Messages
Subject Sender Date Priority
ESInet's Tip of the Month: Eud... Help for ESINet Tue 16:27
Marathon session Gerard P. Learmonth Sr. Thu 9:17
MAKE MONEY FAST! Bryan Pfaffenberger Fri 10:43
Hide: ESInet's Tip of the Month: Eudora E-Mail
Subject: ESInet's Tip of the Month: Eudora E-Mail
Date: Tue, 22 Apr 1997 16:27:49 -0400 (EDT)
From: Help for ESINet <help@esinet.net>
To: All ESInet Customers <ALL@esinet.net>
Welcome to the ESInet Tip of the Month email. This emailing will go out to all ESInet customers once per month in an effort to better your online experience.
This month, we are going to cover Eudora (the email program).
When you set up your ESInet account, you received a copy of Eudora Light, a full-featured email client that allows you to send messages to people all over the world, for free. You can use it to keep in touch with family, friends, and colleagues wherever they may be. All they need is an email account and you can communicate, regardless of the distance.
Here is one important thing you may not know about Eudora: You don't need to be online to use it. You only need to be online when you're actually sending out your mail and when you're actually downloading your mail from your account.
When you get email, it actually comes to a computer here at ESInet, like a post office box. Your mail program acts like a letter carrier, taking the message from your post office box to your computer. Once the letter carrier puts the mail in your mailbox, you do not need to keep sending him back and forth to the post office to keep checking mail, which is what happens when you stay online.

Figure 17.7 The Messenger Mailbox enables you to view the contents of a mail folder.

The Messenger Mailbox window has its own menu and tool bar, which we'll examine in a moment. For now, note that the window is divided into two panes:

- **Message List Pan** Here you'll see the messages that you've received. You'll see the subject of the message, the sender's name, and the date received.
- **Message Pane** Here you see the text of the message that's currently selected in the message header pane.

With the mouse, you can adjust the size of the window panes. Just drag on the borders to do so. You might try decreasing the size of the message list pane—it doesn't need so much room—so that there's more room to display the message pane.

You can quickly hide the message page by clicking the down arrow next to Hide, on the bar separating the two panes. To restore the message pane, click the up arrow on the status bar.

Displaying More Information about Messages

The Messenger Mailbox window displays three or four columns of information about the mail that's stored in the folder. If you click the little left arrow at the right edge of the button bar (just above the message list), you can see more columns, as shown in Figure 17.8.

To sort the mail list, just click one of the buttons at the top of a column. For example, to sort the message list by Sender, click the Sender button. By default, Messenger sorts in ascending order (a, b, c, or 1, 2, 3); if you wish, you can change the sort order to descending order (z, x, y, etc.). To change the sort order, click View on the menu bar, choose Sort, and choose Descending or Ascending from the pop-up menu. If you like to sort your messages by Date (a good choice for e-mail), choosing Descending is a great idea. You'll see your most recently received messages at the top of the list.

- **Thread** This is the first column, and it takes a little explanation. Messenger is capable of *threading* the messages you've received—that is, grouping them by subject. If you see a *thread icon* in the first column, you know that Messenger has grouped two or more messages. The Messages column (the last column to the right) shows how many messages are included in the thread. To see all the messages in the thread, click the plus sign next to the threaded message. When you sort your messages by thread, the overall sort order is by date, except that messages with the same subject are grouped together.
- **Subject** In this column, you see the message's subject. If you click the Subject button, Messenger sorts the list by subject.

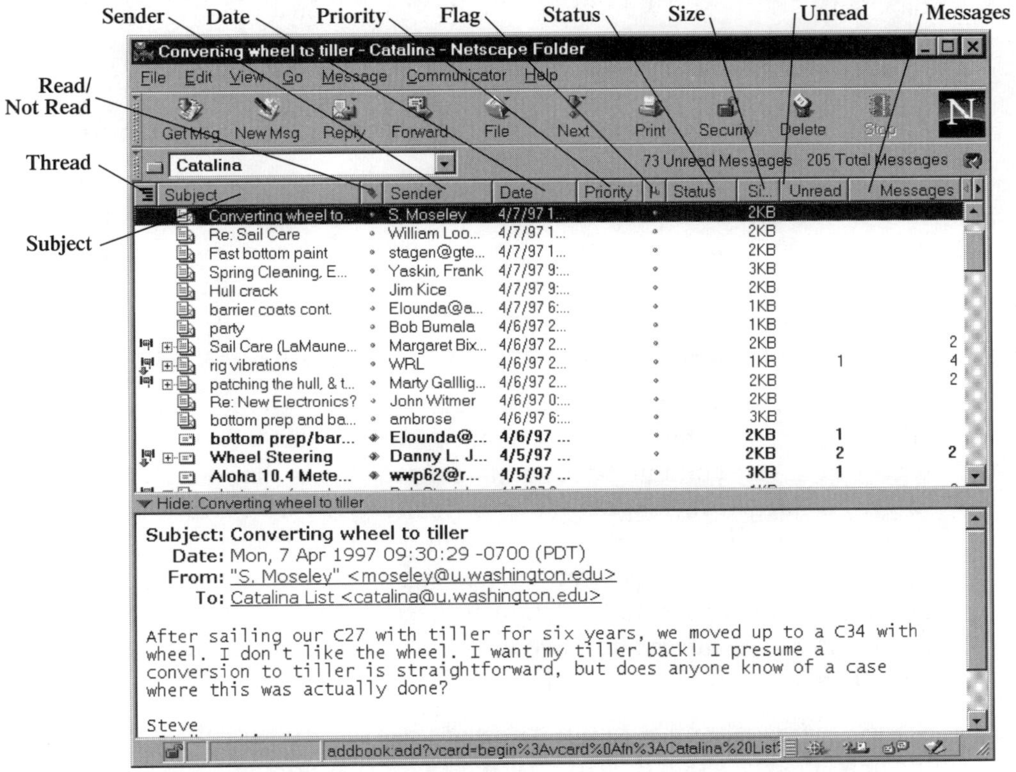
Sender
Date
Priority
Flag
Status
Size
Unread
Messages
Read/ Not Read
Thread
Subject
Converting wheel to tiller - Catalina - Netscape Folder
Subject: Converting wheel to tiller
Date: Mon, 7 Apr 1997 09:30:29 -0700 (PDT)
From: "S. Moseley" <moseley@u.washington.edu>
To: Catalina List <catalina@u.washington.edu>
After sailing our C27 with tiller for six years, we moved up to a C34 with wheel. I don't like the wheel. I want my tiller back! I presume a conversion to tiller is straightforward, but does anyone know of a case where this was actually done?
Steve

Figure 17.8 You can see more information about your messages, if you wish

- **Read/Not Read** This column, headed by a little green diamond, enables you to sort your message list by whether you've read the messages. Messages you've read have a small diamond icon. Messages that you haven't read have a larger diamond icon, and they appear in bold face type. Also, read messages have a different icon in the Subject column. The "read" icon shows a letter that's been taken out of its envelope. The "unread" icon has a little green arrow and a document icon.
- **Sender** This column shows the sender's name or nickname. Unfortunately, there's no standard that would enforce consistency in the order of first and last names, so some people's messages will be sorted by their first name rather than their last name. Also, some people don't configure their e-mail programs properly, so that their e-mail address

appears instead of their names. And then there are the people who use nicknames, such as "Wildcat" or "Caveman," instead of real names. In spite of all this variation, sorting by sender is very useful because it enables you to group all the messages from a particular sender.

- **Date** This column shows the date that the message was sent. Sorting by date is a good choice for e-mail.
- **Priority** Some mail programs enable users to add priorities to their messages. By default, messages have Normal priority, and nothing shows up in the Priority column. Some messages are flagged with Urgent priority; others are flagged with Low priority. If the sender has chosen one of these, you'll find out in the Priority column.
- **Flag** If you wish, you can flag a message (select the message, and choose Flag from the Message menu). After you flag a message, you see a flag in this column. Sorting the message list by flag enables you to group flagged messages. What is this for? It's up to you, really. Keep it in mind as a way to mark and group messages for convenience purposes. For example, suppose I wanted to group all the messages that pertain to a certain project, even though they come from different senders and have all sorts of different subjects. Flagging them enables me to do this.
- **Status** This column is blank for read messages. It contains "new" for new messages or "replied" for messages that you've replied to.
- **Size** This column shows the size of the message, in kilobytes (KB). Click the Size button to sort your messages by size.
- **Unread** This column shows how many unread messages are stored in a thread. This column is needed because, by default, Messenger collapses threads. Without the number in this column, you wouldn't know how many messages are contained in the thread unless you clicked the plus sign next to the first threaded message's subject.
- **Messages** This column shows how many messages, read or unread, are stored in a thread. It's needed for the same reason you need the Unread column.

How many columns do you really need to show? For mail, you don't really need the last two columns—they're useful for mailing lists and newsgroups, though, but they're dispensable even for these. Click the little right or left arrows until you've adjusted the column display to your liking. I prefer to view Subject, Sender, and Date only; this leaves plenty of room for the sender's name and all or most of the subject.

The Mail Window's Menu Bar

The mail window's menu bar differs from the browser window's button bar, although there are some familiar menus (File, Edit, View, Go, Communicator, and Help). As you'll see, these menus contain some unique, mail-related options, and there's a new menu, Message, which gives you message-related options.

As with other Communicator windows, the most frequently used options are available on the toolbar. The menus contain the same commands that the toolbar offers, as well as some less frequently used commands. Take a moment to explore the menus just to get a sense of what these options are and how they're grouped. We'll get into the specifics as they're needed.

I'm getting sick of saving all my message! Don't! There's no need to choose Save from the File menu. By default, Messenger saves your incoming mail in the Inbox folder, and your outgoing mail in the Sent folder. You only need to save a mail message if you'd like to incorporate the message in some other application.

The Navigation Toolbar

The Mail window's Navigation toolbar enables you to choose frequently used options quickly. Here's a quick rundown of what these buttons do; you'll learn more about them later.

Click here to see if there are any new messages waiting for you on the server.

Click here to compose a new message.

Click here to write a reply to the sender. If you hold down the mouse button when you click this button, you'll see additional reply options.

Click here to forward the message to someone.

Click here to display a menu of folders. When you choose a folder, Messenger stores the message in that folder.

Click here to display the next unread message.

Click here to print the message.

Click here to display security information about this message.

Click here to stop downloading a lengthy, unwanted message.

Click here to delete the selected message.

The Folder Toolbar

Below the Navigation toolbar, you see the Folder toolbar. In the list box, you see the name of the folder you're currently viewing. To the left of the list box, you see the folder's icon (different types of folders have their own, distinctive icon, as you'll see by viewing the folder list). These icons help you differentiate between Messenger's built-in folders (such as Inbox, Sent, and Trash), and the folders you create. Also on the Folder toolbar is a list of the number of unread and the total number of messages; the little green arrow icon at the extreme right of the toolbar enables you to return to the Message Center.

You can use the folder list box to change the folder you're viewing. Click the down arrow, and choose the folder you want to see. You'll see that folder's messages in the Mail window.

The Status Bar

At the bottom of the screen, you'll see the status bar. This bar contains a security icon. You can click this icon to see security information about the selected message. There's also a progress indicator, a message area, and the component bar (unless you've moved it).

The Mail Window's Pop-up Menu

As you know, you can right-click just about anything on Communicator's windows, and see a pop-up menu with options relevant to what you're doing. The Mail window's pop-up menu is particularly useful (see Figure 17.9). From this menu, you can choose just about everything you'd want to do to a message. If you like pop-up menus, this one's really useful.

Creating a Signature

You're almost ready to get started with sending and receiving e-mail, as discussed in the next chapter! Before you do, though, take a moment to create a signature. You can do this with Notepad or any other text editor that's capable of saving plain ASCII text (no formatting). Don't use a word processing program for this unless you know how to save your text as plain text.

What should you put in your signature? It depends. If you're using e-mail for professional purposes, you should include professional contact information, such as your full name and title, organizational affiliation, address, work phone number, and work fax number. If you're using e-mail for personal purposes, you could include your name and perhaps a short quotation that sums up your view of life. Don't include your home phone number, though, unless you send mail only to people you can trust.

From Here

- Now that you've configured Messenger and set up your "sig," it's time to get into e-mail! In the next chapter, you'll learn how to send

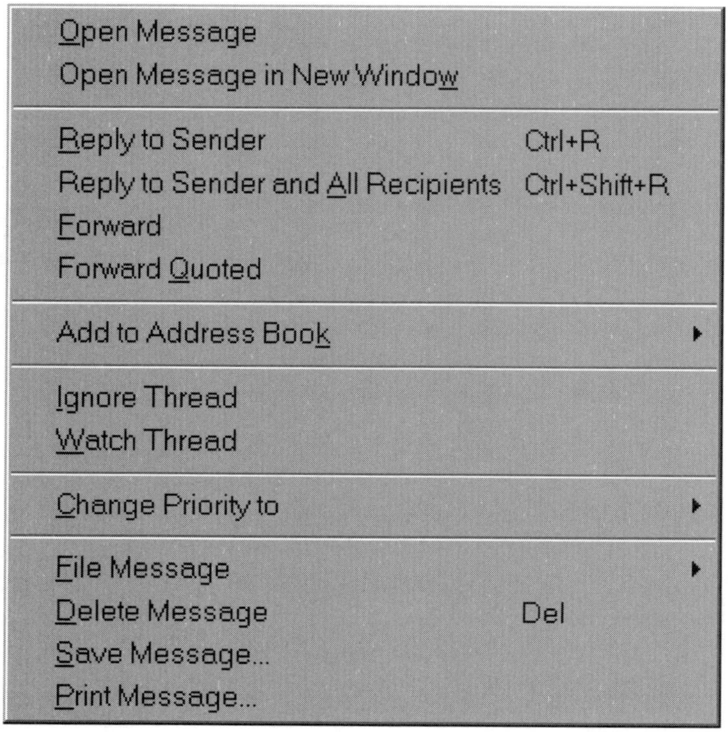

Figure 17.9 To see this menu, right-click a message in the Mail window.

and receive e-mail messages using the cool features of Communicator, including richly formatted (HTML) messages.

- In Chapter 19, you'll get into advanced e-mail. You'll learn how to organize your mail into folders, how to write rules that sort incoming mail automatically, and how to send and receive encrypted (secure) e-mail. Get ready for the next generation of mail technology!

Chapter 18

Sending and Receiving E-mail

The Web is neat, but most people say that e-mail is the most useful thing about the Internet. In this chapter, you'll learn how to make the most out of e-mail with Communicator's convenient but powerful features. Let's get going!

Logging On to Your Server

To log on to your server and download any mail that might be waiting for you, choose Inbox from the Messenger Mailbox window's folder list. Then click Get Msg. (You can also click File on the menu bar, choose Get Messages, and choose New from the submenu, or press Ctrl + T.)

If this is the first time you've logged on, you'll see a dialog box asking you to type your password. Do so, and click OK.

After you log on to the mail server, Netscape checks to see whether you've received any mail. If there's no mail for you, you'll see a dialog box informing you that no mail is waiting for you. Click OK to proceed.

If there is some mail for you, you'll see a new message header in the message header pane. To learn how to read and reply to your mail, see "Reading and Replying to Mail."

Composing and Sending Your First Message

Now that you've configured Netscape Mail and logged on to your server, it's time to send a message! You've probably got somebody's e-mail address—but if not, you can send a message to yourself. Either way, try it out!

For the Time-Challenged

- Messenger's Composition window enables you to create new messages, as well as to reply to or forward existing ones.
- Included is a first-rate spell checker, so you can avoid making yourself look dumb when you send e-mail or post to discussion groups.
- The Address Area has three panes—for addresses, attachments, and options. You can address your message to as many recipients as you wish.
- You can format your e-mail messages using the formatting tools in Messenger. For now, bear in mind that not all e-mail recipients can handle HTML-enhanced mail. Check with your correspondent before sending HTML-enhanced messages.
- You can attach files or Web pages to your message. Depending on the capabilities of your recipient's program, these attachments may appear in line (within the mail message). Otherwise, your recipient can save them and open them with the appropriate program.

To compose your message, click New Msg. (You can also open the File menu, choose New, and choose Message from the submenu. Another way: Choose New Message from the Message menu. Alternatively, use the Ctrl + M shortcut.) You'll see the Composition window, shown in Figure 18.1. If you've added a signature, as explained in the previous section, you'll see the sig text at the bottom of the message area.

We'll look more closely at the fine points of the Composition window in a bit. For now, fire off a message. If you don't have anyone's e-mail address to write to, write to yourself! It's a great way to test Messenger's capabilities.

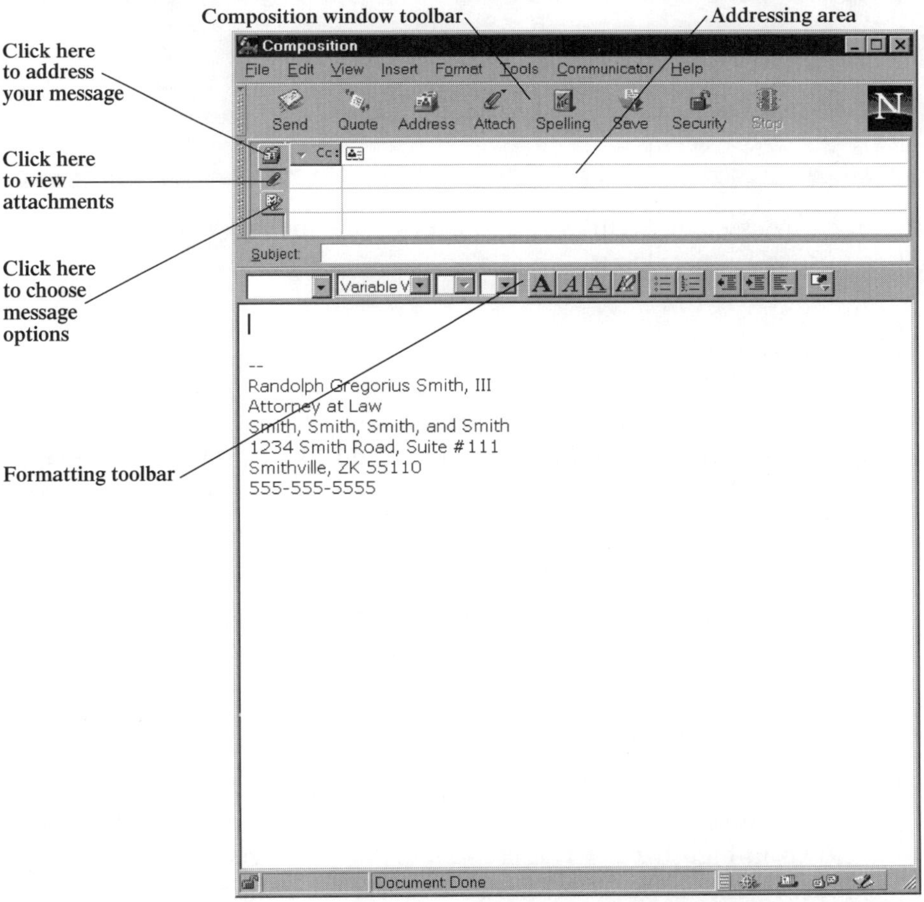

Figure 18.1 Message Composition window.

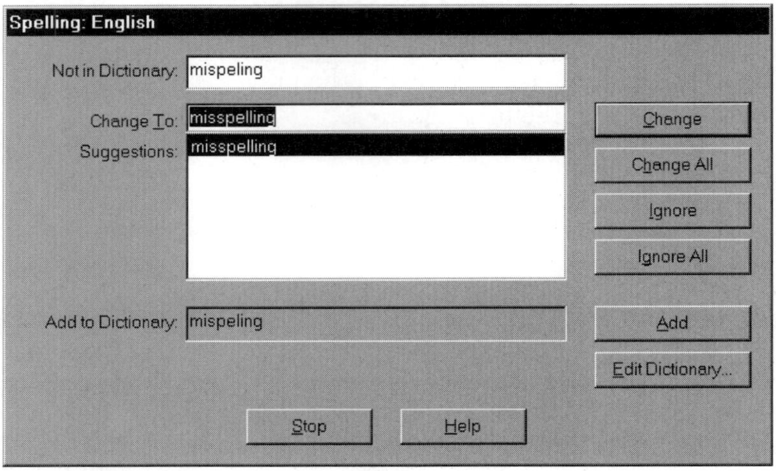

Figure 18.2 Messenger enables you to check your spelling before you send e-mail or post to Usenet. Do it!

To compose your message:

1. In the To box, type the e-mail address of the person to whom you're sending the message. If you would like to send the message to more than one person, type additional e-mail addresses, separated by semicolons (as in this example: jn@snoopy.virginia.edu; rm683e@grumpy.green.edu).
2. In the Subject box, type a subject line for your message. *Note*: Don't forget to do this. People get annoyed when they see messages without subjects.
3. In the message body area, type your message.
4. To check your message's spelling, click the Spelling button on the Composition window's toolbar. You'll see the Spelling dialog box, shown in Figure 18.2. If there's an error, you'll see a list of suggestions. If one of the suggestions is correct, highlight the suggestion and click Change (or Change All to change all instances of that misspelling throughout your letter). To ignore a word, click Ignore (or Ignore All to ignore all instances of the word). To add a cor-

rectly spelled word to the dictionary, click Add. When Messenger is done checking spelling, you'll see a dialog box that tells you that you're finished checking spelling. Click OK to continue.

5. To send your message, click Send to send the message now. After you send the message, Messenger writes a copy to your Sent folder, and you see the Messenger Mailbox again.

If you sent a message to yourself, wait a minute or two, then click Get Msg to receive your message.

I just sent off an angry letter and now I'm really sorry I did! The Send button sends your message right away—it doesn't give you any time to think whether it's really smart to have done this. If you're writing something that you're not sure you should send, do yourself a favor and click File on the menu bar, and choose Send Later. This command routes the message to your Outbox folder, and there it stays until you deliberately send it onward. Sleep on it—look at the message tomorrow, and see how you feel. You can edit the message by double-clicking it to bring it into the Composition window again; you can then click Send to send the message right away. To send all the messages in the Outbox, click File on the menu bar, and choose Send Messages in Outbox.

You've just sent your first e-mail message with Messenger. Congratulations! Now let's look at some of the finer points of sending messages.

Understanding the Composition Window

Netscape's Composition Window consists of several areas, shown in Figure 18.3. Here's a quick rundown of what's on screen:

- **Menu Bar** Like the other Communicator windows you've examined, this one has its own menu bar. There are some familar faces (File, Edit, View, Communicator, and Help), as well as some new ones (Insert, Format, and Tools). The new menus give you loads of commands from Composer, Communicator's HTML composition module.

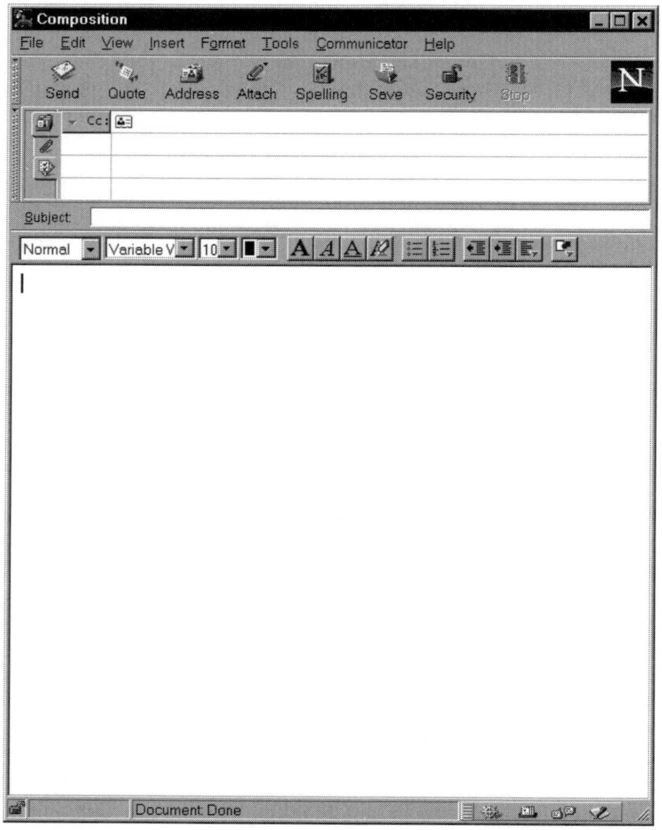

Figure 18.3 The Composition window has its own toolbars, as well as its own version of the Composer toolbar.

- **Message Toolbar** This toolbar contains the Composition windows most frequently accessed commands. You'll learn what these do in the next section.
- **Addressing Area** This area displays three different panes, depending on which of the little buttons you press. The default pane is the Address Pane. You can also display an Attachment Pane (for attachments), or an Options Pane (for choosing message options).
- **Subject** You type the message's subject in this box.

- **Formatting Toolbar** This toolbar includes many of Composer's most frequently chosen HTML commands. You can use these to send richly formatted e-mail messages to people using HTML-capable e-mail programs.

The Addressing Area has three panes, as I just mentioned. To see a pane, click its icon—there are three of them lined up in a column on the left of the Addressing Area. Alternatively, click the View menu, and choose Address Pane, Attachment Pane, or Options Pane.

What's on the Message Toolbar?

Here's a quick guide to the buttons you'll find on the Message Toolbar:

Sends your message right away (without routing it to the Outbox for later sending).

If you're replying to a message, this button inserts the text from the message you're replying to.

Displays the Address Book, so you can retrieve e-mail addresses that you've stored there.

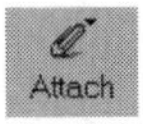

Enables you to add a file (an *attachment*) to send with your message.

Checks the spelling in your letter.

Saves a draft of this message in the Draft folder, so you can work on it later.

Displays security information and options for this message.

Enables you to stop sending a really lengthy message (or one with a lengthy file attachment). This button doesn't remain available very long when you're sending a short message.

I wrote this huge message, but it stinks, and I don't want to send it! You don't have to. Just click the close box in the Composition window. You'll see a dialog box asking you whether you really want to discard this message. Click Yes.

Fancy Message-Sending Tricks

Messenger enables you to do all sorts of cool things when you're sending mail, including formatting your message in rich HTML. This section introduces a lot of the tricks you'll want to use every day (the next chapter goes into the advanced stuff that you'll use less often).

Sending Your Message to More Than One Person

Try this: With the Composition window displayed, click the To button. You'll see a drop-down menu with lots of options. These are *addressing fields*, and you can use as many of these as you like. Here's a quick overview of what these fields do:

- **To** This is the field you use for the main recipient's e-mail address.
- **Cc** If you would like to send a carbon copy of this message to somebody, type the person's address in this field. The recipient will know that there was a carbon copy sent.
- **Bcc** If you want to send a carbon copy to somebody but don't want the recipient to know it, type the carbon copy recipient's e-mail address in this field.
- **Group** If you've created a list of e-mail addresses using Address Book (more about that in the next chapter), you can type the name of the group here to send a message to everyone in the group.
- **Reply-To** If you would like your recipient to reply to a different e-mail address than the one you're sending the message from, type the address in this field.
- **Followup-To** This is used for Usenet posts. More about that in a subsequent chapter!

To address your message, do the following:

1. In the Composition window, the first address pane line has a To label. That's fine—just go ahead and type the recipient's address in the first line.
2. Click the box just below the To box. Messenger adds another To box on the second line.
3. From the second line's To box, choose the addressing field you want to use. For example, to send a carbon copy of your letter to somebody, choose Cc. Type the recipient's name in the second line.

   If you want to send the message as a To message to more than one person, just leave the To box set to To, and type an address. You can repeat this as many times as you wish.
4. Repeat steps 2 and 3 to add as many additional recipients as you like. When you've used up the four standard lines, a scroll bar appears (see Figure 18.4).

Getting a Return Receipt

Like to know whether your message has been delivered? If so, click the Message Sending Options button in the Composition window's Address Area (it's the lowest of the three buttons in this area), and click Return Receipt. You'll get a notice back pretty quick if the message was successfully delivered to the person's mailbox.

I can't get this person to respond! It doesn't necessarily mean that you're being ignored, although that's always a possibility, frankly! It could mean that the person hasn't logged on to his or her mail for a while. A common reason: People go on vacations or out-of-town trips, and can't access their mail for a while. Don't bombard the person with repeat messages; you'll just fill up your recipient's mailbox and create ill will.

Choosing Priorities

By default, Netscape sends messages with Normal priority, which means that—with most mail programs—nothing special pops up in your recipient's message list. You can also send messages with Lowest, Low, High, and

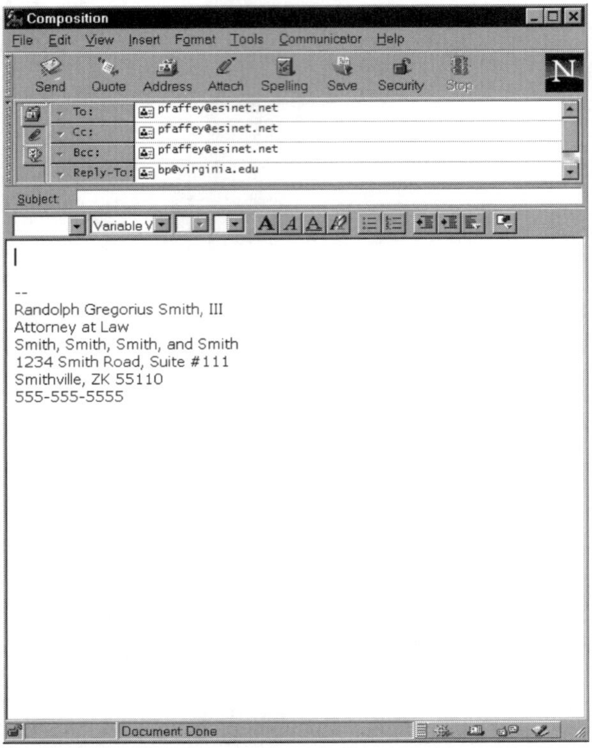

Figure 18.4 In the Address pane, you can add as many addresses as you wish.

Highest priority. Most mail programs can detect the Low and High priorities, which will show up (somehow or other) in the message list. (Messenger displays the text of the priority, such as "Low," in the Priority column; some programs display icons denoting priority levels.)

To choose a priority level for your message other than Normal, click the Message Sending Options button in the Address Area (it's the lowest of the three buttons in this area). In the Priority list box, choose the priority you want (choose from Low or High for compatibility with other mail programs). Human nature being what it is (i.e., egotistical), I don't suppose all that many of you will choose Low, and even fewer will choose Lowest. But then again, you never know.

Don't overuse High priority—that would be like the fable about the boy who cried "Wolf" to the point that nobody listened to him when a real wolf appeared.

Adding Rich Formatting

Are you sending e-mail to somebody whose e-mail program can read HTML? If so, you can add a lot of pizazz to your message by adding formatting. The formatting tools in Messenger are a subset of Composer's tools, which you'll learn about in Part VI of this book. I won't go into the details of these tools now—that's what Part VI is for—but you might want to play around with them a bit. Try sending a richly formatted message to yourself, and see how it looks (see Figures 18.5 and 18.6 for a tasty example).

This message is 161 KB! Well, that's the downside of sending richly formatted messages. If you include graphics, like I did (see Figure 18.5), the message is going to be a lot bigger than one containing just text. If you're concerned about message size, lay off the graphics.

The Formatting Toolbar Here's a quick guide to the formatting tools you'll see on the Formatting toolbar:

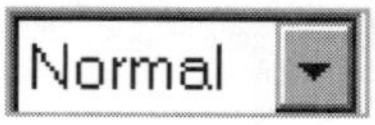

Choose HTML tags here (Normal, Headings 1 through 7, Address, Formatted List Item, Description Title, or Description Text).

Click here to choose a font for your message. Remember, your recipient can't see the font unless it's installed on the recipient's system.

Click here to choose a font size.

Click here to choose a text color.

Click here to format your text in bold.

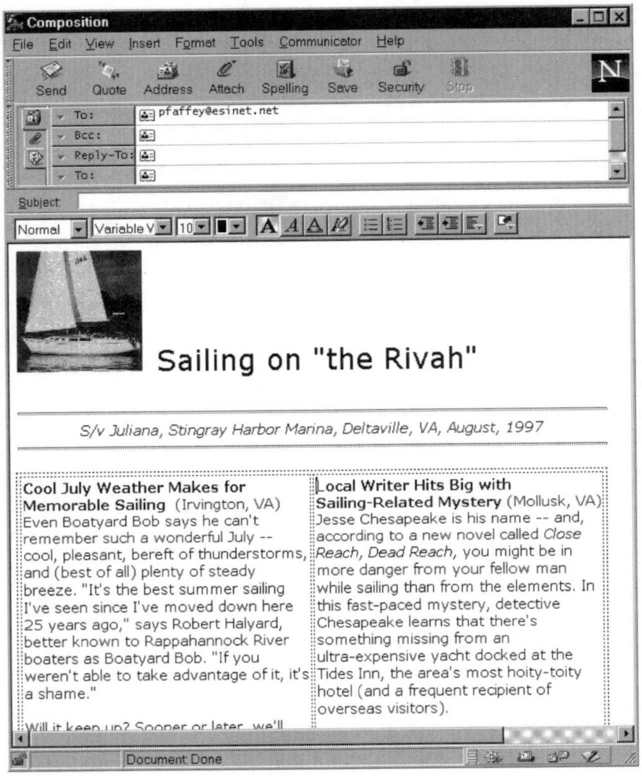
Composition
File Edit View Insert Format Tools Communicator Help
Send Quote Address Attach Spelling Save Security Stop
To: pfaffey@esinet.net
Bcc:
Reply-To:
To:
Subject:
Normal
Variable W
10
Sailing on "the Rivah"
S/v Juliana, Stingray Harbor Marina, Deltaville, VA, August, 1997
Cool July Weather Makes for Memorable Sailing (Irvington, VA) Even Boatyard Bob says he can't remember such a wonderful July -- cool, pleasant, bereft of thunderstorms, and (best of all) plenty of steady breeze. "It's the best summer sailing I've seen since I've moved down here 25 years ago," says Robert Halyard, better known to Rappahannock River boaters as Boatyard Bob. "If you weren't able to take advantage of it, it's a shame."
Local Writer Hits Big with Sailing-Related Mystery (Mollusk, VA) Jesse Chesapeake is his name -- and, according to a new novel called Close Reach, Dead Reach, you might be in more danger from your fellow man while sailing than from the elements. In this fast-paced mystery, detective Chesapeake learns that there's something missing from an ultra-expensive yacht docked at the Tides Inn, the area's most hoity-toity hotel (and a frequent recipient of overseas visitors).
Document Done

Figure 18.5 Here's what a richly formatted message looks like when you're composing it.

Click here to format your text in italics.

Click here to format your text with underlining.

Click here to remove formats from the selected text.

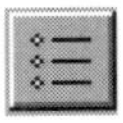
Click here to add a bulleted list to your message.

Figure 18.6 And here's what a richly formatted message looks like on receipt.

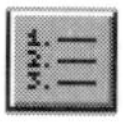

Click here to add a numbered list to your message.

Decrease indent of paragraph one level.

Increase indent of paragraph one level.

Click here to choose paragraph alignments (flush left, centered, or flush right).

Click here to insert something into your letter. You can choose from a hyperlink, a target (a place to jump to within your document), an image, a horizontal line, or a table.

There's a lot to learn about using these tools, but for now, you can use them almost as if you'd use a word processing program's tools. You'll learn about Composer (as well as all the advanced options accessible on the menu bars) in Part VI.

If you know that your recipient can't receive HTML and you don't want to inadvertently send any, click the Message Sending Options button in the Address Area, and choose Plain Text only from the Format box.

Sending a Richly FormattedMessage When you send a message that includes HTML formatting, Messenger jumps in to warn you that your recipient might not have an HTML-capable e-mail program, so you'll see the HTML Mail Question dialog box shown in Figure 18.7. You have the following options:

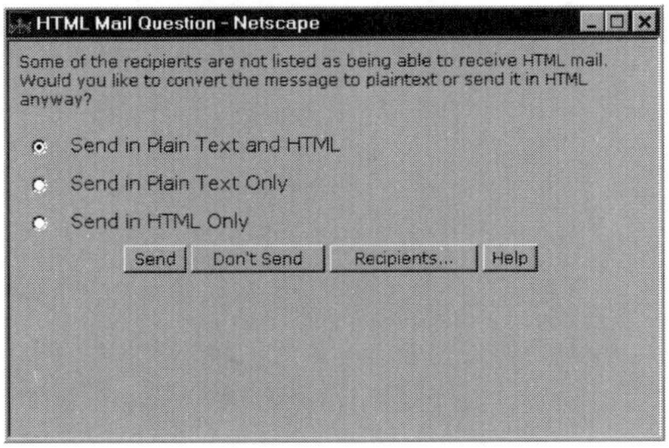

Figure 18.7 This dialog box appears when you send a richly formatted message.

- **Send in Plain Text and HTML** This sends the message in both formats, so the user can pick one.
- **Send in Plain Text Only** This is for people who don't have HTML-capable e-mail programs.
- **Send in HTML Only** This is for people that you know have HTML-capable e-mail programs.

Choose one of these options, and click Send.

Identifying HTML-Capable Recipients If you know that certain recipients of your messages have HTML-capable e-mail programs, you can add their names to an HTML-capable recipient list. Here's how:

1. Prepare the message, and click Send. You'll see the HTML Mail Question dialog box, shown in Figure 18.7.
2. Click Recipients. You'll see the HTML Recipients dialog box shown in Figure 18.8.
3. In the Does Not Prefer HTML pane (the default for all new recipients), select the person's name or e-mail address.

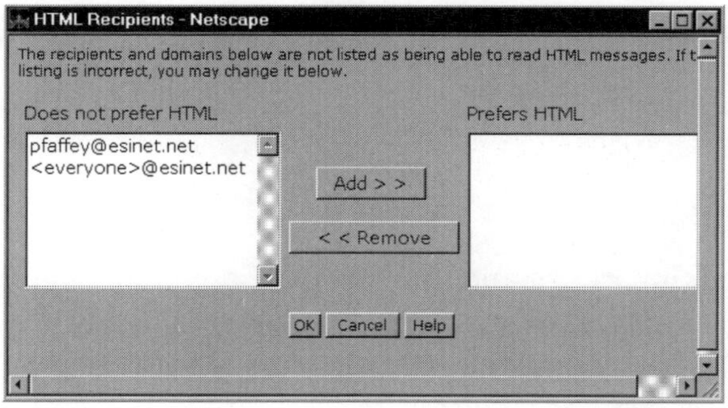

Figure 18.8 You can choose just who gets HTML-formatted mail.

4. Click Add. You'll see the person's name or e-mail address in the Prefers HTML pane.
5. Click OK.

After you identify somebody as HTML-capable, they'll get HTML e-mail automatically when you send them a letter.

You can also specify a recipient's HTML capabilities in the Address Book. For more information, see the section on the Address Book, in the next chapter.

I thought the person could get HTML, but they can't, and they're mad! They're seeing what looks like a lot of garbage on screen. To take the person off your HTML list, just follow the above steps next time you mail this person, and remove the person's name from the Prefers HTML pane.

Saving a Draft and Working On It Later

If you can't finish a message within the time you have available, click the Save button on the Composition window toolbar. (You can also click the File menu and choose Save Draft, or press Ctrl + S.) Then close the message by clicking the close box, or choose Close from the File menu (you can also press Ctrl + W).

To work on the message later, use the Messenger Mailbox window to open the Drafts folder. Select the message, and double-click it. You'll see the message in a Composition window. You can finish it and send it as you normally would.

Attaching a File

Using established Internet standards, Netscape enables you to include an attachment with your e-mail message. An *attachment* is a file that's carried along with your message. The standards that support sending and receiving attachments are called the Multipurpose Internet Multimedia Extensions (MIME). Thanks to these standards, you can send just about any computer file your system can create—formatted word processing files, graphics files (including bitmaps, JPEG, and GIF images), compressed files of any type, and even computer programs.

Will your recipient be able to receive the attachment? That depends. To receive a message that contains an attachment, your recipient must be using a computer that's directly connected to the Internet. In general, people using some outmoded on line services can't receive attachments, although they can receive Internet mail. In addition, the person must be using a MIME-compliant mail program, such as Messenger. Most decent mail programs are MIME-compliant.

To attach a file to your message, do the following:

1. In the Composition window, click the Attach button. You'll see a drop-down menu.
2. Choose File to attach a file. You'll see the Enter File to Attach dialog box.
3. Use this dialog box's navigation controls to locate and select the file you want to attach, and click Open.
4. In the Attachments pane, you'll see a list of the attachments you've added to your message. If you would like to delete an attachment, select it and click the Delete button.

If you're thinking about sending an attachment, bear in mind the capabilities of your recipient's system. Generally, it's pretty easy to send an attachment successfully to somebody who's using the same type of system and the same software you're using; problems occur, though, when Windows users send files to Mac users, and vice versa. A little advance planning can solve these problems. For example, if you're sending a Word for Windows document to somebody using a Macintosh and Microsoft Word 5.1, it might be wise to convert the file to the file format used by the Macintosh version of Word (Word for Windows can do this). The person to whom you send the file will then be able to open it with no problems.

I sent a file to somebody but they said it's garbage! No, they're not referring to the content of what you sent, but rather to the encoding. By default, Messenger uses MIME encoding to send attachments. If your recipient is using an e-mail program that dates to the Lower Paleolithic of e-mail, the program may not be able to handle MIME. Write to your correspondent, and ask whether his or her program can handle the older UUENCODE format. If so, compose a new message, and click the Message Sending Options button in the Address Area (it's the lowest of the three buttons in this area). Select Uuencode instead of MIME for attachments.

Attaching Web Pages and Address Book Cards

In addition to sending files, you can attach Web pages and Address Book Cards to your messages.

To add a Web page, click the Attach button, and choose Web page from the drop-down menu. In the dialog box, type the URL, and click OK. If the reciepient of your message is using an HTML-compliant e-mail program, the Web page appears within the person's Inbox (as shown in Figure 18.9).

To add your Address Book card to your message, click the Attach button, and choose My address book card. You filled out this card when you configured Messenger, as explained in the previous chapter. Also, note that not every mail program can read the Address Book files. They conform to a standard, but it's not very widely supported. At present, an Address Book card is no substitute for a signature.

Searching for Someone's E-mail Address

If you don't know a person's e-mail address, you can try searching one of the big Web-based e-mail directories. You can do this within Messenger. Here's how:

1. In the Composition window, click Address. You'll see the Select Addresses dialog box.
2. In the list box that says Personal Address Box, choose an online e-mail directory, such as Four11 or BigFoot.
3. Type the name you're looking for in the text box. If the service gives you a match, you'll see it in the list box, as shown in Figure 18.10.
4. Select the name of the person to whom you want to mail the message.
5. Click To. (If you want to send this person a carbon copy or blind carbon copy instead, click Cc: or Bcc:.)
6. Click OK.

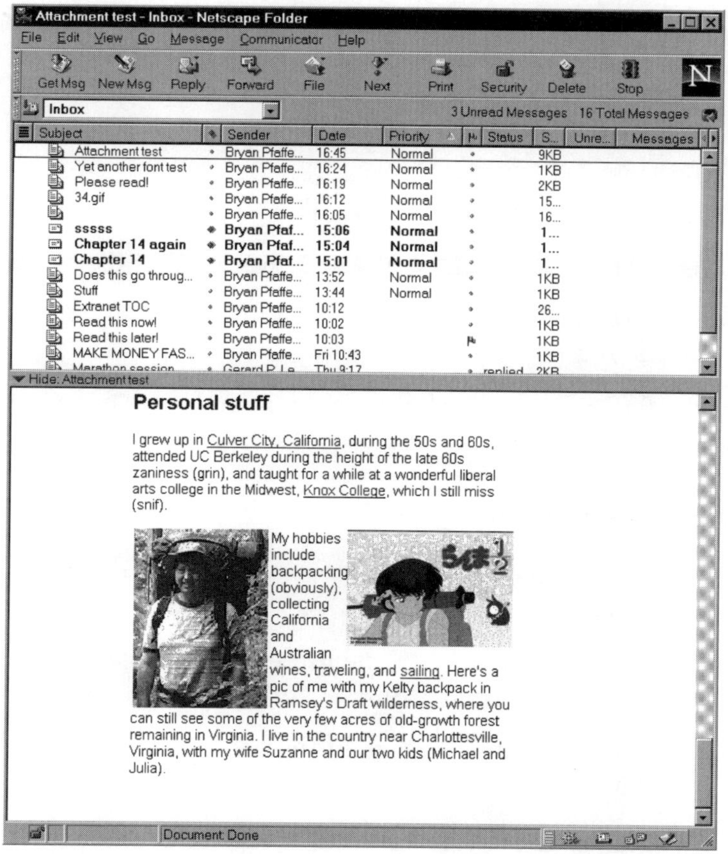

Figure 18.9 You can send a Web page to anyone; if they're using Communicator, the page appears within the mail window!

Reading and Replying to Mail

If you've set up Messenger to check your mail automatically at specified intervals, the program will automatically check for new mail. You can also check for new mail whenever you wish by clicking Get Msg in the Messenger Mailbox window. When you've got some new mail, you can read it, view the attachments (if any), reply to the mail you've received, forward the

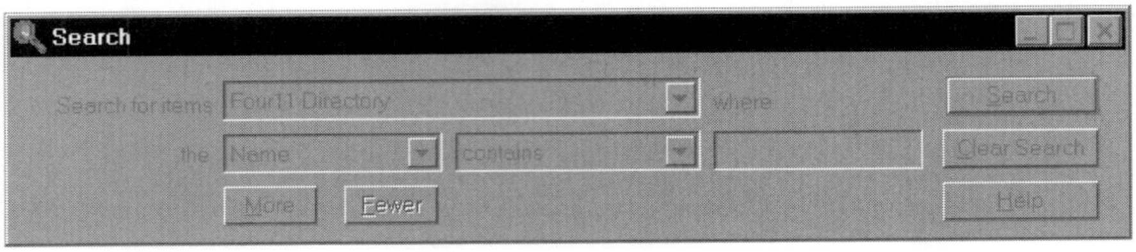

Figure 18.10 You can search for somebody's e-mail address using Four11 and other Internet-based e-mail directories.

mail to others, flag messages for later attention, and print messages. The following sections discuss each of these procedures in detail.

Navigating the Message List

The Next button gives you a great way to navigate the message list—but there are alternatives.

- To view the next message in the list, even if it's read, press Shift + N or choose Next Message from the Go menu.
- To view the previous message in the list, press Shift + P, or choose Previous Message from the Go menu.

Another way to navigate the message list is to open the message reading window, shown in Figure 18.11. To open a message in this window, just double-click it. This window has pretty much the same options as the Messenger Mailbox window. Click Next to go through your messages in this window.

Reading Your Mail

If you've received a new message, select the new message in the message list pane. You'll see the message text in the message pane.

Did you receive more than one message? To read the next unread message, click the Next button.

You'll soon find that your mailbox is filled with messages that you've already read. However, very few of them are worth keeping. Do yourself a favor and delete worthless messages

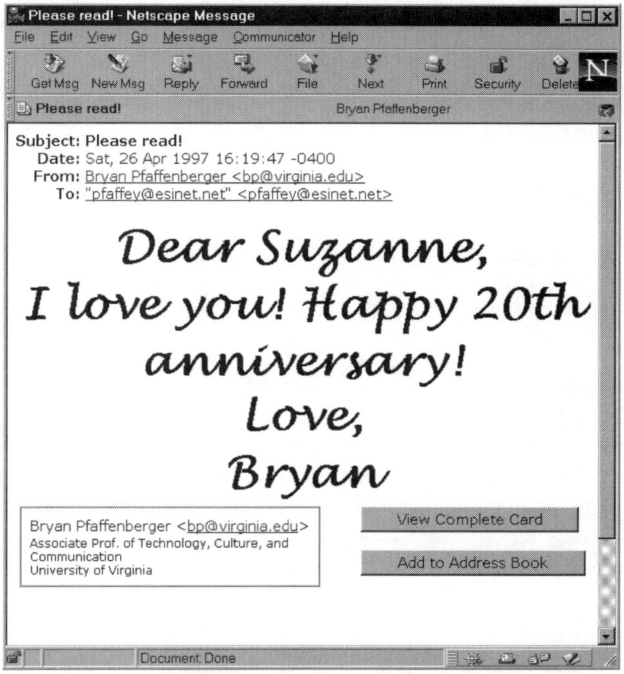

Figure 18.11 The message reading window gives you another way to read your messages.

right after you've finished reading them. To do so, click the Delete button. Note that this button doesn't actually delete the message—instead, it moves the message to the Trash folder, where you can recover it should you later decide that it wasn't so worthless after all.

Viewing Attachments

If you've received a message with one or more attachments, you can view the attachment in line (you actually see the attachment within the mail message, if Netscape can figure out how to display it) or as a link (to see the attachment, you click the link). Unless the attachment is very small, it's much more convenient to view the attachment as a link.

To control the way attachments are viewed, open the View menu, choose Attachments, and choose one of the following: Inline (to view attachments in the same window as the message) or Links (to view the attachment as a link).

Replying to Your Mail

To reply to a message, select the message in the message header pane, and click Reply. The Reply button displays a drop-down menu, with two options:

- **Reply to Sender** (shortcut: Ctrl + R) Send your reply only to the person who actually sent the mail to you.
- **Reply to Sender and All Recipients** (Shortcut: Ctrl + Shift + R) Send your reply to everyone who received a copy of the message, including carbon copy recipients, and other people listed on the To: line.

Normally, you should choose Reply to Sender.

I just sent a VERY personal reply to everyone in my company! Chose Reply to Sender and All Recipients, did you? Didn't notice that one of the addresses was a group list that echoes a copy to everyone on the whole network? Feeling a little embarrassed, are you? Don't let this happen to you. Always choose Reply to Sender unless you have some special, very well-thought-out reason to choose the other option. To stay on the safe side, initiate replies using the keyboard shortcut, Ctrl + R. This eliminates the chance that you'll choose Reply to Sender and All Recipients by mistake.

You'll see a Composition window. Netscape automatically filled in the sender's e-mail address (look at the To box), and the program has proposed a subject (using Re: followed by the original message's subject line). You can change the subject, if you wish. If you've set up Messenger to add your signature, that's added, too.

If you set up Messenger to quote the original message's text automatically, you'll see the text in the window. If not, and if you'd like to quote the text, click the Quote button. You'll see the quoted text in the window. Note that each line is preceded by a vertical bar character. If you send the message in plain text, these will be converted to greater than characters (>), in line with Internet usage. To experienced Internet users, these characters immediately convey that the following text is quoted.

Normally you shouldn't use all the quoted text. Edit the text down to just a line or two that you want to discuss.

When you reply, you can do all the tricks you'd do when writing a new message, such as adding rich formatting. To finish the reply, type your message, check your spelling, and click Send.

Forwarding Mail

To forward a message to someone, highlight the message in the message header panel, and click the Forward button (or press Ctrl + L). You'll see a message composition window. Note that Messenger has automatically included the message as an attachment.

Type text that explains why you're forwarding the message, and click Send.

If you're forwarding mail to somebody whose system can't handle attachments, you can forward the mail as quoted text. To do so, select the message, open the message menu, and choose Forward Quoted (or press Ctrl + Shift + L).

While you're working in the message list, you can use the right mouse key to display a pop-up menu. From this menu, you can reply, reply to all, forward, forward quoted, delete, save, and print messages.

Marking and Flagging Messages

When you're reading your mail, you'll often say to yourself, "I don't want to answer this right now" or "I'd better remember to look at this again, later, and do something about it." With many e-mail programs, the messages you've read disappear into a long, lengthy list of read messages, and you forget about them. With Netscape, though, you can mark messages as unread (even if you've read them). The message then shows up in bold in the message header pane, encouraging you to look at it again. If that's not enough, you can also put a red flag next to a message.

To mark a message as unread (even though you've read it), highlight the message in the message header pane. Then press the U Key (uppercase or lower). If you change your mind, press M.

To flag a message, click on the flag column next to the item's name. Click again to unflag the message.

Don't forget you can sort your message list quickly just by clicking one of the buttons at the top of the message list columns. To see all the unread or flagged messages grouped together, just click Unread or the flag button at the top of the flag column. (If you can't see these buttons, click the little right arrow on the button bar until these buttons come into view.)

Printing Messages

You can easily produce hard copy (printed output) of one or more messages. To see what the message will look like when printed, choose Print Preview from the File menu.

To print the message you're currently viewing, just click the Print button.

By default, Messenger prints your message with the preset headers and footers, including the message title, the message location, the page number, the page total, and the date printed. If you'd like to adjust these or any other print settings, choose Page Setup from the File menu, adjust the settings, and click OK.

Using Netscape Mail Notification

Windows 95/NT users can take advantage of Netscape Mail Notification, a program accessible from the Start menu. After you start this program, you'll see a new mail icon (an envelope) on the taskbar. When you're connected to the Internet, and you've got mail waiting, the icon sports a little red waving flag, alerting you that there's mail waiting. If you move the pointer to this icon, you'll see how many messages are waiting for you. If you right-click the icon, you'll see a pop-up menu with several options, including Check Now, Run Mail, and New Message. To select options, click Options on this menu;

you can change the mail-checking frequency, the sound that's played when mail arrives, and what happens when you click the mail notification icon.

Netscape Mail Notification is a cool accessory, and you might want to think about placing a shortcut to this program in the Startup menu (one of the menu items on the Program menu within the Start menu). This will start Netscape Mail Notification automatically at the beginning of each operating session. I don't really recommend this, though, if you're accessing the Internet by means of a dial-up modem line. Although you ostensibly have unlimited access, you really shouldn't stay connected when you're not actively using the network—doing so makes the service unavailable for others. Most service providers disconnect after a period of inactivity, but Netscape Mail Notification prevents this by sending mail check requests at specified intervals (by default, every five minutes).

Top E-mail Tips

Here's a quick list of my best tips for e-mail, based on what you've learned so far:

- Deal with mail immediately—reply to it or delete it. Don't let it sit around in your Inbox without doing anything to it right away. Otherwise, you may forget about the message.
- Go through your mail by opening the first new message in a mail reading window (to open this window, just double-click the message in the message list). In this window, you can reply to or delete each new message. Clicking Next takes you to the next unread message. In a short time, you'll have dealt with all your new mail.
- Edit quoted text to highlight just the portions of this text to which you'd like to respond. This makes things easier for your recipient, decreases download time, and reduces storage space on your recipient's mail server.
- Be superdiplomatic and nice. E-mail messages can come across as caustic or curt, even when you didn't mean this at all.

- When you're responding to a message with multiple recipients, be sure to reply only to the sender, unless you really want the reply to go to all recipients.
- Think twice before sending a message written in anger. Click the Save button to save it as a draft, get a night's sleep, and read it again in the morning. I'll bet you don't send it!
- Use Messenger's Directory search to hunt for old friends. Renewing friendships from the past is one of the Internet's greatest pleasures.

From Here

- By now, you're an e-mail maven, sending and receiving messages like mad. But it's time to learn the finer points. In the next chapter, you'll learn how to make full use of Messenger's many advanced options, including the Address Book, custom folders, filtering rules, and secure mail. This stuff may sound advanced, but once you've learned how to use it you won't want to work without it!

Chapter 19

Taking E-mail to the Max

You've already learned all the fundamentals of Internet e-mail the Messenger way, but there's more to learn. For example, you're probably having quite a time keeping track of e-mail addresses, and don't you agree that they're a pain to type? In this chapter, you'll learn how to create Address Book entries that enable you to store and enter e-mail addresses very easily. Have you ever spent time searching for a message that you just *know* is hidden somewhere in your message list? In this chapter, you'll learn how to use Messenger's advanced search capabilities to search the text of every message you've ever received, or sent.

And that's just the beginning. The heart of this chapter explains how to set up folders to categorize your incoming mail, and how to write *filters* (rules) that automatically route incoming mail to these folders. With this capability, you can join all the mailing lists you want, without having to worry about clogging up your inbox—where you'll find only those letters that have been addressed to you personally.

This chapter closes by examining Messenger's security features, which enable you to attach digital signatures to messages, as well as encrypting messages so that they cannot be read while they're en route. If you're concerned about your privacy, you'll be delighted to discover these security features, which make it virtually impossible for anyone except your intended recipient to read your mail.

New for 4

If you've used previous versions of Netscape e-mail, be prepared for lots of new stuff—just about everything in this chapter is new, with the exception of portions of the Address Book.

For the Time-Challenged

- Messenger's Address Book enables you to store and retrieve e-mail addresses with ease. Filling out your Address Book enables you to enter recipient's addresses with just a few keystrokes.
- Can't find a message? Messenger can search for messages in a variety of ways, including searches of the full body text of every message you've ever received or sent.
- Set up folders to store your incoming mail. If you've subscribed to mailing lists, for example, set up a folder to store these messages.
- Write filters to route incoming, low-priority mail to the folders you've created. This clears your Inbox so that it contains only your important, personal messages.
- Send your digital certificate to any correspondent who's using an S-MIME-compatible mail program. The signature attests that the mail is really coming from you.
- After you've exchanged digital signatures with your correspondent, you can also exchange encrypted e-mail.

Creating an Address Book

As you'll surely agree after typing a few e-mail address, it's tedious to type all those funny characters, obscure user names, and funny computer names—and what's worse, your message won't reach its destination if you make a typing mistake. For these reasons, it's a great idea to build an Address Book. The Address Book will contain the e-mail addresses of the people with whom you frequently correspond. From the Address Book (Figure 19.1), you can quickly and accurately enter a recipient's e-mail address, and quickly paste this address into the Address Area when you send messages. The following sections show you how to take full advantage of this neat capability.

To access the Address Book from any Communicator window, open the Communicator menu, and choose Address Book. You'll see the Address Book window, shown in Figure 19.1. Yours will be blank (unless you've added some names to it); mine shows four of my buddies, including Bointee and Baloona.

Adding Addresses to Your Address Book

The easiest way to add an address to your Address Book is to display a message that somebody has sent you. Point to the message within the message pane, and click the right mouse button—you'll see a pop-up menu with lots of reply and forwarding options. But what you're after is Add to Address Book. When you select this option, choose Sender from the submenu. You'll see the Address Book dialog box, shown in Figure 19.1.

When you add an address by right-clicking a message from the person and choosing Add to Address Book, Messenger automatically parses the person's first and last name (if these are available) and includes the person's e-mail address in the first page of the Address Book Card for that person, as you can see in Figure 19.2.

If you haven't yet received a message from the person, you can create a new Address Book Card by clicking New Card in the Address Book window. (To display this window, choose Address Book from the Communicator menu in any Netscape Communicator window, or press Ctrl + Shift + 2.

To fill out the Address Book Card for this person, do the following:

1. In the Name and Contact pages of the card window, type all the information you have for this person. Don't forget to include a nickname (such as the person's first name); this will help you retrieve the person's e-mail address easily.

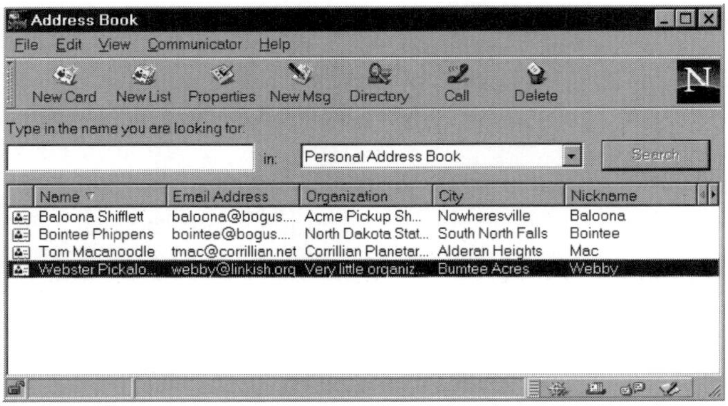

Figure 19.1 Address Book dialog box.

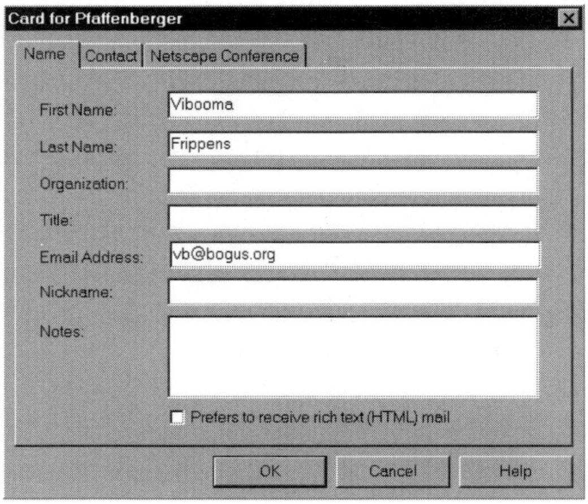

Figure 19.2 When you add an entry by right-clicking someone's message, Messenger fills in the person's name and e-mail address.

Don't worry about the Netscape Conference page just now; we'll get to that in the chapters on Conference.

2. If you know that the person is using an HTML-capable mail program, click Prefers to receive rich text (HTML) mail.
3. Click OK. You'll see the person's name in your Address Book list.

Take a few minutes now to add all your correspondents to your Address Book. You'll be glad you did, because it's much easier to place their addresses into mail (as you'll discover later on in this section).

This guy's address has changed! How do I edit his entry? Simple. In the Address Book window, select the person's name and click Properties. You'll see the person's current information. Edit this information, and then choose OK.

Searching for Addresses

If you'd like to add a card for somebody, but don't know his or her e-mail address, try searching one of the big Web directories such as Four11 or Bigfoot. These directories are nicely integrated with Messenger, as you'll see: When you find the person's e-mail address, you can click a button to add this person's name to your Address Book. Cool!

To search for an e-mail address and add the person's information to your Address Book, do the following:

1. In the Address Book window, click Directory. You'll see the Directory window, shown in Figure 19.3.
2. In the Search for Items list box, choose the directory you want to search. Start with the default option.
3. In the next row, describe the information you know about the person. In the first list box, you can choose from Name, Email, Phone Number, Organization, Organizational Unit, City, and Street.
4. In the second list box, choose a comparison method (the default is Contains). You can also choose Doesn't Contain, Is, Isn't, Begins With, Ends With, or Sounds Like.
5. In the third box, type the text or number you want to match.

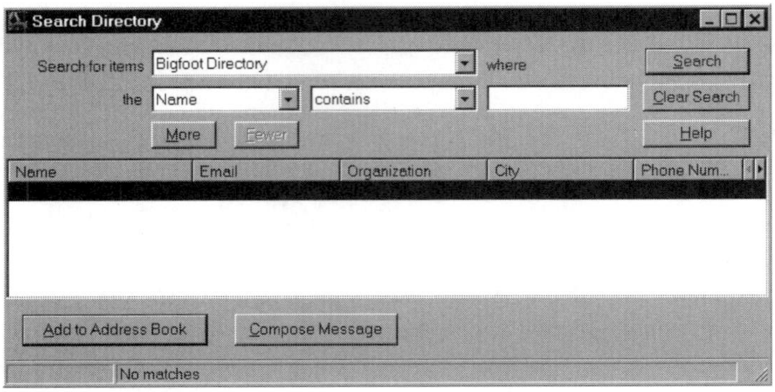

Figure 19.3 If your directory search finds the person's e-mail address, you can quickly add that person's information to your Address Book.

6. If you'd like to add additional conditions, click More, and repeat steps 3 to 5. Adding more conditions narrows the focus of your search, as shown in Figure 19.4.

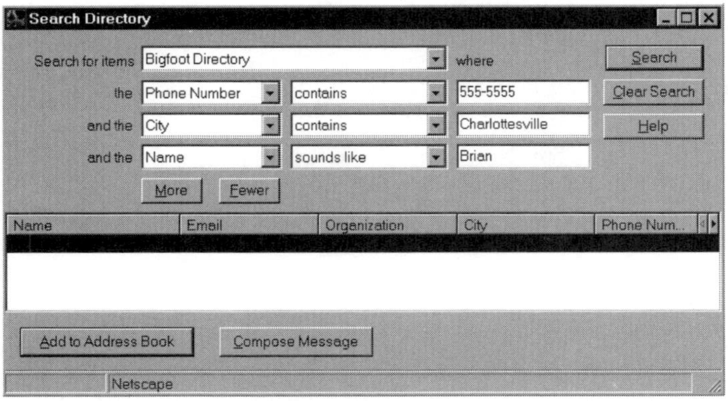

Figure 19.4 Adding conditions can help you pinpoint your search.

7. Click Search. If the service finds one or more matches, you'll see them in the list. If not, you'll be informed that there aren't any matches.

   If you didn't get a match, choose a different directory,and try again.

8. If you've retrieved the correct person's information, select this information, and click Add to Address Book. Messenger will create a card for this person, based on whatever information the directory supplied (you may need to add to this, but the basics will be there). You can also start a new message to this person by clicking the Compose Message button.

Creating a List

If you routinely send e-mail to a group of people, you can save yourself a lot of trouble by creating a *list*. A list is a nickname that's linked to a table of e-mail addresses. To send mail to the list, you just type the list's nickname (instead of all those addresses).

Before creating the list, create Address Book Cards for each person you intend to add to the list. This will make list maintenance easier. When you correct a person's Address Card, the correction will be automatically made to the list as well.

To create a list, do the following:

1. In the Address Book window, click New List. You'll see the New List dialog box, shown in Figure 19.5.
2. In the List Name box, type the list's official name, such as "Graduate Studies Committee."
3. In the List Nickname box, type a short nickname. Nobody but you will see this nickname; it's just for your convenience. Keep it short and use something you'll remember.
4. In the Description box, type a brief description of the list's purpose, if you'd like. This is optional.
5. To add names to the list, begin typing the person's name. Messenger tries to make a match. When it succeeds, just press Enter to go on to the next line.
6. Repeat step 5 until you've typed all the names.

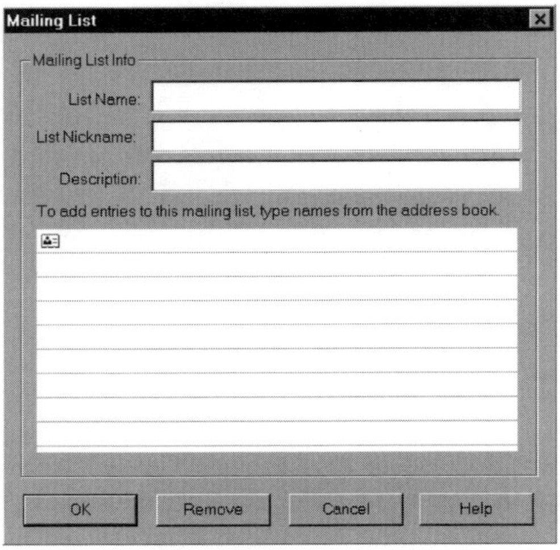

Figure 19.5 Here, you creat a new mailing list.

7. Click OK. Messenger adds the list to the card list, with a special icon that tells you what type of entry this is (a list as opposed to an individual's card).

Remember, once you've created the list, you maintain the accuracy of the e-mail addresses by editing each individual's Address Book Card rather than the list itself. For example, suppose you try to send a message to the group, and one of the messages bounces back with a note that the e-mail address is wrong. To correct this person's address, access the person's Address Book Card, and make the change there. The change will be reflected automatically in the list you've created. The only reason you'd need to edit the list itself is to add or remove a person's name.

If you need to edit the list (to add or remove names), select the list, and click Properties (or just double-click the list name). You'll see the Mailing List dialog box, where you can add or remove names as you please. Click OK to confirm.

Exploring the Address Book Window

Now that you've learned how to add addresses to your Address Book, take a moment to learn more about the Address Book window.

The Address Book Menu This is one of Communicator's least complex menus. Plus, just about everything you'd want to do in the Address Book is better accessed by means of the various buttons and list boxes. There are a couple of exceptions, but we'll get to them later.

The Address Book Toolbar This toolbar contains just about everything you need to use the Address Book. Here's a quick rundown of what the various tools do:

Click here to start a new Address Book Card for somebody.

Click here to create a new, named list of e-mail addresses, so you can send a message to many people with just one address.

To see and edit the current Address Book Card for someone, select that person's entry in the card list, and click here.

To send a new message to someone in your card list, select the person's entry, and click here.

Click here to search for someone's e-mail address in one of the big Web directories such as Four11 or Bigfoot.

Click here to initiate a call to this person using Netscape Conference.

Click here to delete the selected entry.

The Search Toolbar Once your Address Book gets big, it's more convenient to search for someone's name rather than going through the list manually. To search for a name in the Personal Address Book, type the name you're looking for in the search toolbar's textbox. As you type, Messenger scrolls the card list and tries to display a match to the characters you're typing. If this doesn't work, click Search.

The Column Buttons As in other Messenger windows, the column buttons tell you what type of information is in the columns (such as "Name" and "City"), and they also enable you to sort the list in different ways. For example, to sort by e-mail address, click the Email address button.

To change the sort order (ascending or descending), choose Sort Ascending or Sort Descending from the View menu.

Use the arrows on the extreme right side of the column bar to increase or decrease the number of columns shown.

Adding Addresses to Your Messages

Now for the cool part. You've done a lot of work, adding all those addresses to your Address Book. And now it pays off.

Give it a try. From the Messenger Mailbox window, click New Msg to start a new message. In the To box, just start typing the person's name or nickname. Messenger tries to find a match, and it will probably succeed after you've typed just a few letters. When the match is made, you'll see gray letters showing the match. Just press Tab to complete the address automatically.

You can also add addresses by choosing names from the Address Book list, although this isn't as fast or convenient. To do so, click Address, a button on the Composition window's toolbar. You'll see the Select Addresses dialog box, shown in Figure 19.6. To add a recipient, select the name, and click To, Cc:, or Bcc:. (If you can't find the name, you can search for it.) You can add as many recipients as you wish; you'll see them in the recipients list. To remove a name, highlight the name in the recipients list, and click Remove.

Searching Your Mail

Time goes by, and you've accumulated hundreds—nay, thousands—of e-mail messages. You remember getting a message long ago that gave you a hot tip for a job. You weren't interested then, but you are now! *Where's that message?*

Thanks to Messenger's great search capabilities, you can search every part of every message you've received (or sent). This includes body text.

To search for messages, do the following:

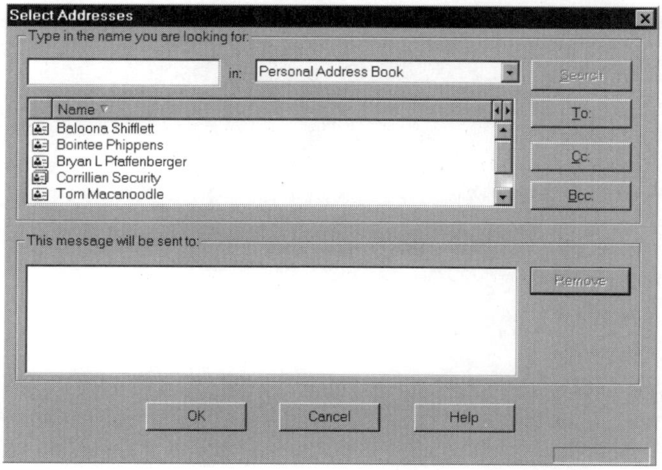

Figure 19.6 You can add addresses to your letter using this dialog box, but it's faster just to type names or nicknames in the Address Area fields.

1. From the Edit menu, choose Message Search. You'll see the Search Messages dialog box, shown in Figure 19.7.
2. Choose the folder you want to search.

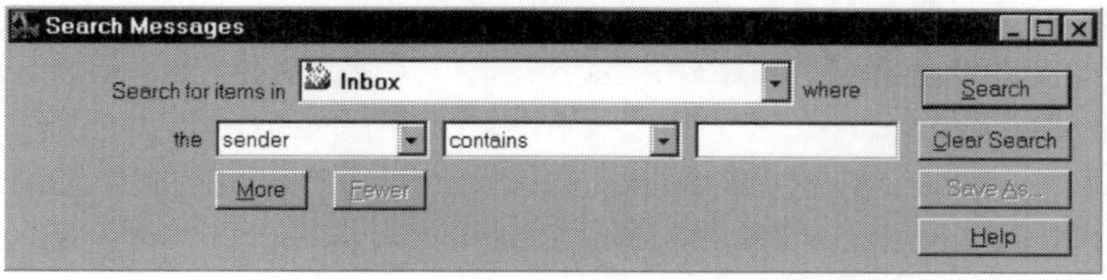

Figure 19.7 You can search for a message using any part of any message you've sent or received.

3. In the next row, describe the information you know about the messge. In the first list box, you can choose from Sender, Subject, Body, Date, Priority, Status, To, Cc:, or To or Cc:.
4. In the second list box, choose a comparison method (the default is Contains). You can also choose Doesn't Contain, Is, Isn't, Begins With, Ends With, or Sounds Like.
5. In the third box, type some text that you *know* is in that message.
6. If you'd like to add additional conditions, click More, and repeat steps 3 to 5.
7. Click Search to begin your search.
8. If the search is successful, you'll see one or more messages that match your search. Highlight the message you want to see, and then click Go to Message Folder. The message will be selected there and you'll see the message's text in the message pane.

If the search didn't work, try a different search strategy. Search a different part of the message, and make sure you've spelled your search text correctly.

Creating New Folders

Once you've got an Inbox full of letters that you really want to keep, you may experience problems navigating through the list and finding letters (despite all of Netscape's neat finding and sorting tools). To keep your Inbox to a minimum, you should create additional folders for storing your messages. For example, I've got folders for messages pertaining to Sailing, Backpacking, Wine, and other hobbies of mine, and then of course I've got one (down at the bottom of the list) called Work.

To create a folder, switch to the Message Center, which makes it easy to see what you're doing (the folders and subfolders are visible in this list). Then choose New Folder from the File menu. You'll see a dialog box prompting you to type the new folder's name.

Start out by creating a folder called something like Personal Folder, and create this folder as a subfolder of Local Mail by choosing this option from the List box. Click OK when you're done.

You can create subfolders within the folders you create. For example, within Personal Folder, I've got folders for various mailing lists that I've joined, as well as projects I'm working on, and some folders for various people whose messages I want to keep permanently (well, they're very interesting people).

Storing Your Messages in Folders

Once you've created folders, you can easily store existing messages (as well as newly received ones) in the folders you've created. Here's how.

In the Messenger Mailbox window, select the message or messages that you want to store. On the toolbar, click File. You'll see a drop-down menu that lists the folders you've created (as well as Messenger's default folders). Choose the folder you want, and release the mouse button. Messenger moves the message or messages to this folder.

Automatically Routing Your Messages to Folders Using Filters

After you've created folders for your mail, you can automatically route mail to these folders. This mail won't appear in your Inbox, but that doesn't mean you can't read new messages easily; just keep clicking the Next button to read the next unread message, and Messenger will move to the next folder until it's found all the new mail.

It isn't difficult to set up folder routing, but it does take a few minutes. Is it worth it? Yes, emphatically. There are few things you can do that will make such a huge difference in your enjoyment of Netscape Communicator.

Planning Your Filters

What sorts of messages should you route to folders? Basically, anything you can categorize. I'm on several mailing lists, including one for my Miata, and I don't like these messages cluttering up my Inbox. They make it hard to see the really important mail that appears there.

But Messenger's filters can do much more than merely move incoming mail to named folders. Before you can really plan your filters, you need to fully understand just what Messenger can do.

Basically, Messenger's mail filters work by matching text or dates in the incoming mail. Here's what Messenger can match:

- **Sender's name or e-mail address** In incoming mail messages, this field contains the sender's name *and* e-mail address. You can match any part of the sender's name, including the e-mail address. Note that you can match a portion of the e-mail address, such as the domain name. This enables you to block all the mail coming from a certain domain, if you wish.
- **Words in the subject line** You can match any text that appears in the subject line. This is a good way to catch unsolicited e-mail (spam), which often includes the word *money* (route this to the Delete folder).
- **Text in the body of the message** This is an advanced feature, not normally found in other e-mail programs.
- **Date** This is the date that the message was sent.
- **Priority** This is the priority setting that the user attached to the message (Low, Normal, or High).
- **To (name or e-mail address)** This is the message's main recipient. You can match the name, e-mail address, or any part of these.
- **Cc (name or e-mail address)** This is the message's carbon copy recipient. You can match the name, e-mail address, or any part of these.
- **To or Cc (name or e-mail address)** With this option, you can match the name, e-mail address, or any part of these, whether they appear in the To or Cc fields.

You can also choose a number of options for matching the text or date you've specified, including Contains, Doesn't Contain, Is, Isn't, Begins With, Ends With, Is Before, or Is After.

Once Messenger has matched some text or a date you specify, you can choose any of the following operations:

- **Move to folder** This is the most commonly chosen option. For example, I move all the incoming mail from the Miata mailing list to the Miata folder, where I read it at my leisure.
- **Change priority** This automatically resets a message's priority. For example, suppose you want all of Karla's messages to be High Priority. You can write a filter that will match Karla's name and change all of her messages to High Priority, even if she didn't choose this priority.
- **Delete** Here's a great way to get rid of mail that you don't want, including junk mail (spam), harassing mail, or any mail containing obscenities.
- **Mark read** This option marks the message as read. This is a really good option for mailing lists; by marking all the messages as Read, the Next button won't display these messages when you're going through your new mail. Of course, you can still read these messages at your leisure by opening the mailing list's folder and reading the messages.
- **Kill thread** This is more useful for newsgroups than for mail; it automatically deletes all subsequent messages that refer to the same subject. This might be useful for mailing lists, though.
- **Watch thread** In newsgroups, this option marks all the subsequent messages having the same subject with a distinctive icon.

Filter Examples

To see what filters can do, here are some plain English examples of filtering rules you can write:

- If the subject line contains "Make Money Fast," then Delete.
- If the sender is Cathy Smith, then route the message to the Cathy folder.
- If the sender is miata@realbig.com, then route the message to the Miata folder.
- If the sender is sail@saillist.org, then mark the message as Read.
- If the date is after 8/8/97 but before 8/21/97, then route the mail to Mail That Came During My Vacation.

- If the body contains "You're a jerk," then route the message to the Revenge folder.

Creating Your First Filter

Ready to get started? You can experiment with this by writing some bogus rules, and then sending mail to yourself to see how the filter works. (It's kind of fun, actually.) Try writing a filter that changes any message from yourself to High priority. Well, naturally!

To create your first filter:

1. From the Message Center or the Messenger Mailbox window, choose Mail Filters from the Edit menu. You'll see the Mail Filters dialog box, shown in Figure 19.8.

   This dialog box shows the filters you've created and enables you to change the order in which they appear.
2. Click New. You'll see the Filter Rules dialog box, shown in Figure 19.9.
3. In the Filter Name box, type a name for your filter.

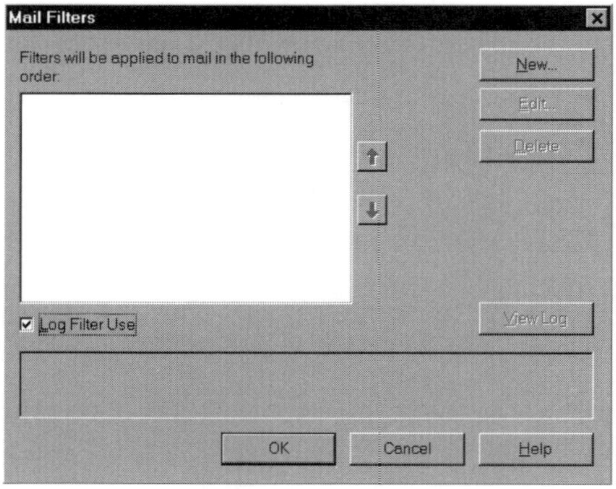

Figure 19.8 This dialog box enables you to change the order of filters you created.

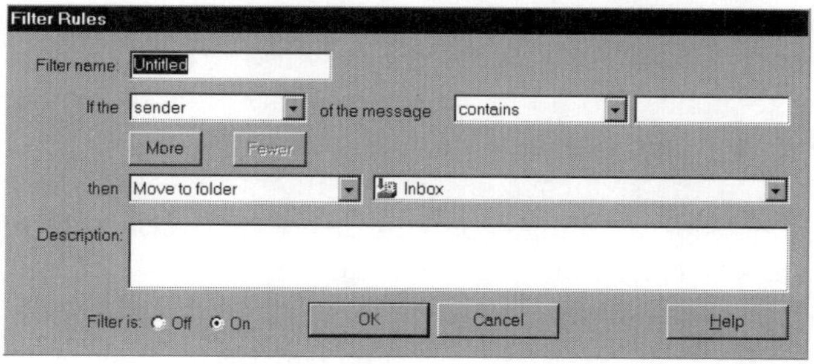

Figure 19.9 Here, you create new filters.

4. In the next line, you write the matching condition. In the first text box, choose the portion of the message you want to match. For example, to match your name, choose Sender.
5. In the next text box, choose the matching technique (the default is "contains," which is good for most purposes).
6. In the third box, type the text you want to match.
7. If you would like to add additional conditions, click More—but be careful, because these additional conditions will narrow the number of messages matched by this filter.
8. Below the More and Fewer buttons, choose an action (the default is Move to folder). If you choose Move to folder, choose a folder in the folder list box. If you choose Change priority, choose a priority in the priority list box. (These boxes appear only if you choose these options.)
9. If you wish, type a brief description of what the filter is supposed to do (although this should be pretty obvious from the dialog box itself).
10. Click OK. You'll see your new rule in the Mail Filters dialog box.

Adjusting Filter Sequence

Messengers applies filters to your incoming mail in the sequence they're listed in the Mail Filters box. To get things working correctly, you may need to adjust the sequence. To do so, choose Mail Filters from the Edit menu. You'll see the Mail Filters dialog box (shown in Figure 19.8). To change a filter's position in the sequence, select the filter, and click the up or down arrow. If a filter isn't working, you can delete it by selecting the filter and clicking Delete—or click Edit, and try changing it.

It's pretty easy to get filters in the correct sequence if you devote a few moments' thought to how they work. Suppose you've written a filter that examines every incoming message for text that says, "You're really cool." These messages are moved to the Ego folder. Subsequently, additional filters look at the sender, and route the messages in various directions according to who sent the message. You want the "cool" filter to come first; after all the "cool" messages have been taken out, the rest of them are parceled out to their folders. If the folder rule came before the cool rule, the cool filter wouldn't work very well because some of these messages might have been directed to folders before the cool filter could get to them.

Help

I can't write a filter that does two things to one message! You're right, and that's too bad. It would be nice, for example, to write a filter that changed a message's priority to High and also routed it to a folder, but you can't do this. Once Messenger finds that a filter applies to a message, it carries out the filter's instructions, and moves on to the next message.

Messenger's filters are neat, but frankly they're not in league with the best e-mail programs (yet). Some programs enable you to write multiple filters for a given message, and even to automatically send replies to certain types of messages. There's a bit more work to do here, Netscape.

SENDING SECURE E-MAIL

Ordinary e-mail is like sending a postcard—anyone can read it while it's en route. And worse, e-mail is easy to forge. A lot of people have gotten into trouble when somebody forged an e-mail message in their name, either as a prank or as a means of getting revenge.

With Netscape Communicator, both of these problems are history. By attaching digital signatures to your mail, you can make sure that your messages are authenticated as actually having come from you. And by encrypting your mail, you can make sure that nobody can read your mail except the intended recipient.

Will your recipient be able to decode your mail? Yes, if your correspondent is using an e-mail program that conforms to the S-MIME standard for secure e-mail. That's the standard that Netscape supports.

Attaching Digital Certificates to Your Mail

To verify that a given message comes from you and nobody else, attach a digital certificate to your outgoing messages. To do so, you'll first need to obtain a digital certificate, as explained in Chapter 10. If you didn't obtain a certificate then, flip back to that chapter and follow the instructions to obtain one. Alternatively, click the Security button, click Yours, and click Get a Certificate. You'll see a Web page listing certification authorities (CAs), from which you can obtain a personal digital certificate.

To attach your certificate to your outgoing mail, do the following:

1. Prepare your message in the Composition window, as you usually do.
2. Click Message Sending Options (the third icon in the Addressing Options area). You'll see the message sending options.
3. Click Signed.
4. Send your message.

Attaching a digital certificate to your e-mail is useful for reasons beyond establishing the authenticity of your message. After you have exchanged digital signatures with a correspondent, you can then exchange encrypted mail, as explained in the next two sections.

Receiving Digital Signatures

When you receive a mail message from someone that contains a digital signature, Netscape automatically detects the incoming signature and adds it to your list of other people's IDs. You also see the ID in the mail message, as shown in Figure 19.10.

If you'd like to examine the digital certificate, just double-click it, or click the Security button, and click View. You'll see the certificate, as shown in Figure 19.11.

Is this certificate *really* from the person who's supposed to have sent it? Good question. As you saw in Chapter 10, there's not much authentication required to get a low-level (Class 1) certificate—you just have to be able to access the e-mail account of the person whose name is on the certificate. That's not hard to do, if you know a little hacking! To make

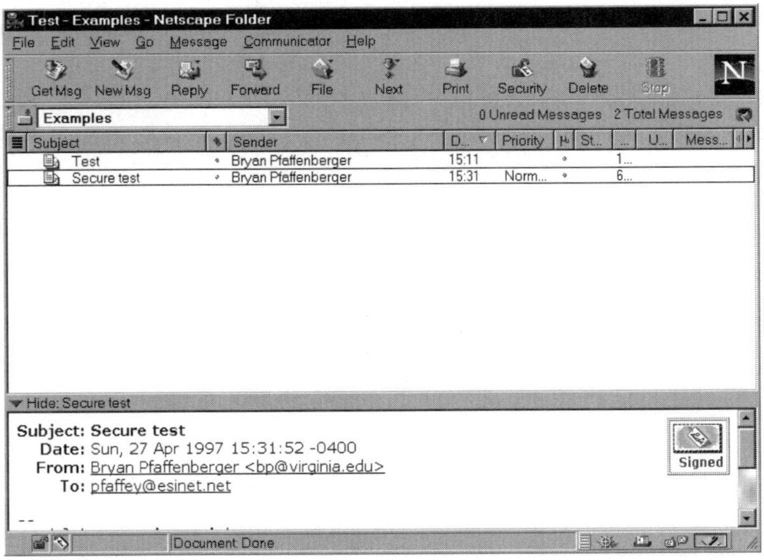

Figure 19.10 If someone adds a digital signature to an incoming message, you see it in the message pane.

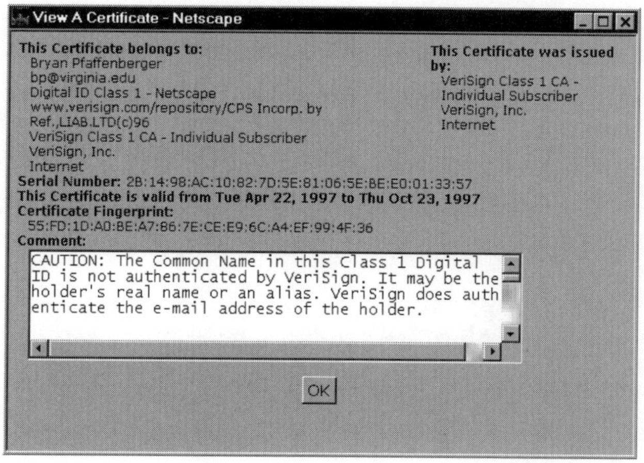

Figure 19.11 Here's what a digital signature looks like.

absolutely sure that this certificate is valid, pick up the phone, ask the person to open his or her certificate, and read you the Certificate Fingerprint (see Figure 19.10 for an example). This should match what the other person is looking at, on screen. If it doesn't, somebody's playing some kind of game with you!

Sending Encrypted E-mail

Once you've exchanged digital certificates with somebody, you can exchange encrypted e-mail with this person. This assumes, of course, that the person is also using an S-MIME compatible mail program. To send encrypted mail, be sure both the Encrypted and Signed options are chosen in the Message Sending Options area.

When you receive an encrypted message, you'll see an icon that says the message is both encrypted and signed. If you click the Security icon, you'll see confirmation that the message was encrypted when it was sent and decrypted when it was received. You don't have to do anything to make all this happen—it's all automatic.

From Here

- You've mastered Internet e-mail. In the next part of this book, you'll learn how to use the Messenger tools you already know to make the most of Usenet newsgroups (and Collabra discussions, if your organization has a Collabra server and makes them available to you).
- Don't like the time delay in e-mail? Talk to other Internetters in real time with Chat, discussed in the next chapter.
- Get into the swing of things on Usenet, and you'll get lots more electronic mail—not all of it friendly! Check out Chapter 21.

Part III

Netscape Collabra: Joining Online Discussion

Chapter 20

Getting Started with Collabra

New for 4

Netscape Collabra is an entirely new feature of Netscape, replacing the News capabilities of the previous version (3.0). Essentially, Collabra is nothing more than the Message Center, which—as you've learned—enables you to view all your communications, whether they're coming from e-mail or from newsgroups, in a single, consistent interface. For most users, Collabra is basically a conjoined e-mail and Usenet newsreading program, and that's its basic benefit: You can use your e-mail skills as a basis for exploring newsgroups. For this reason, you should read Part III before reading the two chapters in this part of the book.

But Collabra's got more going for it. Using Netscape's Collabra server, organizations can set up private newsgroups that employ secure, SSL-based communications to prevent the interception of messages en route. This opens the possibility of creating enterprise-wide discussion groups that are closed to the public, secure, and immensely valuable to all concerned.

Most readers of this book won't be able to access Collabra servers, so this part of the book will feature the use of Collabra to access Usenet newsgroups, which are publicly accessible. It's perfectly good training, after all: Usenet newsgroups work exactly the same way Collabra discussions do, since they're based on the same open technology and agreed-upon standards.

This chapter shows you how to get going with Collabra and Usenet. You'll choose configuration and setup options, explore the various Collabra windows, and download the newsgroup list. In the next chapter, you'll learn how to unleash yourself on the world at large by contributing to Usenet newsgroups!

For the Time-Challenged

- Usenet is a computer-based discussion system that features more than 25,000 topically named discussion fora, called *newsgroups*.
- Collabra can access Usenet newsgroups as well as private newsgroup servers, including Collabra servers, which enable organizations to set up password-protected, SSL-secured discussions. In this and the next chapter, we'll concentrate on the use of Collabra for accessing Usenet.
- Newsgroups are divided into *hierarchies*. There are quite a few top-level hierarchies on subjects such as recreation, science, and computing. Within each hierarchy dozens, or even hundreds or thousands, of newsgroups.
- A newsgroup discussion consists of posts (also called *articles*), which are messages contributed on new subjects, and *follow-up posts* (also called *follow-up articles*), which comment on previous posts. As more people comment on a post, a thread of discussion develops. A thread is a series of messages that all pertain to the same, original post, or subsequent posts on the same subject.
- You need to configure Collabra to access Usenet by supplying the name of your Usenet (NNTP) server. Find this out from your service provider.
- After you configure Collabra to access Netscape, download the newsgroup list.
- Use the Subscribe to Newsgroups window to locate and subscribe to newsgroups of interest.

Introducing Usenet

Usenet is a computer-based discussion system that's widely distributed on the Internet. The idea underlying Usenet is devilishly clever: The Usenet software works behind the scenes, copying and relaying the messages users contribute, so that in time every participating computer (called a *Usenet site*) has an exact copy of every message contributed to the network. The software knows how to organize these messages into topical categories, called *newsgroups*, which you can read. In addition, you can contribute your own messages to these newsgroups. With more than 160,000 Usenet sites connected to the network worldwide, more than 15,000 newsgroups, and an estimated 7 million regular users, contributing to Usenet may be the ultimate act of self-publishing—or self-immolation, if you break any of Usenet's none-too-explicit rules or guidelines. Whatever else you do with Usenet, read newsgroups for a good while before attempting to post your own messages.

Usenet got its start in 1979 as a method of sharing information about UNIX computer systems, and the network still plays a major role in providing computer support. From its earliest days, though, participants showed even more interest in discussing social and political issues, including controversial ones such as abortion and the death penalty. Since then, Usenet has grown wildly, but the growth has not been without controversy. Usenet's strong points lie in the discussions of computer hardware and software, hobbies, entertainment, and recreation. But many people have concluded that Usenet is not very well suited for the discussion of controversial social issues. It's just too easy for obnoxious twerps to ruin the discussion, leading to a "low signal-to-noise ratio," as experienced Usenet hands term it. I'll promise you one thing: After you read Usenet for a while, your estimate of the number of obnoxious twerps in the world will go up by a very substantial percentage.

One of Usenet's worst problems is its own success. Every day, Usenet contributors post the equivalent of 80,000 pages of text—the days are long gone, obviously, when anyone could hope to read all or most of the newsgroups. Most people follow just one or two of them and ignore the rest—but even so, many newsgroups receive dozens or hundreds of messages per day.

Still, Usenet is a wonderful resource. Many newsgroups offer intelligent discussion, particularly the moderated ones, in which all submissions must pass the scrutiny of a human moderator, who checks to see whether they are relevant to the newsgroup's goals. Generally speaking, the technically oriented newsgroups are of the greatest value; there's a real spirit of information exchange and resource sharing. Some of the best things about Usenet are the FAQs (Frequently Asked Questions), which attempt to provide answers to the questions people are most likely to ask. There are hundreds of these, and some of them are among the best sources of information on a topic that you can obtain anywhere.

To read and contribute to Usenet newsgroups, you need software called a *newsreader.* But don't go out on the Net hunting down FTP sites—you already have one of the best newsreaders available: Collabra. Whether you want to join in the hue and cry or just access FAQs, Collabra provides wonderful tools for accessing Usenet. You can read messages, post your own messages on a new subject, or reply—either by a follow-up post or an e-mail message—to messages others have left. Compared to the most powerful newsreading programs, Collabra lacks only a few advanced functions. It's the perfect tool for reading Usenet on a daily basis. This chapter and the next thoroughly explore Collabra's Usenet capabilities.

They flamed me! To be "flamed" means to receive a lot of unfriendly e-mail letters. If you break the rules of Usenet "netiquette," flaming may be the result. Please do not post messages to a Usenet newsgroup until you fully understand the newsgroup's purpose and the range of acceptable discussion subjects. Most of all, please do not post questions that have already been answered in the newsgroup's FAQ (Frequently Asked Questions), if there is one (not all newsgroups have FAQs). This chapter shows you how to access Usenet FAQs; please read this section carefully and obtain the FAQ for any newsgroup to which you're thinking of posting a message. Carefully observe the rules of netiquette, which boil down to good manners, basically: Be polite, don't "shout" (using all capital letters), give credit where credit is due, and don't post anything in anger.

Introducing Usenet Newsgroups

With as many as 25,000 Usenet newsgroups available from most servers, some kind of organization is needed to make sense of the lengthy list of newsgroup names. This organization is hierarchical, and works in the following way:

- Every newsgroup is part of a top-level hierarchy, such as comp (computer-related subjects), rec (recreation), or soc (social newsgroups).
- Every newsgroup has at least one other part to its name, with the parts separated by dots (such as misc.test or alt.censorship).
- Many newsgroups are further subdivided by adding additional names, as in the following examples:

  alt.fan.tolkien
  alt.fan.woody-allen
  comp.sys.ibm.pc.games.action
  comp.sys.ibm.pc.games.adventure

Newsgroups are organized into two broad categories:

- **Standard Newsgroups** These newsgroups have been established by a formal voting procedure. Every Usenet site is expected to carry the standard newsgroups; not all do, however, owing to problems with disk storage space.
- **Alternative Newsgroups** Anyone who knows the correct UNIX command can create a newsgroup in the alternative (alt.*) hierarchy—but no Usenet site is obligated to carry it. However, many sites offer all or many of the alt newsgroups, which range from important and useful (alt.censorship) to completely silly (alt.barney.dinosaur.die.die.die).

The standard newsgroups fall into the following hierarchies:

bionet	Biology and the environment
biz	Business discussions and advertising
ClariNet	A do-it-yourself online newspaper consisting of feeds from major wire services, such as UPI and AP
comp	Computers and computer applications
K12	Primary and secondary education
misc	Anything that doesn't fit into the other categories
news	Newsgroups about Usenet itself
rec	Hobbies and sports
sci	The sciences generally

soc	Social issues and socializing
talk	No-holds-barred controversy, flaming, verbiage—and occasionally, interesting discussion and debate

Usenet may be among the world's most ephemeral communications media: Every article is set to expire after a certain period (usually, two weeks), in which case the message simply disappears from the Net. With hundreds of megabytes of new articles streaming in daily, many Usenet sites have no choice but to decrease the expiration period down to as little as 24 hours. If you don't read the newsgroup regularly, then, you'll miss the action—and you won't have a clue about why a certain topic has become the day's cause célèbre.

What's in a Newsgroup?

A newsgroup consists of articles that have been contributed by Usenet's participants. They fall into two categories:

- **Posts** An original message, with a new topic, that somebody contributed.
- **Follow-up Posts** A reply to the original message, which usually contains some quoted text from the original message. The title of a follow-up post usually echoes the original post's title, with the addition of "re:" at the beginning of the title.

To enhance your ability to follow the thread of discussion, Usenet software can organize posts and follow-up posts into groups (called *threads*). Not all newsreaders are threaded, though, in which case they throw the messages at you in chronological order. Happily, Collabra can thread the messages—and that makes it an above-average newsreader. Other features take it into the "very good" category, as you'll see in the pages to follow.

Why won't Usenet work? To access Usenet, you need access to an NNTP server, a program that makes Usenet newsgroups accessible to newsreading software. Generally, access to an NNTP server is included with Internet service subscriptions. If you're not sure, call your service provider, and be sure to get the NNTP server's domain name. The next section shows you how to tell Netscape which server to use.

Configuring Usenet Access

Configuring Collabra to work with Usenet newsgroup is easy. You'll need one piece of information from your Internet service provider: The address of the computer that enables you to access Usenet news. (Chances are this is something like news.provider.net, where "provider" is the name of your Internet service provider.) That's all the information you need to get connected.

Just follow these instructions to configure Collabra for Usenet news:

1. In any Communicator window, choose Preferences from the Edit menu.
2. In the Category pane, choose Groups Server, under Mail & Groups. (If you don't see this option, click the plus sign next to Mail & Groups.)
3. In the Discussion Groups (news) server box, type the name of your service provider's Usenet computer.
4. In the Discussion Group (news) folder area, Communicator has placed a default folder name. It's fine, so let it be.
5. If you would like Collabra to ask you before downloading more than 1,500 messages, just leave the default settings as they are. This is a good choice for anyone using a modem. If you're connecting from work and have a faster connection, you might want to turn this option off, or specify a higher number.
6. Click OK to confirm.

Downloading the Newsgroup List

After you've configured Collabra to access your news server, you need to download the newsgroup list. This can take a while, considering that many servers offer as many as 25,000 newsgroups! Of course, you're only downloading the names of the groups, but you can probably take at least a five- or ten-minute break after initiating the download (unless you have a superfast connection).

To download the newsgroup list:

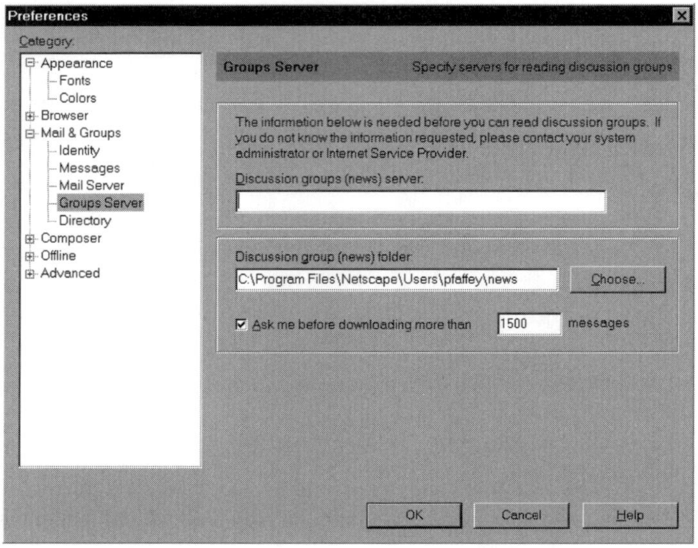

Figure 20.1 In this Preferences page, you identify your service provider's Usenet server.

1. From any Communicator window, open the Communicator menu, and choose Collabra Discussions. Alternatively, press Ctrl + 3. You'll see the Message Center, the same one that you use when you access your mail folders. However, Collabra automatically highlights your news server, as shown in Figure 20.2.
2. On the Message Center toolbar, click Join Groups. You'll see the Subscribe to Discussion Groups window, shown in Figure 20.3.
3. Click Get Groups. Collabra contacts the server, and starts downloading the group list. When the groups have finished downloading, you see a newsgroup list such as the one shown in Figure 20.4.

Let's take a closer look at the Subscribe to Discussion Groups Window.

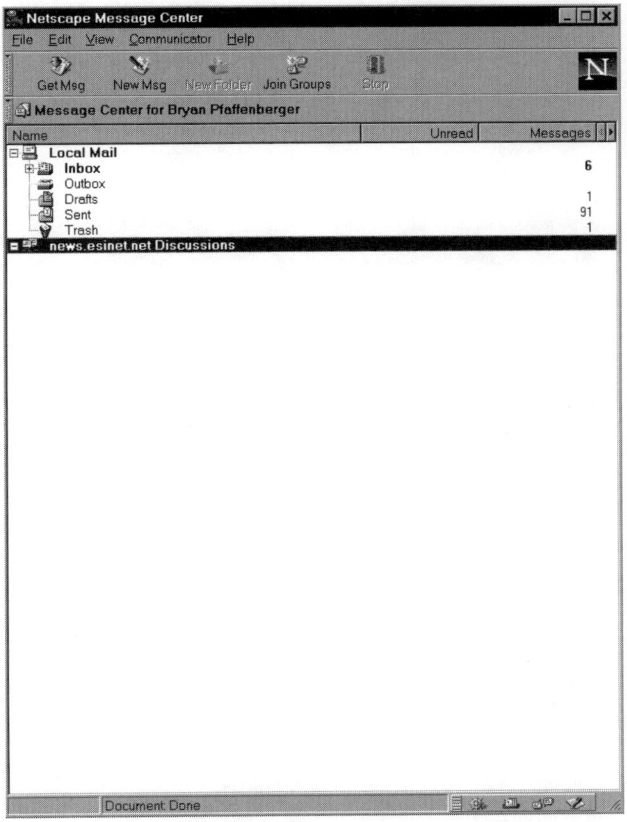

Figure 20.2 When you access Collabra Discussions, your news server's name is automatically highlighted in the Message Center window.

Understanding the Subscribe to Discussion Groups Window

Now that you've downloaded the Subscribe to Discussion Groups Window, you can use this window to find discussion groups of interest to you, and subscribe to these groups. To *subscribe* means to flag the group so that its

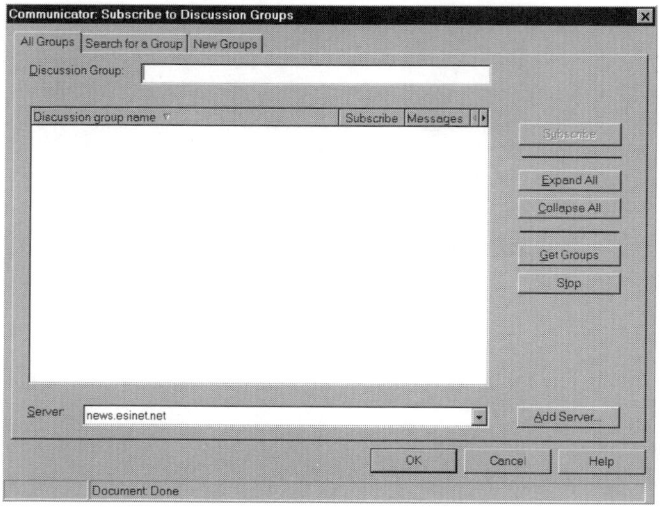

Figure 20.3 This window displays the discussion groups list, and enables you to subscribe to groups of interest to you.

name appears in the Message Center, giving you much more convenient access—you won't have to plough through the entire group list to find this group when you next want to read it. Subscription is a purely local matter, involving settings on your computer (not on your service provider's).

Expanding and Collapsing Hierarchies

As you know, Usenet newsgroups are arranged in hierarchies. For example, the top-level rec *hierarchy* pertains to recreation; within this hierarchy are a number of subhierarchies, such as the following:

rec.antiques
rec.audio
rec.birds
rec.boats

Within some of these subhierarchies, there are further subhierarchies—folders within folders, to use a more familiar metaphor. For example, rec.bicycles.* is broken down into seven groups, such as

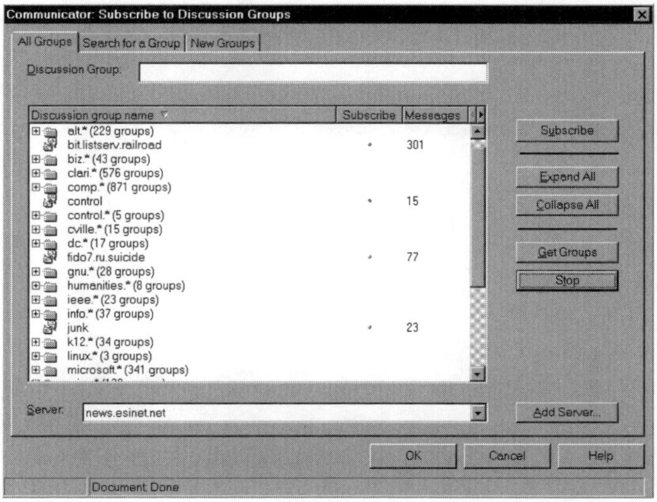

Figure 20.4 Here, you subscribe to newsgroups.

rec.bicycles.marketplace and rec.bicycles.racing. In Usenet nomenclature, an asterisk is a wildcard indicating that there are additional subgroups below this level.

In the Subscribe to Discussion Groups window (see Figure 20.5), you see both newgroups (shown with two conversational balloons) as well as folders containing collapsed newsgroups. If you click on the plus sign next to a folder, you see the newsgroups (and perhaps additional folders) within that folder. In Figure 20.6, you see what the rec.arts.* hierarchy looks like when it's expanded. As you can see, there are a lot of groups in this hierarchy, and there are even some additional subhierarchies within it.

Once you've brought some newsgroups into view, note that the window has three columns (click the arrows to bring them into view, if they're not visible): Discussion group name, Subscribe, and Messages. The Subscribe column uses a distinctive icon to show which groups you've subscribed to, and the Messages column indicates how many new messages are waiting on the server.

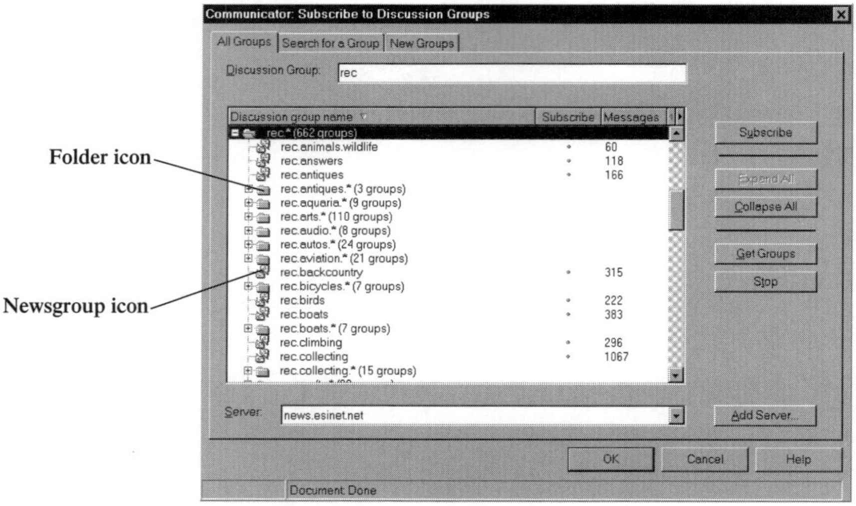

Figure 20.5 In the Subscribe to Discussion Groups window, icons show you whether you're looking at a newsgroup or a folder containing two or more newsgroups.

To collapse a hierarchy that you've expanded, just click the minus sign next to the hierarchy name. To collapse all the hierarchies, click the Collapse All button.

Searching for Groups

With more than 25,000 newsgroups available from many service providers, navigating the group list can be a daunting exercise—even with the expand/ collapse tools you just learned about. Fortunately, Collabra makes it easy to find a newsgroup.

If you know the exact name of a newsgroup, the easiest way to locate it is to type its name in the Discussion Group box. Click Collapse All, and try typing rec.boats.crusing, a group that is carried on almost all servers. As you see, Collabra scrolls down the list and automatically expands the hierarchies as necessary, until the group's name is selected.

If you'd like to find newsgroups pertaining to a topic of interest to you, click Search for a Group, one of the tabs at the top of the Subscribe to Dis-

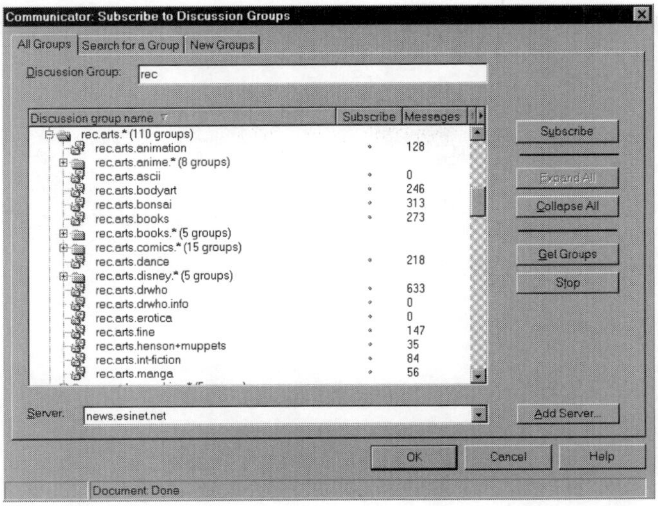

Figure 20.6 Here's what the rec.arts.* hierarchy looks like when it's expanded.

cussion Groups window. You'll see the Search for a Group page, shown in Figure 20.7. I'm going to type my favorite subject—boats—just to see what happens. After clicking Search, I get the results shown in Figure 20.8.

To find out which newsgroups pertain to subjects of interest to you, try typing a word in the Search for box, and see what comes up.

Subscribing to Newsgroups

I'm sure you've already found several groups that interest to you. Go ahead and subscribe to them. In the next chapter, you'll learn how to access these groups, read the news, and join the fray yourself.

To subscribe to a newsgroup, highlight the newsgroup's name, and click Subscribe. After you subscribe to a group, you see a check mark next to the group's name, as shown in Figure 20.9.

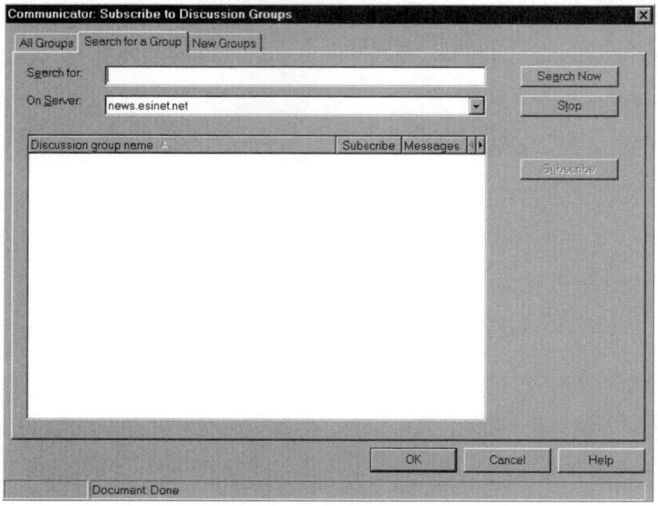

Figure 20.7 This page enables you to search for a newsgroup.

Adding a Server

Suppose you find out that your organization has its own, private newsgroup server—perhaps a Collabra server, which enables secure discussions using SSL encryption.

You can add a server by clicking the Add Server button in the Subscribe to Discussion Groups window. You'll see the New Discussion Groups Server dialog box, shown in Figure 20.10. Type the server name in the Server box. Don't change the Port setting, unless you've been told to do so by your network administrator. If the server is secure, click the Secure option. If the server requires you to supply a user name and password in order to access it, click Always use name and password. When you're done filling out the server information, click OK. You'll see the new server's name in the Message Center. To download the groups list for this server, highlight the server's name, highlight Join Groups, and click Get Groups.

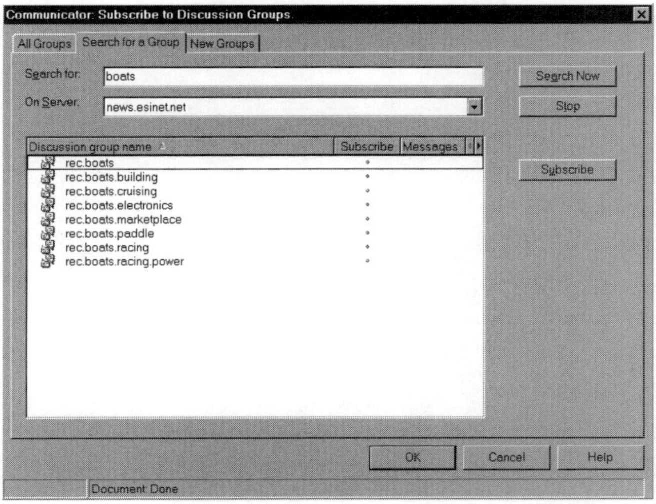

Figure 20.8 Collabra found all of these newsgroups that pertain to boats. Cool!

From Here

- You've configured Netscape to work with newsgroups, you've downloaded the newsgroup list, and you've even subscribed to newsgroups. So what are you waiting for? In the next chapter, you learn how to read newsgroups and contribute your own two cents' worth.

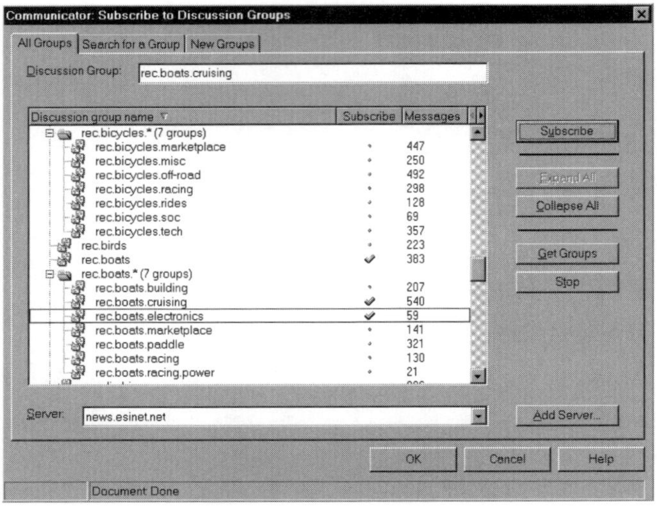

Figure 20.9 After you subscribe to a newsgroup, you see a check mark next to the group's name.

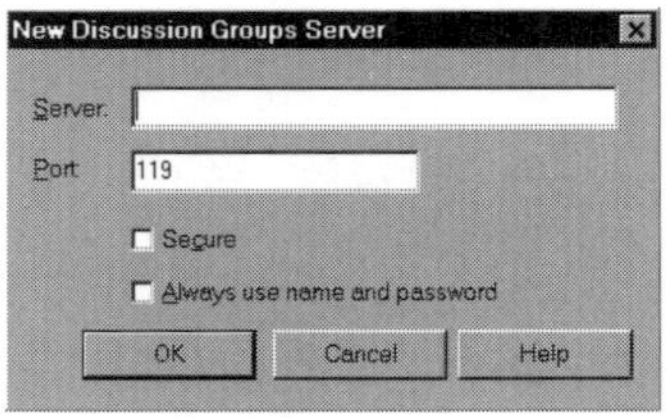

Figure 20.10 To add another server, use this dialog box.

Chapter 21

Reading the News and Joining the Fray

You've configured Collabra to access Usenet, and you've even subscribed to some newsgroups. So have at it! This chapter shows you how to use all of Collabra's useful tools to read the news efficiently. You'll also learn how to post your own messages and reply to existing messages.

Understanding the Discussion Window

The Discussion window (Figure 21.1) is very similar to the Messenger window discussed in Chapter 17—in fact, if you've already learned how to send

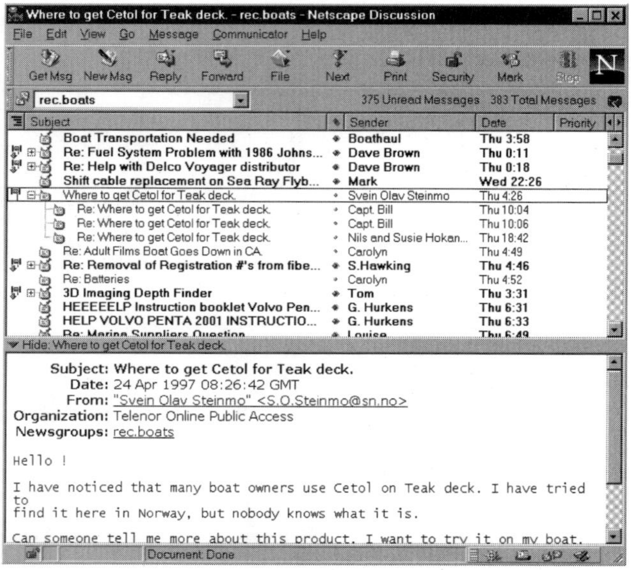

Figure 21.1 The Discussion window.

and receive e-mail with Netscape, you know a lot of how to get into the swing of things on Usenet.

The only difference between the Discussion window and the Messenger Mailbox is the Mark tool, which enables you to mark threads for various purposes. We'll get into the use of this tool a bit later; for now, you need to understand how threading works.

To view the Discussion window, open Collabra Discussions, highlight the name of the group you want to read, and double-click the newsgroup name. Alternatively, choose Open Discussion Group from the File menu.

It says there are more than 1,500 messages! Popular group, huh? If you like, you can download all of them—but I hope you don't have anything to do for a bit. Otherwise, just download the next 1,500. That ought to give you enough of a sense of what's going on the newsgroup.

Understanding Threading

By default, Netscape sorts the messages by *threads*. The term *thread* comes from the phrase "follow the thread of a discussion." In thread sorting, original messages are grouped with their replies.

Here's an example. Suppose I post a message asking people in rec.boats which marinas they recommend in the Deltaville area of the Chesapeake Bay. Soon, several people reply. The message header pane looks like this:

```
Suggestions for marinas near Deltaville?
   Re: Suggestions for marinas near Deltaville?
   Re: Suggestions for marinas near Deltaville?
```

Now suppose somebody responds to one of the Re: messages. Netscape will add the message as follows:

```
Suggestions for marinas near Deltaville?
     Re: Suggestions for marinas near Deltaville?
     Re: Suggestions for marinas near Deltaville?
       Re: Suggestions for marinas near Deltaville?
```

Threading is a great feature. You're going to love it. Without threading, you'd have to search through the message list to find replies—and that really takes the fun out of Usenet.

What's in the Header?

For each message, you'll see a *header*, which contains a lot of information about the message you're viewing, including the message's subject, date, the e-mail address (and sometimes the name) of the person who contributed the message, and the newsgroups to which the message was posted. Sometimes you'll see additional information, including the following:

- **Reply To** This field indicates the e-mail address to which you should reply, if you wish to do so.
- **Followup-To** If the message was posted to more than one newsgroup, this field indicates the group to which you should send the reply.
- **References** If you're viewing a reply, the references identify the original messages. These are links; if you click the first reference

(number 1), you'll see the original message, if it's still available (it might have been deleted by the server).

One of the things you'll notice in Usenet is that some messages are posted to more than one newsgroup. This is called *crossposting*. You'll see a lot of flames about crossposting, a fact that's attributable to new users' misconceptions about it. So let's get this straightened out right now.

Crossposting isn't a bad thing in itself. Often, it makes sense to crosspost. For example, suppose I'm describing marinas in Virginia. I might want to post my message to rec.boats.cruising and crosspost it to a local Virginia newsgroup. Nobody would object to that.

What gets people in trouble with crossposting is overdoing it. People who abuse Usenet—for example, by posting irrelevant advertisements in newsgroups on completely unrelated subjects—tend to crosspost wildly, sometimes crossposting to dozens or even hundreds of newsgroups. There have been several infamous incidents of crass individuals trying to post ads to every newsgroup in existence.

Reading the News

To read an article, just click the article's subject header in the message list. You'll see the article's text in the message pane.

I read this cool article the last time I logged on to this newsgroup, but now it's gone! The article has expired (most Usenet servers keep articles for only a couple of weeks). That's why they call it "news"!

Navigating the Message List

As you read the news, you'll commonly perform the following actions:

- **Go to the next unread article.** Click the Next button or press. If the next unread article is in a collapsed thread, Collabra expands the thread.
- **Read the previous unread message.** This command does something only if you've started reading a message that's not at the top of the newsgroup, but that's just what you'll do, pretty often. To read the previous unread message, press P (or choose Previous Unread Message from the Go menu).
- **Read the next message, whether it has been read or not.** Press Shift + N, or choose Next Unread Message from the Go menu.
- **Go back to the previous message, whether it has been read or not.** Press Shift + P, or choose Previous Message from the Go menu.
- **Skip to the next unread thread.** Is this thread boring? Skip directly to the next unread thread (and mark the current thread as entirely read) by pressing T (or choose next Unread Thread from the Go menu).
- **Read the article that started all this ruckus.** If you're reading a follow-up article, look in the header for a References field, and click the first number you see. The original article may have expired, though.
- **Go to the next group in your list of subscribed groups.** From the Go menu, choose Next Folder.
- **Go to the next group containing unread messages.** From the Go menu, choose Next Unread Folder.
- **See if any new messages have arrived on the server.** Click Get Msg.

This message is all scrambled! I'll bet you don't run into this very often, but it can happen. To prevent youngsters from coming across something risqué, Usenetters sometimes employ a primitive encryption technique called ROT-13. (This technique simply moves all letters of the alphabet thirteen places to the right.) To unscramble a ROT-13 message, choose Unscramble (ROT13) from the View menu. Frankly, this is a holdover from the kinder, gentler days of Usenet; it doesn't seem that people care much anymore about what kids might come across. They should.

Hiding Read Messages

By default, Collabra shows all the messages in the group. However, this really isn't the best setting for convenient reading. To cut down the number of messages you're viewing, choose a setting that hides read messages so that they don't appear the next time you access the server.

To do this, open the View menu in the group's Discussion window, and choose Messages. From the pop-up menu, choose Threads with New. This is really a cool option because it hides all the read messages, except the ones within threads for which there are new contributions. With this option, you get rid of the lion's share of the read messages; you see read messages only when there's a lively discussion still going on.

If you've hidden read messages but decide you'd like to view them again, choose Messages from the View menu, and select All from the pop-up menu.

Marking Messages as Read

Now that you've configured Collabra to hide read messages the next time you access the group, you'll want to take advantage of the Mark button (on the Discussion window's toolbar).

- To mark a message as read, press M, or click the Mark button and choose as Read. You won't see the message the next time you access this group. To mark the entire thread as read, click the Mark button and choose Thread Read.
- To mark a message as unread so that it shows up the next time you access this group, press U, or click the Mark button and choose as Unread.
- To mark all the messages as read, click the Mark button and choose All Read.
- To mark messages read up to a date you specify, click the Mark button, and choose By Date. You'll see the Mark Messages Read dialog

box, which enables you to specify a date (by default, Collabra inserts today's date). Choose a date, and click OK.

Watching and Ignoring Threads

As you're reading a newsgroup, you'll find that some threads are really interesting, but others are just horrifically boring or terminally stupid. Thankfully, you can *watch* interesting threads (flag them with a special icon) or *ignore* the dumb ones. If you choose to ignore a thread, you won't see any new messages that have been contributed to this thread (thank heavens).

To watch a thread, select the first message in the thread, and press W. Alternatively, choose Watch Thread from the Message menu.

To ignore a thread, select the first message in the thread, and press K. Alternatively, open the Message menu, and choose Ignore Thread.

To cut down the verbiage to just the topics in which you're interested, open the View menu, choose Messages, and choose Watched Threads with New. The next time you access this group, you'll see only your favorite threads from before, as well as all the new messages and new threads. Essentially, this option ignores all the old threads except the ones you've chosen to watch.

Many graphic images are posted to the alt.binaries.pictures.* newsgroups—and not just the naughty ones you've heard about. There are plenty of fun and perfectly legal pictures, too (while browsing alt.binaries.pictures.animals, I found a really cute picture of some kittens—and it's now my Windows wallpaper). Netscape can display these images, as long as they're posted in one part (look for 1/1 in the subject line). If the image is posted in two or more parts, Netscape can display only the first part.

Printing a Message

You can print the text of any Usenet post you see. Just open the File menu and choose Print. Alternatively, you can press Ctrl + P or click the Print button.

Posting Your Own Messages

After you've read a newsgroup for a while, you may wish to try posting your own messages. But please be sure you know what you're doing before posting.

Netiquette

Before you post to Usenet, you should make sure you know what you're doing. If you don't, you may find yourself on the wrong end of lots of angry posts and e-mail messages. Usenet people aren't difficult to get along with—as long as you follow the rules. Here's a quick overview:

- Don't crosspost (post to more than one newsgroup) unless there's a compelling reason to do so. Since you're a beginner, you wouldn't know any such reasons, so don't do it.
- Make sure you are posting to the right newsgroup.
- Read the newsgroup for at least two weeks before posting.
- Read the FAQ (Frequently Asked Questions) for the newsgroup. Don't ask questions that have already been answered in the FAQ. To locate the FAQ for a newsgroup, use Infoseek or one of the other search engines discussed in Chapter 4, and search for the newsgroup's name and FAQ.
- Do not criticize anyone's spelling or grammar. Lots of people who post to Usenet speak English as a second or third language.
- Keep your cool. Never post in anger.
- Ignore messages that contain obvious inaccuracies ("Francis Ford Coppola directed *Star Wars*"). These messages may be a trap (called a *troll*) to tempt you to make a fool out of yourself.
- Do not post a follow-up message if an e-mail reply will do.
- Don't post anything you wouldn't want to see on your boss's desk tomorrow morning—or your mother's.
- Do not post "test" messages to an ordinary newsgroup. There are newsgroups for this purpose, such as alt.test.

Posting an Original Message

Assuming you've carefully read the "Netiquette" section above and you're confident you know what you're doing, you can use Netscape to post a message to Usenet. For your first post, use alt.test.

I'm getting junk e-mail! Posted to Usenet, did you? There are programs that automatically scan Usenet for e-mail addresses, which are then packaged and sold to people who hope to make some freebie money by pelting millions of people with junk e-mail. This is called spamming. At present, there's not much you can do about it, except refrain from posting to Usenet. Legislation is needed to make e-mail advertising illegal, just as it's illegal to advertise using fax machines.

Assuming you're willing to put up with spam, and you'd like to post your own message, do the following:

1. Display the Discussion window for the group to which you'd like to post a new message.
2. Click New Msg. You'll see a Composition window, exactly like the one you use to create Messenger e-mail. The only difference is that, in the Addressing area, Collabra has automatically entered the name of the group you're viewing.
3. In the Subject line, type a descriptive but short subject line.

   Please be specific. If you type something like, "Request for Assistance," or "Help with a Problem," you're not going to get very many responses, if any.
4. In the message pane, type your message. If you use rich formatting (HTML), be aware that very few people are using newsreaders that can display HTML natively. Rich formatting is for corporate Collabra or other NNTP servers, running on networks where everyone is using an HTML-capable newsreader.
5. Click Spelling to check your spelling.
6. Click Send to post your message.

I don't see my message on the article list! Don't worry, everything's OK with your post. Usenet software has a low priority for processing; the posts you contribute are kept in a storage area until there's enough computer capacity to take care of them. This might be minutes, or even hours, from the time you actually post the message.

Replying by E-mail

If you want to reply to somebody's post, consider sending an e-mail reply rather than posting to the group. Suppose, for example, that somebody has posted a question and you know the answer. Do you think the whole group would be interested? If so, then post a follow-up reply, as explained in the next section. If you think only the person asking the question would be interested, then send an e-mail reply.

To send an e-mail reply, follow these steps:

1. Display the article to which you want to reply.
2. On the Netscape button bar, click Reply, and choose Reply to Sender from the menu. Alternately press Ctrl + R. You'll see the composition window. Netscape has echoed the person's e-mail address in the To box.
3. If you configured Messenger to display quoted text by default, you see the quoted message. (If not, click Quote.) By all means edit this text down to just the part to which you want to respond. In particular, edit out the person's signature.
4. Type your reply. You can insert this within the quoted text, if you like.
5. Check your spelling.
6. Click Send.

I changed my mind! I don't want to send this! No problem. Just click the close box. You'll see a message asking if you really want to abandon the message. Click Yes.

Posting a Follow-up Message

Post a follow-up message only if you're sure you want the whole newsgroup to see your reply. It's OK to post such a message, as long as you really think that it's worth reading and that it falls within the newsgroup's guidelines.

To post a follow-up message, follow these steps:

1. Display the article to which you want to reply.
2. Click the Reply button, and choose Reply to Group (you can also press Ctrl + D). To reply to the Sender via e-mail as well as post to the group, choose Reply to Sender and Group, or press Ctrl + Shift + D. You'll see the composition window. Netscape has echoed the subject and placed "Re:" before it.
3. Click Quote if you don't see the quoted text. By all means edit this text down to just the part to which you want to respond. In particular, edit out the person's signature.
4. Type your reply. You can insert this within the quoted text, if you like.
5. Check your spelling.
6. Click Send.

Searching Recent Usenet Postings

If you're looking for specific information on Usenet, you can easily go nuts trying to search manually through the thousands of postings that appear each day. Why not let the computer do it for you?

There are several services on the Web that enable you to search Usenet posts. All of these services enable you to view the articles retrieved by the search. Here's a quick overview:

- **Infoseek (www.infoseek.com)** To search newsgroups, select Usenet Newsgroups from the list box. Type the words for which you want to search, and click Seek.

- **AltaVista (altavista.digital.com)** Click the AltaVista link. In the AltaVista page, choose Usenet from the drop-down list box after Search. Type the words for which you want to search, and click Submit.
- **DejaNews Research Service (www.dejanews.com)** In the Search Categories area of Netscape's Internet Search page, click the Newsgroups link, which leads to a page of search services specializing in Usenet searches. Click the DejaNews link. In the DejaNews page, type the words for which you want to search, and click Find.

Searching Usenet FAQs

To make sure you don't post a question that others have asked before, you should read the FAQ for a newsgroup to which you want to post. Not all newsgroups have FAQs, but you should make an effort to find one in case there is.

Happily, it's easy to search for Usenet FAQs. In the Navigator window, click the Search button. In the Search Categories area, click Newsgroups. Choose the List of USENET FAQs link.

From Here

- You've mastered Collabra! It's on to the next of Communicator's modules, Conference.
- If Internet telephony isn't your schtick, flip to Part V, and learn how to create your own Web pages with Compose.

Part IV

Netscape Conference: Chatting It Up Online

Chapter 22

You've Got a Call!

Using Conference

The latest wrinkle on the Internet is Internet-based telephony, which is giving the long-distance phone companies fits. And for good reason: If you've got an Internet connection, you can call somebody for *free*. (A not-so-minor detail: You and the person on the other end will need a computer equipped with a sound card, speakers, a microphone, an Internet connection, and copies of Conference, the Netscape Communicator module that makes all this happen, or another program that conforms to the relevant international telephony standard.)

New for 4 Did you use CoolTalk, the Internet telephony program that was included with Netscape 3.0? It's history, and here's why. Conference conforms to new, recently-adopted international standards for Internet telephony. (This standard is called H.323, and it's supported by the International Telephony Union, a U.N. organization.) This means that you may be able to talk to people who are using certain other Internet telephony programs, as long as these programs conform to the same standards.

Conference is much more than an Internet telephone program. It's also a conferencing tool, complete with shared whiteboard space, a text chat tool, file exchange, and an extremely cool collaborative browsing function, which enables users to browse the Web together (both people see the same sites).

Although Conference is called Conference, you can't talk to more than one person at a time. That's a limitation built into the current Internet telephony standards. It's possible that future versions of Conference will enable multiple-party conference calls, but this will require changes to the standards.

You probably already have a sound card and speakers, but what about the mike? You can use any microphone that can plug into your sound card's microphone input. Most sound cards are designed to accept the same small stereo plugs that fit into portable tape recorders; check your sound card's documentation to make sure. (I'm using the cheap little mike that came with my daughter's Macintosh LC.)

Introducing Conference

Here's a quick overview of Conference's features :

- Full-duplex audio conferencing enables both users to speak and hear at the same time.
- You can adjust the audio quality for the type of modem you're using (14.4 or 28.8 Kbps).
- A chat tool enables you to send and receive text while you're talking.
- A shared Whiteboard, replete with graphics tools, enables both users to think through ideas visually while they're talking. You can import a file (eight formats are supported) into the Whiteboard, and then mark it up with the graphics tools (which function on a separate layer, preserving the original file).

- Simplified call placement by means of e-mail addresses and Web links
- File exchange utility enables users to exchange files while they're connected
- Collaborative browsing tool enables you to browse the Web together; both people see the same sites!

Can somebody listen to my conversation while it's en route? Not very easily. All Conference conversations are sent in compressed form, which would be just so much gibberish if they were intercepted in some way.

Configuring Conference

Before you start Conference for the first time, make sure you've plugged in your speakers and microphone. You'll need them for various tests that the program makes to determine the optimum sound quality for your system.

The first time you start Conference, you'll see the Conference setup wizard (Figure 22.1), which walks you through the installation procedure. You'll be asked to fill out your Business Card (Figure 22.2), which you can make available to callers if you wish.

Do you have a scanned photo of yourself, in bitmap (*.bmp) format? If so, you can include this picture in your Business Card. To do so, click the open folder icon beneath the picture area (look on the right side of the Business Card in the Conference setup wizard). Use the dialog box to locate and select your photo, and click OK. Note: If you've already filled out the Conference setup wizard and didn't do this, you can get another chance by choosing Setup Wizard from Conference's Help menu. If you don't have your photo now, you can get it later and use this command to add your photo to your setup.

After you fill out the Business Card and click Next, you'll see the Directory Preferences page of the setup wizard, shown in Figure 22.3. Here, you indicate the Dynamic Lookup Service (DLS) server that you want to use. By default, Netscape hooks you up to its own DLS server.

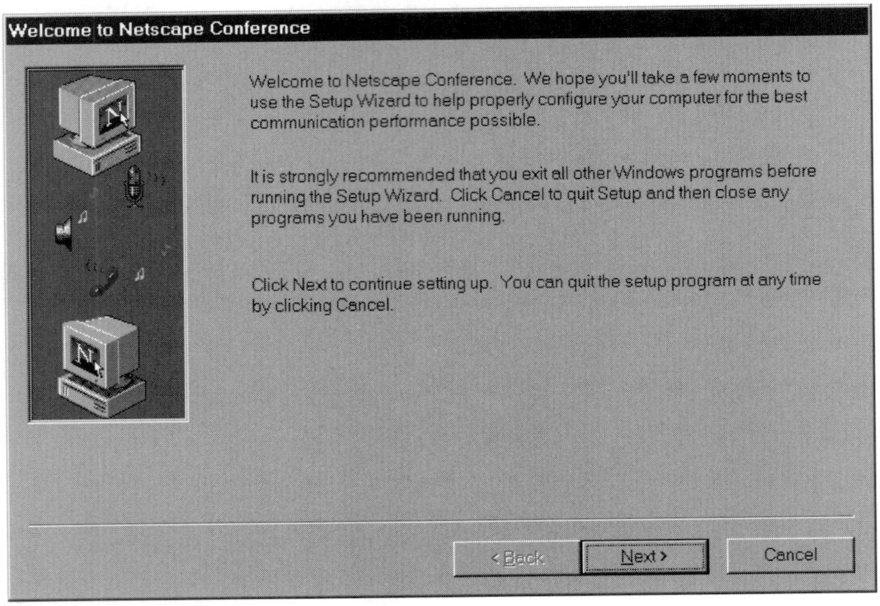
Welcome to Netscape Conference
Welcome to Netscape Conference. We hope you'll take a few moments to use the Setup Wizard to help properly configure your computer for the best communication performance possible.
It is strongly recommended that you exit all other Windows programs before running the Setup Wizard. Click Cancel to quit Setup and then close any programs you have been running.
Click Next to continue setting up. You can quit the setup program at any time by clicking Cancel.
< Back
Next >
Cancel

Figure 22.1 This wizard helps you configure Conference.

Your company might have its own telephony server. Call the computing support staff to find out. If it does, enter the server's address in the DLS server box. If addresses are accessible from a Web page, enter the address of this page in the Phonebook URL box.

Unless your company has its own DLS server, you can pretty much ignore this page—except for the List my name in phonebook option. I'd disable this, if I were you.

I just got this weird, threatening call! Consider very carefully whether you want Conference to publish your name and e-mail address on the Web. This will enable any Tom, Dick, or Harry to call you—and call they will. This is amusing at first—lots of people are trying out Conference, from all over

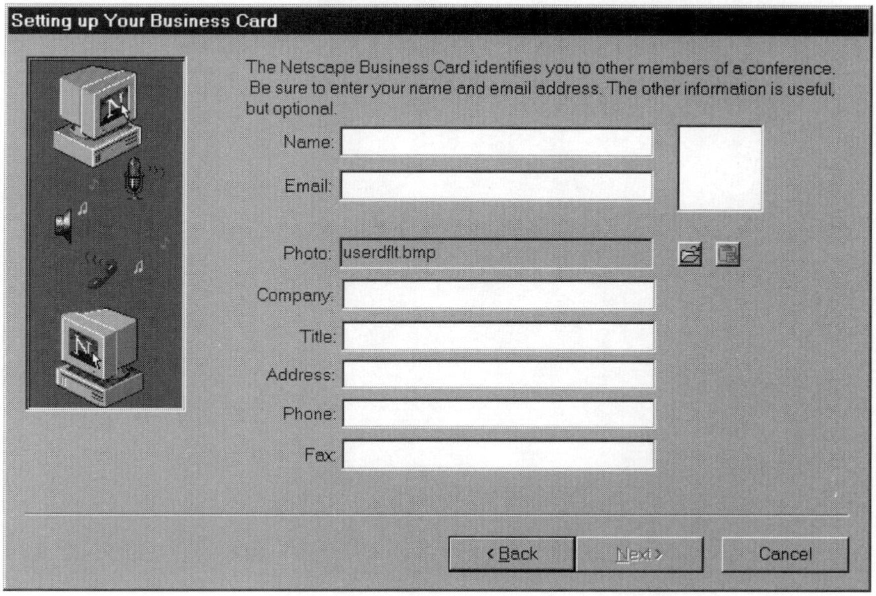
Setting up Your Business Card
The Netscape Business Card identifies you to other members of a conference. Be sure to enter your name and email address. The other information is useful, but optional.
Name:
Email:
Photo: userdflt.bmp
Company:
Title:
Address:
Phone:
Fax:
< Back
Next >
Cancel

Figure 22.2 Your business card can include your picture, if you like.

the world—but it gets tiring. Also, women should carefully consider whether they want to expose themselves to potential harassment. To stop Conference from publishing your information every time you log on, de-select List my name in phonebook (an option on the Directory Preferences page of the setup wizard). If you've already set up Conference, you can disable this option by choosing Preferences from the Call menu, clicking the Network tab, and deselecting List my name in phonebook.

After you click Next, you'll see the Network Type page (see Figure 22.4). Click the type of connection you're using, and click Next. You'll see the sound card page, shown in Figure 22.5. Conference should have automatically detected your sound card; if not, it's not installed properly, so you should quit the setup wizard now and run the sound card's installation program.

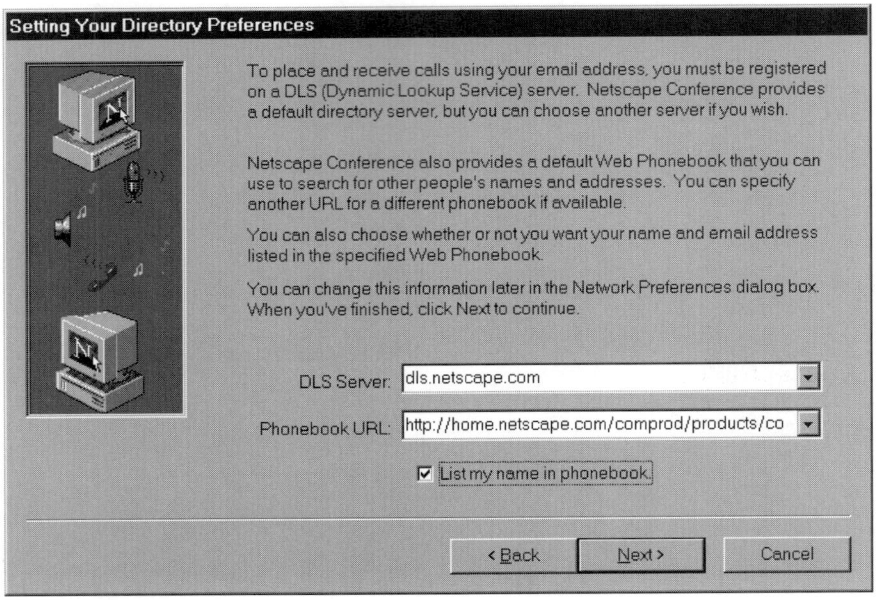
Setting Your Directory Preferences
To place and receive calls using your email address, you must be registered on a DLS (Dynamic Lookup Service) server. Netscape Conference provides a default directory server, but you can choose another server if you wish.
Netscape Conference also provides a default Web Phonebook that you can use to search for other people's names and addresses. You can specify another URL for a different phonebook if available.
You can also choose whether or not you want your name and email address listed in the specified Web Phonebook.
You can change this information later in the Network Preferences dialog box. When you've finished, click Next to continue.
DLS Server: dls.netscape.com
Phonebook URL: http://home.netscape.com/comprod/products/co
List my name in phonebook.
< Back
Next >
Cancel

Figure 22.3 Here, you indicate your directory preferences.

After you click Next from the sound card page, you'll see the start of the audio test. You'll be asked to speak into your microphone. Be sure to position the mike about 5 to 11 inches away from your mouth—don't shout into it close-up—and speak in a normal, conversational tone. To perform the test, click Next, and follow the onscreen instructions.

What's in the Conference Window?

The Conference window includes the following (see Figure 22.6):

- **Menu Bar** The Call menu enables you to place a call, but that's easier to do with the various buttons and tools within the workspace. There are some useful operating options in this menu, though, and we'll get

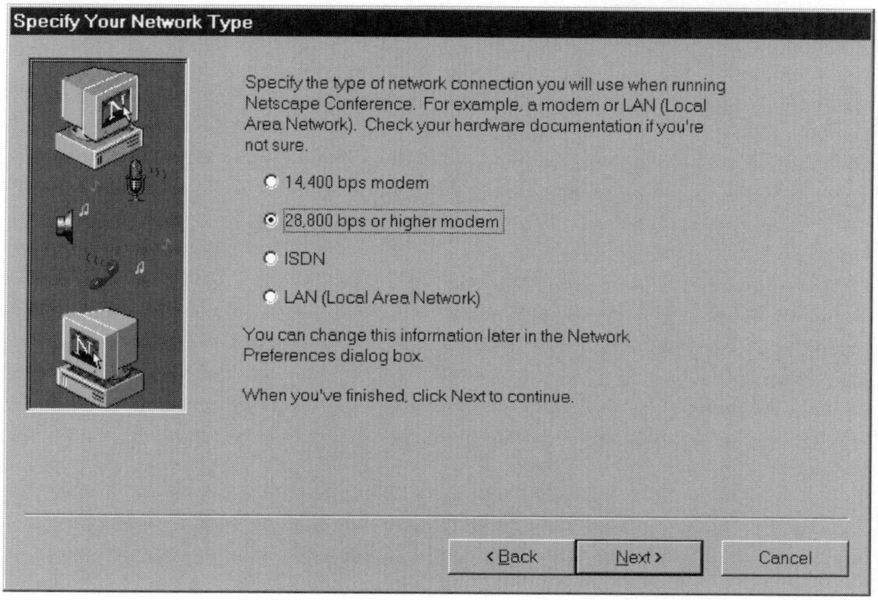
Specify Your Network Type
Specify the type of network connection you will use when running Netscape Conference. For example, a modem or LAN (Local Area Network). Check your hardware documentation if you're not sure.
14,400 bps modem
28,800 bps or higher modem
ISDN
LAN (Local Area Network)
You can change this information later in the Network Preferences dialog box.
When you've finished, click Next to continue.
< Back
Next >
Cancel

Figure 22.4 In this page of the Conference setup wizard, you indicate your connection type.

to these later. The SpeedDial menu enables you to store e-mail addresses for fast calling—but again, that's easier to do with buttons.

- **Toolbar** On the toolbar, you get access to Conference's non-audio tools, including the white board, collaborative browsing, file exchange, and text chat.
- **Make a Call area** In this area, you can place a call in two ways: by using the Web phonebook or by typing (or choosing) an e-mail address. You'll learn more about making a call in the next section.
- **Answer Mode icon** This icon shows what's happening with Conference. If you move the mouse pointer to this icon, you'll see the current answer mode (the default option always notifies you if you're receiving a call). When you're talking to somebody, you see

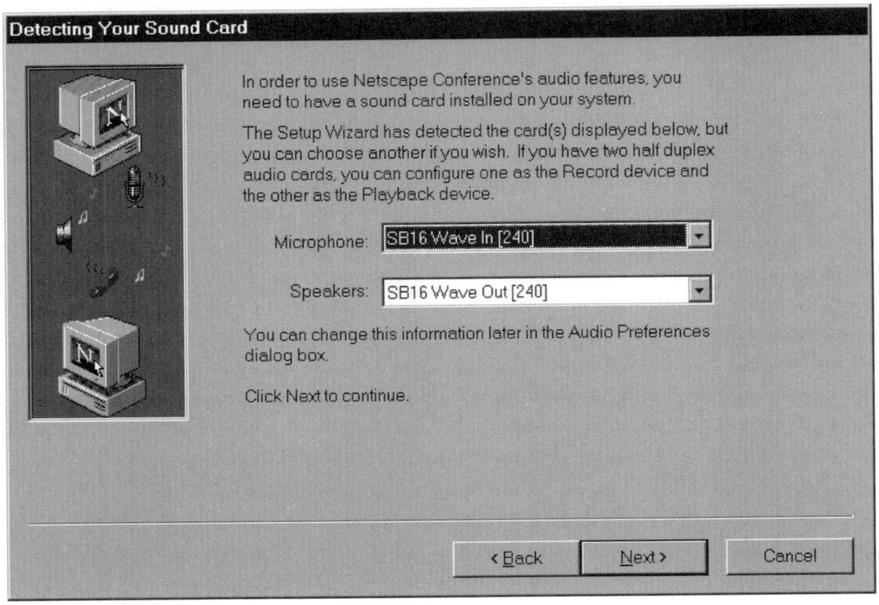
Detecting Your Sound Card
In order to use Netscape Conference's audio features, you need to have a sound card installed on your system.
The Setup Wizard has detected the card(s) displayed below, but you can choose another if you wish. If you have two half duplex audio cards, you can configure one as the Record device and the other as the Playback device.
Microphone:
SB16 Wave In [240]
Speakers:
SB16 Wave Out [240]
You can change this information later in the Audio Preferences dialog box.
Click Next to continue.
< Back
Next >
Cancel

Figure 22.5 If Conference didn't detect your sound card here, there's a problem with the installation.

the person's picture, if they've made a picture available (otherwise, you see an icon showing a person).

- **Speed Dial Toolbar** Normally hidden, you can bring this toolbar into view by clicking the Show Speed Dial button. The Speed Dial buttons
- **Microphone and speaker areas** Here, you can set the volume for recording and playback.

You'll find the following icons on the toolbar:

 Click here to start a collaborative browsing.

 Click here to start a shared whiteboard.

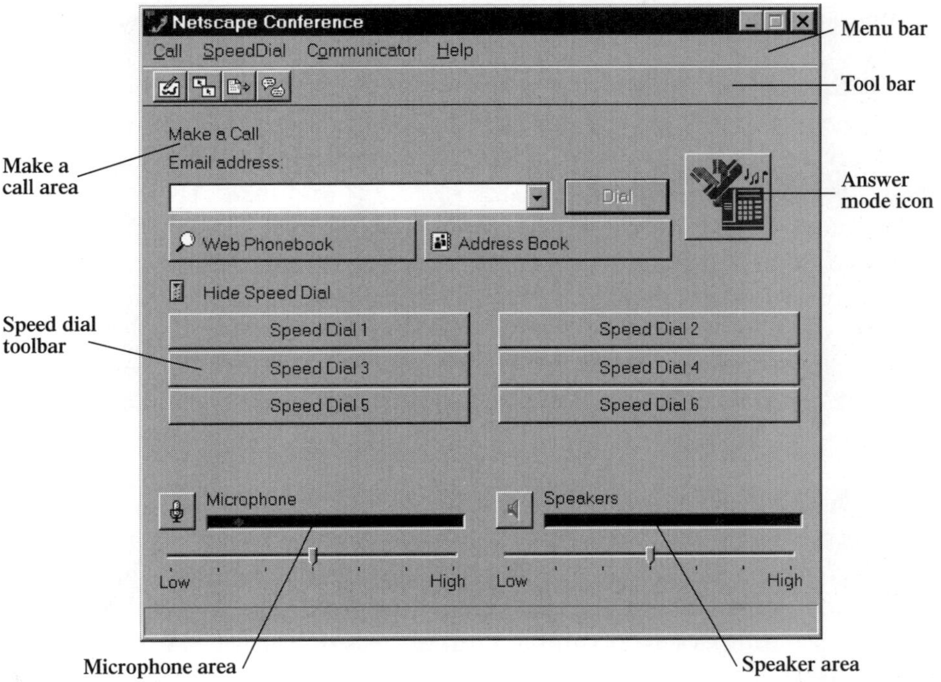

Figure 22.6 Guide to the Conference window.

 Click here to exchange files with the person to whom you're chatting.

 Click here to start a text chat session.

You'll learn about these conferencing functions in the next chapter.

What Number Do I Dial?

I'm sure you're anxious to place a call. But which number do you use? Unfortunately, there isn't one. This section explains how you can place a call even though there's no such thing as an Internet phone number.

Here's the problem with Internet calling. Many people using the Internet have direct connections (often through a local area network at the office), and these lucky individuals have *permanent IP addresses.* (An IP address is a number that uniquely identifies the location of a computer on the Internet. It's something like the address of your house or apartment.) It's no problem for Conference or any other Internet telephony program to link with somebody who has a permanent IP address: You just get the person's address (which will look something like 128.15.299.52) and make the connection. (With Conference, you can do this by choosing Direct Call from the Call menu, and typing an IP address.)

The problem is that many people use modems to connect to the Internet, and most of these people don't have permanent IP addresses. The modem does, but most Internet service providers have lots of modems—hundreds or thousands of them—and you can't control which one you're going to get. So your IP address is assigned temporarily, and differs from session to session.

To solve this problem, computer geniuses came up with the idea of a telphony server. Here's how it works. Your telephony program (such as Conference) creates a unique name for you, a name that doesn't change (for example, "JJ-Chan@saotome.com." When you start your telephony program, the program contacts the server and says (in effect), "Hey, JJ-Chan's using such-and-such IP address for this session." If somebody wants to call JJ-Chan, they look up JJ-Chan in the server's phone number list and select this name. The server takes care of making the connection.

The telephony server, in sum, functions as a global telephone operator, keeping track of changing IP addresses so that somebody wishing to call you can get through.

There's one big problem with the telephony server idea, though. If the person you're trying to call hasn't logged on, there's no current entry for the person. You're out of luck unless you can obtain the person's IP address.

When you start Conference, the program contacts the DLS server and registers your current IP address. Only in this way can somebody type your e-mail address and reach you with Conference.

Placing a Call

To call somebody on the Internet, you first begin by dialing the person's "number"—ideally, this is the person's e-mail address (but this works only if the person you're calling is online and is currently running Conference or a compatible Internet telephone program). If the connection succeeds, you can chat away. (If not, you've the option of sending voice-mail to the person's mailbox.) When you're done chatting, you can terminate the call. The following sections explain the details of placing a call.

Dialing the "Number"

With Conference, you can call somebody in five different ways:

- **Choose a number from the Web Phonebook** If you click the Web Phonebook icon, you see the DLS server that's currently listed in Conference's configuration. Currently, Netscape uses a server that's linked to the Four11 directory service (see Figure 22.7). Use the search box to search for the person's name, or click one of the alphabet letters. When you find the person's name, click the name to initiate the call.
- **Type the person's e-mail address, and click Dial.** This works only if the person is registered at the current DLS server.
- **Choose the person's Address Book Card from Messenger's Address Book, and click the Call button.** Again, this works only if the person is registered at the current DLS server.
- **Click a Speed Dial button.** You need to configure these buttons before you can use them. They're very handy for people you frequently call.
- **Type the person's IP address.** Use e-mail to find out the person's IP address, and then choose Direct Dial from the Call menu. Type this address, and click Dial.

Making the Connection

After you've entered the person's information and clicked Dial, you see a Pending Call Information dialog box while Conference attempts to make the connection. If the person on the other end of the "line" accepts the call, you see the person's picture (if a picture has been provided), and most of the dialog boxes are dimmed (see Figure 22.7). You can start speaking!

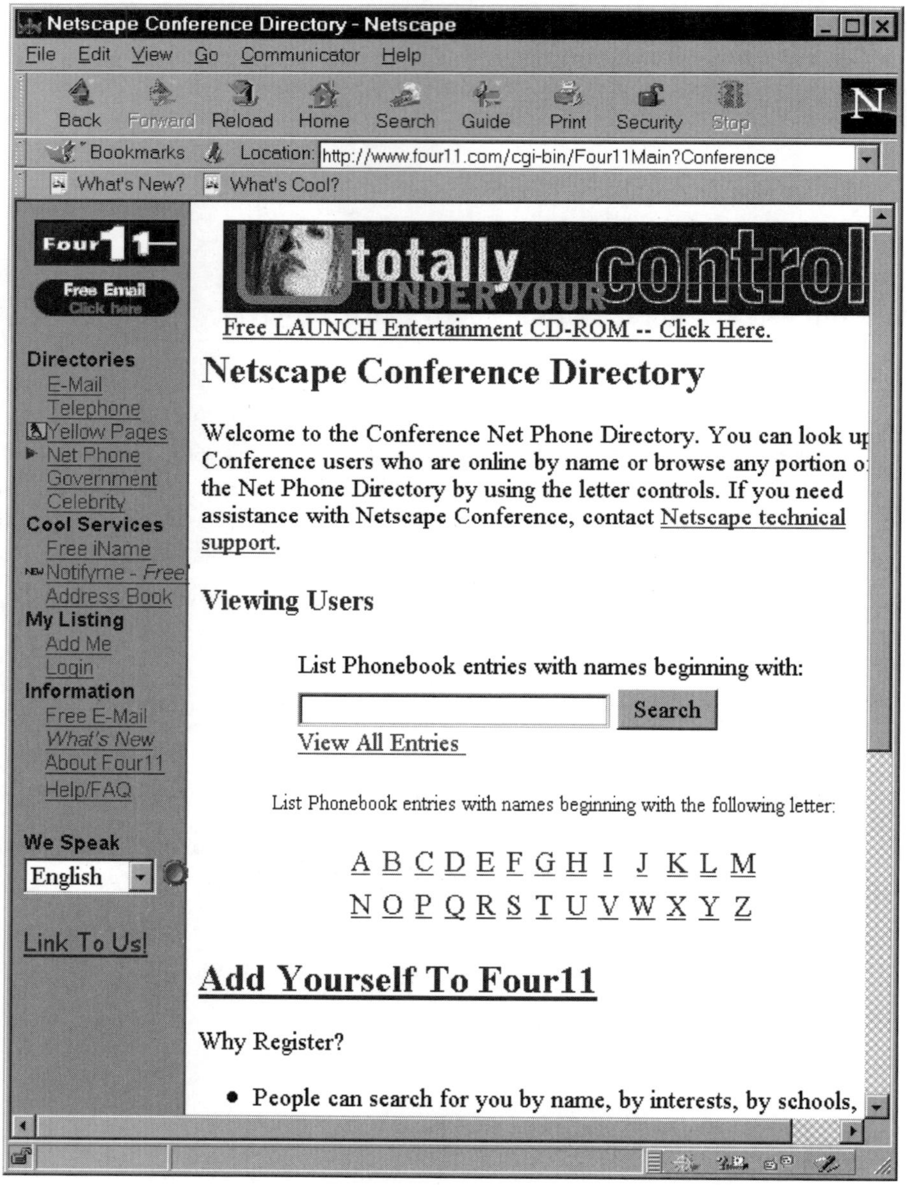

Figure 22.7 Netscape's default DLS server is currently managed by Four11, a Web-based directory service.

It says, "The person you are calling did not answer or refused the call." This means that the person's address is currently registered on the server, but for some reason the person didn't respond. He or she may be away from the computer—or just doesn't feel like talking right now. (You'll learn how to refuse calls later.)

Dealing with a Bad Connection

If you're having trouble understanding the person you're talking to, you may wish to chat via text rather than voice. To start text chatting, click the Text Chat tool, and flip to the next chapter to learn how to use this tool.

Leaving Voice Mail

If the person you're trying to call isn't online and (for this reason) isn't currently registered with the DLS server, you'll see a Voice Mail dialog box stating that the person you're calling isn't available. If you wish, you can leave voice mail. Essentially, what you're doing is sending an e-mail message with a voice attachment. This goes to Messenger, not to Conference.

To record voice-mail, click Yes in the Voice Mail dialog box. You'll see the Netscape Voice Mail dialog box, shown in Figure 22.8. Click the red dot

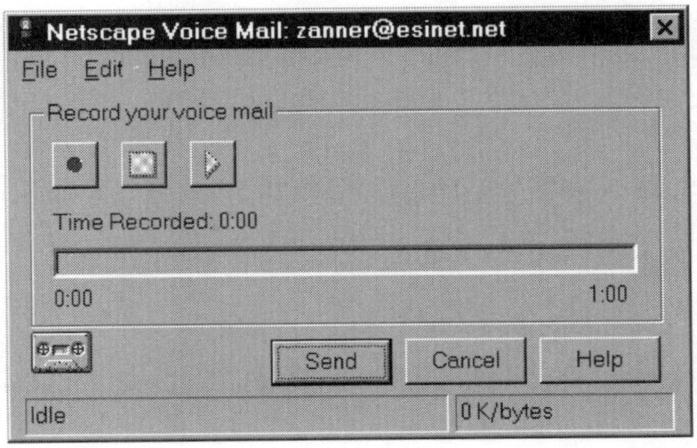

Figure 22.8 If you can't get in touch with Conference, you can send voice mail to the person's e-mail address.

to start recording. Note that you only have one minute of recording time, so make it concise! When you're done, you can click the play button to listen to your recording. If you wish, you can re-record by clicking the red record button again. When you're happy with your recording, click Send.

Terminating a Call

When you're done talking, say "Bye," and click Hang Up.

Receiving a Call

When somebody tries to call you, you'll hear a ringing sound, and you see the name of somebody trying to call you. You'll see the Call Invitation dialog box, which enables you to accept or reject the call. To accept the call, click Accept. To reject it, click Reject.

After you've accepted the call, say "Hello." Well, it isn't quite a phone, but you're still supposed to be nice!

How do I tell if they hung up? If somebody hangs up on you, the person icon changes back to the phone set icon, and the dimmed buttons are undimmed.

Using Netscape Conference Attendant

If choose Netscape Conference Attendant from the Start menu, you can receive calls even if Conference isn't running. This program places an icon on your taskbar. When Conference Attendant detects an incoming call, it starts Conference automatically and notifies you that a call is coming in.

Choosing Answering Options

By default, Conference notifies you when a call is received. From the Call menu, you can choose the following options:

- **Auto Answer** Automatically answer every incoming call. I don't recommend this unless you're using a corporate DLS server.
- **Do Not Disturb** Don't answer any calls.

Configuring Speed-Dial Buttons

If you frequently call somebody, configure a speed dial button so that you can call this person quickly. To configure a speed dial button, just click one of the unconfigured buttons in the Speed Dial area (if this area isn't visible, click Show Speed Dial). You'll see a dialog box (see Figure 22.9) that enables you to type the person's name, e-mail address, DLS server, and direct address (if known). After you click OK, you'll see this person's name on the button face. To call this person, just click the button, or choose the person's name from the SpeedDial menu.

Viewing the Call Log

Conference keeps track of the calls you placed. To see the call log, choose Call Log from the Call menu. In the Call Log dialog box, you'll see a list of all the calls you've placed, including the person's name, e-mail address, DLS server address, time of call, and duration of call.

Are you trying to remember the e-mail address of somebody you talked to previously? Check the call log!

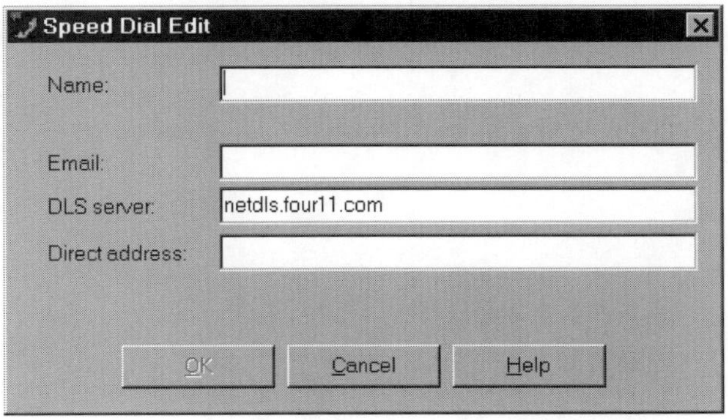

Figure 22.9 Editing a speed dial button.

From Here

- This chapter explored Conference's capabilities for audio calls. In the next chapter, you explore all the cool things you can do while you're talking, including working with a shared whiteboard, browsing the Web together, exchanging files, and text chatting.

Chapter 23

Using the Conferencing Tools

While you're talking in Conference, you can make use of four additional tools: a shared whiteboard space, collaborative Web browsing, file exchange, and text chatting. These tools greatly enhance what you can do with Internet telephony, as you'll quickly discover. Once you've played around with these tools in the context of a conversation, you'll realize why many people believe that audio telephone services will eventually give way to computer-based telephony.

You'll do some fooling around with these tools to see how they work, but I hope I can convince you that they aren't toys. For example, using Whiteboard, you can capture a screen in another application—say, an Excel chart or a spreadsheet—and display this in Whiteboard so that both of you can see it. While you're chatting about it, you can click a pointer tool that displays a big, very noticeable arrow pointing toward some feature you'd like

For the Time-Challenged

- Conference's collaboration tools add to the Internet telephony experience. You can use the shared whiteboard create graphics collaboratively or share graphics files.
- A nifty feature of Conference is collaborative browsing. If you're in control, the other person sees where you're browsing. You can also give up control and let the other person take you for a ride.
- You can exchange files while you're chatting away.
- If the audio connection isn't good, you can use text chat.

to emphasize. And if the person you're calling would like to know more, you can quickly and easily transfer the Excel file to the other person's computer—while you're talking! To illustrate the point you're making, take this person on a tour of some Web sites that you'd like to share. You'll both see the same sites onscreen.

Get started by learning about Whiteboard. From there, this chapter covers collaborative browsing, file exchange, and the chat tool.

Using the Whiteboard

Conference's Whiteboard appears when you click the Whiteboard tool on the Conference toolbar. In the Whiteboard, whatever you do—even making pretty picture (see Figure 23.1)—appears on your interlocutor's Conference screen as well as your own. If you're not much of an artist, you can import bitmap (*.bmp), JPEG, or GIF graphics into the whiteboard, and transmit these (see Figure 23.2). You can also capture screens from other windows, and share these screens with the person you're calling.

This space is collaborative—you see everything that both of you do.

Although you can add text to the whiteboard, this isn't a good place to chat with text. To exchange text, click the Text Chat tool.

Figure 23.1 Whiteboard enables you to send bit-mapped images while you're chatting away in the audio conference.

Understanding the Whiteboard Window

If you've ever used a paint or drawing program before, you already know how to use most of the Whiteboard tools. Here's a quick overview of the tools on the Whiteboard toolbars.

On the Whiteboard toolbar (the one below the menu bar), you'll find the following tools in addition to the drop-down list boxes for font and font size:

Figure 23.2 If you're not a very good artist, you can import bitmap, JPEG, or GIF graphics and share them.

Click here to choose a bitmap, JPEG, or GIF graphic to display in the whiteboard space.

Click here to save the whiteboard's current contents.

Click here to print the whiteboard's current contents.

Click here to copy the selection to the Clipboard. To select something within the Whiteboard, hold down the left mouse button and drag.

Click here to paste the current Clipboard contents into the Whiteboard window. After you click this button, move the mouse

pointer to where you want the image to appear, and click the left mouse button.

Click here to enter bold type.

Click here to enter italic type.

In the drawing toolbar, you find the following tools:

Click here to draw a freehand line. To draw, just hold down the left mouse button and move the mouse.

Click here to erase something you've drawn. Erase by holding down the left mouse button and moving the mouse.

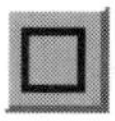
Click here to create a rectangle. To enter the rectangle, click where you want the rectangle corner to appear, hold down the left mouse button, and move the mouse. Hold down the Shift key while dragging if you want to enter a perfect square.

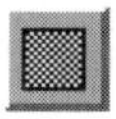
Click here to enter a filled rectangle. This tool works just like the rectangle tool, except that it fills in the rectangle or square with the color and fill pattern that are currently selected in the fill and Color toolbars.

Click here to create a circle. To enter the circle, click where you want the circle to appear, hold down the left mouse button, and move the mouse. Hold down the Shift key while dragging if you want to enter a perfect circle

Click here to make a big, very noticeable pointer arrow appear on the screen where you click the mouse. This is very useful for calling attention to something while you're chatting.

Click here to add text. To enter the text, click where you want the text to appear, and then choose a font and font size from the toolbar. Start typing to enter the text.

Click here to draw a line. To enter the line, click where you want the line to start, and move the mouse.

Click here to draw lines that are straight up and down or level. To enter the line, click where you want the line to start, and move the mouse.

In the Width, Fill, and Color areas, you can choose line widths, fill shades, and colors that affect the appearance of the shapes you enter.

This thing's a mess! How do I erase all this junk and start over? Don't rub away with that little eraser—it takes too long. From the Edit menu, choose Clear Markups to clear any annotations you've made to an image you've pasted, or Clear White Board to start out with a clean slate.

Changing the View

To get a closer look at something on the screen—a look that the person with whom you're talking will also see—choose one of the Zoom In options on the View menu, and click the Zoom pointer (a magnifying glass) where you want the image to be enlarged. To restore normal size, click Original Size in this menu. From this menu, you can also reduce the image's size by clicking one of the Zoom Out options.

Capturing Screen Areas

A neat White Board feature is the ability to capture windows, your desktop, or selected areas in other windows, and display them within White Board (see Figure 23.3).

To capture something you're displaying in another window, click Capture, and choose Window. Switch to the window you want to capture, and click.

Collaborative Browsing

A very cool feature of Conference is collaborative browsing, which enables you to browse with the person you're talking to. Both of you see the same sites on your respective copies of Netscape Navigator.

To browse collaboratively, click the Collaborative Browsing dialog box (Figure 23.4), and click Start Browsing. The person you're calling will see a dialog box asking whether he or she would like to browse collaboratively. Click Yes.

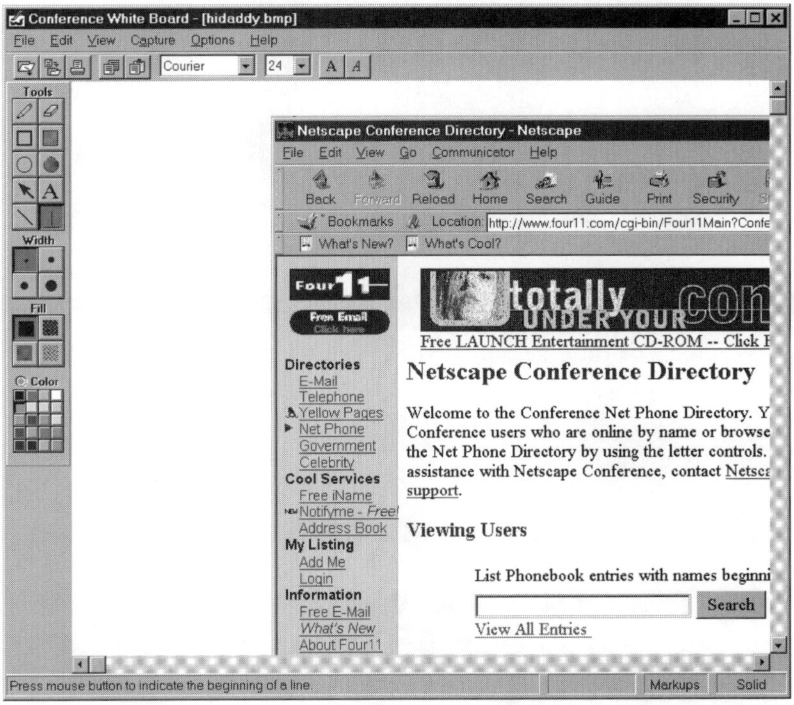

Figure 23.3 Screen captured—and displayed in White Board.

To control the browser, click the check box next to Ctrol the Browsers. To bring both browsers into synchronization, click Sync Browsers. When you're done collaborative browsing, click Stop Browsing.

Exchanging Files

You can exchange files with the person you're chatting with. To send a file, click File Exchange. You'll see the Conference File Exchange dialog box, shown in Figure 23.5. To send a file, click Open, and locate the file you

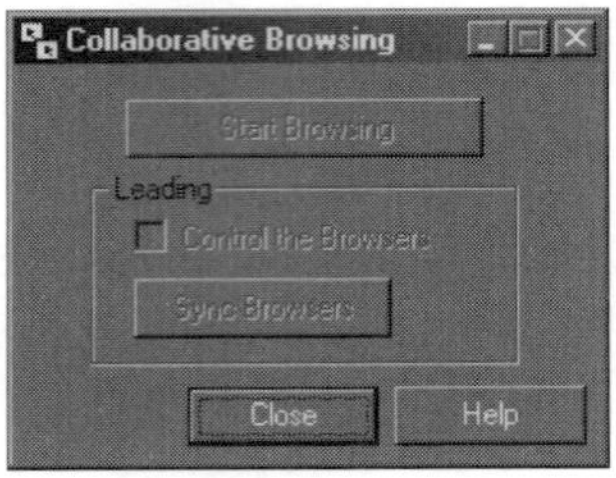

Figure 23.4 You initiate and control collaborative browsing with this dialog box.

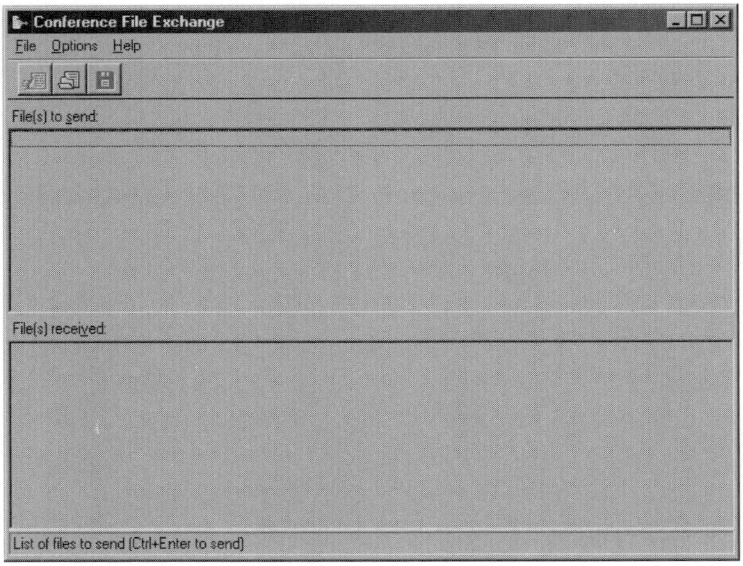

Figure 23.5 You can send a file with this dialog box.

want to send. You'll see the file name in the Files to Send area. To send the file, choose Send from the File menu, or press Ctrl + Enter.

If your correspondent sends you a file, you'll see the name of the file in the Files Received area.

Using Text Chat

If your audio connection isn't working very well, you can chat via Text Chat (Figure 23.6). To use Text Chat, click the Text Chat button. You'll see the Conference Text Chat dialog box. In the Personal Note pad area, type the text you want to send, and press Ctrl + Enter.

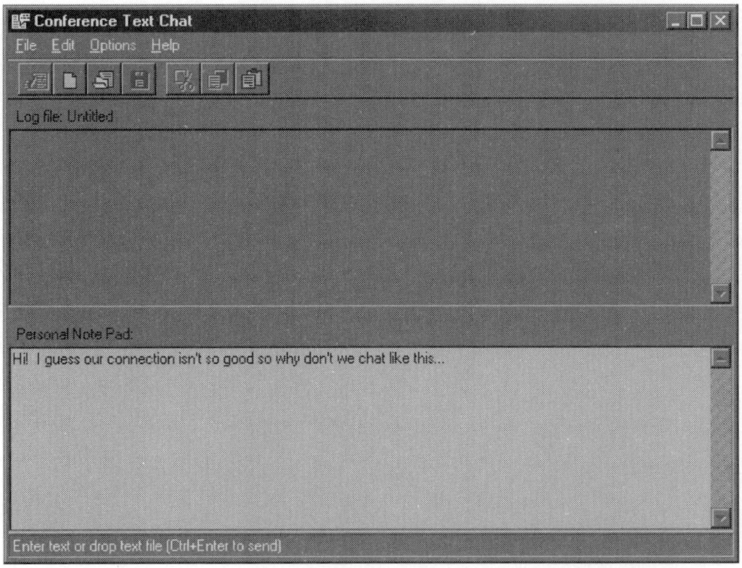

Figure 23.6 Text Chat enables you to chat via text if the audio signal isn't getting through (or if one or both of you don't have sound equipment).

You can send a text file, if you wish. To do so, click the Include button on the text chat toolbar to include a text file. Locate the file, and choose Send.

From Here

- The next Communicator module to explore is Netcaster, discussed in Chapters 24 and 25.

Part V

Netscape Netcaster: Subscribing to Live Content

Chapter 24

Getting Started with Netscape Netcaster

It's the latest thing: Push media. If that sounds something like e-mail spamming, read on—it's a lot more pleasant, and you're always in control. Essentially, push media enables you to subscribe to Web "channels" and receive updates automatically. The subscribed content is downloaded automatically—you don't have to go hunting for it. You can view the content in a Netscape window or, if you'd prefer, in a *webtop*, which is a full-screen window that takes the place of your desktop. You can position other windows over this to keep working, and then switch to the webtop see what's up.

This chapter introduces the basics of working with Netscaster. In the next chapter, you'll learn how to customize Netscaster, control update frequencies, and even browse documents while you're offline.

For the Time-Challenged

- Netcaster enables you to subscribe to *channels*, which are Web sites that pump out new content at intervals chosen by the content provider. You can display the content in Navigator or on the *webtop*, a special window that covers up your desktop.
- After you start Netcaster, you see a Channel Finder and the default webtop. The Channel Finder has two panes, a list of supplied channels and My Channels, a list of the channels to which you've subscribed.
- You can easily add channels to your My Channel list. Look for sites that offer Netscape Netcaster subscriptions, and click Subscribe. Or select a channel in the Channel Finder, and click Add.
- You can place an ordinary Web site on the webtop. Click Options, and then click Add to supply the site's name and URL.

Introducing Channels

Channels are Web sites, created with the same tools that are used to create any Web site. The only difference is that they're automatically delivered to your desktop. You can subscribe to just the channels you want.

In addition to Web site channels, you can also use Netcaster to subscribe to Marimba Castanet channels. Castanet enables you to subscribe to channels that broadcast Java applications—and to receive updates automatically.

You can also subscribe to ordinary Web sites. You can set up Netcaster to check these sites at periodic intervals, and display them within Navigator or on your webtop.

Starting Netcaster

To start Netcaster, do one of the following:

- In the Communicator menu, choose Netcaster.

  or

- In Navigator's personal toolbar, click the Netcaster button.

You'll see Netcaster on screen. Netcaster starts with the default webtop, which is—guess who? Netscape's page. You can change the default webtop, if you wish, but we'll get to that in Chapter 25.

Understanding Netcaster's window

Netcaster consists of two windows, the Channel Finder and the Webtop (see Figure 24.1):

- **Channel Finder** The Channel Finder window includes two panels. The panel that you'll see when you open Netcaster displays the current roster of content providers that have signed up with Netscape. (This list changes, so check it out often.) The second panel, My Channels, shows the channels and sites to which you've subscribed. Right now, you're subscribed only to the default channel, Netscape's channel. You open and close these two channels by clicking the tabs.
- **Webtop** In the Webtop window, you see Netscape's channel. You can add additional channels to the webtop. You see only one channel at a time, but you can add as many channels as you wish to the webtop list. The My Channels panel of the Channel Finder enables you to display your subscribed webtops.

Let's look more closely at the Netcaster window to see how the various parts work.

Displaying and hiding Netcaster

When you start Netcaster, you see the Channel Finder and Webtop. If you'd like to hide these, just click the tab on the side of the window. To bring Netscaster back, just click this tab again.

Understanding Netcaster's buttons and controls

You'll find two rows of options and buttons at the bottom of the Netscape Netcaster window. Here's what the options do:

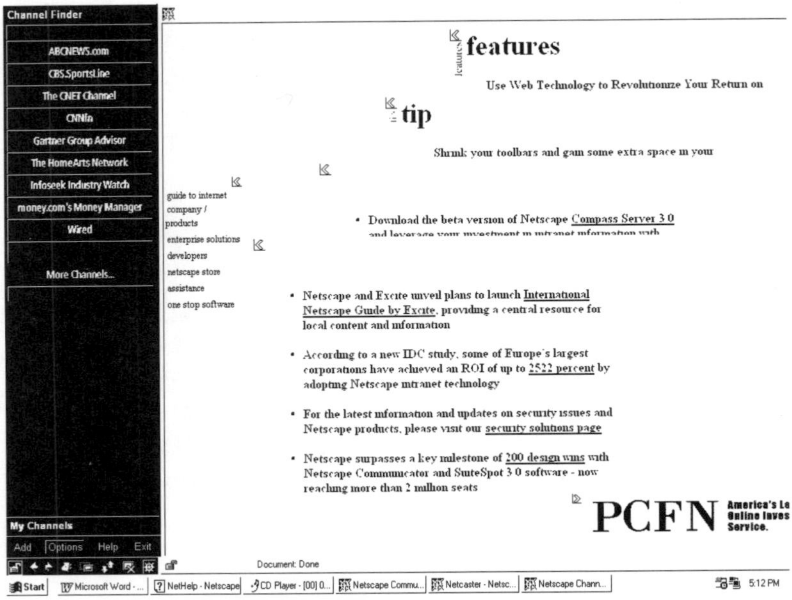
Channel Finder
ABCNEWS.com
CBS.SportsLine
The CNET Channel
CNNfn
Gartner Group Advisor
The HomeArts Network
Infoseek Industry Watch
money.com's Money Manager
Wired
More Channels...
My Channels
Add Options Help Exit
features
Use Web Technology to Revolutionize Your Return on
tip
Shrink your toolbars and gain some extra space in your
guide to internet
company /
products
enterprise solutions
developers
netscape store
assistance
one stop software
Download the beta version of Netscape Compass Server 3.0
Netscape and Excite unveil plans to launch International Netscape Guide by Excite, providing a central resource for local content and information
According to a new IDC study, some of Europe's largest corporations have achieved an ROI of up to 2522 percent by adopting Netscape intranet technology
For the latest information and updates on security issues and Netscape products, please visit our security solutions page
Netscape surpasses a key milestone of 200 design wins with Netscape Communicator and SuiteSpot 3.0 software - now reaching more than 2 million seats
PCFN
Document: Done
Start
5:12 PM

Figure 24.1 Netcaster has two windows, the Webtop and the Channel Finder.

- **Add** Add the currently-selected channel or site to My Channels.
- **Options** Display the Netcaster Options window so you can customize Netcaster. Chapter 26 discusses these options.
- **Help** Display help for Netcaster.
- **Exit** Exit Netcaster, including the webtop.

When you've opened a webtop window, you'll also see the following controls:

 This padlock icon gives you security information about the current channel.

 Displays the previous page in the webtop list.

Displays the next page in the webtop list.

Prints the webtop.

Displays or hides the desktop beneath the webtop.

Places the webtop in front of or behind application windows.

Closes the webtop

Opens a Navigator window.

ADDING CHANNELS TO THE WEBTOP

You can add channels to the webtop in two ways, as explained in this section.

Adding channels at a site

If you run across a site that offers a Netcaster subscription, like the Sandra Bullock site shown in Figure 24.2, just click the Subscribe link to add the site to your webtop.

Adding channels with Channel Finder

You can also add channels using the Channel Finder. Since Netscape demands fairly hefty fees for content providers to be included in Channel Finder, don't expect to find do-it-yourself pages here. Still, there are lots of attractive options here.

To subscribe to a channel, highlight the channel and click Add. You'll see the Member Services Registration wizard which, frankly, gets pretty pushy about asking for personal information. Unless you want to go hunting for your own channel providers, though, you've

If you don't find anything appealing in the Channel Finder list, click More Channels; you'll see the Netcaster Channel Finder page, shown in Figure 24.3, with more channel options. Click the add or subscribe button to subscribe.

Channel Finder
My Channels
Netscape Channel
ABCNEWS.com
Celebguide Channels - Netscape
presents
Sandra.Network is a brand new push channel available for Netscape Netcaster ( ), available with Netscape Communicator 4.0 dedicated to the actress Sandra Bullock. Included is a constantly updated news area, games, puzzles, biographies, filmographies, and more. The channel will update itself or you can do so manually. Currently it is available only for Netscape Communicator 4.0 with Netcaster.
Click the button below to subscribe.
subscribe
Add Options Help Exit
Document: Done

Figure 24.2 Some Web sites will let you subscribe just by clicking a Subscribe button on the site's page.

After you've added the channel, you'll see the Channel Properties dialog box, shown in Figure 24.4. The defaults indicate the channel provider's preferences, so they're probably fine. You can change these, though, by clicking the Display tab (you can choose between a Navigator or a webtop window), Cache (this affects how many levels you download past the site's URL), and the General tab, which specifies the name, location, and download frequency. Basically, you should just click OK here. You'll learn more about customizing channels in the next chapter.

Selecting a Channel to View

Once you've subscribed to two or more channels, you can select the channel to view on the webtop. To do so, click My Channels in the Channel Finder, and click the channel you've added. Alternatively, click the Back or Forward

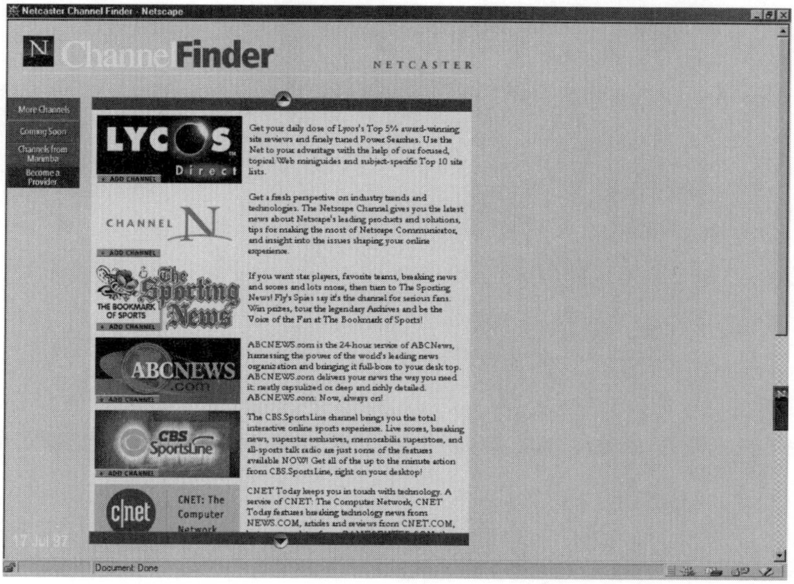

Figure 24.3 Click More Channels to see this page, which lists additional channel options.

buttons in the Channel Finder toolbar until you see the channel you want. Be warned, though, that this is a pretty slow way to select channels! It's better to select the channel in the Channel Finder.

After you've selected the channel you want, you see it on the webtop (Figure 24.5).

Placing an Ordinary Web Site on Your Webtop

One of the coolest things about Netcaster, in my not-so-humble opinion, is not necessarily the flashy content providers you'll find in the Channel Finder. It's that you can put *any* Web site on the Webtop, and specify the update frequency to your heart's content.

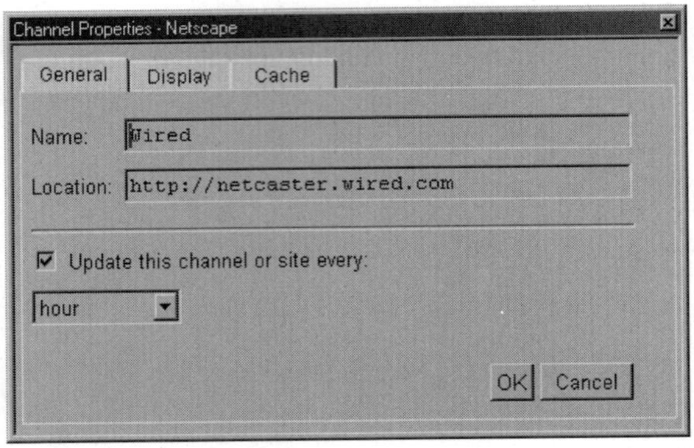

Figure 24.4 Here, you can choose options—but for now, just click OK.

To add an ordinary, garden-variety Web site to your webtop, do the following:

1. In the Channel Finder, click Options. You'll see the Options dialog box, shown in Figure 24.6.
2. Click Add. You'll see the Channel Properties dialog box, shown in Figure 24.7.
3. In the Name box, type the name of the site.
4. In the Location box, type the URL of the site.
5. To update this channel automatically, click the Update box, and choose an update frequency.
6. Click Display, and make sure the Webtop option is checked.

   You don't need to worry about the cache options, which are important only for offline browsing, discussed in Chapter 26.
7. Click OK to add the Web site to your My Channels list.

In the My Channels list, select your site. You've got to love this—your choice, no cheeky advertising, the information you want. I've added my local weather report, updated every three hours (Figure 24.8). I'm starting to like "push"—but only when I "pull"!

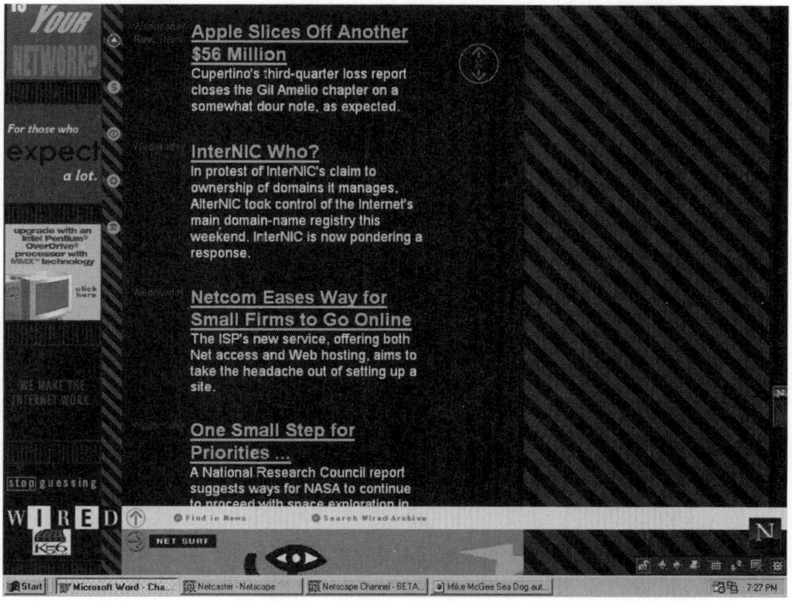
For those who
expect
a lot.
upgrade with an Intel Pentium® OverDrive® processor with MMX™ technology
click here
stop guessing
WIRED
Apple Slices Off Another $56 Million
Cupertino's third-quarter loss report closes the Gil Amelio chapter on a somewhat dour note, as expected.
InterNIC Who?
In protest of InterNIC's claim to ownership of domains it manages, AlterNIC took control of the Internet's main domain-name registry this weekend. InterNIC is now pondering a response.
Netcom Eases Way for Small Firms to Go Online
The ISP's new service, offering both Net access and Web hosting, aims to take the headache out of setting up a site.
One Small Step for Priorities ...
A National Research Council report suggests ways for NASA to continue
Find in News
Search Wired Archive
NET SURF
N
Start
Microsoft Word - Cha...
Netcaster - Netscape
Netscape Channel - BETA...
Mike McGee Sea Dog aut...
7:27 PM

Figure 24.5 Your webtop comes alive! (Um, with advertising)

Managing Channels

Deleting an unwanted channel

To delete an unwanted channel, do the following:

1. In the Channel Finder's toolbar, click Options.
2. Select the channel you want to delete.
3. Click Delete.
4. Click OK.

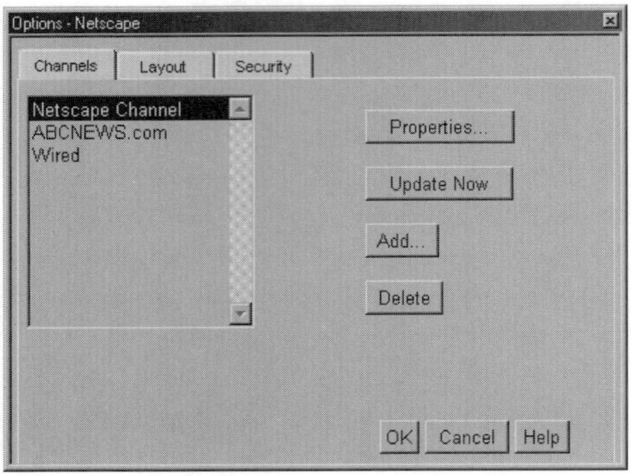

Figure 24.6 This dialog box is your gateway to Netcaster's interesting options.

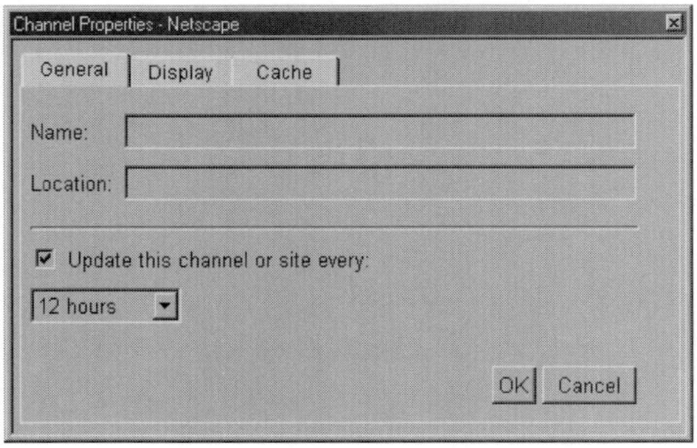

Figure 24.7 Here, you can add any Web site to your desktop.

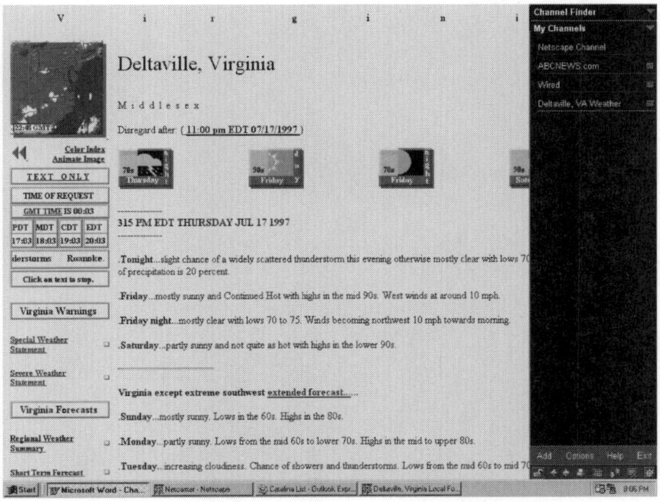

Figure 24.8 Add your favorite Web site to the webtop.

Setting the default channel

To select the default channel to display on the webtop:

1. In the Channel Finder's toolbar, click Options.
2. Click the Layout tab.
3. Under Default Channel, click set default to, and then choose the channel you want to set as the default.
4. Click OK.

From Here

- You've learned the essentials of Netcaster! Polish off your skills in the next chapter, which shows you how to customize Netcaster.

Chapter 25

Taking Netcaster to the Max

Netcaster is easy to use, but there are several nifty options lurking under the surface. If you enjoy playing with options, you can choose a range of customization options for channels. What's really cool, though is that you can use Netcaster to set up offline browsing, in which the program dutifully downloads an entire site while you're not using your computer; you can then browse the site even if you're not connected to the Internet. Another non-obvious but nifty capability of Netcaster is its ability to work with Castanet channels, which bring you Java applications. All of these cool possibilities are discussed in this chapter.

For the Time-Challenged

- You can fiddle with channel customization if you like, but heck—the default settings are fine.
- If you think you're not seeing the latest content, right-click a channel in the Channel Finder, and click Start Update.
- To browse offline, switch to Navigator, open the File menu, and choose Go Offline. You can then browse a downloaded channel in Netcaster.
- You can access any Castanet channel using exactly the same procedures you use to subscribe to a Netcaster channel. You get a Java application instead of a Web site.

Moving the Netcaster Window

If you'd like to rearrange the Netcaster window, you have a few options. Click Options, and click the Layout tab. You can move the webtop and the Channel Finder to the left or right of the screen. To confirm your choice, click OK.

Updating Channels

Don't want to wait for the next update—or not sure whether you're looking at the most recent material? You can update the channel right now.

To update a channel, do one of the following:

- In the Options dialog box, click Channels. In the Channel Properties dialog box (Figure 25.1), click update Now.

  or

- In the My Channels list (Channel Finder), right-click a channel, and click Start Update.

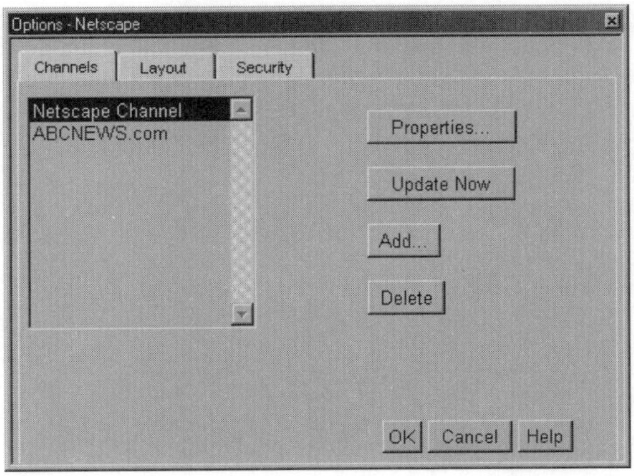

Figure 25.1 This dialog box enables you to choose several options for subscribed channels.

CHANGING THE DEFAULT CHANNEL

The default channel is the one that Netscape displays when you start Netcaster. You can change the default channel, if you wish.

To change the default channel, follow these steps:

1. In the Channel Finder, click Options.
2. Click Layout. You'll see the Layout options, shown in Figure 25.2.
3. Under Default Channel, select Set default to, and choose the channel you want to open by default.
4. Click OK.

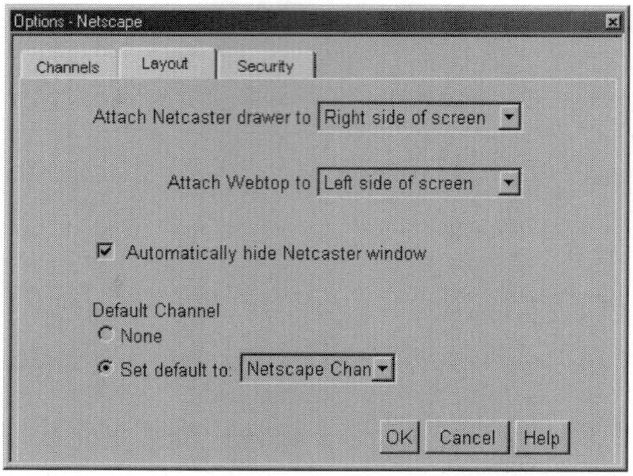

Figure 25.2 Here, you can choose layout options for the webtop.

Specifying Update Frequencies

Channels specify their own update frequencies. Since content providers know how often they update their own sites, you'll be wise to let them dictate the update frequency. However, you may wish to choose your own update frequency if you've added ordinary Web sites to your webtop, as explained in the previous chapter.

To specify an update frequency for a channel:

1. In the Channel Finder, click Options.
2. Select the channel you want to modify.
3. Click Properties. You'll see the Properties dialog box, shown in Figure 25.3.
4. Make sure the Update this channel box is checked.
5. In the drop-down list box, choose the update frequency you want.
6. Click OK.

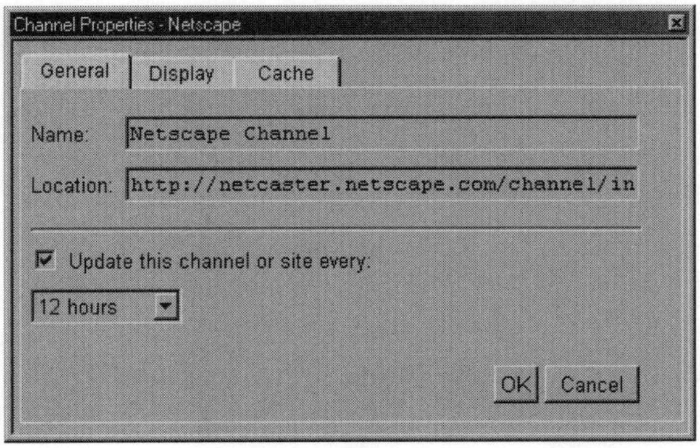

Figure 25.3 In this dialog box, you choose properties for the selected channel.

Browsing Offline

Are you starting to notice that the Web slows down during the day? For me, back here on the East Coast where things are civilized, everything's fine until about noon, when all those people out there in the West Coast start getting out of bed and turning on their computers. I don't know why they get up so late. But when they do, the Web slows down. By 2 or 3 o'clock, it's tough to access sites at all, let alone quickly. By five, happily, we sensible people back here on the East Coast start to flip off our computers and do more important things, and the Web starts to speed up again. There's another draggy period, of course, when all the IRC addicts go online after work, but by midnight the 'Net's pretty fast.

And that's when you should be downloading, or so goes the offline browsing theory. With offline browsing, you set up Netcaster to access sites when you're not using your computer. Netcaster downloads all the site's content, including graphics, JavaScripts, animated GIFs—the works. In addition, it also downloads linked pages, up to a depth you specify. In this way, you can download pretty much a whole site, and it's stored on your hard disk. (You do have lots of disk room?) During the day, when the Web slows to a crawl, you can log off and browse on your desktop. Access is really fast because everything's on your disk.

Offline browsing is also a good option if you're charged for connection time. You can download the site, log off, and view it offline. But why not just find an ISP with unlimited access?

Browsing offline

To browse a site offline:

1. Make sure that Netcaster has updated the site at least once. To do so, select the site in the Channel Finder's My Channels pane, right-click the channel name, and choose Start update. (Do this while you're connected.).
2. Log off, and start Navigator. From the File menu, choose Go Offline.
3. Switch back to Netcaster, and select the site in the Channel Finder. You can now browse the site offline. If you click a link that requires a connection, you'll see a dialog box asking whether you would like to go online.

Choosing offline browsing options

You can specify how much of the site Netcaster downloads for offline browsing. To do so, follow these instructions:

1. In the Channel Finder, click Options.
2. Select the channel you want to modify, and click Properties.
3. In the Channel Properties, dialog box, click Cache. You'll see the Cache page, shown in Figure 25.4.
4. In the Download area, choose the number of levels you want to download. If you specify 1, Netcaster downloads all the pages 1 link away from the referenced page. If you specify 2, Netcaster downloads all the pages 2 links away from the referenced page. Watch out for specifying more than 2 or 3 links; at some sites, this could result in downloading hundreds of Web pages!
5. In the Don't store more than area, specify the maximum amount of data you want to download. This is a stopguard in case you went too far in step 4.
6. Click OK.

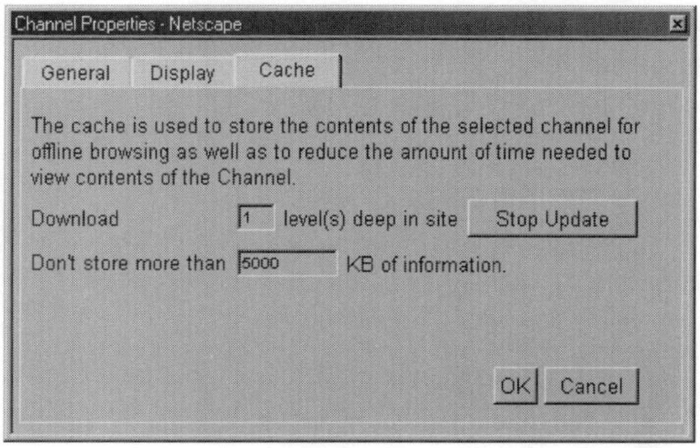
Channel Properties - Netscape
General
Display
Cache
The cache is used to store the contents of the selected channel for offline browsing as well as to reduce the amount of time needed to view contents of the Channel.
Download
1
level(s) deep in site
Stop Update
Don't store more than
5000
KB of information.
OK
Cancel

Figure 25.4 Don't choose more than 1 or 2 levels deep, unless you've tons of disk space.

Shaking it up with Castanet

Castanet is an innovative Web broadcasting technology created by Marimba, a Java-savvy outfit—and rightly so, considering that it was founded by a bunch of Sun Microsystems expatriates. (Sun invented Java.) What's so cool about Castanet is that you can subscribe, not to sites, but rather to software, so that you can automatically, transparently, and—dare I say it?—even unconciously receive software maintenance upgrades (that's uptown talk for "bug fixes"). This is really pretty neat, when you think about what's required to download and install new versions of software manually. This is a significant innovation, and it points the way to how we'll obtain and maintain computer programs in the future.

So what do you get when you download a Castanet channel? It's not just executables, such as the remarkable (and free) Corel Office Suite for Java. Castanet downloads Java executables, which can present multimedia content, including games and other solidly interactive stuff. Explore Castanet—it's really interesting technology.

I love it but it's S - L - O - W! That's the down side of Java. Improvements are being made steadily, but the fact remains that Java software just doesn't execute as fast as code that's been expressly designed for a specific processor. Still, you can enjoy Java applications, such as the ones you'll download with Castanet, if you've got a reasonably fast computer—say, one with a clock speed of at least 166 MHz and tons of RAM (48 MB is nice).

Another nice place to find Castanet channels is Bloke.com (gday.bloke.com). And don't miss the Excite Channel Guide, at trans.excite.com/ExciteChannelGuide.

Finding a Castanet channel

For a nice list of Castanet channels, check out www.marimba.com, and follow the links. You'll see a list of available Castanet channels (Figure 25.5).

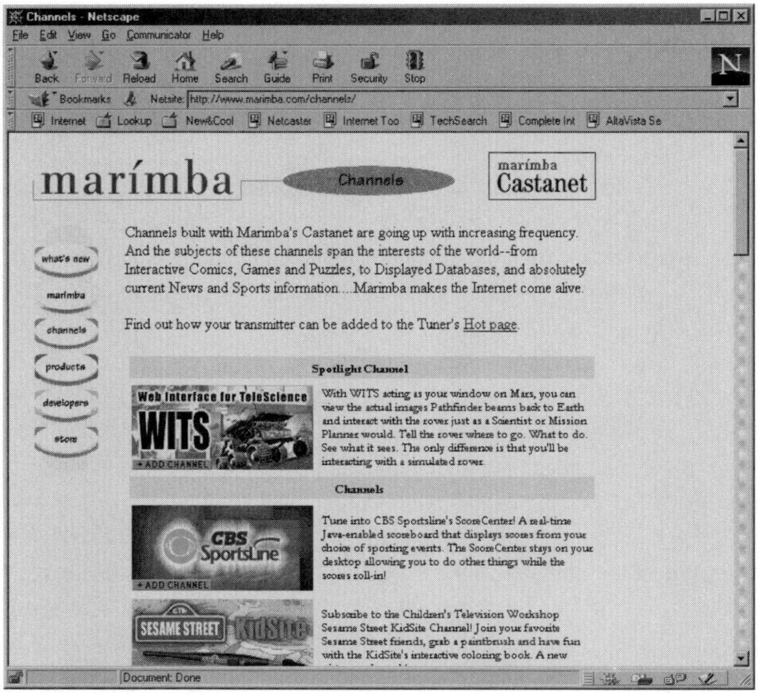
Channels - Netscape
File Edit View Go Communicator Help
Back Forward Reload Home Search Guide Print Security Stop
Bookmarks Netsite: http://www.marimba.com/channels/
Internet Lookup New&Cool Netcaster Internet Too TechSearch Complete Int AltaVista Se
marímba
Channels
marímba Castanet
Channels built with Marimba's Castanet are going up with increasing frequency. And the subjects of these channels span the interests of the world--from Interactive Comics, Games and Puzzles, to Displayed Databases, and absolutely current News and Sports information....Marimba makes the Internet come alive.
Find out how your transmitter can be added to the Tuner's Hot page.
what's new
marimba
channels
products
developers
store
Spotlight Channel
Web Interface for TeleScience
WITS
+ ADD CHANNEL
With WITS acting as your window on Mars, you can view the actual images Pathfinder beams back to Earth and interact with the rover just as a Scientist or Mission Planner would. Tell the rover where to go. What to do. See what it sees. The only difference is that you'll be interacting with a simulated rover.
Channels
CBS SportsLine
+ ADD CHANNEL
Tune into CBS Sportsline's ScoreCenter! A real-time Java-enabled scoreboard that displays scores from your choice of sporting events. The ScoreCenter stays on your desktop allowing you to do other things while the scores roll-in!
SESAME STREET KidSite
Subscribe to the Children's Television Workshop Sesame Street KidSite Channel! Join your favorite Sesame Street friends, grab a paintbrush and have fun with the KidSite's interactive coloring book. A new
Document: Done

Figure 25.5 Cast your net for Castanet (try www.marimba.com).

Subscribing to a Castanet Channel

Subscribing to a Castanet channel is no different than subscribing to a Netcaster channel: Just click the Add Channel or Subscribe link. Netcaster's subscription wizard guides you through the rest of the process.

Once you've subscribed to a Castanet channel, you can manage the subscription in exactly the same way you'd manage a Netcaster subscription. See Chapter 24 for the lowdown on managing channels.

From Here

- You've browsed for content, searched for content, and now you've had content pushed at you. Fight back by creating your own, as explained in the next part of this book.

Part VI

Netscape Page Composer: Creating High-Impact Web Pages

Chapter 26

Netscape Composer Fundamentals

Netscape Composer—or Composer for short—provides the environment you need to create winning HTML pages. Best of all, you don't need to learn HTML (see the sidebar on page 447.)

The cool thing about Composer is that your Web page looks like it does when it's viewed in Netscape's browser window (although, as you'll see, there are a couple of exceptions to this—for example, you can't see text wrapped around a graphic). This is a seriously cool thing, since previously you had to code the HTML and then switch to a browser to view your work, which was a time-consuming pain. For the most part, you see your changes immediately while you're working with Netscape Composer, and your page looks like it does in the browser.

This chapter gets you going with Netscape Composer by introducing all the Composer fundamentals.

For the Time-Challenged

- Netscape Composer enables you to prepare winning Web pages without knowing HTML. However, it doesn't do quite everything, and some formats can't be displayed until you view them in the browser.
- To publish your pages, you first create them with Netscape Composer, and then copy them to a computer that's running a Web server.
- Begin by choosing initial preferences, including supplying your name.
- The menus are useful, but the most frequently accessed commands are more conveniently accessed on the toolbars.
- The toolbars include commands for character formatting, paragraph formatting, filing operations, and editing tasks.
- You can create a new blank document, or you can build one using the Wizard. Alternatively, you can open and modify a template.

Getting Oriented: The Composer Publishing Process

Publishing great-looking Web pages with Composer is a two-step process.

Step One: Creating Your Page with Netscape Composer

First, you create your page using the Composer. You can start with the Netscape Page Wizard, one of Netscape's templates, or a blank document. (A *template* is a sample Web page that you can download and modify for your own purposes.)

After you finish your page, it's stored on your hard disk, which means it isn't accessible to anyone.

Step Two: Publishing Your Page

For other people to access your page via the Web, you *publish* your page. To publish your page means to make it accessible to a *Web server*, a program

HTML—And Why You Don't Need to Learn It

In a recent interview, Web founder Tim Berners-Lee expressed amazement that people were still using HTML to create their Web pages. HTML was never intended for prolonged use, Berners-Lee said; its creators expected programs to come along that would generate the HTML code as the user manipulated text and images in a "what-you-see-is-what-you-get" environment.

Short for HyperText Markup Language, HTML enables Web authors to code text so that browsers (such as Netscape) will recognize the text to be a certain part of a document, such as a title, a heading, or a hyperlink. It's pretty tedious to use. In fact, it's a lot like the formatting codes that writers had to use during the early years of word processing. To make text bold, for instance, you had to type @BOLD(here is the text to be boldfaced). With HTML, the code looks like this: <B>here is the text to be boldfaced</B>. Both are prone to error: If you forget the closing symbol (in HTML, </B>), you get bold all the way to the end of your document. Nuts!

With Composer 3.0, the long-awaited automatic HTML may have finally arrived. I say "may," because Composer can't quite do everything. For example, frames—something that Netscape Communications themselves introduced—can't be created without manual coding. And there are a few tags here and there that Composer 3.0 doesn't enable you to insert unless you're willing to type the HTML yourself. That's why Composer includes a command that enables you to type HTML code directly. In the chapters to come, look for tips concerning some cool HTML that you can plug in here and there!

that knows how to accept incoming requests from the Internet and dole out the requested documents. Unless you have a Web server running on your own computer, you'll need to upload your page to the server's computer. It's easy to do this with Composer's extremely cool one-button publishing, as explained in Chapter 35.

I don't have anywhere to publish my page! Maybe you do and don't know it. Many Internet service providers (ISPs) give you some Web space—up to 5MB's worth, sometimes—for your Web publishing efforts. This is usually included as a freebie with your Internet subscription. Check with your service provider to find out whether you've got some Web publishing space already. Otherwise, it might be time to look for a new ISP!

Choosing Initial Preferences

Before you get started with Netscape Composer, work through some initial preferences and options. Doing so now will help you work with Composer much more productively.

To begin choosing preferences, display the Composer Preferences dialog box by choosing Preferences from any Communicator module's Edit menu. Click Composer to see the Composer options (Figure 26.1).

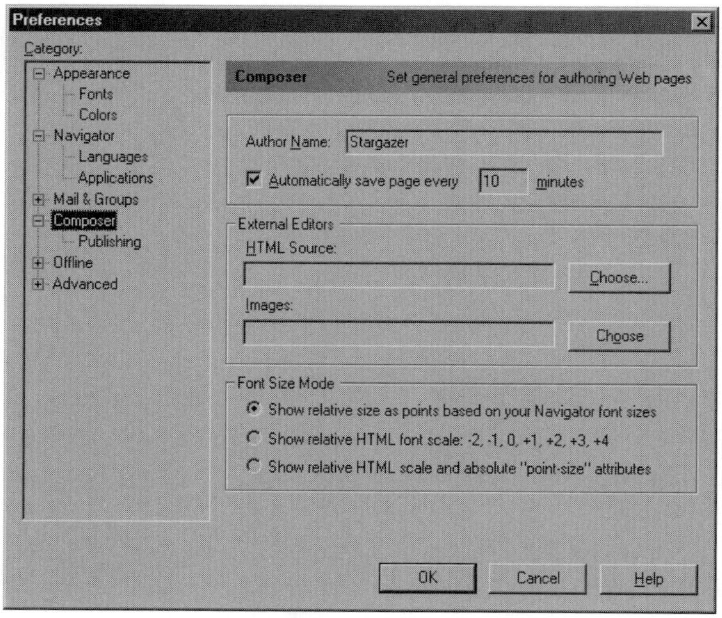

Figure 26.1 Composer Preferences: General options.

Do the following:

1. In the Author Name area, type your name. Netscape will automatically add your name to all the documents you publish. The name won't appear in your documents, but search engines will be able to access it, and they'll index your documents under your name.
2. If you would like Netscape Composer to automatically save your document, check the box under Auto Save and type a time interval. This is highly recommended!
3. In the External Composers boxes, use the Browse button to locate the text and graphics composers that you would like to use. These come in handy when you're doing some direct HTML editing or sizing graphics. For a text composer, I recommend the Windows Notepad utility. For a graphics composer, I recommend Paint Shop Pro, a shareware program that's widely available for downloading from the Net.
4. Click OK to confirm your choices.

Using the Toolbars

Netscape Composer comes with two toolbars: Composition and Formatting toolbars (see Figure 26.2). You'll find these toolbars very helpful and you'll want to keep them on-screen. If you don't see them, choose Show Composition Toolbar or Show Formatting Toolbar from the View Menu.

This section introduces the tools briefly; you'll learn more about what each of them does in the chapters to follow. You'll also find this section handy for quick reference. Don't try to memorize what all of them do; a quick skim is all that's required for now.

If you forget what one of the tools does, just move the mouse pointer to the tool and wait a second or two. You'll see a help box that names the tool.

Understanding the Composition Toolbar

The Composition toolbar contains shortcuts to commands you'll use most frequently. (Additional commands are found in the menus.) Right now, you

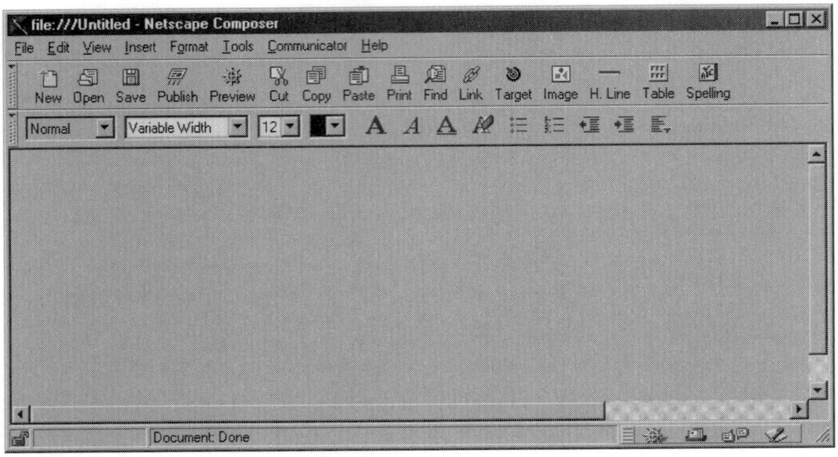

Figure 26.2 The Composer window has a very handy toolbar.

won't understand what all these buttons do; you'll learn about the more mysterious ones (like "Publish" and "Target" in subsequent chapters). The toolbar contains the following buttons:

Creates a new, blank Composer document.

Opens a local document (one you previously created and stored on your computer.

Saves the current document locally (on your hard disk).

Uploads the current document to your Web server.

Displays the current document in Netscape Navigator.

Cuts the selection to the Clipboard.

Copies the selection to the Clipboard.

Pastes the Clipboard contents at the cursor's location.

Prints the current document.

Finds text in the current document.

Inserts a hyperlink at the cursor's location.

Inserts a target for an internal link at the cursor's location.

Inserts an inline image at the cursor's location.

Inserts a horizontal line at the cursor's location.

Inserts a table at the cursor's location.

Checks the document's spelling.

Understanding the Formatting Toolbar

The formatting toolbar enables you to choose appearance options for your document. Note that many of these tools appear in the Messenger window, as well, enabling you to add rich HTML formatting to your mail messages.

Enables you to choose a paragraph style for your document, including headings and list items.

Enables you to choose a font for text entry or for the selected text.

Enables you to choose a font size for text entry or for the selected text.

Enables you to choose a font color for text entry or for the selected text.

Adds bold formatting to the selected text.

Adds italic formatting to the selected text.

Adds underlining to the selected text.

Removes character styles from the selected text.

Creates a bulleted list.

Creates a numbered list.

Reduces paragraph indentation.

Adds indentation to a paragraph.

Enables you to choose alignment options (flush left, centered, flush right).

Using Composer's Keyboard Shortcuts

If you prefer to use keyboard commands rather than fussing with the mouse, you'll be pleased to learn that Composer enables you to use keyboard shortcuts for lots of commands. Here's a list of them; you can keep this page open while you're working in order to learn them.

To do this:	Press this key:
Bold	Ctrl + B
Close the current window	Ctrl + W
Copy	Ctrl + C
Cut	Ctrl + X
Decrease indent	Ctrl + - (hyphen)
Display a new, blank Composer window	Ctrl + Shift + N
Display character properties dialog box	Alt + Enter
Find	Ctrl + F
Find Again	F3
Help	F1
Increase indent	Ctrl + = (equal sign)
Insert hyperlink	Ctrl + Shift + L
Italic	Ctrl + I
Open existing page	Ctrl + O (the letter)
Paste	Ctrl + V
Quit Composer	Ctrl + Q
Remove all styles	Ctrl + K
Save the current document	Ctrl + S
Start a new line without entering a blank line	Shift + Enter

Start a new paragraph with a blank line before it	Enter
Underline	Ctrl + U
Undo	Ctrl + Z

Using Composer's Pop-up Menus

Another way to work with Composer is to use the program's pop-up menus. To display these, point to something on-screen, and click the right mouse button. Here's a quick overview of what's on the pop-up menus that appear when you point to the following items:

Point at the following object:	**Right-click to do the following:**
Text	Change the text's current character, paragraph, or list properties. You can also insert a new hyperlink or paste text from the Clipboard.
Hyperlink	Change the link destination, or change the link's current paragraph or list properties. You can also open the link in a new borwse or edit window, copy the link, remove the link, or add a bookmark for the link.
In-line image	Change the image's link or list properties, add a link using the image, save the image under a new name, make the image the page background, or edit the image (cut, copy, or paste).
Horizontal line	Change the horizontal line's properties, including paragraph or list properties; edit the line (cut, copy, or paste).
HTML tag marker	Change the tag properties, or edit the tag (cut, copy, or paste).
Table	Change the paragraph or list properties for the whole table; change table, row, or cell properties; insert or delete a table, column, row, or cell; insert a link; or paste text.

Dragging and Dropping

Drag-and-drop operations are very convenient, but they're not obvious – many people don't realize they can do the following things (and love these procedures when they finally do discover them). Not all of these will have meaning for you right now, but keep them in mind; I'll remind you of them later, when the context arises.

To do this:	Do the following drag-and-drop maneuver:
Insert a link in your document	Drag the link from any Communicator window (including Navigator and Messenger), or even from the Windows File Manager or Windows Explorer, and drop it into Composer.
Insert an image in your document	Drag the image from a Navigator window and drop it in the Composer window.
Insert a Windows bitmap (*.bmp) image from the desktop and automatically convert it to JPEG format.	Drag the image from the desktop and drop it in the Composer window.

Creating New Documents with Netscape Composer

When you choose New from the File Menu, you'll see a pop-up submenu that gives you three choices:

Blank Page You see a new, blank Web document. This is the best choice when you want to start your page from scratch.

Page From Template When you choose this option, Composer accesses the template location. You can specify a local template location, or access

Netscape's server, which gives you access to lots of templates. After you've chosen a template and opened it, you can modify it and save it to your hard disk.

Page From Wizard — This option accesses the Netscape Page Wizard. It's a great way to create the fundamentals of a good-looking page in very short order. You can then embellish the page by opening it in Netscape Composer (see the next section).

You can also choose these options by clicking the New button.

Opening an Existing File

You can open existing files from your disk or from the Web.

Opening Existing Files from Your Disk

You can open and edit an existing file in a Navigator window by doing the following:

1. Choose Open Page from the File menu. You'll see the Open Page dialog box, shown in Figure 26.3 .
2. Click the Composer option so that you'll open the page in Composer.
3. Click Choose File to open a local file. You'll see an Open window. Locate the file, and click Open.

The above procedure works in a Composer window too, but it's faster to click the Open button. This brings up the Open dialog box directly, without your having to fuss with the Open Page dialog box.

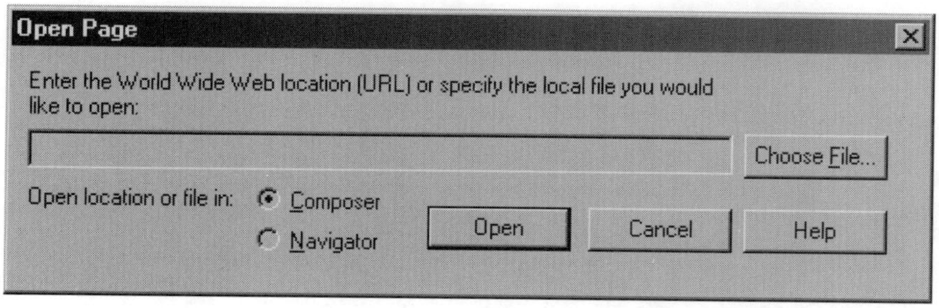

Figure 26.3 If you're using Navigator, you can use this dialog box to open a page in Composer.

Opening Existing Files from the Web

And now for something enormously cool: You can use Composer to open any page on the Web. When you do so, Composer automatically downloads all the related images and additional resources, and saves them on your disk.

Is this a good thing? Yes and no. The good part is that it's easy to go to your own Web site, open your own document, and begin editing the uploaded version. However, this obviously provides a tremendous temptation for ripping off other peoples' creative work. For example, take a look at Figure 26-4: Composer has opened a page at a commercial site (www.news.com) – and not only that, it has downloaded all of the site's graphics and text and stored them on your computer. The page is now ready for modification!

To be sure, you can't *alter* the document that's actually stored on the server unless you have the necessary password – but you can *copy* somebody else's Web design, save it to your hard disk, and modify it as you please. To be sure, some would argue that this isn't plagiarism if you're doing this only to copy some basic HTML, such as a table layout – you could do the same thing by viewing the source HTML and copying it. But copying a truly original Web design, inline images, or text is definitely uncool and could get you into a lot of trouble.

To open an existing document from the Web, use Navigator to display the document, and do the following:

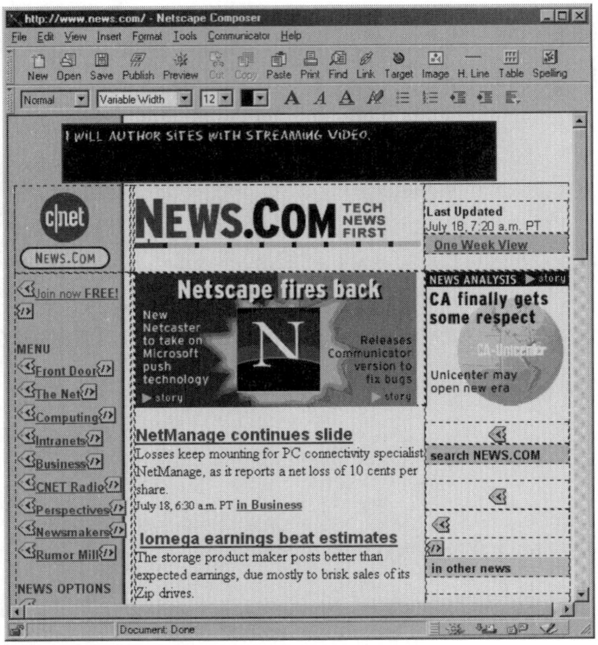

Figure 26.4 With Composer, you can open and edit any page on the Web—but it isn't cool to appropriate somebody else's intellectual property!

1. Choose Open Page from the File menu. You'll see the Open Page dialog box, shown in Figure 26.3.
2. Click the Composer option so that you'll open the page in Composer.
3. Click Open.

Using Templates

A quick way to create a Web document is to begin with a template, which is a generic Web document that you can open and modify. You'll find lots of templates on Netscape's server; they're expressly available for your use and modification without any need for asking permission. To use one of Netscape's templates, choose New from the File Menu, choose Page from Template, and click Netscape's Templates. Click a template link, and then open the page for editing, as described above.

The big advantage of a template is that it enables you to begin with a page that already has a bunch of complicated formats entered. These pages have some text already entered, but you can easily replace this text with your own. Another advantage of using templates is that they were written with good Web page design practices in mind. Since you don't know what these practices are all about just yet, it's wise to use templates.

Figure 26.5 shows one of the templates available from Netscape. It's for a windsurfing page, but you could use it for almost anything.

Before proceeding, you may wish to create a directory on your hard disk to store your Web creations. Call this directory something like WebPages.

Once you've downloaded the template, you can modify it as you please. You can remove the existing text and add your own. You can also add hyperlinks and graphics.

Setting up a Directory for Your Own Templates

Soon, you'll learn how to create your own Web page designs, which you may wish to re-use as you add additional pages to your site. (It's a good idea to establish a consistent design for a presentation that involves several linked pages, and to use this design on each and every page.) First, create the directory where you want to store your templates. Then, in the Composer, choose Options/Composer Preferences, and click the General tab. In the New Document Template area, enter the location of your templates directory in the Location box (for example, c:\Web Sites\Templates). Click OK to confirm your choices. Now you'll see a directory listing for this folder or directory when you choose File/New Document/From Template.

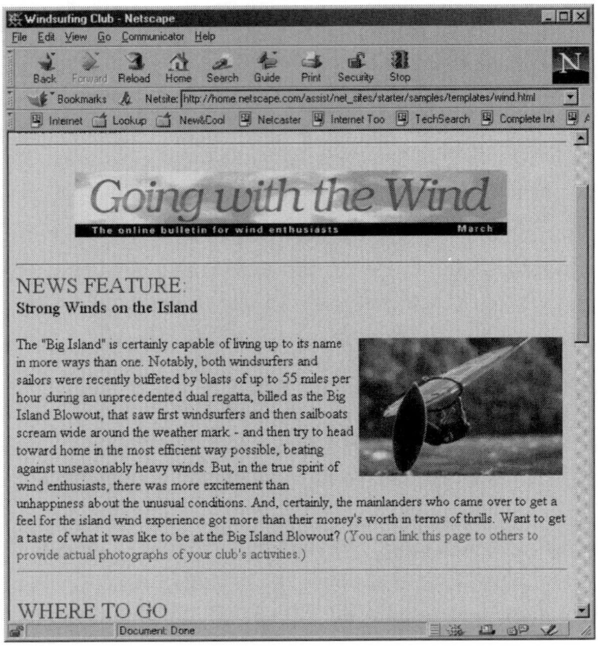
Windsurfing Club - Netscape
File Edit View Go Communicator Help
Back Forward Reload Home Search Guide Print Security Stop
Bookmarks Netsite: http://home.netscape.com/assist/net_sites/starter/samples/templates/wind.html
Internet Lookup New&Cool Netcaster Internet Too TechSearch Complete Int
Going with the Wind
The online bulletin for wind enthusiasts March
NEWS FEATURE:
Strong Winds on the Island
The "Big Island" is certainly capable of living up to its name in more ways than one. Notably, both windsurfers and sailors were recently buffeted by blasts of up to 55 miles per hour during an unprecedented dual regatta, billed as the Big Island Blowout, that saw first windsurfers and then sailboats scream wide around the weather mark - and then try to head toward home in the most efficient way possible, beating against unseasonably heavy winds. But, in the true spirit of wind enthusiasts, there was more excitement than unhappiness about the unusual conditions. And, certainly, the mainlanders who came over to get a feel for the island wind experience got more than their money's worth in terms of thrills. Want to get a taste of what it was like to be at the Big Island Blowout? (You can link this page to others to provide actual photographs of your club's activities.)
WHERE TO GO
Document: Done

Figure 26.5 You can modify this template to your heart's content.

From Here

- Learn the basics of text entry and editing in Chapter 27.
- Add headings, lists, and indents, as shown in Chapter 28.
- Control character and font formatting with Chapter 29 as your guide.

Chapter 27

Working with Text

Writing with Composer is very much like writing with a word processing program. You work in a "what-you-see-is-what-you-get" environment. If you're already familiar with a good word processing program, such as Microsoft Word for Windows, you already know much of what you need to know in order to create and edit text with Composer. This chapter surveys the basics, including positioning the cursor, adding new text, selecting text, copying and moving text, and deleting text.

Positioning the Cursor

To enter and edit text with Composer, you need to move the cursor around. You can do this with the mouse; just click where you want the cursor to

For the Time-Challenged

- You can position the cursor with the mouse, but Netscape Composer also responds to the cursor-movement keys used by popular word processing programs.
- Body text is entered using the Normal paragraph style.
- To start a new paragraph and enter a blank line at the same time, press Enter.
- To start a new paragraph without entering a blank line, press Shift + Enter.
- To select a word, double-click it. To select a line, click just to the left of the line's first letter.
- If you deleted something by mistake and want it back, choose Edit/Undo or press Ctrl + Z.

appear. If you'd prefer to move the cursor with the keyboard, you can use any of the keys listed in the following table.

To move the cursor:	Press this key:
One character left	Left arrow
One character right	Right arrow
One word left	Ctrl + left arrow
One word right	Ctrl + right arrow
To the beginning of the line	Home
To the end of the line	End
One line up	Up arrow
One line down	Down arrow
To the beginning of the document	Ctrl + Home
To the end of the document	Ctrl + End

About the Normal Paragraph Format

To add body text to your document, you use the Normal paragraph format. To do so, choose Normal from the Paragraph Styles list box (in the Formatting toolbar), or choose Format/Paragraph/Normal from the menus. In the next chapter, you'll learn how to enter text in other paragraph formats, including lists and headings.

Adding Text

It's easy to add text with Composer. Just position the cursor where you want the text to apppear, and start typing (see Fifure 27.1).

You don't need to press Enter at the end of every line—the program automatically "wraps" text down to the next line.

Keep the following in mind:

- To start a new paragraph (with a blank line before it), press Enter twice.
- To get rid of a paragraph break, place the cursor at the beginning of the second paragraph and press Del.

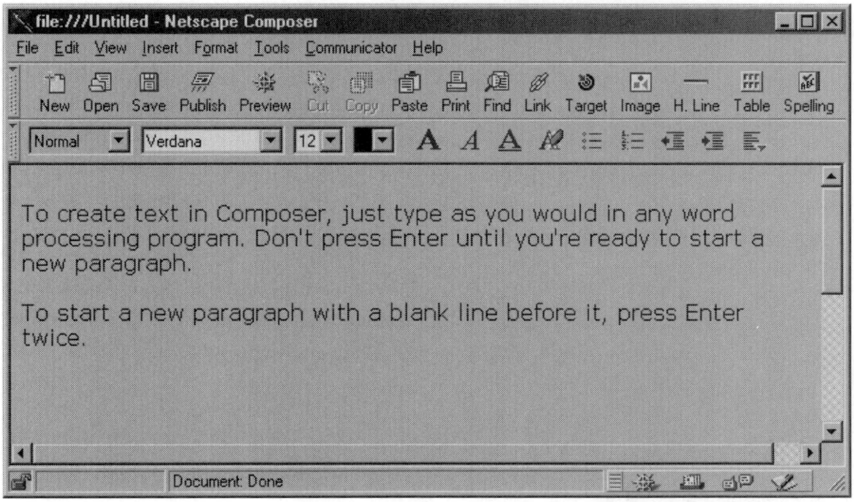
file:///Untitled - Netscape Composer
File Edit View Insert Format Tools Communicator Help
New Open Save Publish Preview Cut Copy Paste Print Find Link Target Image H. Line Table Spelling
Normal Verdana 12
To create text in Composer, just type as you would in any word processing program. Don't press Enter until you're ready to start a new paragraph.
To start a new paragraph with a blank line before it, press Enter twice.
Document: Done

Figure 27.1 To creat text with Composer, just type away.

- Paragraph breaks are marked by symbols, which you can see if you wish. They're ugly, but some people find it easier to edit their documents if they can see the symbols. To display them, choose View/Show Paragraph Marks. Figure 27.2 shows the paragraph marks.

Writing for the Web

Every well-written document is adapted to its medium. You wouldn't put a business report into a newsletter, or a poem into a scientific article! Similarly, you should adapt your writing for the Web. The best Web writing is, above all else, concise. Get right to the point straightaway: Describe your page's purpose and audience at the inception. Write personally, and focus on your reader—use what business writers call the "you" orientation. Wherever possible, break up the text on the page using headings, bulleted lists, and white space. Highlight the terms that convey your document's key subjects: your reader should be able to grasp your page's scope in a quick visual scan.

I added lots of blank lines but Netscape won't let me see them! They show up in the Composer too, but, frustratingly, they don't show up when you view the page in the browser. Why? Here's a very important rule that you need to learn: Web browsers always ignore extra spaces and extra line breaks. You can add all the spaces you want by pressing the spacebar, but your browser only shows one. You can add all the line breaks you want by pressing Enter gazillions of times, but the browser only shows one. You'll have to handle spacing by using commands other than manually entered spaces and Enter keystrokes, as this and the following chapters explain.

Selecting Text

The easiest way to select text is to drag over it with the mouse. Click where you want the selection to start, and then hold down the left mouse button

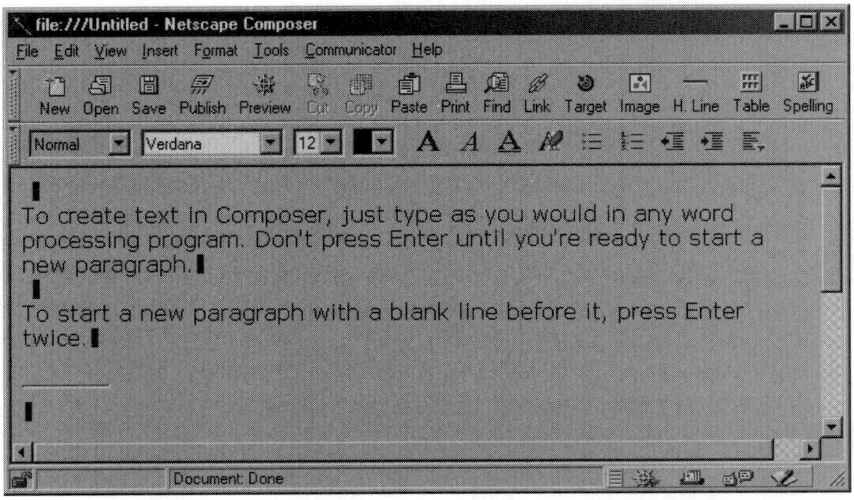
file:///Untitled - Netscape Composer
File Edit View Insert Format Tools Communicator Help
New Open Save Publish Preview Cut Copy Paste Print Find Link Target Image H. Line Table Spelling
Normal Verdana 12
To create text in Composer, just type as you would in any word processing program. Don't press Enter until you're ready to start a new paragraph.
To start a new paragraph with a blank line before it, press Enter twice.
Document: Done

Figure 27.2 You can view the paragraph marks if you want to.

and move the pointer to the end of the text you want to select. If you don't like dragging, click where you want the selection to start, and then move the pointer to the place where you want the selection to end. When you hold down the Shift key and click, Composerautomatically selects all the text between the first and second places you clicked.

Here are some cool text-selection tricks:

- To select an entire word, double-click the word.
- To select an entire line, move the cursor just to the left of the line's first letter, and click the left mouse button.
- To select an entire paragraph, move the cursor just to the left of any line in the paragraph, and double-click the left mouse button.
- To unselect text, just click elsewhere.
- To select the entire document, press Ctrl + A. You can also choose Edit/Select All. Be careful about doing this, though, since it's easy to delete the entire document while everything's selected!

Copying and Moving Text

You can also move text around in the Composer, just as you would in a word processing program.

- To copy text, select the text and press Ctrl + C or choose Edit Copy. Position the cursor where you want the copied text to appear, and press Ctrl + V (or choose Edit/Paste).
- To move text, select the text and press Ctrl + X (or choose Edit/Cut). Position the cursor where you want the text to appear, and press Ctrl + V (or choose Edit/Paste).

Tips for Editing Templates

If you're modifying the text in a template, note that you can replace existing text just by selecting it and typing over it. However, this works best for normal paragraph text. (You can tell if you're working with normal paragraph text quite easily—just position the cursor within the text and look at the style selection box on the toolbar. If it's normal paragraph text, you'll see "Normal" in this box.) Exercise caution when changing headings or list items so that you don't lose the formatting; it's better to type your new text and then carefully delete the old text. Also, don't try to type over link text directly; it won't work. You'll need to delete the template's unwanted links and add new ones, as explained in the next section. Be careful not to press Backspace at the beginning of a section of distinctively formatted text, or Del at the end; if you do, you may wipe out hidden formatting information. To restore a format you've messed up, press Ctrl + Z or choose Edit/Undo.

Deleting Text

If you've made an error, or if you would like to get rid of some generic text in a template, you can delete it using any of the following techniques:

- To delete text to the left of the cursor, press Backspace.
- To delete text to the right of the cursor, press Del.

- To delete the selection, press Del, or just type over it.

I just deleted something by accident! Can I get it back? Sure you can. Just press Ctrl + Z, or choose Edit/Undo. Note that you can only undo your last editing action. If you find that the deletion really deserved to be deleted, choose Edit/Redo to redo your last action.

Checking Spelling

Composer can check your document's spelling—and please, do so before publishing your page.

This is one of the nicest of Composer's features, and you'll love it. In contrast to text editors or HTML editors, which have a tough time distinguishing between HTML code and document text, there's no hassle with using Composer's spell-checking capabilities. You can quickly check your document's spelling without having to skip over HTML tags.

To check your document's spelling, do the following:

1. Click the Spelling tool. You'll see the Check Spelling dialog box. If there are any spelling mistakes in your document, you'll see the first of them in the Word box.
2. If Spelling finds a misspelling, do one of the following:
   - Click Replace to replace the misspelled word with the highlighted suggestion.
   - Click Replace All to replace every instance of the misspelled word with the highlighted suggestion.
   - Click Check to go through your document and underline any misspellings.
   - Click Ignore to ignore the current word.
   - Click Ignore All to ignore all instances of the current word in this document.

- Click Learn to add the current word to the dictionary.
- Click Edit dictionary to edit the words you've added to the dictionary with Learn (this comes in very handy if you click Learn by mistake).

3. Repeat Step 2 until you've dealt with all the suspected misspellings in your document.

This guy wrote me to tell me that there's a spelling mistake on my page, even though I ran a spell-check on it! What gives? Composer can't find every type of spelling mistake. In particular, it can't tell whether you've put a correctly spelled word in the wrong place. For example, Composer will skip over the following sentence: "I doe knot no ware she has gone." Note, too, that Composer can't catch common grammatical errors, such as the following: "*Its* very common to find pages with mistakes these days." (*Its* is the possessive of *it*; *it's* is a contraction of *it is*.) "Its a pane..." but you're document will need a final proofreading by (preferably sharp) human eyeballs.

From Here

- Learn how to enter text in heading and list formats. They're surveyed in the next chapter.
- Add character formatting, such as styles (e.g., boldface) and fonts. Learn how in Chapter 29.
- If you'd like to arrange your text in a table, see Chapter 33.

Chapter 28

Adding Headers, Lists, and Indents

One key to effective Web writing is to break up the text on the page as much as possible. Use headings and lists to provide visual cues to your readers. In this chapter, you'll learn how to add titles, headings, and a variety of lists, as well as how to indent and align text. These tools will help you create eye-catching, readable documents.

Giving Your Document a Title

On the Web, a document *title* doesn't actually appear within the document. It appears on the browser's title bar. A lot of Web authors ignore the title for this reason, but they do so at their peril: the browser may display such pages

For the Time-Challenged

- Your document's title shows up on the title bar. Don't forget to add a title or your document will show up in search engines' lists with the heading "No Title."
- Composer lets you enter up to six levels of headings, each with its own distinctive format, but few Web authors use more than three levels. Heading 1 text is used for a title that shows up in the document (unlike the true title, which appears on the browser's title bar).
- You can align text flush left, center, or flush right by clicking one of the alignment tools on the toolbar.
- Bulleted lists are useful for setting items apart from the text. You can choose from three default bullet styles.
- Netscape numbers the items in a bulleted list automatically, but you don't see the numbers until you switch to the browser.
- Description lists look nice, but they're tedious to enter; you can achieve the same effect by indenting normal text.
- Block quotes are useful for extended quotations and for emphasizing passages of text.
- You can create an outline with Roman numerals, but it's a lot of work.

with the word "Untitled" on the title bar. What's more, if somebody retrieves these documents using a search engine, it will probably list the document under a "No Title" or "Untitled" heading. Either way, it looks unprofessional!

To title your document, choose Page Colors and Properties from the Format Menu. You'll see the Document Properties dialog box. Click the General tab, if necessary, to display the page shown in Figure 28.1.

Do the following:

1. In the Title area, type your document's title. Be as descriptive as possible; indicate the general subject as well as the specific topic of your page ("Recreational Sailing: The Chesapeake Bay").
2. If you set Composer's initial preferences as the previous chapter suggested, you'll see your name in the Author box. If not, type

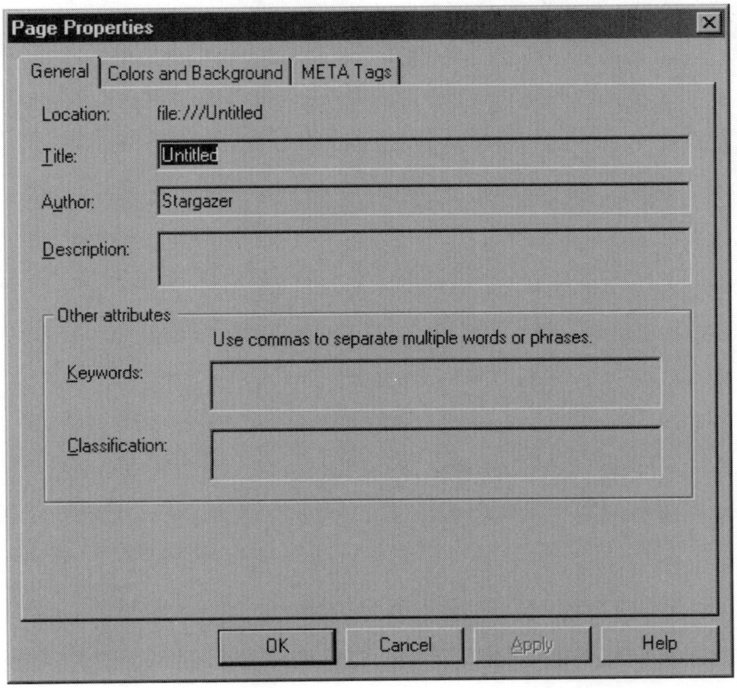

Figure 28.1 Enter your document's title here.

your name. This doesn't show up in the browser window, but it will be seen by search engines.

3. In the Description box, you can type some information about the document. Like the author's name, this information won't be seen by browsers, but it will be taken into account by search engines.
4. In the Other attributes area, you can type keywords and a document classification to improve your document's retrievability by search engines. This is strictly optional. Like the author and description, this information won't show up in the browser, but it will be seen by search engines.
5. Click OK to confirm your title.

After you've entered your title, you'll see it on the title bar of the windows. In the window, the title is accompanied by the file name and location of the document on which you're working, as shown in Figure 28.2.

Although the title, strictly speaking, is the text that appears on the title bar, you still need to give your document something that will *look* like a title when people read your page. You do this by adding a Level 1 heading, as described in the next section.

Adding Headings

You can add up to six levels of headings to your document, each with its own distinctive formatting (Figure 28.3). You can use these headings to add what appears to be a document title (Level 1), major headings (Level 2), and subheadings (Level 3). Very few Web authors use the other levels.

Figure 28.2 Your document's title appears on the title bar.

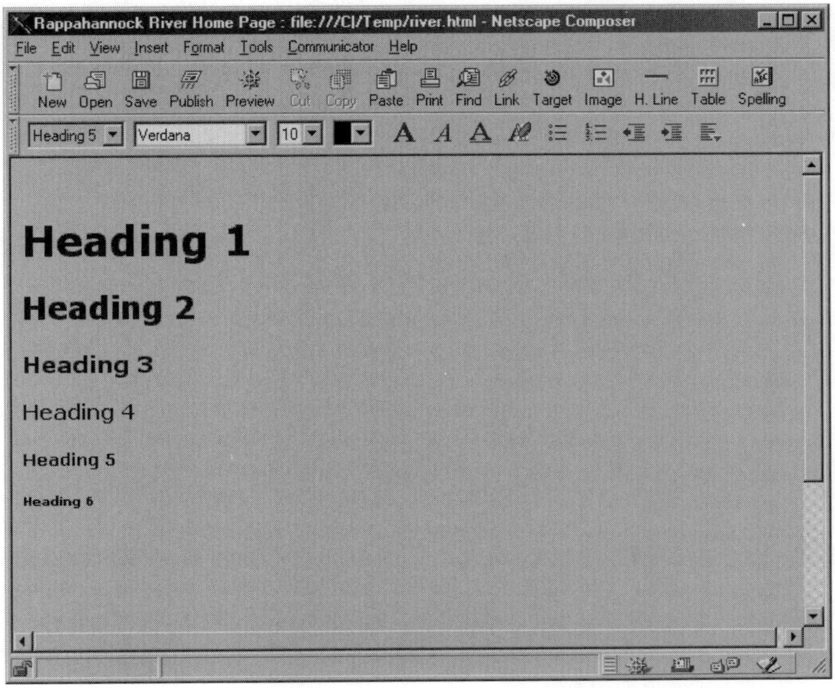

Figure 28.3 Each heading level has its own distinctive format.

Do you have to use the headings? Why not just add text using the Normal paragraph format and choose the formats you want? Go ahead, if you like, but bear in mind that most search engines give extra weight to terms found in heading formats. If you would like to maximize your document's retrievability, use headings.

To give your document a title that's visible in your document, not just the title bar, use a Heading 1 paragraph format, as shown in Figure 28.4.

Figure 28.4 Use a Heading 1 format to provide an apparent title for your document.

Aligning Text

You can align a heading (or any other text you enter) by just selecting the text and clicking the Alignment tool on the Formatting toolbar. Figure 28.5 shows the effect of clicking the Center tool, while Figure 28.6 displays text aligned flush right with the Align Right tool.

If you'd prefer to use the menus, you can align text by selecting it and choosing Align from the Format Menu, and then choosing Left, Center, or Right. Click OK to confirm. Alternatively, you can press Ctrl+L (flush left), Ctrl+E (center), or Ctrl+R (right).

You can press Tab or Shift + Tab to indent or unindent the selected text.

Figure 28.5 Text centered with the Center tool.

Figure 28.6 Text aligned flush right with the Align Right tool.

Creating Lists

To improve your document's readability, break up the text on the page. Composer gives you several list formats from which you can choose: bulleted lists, numbered lists, menu lists, directory lists, and description lists. As you'll see, you can combine list formats to produce precisely the effect you're looking for. The following sections describe each of these options.

Adding a Bulleted List

When you would like to list a number of items without implying that they're in a particular sequence, use a bulleted list. The bullets call attention to the items, as if to say, "These are all important." The eye naturally gravitates to a bulleted list.

To create a bulleted list, position the cursor where you want the list to begin, and click Bullet List. Alternatively, type the list, select it, and choose Bullet List. Composer adds the bullets automatically, as shown in Figure 28.7.

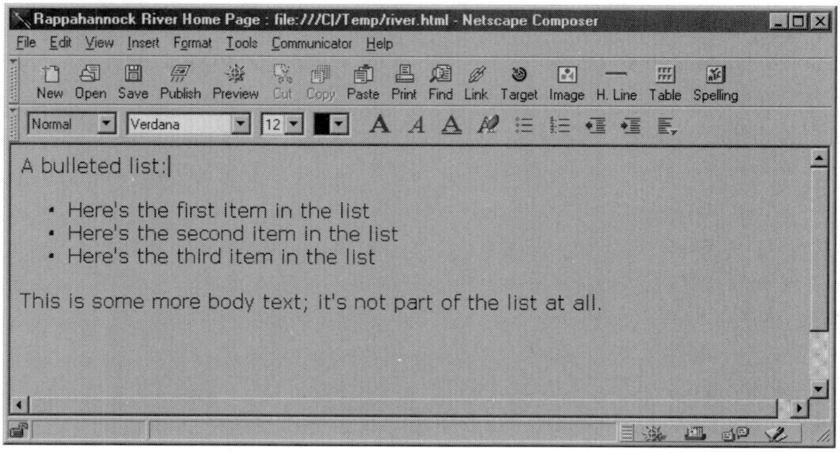

Figure 28.7 Bulleted list created with the Bullet List tool.

To stop typing in a bulleted or any other list format, press Enter to start a new line, and then choose Normal from the paragraph styles list box.

Changing the Bullet Style

By default, Composer adds a solid circle in front of each bullet list item. However, you can choose from two other formats: an open circle (see Figure 28.8) or a solid square (Figure 28.9). To change the bullet style, select the list items and choose Character Properties from the Format menu, or press Alt+Enter. Click the Paragraph tab, and choose a bullet style in the Bullet Style list box. Click OK to confirm.

Instead of creating a bulleted list, you may wish to create an unbulleted list and add small graphics that look like bullets. You'll find out how in Chapter 33.

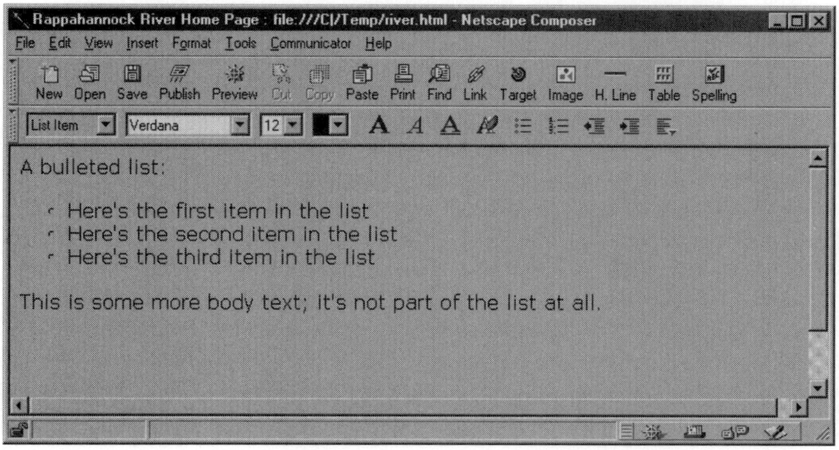

Figure 28.8 Bulleted list using open circles as the bullet style.

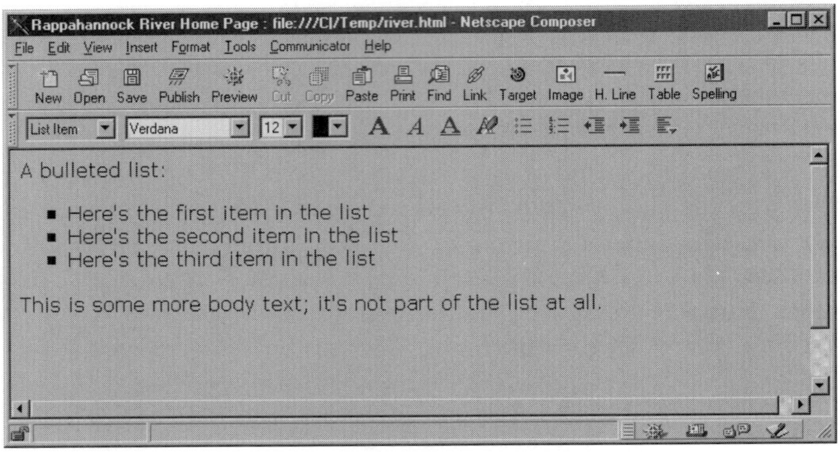

Figure 28.9 Bulleted list using solid squares as the bullet style.

Adding a Numbered List

To create a numbered list, type the items but don't type any numbers! Your browser will number the items for you. When you're done typing the list, select the list and click the Numbered List tool.

I don't see any numbers! You won't see the numbers in Composer—all you'll see are # symbols. To see the numbers, click View in Browser. You'll see the numbers there (see Figure 28.10).

Adding a Description List

A description list, or glossary list, is often used to list and define terms, as shown in Figure 28.11. Such a list consists of two formats:

Description Item This format is used for the term.

Description Text This format is used for the definition. As you can see in Figure 28.11, it's indented.

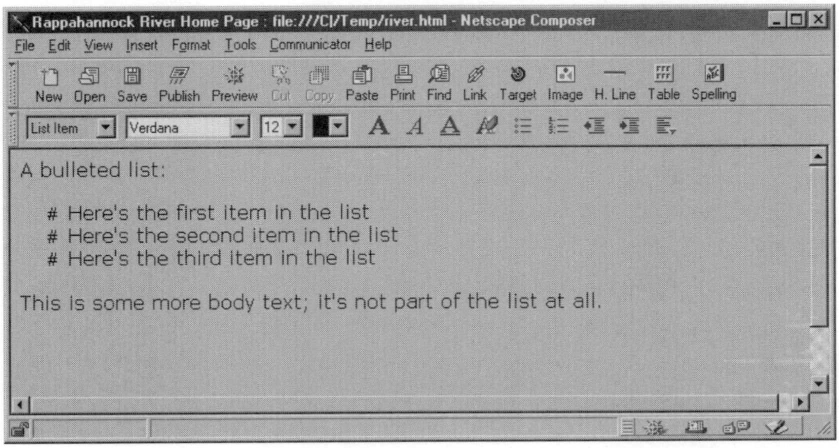

Figure 28.10 To see the numbers in a numbered list, you must switch to the browser view.

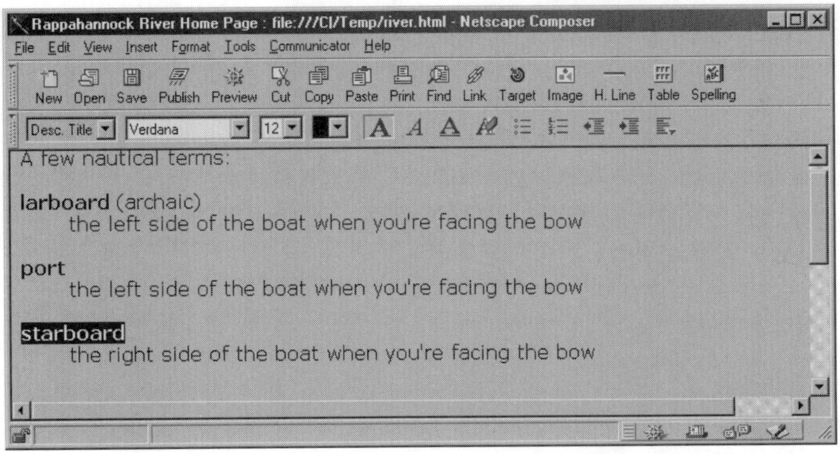

Figure 28.11 Description lists are useful for glossaries of key terms.

It's somewhat tedious to create a description list. To enter the first description item, you choose Description Item from the paragraph style box and type the item. To enter the definition text for this item, you choose Description Text and type the text. You have to repeat these commands for each item you enter.

If you're creating a lengthy list, consider using the Normal text style plus indents to do the job. It's easier to enter the formats because you can just click the Increase Indent tool to indent the description text.

It says I can create menu lists and directory lists, but these just look like bulleted lists! That's right. These two formats stem from the early days of HTML, and they aren't often supported in most browsers—including Netscape! You'll see these two options in the Paragraph Properties dialog box, but just ignore them.

Creating Block Quotes

When you insert an extended quotation in your text—we're talking about three or four lines here—you should indent the text so that it's set apart from the body text. You can use the Block Quote format for this purpose (see Figure 28.12).

To create a block quote, select the text, and choose Paragraph from the Format Menu, and choose BlockQuote from the submenu.

The Block Quote format is useful for purposes other than typing extended quotations. For example, it's a great way to set important text off from the rest of the text. In Figure 28.13, you see a Block Quote format that's been set apart from the body text with horizontal lines; it's an effective way to call attention to something really important.

Indenting Text

It's easy to indent text using the Increase Indent and Decrease Indent tools. Try entering a paragraph of normal text, and click these tools to see what

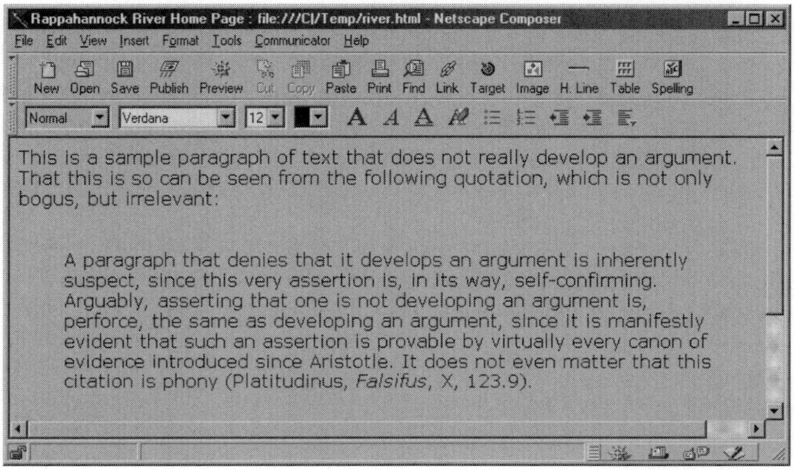
Rappahannock River Home Page : file:///C|/Temp/river.html - Netscape Composer
File Edit View Insert Format Tools Communicator Help
New Open Save Publish Preview Cut Copy Paste Print Find Link Target Image H. Line Table Spelling
Normal
Verdana
12
This is a sample paragraph of text that does not really develop an argument. That this is so can be seen from the following quotation, which is not only bogus, but irrelevant:
A paragraph that denies that it develops an argument is inherently suspect, since this very assertion is, in its way, self-confirming. Arguably, asserting that one is not developing an argument is, perforce, the same as developing an argument, since it is manifestly evident that such an assertion is provable by virtually every canon of evidence introduced since Aristotle. It does not even matter that this citation is phony (Platitudinus, Falsifus, X, 123.9).

Figure 28.12 Block Quote format is used for extended quotations.

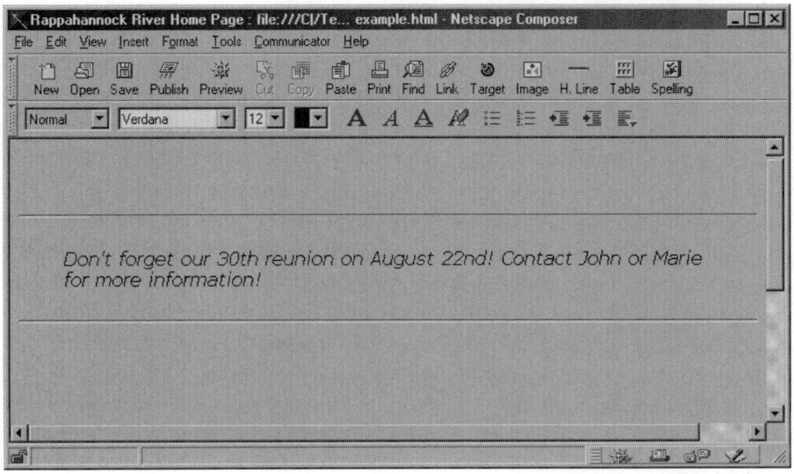
Rappahannock River Home Page : file:///C|/Te... example.html - Netscape Composer
File Edit View Insert Format Tools Communicator Help
New Open Save Publish Preview Cut Copy Paste Print Find Link Target Image H. Line Table Spelling
Normal
Verdana
12
Don't forget our 30th reunion on August 22nd! Contact John or Marie for more information!

Figure 28.13 Block Quote format used with horizontal lines for emphasis.

they do. When you click Increase Indent, the text moves about a half-inch right; clicking Decrease Indent moves the text back to the margin.

When you finish typing in some formats (such as Block Quote), the only way you can get back to the true Normal (body text) format is to click Decrease Indent. That's because the indent is separate from the paragraph style.

Creating an Outline

By combining indents with numbered list formats, it's possible to create a school-type outline, replete with Roman numerals. It isn't easy, though.

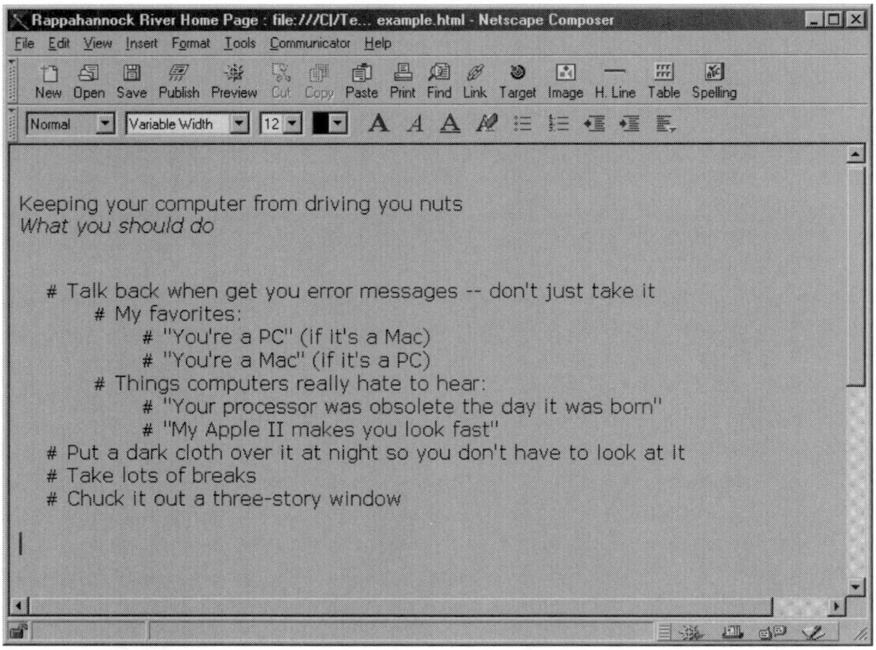
Rappahannock River Home Page : file:///C|/Te... example.html - Netscape Composer
File Edit View Insert Format Tools Communicator Help
New Open Save Publish Preview Cut Copy Paste Print Find Link Target Image H. Line Table Spelling
Normal
Variable Width
12
Keeping your computer from driving you nuts
What you should do
Talk back when get you error messages -- don't just take it
My favorites:
"You're a PC" (if it's a Mac)
"You're a Mac" (if it's a PC)
Things computers really hate to hear:
"Your processor was obsolete the day it was born"
"My Apple II makes you look fast"
Put a dark cloth over it at night so you don't have to look at it
Take lots of breaks
Chuck it out a three-story window

Figure 28.14 Outline viewed in Composer.

To start your outline, type all the major items, the ones that get capital Roman numerals (I, II, III, etc.). Select the whole list, and click the Numbered List tool. Then press Alt+Enter, click Paragraph, and choose I, II, III in the Number style box.

To add the second level of headings, the ones that start with capital letters, press Enter after one of the first-level headings. *Important*: Click the Increase Indent tool. You must indent this heading or you can't give it a different number style. Then press Alt+Enter, click Paragraph, and choose A, B, C in the Number style box.

Continue adding more headings by indenting, where necessary, and choosing the number format from the Number Style box. You don't see the numbering in the window, except that the program uses large and small X marks to denote Roman numerals, while it uses large and small A marks to denote letters (see Figure 28.14). You don't see the numbering until you view your document in the browser (Figure 28.15).

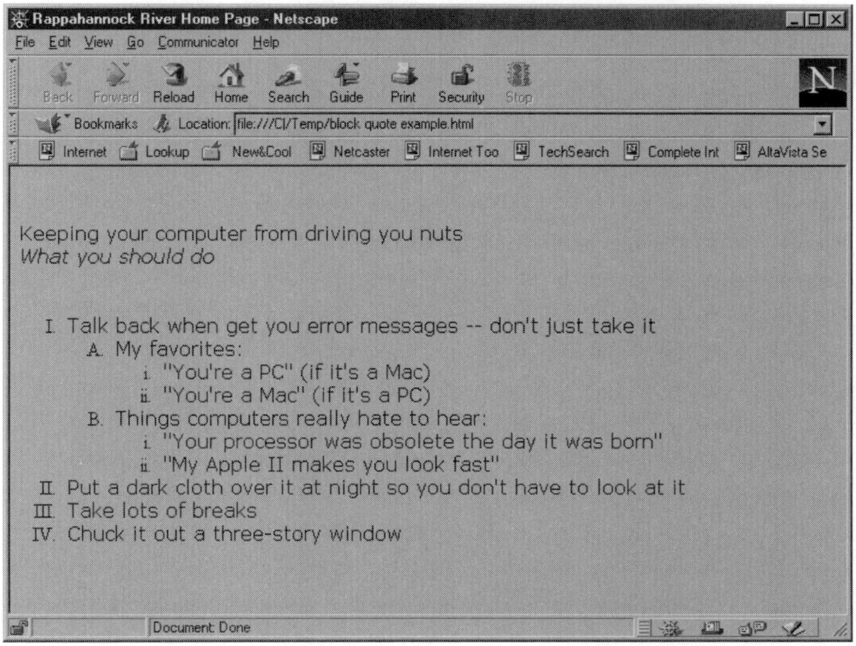
Rappahannock River Home Page - Netscape
File Edit View Go Communicator Help
Back Forward Reload Home Search Guide Print Security Stop
Bookmarks Location: file:///C|/Temp/block quote example.html
Internet Lookup New&Cool Netcaster Internet Too TechSearch Complete Int AltaVista Se
Keeping your computer from driving you nuts
What you should do
I. Talk back when get you error messages -- don't just take it
A. My favorites:
i. "You're a PC" (if it's a Mac)
ii. "You're a Mac" (if it's a PC)
B. Things computers really hate to hear:
i. "Your processor was obsolete the day it was born"
ii. "My Apple II makes you look fast"
II. Put a dark cloth over it at night so you don't have to look at it
III. Take lots of breaks
IV. Chuck it out a three-story window
Document: Done

Figure 28.15 Outline viewed in Netscape Navigator.

From Here

- You've mastered paragraph formats; let's tackle characters and fonts. On to the next chapter!
- Like to play around with fancy backgrounds? See Chapter 30.
- If you'd like to learn how to create bulleted lists with small graphics instead of bullets, flip to Chapter 31.

Chapter 29

Working with Characters and Fonts

To jazz up your document a bit, you may wish to add character styles (such as bold or italic), font colors, and varying font sizes. It's also possible nowadays to specify font typefaces, such as Helvetica, Garamond, or Times Roman, since the two leading browsers (Netscape Navigator and Microsoft Internet Explorer) can both read and respond to your typeface choices. This chapter tells you everything you need to know to make your characters and fonts look attractive.

Adding Character Styles

Character styles (such as boldface and italic type) can add emphasis and meaning to your document—as long as they're not overused. Figure 29.1 goes

For the Time-Challenged

- You can add bold and italic quickly by selecting text and pressing Ctrl + B (bold) or Ctrl + I (italic). Other character styles—including superscript, subscript, strikethrough, and the dreaded blink—can be chosen from the Properties/Character menu.
- You can add color to selected text by clicking the Font Color tool, but you might want to wait until you've decided on a color scheme for your document (see Chapter 30).
- To size selected text, click Increase Font Size or Decrease Font Size, or use the Font Size list box.
- You can add distinctive typefaces to your document by inserting the <FONT FACE> tag directly into your document.

overboard. The character formatting really isn't necessary because the paragraph formats guide the eye sufficiently.

Still, there are valid reasons for using bold and italic, and it couldn't be easier to apply these formats with Composer. To add bold, for example, select the text you want to format, and click the Bold tool. If you prefer, you can choose Properties/Character/Bold from the menus, or press Ctrl + B.

You can add character styles while typing, if you prefer. For example, to start typing something in bold, click the Bold tool and type away. When you want to switch back to normal text, click the Bold tool again to turn bold off.

In addition to bold, Composer enables you to add the following character styles to your document:

Italic Click the Italic tool, Format Style/Italic, or press Ctrl + I.

Underline Click the Italic tool, choose Format Style/Underline, or press Ctrl + U. *Note:* Not many browsers recognize underlining, for the simple reason that

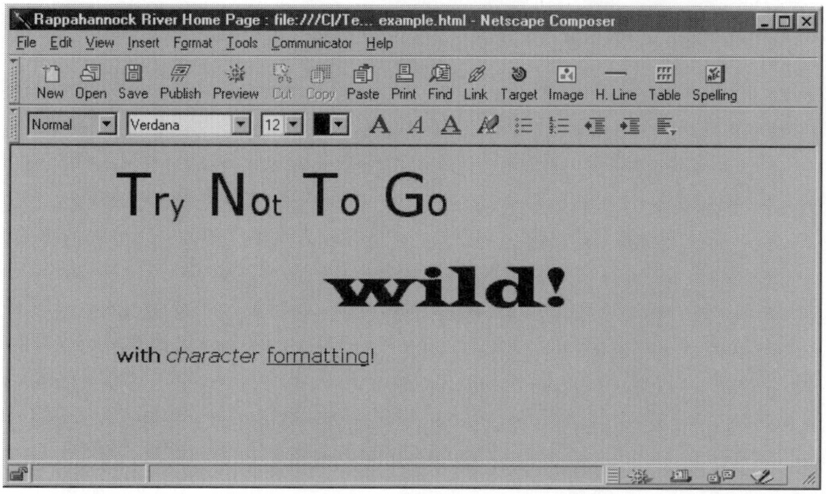

Figure 29.1 A bit too much character formatting.

	underlined text might be confused with a hyperlink.
Superscript	Choose Format/Style/Superscript.
Subscript	Choose Format/Style/Subscript.
Strikethrough	Choose Format/Style/Strikethrough.
Blink	Choose Format/Style/Blink.

If you went overboard in your character formatting, you can clear all the styles from a selection with just one click. Select the over-formatted text and click the Clear All Styles tool.

Figure 29.2 shows the appearance of each of these formats in the Composer (except that we can't really show the Blink format in this medium—no great loss!).

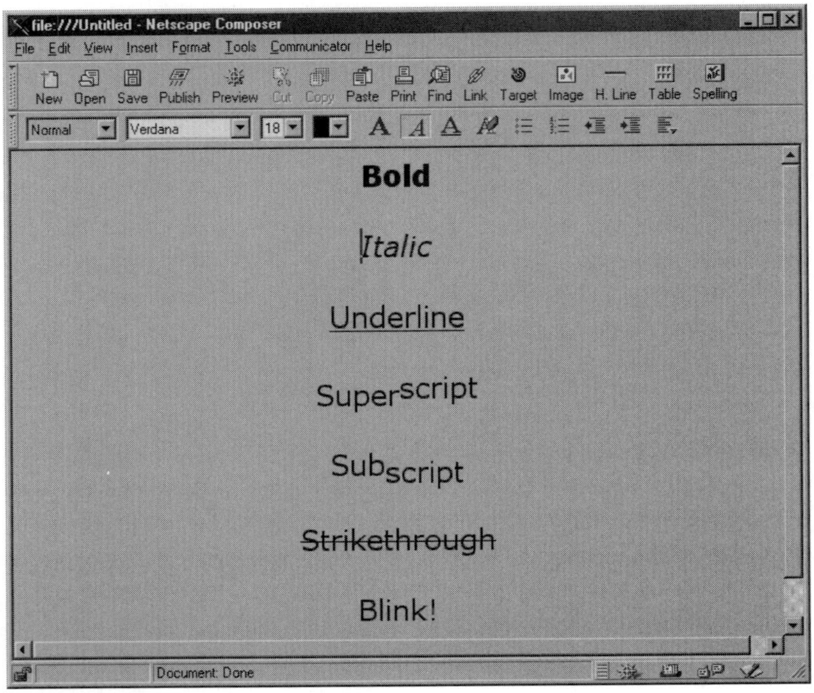

Figure 29.2 Character styles.

This guy flamed me for using Blink! Frankly, the blink character style isn't too popular, largely because it was overused when first introduced. Use it only when it's absolutely necessary to call attention to something really, really important—and use it only once in a document.

Adding Color

You can add color to your text. Since many people browsing the Web are using color monitors, this is a great way to add emphasis and meaning to your text.

Before adding color willy-nilly to your text, you may want to think through the color scheme for your whole document. Get the lowdown in Chapter 31.

To add color to your text, select the text and click the Font Color tool. You can also choose Color from the Format menu. You'll see the Color dialog box, shown in Figure 29.3. Just click a color and click OK.

If you're not happy with the colors you see in the Basic Colors or Custom Colors lists, you can create a new custom color by clicking Other, in the Color dialog box. This produces an expanded dialog box. To define a custom color, drag the color cursor around until you've found the hue you want, and then drag the slider up and down to control the amount of white and black in your color. When you've finished choosing your color, click Add to Custom Colors.

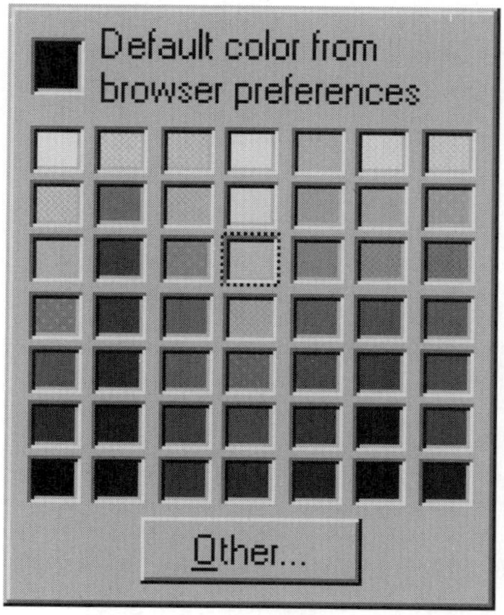

Figure 29.3 Use the Color dialog box to add color to your text.

Controlling Font Sizes

When you choose configuration options for Composer (in the Preferences dialog box), you choose the type of font size configuration you want. Your options are as follows:

- **Show relative size as points based on your Navigator font sizes** This is the default option, but it isn't a very good choice, because not all browsers can deal with font sizes specified in points.
- **Show relative HTML font scale (–2 through +4)** This is the recommended setting.
- **Show relative HTML font scale and relative sizes** This option places both types of font sizes in the font size menu in the Formatting toolbar, enabling you to choose between the two on the fly. But the use of fixed point sizes still has the same disabilities.

You can enlarge or decrease the size of selected text by means of the Font Size list box, located in the Formatting toolbar. You can also change the size of selected text by clicking the Increase Font Size and Decrease Font Size tools, which are in the same toolbar. These controls enable you to choose a *relative* size for your text. It's up to the browser to determine just how large or small the text actually looks on-screen. By default, all text is set to the size +0. You can choose sizes up to +4, the largest size, or down to –2, the smallest. Figure 29.4 shows how Composer displays these font sizes.

Using the Fixed Width (Typewriter) Font

In standard HTML, your font choices boil down to two:

- **Proportionally spaced (variable width) type** This is the type of font used for body type. In a proportionally spaced typeface, each letter's width is proportional to its size (a "w" gets more horizontal space than an "I").

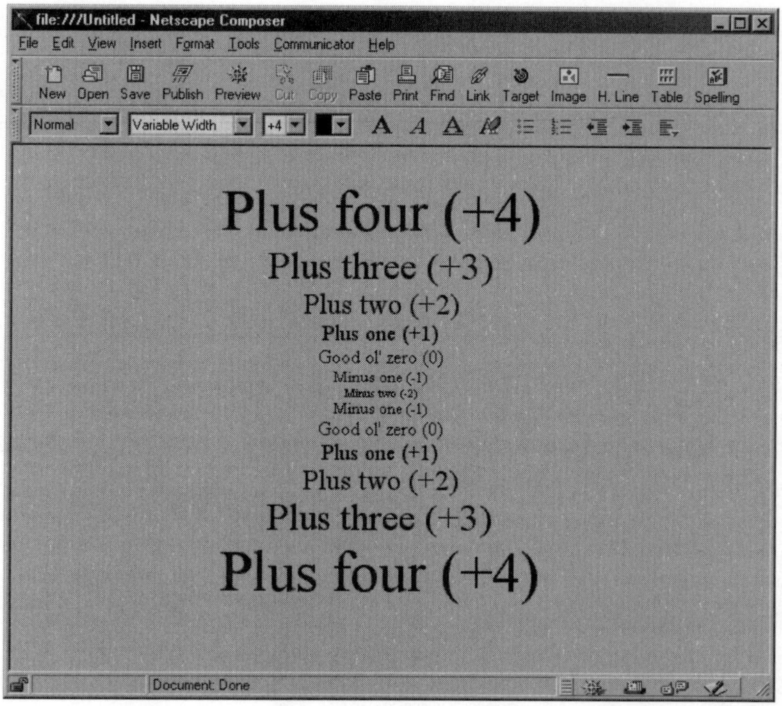

Figure 29.4 Relative font sizes (+4 to –2).

- **Fixed-width type** This type of font resembles typescript. Each letter gets the same width.

Figure 29.5 shows the difference. Normally, your document is formatted in proportionally spaced type; the exact font (such as Times Roman) is chosen by the user, who configures the browser to display this type using one of the typefaces installed on the user's system. You may wish to use the fixed-width font to show an example of computer code. Some Web designers like to use it for special effects.

Figure 29.5 Proportional vs. fixed-width type.

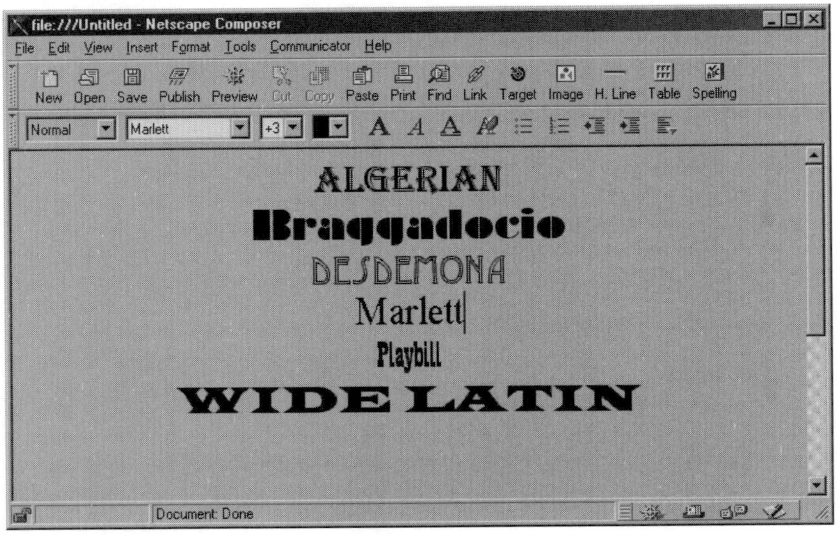

Figure 29.6 You can see your font choices in the browser.

Using Fonts

Composer enables you to use any of the fonts installed in your system, as you can see by pulling down the font list box in the Formatting toolbar. They look great in your document (see Figure 29-6). But there's a big problem. When sombody access and views your page, they won't see the fonts unless they've got them install on *their* system.

Which fonts do all users have installed on their systems? Times Roman and Helvetica? But sometimes these fonts are called by different names. Will the user's browser know how to map your font choices to fonts that are actually installed on their systems? Probably not.

From Here

- It's time to work out your document's color scheme. For the lowdown on this and other document formats, see Chapter 30.
- Add some hyperlinks, already! Find out how in Chapter 31. And how about some graphics, while you're at it? See Chapter 32.

Chapter 30

Choosing a Color Scheme

To put together a good-looking Web page, you need to devote some thought to color. You can choose distinctive colors for normal text, link text, visited link text, and backgrounds. Ideally, these colors will work harmoniously together. And if they do, you can use them on all the pages of your site, lending your creative efforts a level of consistency that users will appreciate.

This chapter shows you how to use one of Netscape's predefined color schemes—and how to create your own, if you wish. It also covers background graphics.

Using Predefined Color Schemes

You've already spent some time browsing the Web, and I'm sure you've been shocked by some of the weird color combinations you've seen, such as green

For the Time-Challenged

- Netscape's predefined color schemes are tasteful and, well, pedestrian.
- You can create your own color scheme, but please make sure that the text is legible against the background.
- If you create a color scheme you really like, you can make it the default for every new page you create.
- You can add a background graphic, but once again, please make sure that the text is legible.

text on purple backgrounds or blood-red type on a sickly lurid yellow. Often, there's not enough contrast between the text and the background, making the documents hard to read as well as repulsive. Yuk!

Perhaps aware of the need to provide some gentle guidance here, Netscape has set up Composer with a selection of nice-looking color schemes, all of which have commendable contrast.

To choose a color scheme for your document, do the following:

1. From the Paragraph menu, choose Page Colors and Properties, and click the Colors and Background tab. You'll see the Colors and Background options (shown in Figure 30.1).
2. In the Color Schemes box, choose a color scheme. You'll see what the color scheme looks like. You may wish to change the text and link colors (see "Choosing Text and Link Colors," in the next section) but give these a try, for now.
3. Click OK to confirm your choice.

Choosing Your Own Text, Link, and Background Colors

Now that you've chosen a responsible color scheme—a conservative, well-designed, respectable color scheme, mind you—you surely want to experiment a little. Perhaps you've got something a little wilder in mind?

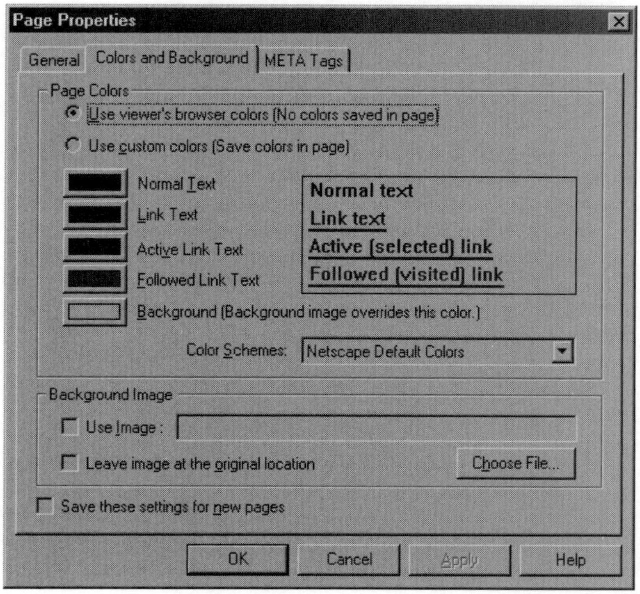

Figure 30.1 Choosing Colors and Background.

You can choose your own text, link, and background colors. But please, try to choose colors that work well together. Above all, make sure your page is readable. If there's too little contrast between the text and the background, your page will be hard to read.

To choose text, link, and background colors for your document, do the following:

1. From the Format menu, choose Page Colors and Properties, and click the Colors and Backgrounds tab (shown in Figure 30.1).
2. Click the Background button. You'll see the Color dialog box, shown in Figure 30.2.
3. If you'd like to choose a custom color, click Define Custom Colors, and move the hue control and black/white slider until you've created the color you want. Click Add to Custom Colors to add your color to the custom color list. When you've decided on your color, click OK. You'll see your color choice. You will probably need to choose new text colors now!

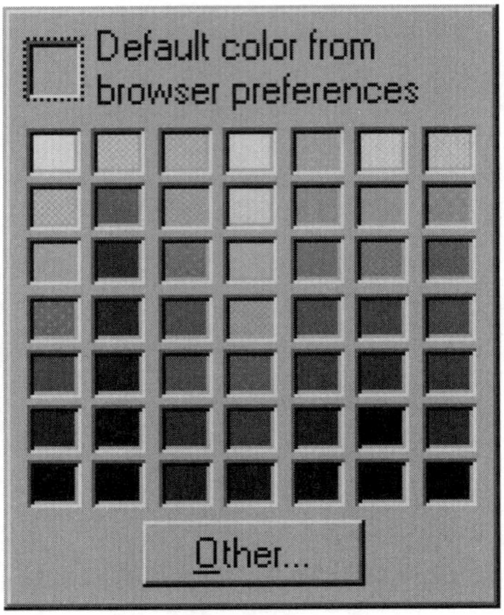

Figure 30.2 Color dialog box.

4. Click Normal Text, and choose a color using the same Color or Custom Color dialog box that you used in step 3.
5. Make color choices for Link Text, Active Link Text, and Followed Link Text. Your Link Text choice should be brighter than your Followed Link Text choice.
6. Choose OK when you've finished making your choices.

Adding a Background Graphic

Instead of a solid color, you may wish to display a tiled background graphic. Such graphics are actually rather small—typically, the files are just a few kilobytes in size—but the browser automatically places them side by side until they fill the whole screen.

Before you add a background graphic, though, think about all the pages you've seen that were hard to read because the background graphic was so busy.

Let's look at some good backgrounds before proceeding. In Figure 30.3, you see what happens when a busy background graphic almost completely obscures the text. Ugly! Figure 30.4 shows a much better choice—it's a low-key yellow fabric that doesn't obscure the text at all. In fact, it adds legibility.

To add a background graphic to your document, do the following:

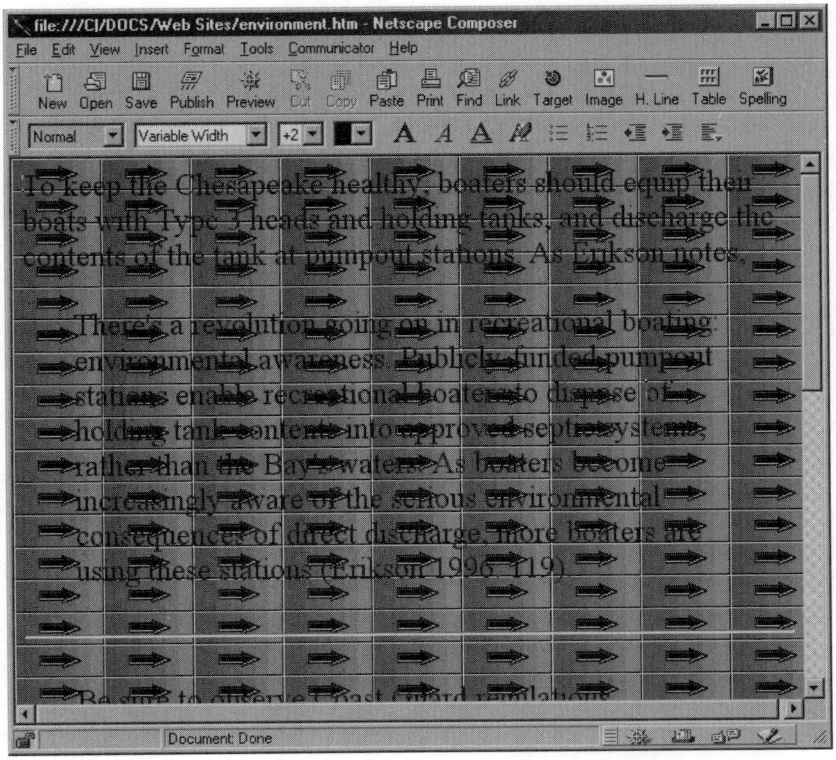

Figure 30.3 Horrible background graphic.

1. From the Format menu, choose Page Colors and Properties, and click Colors and Backgrounds.
2. In the Background Image area, click Use Image, and use the Browse button to locate your background graphic.
3. Click OK to confirm your choice.

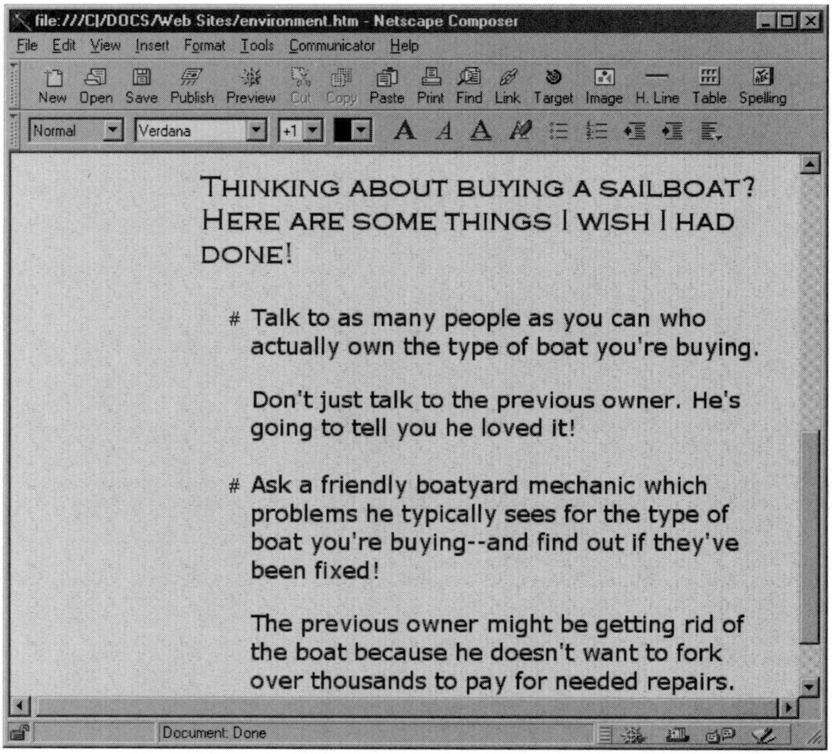
file:///C|/DOCS/Web Sites/environment.htm - Netscape Composer
File Edit View Insert Format Tools Communicator Help
New Open Save Publish Preview Cut Copy Paste Print Find Link Target Image H. Line Table Spelling
Normal
Verdana
+1
THINKING ABOUT BUYING A SAILBOAT? HERE ARE SOME THINGS I WISH I HAD DONE!
Talk to as many people as you can who actually own the type of boat you're buying.
Don't just talk to the previous owner. He's going to tell you he loved it!
Ask a friendly boatyard mechanic which problems he typically sees for the type of boat you're buying--and find out if they've been fixed!
The previous owner might be getting rid of the boat because he doesn't want to fork over thousands to pay for needed repairs.
Document: Done

Figure 30.4 Beautiful background graphic.

> Looking for background graphics? You'll find tons of them on the Web. Assuming you ask permission to do so, you can copy a background to your hard disk—and use it in your pages—by right-clicking the background in the browser, and choosing Save Background As. You'll also find lots of sites that collect background graphics; one of the best is Pattern Land (http://www.netcreations.com/patternland/). For more great links, check out Yahoo's Backgrounds page (http://www.yahoo.com/, and search for Backgrounds). Texture Woild (http://www.websharx.com/~ttbrown/txtwoild.html) has lots of beautiful background graphics. If you hate my advice about tasteful backgrounds, please go directly to Jeffrey Zeldman's remarkable Jeffrey Zeldman Presents (http://www.zeldman.com), which is loaded with background graphics that go very far off the deep end.

From Here

- Enough with the aesthetics—let's get down to business. Add some hyperlinks! Learn how in Chapter 31.
- And how 'bout some graphics? Become a master of in-line images in Chapter 32.

Chapter 31

Adding Hyperlinks

A *hyperlink* is a distinctively formatted word or phrase that, when clicked, takes the user to another document (or another location within the same document). Graphics can be hyperlinks, too. In this section, you'll learn how to add hyperlinks to your document.

Adding Hyperlinks Using the Character Properties Dialog Box

To add a hyperlink to your document, position the cursor where you want the hyperlink to appear, and click Link on the toolbar (it looks like part of a chain). Alternatively, choose Insert/Link, or press Ctrl + L. You'll see the Character Properties dialog box, shown in Figure 31.1, with the Link page displayed.

Follow these instructions to add a link using the Link Properties dialog box:

1. In the Link Source box, type the text (called the *link text*) that you want the user to see.
2. In the Link To box, type the URL.
3. Click OK to add the hyperlink to your document. To see if it's working OK, click View in Browser on the toolbar, or choose File/ Browse Document.

If you prefer, you can type the link text in your document, and select it. When you click Link, you'll see that Composer has automatically entered this text in the Character Properties dialog box.

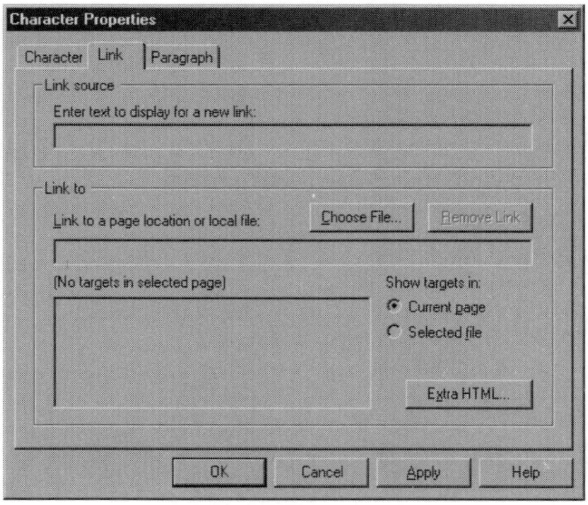

Figure 31.1 Use this dialog box to add new hyperlinks to your document.

It doesn't work! You switched to the browser window and clicked your link—but it doesn't work! What went wrong? Lots of possibilities here:

- Probably, you typed the URL wrong. Note that URLs are case-sensitive; you have to duplicate the capitalization pattern exactly. Also, don't leave any spaces within URLs. Be sure there are two slashes and a colon after "http." Edit the hyperlink (see "Editing Hyperlinks," later in this chapter).
- The page may have moved or no longer exists. If it's moved, edit the link with the page's new location (see "Editing Hyperlinks," later in this chapter).
- Last but not least? Maybe you're not connected to the Internet. Log on!

Adding Links Using Drag-and-Drop

You can add hyperlinks just by dragging the link from a browser page to the Composer page. This enables you to build up a list of links very quickly!

You can use this technique to add a link on your page to the page currently displayed in the browser window:

1. Display the browser window as well as the window. In the browser window, display the document to which you want to link.
2. In the Composer window, position the cursor where you want the new hyperlink to appear.
3. Drag the chain link icon (next to the Location box) from the browser window to the Composer window, and release the mouse button. Composer adds the link to your document at the cursor's location.

To test your hyperlinks at any time, click Preview (on the toolbar). If you haven't saved your page, you'll be prompted to do so—and you should. You'll then see your page in a

Netscape browser window. Log on to the Net, if you haven't done so, and click your hyperlinks to test them.

Follow these instructions to add a link within a displayed page:

1. Display the browser window as well as the Composer window. In the browser window, locate a document that contains the link you want to include in your Composer document.
2. In the Composer window, position the cursor where you want the new hyperlink to appear. If you want the hyperlink to appear on a new line, press Enter or Shift + Enter.
3. Drag the hyperlink from the browser window (see Figure 31.2). As you do, you'll see that the pointer changes shape to indicate that you're "carrying" a hyperlink. When the pointer reaches the Composer window, release the mouse button. You'll see the new hyperlink at the cursor's location.

Creating Internal Links

Internal links enable users to move to a specific location within a document. In order to create internal links, you must first define *targets*, which are named places within a document. Targets serve as destinations for internal links.

Here's an example. Suppose you're creating a lengthy document that contains a lot of text. You could place a table of contents at the beginning, one that listed the major headings in the document. You could then define each of the major headings as a target, and make each entry in the table of contents serve as an internal link. Readers can then click an item in the table of contents, and they'll jump right to the section they want.

In the following sections, you learn how to create targets and how to link to targets using internal links.

Defining Targets

It's easy to define targets in your document. Wait until you've finished writing it and then do the following:

Figure 31.2 Dragging and dropping a hyperlink.

1. Select a word at the beginning of the text that you want displayed when your reader selects the internal link. This word will be positioned at the top of the screen when your users jump to this target.
2. Click Target or choose Target from the Insert menu. You'll see the Target Properties dialog box, which automatically contains the text you've highlighted. In Figure 31.3, the phrase "sailing pages" had

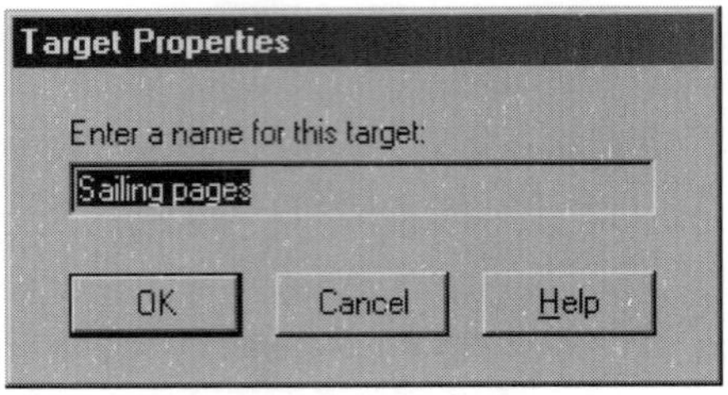

Figure 31.3 Defining a target.

been selected to serve as the target, and that's what appears in the Target Properties box.

3. Repeat step 2 to define all the additional targets that you want to create in this document.

After you define targets, Composer shows you where you've placed them by means of a little icon (see Figure 31.4).

Creating Links to Targets

Now that you've created targets in your document, it's easy to create links to them. Do the following:

1. Type and select the text that you want to serve as the linking text.
2. Click Link. You'll see the Link page of the Character Properties dialog box. Note that all the targets in your document are listed (look at the area called "Select a named target in current document"; see Figure 31.5).
3. Select the target to which you want to link.
4. Click OK.

Linking to a Target on a Different Page

You can also link to targets in another document. To do so, follow these instructions:

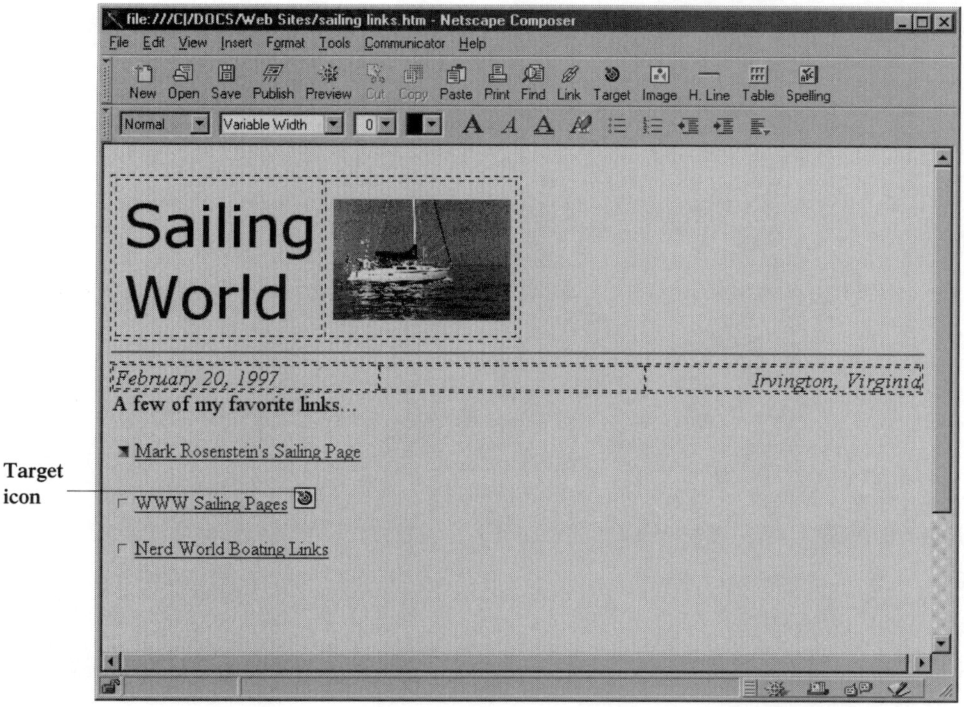

Figure 31.4 The icon shows you where you've entered a target.

1. Type and select the text that you want to serve as the linking text.
2. Click Link. You'll see the Link page of the Character Properties dialog box.
3. In the Link To area, use the Browse button to select the file that contains the targets.
4. Under the area called "Show targets in," click Selected File. You'll see the target names.
5. Select the target to which you want to link.
6. Click OK.

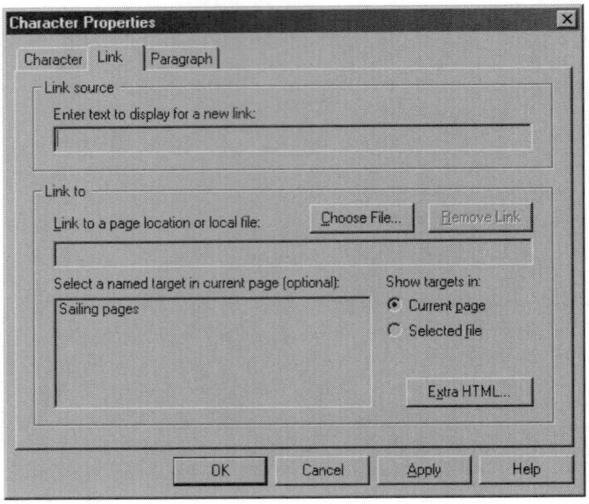

Figure 31.5 After you define targets, you'll see the target names in the Link Properties dialog box.

Adding a Mailto Hyperlink

Chances are you'll want to hear from the people who access your page; they may make suggestions, tell you about dead links, or just tell you how much they enjoyed your page! You can add a link, called a *mailto hyperlink,* to your page that automatically brings up a mail window if the user is using a reasonably up-to-date browser. The mail window automatically contains your e-mail address in the To box.

To create a mailto hyperlink, follow these instructions:

1. Type and select the text that you want to serve as the linked text. Normally this is your e-mail address. This will enable people who don't have mail-capable browsers to see your e-mail address.
2. Click Link. You'll see the Link page of the Character Properties dialog box.

3. In the Link To box, carefully type *mailto*: followed by your e-mail address, with no spaces, as in the following:

   mailto:julia-bear@nowhere.net

4. Click OK.

Editing Hyperlinks

If you've already entered a hyperlink and it doesn't work (or the site's moved), you can edit the URL. To do so, select the hyperlink and then click Object Properties on the Toolbar, or choose Properties/Link, or click Ctrl + L. You'll see the Properties dialog box. Edit the URL, and click OK.

From Here

- You've got the links. Now get the pix! Find out how in the next chapter.
- Want to achieve the ultimate in Web page design? Learn how to use tables and frames, as explained in Chapter 33.

Chapter 32

Adding Images to Your Page

Enough text! You want pictures! Well, you came to the right place. In this chapter, you'll learn how to jazz up your page by adding images. Like hyperlinks, images can be added in two ways: with the Image Properties dialog box or by dragging and dropping. Before getting to the specifics, though, let's take a quick look at the sorts of images you'll be adding, including how you can obtain them if they're freely available.

A Quick Introduction to Web Graphics

Graphics are stored in lots of differing file formats. For Web publishing, though, there are really only two kinds of graphics in wide use:

For the Time-Challenged

- You can insert GIF or JPEG graphics into your page. GIF graphics are best for small, geometric graphics with up to 256 colors, while JPEG graphics are best for photographic-quality images.
- If you've located some public domain art, or you have permission to copy some art, you can download a graphic by right-clicking the graphic in Netscape's browser and choosing Save Image As from the pop-up menu.
- When you add images, be sure to add alternate text for the benefit of those who have switched off graphics or use text-only browsers.
- The easiest way to add graphics to your Composer page is to drag them from a browser window!
- Once you've added a graphic to your document, you can align it, copy it, move it, or delete it. You can also choose how you want text positioned relative to the graphic, including text wrapping, and you can add white space or a border around it.

GIF	This graphic file format stores images in up to 256 colors. It's best used for graphics with a limited range of colors and geometric shapes.
JPEG	This graphic file format can store millions of colors. It's best used for photographic-quality graphics.

Where can you obtain graphics for your Web page? Lots of places, but make sure the image isn't copyrighted before using it on your page. Just because somebody makes a graphic available on the Web doesn't imply that the graphic can be freely reused elsewhere! That said, there are lots of image archives, and some of them are expressly in the public domain.

A great source of free graphics is Laurie McCannas' Free Art Website (http://www.mccannas.com). Laurie is the author of *Creating Great Web Graphics*, published by MIS Press. The site offers some particularly beautiful icons and bullets.

Getting Graphics with Netscape

If you've located a graphic that you want to use, and you're sure you can do so without violating copyright, you can save it to your hard disk. Later, you can add the image to your page using Composer.

The Virtual Image Archive (http://imagiware.com/via/) lists hundreds of links to image archives on the Web. Note that many of these images are copyrighted and can't be reused without permission; others are in the public domain. If you have any question about whether you can use any of the images accessible through this archive, contact the person who maintains the page containing the image.

To save an image to your hard disk, use the browser to display the page containing the graphic. Then hold down the right mouse button and choose Save Image As. In the Save As dialog box, choose the directory that contains the Web page on which you're working, and click OK.

Do you have access to a scanner? It's another great source of graphics. To learn how to get the most out of a scanner for Web publishing purposes, check out Sullivan's Scanning Tips Online (http://www.hsdesign.com/scanning/tipswelcome.html). It's a truly great site.

Adding Images Using the Image Properties Dialog Box

To add an image to your document with the Image Properties dialog box, follow these instructions:

1. Position the cursor where you want the image to appear.
2. On the toolbar, click Image, or choose Image from the Insert menu. You'll see the Properties dialog box, with the Image page displayed (see Figure 32.1).
3. In the Image location area, type the location and name of the image file, or use the Browse button to locate the file.
4. Select "Copy image to document's location." This will ensure that the graphic is located in the same directory as your Web page.
5. Click OK.

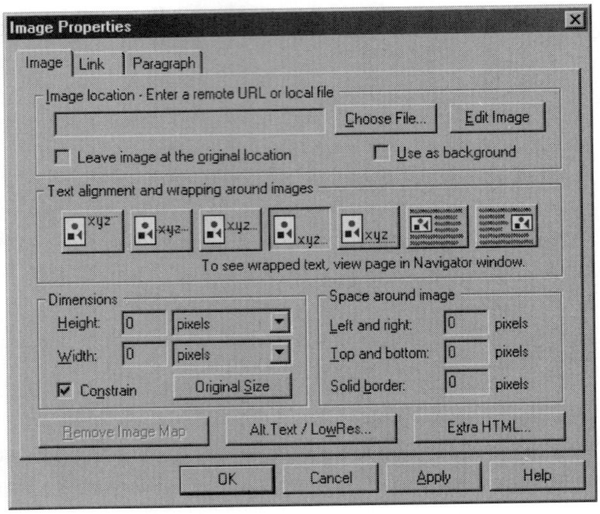

Figure 32.1 Image Properties dialog box.

You'll see your graphic in your Web page (for an example, see Figure 32.2). For information on sizing the graphic and specifying its relationship with surrounding text, see "Sizing Graphics and Aligning with Text," later in this chapter.

Adding Images Using Drag-and-Drop

By far the easiest way to add images to your page is simply to drag them from a browser window into your document. Adjust the two windows (the browser and Composer) so that you can see both the source graphic and the general area where you want the graphic to be positioned. In the Composer window, position the cursor where you want the graphic to appear. Drag the source graphic into the window and release the mouse button. Composer automatically copies the source graphic to the Composer document's location.

Figure 32.2 Graphic added to page.

Editing Graphics

Once you've added a graphic to your page, you can copy it, move it, or delete it.

Copying a Graphic

If you've just entered a graphic in a document and would like to use it more than once, you can copy it and paste as many copies as you like. This is exactly what you'll do when you insert a small graphic to serve as a bullet (see "Using Graphics as Bullets," later in this chapter). Just select the graphic and press Ctrl + C to copy the graphic to the Clipboard (you can also choose Edit/Copy from the menu bar, if you wish). Position the cursor where you want the graphic to appear and press Ctrl + V (or choose Edit/Paste).

Moving a Graphic

If you don't like the graphic's position, you can move it. Just select the graphic and press Ctrl + X, or choose Edit/Cut. Move the cursor to the place in which you would like the graphic to appear and press Ctrl + V, or choose Edit/Paste.

Deleting a Graphic

If you'd like to delete a graphic you've inserted, just select the graphic and press Del.

Positioning and Sizing Graphics

Once you've entered a graphic in your document, you can align it left, center, or right. You can also specify the relationship to the surrounding text and even "wrap" text around a graphic for a cool desktop-publishing effect.

Aligning Graphics

You can align your graphic simply by selecting it and clicking the Left, Center, or Right icons on the toolbar. In Figure 32.3, you see a graphic that's been aligned flush right.

Specifying the Relationship to Surrounding Text

If you would like to position one line of text next to your graphic, you can align it at the top, middle, or bottom of the graphic. By default, text appears to the right of the graphic, no matter how you've aligned the graphic. Figure 32.4 shows the text positioned at the top of the graphic, while Figure 32.5 shows text aligned at the middle and Figure 32.6 shows text aligned at the bottom.

Note that for the middle and bottom positions, you can choose to position the text so that the text is either aligned with or above a line drawn through the graphic's middle or the graphics's bottom line. (You can't see the difference unless you display the page in the browser.)

To choose an alignment option, click the appropriate icon in the Alignment area of the Image Properties dialog box.

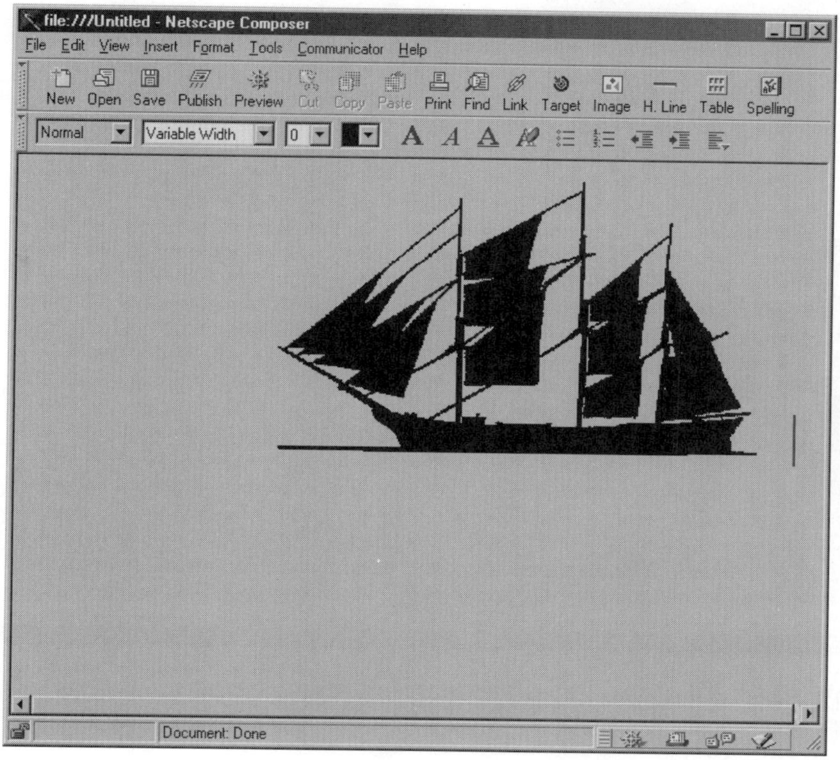

Figure 32.3 Right-aligned graphic.

Wrapping Text around a Graphic

If the graphic is positioned next to a paragraph of text, you can wrap the text around it, as shown in Figure 32.7. To wrap text left or right around the graphic, click the appropriate icon in the Alignment area of the Image Properties dialog box.

The text wrapping won't work! You have to switch to the browser window to see the wrapped text. To do so, click View in Browser.

Figure 32.4 Text positioned at top of left-aligned graphic.

If you want to add some text below the graphic that isn't wrapped, choose Insert/Break Below Images from the menu bar. Then start typing the text. This text won't be included in the wrapped text. In Figure 32.8, note the text "A few of my favorite links" below the graphic; this text is preceded by Break Below Images.

Sizing Your Graphic

By default, Composer uses the graphic's original size, in pixels. However, you can specify a different size, and both the Composer and most browsers that access your page will size the graphic accordingly. To change the size, type a new height and width in the Dimensions area of the Image Properties dialog box, but be sure to preserve the original graphic's aspect ratio (the height divided by the width). Or better yet, skip sizing your graphic entirely.

Figure 32.5 Text positioned at middle of left-aligned graphic.

I changed the size and now it looks terrible! You probably changed the aspect ratio. It's a much better idea to resize the graphic using a graphics program such as Paint Shop Pro. Note that there's a link to a graphics program in the Images Properties dialog box. You can use this link to open a graphics editor, such as Lview Pro, in which to resize the image correctly.

Adding a Border

If you would like to place a border around your graphic, specify the width in the Solid Border box of the Image Properties page. Try 2 pixels, if you like. Frankly, I think most graphics look better without borders.

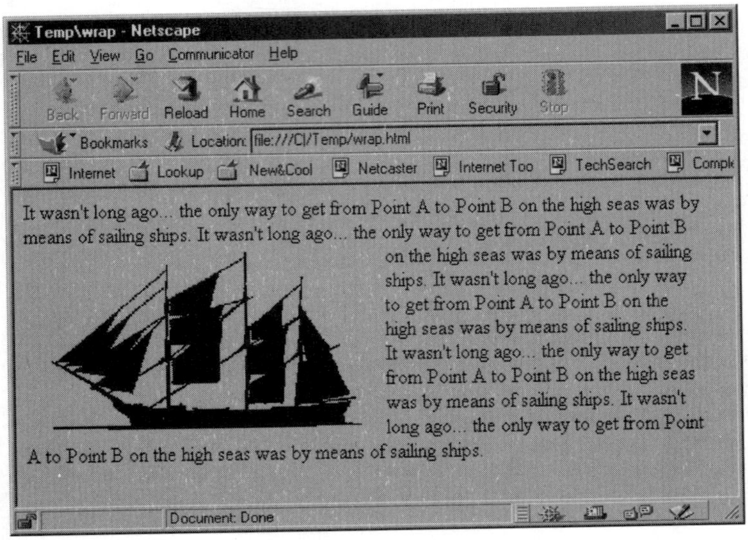
Temp\wrap - Netscape
File Edit View Go Communicator Help
Back Forward Reload Home Search Guide Print Security Stop
Bookmarks Location: file:///C|/Temp/wrap.html
Internet Lookup New&Cool Netcaster Internet Too TechSearch
It wasn't long ago... the only way to get from Point A to Point B on the high seas was by means of sailing ships. It wasn't long ago... the only way to get from Point A to Point B on the high seas was by means of sailing ships. It wasn't long ago... the only way to get from Point A to Point B on the high seas was by means of sailing ships. It wasn't long ago... the only way to get from Point A to Point B on the high seas was by means of sailing ships. It wasn't long ago... the only way to get from Point A to Point B on the high seas was by means of sailing ships.
Document: Done

Figure 32.6 Text positioned at bottom of left-aligned graphic.

Adding Space around the Image

If you don't add any space, the text can be positioned right up against the image, which might not look good. To increase the space, add 1 or 2 pixels to the "Left and right" or the "Top and bottom" boxes, which you'll find in the Space Around Image area of the Image Properties dialog box.

Adding Horizontal Lines

In publishing, a *rule* is a line that's used to separate text areas. You can easily add horizontal rules with Composer. Too easily, perhaps—it's easy to get carried away. Use horizontal lines like a spice: just a little does it!

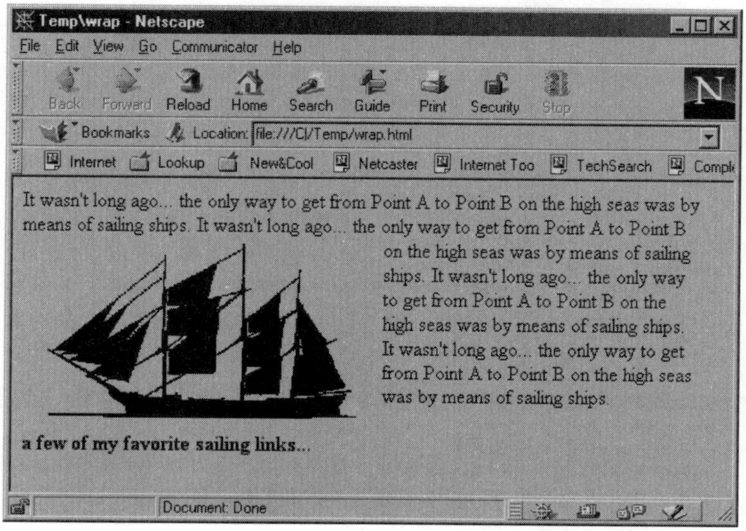
Temp\wrap - Netscape
File Edit View Go Communicator Help
Back Forward Reload Home Search Guide Print Security Stop
Bookmarks Location: file:///C|/Temp/wrap.html
Internet Lookup New&Cool Netcaster Internet Too TechSearch
It wasn't long ago... the only way to get from Point A to Point B on the high seas was by means of sailing ships. It wasn't long ago... the only way to get from Point A to Point B on the high seas was by means of sailing ships. It wasn't long ago... the only way to get from Point A to Point B on the high seas was by means of sailing ships. It wasn't long ago... the only way to get from Point A to Point B on the high seas was by means of sailing ships.
a few of my favorite sailing links...
Document: Done

Figure 32.7 Text wrapped around left-aligned graphic.

Adding a Rule

To add a rule to your document, position the cursor where you want the rule to appear, and click H. Line on the toolbar, or choose Horizontal Line from the Insert menu.

Choosing Rule Options

To change the appearance of the rule, select the rule, click the right mouse button, and choose Horizontal Line Properties. You'll see the Horizontal Line Properties dialog box, shown in Figure 32.8.

In this dialog box, you can choose the following options:

Height The default line is 2 pixels high. Try changing this number to see the effect of narrower or wider rules.

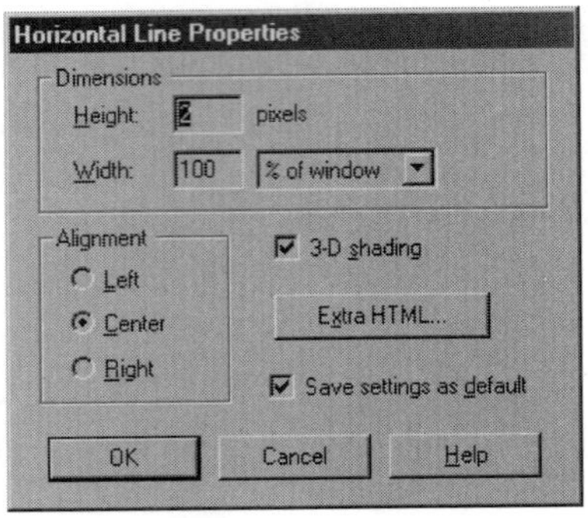

Figure 32.8 Horizontal Line Properties dialog box.

Width	By default, the line spans 100% of the window. You can specify the exact width in pixels or specify a different window width percentage.
Align	Lines are centered by default. Your page design might work with left or right alignment.
3-D Shading	Selected by default, this option produces a mannered line that calls attention to itself. Try turning it off!

Using a Graphic as a Rule

You can use a graphic as a rule—it's simple. You just add a rule graphic in the same way that you'd add any other graphic. There are lots of places on the Web where you can find graphics to suit every taste, or lack of taste.

Looking for cool rules? You'll find a nice collection at The Clip Art Collection (http://www.acy.digex.net/~infomart/clipart/) and most of them are in the public domain.

Using Graphics as Bullets

The bullets inserted into your document by Composer's Bullet List command are pretty boring. You've seen them zillions of times around the Net. To spice up your pages, it's better to use small graphics instead of those boring old default bullets. For an example, see the list in Figure 32.9.

Looking for bullets? Look no further than Bullets by Jen (http://ww2.cynernex.net/~jen/webpages/bullets/bullets.html). You'll find hundreds of graphics for every conceivable use. They're free for individual publishing or non-profit use.

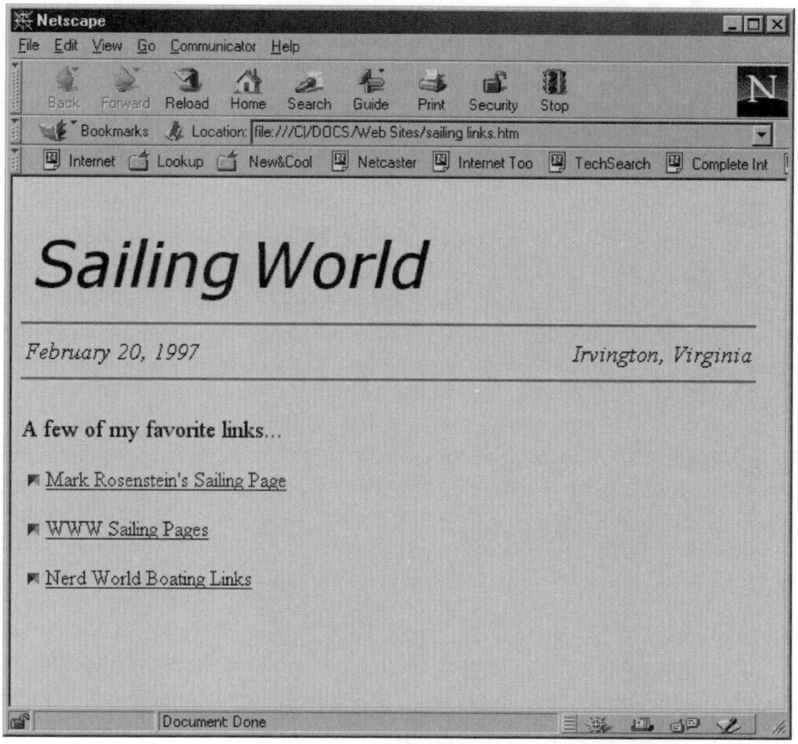

Figure 32.9 Small graphics make nice bullets.

What will you find? Everything from the ace of spades to the yin-yang symbol.

To create a bulleted list with graphics serving as bullets, type the list in a Normal paragraph format. Press Shift + Enter at the end of each item, unless you would like to separate the items by blank lines. Add the first graphic by positioning the cursor at the beginning of an item and choosing Insert Graphic.

Consider adding some space on the left and right of the graphic so that it doesn't look so crunched-up at the beginning of the line. To add space, double-click the graphic; you'll see the Image Properties dialog box. In the "Space around image" area, try 5 pixels in the "Left and right" box. Click OK to confirm.

After inserting the graphic, you can copy it to the Clipboard and insert it at the beginning of each line.

This graphic has an ugly border around it! To get rid of the border, double-click the graphic so that the Image Properties dialog box appears. In the "Space around image" area, make sure the Solid Border box contains 0, and then click OK.

Making a Graphic a Hyperlink

You can convert any graphic into a hyperlink. To do so, simply select the graphic and click Make Link. You'll see the Link Properties dialog box. Specify the page to which you want to link, and click OK. That's all there is to it!

After you define a graphic as a hyperlink, users won't have any way of knowing that it's a link unless they move the mouse pointer over the graphic. Then, the pointer changes to a hand shape, indicating that the user can click there to jump to a different document. But this may take a bit of explaining, if the picture doesn't say it all.

Can I Create an Imagemap with Composer?

You can't create one with Composer, but you can easily insert one. An *imagemap* is a graphic that contains multiple URLs. Just where you go when you click depends on precisely where the mouse pointer is positioned. Imagemaps used to be a pain to create, requiring all kinds of programming. Now it's easy to make them, but you'll need additional software to do it. A great program for creating imagemaps is Map This, which is available from the Map This home page (http://galadriel.ecaetc.ohio-state.edu/tc/mt). Map This enables you to open a GIF graphic, define "hot spots" that are associated with specific URLs, and paste the requisite code (automatically generated by the program) into your HTML source. It's really easy, and the results are spectacular.

From Here

- Tables and frames add organization and visual interest to your page. Composer doesn't work with frames, but you can create tables. Find out how in Chapter 33.
- Jazz up your document with animated GIFs, JavaScript, and other bells and whistles. See Chapter 34.
- Publish your document on the Web! See Chapter 35.

Chapter 33

Creating Tables

Before Composer, creating a table with HTML was a mind-numbing exercise; you had to use table tags that were actually never designed for human use—something like Composer was envisioned from the beginning. Now that Composer is here, you can easily add a table to your Web page.

This chapter fully covers Composer's table capabilities, which are pretty impressive. You'll learn how you can use tables for layout purposes as well as for organizing information. You'll learn how to insert and add text to tables and how to modify a table's structure after you've created it.

For the Time-Challenged

- You can use tables for more than organizing information in a tabular form. They're also fantastic tools for layout purposes.
- Plan your table's layout of rows and columns before starting.
- By default, your table is sized dynamically as you type. You may wish to fix the size for special applications, such as a page design with a thin vertical column of navigation aids.
- You can choose a variety of appearance options for your table, including borders, cell spacing, cell padding, colors, and alignments.
- You can add a caption above or below your table.
- If you need to add rows, columns, or cells after creating your table, it's easy to do so. You can also delete rows, columns, or cells—and even the whole table. To create banners, you can define a cell so that it spans two or more rows or columns

What Are Tables For?

Tables provide a convenient way to organize material (see Figure 33.1). Here, borders make the information easy to follow.

Clever table design provides a means to provide layout control (see Figure 33.2), producing desktop-publishing-quality Web page designs. You can turn the borders off to achieve cool-looking layout effects.

Planning Your Table

Although it's possible to alter the structure of your table after inserting it, you will save time and trouble if you do some planning first. Begin by deciding how many rows and columns your table will have.

Rows are horizontal; they go across the table. *Columns* are vertical. Where a row and a column come together, they form a *cell*. At the top of

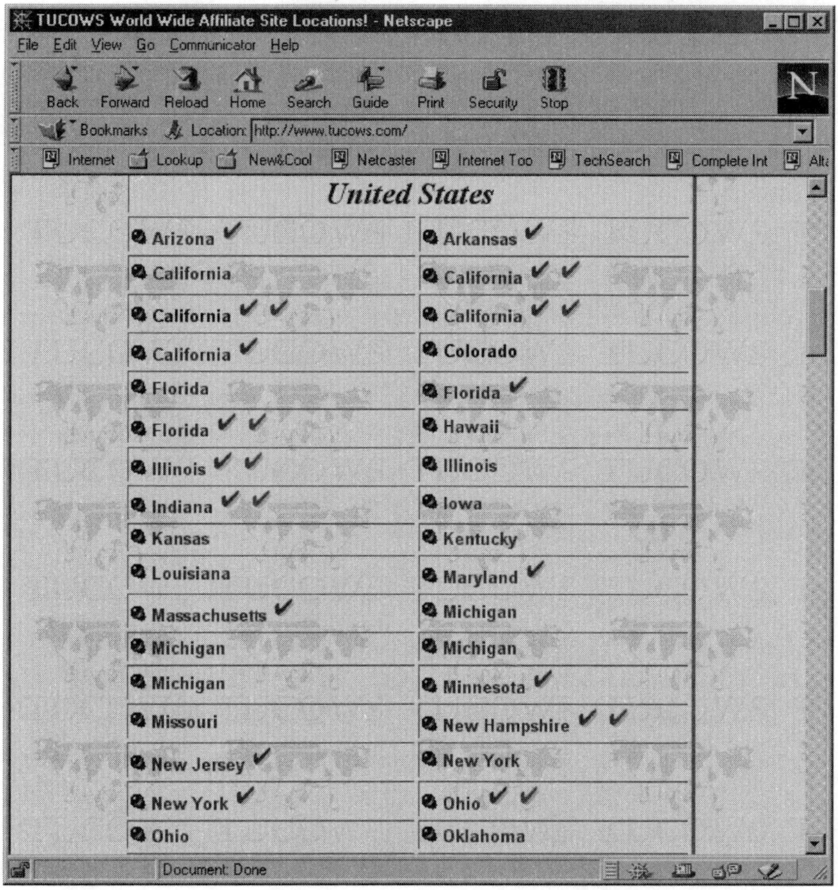

Figure 33.1 Tables can be used to organize material on-screen.

each column, you can define the cells as *header cells*, if you wish. Header cell text appears in bold. Figure 33.4 shows the basic table layout. Sometimes tables have rows or columns that *span* two or more cells (see Figure 33.5).Take a few moments now to plan your table. For your first table, don't include row or column spanning—learn the basics first. You'll get to spanning later in this chapter.

Figure 33.2 Tables can also be used for layout control.

Inserting a Table

To create your first table, click the Table button, or choose Insert/Table/Table from the menu bar. You'll see the New Table Properties dialog box, shown in Figure 33.3.

This dialog box has lots of options, but the only ones you should worry about now are the number of rows and columns you want. Try creating a

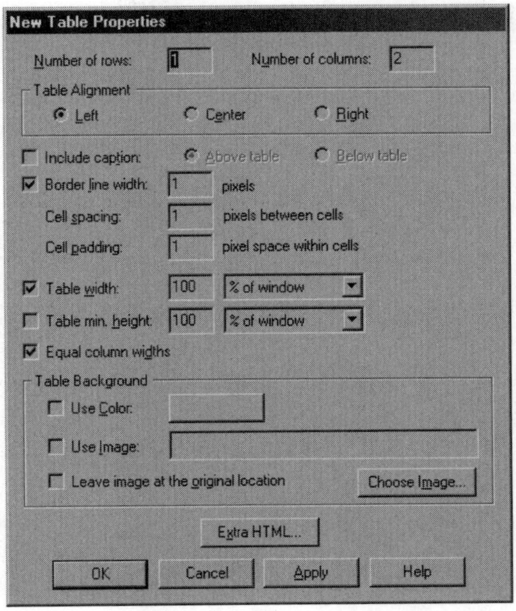

Figure 33.3 New Table Properties dialog box.

table with three rows and columns. Type 3 in the Number of Rows box and in the Number of Columns box, and click OK.

The table doesn't look like much after you insert it (see Figure 33.6) . That's because you haven't added any text yet.

Adding Text to a Table

Now try adding some text to your table. To select a cell, just click in it. Figure 33.7 shows a table with some text added.

Typing in a table is a little disconcerting, since Composer expands the cell dynamically to accommodate your typing. By default, the program sizes the cells to fit the longest line you type, except that the whole table won't expand beyond 100% of the window width.

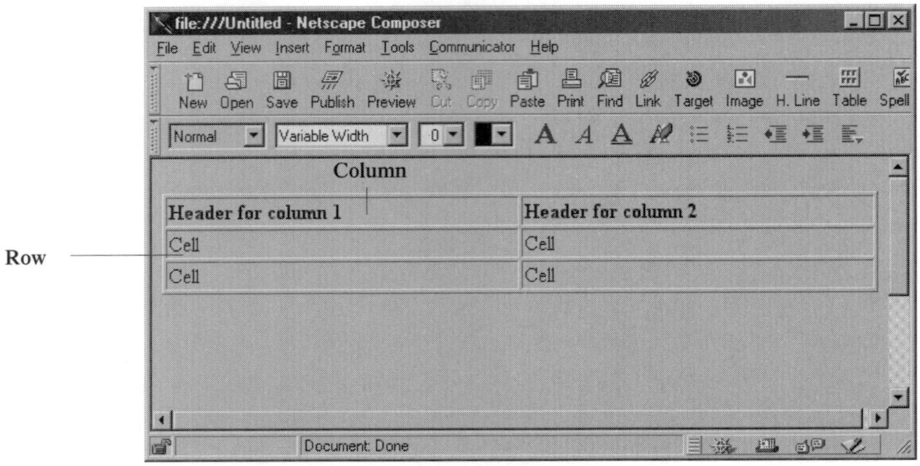

Figure 33.4 A table consists of rows, columns, and cells.

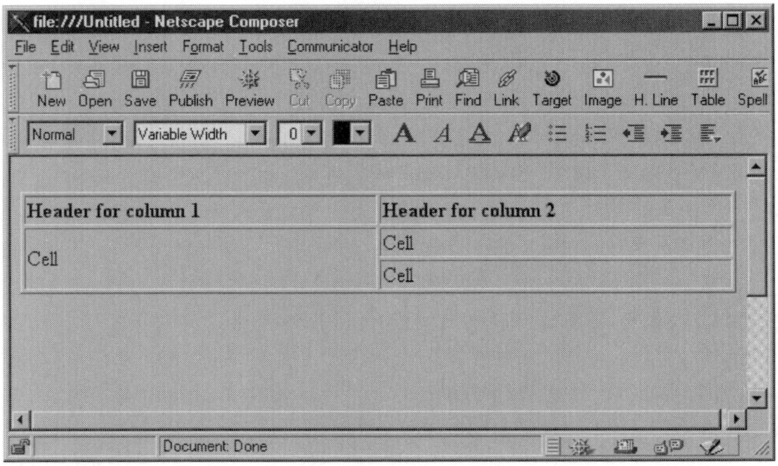

Figure 33.5 Cells can span rows or column.

Figure 33.6 Table before adding any text.

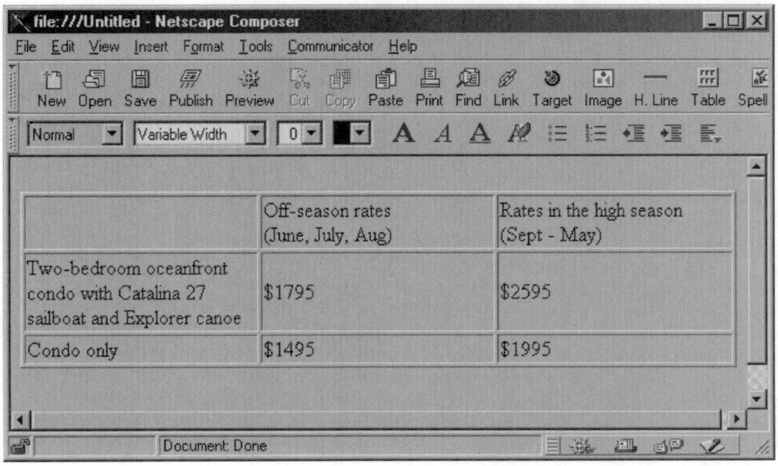

Figure 33.7 Table with text added.

You can press Enter within cells to break lines. In Figure 33.7, Enter was used to create a line break after "Off-season rates" and "Rates in the high season."

I tried pressing Tab and Shift + Tab to move from cell to cell, but it didn't work! If you're used to moving from cell to cell in a spreadsheet by pressing these keys, you need to unlearn this habit. In Composer, you press Tab to indent text, and Shift + Tab to unindent. If you accidentally indented some text, just select the cell and press Shift + Tab.

Changing Your Table's Look

Now that you've created your table, you can take advantage of commands that change your table's appearance. For example, you can turn off table borders. Figure 33.8 shows how much more attractive the example table looks with borders turned off.

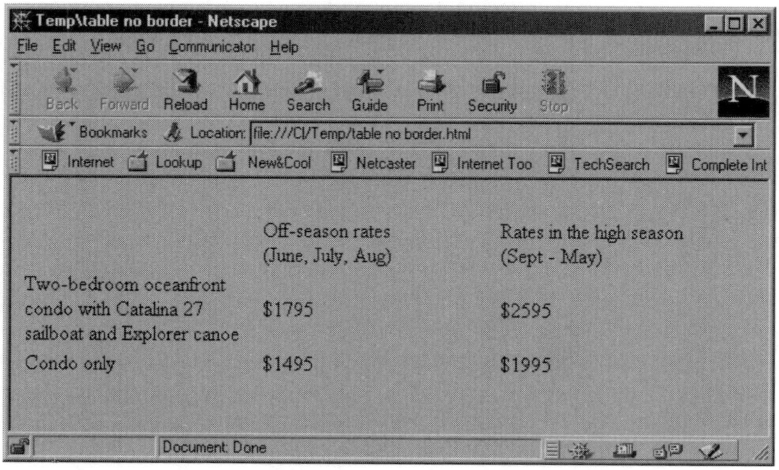

Figure 33.8 Table with no borders.

You can choose appearance options for the entire table, for individual rows, or for individual cells. The following sections explain these options.

Appearance Options for the Entire Table

To change appearance options for the entire table, place the cursor within the table, and choose Format/Table Properties and click the Table tab. You'll see the Table Properties dialog box, shown in Figure 33.9.

You can change the following:

- **Borders** Type the width of the table border in pixels. To remove borders, type 0.
- **Cell Spacing** This controls the amount of white space that is inserted between cell boundaries.
- **Cell Padding** This controls the amount of white space that is inserted within the cell, between the text and the cell boundary.

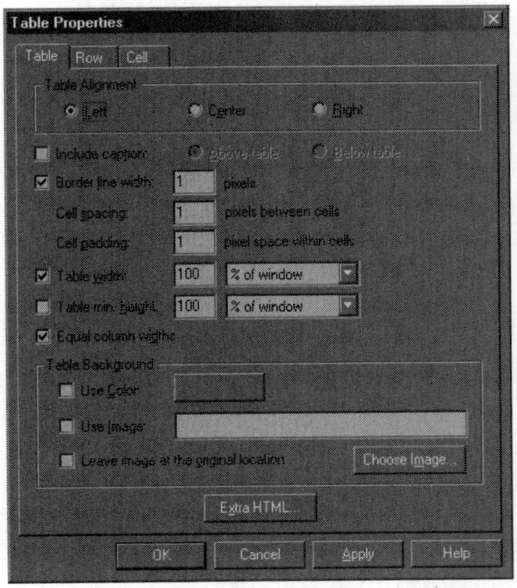

Figure 33.9 Table Properties dialog box.

- **Table Color** You can choose a background color for the whole table. *Note:* You can also choose colors for rows and individual cells. To choose a color, click the Table Color check box and choose a color by clicking the Choose Color button.
- **Table Alignment** Here, you choose a default text alignment for the whole table (left, center, or right).

To see what these options do, try playing around with them and clicking Apply. This leaves the dialog box open so you can experiment more, but you see the changes in the table. (If you can't see the table, adjust the location of the Table Properties dialog box so that you can.)

In addition to the formatting options in the Table Properties dialog box, you can format the text with font sizes, styles (such as bold or italic), and font colors. For more information on these options, see Chapter 29.

To choose formatting options for the whole table, choose Edit/Select Table from the menu bar. This selects every cell. Now you can choose alignment, font, font size, and style options that will affect the whole table.

Adding a Caption

To add a caption to your table, click Include Caption in the Table Properties dialog box, and click Above or Below table. After you click OK, you'll find that Composer has created a format for a table caption; just click above or below the table and start typing. Figure 33.10 shows the example table with a caption added. The caption is centered by default. The figure shows the caption's appearance with increased font size and bold added.

Choosing Row Options

To choose row appearance options, position the cursor within one of your table's rows, choose Properties/Table, and click the Row tab. You'll see the Row page, shown in Figure 33.11. Here, you can choose the following:

- **Horizontal Text Alignment** This option enables you to choose text alignment for each cell in the row. If you choose an option other

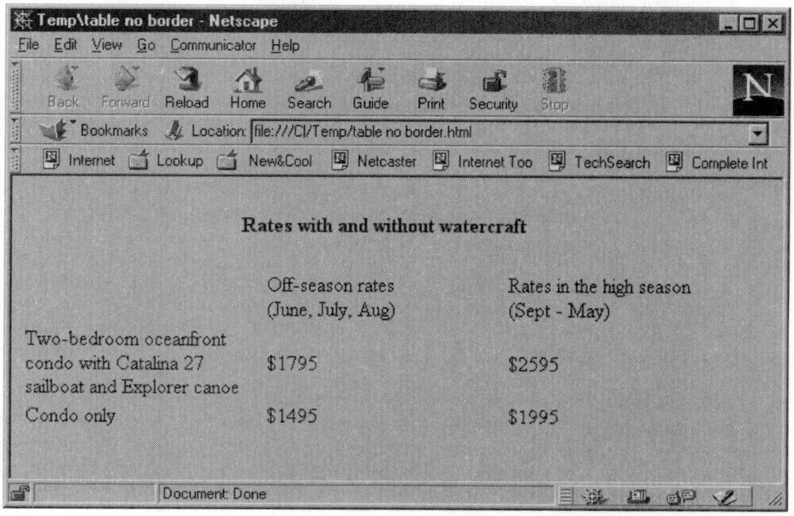

Figure 33.10 Table with caption added.

than Default, your choice here overrides the default alignment. You can choose Left, Center, or Right.

- **Vertical Text Alignment** This option enables you to position the text vertically within each cell in the row. By default, text is positioned according to the browser's default settings You can also choose Top, Center, Bottom, or Baselines (text is aligned so that the baselines of text are even).
- **Row Color** This color choice affects the whole row. To choose a color, click the Color checkbox and choose a color by clicking the Choose Color button.

Choosing Cell Options

To choose cell appearance options, position the cursor within one of your table's cells, choose Properties/Table, and click the Cell tab. You'll see the Cell page, shown in Figure 33.12. Here, you can choose the following:

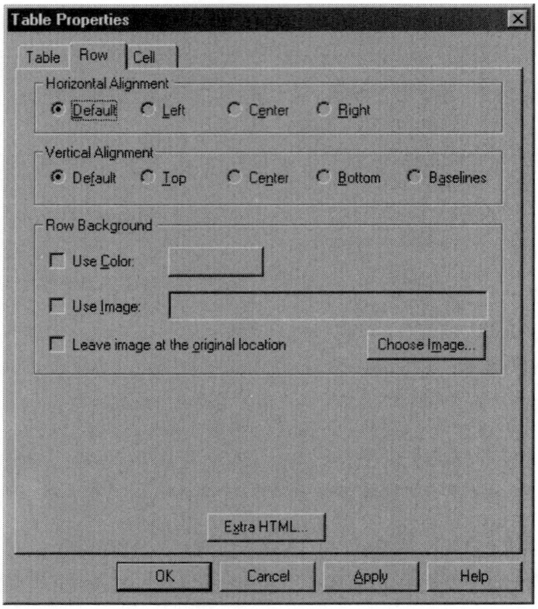

Figure 33.11 You choose row appearance options here.

- **Horizontal Text Alignment** This option enables you to choose an alignment option for the current cell only. If you choose an option other than Default, your choice here overrides the default alignment. It also overrides any choice you might have made for the row in which the cell is positioned. You can choose Left, Center, or Right.
- **Vertical Text Alignment** This option enables you to choose vertical alignment options for the current cell only. By default, text is positioned according to the browser's default settings. If you choose an option other than Default, you override the row alignment setting. You can also choose Top, Center, Bottom, or Baselines (text is aligned so that the baselines of text are even).
- **Text** To define a cell as a header cell (with bold, centered type), click Header Style. By default, text is wrapped within cells—which is good, since people might display your table using a narrow window. Leave this setting as it is.

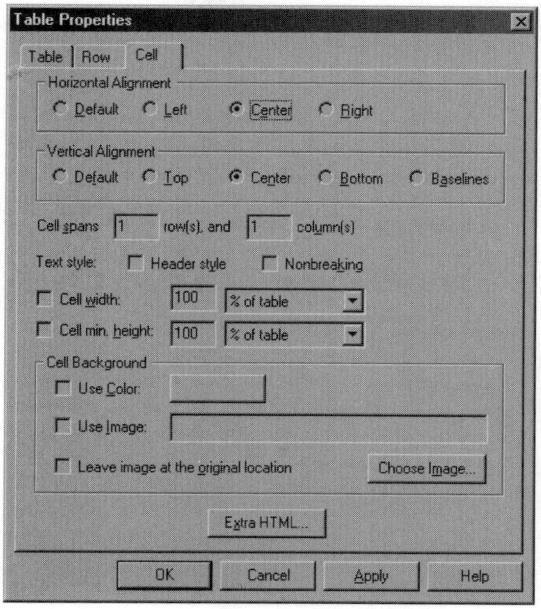

Figure 33.12 Cell appearances page of Table Properties dialog box.

- **Cell Color** This color choice affects only the current cell. To choose a color, click the Color checkbox and choose a color by clicking the Choose Color button.

Figure 33.13 shows the example table after choosing a number of table, row, and cell appearance options, including row and cell colors and vertical and horizontal alignment options. The two cells in the top row are formatted with the Header Cell option.

Note that the table in 33.13 actually has nine cells. However, the blank cell doesn't show up because borders are turned off and it has no color. This cell would show up, though, if you used borders—in which case you'd need to get rid of it. To delete an unwanted cell, position the cursor in the cell and choose Edit/Delete/Table Cell.

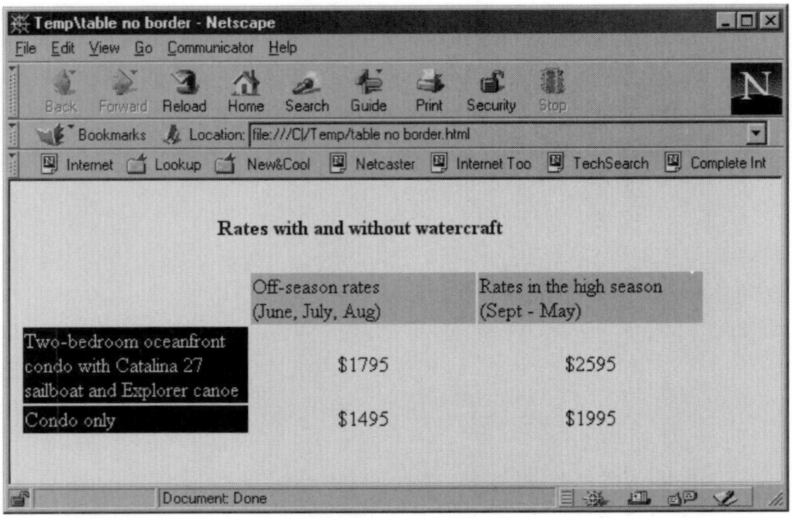

Figure 33.13 Table after choosing appearance options.

Sizing Your Table

By default, Composer dynamically sizes your table. For most purposes, that's fine. When people view your table with a browser, the browser will also dynamically size it, adjusting the table and cell width according to the window width that the user has chosen. With the default sizing setting, you'll know that all portions of your table will remain visible, although it might look funny if somebody chooses a ridiculously narrow window width.

But you may wish to specify the exact width of your table or of individual cells within it. For example, you can set the width of a column by specifying a fixed width for all the cells in the column. In Figure 33.14, for example, there's a very simple table—it only has one row and two columns—and the left column is sized so that its contents fit within the dark part of the background graphic.

You can control the size of your table in the following ways:

> ### *Creating a Page with a Vertical Row of Navigation Buttons*
>
> The secret to creating a page such as the one shown in Figure 33.14 is to use a background graphic like the one shown in Figure 33.15—very long and thin! You can easily make such a graphic using any good graphics program. Cool, huh?

- **Table Properties** In the Table page of the Table Properties dialog box, you can choose a table width or a minimum table height. You can specify the width or minimum height in a percentage of the window or in pixels.
- **Cell Properties** In the Cell page of the Table Properties dialog box, you can choose a cell width and a minimum cell height. You can specify these in a percentage of the table width or in pixels.

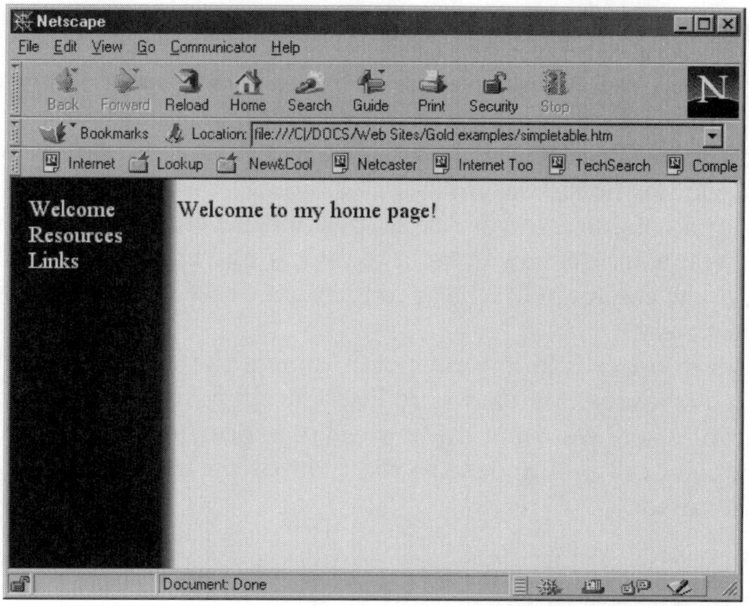

Figure 33.14 A simple 1 x 2 table.

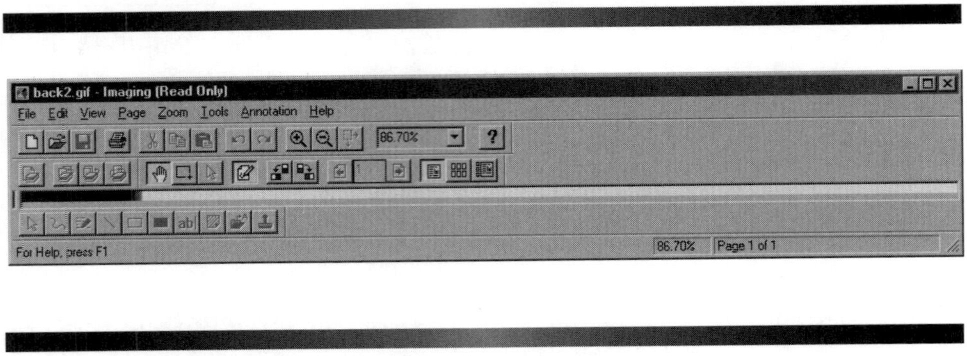

Figure 33.15 A long, thin background graphic for creating a table.

Changing the Table Structure

Need more columns or rows? You can insert them. Got some extras? You can delete them. And as this section shows, you can also span columns or rows.

Inserting Rows, Columns, and Cells

To insert a row into your table, position the cursor one row above where you want the row to appear (you must position it somewhere within the table) and choose Insert/Table Row. The new row will appear below the cell in which you positioned the cursor.

To insert a column into your table, position the cursor one cell to the left of where you want the new column to appear and choose Insert/Table Column. The new column will appear to the right of the cell in which you positioned the cursor.

You can insert cells in any row, even though the number of cells in that row exceeds those of other rows. To insert a cell, position the cursor one cell to the left of where you want the new cell to appear, and choose Insert/Table Cell. The new cell will appear to the right of the cell in which you positioned the cursor.

Deleting Rows, Columns, and Cells

You can delete rows, columns, or cells. Just position the cursor in the cell you want to eliminate and choose Edit/Delete/Table. From the pop-up menu, choose Row, Column, or Cell.

Deleting the Whole Table

If your table didn't work out, you can delete the whole table. Just position the cursor somewhere within it, and choose Edit/Delete/Table/Table.

Spanning Rows and Columns

To span a row or column, you format a cell so that it spans a specified number of rows or columns (for an example, see Figure 33.16). It's simple to format a cell so that it spans columns, but doing so will push the other cells in the row or column out of the way—you'll have to delete them using the Edit/Table/Delete Cell command.

To format a cell to span two or more rows or columns, position the cursor in the cell that you want to do the spanning, and choose Properties/Table. Click the Cell tab, if necessary, and type a number greater than 1 in the "Cell spans X rows" or "Cell spans X columns" box. Click Apply to make sure this makes sense; if not, change the settings. Click OK to confirm.

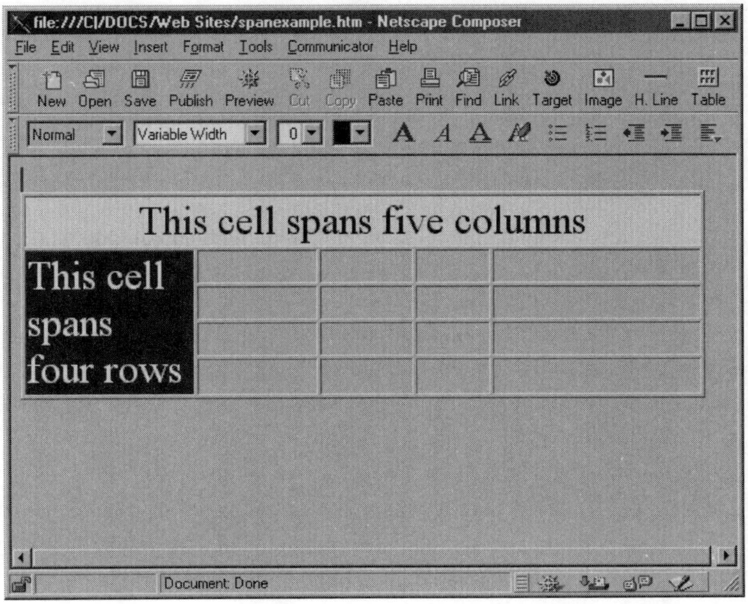

Figure 33.16 Table with cells spanning multiple rows and columns.

Awesome Table Tricks

Experienced Web designers use tables to pull off all kinds of things that aren't possible with ordinary HTML—and you can do them, too.

Ever wanted to place your document's title to the *left* of a graphic? You can't do it with ordinary HTML, but you sure can with a simple two-cell, no-border table. Get it? Take a look at Figure 33.17.

Publishing an on-line newsletter? You may want to include a *banner*, which indicates the date and place of publication. Ideally, this would be a single line of text that mixes alignment (flush left and flush right). You can't do that with ordinary HTML, but you can do it with a one-row, two-column table, as shown in Figure 33.18.

See why Web designers love tables?

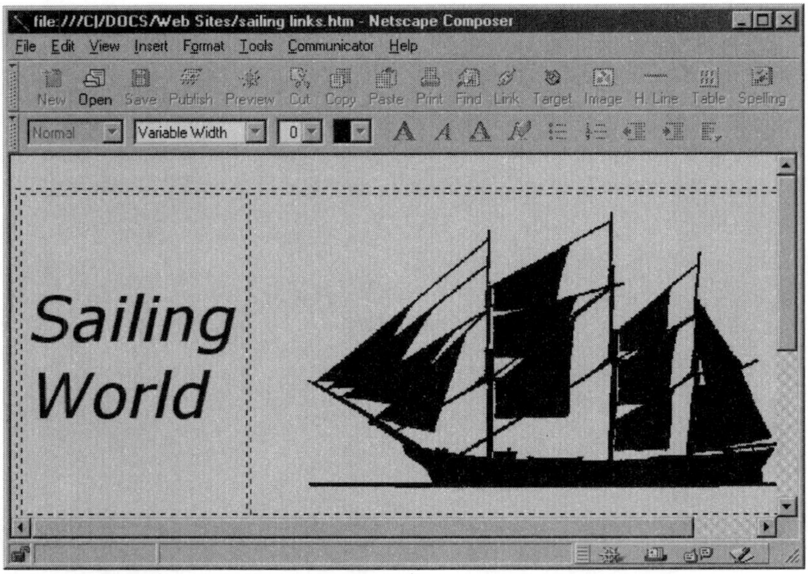

Figure 33.17 This document's title and graphic are positioned within a two-column table with no borders.

Figure 33.18 This newsletter's banner was created with a one-row, two-column table.

From Here

- You're just about done with Composer! In the next chapter, "Bells and Whistles," you'll learn how to add links to multimedia and other live content, including Java applets.
- Chapter 35, "Publishing Your Page," shows you how to publish your page using Composer's fantastic one-button publishing.

Chapter 34

Bells and Whistles

If you're like most aspiring Webmasters, you want your page to come alive—specifically, with live action (such as animations and movies), sounds, and Java programs. This chapter shows you how to incorporate these "bells and whistles" (cool, advanced features) into your pages.

This chapter doesn't try to teach you how to create animated GIFs, record sounds, digitize movies, or write JavaScript or Java programs. Those are subjects that would require a book in themselves (or several!). Instead, it focuses on incorporating these features into your pages. As you'll discover, you'll find thousands of animated GIFs, sounds, movies, JavaScript scripts, and Java applets available on the Web, many of

For the Time-Challenged

- Even if you're not a whiz at graphics, sound recording, or programming, you can find active content all over the Web and incorporate this content into your document.
- You can easily add animated GIFs to your Web documents. Just copy one from a site that makes these GIF files freely available and add it to your document just like you'd add any other GIF.
- To make a sound or movie file accessible from your document, you simply make a hyperlink to the sound or movie file, just like those you would create to link to a document. There's a neat and easy trick you can do that makes a sound play in the background automatically when the user opens your document.
- JavaScript is a programming language that can make things happen on a Web page, such as displaying a clock, calendar, or scrolling banner. Without learning any JavaScript, you can copy and paste JavaScript code snippets into your documents, as this chapter explains.

which are free for the downloading. Simply by downloading these files and incorporating them into your pages following this chapter's instructions, you'll look like you're an absolute whiz at multimedia production!

Adding Animated GIFs

A quick 'n' easy way to add impressive animation to your site is to download and insert an *animated GIF*. In brief, an animated GIF is a graphic that contains several variants on a picture, together with information about the order in which they are to be displayed and the timing between frames. The leading browsers can display animated GIFs without any trouble, and they're equally easy to add to your document—you just add them as if they were any other graphic!

You'll find many animated GIFs on the Net, but bear in mind that not all are free for unrestricted use. Many of the artists who make animated GIFs available state that they want you to ask permission via e-mail, provide a link back to their site, or pay a modest fee.

To add an animated GIF to your page, simply insert the graphic into your document as you would an ordinary GIF or JPEG graphic: Click Insert Image on the toolbar, or choose Insert/Image from the menus. That's all there is to it!

A great place to see what people are doing with animated GIFs is the 1st Internet Gallery of GIF Animation, located at

http://www.r4eiworld.com/royale/galframe.htm

Please note: These aren't for downloading or reuse without permission.

For the latest free animated GIFs on the Web, see Yahoo's animated GIFs page (Computers and Internet:Graphics:Computer Animation:Animated GIFs:Collections), which you can access from Yahoo's home page (http://www.yahoo.com). One of the linked sites is the GIF Animation Site (http://www.cswnet.com/~ozarksof/), shown in Figure 34.1. You'll find dozens of animated GIFs on Debby's Animated GIFs page, located at

http://www.hooked.net/~jpadilla/animate.htm

For information on creating GIF animations, check out Scot Hacker's GIF 89a: Creating Dynamic Web Imagery and Animations Without Fancy Tools (http://www.zdnet.com/aci/articles/gif89a.html).

Adding a Link to a Sound or Movie

Adding a sound or movie file to your page is as easy as adding a hyperlink—in fact, you add it in exactly the same way!

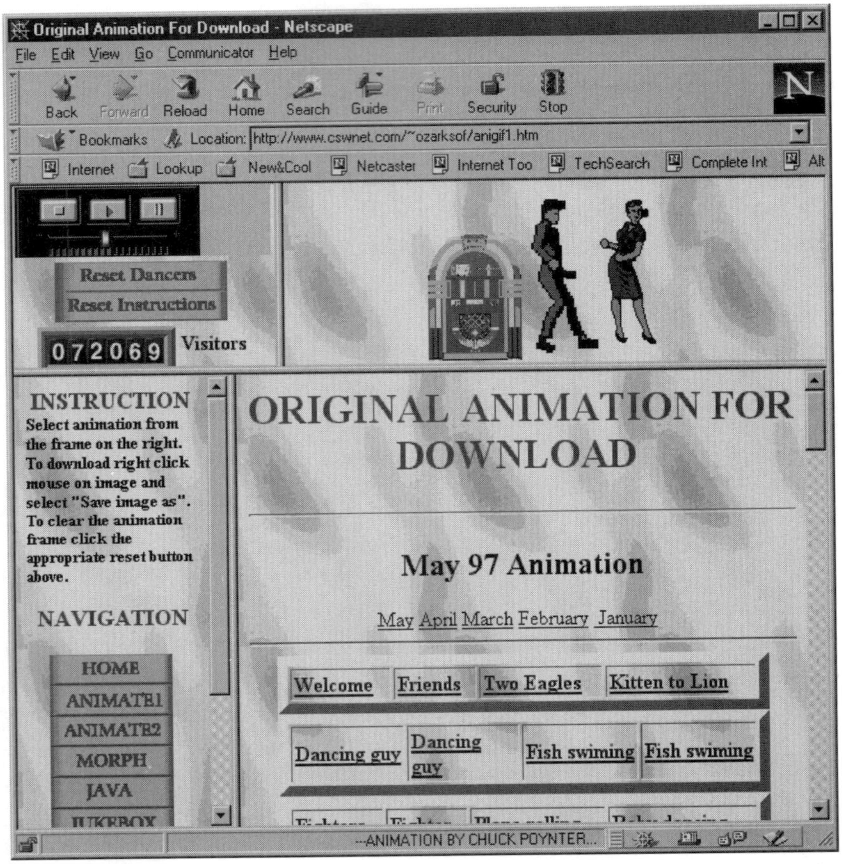

Figure 34.1 The GIF Animation Site has lots of cool animated icons.

When you're adding a link to a sound or movie, it's good manners to tell your users how large the file is (in K, such as 564K or 1024K). Some users have very slow connections, so they might want to skip the file if it's too large. By the same token, they're more likely to click the link if they know the file is fairly small (200K or less).

If you've obtained a sound or movie file and want to add it to your page, do the following:

1. Place the sound or movie file in the same directory as your Web page.
2. Open your Web page in Composer.
3. Select the text or graphic that you would like to serve as the linked source visible in your Web page.
4. Click Link, or choose Insert/Link from the menu bar, or just click Ctrl + L.
5. Click the Browse File button, and locate the sound or movie you want to add.
6. In the Files of Type box, choose the type of file you want to add. (For the types of sound and movie files you can use, see the sidebar.)
7. Select the sound or movie you want to use, and click Open.
8. Click OK.

For tons of sounds you can download and add to your site, see Yahoo's Sound Archives page (Computers and Internet:Multimedia:Sound:Archives), accessible from http://www.yahoo.com.

What Types of Sound and Movie Files Can You Use?

You can add the following sound and movies files to your Composer documents: QuickTime for Windows movies (*.mov files), Sun/NeXT sounds (*.au files), Silicon Graphics/Apple sounds (*.aiff files), Windows WAV sounds (*.wav files), MIDI music files (*.mid and *.midi files), and Video for Windows (*.avi files).

Playing a Sound in the Background

Here's a cool trick that you'll enjoy—and so will the people accessing your page. You can use the HTML <EMBED> tag to place a sound in the background of your document. It will begin playing automatically when your page opens. You can add a Windows WAV sound (*.wav), Sun/NeXT sound (*.au), or a Silicon Graphics/Apple sound (*.aiff).

This tag requires a browser that recognizes the <EMBED> tag. Not all do, including Netscape 1.0! Also, some of the advanced functions require a browser equipped with a sound-playing plug-in or helper program. Netscape Navigator 3.0 and Microsoft Internet Explorer 3.0 can handle the <EMBED> tag just fine.

To play a sound in the background, do the following:

1. Copy the sound file to the directory or folder containing your Web page. Make a note of your sound file's exact name, such as hello.wav.
2. Click in an empty area of the page, near the top.
3. From the menu bar, choose Insert/Tag.
4. In the HTML Tag dialog box, type the following carefully, but substitute your sound's file name in place of the example (hello.wav):

   <EMBED SRC="hello.wav" autostart = true hidden = true>

   If you would like the sound to loop endlessly, add a loop = true statement, like this:

   <EMBED SRC="hello.wav" autostart = true hidden = true loop = true>
5. Click OK to insert the tag.

Adding JavaScript to Your Page

JavaScript is a Netscape-developed *scripting language* that enables Web authors to make things happen on their pages. JavaScript resembles HTML in that you type various commands, which aren't visible to the person reading the page. However, JavaScript is a true programming language, unlike HTML. JavaScript enables an amateur programmer to create simple programs, such as an on-screen clock that displays the current date and time, a scrolling banner, or a calendar. (Java, in contrast, is a professional programmer's language that requires considerable expertise to learn.)

It's beyond the scope of this book to teach JavaScript, but it's easy to learn how to copy snippets of JavaScript code and paste them into your pages! (A *snippet* is a mini-program that does something, such as displaying an on-screen banner.)

Finding and Selecting a Snippet

If you find a page that has a JavaScript snippet that's been made available for downloading, choose View/Document Source (or, if you're viewing a framed document, select the frame and choose View Frame) to display the document in your default source viewer. (If you haven't selected a source viewer, choose Options/General Preferences, click the Apps tab, and use the Browse button next to the View Source box.)

You'll see that confusing HTML code in your source viewer, as shown in Figure 34.2. What you're looking for is everything between the <SCRIPT language = "JavaScript"> and closing </SCRIPT> tags. Select all of this text, including the <SCRIPT> and </SCRIPT> tags, and copy this text to the clipboard by pressing Ctrl + C.

Inserting the Code into your Composer Document

To insert the code into your Composer document, choose View/Edit Document Source. Go through your HTML code until you find the place where you want the applet's product (such as a clock or calendar) to appear. Press Ctrl + V to paste the code from the Clipboard. Then choose File/Save and click the close box to close this document.

When you return to Composer, you'll be asked whether you want to save the document. Choose Yes.

Testing the Script

To see whether your script is working right, click View in Browser.

It doesn't work! If you see an error box, something must have gone wrong in the cutting and pasting. From Composer, redisplay the source, delete the JavaScript, and resave your document. Then repeat the whole process, making sure that you select the original script correctly.

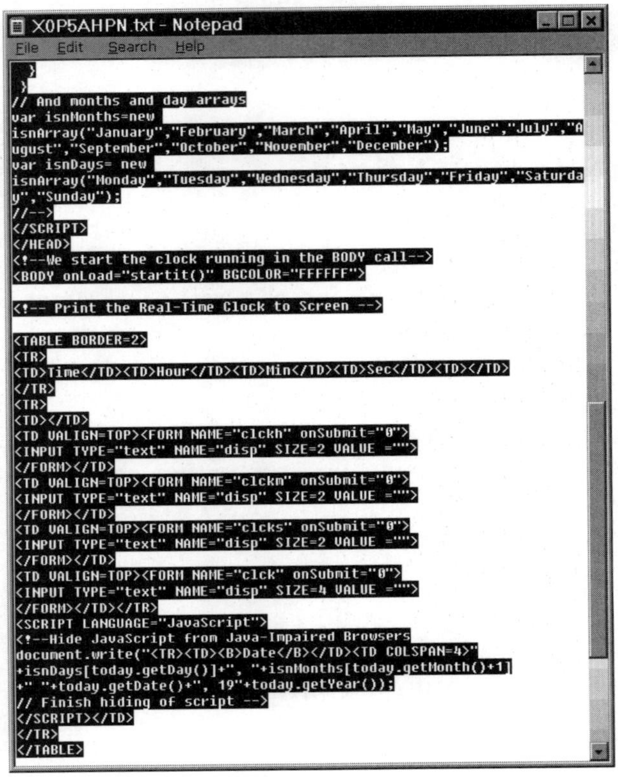


```
    }
  }
// And months and day arrays
var isnMonths=new
isnArray("January","February","March","April","May","June","July","A
ugust","September","October","November","December");
var isnDays= new
isnArray("Monday","Tuesday","Wednesday","Thursday","Friday","Saturda
y","Sunday");
//-->
</SCRIPT>
</HEAD>
<!--We start the clock running in the BODY call-->
<BODY onLoad="startit()" BGCOLOR="FFFFFF">

<!-- Print the Real-Time Clock to Screen -->

<TABLE BORDER=2>
<TR>
<TD>Time</TD><TD>Hour</TD><TD>Min</TD><TD>Sec</TD><TD></TD>
</TR>
<TR>
<TD></TD>
<TD VALIGN=TOP><FORM NAME="clckh" onSubmit="0">
<INPUT TYPE="text" NAME="disp" SIZE=2 VALUE ="">
</FORM></TD>
<TD VALIGN=TOP><FORM NAME="clckm" onSubmit="0">
<INPUT TYPE="text" NAME="disp" SIZE=2 VALUE ="">
</FORM></TD>
<TD VALIGN=TOP><FORM NAME="clcks" onSubmit="0">
<INPUT TYPE="text" NAME="disp" SIZE=2 VALUE ="">
</FORM></TD>
<TD VALIGN=TOP><FORM NAME="clck" onSubmit="0">
<INPUT TYPE="text" NAME="disp" SIZE=4 VALUE ="">
</FORM></TD></TR>
<SCRIPT LANGUAGE="JavaScript">
<!--Hide JavaScript from Java-Impaired Browsers
document.write("<TR><TD><B>Date</B></TD><TD COLSPAN=4>"
+isnDays[today.getDay()]+", "+isnMonths[today.getMonth()+1]
+" "+today.getDate()+", 19"+today.getYear());
// Finish hiding of script -->
</SCRIPT></TD>
</TR>
</TABLE>
```

Figure 34.2 Selecting a snippet of code in the source viewer.

A fantastic place to find JavaScript snippets is JavaScript Planet (http://www.geocities.com/SiliconValley/7116/), shown in Figure 34.3.

FROM HERE

- There's only one place to go from here, as far as Composer is concerned: Chapter 36, which shows you how to make your documents available to others on the Web.

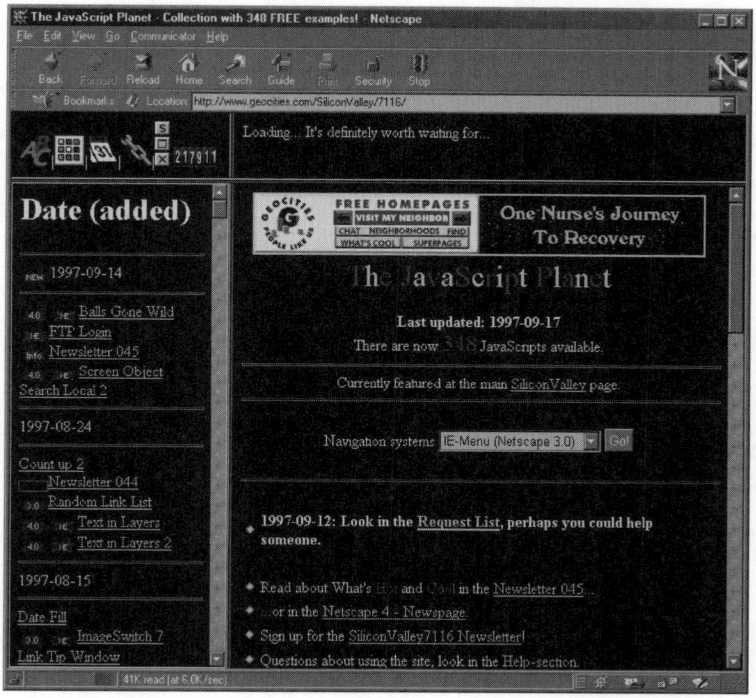

Figure 34.3 JavaScript Planet has lots of JavaScript you can borrow.

Chapter 35

Publishing Your Page

Now that your page is finished, it's time to publish it! This means that you need to place your page on a computer that's running a Web server, a program that knows how to make your page available to others on the Web. You need to understand a few simple concepts, get some information, and configure Composer to do the job. After that, publishing is easy!

Introducing Web Servers

To make your Web page available so that others can access it, you must place your page on a computer that's running a web server. A *web server* is a program that intercepts incoming requests for Web documents and doles them out over the Internet.

For the Time-Challenged

- A *Web server* is a program that knows how to make your Web page available to the Internet. To run a Web server, a computer requires a permanent connection to the Internet, which is an expensive proposition. For this reason, you'll probably want to publish your page using Web space provided by your Internet service provider (ISP).
- To get your page to your ISP, you need to transfer it using the File Transfer Protocol (FTP). You could use an FTP program to do this, but Composer makes it much easier. Composer automatically transfers all of the images in your document. With an FTP program, you'd have to transfer these files manually.
- Once you've configured the Publish page of Editor's Preferences dialog box, publishing your pages is as easy as clicking the Publish button!

Can you set up your own Web server? Only if you have a permanent Internet connection and a permanent Internet address. Most people (including your author) connect to the Internet by means of a modem, telephone line, and a friendly local Internet service provider (ISP). In most cases, you don't get a permanent connection or address with this service. You could arrange for a permanent connection and address, but it would cost you some serious money: as much as $200 per month for a *leased line*, a specially conditioned telephone line that's connected 24 hours per day.

For most people, shelling out the money for a permanent Internet connection just isn't worth it. Besides, most Internet service providers give you some free space on their computers to place your Web page, and their Web server makes your page available to the rest of the world. Check with your ISP to find out whether Web publishing services are available and whether they're included with your basic subscription fee.

The only rub with publishing via your ISP is that you need to copy your Web page and images to your ISP's computer. That's where FTP, the File Transfer Protocol, comes in.

Introducing FTP

The File Transfer Protocol enables Internet users to copy files between dissimilar computers. If you've created your Web pages on a Windows 95 system, you can copy your pages—and all the images they contain—to a UNIX or Macintosh system, thanks to FTP.

Before Composer came along, the only way you could transfer your Web pages to your ISP's computer was to use an FTP program. There are several good Windows FTP programs that make transferring files to another computer on the Internet as easy as transferring files between folders on your computer. Still, it's a tedious job. You must manually make sure that you're copying all the images associated with each page. If you forget just one of them, your page will show a placeholder instead of a graphic, and the page will look unprofessional.

That's where Composer comes in. One of the coolest of Composer's many excellent features is one-button publishing. Once you've set this up, as explained in the next section, you can send your completed page to an FTP server just by clicking one button, the Publish button.

Setting Up One-Button Publishing

Most people publish their Web pages by sending their pages (and associated images) to an Internet service provider via FTP. If you can publish your pages this way, you can take advantage of Composer's one-button publishing. To do so, you must first obtain information from your Internet service provider, as explained in the following section. Then you type this information into the Publish page of Composer Preferences. The following sections detail these procedures.

Obtaining FTP Information

To get started with one-button publishing, obtain the following information from your Internet service provider:

- The exact address of the location where you are supposed to store your Web pages and graphic images. This address should be phrased as a URL, such as ftp://www.fictititious.com/~barney/. Be *sure* to tell your ISP that you need this address phrased as a URL.
- The exact Web address of pages in your directory—that is, the address that people will use to access your pages. This address should be a URL, such as http://www.fictitious.com/~barney/.
- The name you should give your home page, or any other page that you want to be displayed automatically when users access your directory (this will probably be *default.html* or *index.html*).

- Your *user name* or *login name* for FTP access. This might be the same as your login name for e-mail, but it might differ.
- Your *password* for FTP access. This might be the same as your e-mail password, but it might differ.
- Any file name restrictions that your ISP might have.

Make sure all your file names conform to these basic restrictions. In general, don't use more than eight characters (not including the extension .htm or .html) to name your files and don't include spaces. Also, use lowercase letters for all your file names. URLs are case-sensitive. If you include capital letters, users may have to remember to type capital letters to retrieve your files.

Using the Publish Page of Composer Preferences

Once you've gotten the information you need from your Internet service provider, you're ready to give this information to Netscape. Click the Publish button on the composition toolbar. You'll see the Publish page of the Composer Preferences dialog box, shown in Figure 35.1.

In the Links and Images area, you'll see a couple of options concerning how Composer deals with the links included in your document as well as the images you've included:

- **Maintain links** By default, Composer automatically adjusts the hyperlinks in your document so that they will work from the document's new location. You should keep this option selected.
- **Keep images with documents** By default, Composer automatically uploads the images you've added to your document. You should keep this option selected.

To finish filling out this dialog box, do the following:

1. In the Publish To box, type the exact URL you were given for uploading your pages via FTP.
2. In the Browse To box, type the exact URL you were given for people to access your page.
3. In the User Name box, type your user or login name.

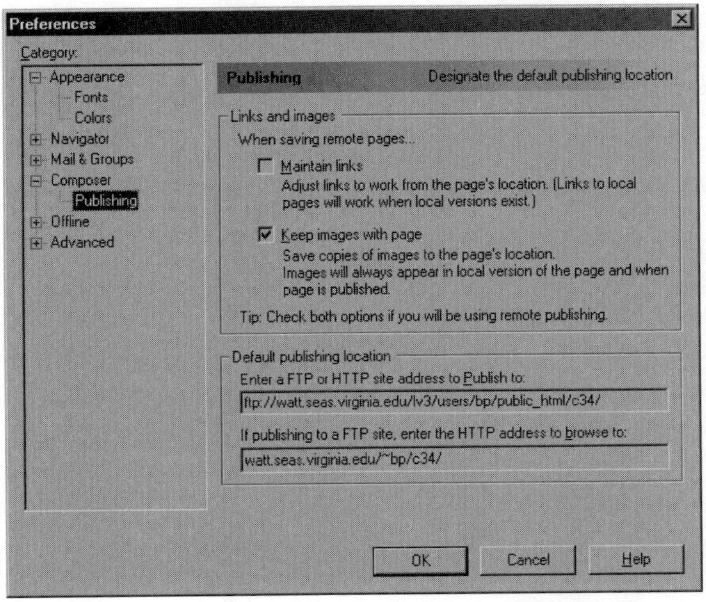

Figure 35.1 Provide your FTP information in this dialog box.

4. In the Password box, type the password you were given for FTP access. Note that you can leave this box blank if you wish, and supply your password manually each time you publish. You should leave the box blank if your computer is used by other people.
5. Check what you've typed carefully! Remember that URLs are case-sensitive and you can't place any spaces within them.
6. When you're done, click OK.

Uploading Your Page to the Server

Once you've filled in the Publish page of the Composer Preferences dialog box, you can publish your Web documents!

To publish your page, do the following:

1. Click the Publish button, or choose File/Publish. You'll see the Publish Files dialog box, shown in Figure 35.2. This dialog box automatically shows the publishing location, user name, and password that you typed in the Editor Preferences dialog box (Publish page). In addition, it lists all the images you've included in your document.
2. In the Include Files area, choose whether you want to upload only the images in the document (the default option) or all the files in the current folder. The default option is fine for your first upload. For more information on the other option, see the next section.
3. In the Save Password box, uncheck this box if your computer is used by others. You'll have to supply your password manually every time you publish, but this will prevent someone from uploading something to your directory without your knowledge.
4. Just click OK to start uploading your files!

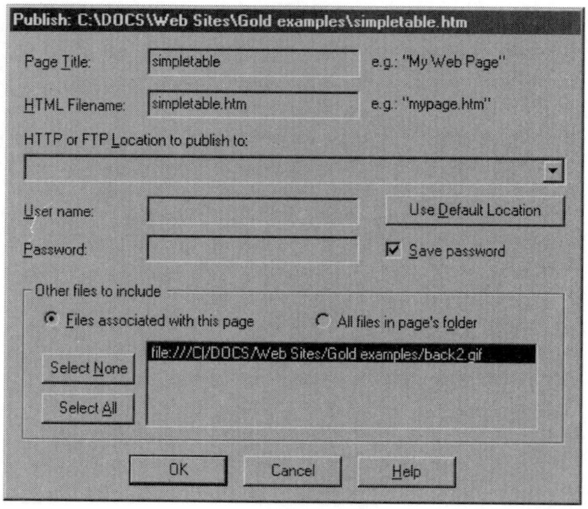

Figure 35.2 This dialog box enables you to publish your Web page.

It didn't work! Problems, huh? Check the error message you're getting. Chances are you didn't type the FTP address, password, or user name correctly. Call your ISP and verify these.

I just uploaded my page, but then I found a mistake! Don't worry, you can correct it. Just make the correction with Composer and publish the page again. Your action will overwrite the old copy.

Publishing a Web Presentation

If you created a Web presentation that includes several linked HTML files, you can take advantage of special features of the Publish Files dialog box that enable you to upload the entire presentation easily.

To publish a Web presentation:

1. Click the Publish button, or choose File/Publish. You'll see the Publish Files dialog box, shown in Figure 35.2.
2. In the Include Files area, click "All files in document's folder." You'll see all the graphics and HTML files in this folder.
3. Click Select All if you want to upload all the files. Otherwise, click Select None and select only the files that are part of your presentation. (You don't have to hold down the Ctrl or Shift key to select more than one file—just click the ones you want.)
4. Click OK to publish your presentation.

From Here

- Thinking about setting up your own business on the Web, or just ordering something on-line? Understand the security issues, which are explained in Chapter 36.
- Check out the shopping opportunities on the Web in Chapter 37.

Part VII

Netscape Communicator in the Enterprise

Chapter

36

Using Netscape Communicator on an Intranet

An *intranet* is an internal network, walled off to some degree (or sometimes totally) from the outside Internet, that uses the same technology the Internet does—including Web servers and Web browsers such as Netscape Communicator. Although Communicator is an excellent program for making full use of the external Internet, it also contains some very well thought-through features for use on intranets, as well. Some of Netscape's features that work quite well on the external Internet take on special, advanced features when they're used with Netscape's intranet servers, such as Netscape Collabra Server, Netscape Calendar Server, and Netscape Directory Server.

This chapter provides a brief introduction to the special uses of Communicator in an internal corporate network. The following chapter introduces the three Netscape Communicator Pro tools that are specifically designed

For the Time-Challenged

- If you're using Communicator behind a firewall, you'll need to specify the location of proxy servers. Get the addresses of these servers from your network administrator.
- If your company is running Netscape Directory Server or some other LDAP-compatible white pages server, configure Communicator to include this server in the white pages directory lists.
- Does your company offer an IMAP mail server as an option? Consider using it instead of POP3 if you're a mobile computer user.
- If your company is using a Collabra news server, configure Collabra to access it so that you can take full advantage of the advanced Collabra functions.

for intranet use: Calendar, AutoAdmin, and IBM Host-on-Demand. The focus here is the end-user's angle rather than the administrator's; in this and the following chapter, you'll learn enough about these facets of Communicator to deal with the program on the user's end.

Before configuring Communicator to work on your internal network, be sure to check with your networking staff. They'll give you the information you need to do this job correctly.

Configuring Proxy Servers

To protect the assets of internal computer networks, many organizations use *firewalls*. In brief, a firewall is a set of programs, often housed on a computer set aside for security purposes, that intervenes between external and internal network traffic. Firewalls perform a number of tasks, but one of the most important of these is the role they play in hiding the specific IP addresses of computers within the internal network. If computer criminals knew these addresses, they would have an easier time overcoming the network's defenses against unauthorized access.

The job of hiding internal computer addresses is done by means of proxy servers. Essentially, a proxy server works by receiving external requests for information that is housed within the internal network, and then translating this request so that it goes to the right server within the internal network. There are proxy servers for all the major Internet services, such as the Web, FTP, e-mail, and Usenet. So far as anyone on the outside of the network knows, they are accessing your company's internal Web site at "www.company.com." What they don't realize is that the proxy server is redirecting their request to an internal server that has a completely different name.

Proxy servers help to insulate the internal network from unauthorized access, but they are inconvenient for internal users who wish to access the external Internet. Proxy servers prohibit any direct connection bewteen the outside and the inside. In order to access the external Internet, you or your network administrator will need to tell Communicator which proxies to use.

I configured proxies and now Communicator doesn't work! Don't do this without getting help from your company's computer staff. They'll tell you which addresses to type and which options to use.

To configure Netscape Communicator to use proxies, do the following:

1. From the Edit menu, choose Preferences. In the Category list, click the plus sign next to Advanced, and then select Proxies. You'll see the Proxies page, shown in Figure 36.1.
2. Do one of the following:

   If your network administrator has given you the URL of an automatic proxy configuration, select Automatic proxy configuration, and type the URL in the Configuration Location box.

   or

   If your network administrator has given you the addresses of proxy servers to use for the Web, FTP, and other Internet services, click Manual proxy configuration, and click the View button. You'll see the Manual Proxy Configuration dialog box, shown in Figure 36.2. Type the addresses and port numbers of the proxy servers you want Netscape to use. (If you don't know these addresses, call your network administrator to get them.) Also, be sure to add internal domain names to the Exceptions box, separating each of them with commas. This tells Communicator to skip

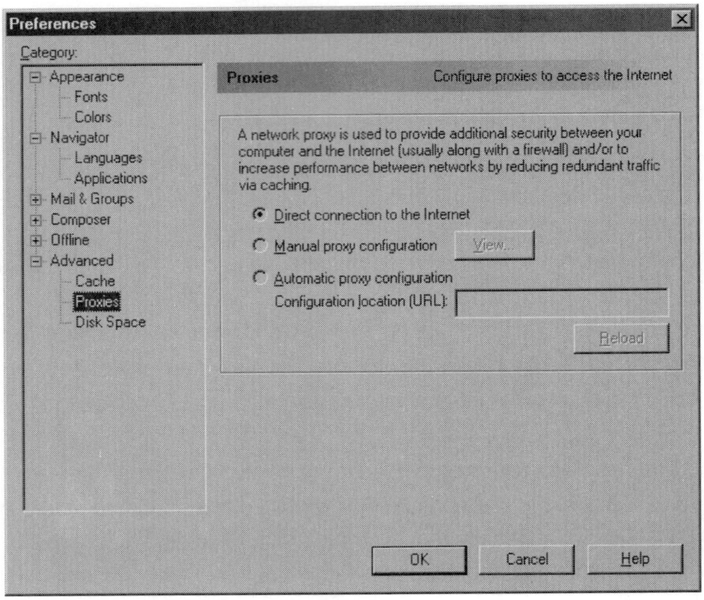

Figure 36.1 Use this dialog box to configure proxies.

the proxy for these addresses, which are inside your company's intranet and are (presumably) secure.

3. Click OK to confirm your choices.

Configuring Internal Servers

Ask your network administrator whether you can take advantage of any of the following:

- White pages directory (LDAP protocol). If your company has a white pages directory that's set up with the Lightweight Directory

Access Protocol, you can configure Communicator so that this directory is one of the directories that Messenger searches when you're hunting for people.

- IMAP e-mail server. If your company uses IMAP instead of POP3 to store your mail, you can take advantage of Communicator's support of this new and convenient protocol. It's especially nice for mobile users, since your mail doesn't get downloaded to your desktop computer (except for reading and replying); your mailbox stays on the IMAP server, where you can access it from any computer that's connected to the Internet.
- Collabra news server. If your company is running a Collabra news server, you can take full advantage of Collabra's advanced features, including user-friendly newsgroup names, SSL security, cross-newsgroup searching, and much more.

If you can make use of these services, get the address of the computer that supplies them, and read on.

Configuring Communicator to Work with an Internal LDAP Directory

To configure Communicator to work with an internal LDAP directory, follow these steps:

1. From the Edit menu, choose Preferences. In the Preferences dialog box, click the plus sign next to Mail & Groups, if necessary, and choose the Directory option. You'll see the Directory page, shown in Figure 36.2.
2. Click New. You'll see the Add Directory Server dialog box, shown in Figure 36.3.
3. In the Description box, type the name of the server, such as "Acme, Inc. White Pages."
4. In the LDAP Server box, type the computer address of the LDAP server. If you don't know this exactly, call your network administrator.
5. In the Search Root box, you can type an expression that limits the search to a certain area. If your network administrator told you to type something here, do so.

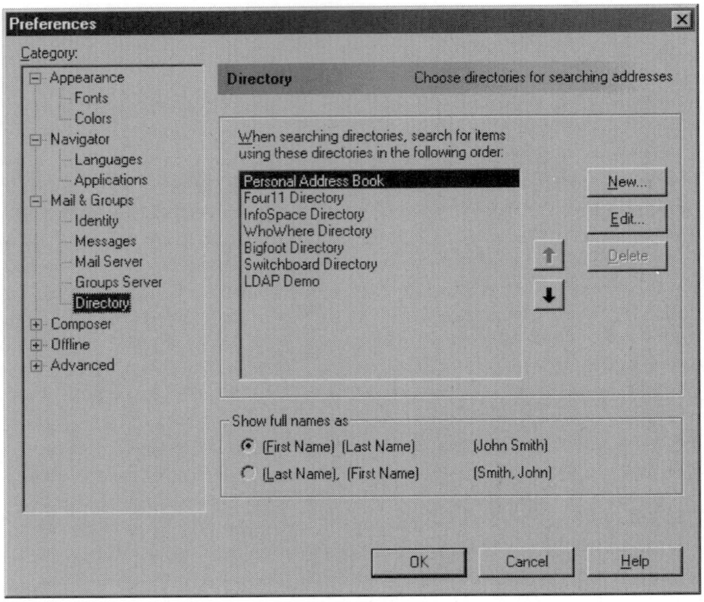

Figure 36.2 You can add an LDAP Directory server by clicking New.

6. If the server you're accessing uses encryption, click Secure.
7. Click OK to confirm your choices.

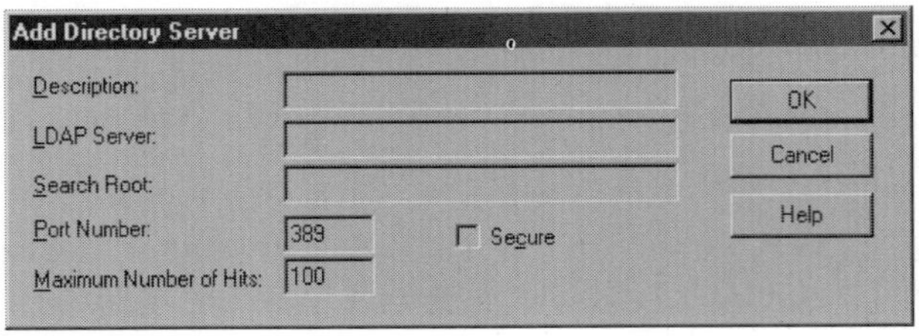

Figure 36.3 Here, you supply the LDAP Directory server information.

After you add the server, it will become available in the various dialog boxes and options that let you search for people. Use it to search for internal e-mail addresses and phone numbers.

Configuring Communicator to Work with an IMAP Mail Server

You're probabably used to a POP3 mail server. You log on, download your mail, and log off. You can leave some of your mail on the server, to be sure, but a lot of ISPs get mad if you use too much disk space for this—they're not set up for it. POP3 is fine, but it's really inconvenient when you travel. Suppose you'd like to access a message that you've downloaded to your home computer. There's no way to get it—unless you can call one of your kids to go into your home office, turn on your computer, look for it, and read it to you!

IMAP is designed to cure this problem by enabling you to store your mail on the mail server. It's accessible if you want to access it from your office at work, your office at home, or Timbuktu. All that's downloaded are the message headers; the message bodies always stay on the server.

To configure Communicator to work with an IMAP mail server, do the following:

1. From the Edit menu, choose Preferences. In the Preferences dialog box, click the plus sign next to Mail & Groups, if necessary, and click Mail Server. You'll see the Mail Server options, shown in Figure 36.4.
2. Click IMAP.
3. If you would like Communicator to copy the folder structure that you create on the IMAP server, check When creating new folders, select them for download when I go offline.
4. If the server supports SSL for secure connections, check the Server supports encrypted connections (SSL) box.
5. Click OK to confirm.

After you've configured Communicator to work with an IMAP server, you can use the Manage Mail Account command on the Edit menu to manage your mail on the server.

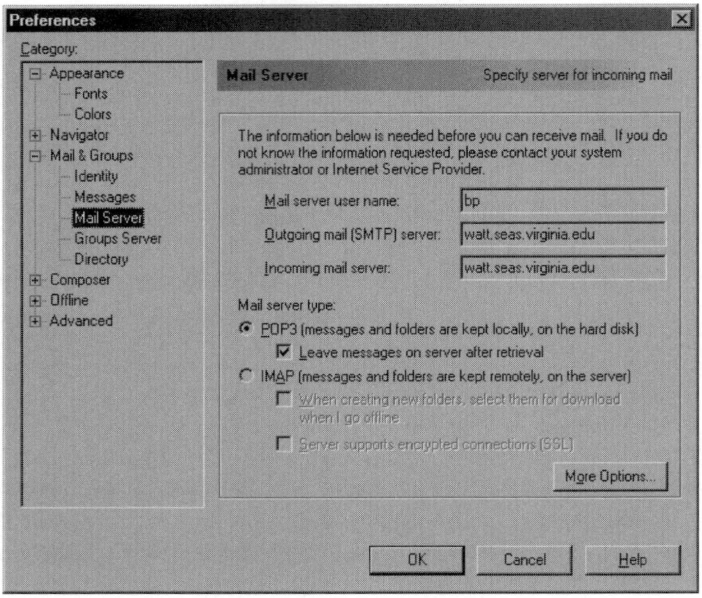

Figure 36.4 Here, you can set up an IMAP server.

Configuring Communicator to Work with a Collabra News Server

If your company has a Collabra server, do the following to add it to your server list:

1. In Collabra, click the File menu, and choose New Discussion Groups Server. You'll see the New Discussion Groups Server dialog box, shown in Figure 36.5.
2. In the Server box, type the address of the Collabra server.
3. If the server uses SSL security, click secure.
4. If the server requires a password, click Always use name and password.
5. Click OK to confirm your choices.

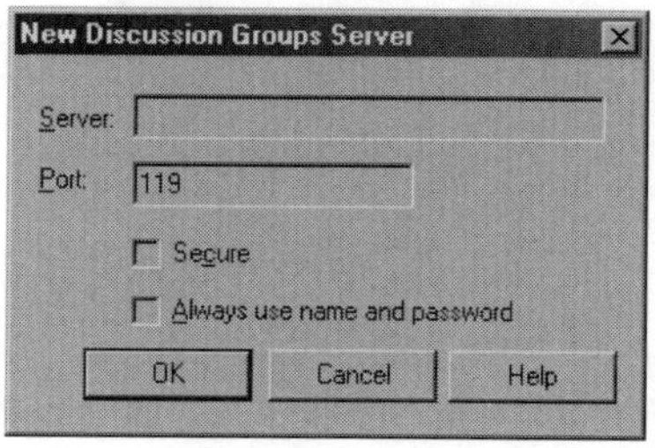

Figure 36.5 Here, you can add a Collabra news server.

After defining the server, you can access it by opening the Message Center and selecting the server.

More Intranet Tips

Here are some tips that will make the use of Netscape Communicator on an intranet a genuine pleasure:

- Change the home page to your intranet's home page. To do so, open the Edit menu, choose Preferences, click Navigator, and type your intranet home page's URL in the Location box. Click OK to confirm.
- Configure the Personal Toolbar with local sites that you'll use often, such as your local intranet search site, employee directory, employee manual, etc.
- Ask your network administrator if there's a bookmarks file containing key intranet sites. If yes, obtain a copy, and install it by opening the Bookmarks window, and choosing Import from the File menu.

From Here

- There's only one place to go: The last chapter, which discusses Calendar, AutoAdmin, and IBM Host-on-demand.

Chapter 37

Introducing Calendar and Host On-Demand

For enterprise computing, Communicator contains two exceptionally useful programs: Calendar and IBM Host On-Demand. Calendar doesn't come into its true functionality until it's teamed with Netscape Calendar Server, but you can use it as a personal information manager even if Calendar Server isn't available. With Calendar Server, Calendar becomes part of an enterprise-wide scheduling system that's very impressive indeed. Host On-Demand, meanwhile, gives you access to important data stored on Big Iron—that is, legacy mainframe systems. This chapter introduces both of these applications.

Introducing Netscape Calendar

In today's enterprises, it's essential to coordinate teamwork—especially now that people from different parts of the company so often work together. When paired with Netscape Calendar Server, Netscape Calendar (Figure 37.1) is a well-designed application that's capable of supporting scheduling in any organization ranging from a small business to a large, complex corporation.

Calendar is an impressive application, but like similar products (including Lotus Notes), it only succeeds if all or most people are using it—and what's more, using it knowledgeably. Companies that plan to use Calendar will need to train employees how to make the most of it. However, the pages to follow should help you gain an initial familiarity with the program that will speed learning when training occurs.

For the Time-Challenged

- Netscape Calendar is very much like a personal information manager (PIM), but it's designed to work on an intranet or extranet. You can make appointments involving other people, and they receive notices of these appointments, which they can accept or reject.
- Netscape Calendar requires Netscape Calendar Server to function. However, you can learn a lot about the program by using it as a personal information manager. Try setting up a few agenda and To Do items.
- IBM Host On-Demand enables Communicator users to access legacy data. You get a window into text-based applications, but these often contain indispensable data.

How does Calendar Differ from a Personal Information Manager (PIM)?

Essentially, Calendar is a personal scheduling program very much like those that you've probably seen on personal computers, but there's a difference. With Calendar, your scheduling information is kept on the server, and it's accessible to others, if they have the clearance to access it. For example, suppose Mary is trying to make an appointment to see Beth. Mary can access

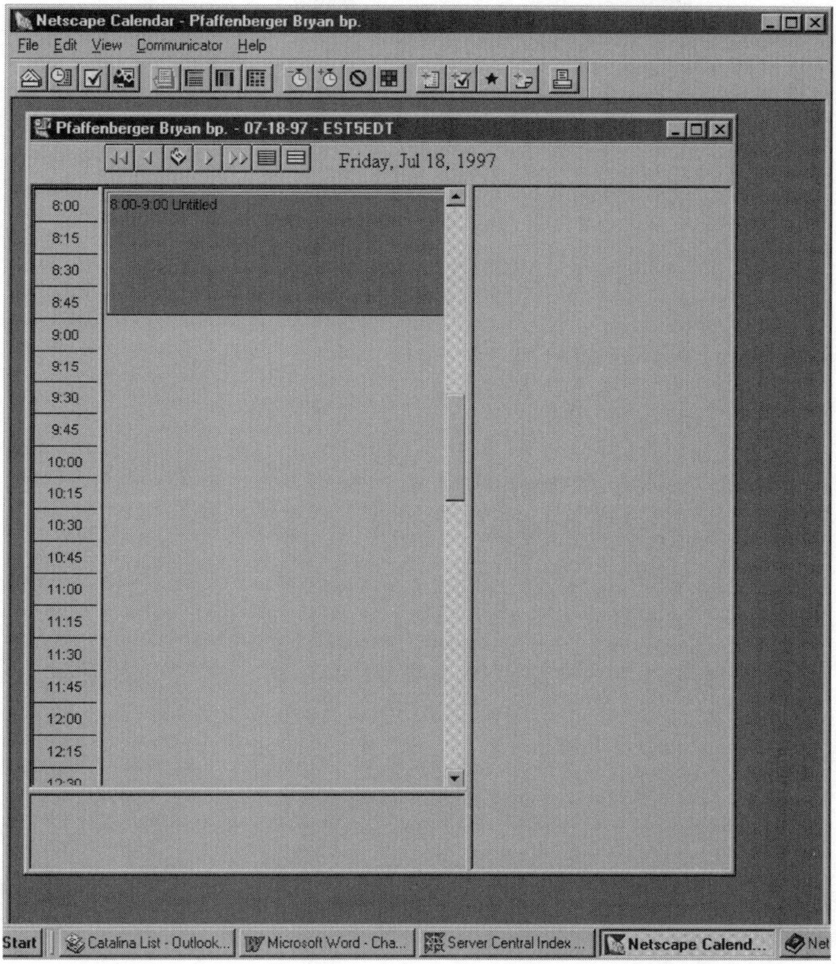

Figure 37.1 Netscape Calendar supports teamwork scheduling in the enterprise—but it looks and works just like a personal information manager.

Beth's schedule, and see which times she's free. By proposing a message when Beth is free, Mary has a much better chance of arranging the meeting successfully without a prolonged back-and-forth negotiation.

This works at the group level, too. By creating a Group Agenda, you can open the Day Views of several people side by side, and schedule an event with the group at times when everyone is available. All without having to call them and poll them on when they're free! Cool, huh?

There's more. By enabling others to be *designates,* Calendar users can allow other people to actually make scheduling entries in their calendars. For example, suppose the team members agree to let the team leader function as a designate for their calendars. The team leader can just go ahead and schedule the meeting right there and then—and the meeting shows up in everyone's calendars, as if they typed it in themselves.

Controlling Access Rights

If the idea of other people writing to your schedule makes you nervous, you're in plenty of company—it's not something you'd want just anyone to do. That's why Calendar enables users to designate access rights. For each individual, you can designate any of the following levels of access:

- **View times only** The designate can only see when you're free or busy.
- **View/reply** The designate can view all of your entries and has the right to reply to invitations in your name.
- **Modify** The designate can actually edit your entries.

For any designate, you can also define access to different types of entries:

- **Normal entries** These include Agenda entries, Day Events, and Notes.
- **Confidential entries** These are the same as normal entries, but you've defined them as confidential.
- **Personal entries** You can make these off limits.
- **Public entries** These can be seen by anybody.

Scheduling an Agenda Entry

To describe Calendar fully would require a book as long as the one you're reading—it's that complex. Still, you can get started with Calendar by using it as a personal information manager (PIM), even without a network connection. From there, it's an easy matter to master the rest of the program, should your company decide to go the Netscape Calendar Server route. (Netscape Calendar Server is required to take full advantage of Calendar's network functions.)

To use Calendar as a PIM, start the program by choosing Calendar from any Communicator menu. You'll see today's agenda, like the one seen in Figure 37.1.

Try scheduling an agenda entry by following these instructions:

1. From the File menu, choose New Agenda Entry. You'll see the New Agenda Entry dialog box, shown in Figure 37.2.
2. In the Title area, type a title for the entry.
3. Use the slider controls to specify the date, start time, duration, and end time.

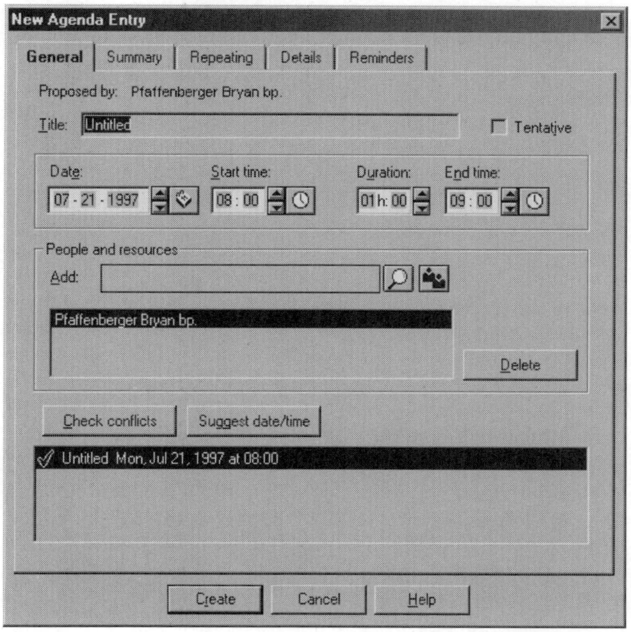

Figure 37.2 Here, you begin scheduling an agenda entry.

4. If you were using Calendar on a network and you had set up names and groups, you could include these in the People and Resources area. By selecting a name, you'd invite this person to the meeting automatically (the invitation goes out via e-mail). By selecting a resource, such as a file, you make this available to everyone who receives an invitation.
5. Once you've chosen names in the People and resources area, you could click Check Conflicts, if you were connected to the network, to see whether your schedule choice conflicts with the schedules any of the people you've invited. If so, you could click Suggest date/time to find a slot that's open for everyone.
6. Click Summary. You see the Summary page, shown in Figure 37.3.
7. In the location box, type the meeting's location. You can also change the importance level, if you wish. The access level list box lets you define the entry as public, normal, or confidential.

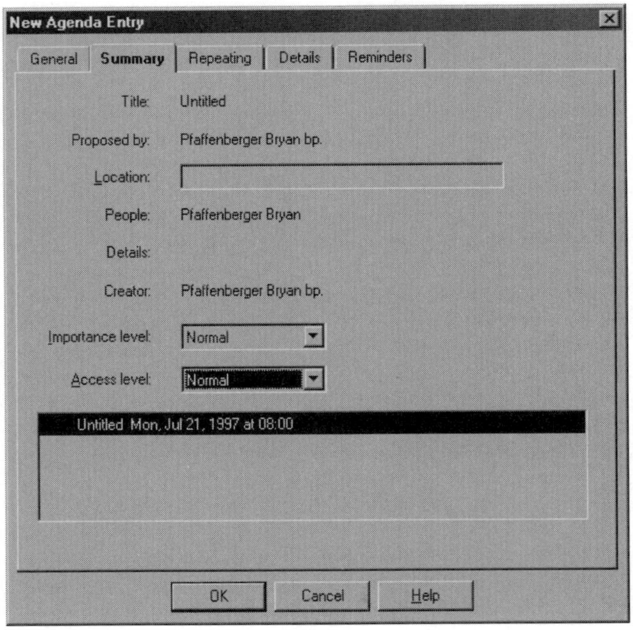

Figure 37.3 You specify the meeting's location here.

8. If the event is a repeating event, click the Repeating tab. You'll see the Repeating page, shown in Figure 37.4.
9. You can use the Details and Reminders pages to add notes about the meeting and set up onscreen notifications, with pop-up dialog boxes and alarms, if you wish.
10. Click Create to confirm your agenda entry.

Exploring Other Calendar Functions

As you can see from the preceding, using Calendar is exactly like using a personal information manager (PIM), except that Calendar Server enables some very powerful teamwork management functions. Here's a quick overview of some additional features of the program:

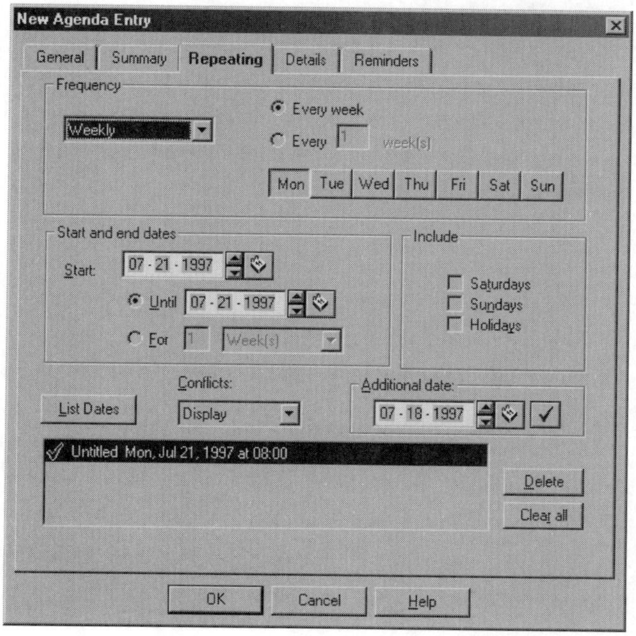

Figure 37.4 You can set up repeating events here.

- To create a Daily Note, click Daily Note on the toolbar. In the same way that you can add people and resources to an agenda item, you can do the same for a Daily Note, which means that your Daily Note will appear as a Daily Note on their calendars, too. The same goes for other peoples' Daily Notes, if they've included you.
- You can define To Do items, indicating the percentage you've gotten done and the finish date. This information is available to others so they can see how busy you are. To add a To Do item, click New Task on the toolbar, and use the New Task dialog box to name the task, specify dates and completion percentages, and choose other options.
- You can also define Day Events, which take up the whole day. These are exactly like agenda items; you can invite other people and search schedules to find out when everyone's free.
- To get a quick overview of all your agenda items, try clicking View Day (or press F8), View Week (or press F9), or View Month (or press F10).

Understanding the In-Tray

As you've just seen, you can send agenda entries to others. But they don't automatically appear in people's schedules, unless they've given you rights as a designate. Normally, users look in the In-Tray to see which entries they've received. There, they can accept them or refuse them, as they wish. Your reply goes out via e-mail.

Defining Groups

In addition to working with individuals' names, you can also define groups (to do so, you choose Manage Groups from the Edit menu). There, you can create a new group, add members to the group, indicate the type of group, and delete members. After creating the group, you can choose the group's name when you're creating an agenda item. This saves you the trouble of having to select all the names individually.

Introducing IBM Host-on-Demand

In many organizations, important data is housed on *legacy systems,* which is a polite way of referring to mainframe-based applications that can be accessed only by means of not-very-user-friendly text interfaces. Many of these systems were designed to be used with a proprietary terminal, equipped with a keyboard having all sorts of strange keys (such as PF1, PF2, Attn, SysReq, and NxtPad).

To enable Communicator users to access this data, Netscape Communicator includes IBM Host-on-Demand, a Java application that simulates an IBM 3270 terminal.

To use IBM Host-on-Demand, you'll need to know the address of the IBM 3270 host, and you'll also need information about how to work the program you're accessing. Once you've got this information, start IBM Host-on-Demand by choosing this option from any Communicator menu. You'll see the Host-on-Demand page, shown in Figure 37.5.

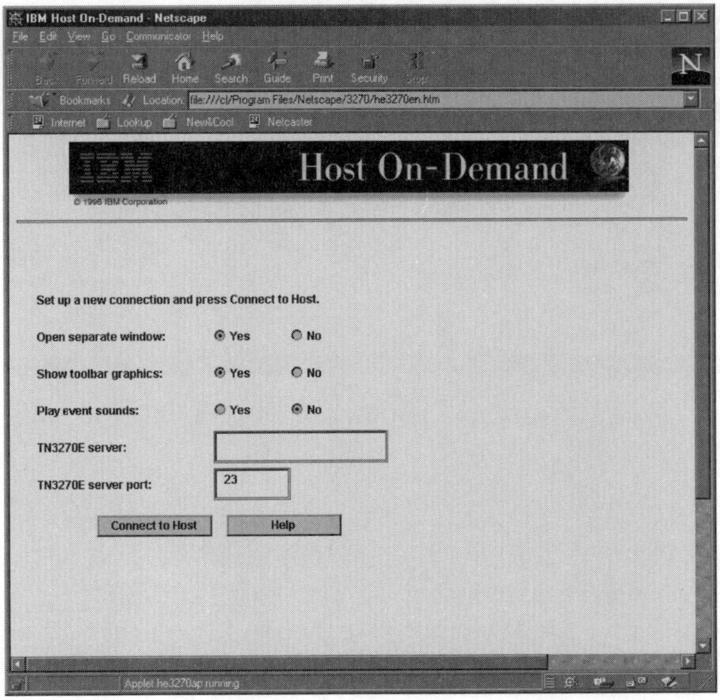

Figure 37.5 IBM Host-on-Demand is a neat Java application that enables you to access data kept on Big Iron—IBM mainframe computers.

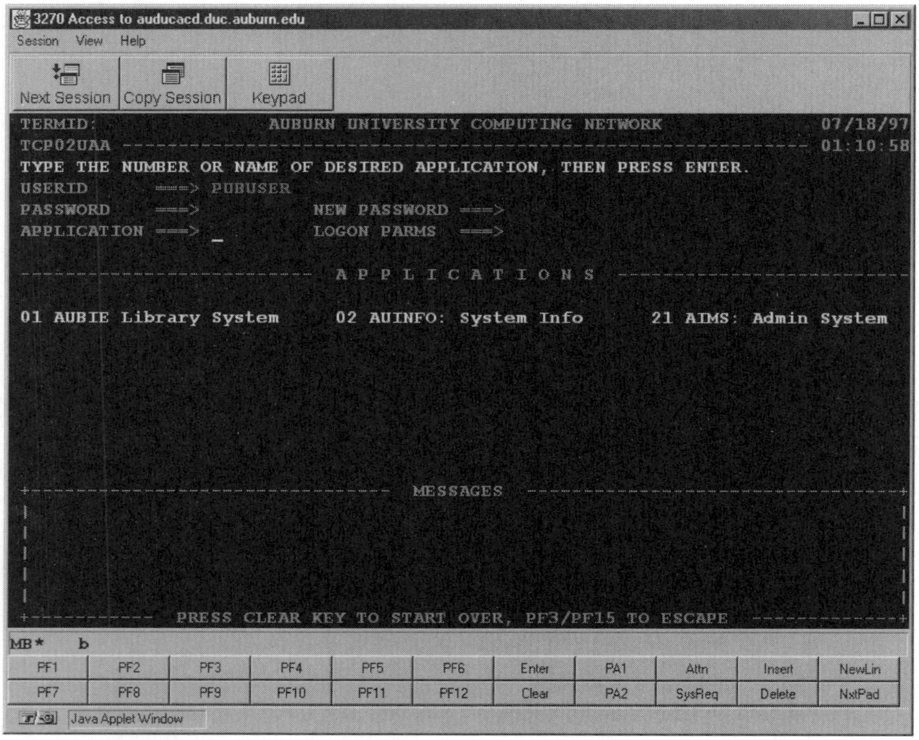

Figure 37.6 You're connected! Follow the onscreen instructions, and good luck.

In the TN3270E server box, type the address of the IBM 3270 computer you want to connect to, and click Connect to Host. If all goes well, you'll see the Host On-Demand window (Figure 37.6), with the text-based interface in all its glory.

Index

A

B

C

D

E

F

G

H

I

J

K

L

M

N

O

Q

R

S

T

U

V

W

X

Y